BIBLE TRUTHS

Learning from the Life of Christ

Stephen J. Hankins

Third Edition

BJU PRESS

Greenville, South Carolina

Advisory Committee
from the faculty and staff of Bob Jones University

Michael P. V. Barrett, PhD

James Frederick Creason Jr., PhD

Marshall P. Neal, PhD

Daniel P. Olinger, PhD

M. Bruce McAllister, DMin

John B. Barnett IV, MA

Note:

BIBLE TRUTHS: LEVEL A Teacher's Edition
Learning from the Life of Christ
Third Edition

Stephen J. Hankins, PhD

Editors
Thomas Parr, MA
Dennis Cone, MA

Designer
John Bjerk

Composition
Carol Ingalls

Photo Acquisition
Susan Perry

Project Manager
Dan Woodhull

Cover Designers
David Siglin
Caroline George

Illustrators
John Bjerk
Paula Cheadle
Preston Gravely
Jim Hargis
Jonathan Johnson
Kathy Pflug
Dave Schuppert
Megan Strand

Photograph credits appear on page TE263.

CD installation instructions appear on page TE264.

© 2006 BJU Press
Greenville, South Carolina 29614
First Edition © 1978 BJU Press

ISBN 1-59166-338-5
ISBN 978-1-59166-338-6

15 14 13 12 11 10 9 8 7 6 5 4 3 2 1

CONGRATULATIONS!

Your search for the very best educational materials available has been completely successful! You have a textbook that is the culmination of decades of research, experience, prayer, and creative energy.

The Facts

Nothing overlooked. Revised and updated. Facts are used as a springboard to stimulate thoughtful questions and guide students to broader applications.

The Foundation

Nothing to conflict with Truth and everything to support it. Truth is the pathway as well as the destination.

The Fun

Nothing boring about this textbook! Student (and teacher) might even forget it's a textbook! Brimming with interesting extras and sparkling with color!

BJU PRESS
Learning for Life™

1.800.845.5731   www.bjup.com

Contents

To the Teacher

Learning from the Life of Christ is the seventh book in the Bible Truths series. The book is intended for junior high school students, seventh graders specifically. The lessons are based on material from the four Gospels.

The process of deciding what to include from the Gospels was governed by two factors: thoroughness in presenting the life of Christ and relevance to students in this age group. The chronology and geography of Christ's life are mentioned when they contribute to an understanding of Christ's teachings and actions. This approach is consistent with the emphasis of the Gospel writers in their attention to these matters. Cultural and historical details receive similar attention. Together, the student text and teacher's edition discuss (at least in summary form) every part of the Gospels.

Each unit of the student text treats a different type of material, as the unit titles imply. Organizing the material this way allows the teacher to capitalize on the variety of content in the Gospels. It also provides a simple structure for the class.

For variety, efficiency, and applicability, several different approaches have been used in the lessons themselves. Some lessons are in-depth treatments of a single passage. Others examine several passages that develop the same concept. Several of the lessons on miracles are examples of this second approach.

The purpose of *Learning from the Life of Christ* is two-fold: to help the student glorify God by being conformed to the image of Christ presented in the Gospels and to teach the student to apply Scripture to his daily life. Each lesson emphasizes a character quality the student is to develop, an action he is to carry out, or a truth he is to believe. After establishing the scriptural basis for each, the lesson explains specific applications.

As you read about the following features, you may wish to glance through the material to see the features and how each contributes to the whole lesson.

The Student Text

Learning from the Life of Christ has fifty-seven lessons. For a two-semester course, two or three lessons per week is an appropriate pace. If the class meets every day, the material could be covered in one semester. (See the suggested schedules on page TEviii.) If you end up with extra time some weeks, a class period can be spent discussing one of the seven "Christ's World" sections. A discussion of the major maps in the student text (pp. 5, 25, 30, 75, 130, and 186) with the map exercises from the CD could also be a single lesson.

The student lessons are designed to be interesting and applicable. Usually each lesson begins with a story or illustration teaching the theme of the lesson. Then the lesson draws main points from the Scripture passage. Details from the passage are usually covered in the Teacher's Edition rather than the student text.

Unit Openers

Each unit begins with a colorful two-page spread. Details from the photographs and illustrations in the unit are designed to stimulate student interest in the lessons ahead. The brief introductory paragraph highlights some of the major concepts that will be presented.

Read & Memorize

The student should read the Scripture passage(s) assigned for each lesson before he reads the lesson itself. Usually brief, these readings should only take an average of five minutes to complete. (Even the longest assigned reading—Lesson 40—can be done in less than ten minutes.) Without reading the Scripture carefully, the student will not be able to understand the lesson completely or to answer many of the questions at the end of the lesson.

Each memory verse captures the central thought of the lesson. Memorization of these verses provides the student with a summary of the main point. (For the teacher's convenience, the chart on page TE257 lists the memory work for all the lessons.)

Bible Expressions to Understand

In the King James Version, most of the Scripture passages selected for the students to read contain terms the students may not know. These terms are listed and defined at the beginning of the lesson to help them understand the biblical text.

Summary Boxes

The short summary at or near the end of each lesson succinctly restates the major idea of the lesson and summarizes the applications.

Do You Remember?

These exercises are designed to assist in immediate review of the lesson. With a few exceptions, the questions are drawn from the Scripture reading rather than the student text or material in the Teacher's Edition. Answers are shown in magenta on the reduced student pages in the Teacher's Edition.

Christ's World

These feature essays appear in the text, one in each unit except in Unit 7 (where the "Master Chart of Christ's Miracles" appears instead). They provide historical, cultural, and geographical background information for the study of the life of Christ.

Charts & Maps

Nineteen charts placed throughout the text provide clear presentation of large amounts of information. In some cases the charts summarize information discussed in a unit. Other charts add to the information presented in a single lesson.

Several maps in the text underscore the historical and geographical reality of the incarnation of Christ. These maps also help the student understand the full significance of Christ's words and actions.

Art & Photographs

Almost every lesson contains photographs or original art that helps the student visualize what is discussed. Many of these pieces have captions that provoke thought or draw the reader into the text.

Indexes

Three indexes are included to help the teacher and student find specific information in the text. The Topical Index provides a thorough listing of important people, places, scriptural terms, and concepts found in the book. The Scripture Index lists all the major passages on which the lessons are based as well as other verses and passages referred to. The Memory Verse List shows all the memory verse references in Bible book order and the lessons in which they are found. This list could be used to create a progress chart for the student to keep a record of the verses he has learned.

Exercises

An exercise or two for each lesson may be found on the CD accompanying this Teacher's Edition. The format varies from lesson to lesson, as does the number of questions. These exercises help the student meditate on the concepts he has read. He can answer them only if he has studied both the Scripture passage and the lesson. The questions address both facts and principles. Answers are also found on the CD.

The Teacher's Edition

The Teacher's Edition of *Learning from the Life of Christ* has been designed with two kinds of teachers in mind: the one who teaches Bible as his primary subject and the one who teaches Bible as his second discipline. The detail in this edition should help the instructor to be prepared without the aid of a large library. However, use of additional sources is both suggested and encouraged. The growing teacher never restricts himself to merely one source for his teaching.

Reading the student text will help the teacher know what to emphasize from the teacher's edition and how to supplement what the student has already read.

Unit Introduction

These short paragraphs give an overview of the material to be covered in the unit. They also alert the teacher to any special features in the unit that may require an adjustment in teaching strategy.

Lesson Heading

Three items are shown in a small chart at the top of each lesson: "Theme," "Scripture," and "Memory Work." "Theme" states briefly the central topic of the lesson. "Scripture" is the passage from the Bible the student is assigned to read. In some cases, parallel or supplementary passages are listed in parentheses. The teacher should read these as part of his preparation. "Memory Work" lists the verse(s) the student is to memorize.

Objectives

Presented in chart form, the objectives for each lesson are divided into two categories: knowledge and application. Knowledge objectives are facts the student should learn. Application objectives are truths the student should strive to implement in his Christian life.

Lesson Outline

An outline that shows at a glance the structure of the lesson material presented in the Teacher's Edition appears on the first or second page of the lesson. It gives the

Contents

teacher an overview of the points to be presented and may also serve as a useful tool for classroom presentation. The CD includes printable copies of the outlines to use as handouts or overheads.

Icons

Some sections have icons to help the teacher spot those sections at a glance.

Approach to the Lesson

All three of the items in this section orient the teacher to the material to be covered. "Theme" provides a detailed definition of the theme listed earlier. "Rationale" helps the teacher see the relevance of the lesson for teenage Christian living. "Background" offers any necessary explanatory comments about the arrangement or selection of material being considered in the lesson. It also explains the relationship of this material to the life of Christ in general.

The Lesson

The content of this section, organized according to the outline, explains the biblical material from a factual perspective. Application notes (set in a smaller font) are sprinkled throughout the lesson. These application sections help the teacher apply the factual information from the lesson. Since our faith and conduct are based on revealed, factual information, striking a balance is essential to effective Bible teaching.

Throughout the Teacher's Edition, key statements are highlighted so the teacher can easily notice the main idea of the unit, section, or paragraph.

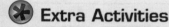

Special Problems and Topics

This feature appears in only a few lessons. Any apparent contradictions in the biblical material are explained, as are varying interpretations of the passage. When a passage suggests a topic of interest that is not central to the discussion, it may be developed here.

Extra Activities

A number of suggestions are presented to make your teaching more interesting. Sometimes complete case studies and discussion outlines are given. Some of these suggestions may be used as additional homework.

Test Packet

A set of unit tests (available for purchase separately) includes six tests: one for Units 1–3 and one each for the remaining units. Each test is comprehensive (five to seven pages in length), but not cumulative. The questions are based primarily on material in the student text and Scripture readings, with a few questions coming from the Teacher's Edition material. In the answer key, a page number or Bible reference is given with the correct answer to indicate where it may be found.

Support Materials CD

The CD contains the following support materials as PDFs:

- Bible Reading Program (see below)
- Exercises for each student text lesson
- Map exercises
- Copies of the charts for use in class as handouts or overheads
- Outlines of each teacher edition lesson for use as handouts or overheads
- Doctrine charts

(See page TE264 for instructions regarding using the CD.)

Bible Reading Program

New to this edition of *Bible Truths*, this program assists students in regular Bible reading. Systematic reading of the Scriptures is a lifelong habit you want your students to develop. As the students read, the program helps them interpret the Bible and see the big picture. It helps them discover how each passage fits into the larger message and broad sweep of the Bible. The program includes instructions for teachers, an explanation of three methods for interpretation, and a schedule for daily reading.

The Bible Reading Program functions well as a semester or year-long homework project for students. Teacher involvement can be limited to a weekly in-class help session. See instructions in the program for further details.

The eighth-grade (Level B) edition of *Bible Truths* (third edition) contains the same version of the Bible Reading Program as the seventh-grade edition. However, starting at Level C (ninth grade), each grade level includes more advanced versions, which move the student to greater levels of understanding. Ideally, by the end of his senior year, the student will have read through the Bible six times.

Suggested Teaching Schedules

One-Semester Course
(five class periods per week)

Week	Lessons & Tests
1	L.1–3
2	L.4–7, Quiz
3	L.8–11
4	L.12–13, U.1–3 Test, L.14
5	L.15–18
6	L.19–20, U.4 Test, L.21–22
7	L.23–26, Quiz
8	L.27–31
9	U.5 Test, L.32–34
10	L.35–39
11	L.40, U.6 Test, L.41–42
12	L.43–46
13	U.7 Test, L.47–50
14	L.51–54
15	L.55–57, U.8 Test

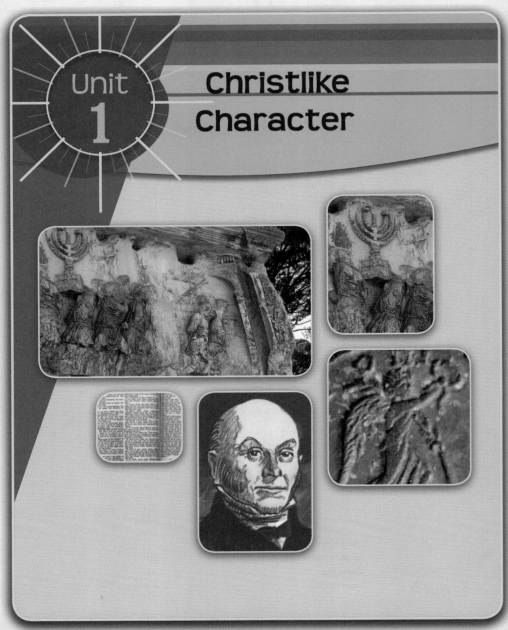

Unit 1

Christlike Character

Two-Semester Course
(two or three class periods per week)

Week	Lessons & Tests	Week	Lessons & Tests	Week	Lessons & Tests
1	L.1–2	11	L.20, U.4 Test, L.21	21	L.37–39
2	L.3, Quiz	12	L.22–23	22	L.40, U.6 Test, L.41
3	L.4–5	13	Quiz, L.24–25	23	L.42–43
4	L.6–7, Quiz	14	L.26–27	24	L.44–45
5	L.8–10	15	Review and Semester Test	25	L.46, U.7 Test, L.47
6	L.11–12	16	L.28–29, Quiz	26	L.48–50
7	L.13, U.1–3 Test	17	L.30–31	27	L.51–52, Quiz
8	L.14–15	18	U.5 Test, L.32	28	L.53–54
9	L.16–17, Quiz	19	L.33–34	29	L.55–57
10	L.18–19	20	L.35–36, Quiz	30	Review and U.8 Test or Final

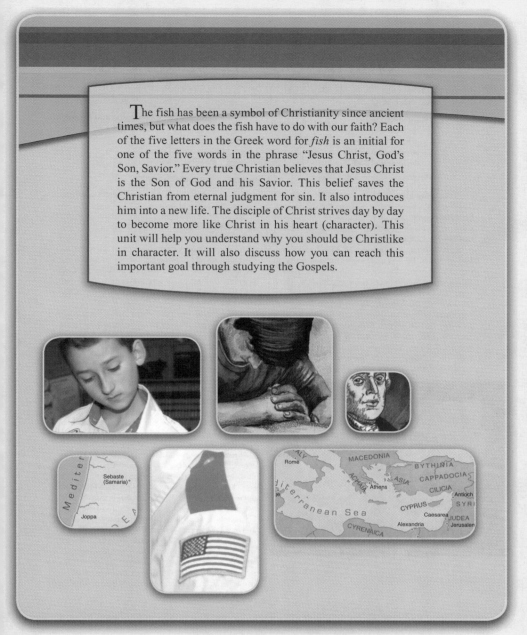

The fish has been a symbol of Christianity since ancient times, but what does the fish have to do with our faith? Each of the five letters in the Greek word for *fish* is an initial for one of the five words in the phrase "Jesus Christ, God's Son, Savior." Every true Christian believes that Jesus Christ is the Son of God and his Savior. This belief saves the Christian from eternal judgment for sin. It also introduces him into a new life. The disciple of Christ strives day by day to become more like Christ in his heart (character). This unit will help you understand why you should be Christlike in character. It will also discuss how you can reach this important goal through studying the Gospels.

Unit 1
Christlike Character

This opening unit lays the groundwork for the rest of the book. It answers three questions: Why develop Christlike character? How does the believer develop Christlike character? How may the Gospels be used as a tool in the development of Christlike character?

Each of the three lessons in the unit each gives a Scripture passage to be read. These passages suggest what is discussed in the lessons but are not discussed in great detail. The passages serve as a foundation for a wider discussion that takes many passages into consideration.

This unit includes a special essay in the student text entitled "The Romans" (following Lesson 1). This discussion will help your students understand the political environment in which Christ lived.

Lesson 3 in the student text includes two charts designed to give students an overview of the four Gospels. Both are reproduced in the *Charts* section on the CD accompanying this Teacher's Edition.

Lesson 1

Why Develop Christlikeness?

Theme	The Need for Christlike Character
Scripture	Ephesians 3:14–21
Memory Work	Colossians 3:8–10

Approach to the Lesson

Theme: Humans have been like God since the beginning. Even before our Creation, God foresaw making man in His own image (Gen. 1:26). The rest of Scripture is the story of man's fall and restoration by God's grace. Our whole purpose, then, is to be like Christ, our Creator (John 1:3). Through growth in grace, we can become what He expects us to be.

Rationale: The primary goal of this lesson is to justify the theme of the entire book. Stress that your students need to become more like Christ. Point out that throughout this year they will be learning specific lessons to help them do that.

Christ is looking for better people, not better programs. Where will He find such people? There will not be any unless the character of our children and teens is molded into the image of Christ. As a Bible teacher, you can be a part of that process. By example and by fervent presentation of Christ, you can see your students' character change. It may be gradual, even virtually imperceptible. Patience is essential for all who build lives for Christ.

Background: Both what a person says and what he does spring from his inner qualities or, to use biblical terminology,

Objectives

Knowledge (concepts students need to grasp)	the meaning of the phrase *Christlike character*
	the priority God gives to developing Christlike character in us
Application (principles students should put into practice)	The image of God in us has been seriously marred by sin.
	We must be saved before the process of character transformation can begin.
	We must commit ourselves to a lifelong process of character transformation.

Bible Expressions to Understand

riches of his glory—God's store of power and perfect character
inner man—the nonphysical part of a person
the fulness of God—the character qualities God possesses that humans may develop

"Like father, like son." "Like mother, like daughter." These often-repeated sayings stress the similarities between parents and their children. A remarkable example of this in American history is John Adams and his son John Quincy Adams.

John Adams was the second president of the United States. He was a personal friend of many of the men who founded our country. His oldest son, John Quincy Adams, also became president. They were the first father and son who both served as president of the United States. Before becoming president, John Adams was successful as a foreign diplomat. So was his son. Adams loved to read, liked farming, and was convinced he was right about politics. All these qualities were true of his son as well. Both father and son were known for being reserved. Both men were driven by a strong sense of

John Adams served as the second president of the United States (1797–1801), and John Quincy Adams was the sixth (1825–1829).

2

duty to America. Both men made great contributions to our political system.

In many ways John Quincy Adams was the image of his father. He was "a chip off the old block." You may have heard friends and relatives say that about you. Children are expected to be like their parents. This principle carries over into the spiritual realm. Children of God should be like their heavenly Father. Christians are to be shaped into the image of Christ. They are to develop Christlike character.

Why should you care about being Christlike? There are several reasons. First, the Bible emphasizes its importance. From the beginning, God has wanted people to be like Himself. Genesis 1:27 says, "So God created man in his own image, in the image of God created he him; male and female created them." Man was created like God in character. He was created in the image of God in his spirit—the inner, unseen person. He had intelligence and feelings like God. He had the ability to choose like God and to communicate with and understand his Creator. He was like God because God wanted him to be that way. And God wants you to be like Him today.

Another way the Bible emphasizes Christlike character is by telling us that our character is the most important part of us. Jesus taught that a person's heart, or character, is like a fountain that pours out all his thoughts, words, and actions. Jesus said, "A good man out of the good treasure of the heart bringeth forth good things: and an evil man out of the evil treasure bringeth forth evil things" (Matt. 12:35).

Why else is Christlike character important? It is the only way you can overcome your greatest enemy—sin. When Adam disobeyed God in the garden, his sin marred the image of God in him and in all his descendants. You are one of Adam's descendants, so

from his heart. One who has Christlike character has inner qualities like Christ's. The development of Christlike character begins with conversion—that point in time when the person becomes a new creation by the transforming power of the Holy Spirit. This is the beginning of a lifelong process called sanctification, which is like the weaving of a tapestry. Removing the strands of sin from the tapestry of the heart is a tedious task. Over the years God removes them through sickness and health, through enemies and friends, through poverty and prosperity. In their place He weaves the threads of Christlikeness. The Spirit of God accomplishes this transformation through the Word of God and prayer. Gradually the beauty of the work begins to show. Where once there was pride, there is now

humility. Where there was rebellion, there is now meekness. Where there was a short temper, now there is patience. In time the individual is more like Christ; he becomes Christlike in character. What is left undone in this life Christ will transform in the next. By the power of Christ and for the glory of Christ, every child of God will be all he can ever become. This is the goal of Redemption, the ultimate triumph of Christ.

The Lesson

I. A Biblical Priority

God's purpose for humans. God's very creative act announced boldly what He has always had planned for the human race. "So God created man in his own image, in the image of God created he him;

sin has marred the image of God in you. The image has been marred so seriously that there is no hope for you to become like Christ through your own efforts. Only God in His power could correct the terrible consequences brought on by Adam's sin. Christ's death and Resurrection for human sin is the solution to the problem. When you trust in Christ's death and Resurrection, you become a new creation in Christ and can begin the process of Christlike character development. From the day you are saved, you can have victory over the sin nature you were born with as well as over the temptations you will face for the rest of your life. The process will come to completion when you see Christ face-to-face in heaven.

A third reason Christlike character is important is that it's the only way you can reach your goal. What goal is that? The Bible says that our aim should be love—for God and for other people. Jesus said, "Thou shalt love the Lord thy God with all thy heart, and with all thy soul, and with all thy mind. This is the first and great commandment. And the second is like unto it, Thou shalt love thy neighbor as thyself" (Matt. 22:37–39). You will be able to reach this goal only if you have become a new creation in Christ and are becoming more and more like Him in character.

What's the Big Deal About Being Like Christ?

Your character is the combination of all your inner qualities—your personality, the way you think about right and wrong, your likes and dislikes, and your ambitions. All of these factors influence the choices you make. If you're a Christian, you should be like Christ in character. The Bible teaches that God has always wanted people to be Christlike in character. Jesus taught the importance of your character when He said that everything a person says or does is a result of inner qualities. Christlike character is the solution for the problem of sin in your life. When you are born again, your heart (character) is made new by Christ. Once you have that new heart, God will help you become more and more like Christ and less and less sinful.

Do You Remember?

1. Who was Adam designed to resemble? _God_

2. What serious problem is resolved by Christ's death and Resurrection? _the problem of sin_

3. When can you begin developing Christlike character? _when you are saved_

4. When will the process of Christlike character development be complete? _when the believer sees Christ face-to-face in heaven_

5. According to Ephesians 3:14–21, who will strengthen you in the inner man? _the Holy Spirit_

6. According to Ephesians 3:14–21, what will the Holy Spirit help you comprehend? _the love of Christ_

7. On the basis of Ephesians 3:14–21, what makes the development of Christlike character possible for the Christian? _the willingness and power of God_

3

Outline

I. A biblical priority
   A. God's purpose for humans
   B. The basis for all Christian conduct
II. The solution for sin
   A. Regeneration—the beginning
   B. Sanctification—the continuation
III. The goal—love
   A. Doctrine of love
   B. Love for God
   C. Love for others

image to be re-created in man. Christ's death satisfied the wrath of God against sin and provided the way of salvation. When a person places faith in Christ's work, he is born again, and the image of God begins to be restored. This process continues throughout the Christian's life and culminates in heaven when, in an instant, he becomes like Christ (1 John 3:2).

The most critical issue in Christian character development is regeneration. Without it your students cannot develop Christlike character. You may teach them some proverbs for living or practical verities that work for all people. Such common-sense instruction is good and necessary, but it is not enough, and it will not make a student like Christ. The importance of regeneration cannot be over-emphasized. Your efforts in Bible teaching are all but wasted on an unregenerate teen. Frequent and clear presentations of the gospel are appropriate in your Bible class.

The basis for all Christian conduct. The Bible affirms that a person's heart determines his conduct. Solomon said, "Keep thy heart with all diligence; for out of it are the issues of life" (Prov. 4:23). The heart is like a fountain from which flow words and actions. Christ reiterated this idea: "A good man out of the good treasure of the heart bringeth forth good things: and an evil man out of the evil treasure bringeth forth evil things" (Matt. 12:35). If a Christian hopes to please God with his words and actions, he must have a cleansed and well-developed inner person, or character.

It is possible to do and say the right things with the wrong motive. When the attitude is wrong, God rejects the words and actions as hypocritical. This is why Christ so severely criticized the Jewish religious leaders during His public ministry. His actions teach us that the condition of the heart is what really matters. Good words and deeds are to proceed from good character.

male and female created he them" (Gen. 1:27). Man was created in the image of God—like God in character. He was like God in his spirit, the inner person. He had intelligence and feelings like God. He had the ability to choose like God and the ability to commune with and understand his Creator. Man was, in these respects, unlike all the rest of God's creation. The psalmist asks, "What is man, that thou art mindful of him? and the son of man, that thou visitest him? For thou hast made him a little lower than the angels, and hast crowned him with glory and honour. Thou madest him to have dominion over the works of thy hands" (Ps. 8:4–6). God made man superior to all the rest of His handiwork.

But the sequel to this glorious chapter of history is all too familiar. Adam chose to disobey God and plunged into sin. As Paul eloquently stated, "Wherefore . . . by one man sin entered into the world, and death by sin; and so death passed upon all men, for that all have sinned. . . . For . . . by one man's disobedience many were made sinners" (Rom. 5:12, 19). The marring of the image of God in man came by Adam's fatal choice. Human character, intended to reflect the character of God, became a shattered mirror, offering a distorted portrait of the image.

Would God let man remain a tribute to the destructive power of Satan? He certainly owed nothing to man. He had given him all, and man had thrown it away. But the same divine character that man had originally reflected would be the source of salvation. God's grace made a way for His

Since this is the first lesson of the year, you should take some time to go over the plan of salvation. You may have students in your class who do not know Christ. You should also go over some evidences of salvation for those who claim to know Christ but do not manifest it in their words and actions.

II. The Solution for Sin

Regeneration—the beginning. Regeneration, or the new birth, is the beginning of the solution to the problem of sin. Though man is born with a sinful nature, at regeneration God imparts to him a new ruling disposition—a love for God and righteousness. The Lord described this to Nicodemus when He said, "Ye must be born again" (John 3:7). Paul explained regeneration when he wrote, "Not by works of righteousness which we have done, but according to his mercy he saved us, by the washing of regeneration, and renewing of the Holy Ghost; which he shed on us abundantly through Jesus Christ our Saviour" (Titus 3:5–6). Regeneration is a renewal, a change in appetite. "Therefore if any man be in Christ, he is a new creature: old things are passed away; behold, all things are become new" (2 Cor. 5:17).

Sanctification—the continuation. In sanctification the believer more and more ceases sinning and is more and more set apart to God for His glory. Regeneration is the instantaneous event that begins the development of Christlike character. Sanctification is the gradual process that follows. Paul portrayed this process as a transforming work performed by the Spirit of God as the believer meditates on the Word of God (2 Cor. 3:18). He also presented it as clothing yourself with Christ (Gal. 3:27) or with the new man, "which after God is created in righteousness and true holiness" (Eph. 4:24). This putting on of the new man is clearly an internal process: "And [you] have put on the new man, which is renewed in knowledge after the image of him that created him" (Col. 3:10). This new Christlike image contrasts with the older sinful character that manifested itself in wrath, malice, blasphemy, filthy communication, and lying (Col. 3:8–9).

What is this new Christlike image like? Christ is the "image of the invisible God" (Col. 1:15), a perfect representation of God's character. Jesus said, "He that hath seen me hath seen the Father" (John 14:9). To be Christlike in character, then, is to be Godlike in character.

The Romans

The Gospels record events in the first century AD, when Rome ruled a vast empire that included Palestine. In 31 BC Octavian, Julius Caesar's adopted son, had defeated Mark Antony and Cleopatra to become Rome's first emperor. He took the name Augustus ("the exalted one") and brought Rome to its peak through his organizational skills.

It was Caesar Augustus who appointed Herod the Great as governor over Palestine. It was Caesar Augustus who began conducting a census every fourteen years for the purpose of taxation. One of these brought Joseph and Mary to Bethlehem (Luke 2:1). In AD 14 Caesar Augustus died, leaving the empire to Tiberius, who reigned during Christ's earthly ministry and at the time of His death.

This bas-relief shows Roman soldiers carrying off temple utensils after the destruction of Jerusalem in AD 70.

Caesar Augustus was a shrewd politician who brought peace to the Roman Empire and greatly expanded its territory.

4

The Romans were practical. They often allowed conquered countries to rule themselves. They had two simple rules. First, they expected absolute loyalty. Second, they expected all conquered nations to pay taxes to Rome. As long as a subject nation followed these rules, life went on as usual. But if a nation dared to rebel, punishment was swift and violent.

To make sure Roman laws were upheld, Caesar and the Roman senate appointed governors over the regions. The governor worked with local officials to collect taxes and keep the peace. Each governor had a legion (5,400 soldiers) to help him. In Palestine there were two legions, one in Samaria and the other in Caesarea, the

seaport which Herod the Great built to honor Caesar Augustus. Pilate, the governor of Judea, lived in Caesarea.

Rome reserved for itself the privilege of reviewing cases of capital punishment; only a Roman official could consent to having a person executed. This is why Pilate got involved in the Crucifixion of Christ.

Rome allowed the Jews to continue their worship of Jehovah with official approval. Judaism had the status of *religio licita* ("legal religion"). Christianity was not given that title, however, until the fourth century under Emperor Constantine.

Certain qualities make God distinct from man—for example, omniscience, omnipotence, omnipresence, and eternality. Man can never possess these attributes. However, he can possess some of the character traits of God. These traits we call *moral* or *communicable attributes*, since they can be communicated to man. These qualities are many, but they fall into several groups:

a. *Holiness*—separation from sin and dedication to spiritual purposes

b. *Righteousness*—conformity to God's standard

c. *Justice*—fairness in dealing with others

d. *Love*—willingness to sacrifice oneself for the good of others

e. *Benevolence*—kind words and acts

f. *Mercy*—pity and aid given those in desperate spiritual or physical condition

g. *Grace*—unmerited favor and spiritual strength given to the humble

h. *Truth*—honesty and sincerity with God and others

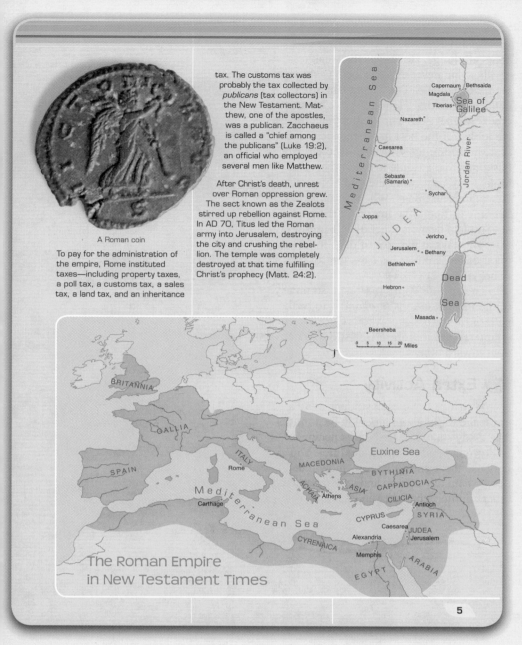

A Roman coin

To pay for the administration of the empire, Rome instituted taxes—including property taxes, a poll tax, a customs tax, a sales tax, a land tax, and an inheritance tax. The customs tax was probably the tax collected by *publicans* (tax collectors) in the New Testament. Matthew, one of the apostles, was a publican. Zacchaeus is called a "chief among the publicans" (Luke 19:2), an official who employed several men like Matthew.

After Christ's death, unrest over Roman oppression grew. The sect known as the Zealots stirred up rebellion against Rome. In AD 70, Titus led the Roman army into Jerusalem, destroying the city and crushing the rebellion. The temple was completely destroyed at that time fulfilling Christ's prophecy (Matt. 24:2).

The Roman Empire in New Testament Times

5

To these broad categories we must add the specifics, which the Christian finds in Scripture. He may see them in a life recorded there, in the words of Christ, in a miracle of an apostle or of the Lord Himself. They may be etched on his heart as he reads about the birth of the Savior or the glorified Christ in Revelation. Embracing virtues and shunning vices work together to mold believers into the image of Christ, i.e., to create in them the character of Christ and the consequent conduct that glorifies Him. This is the process of sanctification, the ultimate solution to the problem of sin in the believer's life.

III. The Goal—Love

The doctrine of love. The way sanctification solves the sin problem is by developing in the believer various traits summarized under the general heading of love. What is biblical love? Two Greek words are translated "love" or "charity" in English: *philia* and *agapē*. *Philia* is a word that describes mutual trust and affection. Such love can exist between two people (Titus 3:15), between the believer and God (John 21:15–17, Peter's responses), between God and the believer (John 16:27), and even between the Father and the Son (John 5:20). *Agapē* includes not only this kind of affection but the additional idea of self-sacrifice as well. The one who shows *agapē* toward another places the interests of the recipient above his own. This involves volition, a deliberate choice by the one who extends it. God loves the world in this sense (John 3:16).

Grasping the subtle differences between these terms is more than an exercise in vocabulary. It is necessary for a proper understanding of the high standard God sets for the believer in his relationship with God and with others. In response to the questioning of an expert in the Old Testament Law, the Lord pinpointed the two greatest commands in the Law. He said, "Thou shalt love the Lord thy God with all thy heart, and with all thy soul, and with all thy mind. This is the first and great commandment. And the second is like unto it, Thou shalt love thy neighbour as thyself. On these two commandments hang all the law and the prophets" (Matt. 22:37–40). *Agapē* for God and for your neighbor is the standard God sets for you. All other standards are subsumed under this one general standard. Without Christlike character, however, there is no possibility of obeying these commands.

Love for God. Jesus said that the believer is to love God with all his heart, soul, mind, and strength. To love God with your strength is to devote your physical energies to His service. Loving Him with your heart, soul, and mind is loving Him with everything in you, all your being. The term *heart* in this commandment refers to the whole of a person's spiritual being. The word *soul* is also general, but at times it means the self-consciousness or self. This encompasses the will. We must subjugate all our choices to love for God. The word *mind* can refer to the human ability to reason and acquire knowledge. Everything a person thinks or learns should contribute to his love for God, either directly or indirectly. The accumulation of these similar terms in this command tells us that we are to love God with every capacity.

This commandment leaves no room for halfhearted devotion to the Lord. This is the standard to which your students are to adhere in their love for God.

Love for others. The second great commandment is to love your neighbor as yourself. We are not commanded to love ourselves. It is something that people (even Christians) do naturally. We appreciate our own admirable qualities of body and spirit. We provide for our own physical and spiritual necessities. Just as a Christian loves himself in these ways, so he should love others. He should appreciate his neighbor's admirable qualities of body and soul. He should seek to help him in times of physical and spiritual need. He should go to the same lengths of sacrifice to help his neighbor as he goes to for himself.

How does love for a neighbor show itself? The most detailed answer is found in the 1 Corinthians 13 description of *agapē*. Because love suffers long, a person who loves is patient with the shortcomings of others. Love is also kind. Love does not envy and is not jealous of the good fortune or accomplishments of others. Love does not vaunt itself, so a loving person does not brag about his accomplishments. That love is not puffed up means that you must have a proper estimate of yourself in order to love your neighbor. An inflated opinion of your own importance will cause you to mistreat others (13:4).

Love does not behave itself unseemly because rudeness and love do not mix. Love does not seek its own means—it is not self-centered. It is not easily provoked and does not lose its temper. It thinks no evil of others and therefore keeps no record of wrongs (13:5).

Love does not rejoice in iniquity, but rejoices in the truth. A Christian who meets the standard of love takes pleasure in the Word of God and shuns sinful thoughts and practices. He knows that following this standard will lead to the glory of God and the benefit of his neighbor (13:6).

A Christian characterized by *agapē* bears all things. He knows the weaknesses of others but never exposes them to ridicule. He protects them. The loving Christian believes all things. He is not naive but trusts others whenever he can. He hopes all things. He looks for the best in others and trusts that shortcomings will be corrected. He has a positive attitude toward others and looks forward to what they will become. He endures all things. When circumstances become difficult, the loving Christian does not run in a desperate act of self-preservation. He stays at his post of duty for the good of those under his care and for the honor of Christ (13:7).

The apostle Paul's masterful summary of the manifestations of *agapē* is to be the pattern for the believer who is Christlike in character and therefore Christlike in conduct toward others.

✳ Extra Activity

Writing: Have each student write a one-page essay about a person he admires. The essay should describe this person's background and character qualities. You may use these essays later to show that people naturally admire and seek to emulate others in their character and actions.

Lesson 2
How to Develop Christlike Character

THEME	Ways to Develop Christlike Character
SCRIPTURE	John 1:1–18
MEMORY WORK	John 1:14, 16

⏱ Approach to the Lesson

Theme: Developing Christlike character is the greatest challenge of the Christian experience. How to accomplish this task is the subject of this lesson.

The process is both human and divine. No Christian will ever develop Christlikeness without cooperating with the Lord. However, human effort is not the only element in the process. Christ must impart His grace to the believer for character transformation to occur. Thus, the outline for this lesson focuses on character-transforming grace.

Rationale: In the previous lesson, you gave your students reasons *why* they should develop Christlike character. Now you are in a position to discuss *how* they can reach this goal. This lesson is fundamentally important to the rest of the book. Here your students can learn a basic method by which to apply the spiritual truths discussed in each lesson.

Background: You will notice that this lesson does not work through a single passage of Scripture verse by verse. This is out of necessity and by design. The subject under discussion is in far too many passages in Scripture and is far too broad in scope to be limited to that approach. Underlying this lesson are more than 150 passages in the New Testament that discuss grace. Like the other two lessons in this first unit, it does not draw primarily from the Gospels, but rather provides a basis to make later examination of the Gospels profitable.

★ The Lesson

I. What Is Grace?

God's goodness to the undeserving. Paul discusses briefly the salvation of some Israelites even though the nation as a whole has rejected Christ (Rom. 11:5). He uses himself as an example of this truth and explains that salvation has nothing to do

with something we deserve, but everything to do with God's grace. No one has ever earned salvation or anything else from God. God has demonstrated His grace in many ways. He provides food for the saved and unsaved alike. He has delayed the punishment of the wicked. He has sent the Spirit of God to convict us of sin. He has preserved His Word for our instruction. The list of God's blessings on us is endless, and we have not earned a single item on the list. Each is a demonstration of God's goodness to the undeserving.

> Your students who have trusted Christ as their Savior have been saved by God's grace. They did not deserve that grace. If they are to be transformed into the image of Christ, this will also be by the grace of Christ, which they do not deserve.

Divine power. Grace is not only an attitude God has, but the power God imparts to people as a result of His attitude. During his ministry Paul suffered from a physical infirmity, from which he asked God three times to deliver him. The Lord's response was to instruct him about grace (2 Cor. 12:7–10). The three terms *grace*, *strength*, and *power* in these verses are synonymous.

> The points where your students feel they are particularly weak spiritually are the Lord's invitation to seek His grace. He alone can change these weaknesses into strengths. He alone can change their character, no matter how seriously lacking, to be Christlike.

Paul concluded that his weaknesses were not actually a problem, whether physical or spiritual, because they provided

Objectives

KNOWLEDGE (concepts students need to grasp)	the biblical definition of the term *grace*
	that sanctification is a process, not a one-time decision
	the means of grace: the Word of God, prayer, and the ministry of other Christians
APPLICATION (principles students should put into practice)	Grace, the undeserved power of God, comes only to those who demonstrate humility.
	Salvation is the beginning and most important step of character transformation.
	Transformation into the image of Christ comes only by the grace of God and the cooperation of the believer.

Outline

I. What is grace?
  A. God's goodness to the undeserving
  B. Divine power
  C. Found in Christ
II. Who receives grace?
  A. The saved
  B. The humble
    1. In submission to God
    2. In submission to others
III. How can I get grace?
  A. The Word of God
  B. Prayer
  C. The ministry of other Christians

him with an opportunity to trust God to impart power to him. Through the avenue of his infirmities, Paul realized he could continually experience the grace of God.

> The believer needs to have an increasingly honest appraisal of himself so that he can call on Christ for the grace he needs. Without honestly appraising himself, the believer will not see himself as who he really is—a sinner who constantly needs grace in order to grow in Christlikeness.

Found in Christ. The transforming grace of God cannot be experienced apart from Christ. The power of God that helps in time of need is available only to the Christian. Grace is not an impersonal force that comes on the believer to help him. It is not some magical power. It is the strong hand of the living Christ, reaching down to shape the misshapen heart, to bind up the broken life, or to strengthen the faltering step. Christ and grace are inseparable. He is the fountain from which grace flows. Christ is "full of grace" and "of his fulness have all we received, and grace for grace" (John 1:14, 16). Every believer has experienced the saving power, i.e., grace, of Christ. It is the will of Christ to add more and more grace—"grace for grace"— to the believer's life. The New Testament repeats this truth frequently. Virtually every one of Paul's epistles begins with a prayer that the recipients will receive the grace of Christ, and most of his epistles end the same way.

> The student text pages for this lesson begin on the next page.

The truth that an inexhaustible supply of grace is ours in Christ should be an encouragement to every believer. Sin and weakness are never necessary. The grace to be strong is always available in Christ. Encourage your students to maintain a close relationship with Christ, Who is the God of all grace.

II. Who Receives Grace?

The saved. By God's goodness and power those who place their faith in Christ are saved from their sins. "For by grace are ye saved through faith; and that not of yourselves: it is the gift of God: not of works, lest any man should boast" (Eph. 2:8–9). This passage presents what we call *saving grace*. Once a person has experienced it, he is able to receive *transforming grace*. This grace will empower him for the work that Christ has for him. As the very next verse goes on to say: "For we are his workmanship, created in Christ Jesus unto good works, which God hath before ordained that we should walk in them" (2:10).

Every believer can receive the grace he needs to serve the Lord acceptably. In fact, he cannot render that service without this grace (Heb. 12:28–29). Once the believer receives this empowering, character-transforming grace, he must be a good steward of it. We should not waste or abuse it (1 Pet. 4:10).

Remind your students that salvation is essential if they are to experience changes by the Lord's grace. It is also necessary if they want to know how they are to use their lives for the Lord and draw on His power in serving Him.

The humble. Proud, self-sufficient Christians are not candidates for character-transforming grace. The basis for the New Testament instruction on this point is Proverbs 3:34: "Surely he scorneth the scorners: but he giveth grace unto the lowly." This general principle applies to both believers and nonbelievers. A proud, self-sufficient man or woman will not see the need of trusting Christ's saving grace. A proud, self-sufficient Christian will not seek Christ's character-transforming grace. Two New Testament passages allude to this statement (James 4:6; 1 Pet. 5:5), each with a slightly different perspective on the importance of humility as a condition for grace.

Help your students understand that ignoring the will of God in order to engage in activities that will bring glory to themselves is pride. In a sense they are say-

Bible Expressions to Understand

the Word—a name for Christ that stresses that He tells us what God is like

the only begotten of the Father—an expression that describes Christ as the Son of God in a sense that is different from all other people

grace—the undeserved gift of Christ's power, which strengthens and transforms the believer's character

The Bible teaches that Jesus Christ is "the image of the invisible God" (Col. 1:15). Jesus is, in character, everything God is. As the passage you read for this lesson says, He is the Word of God. This means that by His character and life Jesus expresses everything you need to know about God. The striking truth of the New Testament is that you, as a believer, are to become the image of Christ (Rom. 8:29). You are to become Christlike and therefore godly in character. How are you going to reach this goal? The Scriptures teach you how.

The first step is salvation. The good news about Jesus Christ is that He died, was buried, and rose again to save you from your sins. If you place your trust in what Christ did for you, God will make you a new person by His grace and through His power (2 Cor. 5:17). Unless you become a new person through Christ's saving grace, you will not want to be Christlike. Having that desire is essential to becoming Christlike. Jesus said, "Blessed are they which do hunger and thirst after righteousness: for they shall be filled" (Matt. 5:6). Only the person who hungers and thirsts after righteousness will be filled and become like Christ. If there is no desire, there will be no transformation. If there is no salvation, there will be no desire.

Once you have been saved, then you can be transformed into the image of Christ by His grace. Christ's grace is the undeserved gift of His transforming power. The apostle Paul wrote, "And he said unto me, My grace is sufficient for thee: for my strength is made perfect in weakness. Most gladly therefore will I rather glory in my infirmities, that the power of Christ may rest upon me" (2 Cor. 12:9). If you look carefully at this verse, you will learn that grace, strength, and power are all the same thing. Jesus Christ is ready to take your weaknesses and turn them into strengths by His grace (power).

Even though the Lord is the one who will transform your character into His image, He wants you to be part of the process. The New Testament presents several channels through which you can receive the transforming grace of Christ. You must use these

This young man wants to receive God's transforming grace. What means is he using to do that?

6

ing that they know what is best for themselves and that they can manage their own lives without God's help. Any believer who takes that approach to life will eventually be chastened.

In submission to God. We show true humility by submitting to the will of God and rejecting the approbation the world offers (James 4:5–7). Sadly, it is natural even for the Christian to have a spirit that wants to be jealous ("lusteth to envy"). There is an inclination in even the most spiritual believer to envy the praise others receive. The believer who resists that temptation and dedicates himself to doing the will of God is a candidate for the transforming and empowering grace of God. The one who proudly and foolishly goes his own way will not receive grace to serve or improve in character. He may receive the glory the world offers, but that's all.

In submission to others. Another way the believer exemplifies true humility is through submission to others. This submissive attitude enables the Christian to receive the grace of Christ (1 Pet. 5:5–7). Every Christian in the will of God finds himself subordinate to other believers. In the church those believers are the mature saints God has chosen to be overseers of the flock. A good Christian has a respectful, obedient attitude toward these leaders. This doesn't mean that he no longer needs to think for himself or be responsible for his own choices, but it does mean that he recognizes the wisdom and maturity of these leaders and considers their advice and instruction carefully. God is ready to grant such a believer grace.

channels if you want to experience character transformation. What are the channels through which Christ's grace will come to you?

One of them is the Word of God. Acts 20:32 says, "And now, brethren, I commend you to God, and to the word of his grace, which is able to build you up, and to give you an inheritance among all them which are sanctified." In this verse the Bible is called the "word of his grace." The "word of grace" builds up the believer and changes him into the image of Christ. This happens by exposure. As you study the Scriptures, you learn more and more about God and the way He thinks. You learn what He expects of you. You learn what He likes and dislikes. If you read with an open mind and a heart that is willing to change, God's words will change the way you think. They will change your character, and you will become more Christlike.

Another channel through which the Lord sends His grace is prayer. Hebrews 4:16 says, "Let us therefore come boldly unto the throne of grace, that we may obtain mercy, and find grace to help in time of need." When you are faced with temptation to sin or with difficult circumstances that you don't think you can stand, the Lord is ready to send you His power to help. He'll change your character so that you can resist the temptation and endure the trial you are facing.

The Lord will also send His grace to you through other Christians—parents, pastors, teachers, mentors, coaches, and others. Having the right friends is also important. If your friends are faithful Christians, then the Lord will use them to impart His power to you. The apostle Paul wrote, "Let no corrupt communication proceed out of your mouth, but that which is good to the use of edifying, that it may minister grace unto the hearers" (Eph. 4:29). Even the words that a good Christian friend says can help you become more conformed to the image of Christ.

Since the Bible is "the word of grace," many churches use programs such as Sunday school and Awana to encourage children and teenagers to study and memorize it.

Can You Get There from Here?

To become Christlike, you must first be saved from your sins and be given a new heart by the grace of Christ. Scripture teaches, "For by grace are ye saved through faith; and that not of yourselves: it is the gift of God" (Eph. 2:8). Once you are saved, then you must continually receive the grace of Christ to become more Christlike. This power of Christ comes through the Word of God, prayer, and the ministry of other Christians.

Christ is the one who has all the power to remake us in His image. The Bible says, "And the Word was made flesh, and dwelt among us, (and we beheld his glory, the glory as of the only begotten of the Father,) full of grace and truth. . . . And of his fulness have all we received, and grace for grace" (John 1:14, 16). Christ has saved us by His grace. He will transform us into His image by His grace, which He is willing to give us if we are willing to receive it.

expects of them and what He likes and dislikes. If they read with open minds and willing spirits, God will change the way they think. And if the way Christians think changes, the way they talk and act will change also.

Reading the Word of God is not an end in itself. The purpose behind exposure to the Word is a changed life, serving and glorifying God.

A promise is connected with this process. God will grant to the believer "an inheritance among all them which are sanctified." There is both a present and a future dimension to this inheritance; the believer will receive blessings in this life and in the life to come. These blessings are available to all the sanctified—those who have trusted Christ as Savior and have continued to be more and more set apart from sin and unto God for His service and glory.

Prayer. Prayer is also a way to receive grace (Heb. 4:15–16). Since Jesus experienced the same temptations believers face, He is the one to go to for help in dealing with them. He is sympathetic to His followers and ready to provide help when we need it. Christ invites the believer to come to the throne of grace. Kneeling at this throne, the Christian can request the power or grace he needs with confidence that the strengthening from the Lord will perfectly meet his need.

Seeking help in times of spiritual need is one of several important facets of prayer. Strength is available to your students through prayer. This should be a strong motivation for them to maintain a regular prayer time.

The ministry of other Christians. The Lord intends for Christians to build one another up in the Faith. We are to be sources of grace or strength for our fellow believers. This is why the Scriptures say, "Let no corrupt communication proceed out of your mouth, but that which is good to the use of edifying [building up], that it may minister grace unto the hearers" (Eph. 4:29). The Lord imparts grace to every believer for ministry to other Christians. The Christian is to be a good steward of this grace (1 Pet. 4:10–11).

Your students are to be a source of grace for their friends. Their friends should be the same for them. If they choose the wrong friends (those who do not know and love the Lord), they will miss out on the grace they need to de-

Your students must have a submissive attitude toward all their spiritual authorities. Besides their parents, this includes their pastor, youth pastor, and other leaders at their church. It also includes their teachers and principal.

Believers should be submissive not only to leaders in the church but also to one another, according to Peter. If the body of Christ is to work together in harmony, each saint must humbly recognize the value of every other. He must also recognize his own limitations.

Warn your students that if they think they are better than their friends and treat them inconsiderately, they cannot receive the grace that they need from the Lord.

III. How Can I Get Grace?

Only the Lord can transform a person into His likeness. That does not mean, however, that the believer is not responsible for his progress in Christlikeness (2 Pet. 1:5). The Christian must take the initiative to avail himself of the channels through which grace comes.

The Word of God. The written revelation of God is a primary means of acquiring grace. Paul described the Bible as literally the "word of grace" (Acts 20:32). The Word of God is able to build up the believer and change him into the image of Christ (2 Cor. 3:18). This happens by exposure to the Word. As Christians study the Scriptures, they learn more and more about God and the way He thinks. They learn what God

velop and be strong believers. The influence of their friends will be negative. Paul wrote, "Be not deceived: evil communications corrupt good manners" (1 Cor. 15:33). This is a plain statement that wrong friends will have a bad effect on the life of a Christian. No student can rightly assert that he is not becoming like the company he keeps. He will become like his companions if the exposure is significant.

As the Christian takes responsibility to use these means of grace, the Spirit applies the grace to the inner person. The result is spiritual strengthening. Paul's prayer for believers was that Christ's Spirit would strengthen them "in the inner man" (Eph. 3:16). To that prayer he added the remarkable benediction: "Now unto him that is able to do exceeding abundantly above all that we ask or think, according to the power that worketh in us, unto him be glory in the church by Christ Jesus throughout all ages, world without end. Amen" (Eph. 3:20–21). What can the believer expect as he uses the means of grace and relies on the Spirit of Christ? He will be transformed into the image of Christ beyond his greatest expectations.

✳ Extra Activity

Case study: Mark attended a Christian school from the time he was in kindergarten. He was always a good student, and no one could outplay him on the soccer field. In his church and school he had learned the importance of good friends, prayer, Bible reading, and a life honoring the Lord. Even though he was saved and worked hard at all these things, he was a weak Christian. He regularly failed the Lord. Being competitive by nature, he even worked hard to be the best Christian in his senior class, but he failed miserably.

Which of the following factors is most likely the reason Mark has experienced difficulty in his Christian life?

a. His environment

b. His friends

c. His pride

d. His failure to pray

e. His failure to read the Bible

f. Poor instruction from his Bible teachers and pastor

The best answer is c.

Do You Remember?

1. What is the first step in the process of becoming Christlike? _salvation_

2. What does a person become at salvation? _a child of God_

3. What will a child of God desire? _righteousness; to become Christlike_

4. What does the term *grace* mean? _undeserved, transforming power of Christ_

5. Who can give all the grace any person needs? _God through Christ_

6. How does the Bible serve as a source of Christ's transforming grace? _____
   It reveals the will of God and changes the way we think.

7. Why is having the right friends important to Christlike character development? _____
   Christ's transforming grace can come through the ministry of Christian friends.

8. How is prayer an important part of Christlike character development? _____
   Prayer is a channel through which the Christian can receive Christ's grace.

9. What will happen to a Christian who does not pray, read his Bible, or have friendships with other good Christians? _____
   He won't become Christlike.

8

Read: Luke 1:1–4;
John 20:30–31; 21:25

Memorize: 1 Timothy 3:16

Bible Expressions to Understand

perfect understanding—complete or full understanding
most excellent—an address of honor often given to government officials in the first century
signs—miracles that say something about the nature of Christ as God
Christ—("anointed one") the spiritual deliverer prophesied in the Old Testament

The Lord has given us the Bible so that we can understand the way He thinks. The Bible is like a yardstick. A yardstick measures the length of things. If you want to know how long something is, you can use a yardstick as an authoritative guide to find out. Without a yardstick or some other tool for measuring, you would have to guess if you needed the measurements of something. The Bible is a measure too, but the Bible measures morals and truth. It is the authoritative guide we rely on to find out what's true and false, right and wrong. Without the Bible, we would have nothing but human opinions about right and wrong, but in the Bible we have God's always-right testimony about truth.

As you learned in the previous lesson, the Bible is central to Christlike character development. It tells you God's thoughts about what your character should be like. And since His thoughts are the thoughts that are always right, you must let the Bible shape your character. The lessons in this book are based on the four Gospels: Matthew, Mark, Luke, and John. These first four books of the New Testament are a good place to begin the study of Christlike character development.

The Gospels	Present the person and the work of Christ
Book of Acts	Proclaims the person and the work of Christ
The Epistles	Explain the person and the work of Christ
Revelation	Foresees the future work of Christ

What are some ways Scripture is like a ruler or yardstick?

The Gospels are the foundation of what follows in the rest of the New Testament. Together they're a presentation of the words and the works of Jesus Christ. After studying them, you will be ready to appreciate the proclamation of Christ in the next book: the Acts of the Apostles. You can then move on to the explanation of the words and the works of Christ, which are found in the twenty-one epistles. The New Testament then closes with Revelation. This book, written by the apostle John, presents the completion of Christ's work in time and the continuation of His work in eternity.

9

Objectives

KNOWLEDGE (concepts students need to grasp)	the structure of the New Testament
	the emphasis of the Gospels on salvation
	the theme of each Gospel
APPLICATION (principles students should put into practice)	We must submit to Christ the King.
	We must obey like Christ the Servant.
	We must show compassion on sinners as Christ, the Perfect Man, did.
	We must trust in Christ, the Divine Son.
	We must study the Gospels to develop Christlikeness.

ically, they are a selective record of the life of the incarnate God, Jesus Christ. No fuller record of His life exists. They give special emphasis to His death, burial, and Resurrection as the means of our salvation. They also provide an opportunity to scrutinize the life of a Perfect Man, "leaving us an example, that ye should follow his steps" (1 Peter 2:21).

Some important teaching aids, including reproducible copies of the charts from pages 9 and 10 of the student text, are found on the CD accompanying this book.

 The Lesson

I. The Gospels and the New Testament

The Gospels are the first of the four main divisions of the New Testament. Each later division builds on the preceding one(s). This means that the New Testament displays a design that is beyond the ability of any human author to produce. This design is a part of what theologians call the *teleological argument* for the existence of God. This argument asserts that the design of creation implies the existence of a Designer-Creator. Considering that the twenty-seven books of the New Testament were written by several authors over about forty years, the design of the document as a whole is remarkable. Thus the teleological argument testifies also to the inspiration of Scripture, a doctrine the writers themselves forcefully asserted. How do the Gospels fit into this design?

The Gospels—presentation. The Gospels present the person and work of Christ.

Lesson 3
Where Do I Start?

THEME	Learning Christlikeness from the Gospels
SCRIPTURE	Luke 1:1–4; John 20:30–31; 21:25
MEMORY WORK	1 Timothy 3:16

 Approach to the Lesson

Theme: Understanding the Gospels is foundational to the development of Christlikeness. Their purpose, structure, and position in the New Testament are all important. This lesson ties the purpose of this textbook, developing Christlikeness, to its content, the Gospels. It shows why we must begin the journey toward God's image by learning about Christ in the Gospels.

Rationale: You have addressed the *why* and the *how* of the development of Christlikeness in the first two lessons. This last orientation lesson introduces the books of the New Testament from which the rest of the lessons are drawn. This is your opportunity to pique your students' interest in the Gospels as a whole.

This lesson is much longer than the others in this book. It is intended to provide material—facts and figures from which you can select. Do not feel obligated to teach everything here.

Background: The Gospels are a unique literary genre from the first century. They contain "good news" about Christ. Specif-

Outline

They are the most complete record of His life. However, the Gospel accounts are selective. They do not include everything Jesus said and did (John 21:25). God in His wisdom has given us a selective record. Without an inspired partial record, the believer would be lost in a mass of eternally significant truth that no mastermind could sort through.

The Gospels provide an overview and general chronology of the life of our Lord. They identify the following stages of Christ's life:

1. Birth and childhood
2. Preparation (including baptism and temptation)
3. Early Judean ministry
4. Samaritan ministry
5. Galilean ministry
6. Late Judean ministry
7. Perean ministry
8. Passion week
9. Resurrection and post-Resurrection ministry

However, the Gospels subordinate chronology to a greater purpose of communicating eternal truth about Christ and His will. Only when the chronology of Christ's life contributes to this greater goal does it seem important to the authors.

The variety of material in the Gospels makes them a source of inspiration and instruction. They record thirty-five specific miracles of Christ. These miracles were usually acts of compassion and also proved that Jesus was God. Often Jesus intended to give instruction through them. In addition, the writers include parables, in which Christ used scenes from everyday life to teach spiritual truth. The Gospels also record longer sermons of Christ, such as the

As you can see, the New Testament has an overall structure, and the Gospels are an important part of it. If you don't know the contents of the Gospels, it's difficult to understand why the early Christians spread the truth about Christ around the world as recorded in the book of Acts. Again, if you don't know about the words and works of Christ in the Gospels, what's explained in the Epistles doesn't make much sense. And the power and majesty of Christ in Revelation can be fully grasped only against the backdrop of our Lord's ministry and suffering.

The Gospels focus on the good news of salvation. Matthew, Mark, Luke, and John don't give us a

Gospel	Theme	Written To
Matthew	The Promised King	The Jew
Mark	The Obedient Servant	The Roman
Luke	The Perfect Man	The Greek
John	The Divine Son	The World

day-by-day discussion of the life of Jesus. Their works aren't mere biographies. Each author carefully chose what to include. No single Gospel tells us everything Jesus did. In fact, all the Gospels together don't present everything Jesus said and did. We don't learn, for example, anything about the life of Christ between the time He was twelve (Luke 2:42) and the time He began His public ministry at age thirty (Luke 3:23).

The Gospels concentrate almost exclusively on the three-and-a-half-year period of His public ministry which ended at His ascension. About one-third of the material in the Gospels deals with the last week of Christ's life, focusing on His death, burial,

and Resurrection. Christ accomplished our salvation through these events. Salvation is where Christlike character development begins. Since that's the emphasis of the Gospels, they're a good place to begin Christlike character development.

In addition, the Gospels are a good source for the study of character development because they present many views of Christ. Jesus is your example and the one in Whom you are to believe. Matthew presents Christ as the Promised King, to Whom you must submit. Mark presents Him as the Obedient Servant, Whose example you should follow. Luke stresses that Christ was the Perfect Man, Who was concerned for sinners. You ought to have the same concern for others who aren't Christians. John proves that Jesus is the Divine Son, in Whom you must trust.

Each author carefully selects the sermons, parables, miracles, and incidents in Christ's life to create his special emphasis. From each detail in each Gospel, you can learn something about what you ought to be as a follower of Christ.

Where Does the Journey Begin?

Once you have decided to be more Christlike, you should start by studying the Gospels. These four books are not merely biographies of Jesus Christ. They lay the foundation for the rest of the New Testament. The book of Acts tells about the spreading of the message of the Gospels to the world. The Epistles explain that message. And the book of Revelation looks ahead to the day when Christ will rule as King.

To understand the New Testament, then, you need to understand the Gospels. Besides that, they're a good place to start because they tell us directly about Christ: what He is like, what He wants, and how He works. If you want to be more like Him, you can find the pattern in the Gospels.

Sermon on the Mount and the Olivet Discourse, as well as some of Christ's shorter discourses. Woven into the fabric of this material is the historical and cultural setting. The Gospels record the names of both the famous and the obscure. They mention actual places and events substantiated by archaeological finds. These Gospels tell us about a person who really lived, taught, died, and rose again. The Gospels present an impressive and inspired introduction to the person and work of Christ.

Acts—proclamation. The book of Acts shows the early proclamation of Christ by the words and actions of His followers. It describes the actions of the proclaimers as a continuation of the works of Christ through them. After Peter preached at Pentecost, "the Lord added to the church daily

such as should be saved" (2:47). The Lord was working through the apostles and the other believers. Another example is Peter's healing of Aeneas (9:34).

A major emphasis of Acts is the coming of the Holy Spirit at Pentecost, fifty days after Passover, to indwell and empower believers. This was a fulfillment of Christ's promise in the Gospels (John 7:38–39; 14:16–17). Plainly, without an understanding of the Gospels, a reader will miss the significance of much that is recorded in the book of Acts.

The eight apostolic sermons recorded in Acts center on the Christ of the Gospels. They encourage belief in Christ because of His miracles. They argue that a proper response to the good news of Christ is repentance and faith in Him. The major

Do You Remember?

1. How are the Gospels the foundation of the rest of the New Testament? _____
   They are a presentation of Christ's words and works.

2. What does the book of Acts present concerning the words and works of Christ found in the Gospels? *It presents the proclamation of them by the apostles and other first-century Christians.*

3. What do the Epistles in the New Testament present about the life of Christ found in the Gospels? *They explain the meaning of His life for the salvation and spiritual progress of believers.*

4. What does the book of Revelation present about the Christ of the Gospels? _____
   His power and majesty at the end of time and in eternity; the completion of His work on earth and the continuation of His work in eternity

5. What is the major emphasis of the Gospels? _____
   They emphasize Christ's work of salvation through His death, burial, and Resurrection.

6. How much material of the Gospels concentrates on the last week of Christ's life? _____
   about one-third

7. What is the special role of Christ as Matthew describes Him? *Promised King*

8. What is the special role of Christ as Mark presents Him? *Obedient Servant*

9. How is Christ presented by Luke? *Perfect Man*

10. How is Christ portrayed by John? *Divine Son*

11

---

events underlying the gospel, according to these sermons, are the death, Resurrection, and exaltation of Christ. These preachers proclaimed Christ as the promised Messiah, the Holy and Just One, the Lord of All, and the Author of Life—God Himself. None of this sermonic material is clear and convincing without a knowledge of the Gospels. Acts clearly builds on this foundation.

The Epistles—explanation. The New Testament contains twenty-one epistles, thirteen written by Paul and eight written by others, assuming non-Pauline authorship of Hebrews. These letters give a detailed interpretation of the teachings and actions of Christ found in the Gospels. They develop a complete doctrinal system and tell how to live in light of Christ's incarnation, atonement, and Resurrection.

Paul's epistles fall into four groups:

1. *Doctrinal epistles*—Romans, 1 and 2 Corinthians, and Galatians (with the exception of Galatians, all written at the height of his missionary career)

2. *Prison epistles*—Ephesians, Philippians, Colossians, and Philemon (all written during his first Roman imprisonment)

3. *Prophetic epistles*—1 and 2 Thessalonians (both written to answer questions about future events)

4. *Pastoral epistles*—1 and 2 Timothy and Titus (written to two of Paul's protégés)

Each epistle develops a different dimension of the teachings and life of Christ, in either a theoretical or a practical way.

Romans gives a detailed development of the doctrine of salvation through Christ. In 1 Corinthians Paul confronts problems that arise in the church and helps Christians see how to live a life that is consistent with faith in Christ. Second Corinthians presents the life and practice of the minister of Christ. Galatians shows that salvation and growth in Christ are not by the law, but through the power of the Holy Spirit made available by the grace of Christ.

The prison epistles also build on this foundation. Ephesians explains God's overarching purpose for the church's existence and His gracious provisions for and expectations of it. Philippians portrays both Christ and His followers as examples of servanthood and teaches that believers are responsible to follow their example. Colossians shows that Christ is the Preeminent One in the creation and the church and thus no believer should expect or seek for any blessing unrelated to Him. Philemon encourages one brother in Christ to forgive another. All these ideas originate primarily in the Gospels.

The prophetic epistles both discuss the Second Coming of Christ. First Thessalonians focuses the Christian's responsibility in light of the coming Rapture. Second Thessalonians explains the events that precede the Day of the Lord. Christ mentioned both these events in the Gospels, and these epistles give a fuller exposition of them.

The pastoral epistles offer instruction to shepherds of Christ's flock. First Timothy offers pastoral instruction and warns against false teachers. Second Timothy exhorts pastors to continue in the Faith. Titus gives pastoral instruction and exhorts believers to do good works. Men receiving responsibility to oversee the body of Christ is not a new idea; Christ taught it in the Gospels.

The other eight New Testament epistles complement the teachings and life of Christ presented in the Gospels. The epistle to the Hebrews was written to convince Jews that the person and work of Christ were the fulfillment of the ceremonial worship of the Old Testament. Only through Christ could they know God and live for Him. James develops the truth, often presented by Christ, that a man proves his faith by his works. Jesus warned that believers would suffer persecution, and 1 Peter follows up that instruction by consoling suffering saints. In the Sermon on the Mount, Jesus warned about false teachers; 2 Peter, 2 John, and Jude elaborate on that theme.

John's first epistle explains the evidences of eternal life in all believers' lives, so that all professing believers may examine their lives for proof of the Spirit's working. Once Jesus instructed John and James about the problem of desiring preeminence among believers; years later the same John wrote 3 John to deal with the problem of a Christian named Diotrephes, who loved to have preeminence over others. Jude, a half-brother of Jesus, wrote a short epistle exhorting Christians to contend for the Faith, which centers on the person and work of Christ.

All these epistles are clearly founded on the record of the Gospels. A careful examination of the Gospels is basic to an appreciation of this array of instructive material.

Revelation—consummation. The book of Revelation gives the consummation of history as "the kingdoms of this world are become the kingdoms of our Lord, and of his Christ" (Rev. 11:15). Christ reclaims the earth from all those who resist His will. The opening chapter of Revelation presents the vision of John, the son of Zebedee, one of Christ's disciples, imprisoned on the island of Patmos for his faith in Christ. Jesus appeared to him in glorified form and commanded him to write the book. Chapters 2 and 3 are letters from the Lord to seven churches in Asia Minor. John describes Him as being in the midst of the churches and caring for their pastors. None of this would have been possible had it not been for the Resurrection of Christ as recorded in the Gospels. Chapters 4–19 present Christ as the Judge, administering justice to a debauched world gone mad in wickedness. His right to judge is based on His Creation of the world and the Redemption He brought to human beings, as recorded in the Gospels. Chapters 20–22 describe the millennial reign of Christ and His eternal reign in the New Jerusalem. Christ prophesied His coming kingdom in the Gospels. Acts records the proclamation of that kingdom. The epistles teach how to live as a member of that kingdom now. Revelation shows the magnificent glorified Christ conquering His enemies and establishing that kingdom eternally on earth. Twenty-five different titles are ascribed to the Lord in Revelation. The dominant one is "the Lamb," which occurs twenty-seven times. This reminds the Christian of John the Baptist's statement, "Behold the Lamb of God, which taketh away the sin of the world" (John 1:29). Full appreciation of the Revelation is possible only against the backdrop of the Gospels.

II. The Emphasis of the Gospels

Purpose—not biographical. The Gospels are not biographies in the strict sense. A biographer writes to reveal as much of his subject as he can. The Gospel writers, on the other hand, wrote not to reveal everything about Christ, but to prove a point about Him (John 20:31; 21:25).

Events preceding Christ's birth, the birth itself, and events immediately following appear in Matthew 1–2 and Luke 1–2. A brief presentation of a single incident from Christ's youth appears at the end of Luke 2. The Gospels give no record of the specific events of the Lord's life from that point until He began His public ministry when He was about thirty years old (Luke 3:23). His life during this period is described only generally by Luke, who states, "And Jesus increased in wisdom and stature, and in favour with God and man" (2:52). The Gospels are arguments rather than biographies.

Theme—Christ's earthly ministry. Each of the Gospels becomes more detailed as the end of Christ's life draws near. Matthew 1–18 (64% of the book) presents all but the last six months of Christ's life. Thus over one-third of the book focuses on those last six months. Mark follows a similar pattern. Chapters 11–16 (37%) present the last six months. Luke's attention to this period is even more intense (chapters 11–24, or 58%). John devotes chapters 10–21 (57%) to the subject.

Focus—passion week. A surprising feature of the Gospels is the focus they have on just one week in Christ's life. Whatever happened during that week must be highly significant. The week climaxes with the saving death of the God-man. No event in human history supersedes this one.

Matthew devotes 25% to the last week of Christ's life (chapters 21–27). Mark discusses it in chapters 11–15 (31%). Luke gives it over 21% (chapters 19–23). John emphasizes this week more than the others; he spends chapters 12–19 (38%) presenting it. Furthermore, chapters 13–19 present the events of a single day during that final week.

Overall, the Gospel writers intended to focus on the good news of Christ's perfect life and atoning death. The Gospels made no attempt to be comprehensive biographies. They are carefully composed, selective records of the greatest life and death of all time.

III. Unique Portraits of Christ

The Gospels overlap; many times they repeat the same teachings and incidents. But each Gospel also has unique information. It is this unique material and its arrangement that give each Gospel a distinctive emphasis.

The Promised King in Matthew. Matthew presents Christ as the Promised King, to whom the believer is to submit. Israel was anticipating the appearance of the Anointed One of God, as foretold in the Old Testament. Matthew was a Jew writing to convince his countrymen that Christ was the King they were looking for. Several things in the Gospel make this clear.

Matthew begins with a genealogy that follows the standard rabbinic format of three sets of fourteen names. Here Matthew establishes Christ's racial and legal right to kingship by identifying Him as a descendant of Abraham and David. Matthew calls Jesus the son of David eight times in the book.

This Gospel repeatedly presents the concept of the King and His kingdom. This contrasts with the emphases of the other Gospels. Thirty-three times the phrase *kingdom of heaven* appears; four times the phrase *kingdom of God* appears. When John the Baptist preached, "Repent ye: for the kingdom of heaven is at hand" (3:2), he was exhorting his listeners to prepare spiritually for the appearance of the Promised King. Jesus also preached the same message of Himself (4:17).

Matthew's Gospel is full of Old Testament references. Including forty Messianic promises, the Old Testament allusions and citations in this book number about 130 and are drawn from twenty-five of the thirty-nine books of the Old Testament.

In His teaching as recounted by Matthew, the Lord gave great emphasis to the importance of coming under His rule as King. He stated, "But seek ye first the kingdom of God, and his righteousness; and all these things shall be added unto you" (6:33). Christ claimed His right to demand this allegiance. Matthew ended his Gospel with the Lord's claim to absolute authority over all things: "All power is given unto me in heaven and in earth" (28:18). Because of this authority, everyone ought to submit to Christ the King.

The Obedient Servant in Mark. An examination of Mark's Gospel reveals support for the idea that he presents Christ as the Obedient Servant, whose example the believer should follow. Of the population of nearly 100 million in the Roman Empire, about 60 million were slaves. Church history suggests that Mark wrote his Gospel as a record of the preaching and teaching of Peter while they were both in Rome. Peter wrote, "The church that is at Babylon, elected together with you, saluteth you; and so doth Marcus my son" (1 Pet. 5:13). This is likely a cryptic reference to the church at Rome. (John uses similar symbolism in Revelation 17:5, 9.) Mark's portrait of Christ as a servant would be highly appropriate and instructive to a culture so familiar with servitude and so misled about greatness.

Mark used the Greek terms translated "straightway," "forthwith," and "immediately" forty-two times referring to Christ and His ministry. This gives special emphasis to His incessant activity as He ministered to others. The book contains frequent allusions to the Servant of the Lord passages in Isaiah 42 and 53, referring to Christ. This contrasts with the infrequency of Mark's allusions to other Old Testament books. Also conspicuous is the absence of any birth and infancy account. The birth and infancy of a servant is not significant. Mark also stresses Christ's teaching on servanthood (9:33–37; 10:35–45). These observations lend weight to the suggested theme.

The Perfect Man in Luke. Luke gives considerable emphasis to the humanity of Jesus, the Perfect Man, concerned for sinners. He gives the fullest account of the birth and infancy of Christ. His genealogy goes back to Adam, the head of the human race, rather than to Abraham, the head of the chosen race. Luke often shows Jesus in prayer, a distinctly human means of fellowship with God. Seven of the nine times Luke pictures Christ in prayer do not appear in the other Gospels.

Christ's compassion for men as Luke records it seems to cross all boundaries. Twenty of the thirty-five recorded miracles of Christ appear in this Gospel. Luke mentions the Greek term for *woman* or *wife* forty-three times, an emphasis not typical of other first-century literature. Thirteen women are mentioned that appear nowhere else in the Gospels. Only Luke tells of Christ sending the seventy disciples into all Israel, evidence of His concern for all people. Three times Jesus refers to Samaritans favorably. Christ's wide concern and open compassion is a strong focus of this Gospel.

Our Lord's great concern for the lost appears nowhere more clearly than in Luke 15. Here He gives a trilogy of parables, all presenting the plight of someone lost in sin and the responsibility of the Christian to recover him. This chapter reflects the concern voiced by Christ throughout the Gospel. (See Lesson 51.) Luke's record calls people *sinners* sixteen times, in contrast to fourteen times in all the other Gospels combined. It is the Perfect Man who will redeem sinful humans from their sin (1:68–69; 2:38; 24:21).

The Divine Son in John. John stands alone as the Gospel writer who clearly states his intent. "These are written, that ye might believe that Jesus is the Christ, the Son of God; and that believing ye might have life through his name" (20:31). John recorded the "signs" or miracles that prove the deity of Christ. He recorded the turning of the water to wine (2:1–11), the healing of the nobleman's son (4:46–54), the healing of the impotent man (5:1–14), the feeding of the multitudes (6:1–14), the bringing of the boat to land (6:16–21), the healing of the man born blind (9:1–7), and the raising of Lazarus (11:1–44). In all, he presents seven miracles that communicate the divine nature of Christ.

These signs validate Christ's descriptions of Himself recorded in this Gospel. He called Himself the bread of life (6:48); the light of the world (9:5); the door (10:9); the good shepherd (10:11); the resurrection and the life (11:25); the way, the truth, and the life (14:6); and the vine (15:5). What most incensed the Jewish leaders was His self-description in John 8:58—"Verily, verily, I say unto you, Before Abraham was, I am." In this statement Jesus asserted that He is the Jehovah (Hebrew *YHWH*) of the Old Testament. The evidence in this Gospel supports this assertion.

✳ Extra Activity

Quiz: After presenting the lesson, ask the following "number" questions.

1. Which Gospel uses the phrase "kingdom of God" or "kingdom of heaven" thirty-seven times?
   Matthew

2. Which Gospel presents seven names that Jesus used to describe Himself?
   John

3. What is the estimated number of Old Testament quotations and allusions in Matthew's Gospel?
   130

4. Which Gospel presents Samaritans favorably three times?
   Luke

5. How many times is Christ described in the Gospel of Mark as actively serving?
   forty-two

6. Which Gospel mentions women over forty times?
   Luke

7. Which Gospel contains forty Messianic prophecies?
   Matthew

8. Which Gospel describes humans as sinners more than all the others combined?
   Luke (sixteen times)

9. How many missionaries did Jesus send out, according to Luke 10?
   seventy

10. Which Gospel presents seven miraculous signs?
    John

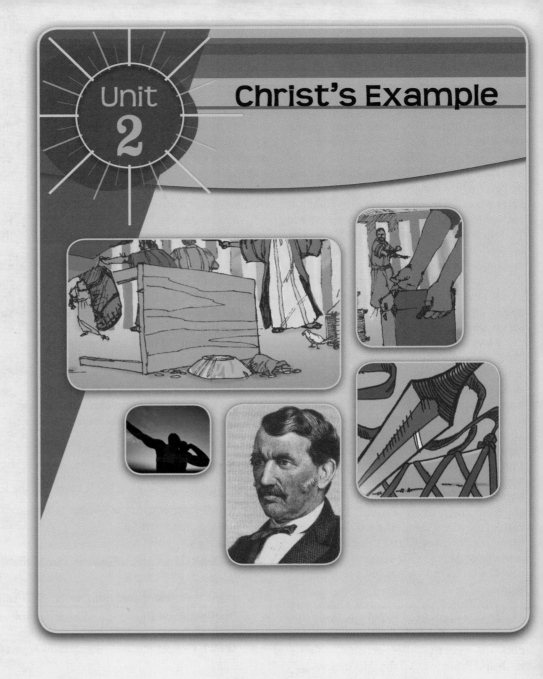

Unit 2

Christ's Example

Jesus Christ became a man to accomplish our salvation through His death and Resurrection. He also lived as a man to set an example for believers to follow. He served His heavenly Father by serving others. The life of our Lord is the answer to the question "How would a perfect man live in relation to God and others?" Jesus taught about qualities you should possess to live that exemplary life. He also demonstrated those qualities. Remember the words of Peter as you read the lessons that follow: "Christ also suffered for us, leaving us an example, that ye should follow his steps" (1 Pet. 2:21).

Christ's Example

The purpose of this unit is to introduce your students to four major qualities of Christ that they should emulate. These lessons will help them see how to study the Gospels in a way that will allow them to formulate goals for improving their character. Christ must first be our Savior; then He becomes our example of how to properly related to God and to other people.

Each lesson has been organized around a different quality of Jesus Christ. The discussion of the meekness of Christ centers on three incidents in the life of Christ. The lesson on zeal is drawn from Christ's first cleansing of the temple. Christ's compassion is shown through three different events recorded in the Gospels. The treatment of Christ's holiness is a topical investigation of how Jesus demonstrated His holiness throughout His life.

This unit includes two special features in the student text.

(1) A map is provided to help your students get an idea of the area where Christ lived (page TE33).

(2) The other feature is an essay focusing on the religious and political leaders of first-century Judaism (pages TE34–35).

Lesson 4
Christ's Meekness

Theme	Meekness
Scripture	Matthew 26:30–46; Luke 2:41–52; John 13:1–17
Memory Work	Matthew 5:5

 ## Approach to the Lesson

Theme: Meekness is gentle submission to God and others. It is not the result of weakness or inferiority; a meek person may be superior to others in power and ability and yet submit to their authority, recognizing God's overruling control. Because of his confidence in God, the meek person does not retaliate for wrongs. He rests in the confidence of God's ability to redress those wrongs. Furthermore, someone who is meek understands that at times God can use even the sins of others to work some spiritual advantage in his life. A meek individual does not ask "Why?" in frustration when authorities request things of him that he does not understand. He calmly obeys, trusting God to work out the situation for His glory.

No one was ever meeker than the Lord Jesus Christ. He was a pattern of gentle consideration and submission from His childhood to the day of His ascension. We should all be meek like the Master.

Rationale: Most teens respond to the driving force in their lives, peer pressure, by trying to impress others in one way or another. You should challenge them to turn their attention outward. If Christ Himself was meek, we should be as well.

Objectives

Knowledge (concepts students need to grasp)	the symbolic meaning of Christ's washing of the disciples' feet
	the purpose of Christ's sweating great drops of blood in the Garden of Gethsemane
Application (principles students should put into practice)	We should submit to our authorities as Christ did.
	We should be meek even though we may excel in sports, academics, or popularity.
	We should show our meekness toward God by obeying His commands.

Bible Expressions to Understand

Gethsemane—("oil press") a garden near Jerusalem where olive trees grew
cup—a symbolic reference to sufferings that Christ would experience in bearing the sins of all mankind
the feast—the Passover
doctors—specialists in the interpretation of Scripture

Some people are born, grow up, and live all their lives in a single small community. This wasn't God's will for a man named David Livingstone. Livingstone was born in Blantyre, Scotland, in 1813. He went to school only until he was ten and then worked long hours in a mill to help support his family. However, he always kept a book nearby so he could read to increase his knowledge while he worked.

 Of his call to mission work, David Livingstone wrote, "In the glow of love which Christianity inspires I soon resolved to devote my life to the alleviation of human misery."

14

When he was seventeen, Livingstone trusted Christ as his Savior and dedicated himself to spreading the gospel in other countries. After attending college to prepare for the ministry and getting medical training, Livingstone arrived in Africa in 1841. During the following three decades, he traveled thirty thousand miles through unexplored and unevangelized territory. During his life he wrote books and poems. He was a scientist, physician, geographer, and specialist in languages. Most important, he was a Christian and a missionary. He had a call from God to reach the unsaved in Africa. This he did with great success. What was the secret of that success?

Perhaps one incident from his early missionary life gives us a glimpse of what made him successful. Not long after Dr. Livingstone arrived in Africa, he joined several other missionaries working there. His natural leadership abilities and Christian character made him a favorite with the missionaries—with one exception. The head of the mission station became jealous of Livingstone and began to slander him and question his motives. Livingstone had just built a lovely home at the mission station, which took a great deal of work and money. Rather than cause further problems and damage the work of Christ, Livingstone left the mission station for another area, leaving his new home behind. He never slandered the other man. Many years later, that man realized his wrong and admitted it to Livingstone, who forgave him without hesitation.

David Livingstone was a meek man. He accepted Christ's authority over his life. He knew how to be submissive toward others for the glory of Christ

Background: The three incidents treated in this lesson are unrelated in terms of time and place. The visit in the temple occurred when the Lord was only twelve years old (Luke 2:41–52). The washing of the disciples' feet (John 13:1–17) and the prayer in the Garden of Gethsemane (Matt. 26:36–46; Mark 14:32–42; Luke 22:39–46; John 18:1) occurred the night before His Crucifixion.

These three occasions are closely related, however, in the spirit of meekness that Christ demonstrated in each case. They are even more significant in that they occur early in Jesus's earthly life as well as near the end of it. Meekness characterized Christ's life throughout His earthly sojourn. These occasions are also significant since they demonstrate three different human relationships.

★ The Lesson

I. Meekness Toward Authority (Luke 2:41–52)

Christ's visit to the temple at age twelve is the only incident from His adolescence that Scripture records. This experience gives a succinct lesson about the proper relationship of a teenager to his parents. Of course, there are details about our Lord's conduct and character given in the account that are unique to Him as the God-man. Therefore, not all that He did can or should be duplicated in the life of the average teenager; however, in principle, Jesus set a pattern for every young person.

Meekness and independence (2:41–47). Although God had commanded Israelite males to attend all three major religious

even when others were wrong. He was gentle and considerate of others. He always desired to be a credit to the work of Christ.

Livingstone had learned well from the Lord Jesus Christ. The Gospels present Christ as a meek man. Meekness is not weakness. It's a gentle, submissive attitude toward those in authority and toward even those who have no authority over you. The Lord Jesus was meek in His relationship with His earthly parents, His disciples, and His heavenly Father. He had great authority because He was God. He had great abilities. None of His personality traits or natural talents were hindered by sin. Yet He was never demanding or rude. He was considerate of the feelings and ideas of others. He listened to their opinions when they were expressed sincerely and honestly.

When the Lord was twelve years old, He went to Jerusalem with His parents for an annual religious celebration called the Passover. Afterwards, Joseph and Mary and others left to return to Nazareth, but Jesus was left behind. Since the group was large, Joseph and Mary did not realize that Jesus wasn't with them until they had traveled a whole day. They returned to Jerusalem, which took another day. On the third day they found Jesus in the temple, talking with the men who were experts in the Old Testament Law. Jesus had surprised these men with His knowledge of the Scriptures.

Jesus's mother was upset with Him because of all the worry they had experienced in trying to find Him. The Lord responded to her by saying that He thought she would know He was in the temple, doing the business of His heavenly Father.

Christ was not rebellious toward His parents. What would you have done for two days by yourself in a big city like Jerusalem? Christ was so obedient to His parents and to God that He spent His time in the temple, the place that would be the most pleasing to them.

Christ was also respectful toward the teachers, the experts in the Scriptures. He was God, and He knew more than any of those men. Yet not once was He disrespectful toward them. He was teachable and submissive. That is true meekness.

If Jesus hadn't been meek as He listened to the teachers of the law and asked them questions, they probably wouldn't have been "astonished at his understanding and answers" (Luke 2:47).

Meekness toward teachers, whether they're your parents or your schoolteachers, honors Christ. There's never any reason to be argumentative with people in authority over you.

At the end of His earthly ministry, the Lord had a special meal with His disciples. He chose this occasion to teach them the importance of having a meek attitude toward other Christians. He acted like a slave and washed the disciples' feet after supper. Peter objected at first, but Jesus taught him that once a person is saved he must become the servant of other Christians.

For the Lord Jesus to make Himself the servant of others was remarkable. If anyone ever had the right to have others serve him, it was the Lord. But He understood the value of serving people who had less knowledge and ability than He had. He understood that showing respect, consideration, and helpfulness to others who have less authority is an important ingredient in true leadership. Christ was both great and meek. Anyone who has both these qualities is attractive to others. Christ has been attracting people to Himself for two thousand years.

If God has given you a good mind, an attractive personal appearance, or a pleasant personality, you will be tempted to think of yourself as better than others and thus be unwilling to serve them. This is the opposite of meekness. It is a proud, inconsiderate spirit, which is not pleasing to Christ. Never let the qualities God has given you allow you to become conceited.

15

---

festivals in Jerusalem each year (Exod. 23:14–17; Deut. 16:16), most Jews in the first century went only to the Passover, which concluded the week of Unleavened Bread. Joseph and Mary went to Jerusalem each year for the Passover. How often Jesus went with them is not indicated in Scripture. For Him to attend at age twelve was appropriate, however, considering the ceremony which He would be a part of the following year. At age thirteen a Jewish boy joined the religious community as a responsible member. He became a "son of the commandment" (*bar mitzvah*).

After attending the seven-day festival (Exod. 13:6), Mary and Joseph left for Nazareth. They assumed that Jesus was among the many friends and relatives traveling together, which suggests the confidence that Jesus's parents had in Him. They had no reason to believe He would be anywhere but among them. Why was He not with them? Since He was sinless, we must conclude that while He was away from His parents, He would be in the right place doing good. According to the biblical account, the Lord spent the time away from His parents in the most profitable way possible. His independent thought and action in this situation were not rebellious; He remained an example of meekness under the circumstances.

Most young people spend considerable time thinking, *If only I could get out from under these restraints . . .* They suppose that if they were away from their parents and other authorities, they would be different people. Jesus did not think this way.

Outline

I. Meekness toward authority (Luke 2:41–52)
  A. Meekness and independence (2:41–47)
  B. Meekness and personal growth (2:48–52)

II. Meekness toward friends (John 13:1–17)
  A. The foundation for meekness (13:1–11)
  B. The incentive for meekness (13:12–17)

III. Meekness toward God (Matt. 26:36–46)
  A. Meekness in suffering (26:36–39, 42)
  B. Meekness as preparation (26:40–41, 43–46)

While in the temple with the "doctors" (specialists in the interpretation of the Law) Jesus showed remarkable spiritual perception. Yet this fact did not lessen His need to be submissive to the teachers. He listened to their instruction and responded to their questions. He did not pose as their teacher even though He certainly had the ability to teach them. These men were astounded at what He understood.

Jesus demonstrated that part of being meek is being teachable. A person who lacks meekness does not see his need of instruction from anyone; he just boldly asserts himself and his ideas, regardless of the thoughts and feelings of others. Jesus never did this with either His parents or His teachers. Some of your students may show astounding spiritual perception for their age. The danger for these students is spiritual pride that casts aside submission and takes an authority to which it has no right. A student who challenges a teacher inappropriately or flouts the judgment of his parents is suffering from this problem and is in need of sobering reproof.

Meekness and personal growth (2:48–52). Jesus's response when His parents found Him proves that meekness enhances personal growth. His mother was the first to speak, rebuking Him in the form of a question. She asked why He had treated her and Joseph as He had. Jesus's answer is surprising for two reasons. First, He asked why they had been searching everywhere. Didn't they realize that He would come immediately to the temple, where He would be serving His heavenly Father? This first statement recorded from Christ's youth evidences an awareness of His unique relationship with the Father. The other surprising element is that He did not indicate any remorse for the "problem." His parents did not understand His words, but apparently the respectful attitude in which they were spoken caused His parents to see that He had not been at fault in the situation. His spirit of submission to them eliminated all questions about a rebellious attitude as He immediately went to Nazareth with them and lived under their authority.

> Every parent must accept his child's growing spiritual independence. God works directly with young people. He is not restricted to working solely through parents and teachers even though this is His primary approach. There are some spiritual incidents in a child's life that a parent will never understand.

The connection between Christ's submission to His parents and His increase in "wisdom and stature, and in favour with God and man" (2:52) should not be overlooked. Certainly Christ's intellectual development (wisdom), physical development (stature), spiritual development (favor with God), and social development (favor with man) cannot be separated from the fact of His sinlessness. Every dimension of His growth continued unimpeded by inherent sin. On the other hand, the natural process of human maturing was enhanced by a right relationship to His parents.

> Christ set the right example and established a right pattern for all Christian young people to follow. If they fail to follow it, trouble will result. Their own growth and development will be hindered.

II. Meekness Toward Friends (John 13:1–17)

John 13 presents one of the most astounding scenes in the Word of God. Jesus Christ, the Lord of the universe, is on His knees before His own disciples, performing a servant's task. The scene takes place at the Last Supper. It was the night that Jesus would be betrayed. The Lord had many things to say to His "own" before the night was over.

The washing of the disciples' feet reflects two customs of the first century. The first was necessary after someone returned from the public baths. Although most of his body was clean, dust from the streets would cling to his feet. This dust made the washing of his feet a necessity when he arrived home.

Why was Christ able to show meekness to His parents and His disciples? Because He was meek toward His heavenly Father. As God the Son, Jesus was sinless, but He was also a man, and as a man He was submissive to God. Few incidents in Christ's life show this submission as clearly as His experience in the Garden of Gethsemane. There He struggled in great sorrow over the approaching time when He would bear the sins of mankind on the cross. His taking our sin upon Him would mean separation from God, a separation He had never experienced before. This suffering was God's will, and Christ submitted to it.

If a person isn't considerate of God and His will, he's not likely to be considerate of other people. A right relationship with your parents and friends always grows out of a right relationship with God. The first and greatest commandment in the whole Bible is to love God with all your heart, soul, mind, and strength. The second commandment is to love others as you love yourself (Matt. 22:36–40). You cannot love God and be unkind, inconsiderate, and selfish toward others. Love for God demands that you be meek.

Are You Meek or Weak?

Meekness is gentle submission to God and others. It is a result of obedience to God's commands. Your meekness is a sign of your spiritual strength. It is not a sign of weakness or inferiority to others. If you have the character quality of meekness, you may be superior to others in your abilities, but you choose to submit yourself to them, recognizing God's over-ruling control of circumstances and people.

To be meek like Christ, you must be considerate of your parents and your teachers, responding wholeheartedly to their desires. Even though you may not understand why they ask you to do certain things, you still obey cheerfully. A meek person never tries to retaliate for wrongs done against him. To be meek, you must submit yourself to God and leave vengeance to Him. Meekness is spiritual strength under God's control.

Do You Remember?

1. What did Mary and Joseph find Jesus doing when they returned to Jerusalem? _____
   listening to and asking questions of the teachers

2. What did Christ do after His parents returned to Jerusalem? _____
   He submitted Himself to them and went with them to Nazareth.

3. How did Jesus grow as a result of His submission to His parents? _____
   "in wisdom and stature, and in favor with God and man" (Luke 2:52)

4. How was Jesus feeling when He entered the Garden of Gethsemane? _____
   "exceeding sorrowful even unto death" (Matt. 26:38)

5. Did Christ want to die and be separated from His Father for a time? *no*

6. What was Christ's goal? *to be submissive to the will of His Father*

7. What did He tell His disciples that they should do to follow His example? _____
   serve and submit themselves to one another

16

The second custom is the role of a household servant in washing the feet of guests who came to dinner. Since the disciples had gathered in the upper room, the usual provisions of a household were lacking, and this task had been left undone. Jesus took on the task Himself and thereby taught the disciples the importance of meekness.

The foundation for meekness (13:1–11). While Jesus was washing the disciples' feet, He taught the importance of regeneration and spiritual cleansing as a foundation for meekness. In response to Peter's objection, Jesus explained that a person who had been cleansed or bathed had only to have his feet washed, referring to the custom of washing after returning home from the baths. The Lord used this imagery to describe regeneration and subsequent daily cleansing from sin through confession. Referring to Judas, Jesus noted that not all the disciples had been bathed in the sense of regeneration.

> Peter's reaction reflected the spirit that Christ was teaching the disciples to avoid. Peter was not being meek in his response to Christ; he was being stubborn and assertive. Self-will (the stubborn unwillingness to surrender all to Jesus daily) makes the believer useless in the service of Christ, just as Christ warned Peter it would.

The incentive for meekness (13:12–17). After completing the washing, Jesus stressed that His example was the incentive they needed to be meek. He had willingly submitted Himself in service to them, which He certainly did not have to do. He was greater than they were in every regard, but He put Himself in the position of a servant to them. This submissive spirit was the attitude they were to show toward one another. To give extra force to this teaching, Jesus said that those who not only know but also practice this truth will be happy (13:17).

> Happiness for Christians is determined largely by our ability to be content as servants, not envying others with greater responsibilities and not becoming angry with the insubordination of others. Emphasize to your students the importance of not thrusting themselves into the limelight. Stress that being meek means taking the role of the servant. In Christ's eyes, the Christian who has the greatest position of ministry to others is better off than the person with great authority over others.

III. Meekness Toward God (Matt. 26:36–46)

The Garden of Gethsemane was a place the Lord often went for prayer and communion with His Father (Luke 22:39). The name *Gethsemane* means "oil press," a reference to the valuable oil pressed from the olive trees that grew there. After the Last Supper, Jesus went there with His disciples.

Meekness in suffering (26:36–39, 42). The first part of our Lord's experience in the garden stresses the necessity of meekness in the course of suffering in the will of God. As Jesus entered the garden, He left most of the disciples and went on to a more private place with Peter, James, and John. He became full of sorrow and was deeply troubled, telling the three disciples of the extreme nature of His sorrow. It was the kind that could cause a person to die. He asked them to watch or stand guard so that His time might be free from intrusion. That they were expected to pray was implicit in the command to watch.

Finally alone, Jesus prayed that the cup He was about to drink would be taken away if it were the Father's will. The emphasis of His prayer is absolute submission to the Father's will. While Jesus prayed, an angel appeared and strengthened Him. He then prayed with even greater earnestness, to the extent that large drops of blood oozed through the pores of his skin (Luke 22:43–44). Even in the middle of suffering and personal anguish, Christ's supreme meekness triumphed. He did not throw off the yoke of the will of God. The "cup" to which Jesus referred three times has been variously described. It likely refers to the sin He was to bear and the consequent separation from God that He would experience.

> A Christian's meekness or lack of it shows when circumstances get difficult in the will of God. Arm your students against the mistaken idea that life is a "bed of roses" once they trust Christ as Savior. A person's real submission to God is not proved when everything is pleasant. It is when life gets difficult and God seems silent that a true testimony of meekness is given. It is just as right for a student to stay in a Christian school when he gets bad grades as when he gets good ones. Witnessing is pleasing to God both when the harvest is great and when it is lean. Obedience to God is just as right when friends and family support you as when they do not. A meek believer understands these truths and lives accordingly in the will of God.

Christ went back to the three disciples, found them asleep, rebuked them, and returned to pray. In His second prayer the Lord again expressed His commitment to the will of God. On returning a second time, He found the disciples asleep again. He left them and prayed the same prayer as before. Three times the Lord found it necessary to express His submission to the Father.

Meekness as preparation (26:40–41, 43–46). The conduct of the three disciples and the words of our Lord during this incident teach the necessity of spiritual alertness in maintaining a spirit of meekness. The disciples fell asleep while Jesus went to pray the first time because of their emotional fatigue over the prospect of Christ's coming death and the difficult future facing them (Luke 22:45). Jesus rebuked them, speaking to Peter, who was often the spokesman for the disciples. He then exhorted them to watch and pray to avoid falling into temptation, explaining that often the spirit is willing but the flesh is weak. They might find themselves running away from the will of God because of the suffering to come if they did not pray to remain meek.

When the Lord returned the third time and woke them, the opportunity to pray about the coming trial was past— the band of soldiers was coming with Judas. Eventually all the disciples fled in fright. They were not prepared spiritually for what befell them. Instead of faithfully and deliberately following the will of God, they ran pell-mell in fear for their lives.

> Jeremiah warns that "the heart is deceitful above all things, and desperately wicked" (17:9). A believer cannot trust himself just because of a previous track record in the Lord's service. He must watch and pray that he will meekly remain in the will of God. The Lord Jesus taught that the meek would inherit the earth. The teenager who loses himself in the will of God will live life to the fullest. The rebellious, self-willed teenager cannot fulfill God's will in his life. He also loses the potential of a life of spiritual service to others. The rebel is the real loser. The meek inherit the earth.

✳ Extra Activity

Writing: Numbers 12:3 states, "Now the man Moses was very meek, above all the men which were upon the face of the earth." This remarkable statement about Moses raises a question. How did Moses demonstrate meekness toward God and others? Have your students answer this question in writing, using the material in Exodus and Numbers as the major source. They may also want to do research in Bible dictionaries and encyclopedias.

Lesson 5
Christ's Zeal

Theme	Zeal
Scripture	Matthew 21:12–17; John 2:13–25
Memory Work	John 2:17

Approach to the Lesson

Theme: Zeal is enthusiastic and diligent devotion in the pursuit of a goal or ideal. The world is full of zealots; however, zeal is to be admired and imitated only if its purpose is right. Some are zealous about making money. Others are zealous about sports. Still others pursue leisure and pleasure with great enthusiasm. Zeal for the glory of God is the right type of zeal. And zeal against evil is a necessary complement to zeal for God. A Christian cannot be for something and against nothing.

It is not enough merely to believe the right doctrines, fellowship with God's people, think the right thoughts, and do the right things. All these things must be done with enthusiasm and devotion for the glory of Christ. Cool hearts and calm lives may be as sinful as corrupt doctrine. Dead truth can condemn a soul as certainly as any heresy.

Rationale: Most teens want to be accepted more than anything else. It is not considered "cool" to be spiritually zealous. You must overcome this aversion to godliness by presenting admirable examples of spiritual zeal—Christ Himself and, as you teach, your own zeal.

Background: Christ cleansed the temple twice. The first time (John 2:13–25) was at the beginning of His ministry, just a few days after His first miracle at the wedding feast of Cana. The second was during passion week, which culminated in Christ's death and Resurrection (Matt. 21:12–17; Mark 11:15–19; Luke 19:45–48). The Lord's zeal for the purity of the worship of God never waned. He was as intense in His pursuit of God's honor at the end of His earthly ministry as He was at the beginning.

Both cleansings came just before the Passover. All Jewish males were required to be in Jerusalem at this time (Exod. 23:14–17; Deut. 16:16; cf. Lesson 4). Thus Jesus traveled the ninety miles from Capernaum, on the shore of the Sea of Galilee, to Jerusalem. For the second cleansing He came from Bethany, a suburb of Jerusalem, into the city in the triumphal entry (Matt. 21:1–11). The timing is suggestive since we know that through His death the Lord Jesus Christ became our Passover (1 Cor. 5:7). Perhaps His own role and the season of the year combined to bring His zeal for the Father's will to a peak at those times.

The temple itself was not open to the public. The inner court surrounding it was largely restricted to priestly use. Only a small section at the eastern end, the end farthest from the temple proper, was open to Israelite men. Beyond it was the women's court. Despite its name, it was open to both men and women. Surrounding it was the outer court, where the cleansings took place. Although this area was open to both foreigners and the unclean, Jesus viewed it as part of the temple and, hence, an area to be kept free from the desecration of the business that was being conducted there.

The outline for this lesson uses the structure of the account of the first cleansing in John's Gospel. Since there is considerable duplication in the two accounts, this is the most efficient way to treat the material. Where the second cleansing varies from the first, the material has been woven into the discussion without confusing the two accounts.

⭐ The Lesson

I. Zeal Opposes Sin (John 2:13–17)

The sin (John 2:13–14, 16). From our Lord's statements in the temple, we can learn the nature of the sin He was reacting to. Not only had the transgressors turned the temple into a marketplace, but they were

Objectives

Knowledge (concepts students need to grasp)	the differences between the two cleansings of the temple
	the practice of buying, selling, and exchanging money that prompted Christ's actions in cleansing the temple
Application (principles students should put into practice)	Avoid the typical teen nonchalance because it is not biblical.
	We should oppose sin, overcome challenges, and beware that our zeal doesn't become misguided.

Outline

I. Zeal opposes sin (John 2:13–17)
   A. The sin (2:13–14, 16)
   B. The zealous opposition (2:15, 17)
II. Zeal overcomes challenges
   A. The authority of the Resurrection (John 2:18–22)
   B. The authority of Scripture (Matt. 21:14–16)
III. Zeal can be wrong (John 2:23–25)

also unconcerned about the worship going on there. Christ was combating this attitude when he forbade people to carry vessels through the temple (Mark 11:16). This meant that He would not permit anyone to use the large court of the Gentiles as a shortcut to get from one part of the city to another. This irreverence was more than the Lord would tolerate.

> Making light of the things of God is a serious sin. The spiritual should never be treated as if it didn't matter.

In the second cleansing, Jesus said the moneychangers and merchants had turned the house of prayer into "a den of thieves" (Matt. 21:13). In the first cleansing, they had made it a marketplace; now they were condemned for their dishonesty. What had they done to deserve this designation? First, they charged a high exchange rate for Jewish coins, the only money accepted in the temple. If a faithful Jew wanted to buy a sacrifice or make a donation, he had to do it with these coins. With pilgrims coming from all over the Roman Empire, the moneychangers had a great opportunity to profit. They took advantage of people. This was tantamount to theft in the mind of the Lord.

The temple inspector was another part of the corrupt system. He charged a fee to inspect sacrifices to ensure that they were acceptable. If he disapproved of a sacrifice for any reason, then a worshiper would have to buy an acceptable animal. Plenty of animals were available right in the temple, but the venders charged high prices. The worshiper had little choice but to pay the price in Jewish coins, which he had to obtain at exorbitant exchange rates. To put it simply, people weren't just doing business in the temple; they were running a racket. (For a full discussion of the financial system within the temple, see Edersheim's *The Life and Times of Jesus the Messiah,* pages 111, 366–76.) These transactions not only desecrated the temple but also provided

Christs Zeal

Read: Matthew 21:12–17;
John 2:13–25

Memorize: John 2:17

Bible Expressions to Understand

merchandise—items bought and sold
moneychangers—people who exchange one currency for another
sucklings—nursing infants

What would you be willing to fight for? Are there things or people so important to you that you would fight before letting someone hurt them? How about your family members? A special friend? A coin collection? A pet?

Some things are worth fighting for. In the previous lesson, we studied Christ's meekness. Many people would be surprised to learn that the meek Christ was also the Christ who believed in fighting for a cause.

This character trait is zeal—energetic devotion to a cause, principle, or person. What was Christ zealous about? What was He willing to fight for?

One cause was the holiness and purity of worship in the temple, His Father's house. He was grieved when He saw men turning the temple into a place of business. On two separate occasions, once at the beginning of His public ministry and once near the end, Christ literally drove the merchants out of the temple and overthrew their tables.

Why did Christ respond to these businessmen with such zeal? To understand Christ's actions, you must understand the situation at that time. At the Passover, Jews had to come to Jerusalem. Some came from faraway places where a different type of currency was used. Some families brought their own animal to be sacrificed, and others bought an animal after they arrived in Jerusalem. The local Jews saw this as a good money-making opportunity. They knew they had the outsiders "over a barrel." Visitors had to buy an animal, and they had to use Jewish currency. The temple inspector could even pronounce a Jew's animal brought from home as unfit for sacrifice and thereby force him to buy a more expensive animal. Furthermore, the moneychangers (those who exchanged foreign and Roman currency for Jewish coins) could make a healthy profit by the exchange rates they charged. Supposedly all of this was done for the greater purpose of worshiping God. The merchants' thoughts, however, weren't on God but on their own financial gain. They were stealing from their fellow Jews! (See Matt. 21:13.)

These conditions enraged Christ. The Scripture says of Him, "The zeal of thine house hath eaten me up" (John 2:17). Christ's anger was righteous because it was properly focused: He was angry at the right thing. He knew that God was not being honored by the temple being used as a marketplace. The Bible says, "And when he had made a scourge of small cords, he drove them all out of the temple, and the sheep, and the oxen; and poured out the changers' money, and overthrew the tables" (John 2:15).

"Take these things hence; make not my Father's house an house of merchandise" (John 2:16).

Like Christ, you need to show your zeal for righteousness by opposing sin. It's not enough just to keep yourself from sinning. You need to oppose the

17

---

many opportunities for the dishonesty that prompted Christ's remarks.

The zealous opposition (John 2:15, 17). In both the first and the second cleansings, the Lord took forceful but methodical action. In the first cleansing He took time to make a whip of small cords and then chased those involved out of the temple. The whip was probably for the sheep and the cattle. He poured the changers' money on the floor and overthrew the tables. He then told those who sold doves to take them out. He probably did this because the doves were in cages, and overturning them might have injured the birds. His actions in the second cleansing were virtually identical, except that there is no comment about a whip or about His driving the livestock out (Matt. 21:12).

Few teenagers get angry about sin. They think it is fine to be a sports fanatic or to be devoted to a movie star or music group, but to get stirred up over Christ's honor is not "cool." Sin should trouble us. If there is something we can do to stop it, we should do it. Our zeal for the Lord should prompt us to action, whether against sin or for righteousness. Ephesians 4:26 says, "Be ye angry, and sin not." Anger stirred up by pride is wrong. But to be stirred up over serving Christ and opposing sin is the Christian's responsibility.

In both cases the Lord was angry, but He was not sinning. His zeal for holiness and against sin prompted the action. He knew that what He saw was not glorifying to God, so He took action. When the disciples witnessed His actions and heard His words of denunciation (John 2:17), they were immediately reminded of Psalm 69:9, "The zeal of thine house hath eaten me up." They saw a burning, holy enthusiasm for God and His cause in the actions of their Master.

Anger is often, but not always, a sin. It is not wrong to be stirred to action against unrighteousness. Moses got angry when the Israelites sacrificed to the golden calf (Exod. 32:19), and he broke the tablets of the law and ground the calf to powder. Nehemiah was angry with those who did business on the Sabbath (Neh. 13:16–21) and threatened them with force. Christ acted out of righteous anger, but He did not lose His temper.

II. Zeal Overcomes Challenges

A believer's zeal is likely to be challenged. The surprising thing about the reaction of the Jewish leaders is that it was only verbal. They did not imprison Christ. Why? Because the injustice of the temple system was common knowledge, and the sentiments of the people were with Jesus. Furthermore, His unexpected boldness may well have left them dumbfounded. In any case, Christ used two sources of authority to respond to their challenge.

The authority of the Resurrection (John 2:18–22). After the first cleansing, the leaders asked Jesus by what authority He was doing these things. He responded with an enigmatic reference to His future death and Resurrection, using the destruction of the temple as an analogy for His body. Not understanding this, they assumed He meant He would actually destroy the temple in Jerusalem and raise it up in three days Later, after His Resurrection, His disciples remembered His remarks.

> As Christ's followers, commissioned in the power of the Resurrection, we too have authority in the face of opposition. We should be bold, knowing that the authority of the risen Christ is behind us (Matt. 28:18–20).

Christ's use of His Resurrection as a means of establishing His right to do what He did in the temple was entirely appropriate. His Resurrection was proof that He was God and therefore the One to Whom the temple belonged. He had every right to cleanse it.

The authority of Scripture (Matt. 21:14–16). Christ's authority was also questioned after the second cleansing. When little children began singing His praises in the temple, the leaders objected. Jesus responded by quoting Psalm 8:2, saying, "Out of the mouth of babes and sucklings thou hast perfected praise" (21:16). He used Scripture to establish His right to receive praise for His activities in the temple. In a parallel account, He said that if the children did not sing His praise, the very rocks would cry out (Luke 19:40).

> The living Christ and the Scriptures that reveal Him are all the authority the believer needs for zealous activity for His glory. It is right for a believer to stand up for what he knows to be right. To do otherwise is cowardice. A Christian young person can never afford to be casual about sin and righteousness. Christians should zealously denounce the one and embrace the other.

III. Zeal Can Be Wrong (John 2:23–25)

After the first cleansing, many believed on the Lord because of the miracles they saw Him do. They had great zeal and enthusiasm for the spectacular. Devotion to Christ solely because of His miracles was a wrong motive. Christ performed His miracles when it best served His purpose of communicating Who He was. He was selective about where and for whom He did miracles. These followers left Him when He stopped performing wonders. Theirs was a devotion not to Christ so much as to what He could do. The object of their faith was faulty, and these people remained lost. Seeing right through this kind of zeal, the Lord knew what was in their hearts and did not expect them to become His faithful followers.

> Some who seem zealous for Christ actually do not know Him at all. They have put their trust in some facet of Christian truth, but not in Christ's work on the cross for them. Because of His omniscience, the Lord is not surprised or frustrated by falsehood. When some who are fervent in their profession later wander from the Lord, we should not be surprised or get frustrated in our efforts to serve Christ. Our zeal, rightly placed in the Son of God Himself, should remain fervent, undaunted by the failures of others.

✳ Extra Activity

Storytelling: The best way to illustrate the profiteering that was going on in the temple is to explain it in story form. Have the students pretend they are Jews from Asia Minor who make a long journey to Judea to sacrifice at the Passover. Because

sins of others, especially the sin of hypocrisy. What do you do when a church youth group camping trip turns into a late night "dirty story time"? How do you act when someone steals something from the school or church?

Christian zeal is not often popular among young people. Your friends may not always appreciate your zeal for Christ. They may misunderstand it. You may even find that your "friends" are really not your friends after all. They may turn from you or turn on you. But your first loyalty is to Christ and His cause. At the same time, you should be careful not to give the impression that you think you're better than others. You shouldn't "look down your nose" at others who are not fervently serving Christ.

Beware of false zeal. Some people dedicate themselves to Christ when others get on the "bandwagon." They respond when, for example, a popular evangelist comes to town and stirs up religious zeal or a natural disaster or terrorist attack strikes the fear of God into the hearts of people. The test of genuine zeal is time. Do people just "go with the flow" for a few weeks, or will they stay fervent for Christ? Genuine zeal will last.

Another danger is misdirected zeal. Perhaps you have known someone who "went off the deep end" over some small issue that the Bible doesn't emphasize. Or perhaps he was so aggressive in his witness that he got too pushy. God's Word doesn't condone foolishness or rudeness. You should be sure to focus your zeal in the right place and in the right way. Just because Jesus used force on these two occasions doesn't mean that using force should be standard practice in ministry.

But zeal itself is a good thing. No one respects a person who doesn't stand for anything, and neither does God. If we are to be like Christ, we must be zealous for His cause.

Are You Gung Ho for God?

Zeal is enthusiastic and diligent devotion to a goal or ideal. You need athletic, academic, and musical zeal, but most importantly you need spiritual zeal. Christ rebuked the lukewarm Laodicean church for its lack of zeal (Rev. 3:15). Christ demonstrated spiritual zeal, not only by His actions toward the Jewish temple merchants, but also throughout His ministry. He prayed, preached, taught, witnessed, healed, and performed miracles with zeal. If you want to be Christlike, you must be full of holy zeal!

Do You Remember?

1. What two profit-making ventures were being carried on in the temple? _____
   exchanging money; selling animals

2. What did Jesus say His Father's house was to be? *a house of prayer*

3. What Jewish holy day was approaching? *Passover*

4. Name three actions Christ performed to cleanse the temple. _____
   He drove the merchants and animals out; He poured out the changers' money; He overthrew the tables.

5. What do these actions suggest about Christ physically? *He was physically strong.*

6. What kind of zeal really pleases the Lord? _____
   (Answers may vary.) genuine zeal for the Lord and His cause

18

lambs are so expensive in Jerusalem at this time of year, they decide to buy one at home. The going rate for a lamb fit for sacrifice is $20.00. (Use dollar amounts so that students can relate to the story more easily.) The travelers then herd this lamb over two hundred miles to Jerusalem to use in their worship of God.

When they arrive, they take the lamb to the temple inspector to get his approval to sacrifice it. After they pay the man $5.00, he tells them that the lamb is unacceptable and that they will have to buy another. The travelers go to the section of the temple where "approved" lambs are sold. The going price is $40.00. When they argue about the price, the man insists that it is the current rate because of supply and demand.

What can they do—go home? So they pull out their money to pay for the lamb. But the salesman refuses it because it is Roman money, not the prescribed Jewish money. The Asian Jews are directed to the moneychanging tables. They ask for $40.00 in Jewish currency, and the exchanger says, "That will be $50.00, please." When they argue, he says that is the going rate of exchange. So they have now spent a total of $75.00 for what should have cost them only $20.00. What type of mood are these Jews in as they enter the temple to worship? This scene occurred hundreds of times a day, and it angered Christ, "the Passover Lamb."

Christ's Compassion

Read: Luke 7:36–50; 19:1–10; John 4:1–42

Memorize: Matthew 5:7

Bible Expressions to Understand

alabaster box—small cylindrical flask made of opaque white stone
creditor—one who lends money to another
ointment—perfume
press—crowd
publican—tax collector

The busload of Christian young people wound its way through the busy streets of New York City. In an all-around one-day tour they saw people from practically every race, religion, and social status. Every intersection offered some strange sight. The bus turned onto the Bowery, one of the oldest streets in America. Once the center of the theater district, today this street and the surrounding neighborhood are home to thousands of drunks and drug addicts.

As the bus moved up the street, the teens stared at both old and young men, wearing ragged clothes and using newspapers as blankets, asleep on the sidewalks. The hollow eyes and haggard faces reflected lives given over to the excesses of sin. The men had broken the law of God and had reaped bitter consequences. The young people got off the bus and began to go up and down the street, passing out gospel tracts and trying to lead some of these men to Jesus Christ.

Imagine yourself about to step off that bus. What would you be feeling and thinking? Some might think, "I don't want to have anything to do with these horrible people," or "I don't want to get near them." Others might reason, "They've rejected God's way, so why should I bother to talk to them?" But what is the right response? Compassion. Honest tears should well up in your eyes, not hatred in your heart. What if one of those men were your own father or brother? Or what if you yourself were a homeless man or woman? You would want someone to tell you about the mercy and love of Jesus Christ. Jesus encountered both the downtrodden and the powerful in His earthly ministry. This lesson focuses on how Christ showed compassion to three people—the woman at the well, the woman at Simon's house, and the tax collector at Jericho. All three were notorious sinners—an adulteress, a prostitute, and a thief. In

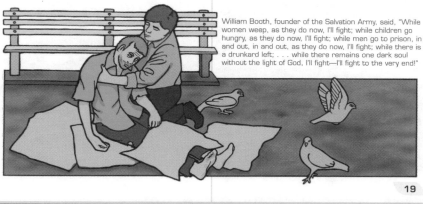

William Booth, founder of the Salvation Army, said, "While women weep, as they do now, I'll fight; while children go hungry, as they do now, I'll fight; while men go to prison, in and out, in and out, as they do now, I'll fight; while there is a drunkard left; . . . while there remains one dark soul without the light of God, I'll fight—I'll fight to the very end!"

19

LESSON 6
Christ's Compassion

THEME	Compassion
SCRIPTURE	Luke 7:36–50; 19:1–10; John 4:1–42
MEMORY WORK	Matthew 5:7

Approach to the Lesson

Theme: To treat someone with kindness is to show compassion. Christ often responded to the pathetic spiritual condition of people with great kindness and concern. He showed that a person's sinful condition, no matter how bad, is never cause for

avoiding him. Instead it is a reason to minister to his needs.

A believer cannot afford to allow his own separation from sin to conflict with his responsibility to win sinful people to Christ. These two commands are harmonized by compassion. Compassion allows a Christian to feel concern for people without approving of their sin or becoming involved in it himself. Compassion also adds tenderness to the message that a person is lost without Christ, and it gives the believer eyes to see beyond the warped character of an unbeliever to what that person can become by the power of Christ.

Rationale: Many Christians react to sin wrongly. Either they reject the sinner along with his sin, or they accept the sin along with the sinner. Help your students

Objectives

KNOWLEDGE (concepts students need to grasp)	the racial tension between Samaritans and Jews
	the significance of Jacob's well in Sychar
	the cultural background of the woman's anointing of Jesus
	the role of a chief publican like Zacchaeus
APPLICATION (principles students should put into practice)	No one should be considered "untouchable."
	Unsaved friends are not in an enviable position and are in need of the gospel.
	We should avoid a pharisaical, unmerciful attitude in dealing with the faults of others.

learn to recognize the destructive power of sin and to react out of compassion to help the sinner.

Background: The woman at the well, the woman at Simon's house, and Zacchaeus are all case studies in compassion. Each was a great sinner, and Christ had compassion on them all.

The Lord ministered to the woman at Jacob's well in Sychar early in His public ministry. He dealt with the woman in Simon's house about eight months later. His dealing with Zacchaeus came during a visit to Jericho more than a year after that. As the main points of the Lesson Outline show, each of these incidents also teaches a specific truth about compassion. (See page TE26.)

The Lesson

I. Compassion Breaks Down Barriers (John 4:1–42)

Racial and cultural barriers (4:1–10, 27–42). Christ's encounter with the woman at the well shows the power of compassion to overcome obstacles. The first barrier was Jewish-Samaritan animosity. Centuries before, in 722 BC, the Assyrian ruler Sargon had deported 27,290 of the inhabitants of the Northern Kingdom of Israel and started a colony of foreigners in the area (2 Kings 17:6, 24). These foreigners intermarried with the Jews that had been left behind, resulting in a racially and religiously mixed populace. The people were called Samaritans because Samaria had been the capital of the Northern Kingdom. The Jews looked down on them. When

Outline

Zerubbabel returned to Jerusalem from Babylon 185 years later, he refused help from Sanballat, the ruler of Samaria, in rebuilding the temple (Ezra 4). Animosity between the Jews and the Samaritans was still prevalent during the time of Christ.

The Lord determined to minister to the Samaritans despite this long-standing problem. In traveling from Judea to Galilee, He took the nontraditional route, directly through Samaria. Normally Jewish travelers detoured through Perea, on the east side of the Jordan River, to show their antagonism toward the Samaritans. When Jesus began talking to the woman, she immediately raised the issue of the hostility between the Jews and Samaritans, but the Lord did not even address the matter. Instead He turned the discussion to her spiritual need. He was determined to overcome the obstacle of racial animosity.

The disciples were away buying food when Jesus struck up a conversation with the woman. When they returned, the disciples were shocked to find the Lord talking with her. After the woman had left, Christ challenged the disciples to do the will of God by reaping the harvest of souls that was before their eyes, referring to the Samaritans. Some of the Samaritans believed because of the woman's testimony, while others believed because they heard Jesus Himself speak. The disciples are not mentioned in the section that discusses the conversion of the Samaritans. A long time would likely pass before their lifelong prejudice would be overcome, but Christ refused to allow this barrier to stand in the way of compassion.

Personal barriers (4:11-26). The second barrier in this incident was the woman's lack of spiritual understanding. When Jesus talked about the water that would end all thirst, she misunderstood completely; she thought He meant physical water. To

each case, others looked on with dismay, shocked that Jesus would have anything to do with these sinners. In spite of their criticism, Christ forgave the sinners. In the process, He taught us about compassion.

In Luke 7:36–50 we read that Jesus went to the home of Simon the Pharisee for dinner. It was customary for a religious teacher to have discussions during and following a meal. The public, though not invited to the meal, could enter the home to hear the teacher. In the midst of this discussion, a woman considered a sinner (probably a prostitute) entered the room. Apparently, Christ had recently forgiven her for her many sins. Now she had come to demonstrate her deep appreciation and love for Him. Her presence and actions offended Simon. Jesus explained to him that those who receive more forgiveness are capable of greater love. And He made it clear that He had the power to forgive sins.

The world is full of people like this woman. All around you are young people who are involved in illicit sex, perversion, and drugs. Should we merely denounce them and be satisfied with our own "pure" lives? While we must be careful not to call their sin acceptable or to be pulled into it, surely we can point them to the mercy of Christ. We cannot win them to the Savior if we stay isolated from them. He died for them, just as He died for us. "Christ Jesus came into the world to save sinners; of whom I am chief," Paul wrote in 1 Timothy 1:15.

The second example is Christ's successful soul-winning effort with an adulterous Samaritan woman (John 4:1–42). Jesus refused to let racial and cultural barriers stop Him from showing her mercy. He set aside her distracting questions about religious differences. He went right to the heart of her need. She was a sinner needing a drink of "living water." He identified Himself as the Messiah, the One Who could forever quench the spiritual thirst of sinners. His disciples didn't understand His actions at first, but in spite of the social obstacles and the disciples' prejudice, Christ showed the woman compassion.

It takes determination to show compassion. You have to overcome your own prejudices and wrong attitudes toward others who are not like you. You have to look past the superficial differences and realize that sinners of any race, culture, or status are people Christ died for. You have to forget about the

misunderstanding you might face by showing compassion to sinners. If Christ, the sinless One, did not consider it beneath Him to evangelize down-and-outers, then neither should we.

A third story about compassion appears in Luke 19:1–10. Here Christ reached out to someone from the upper class. Zacchaeus, a rich chief tax collector, could well be called a white-collar criminal. He probably gained his wealth by overcharging the local Jews and keeping part of the tax money for himself. This common practice certainly contributed to the hatred the Jews had for their Roman overlords and their feeling that tax collectors were like traitors.

When Christ announced He was going to the tax collector's house, the crowd murmured. The people didn't understand why He would fellowship with a thief. But Christ knew that Zacchaeus was more than a curiosity seeker. The compassion Christ showed resulted in a changed life—a life of dishonesty changed into one of generosity and Christian zeal, as Zacchaeus promised to return four times the amount he had stolen.

How can we claim to be Christlike when we fail to show compassion? If we want to be like our Savior, then we must follow His example of showing compassion. We may be repulsed by the sinfulness of lost people. We may not like the way they look or smell nor appreciate the way they have treated others. We may not like what others say about us for being around such people. But compassion must be greater than all these obstacles. John Newton, the converted slave trader who wrote the hymn "Amazing Grace," reportedly said when his memory began to fail, "Two things I do remember: the great sinfulness of man and the greater grace of God."

Do You Really Care?

To treat an offender with kindness is to show compassion. Christ never condoned sin, but He did show compassion even to those who had repeatedly broken the law of God. All of us are repeat offenders. None of us deserves anything but God's wrath.

clear up her confusion, Jesus confronted her with her own immorality to make her "thirsty" for spiritual water. The woman either remained confused or thought she could satisfy Jesus's concern for her by talking about the religion of the Samaritans. Or perhaps she was intentionally trying to turn the discussion away from her sin. For whatever reason, she brought up the conflicting views of the Jews and Samaritans concerning the place of worship. The Samaritans worshiped at Mount Gerizim, and the Jews at Jerusalem. The Lord skillfully avoided the diversion, telling her that the important aspects of worship were the spirit of the worshiper and the One being worshiped. The Lord told her plainly that He was the Messiah.

In many ways these barriers are typical of the barriers all people erect. Compassion must overcome racial, political, and cultural differences. But the greatest barriers are personal. As a teacher you must work at overcoming such barriers as you minister to your students. Facing one's own sin is never easy. The compassionate Christian, whether helping a believer overtaken in a fault or helping an unsaved person, must gently bring that person to see his spiritual need.

II. Compassion Results in Gratitude (Luke 7:36–50)

Luke alone records the account of the sinful woman who came to the house of Simon the Pharisee while Jesus dined there. (A similar incident recorded in Matt. 26:6–13, Mark 14:1–11, and John 12:3–9 occurred more than a year later in Bethany at

Do You Remember?

1. What kind of response did Christ receive from the woman at Simon the Pharisee's house? _____
   gratitude and love for His forgiveness

2. What question did the woman at the well have about worship? _____
   Which is the right place of worship?

3. What illustration from everyday life did Jesus use when He was witnessing to the woman at the well? *water quenching thirst*

4. Who did not understand Christ's demonstration of mercy to the woman at Simon's house? _____
   Simon and the others at the table (Luke 7:47), possibly other Pharisees

5. What group did not understand why Jesus was talking with the Samaritan woman? _____
   His own disciples

6. Who was Zacchaeus? (Mention his social status, occupation, and crime.) _____
   He was a rich chief tax collector who apparently stole from the people by taking too much tax money from them.

7. How did Zacchaeus demonstrate a changed life? _____
   He said that he would make generous restitution.

8. What great truth is stated at the conclusion of the story about Zacchaeus? _____
   Jesus came to seek and save the lost.

21

---

the home of Simon the Leper.) It was customary for people to come for conversation during a meal like this, even if they were not eating. Even so, this woman's conduct was unusual. It shows that the gratitude expressed is often in proportion to the compassion experienced. The language suggests that the woman was a prostitute until her recent conversion. She was so overwhelmed by Christ's compassion that she went to great lengths to express her gratitude.

First, she entered the home of a Pharisee, a bold step for a sinful woman. She then wept over Christ's feet while He was at the supper table. What was even more unusual was her use of her hair to wipe Jesus's feet. Further, she anointed His feet with an aromatic ointment, often worn around the neck in an alabaster flask for use as a perfume and breath deodorizer. Finally, she kissed Christ's feet, a customary act of respect for an honored teacher.

These acts showed deep gratitude. Yet all Simon could do was object to the fact that Jesus had let a sinner touch Him. It is sad that his religion had completely drained him of tenderness. Knowing what was in Simon's heart, the Lord gave a brief parable that showed His appreciation for the grateful response to His compassion.

Jesus told of a creditor who had two debtors. One owed ten times as much as the other. The creditor canceled both debts. Jesus then asked Simon which one would love his benefactor more, and Simon answered correctly that the one forgiven more would love more. Then with a stinging rebuke the Lord revealed that the less grateful debtor was Simon and the other was the woman. Simon had done nothing to show gratitude for Christ's compassion. The reader is left to conclude that He had not experienced the mercy of Christ. Jesus specifically told the woman that her sins were forgiven and that her faith had saved her, but to Simon He gave no such assurance.

An apathetic attitude toward salvation is symptomatic of one who has never known salvation. Do not assume that all your students know Christ. Their attitudes and actions will often be more revealing than their occasional testimonies. The context of this passage is salvation, but the principle of gratitude for compassion extends into other areas.

Whenever we are compassionate toward others in their personal weaknesses, most people will be grateful in return. None of us is without faults, spiritual or otherwise. You naturally appreciate someone who accepts you as you are and helps you improve. Your students will respond well to this treatment although they may not do as well as you would like. You cannot afford to be too lenient, but it is often wise to show some mercy in the classroom.

III. Compassion Brings Change (Luke 19:1–10)

Zacchaeus is one character your students have been familiar with since they were little children. What they often do not realize is that he was a wicked man. As chief publican (tax collector) for the Romans in the area of Jericho, he was despised by his countrymen as a traitor. This passage also reveals that he had been fraudulent in his tax collecting. The position lent itself to extortion since any amount a publican could collect above what the Romans required was profit; Zacchaeus had fallen prey to the temptation. When he met Christ, however, his life changed.

Sudden change (19:1–7). The change in Zacchaeus in response to Christ's compassion was sudden. While Jesus was passing through Jericho, Zacchaeus climbed a tree to see Him. This urgency in a rich man shows an unusual spirit for an otherwise self-sufficient, conniving thief. When Jesus invited him to come down and take Him to his house, Zacchaeus was thrilled. There was no false air of dignity in his manner.

What is to account for these uncharacteristic responses from a man of such position, religious cynicism, and wealth? The people in the town still knew him as a sinner. It was Christ's compassion that had quietly and suddenly caused the change.

Radical change (19:8–10). After they had come to his house and apparently had reclined to eat, Zacchaeus stood up and made a shocking announcement—he was going to give away half of his wealth to the poor. Anyone whom he could remember defrauding specifically, he would reimburse four times the amount he had wrongly collected. Zacchaeus viewed his fraudulent conduct as theft. Instead of returning all that he had gained dishonestly, plus one-fifth, as the Law required (Lev. 6:5; Num. 5:6–7), he said he would make four-fold restitution as required for outright theft (Exod. 22:1). That day the Savior brought him salvation, resulting in sweeping changes.

> Why would one who understands and accepts Christ's salvation want to remain in his former condition? He wouldn't. What about those who profess to be saved and never change? The evidence suggests that they haven't really been saved. Again, by extension, the principle of change applies to areas other than salvation. If you extend compassion to students who are late with an assignment, it is right for them to respond by changing their habits in the future and turning assignments in on time. If children are not disciplined for an offense, that mercy should be an incentive for them to avoid that sin in the future. Justice and mercy are both strong incentives to do right. As the authority in the classroom, the teacher is using powerful motivators when he mixes justice and mercy.

Special Problems and Topics

• **Does separation mean you can't show compassion?**

Paul discusses separation in 1 Corinthians 5:9–11. He makes it clear that we should separate from a believer who is practicing sin, but that we are not to separate from unsaved people even though they are living in obvious sin. They are in bondage to their sin, and they need Christ. Paul even says that a Christian is free to go to an unsaved person's house for dinner (1 Cor. 10:27). The Bible emphasizes personal separation from *sin,* but never personal separation from *sinners.*

 ## Extra Activities

Discussion: To begin the lesson, ask your students, "Is it right to have a known sinner over to your house to eat?" Allow several students to voice their opinions. After the lesson ask the same question again to see how many have changed their minds. Most students who answer "No" do so because of the words *known sinner.* (See 1 Cor. 5:11 on this point.) Because many students in Christian schools are isolated from flagrant sinners, they fear them or despise them. Some think, "If the sinner will clean himself up and be respectable, then I'll take the gospel to Him." But Christ makes it clear that He came to save sinners (Matt. 9:12–13). Typically, sinners are not going to come knocking on our doors, looking for the truth. It is our responsibility to take the gospel to them (Matt. 28:18–20). It is only when God breaks our hearts over sinners and we cultivate this Christlike attitude of compassion that we will reach out to them. Remember to warn students, however, about the danger of making unbelievers their best friends. The students could be drawn into sin themselves.

Survey: Ask your students how many of them came to Christ through (1) printed material (tracts, books) or mass media (television, radio); (2) someone who knocked on their door or witnessed to them on the street; or (3) someone with whom they had a friendship or a personal relationship. These are all legitimate means of evangelism, but most people come to Christ through a friend or relative. One of the great hindrances to evangelism is that we have involved our students in so many Christian activities that they have no contact with the lost and consequently no burden for them. Help them draw the conclusion that if many of them were won to Christ by a friend, it follows that they need to befriend others to win them.

LESSON 7
Christ's Holiness

THEME	Holiness
SCRIPTURE	John 8:31–47
MEMORY WORK	1 Peter 1:15–16

 Approach to the Lesson

Theme: Stated positively, holiness is complete commitment to God and His purposes. Stated negatively, it is separation from sin, which makes the believer more fit for worship of and service for the Lord. The two sides of holiness complement each other (2 Tim. 2:21).

Christ is the perfect example of holiness. He was both sinless and absolutely devoted to the will of God. Christ's holiness is the goal toward which the Christian strives. "But as he which hath called you is holy, so be ye holy in all manner of conversation; because it is written, Be ye holy; for I am holy" (1 Pet. 1:15–16).

Rationale: Most teens reject mindless "dos and don'ts," and one can hardly blame them. Stress the positive aspect of holiness without slighting the negative. We are to be separated *to* God as well as *from* sin, much as a husband is separated *to* his wife as well as *from* other women. A proper focus on the positive aspect—love for his spouse—makes the separation-from-others aspect no great sacrifice.

While considering holiness as exemplified by the Lord, remind the students that Jesus was fully human as well as fully God. To attribute His holiness to His deity is to miss the emphasis of the New Testament. Christ was holy in His *human* nature. He obeyed God's will explicitly, and He remained absolutely pure in the face of severe temptation. Though no theologian has adequately explained the effect Christ's deity had on His humanity, we can see when His humanity and His deity are being emphasized. When holiness is under discussion, Christ's humanity is usually the focal point. Thus the believer can derive great encouragement from the example of Jesus. As our Leader, Christ overcame every sin and was perfectly conformed to God's

will. He has set a high standard toward which we should all strive.

Background: The purpose of this lesson is to show that Christ's life on earth evidenced His holiness. At appropriate points, passages from outside the Gospels that prove Christ's holiness are woven in.

The lesson proceeds chronologically, showing that holiness was foremost from the beginning to the end of the Lord's life.

 The Lesson

I. Christ's Commitment to the Father

In His youth. Christ demonstrated commitment to God and His will throughout His life, beginning in His youth. When only twelve years old, He went to the temple and talked with the teachers of the Law. (Refer to Lesson 4.) When His parents found Him, He told them He had been about His Father's business (Luke 2:49). This is the first of Christ's recorded statements. Even at this young age, He was completely committed to God and His purposes. This is holiness in the positive sense.

> Christ's dedication when He was so young is an important example for your students. They are not too young to be totally devoted to the Lord and His cause. The younger a person is when he gives himself wholly to God's will, the better it is for him. Beginning young is good, but as time goes by he must remain faithful. This was true of Christ: "And Jesus increased in wisdom and stature, and in favour with God and man" (Luke 2:52).

Objectives

KNOWLEDGE (concepts students need to grasp)	the New Testament teaching that Jesus was sinless
	the two dimensions of holiness
	the Bible as the source book for holiness, naming sins to avoid and giving commands to obey
APPLICATION (principles students should put into practice)	We must set high standards of holiness because God requires it.
	We must not be one-sided; we must both shun sin and embrace holiness.
	We must not allow recreation or entertainment to cause us to sin or to distract us from other aspects of God's work.

Outline

I. Christ's commitment to the Father
   A. In His youth
   B. In His ministry
      1. His priorities
      2. His conformity
      3. His obedience
   C. In His death
II. Christ's separation from sin
   A. In His youth
   B. In His ministry
      1. His friends' testimonies
      2. His enemies' testimonies
   C. In His death

In His ministry. Christ showed the same commitment during the years of His public ministry. Some who are in the ministry begin well, but then fall into half-heartedness. Jesus was not this way.

His priorities. The Lord remained zealously committed to God's purposes and priorities. From early in His ministry He closely followed the commission God had given Him: "And he said unto them, Let us go into the next towns, that I may preach there also: for therefore came I forth" (Mark 1:38). He was commissioned of God to preach to the Israelites, and He determined to accomplish that goal. He did minister to Gentiles, but this was not His primary ministry. He said to the Syrophoenician woman, "I am not sent but unto the lost sheep of the house of Israel" (Matt. 15:24). But the woman persisted, and the Lord responded to her faith. In every detail He was committed to God and His purposes.

> What is most important to your students? Where are their priorities? Probably not where they should be. If they live for entertainment, popularity, or material things rather than for serving God, they have failed to keep their priorities holy.

His conformity. Another incident that shows the Lord's commitment is the questioning by John the Baptist from prison (Matt. 11:1–5). John needed confirmation that Jesus was the promised Messiah. Jesus said to John's emissaries, "Go and shew

> **The student text pages for this lesson begin on the next page.**

John again those things which ye do hear and see: the blind receive their sight, and the lame walk, the lepers are cleansed, and the deaf hear, the dead are raised up, and the poor have the gospel preached to them" (11:4–5). Christ's ministry so closely and completely conformed to the scriptural teaching about the ministry of the Messiah that there could be no doubt that He was the Anointed One. He was totally devoted to God. He was holy in a positive sense.

> Your students are not supposed to conform to the pattern for the Messiah, of course, but they do have a biblical pattern. How closely do they resemble it? To the degree they fall short they demonstrate a lack of holiness.

His obedience. Jesus's own words testify that He completely obeyed God. When He was in Jerusalem during the Feast of Dedication near the end of His ministry, the Jewish leaders opposed Him as a blasphemer. In His own defense, the Lord said, "If I do not the works of my Father, believe me not. But if I do, though ye believe not me, believe the works: that ye may know, and believe, that the Father is in me, and I in him" (John 10:37–38). Jesus was the perfect Servant of the Lord. He was completely committed to God and His purposes. They could not deny that truth. Later, during the week before His death, the Lord affirmed that He had lived in obedience to God's will: "As the Father gave me commandment, even so I do. . . . If ye keep my commandments, ye shall abide in my love; even as I have kept my Father's commandments, and abide in his love" (John 14:31; 15:10). No one was ever more committed to God's will than Christ. He was absolutely holy.

> By His ministry Jesus showed that a Christian in the ministry can be holy in fulfilling God's will. Your students should want to know God's will and to throw themselves into doing it. It is part of being holy.

In His death. Christ's death for lost people was the crucial part of God's will. Christ did not allow anyone to divert Him from this task. Six months before His death, He told His disciples that He was going to die (Matt. 16:21). When Peter began to object to the idea, Jesus reproved him: "Get thee behind me, Satan: thou art an offence unto me: for thou savourest not the things that be of God, but those that be of men" (Matt. 16:23). Just before this incident He had said, "Therefore doth my Father love

Bible Expressions to Understand

Abraham's seed—a descendant of Abraham
convinceth me of sin—proves me guilty of sin

Have you ever watched a star athlete in action and wished you could perform as well as he does? Maybe you've watched a daring halfback break tackle after tackle on his way to the goal line. The Olympic runner who wins the gold medal and sets new records is admired by all.

In sports, as in other endeavors, those who achieve the greatest heights have usually paid the greatest price. They have subordinated everything in their lives to the one purpose of achieving athletic superiority. For years they train by running, lifting weights, and practicing. Even their eating and sleeping habits are subordinated to their athletic goals. You might say that they are "set apart" to athletics.

To excel in sports, athletes undergo rigorous training. (See 1 Cor. 9:25.)

22

Believers are also set apart— but unto God. They are "saints" (1 Cor. 1:2). The word *saint* means "one who is set apart" or "holy one." When a person is saved, he is set apart from sin and the world. He's different! A Christian shouldn't think that he's better than others, but he is to act as though he has a new Master. He shouldn't be "holier than thou," but he should be holy.

The supreme example of holiness is the Lord Jesus Christ. How was He holy? First, He set Himself apart to achieve God's purposes for His earthly ministry, and, second, He never sinned. Let's look at both aspects more closely. What was Christ's great purpose in coming to earth? "For even the Son of man came not to be ministered unto, but to minister, and to give his life a ransom for many" (Mark 10:45). "Christ Jesus came into the world to save sinners" (1 Tim. 1:15). Christ's purpose was to give Himself as a perfect, sinless sacrifice for man's sin.

What happens when you dedicate yourself to doing the will of God? You face distractions— things or people that might turn you away from that purpose. Christ did too. His own brothers once tried to get Him to reveal Himself prematurely to the hostile Jews in Jerusalem (John 7:2–10). Sometimes relatives try to get Christian young people off the path of God's service. Jesus said that in the Christian life "a man's foes shall be they of his own household" (Matt. 10:36).

Once Peter tried to deter Christ from going to the cross (Matt. 16:22–23). "Be it far from thee, Lord," Peter said, "this shall not be unto thee." The Lord was so determined not to be distracted that He rebuked Peter by saying, "Get thee behind me, Satan: thou art an offence unto me: for thou savourest not the things that be of God, but those that be of men." Though Peter was one of His closest associates, Jesus didn't allow him to get in the way of His

me, because I lay down my life, that I might take it again. No man taketh it from me, but I lay it down of myself. I have power to lay it down, and I have power to take it again. This commandment have I received of my Father" (John 10:17–18). Both the Crucifixion and Resurrection were in the will of the Father, and Jesus determined to fulfill that will. Christ was holy, even to the point of great personal sacrifice.

> Your students have probably never faced the possibility of dying for Christ. Their death is not nearly as significant as His, of course, but they should be willing to die if that is God's will.

At the beginning of His high priestly prayer for the saints in the last week before His death, Jesus affirmed that He had always done the Father's will and soon

would continue to do so by dying. He even spoke of His death as an accomplished fact: "I have glorified thee on the earth: I have finished the work which thou gavest me to do" (John 17:4). At the moment of His death, the Lord said, "It is finished" (John 19:30) and then "gave up the ghost"—literally, "delivered over His spirit." His death was no accident; it was a choice of His will, a decision to be positively holy.

II. Christ's Separation from Sin

In His youth. The Lord was separate from sin from the moment of His conception. The announcing angel said to Mary, "The Holy Ghost shall come upon thee, and the power of the Highest shall overshadow thee: therefore also that holy thing which shall be born of thee shall be called

purpose. Sometimes friends try to get us off the right path. They may mean well, but we must be discerning. No friend is worth leaving the will of God for.

Christ's enemies also tried to deter Him from His mission. The Jewish leaders plotted to stop Christ's teaching ministry. They wanted desperately to kill Him. Christ had come to die, but He knew that God's will involved not only doing the right thing but also doing it at the right time. Christ showed that He was holy—set apart to accomplish the Father's will perfectly—by not allowing His enemies to side-track Him. Twice He slipped away from them when He knew they were after Him (John 8: 59; 10:39). But when the perfect time came for His death, He gave Himself willingly and even told Peter not to defend Him (John 18:11). How interesting that His enemies, who thought they were stopping Him, were unknowingly used by God to accomplish the purpose of His coming: "to give His life a ransom for many."

All believers should follow Christ's example by not letting family, friends, or enemies turn them from God's will. You have a God-given task to perform and God-given gifts and talents to develop. Don't let anything stop you from doing God's will. Satan will try to ensnare you through his subtle temptations. The world will try to allure you to its pleasures. In the face of temptation, be holy. Say to yourself, "I belong to God. I must please Him!"

Christ showed His holiness not only by His determination to do His Father's will but also by His sinless life. Hebrews 4:15 declares, "For we have not an high priest which cannot be touched with the feeling of our infirmities; but was in all points tempted like as we are, yet without sin."

Are You Set Apart?

Holiness is separation—separation from sin and complete commitment to God and His purposes. When we're saved, we're set apart to God. God tells us that we're already holy or sanctified (1 Cor. 6:11). In practice, we need to become what He has declared us to be. We need to act in accordance with our true identity as saints. In simple and direct words, "If you're a saint, then act like one!"

Jesus never sinned in thought, attitude, word, or action. Can you imagine never thinking a wrong thought, never having a sinful attitude, or never saying a wrong word? Christ never did one thing to sin against God or others.

> "It is a great deal better to live a holy life than to talk about it. Lighthouses do not ring bells and fire cannons to call attention to their shining—they just shine."
> —Dwight L. Moody

When God says, "Be ye holy; for I am holy" (1 Pet. 1:16), He is telling us to be like Christ. John wrote, "My little children, these things write I unto you, that ye sin not" (1 John 2:1). We should try, by the power of the Holy Spirit, to avoid sin. Never should we make provision for sin or make excuses when we do sin. When we're convicted of sin, we should confess it to God immediately. God has made provision for our forgiveness when we have sinned (1 John 1:9).

When tempted to sin, we should focus on the way Christ would have responded: "For consider him that endured such contradiction of sinners against himself, lest ye be wearied and faint in your minds. Ye have not yet resisted unto blood, striving against sin" (Heb. 12:3–4). Christ's agonizing prayer in the Garden of Gethsemane demonstrated His fervent resistance to sin. "And being in an agony he prayed more earnestly: and his sweat was as it were great drops of blood falling down to the ground" (Luke 22:44). His bloody scourging and gruesome Crucifixion revealed His determination to accomplish our Redemption. He didn't sin by giving in to the temptation to quit.

What sins most often cause teens to stumble? The desire to win a friend's approval ensnares many. Some will smoke or drink, for example, just to be accepted. Others will be immoral or use bad language. Many teens have trouble with sins of the spirit, such as pride, envy, hatred, or malice. These sins destroy a person from the inside, like a cancer. Sins of the tongue, such as gossiping or insulting others, greatly hurt the body of Christ and hinder the effectiveness of the gospel. When tempted to sin in any of these areas, remember to resist temptation as Jesus would have.

23

In His ministry. During His ministry Jesus was subject to what are called sinless human infirmities. He experienced weariness (John 4:6), hunger (Matt. 4:2), thirst (John 19:28), and sleepiness (Matt. 8:24). These sinless infirmities are in part the very things that make temptation a possibility. Because of such physical factors, the pressure of temptation to satisfy needs for the wrong motives was strong. The temptation to eat too much or to drink too much or just to place too high a priority on physical needs was always present. But the Lord never succumbed to these temptations.

His friends' testimonies. Christ's disciples never saw sin in Him. Peter, Christ's close friend and disciple, wrote that He "did no sin, neither was guile found in his mouth" (1 Pet. 2:22). The New Testament records not a single word from Christ's family members accusing Him of sin. On the contrary, James and Jude, two of His half brothers, became faithful followers (James 1:1; Jude 1; Matt. 13:55). Had Christ been a sinner, His brothers would have seen His hypocrisy and never followed Him. Why did John the Baptist hesitate when Jesus came seeking baptism? It was because John's baptism was a baptism of repentance from sin, and he knew Jesus was sinless. At Christ's insistence, he baptized Him "to fulfil all right-eousness," i.e., to set an example (Matt. 3:14–15).

His enemies' testimonies. Christ's enemies could never establish any charge of sin. They accused Him but could never come up with evidence to make their case. When the Jewish leaders accused Jesus of being demon possessed, He challenged them to prove one sin He had ever committed: "Which of you convinceth me of sin?" (John 8:46). None of them stepped forward with evidence. Even demons acknowledged His holiness (Mark 1:24).

Can your students' friends—even their enemies—find no fault in them? This is the standard Christians should strive for.

In His death. The Lord lived without sin to the very end of His stay on earth. He is the prime example of persistence in holiness. He continued to strive against sin even unto death. He then conquered both sin and death for us.

The evidence for Christ's sinlessness during His trials is overwhelming. The leaders of Israel tried to convict Him of some sin or crime: "Now the chief priests, and elders, and all the council, sought

the Son of God" (Luke 1:35). The virgin birth of Christ was as much a moral miracle as a physical one; no sinless man had ever been born before.

The Lord grew up in holiness. Faced with all the temptations of youth, He remained absolutely without sin. How do we know this? We have no thorough record of those thirty years, just a verse or two. But those brief sentences speak volumes. Notice again what Luke records of His childhood: "And the child grew, and waxed strong in spirit, filled with wisdom: and the grace of God was upon him" (Luke 2:40). This verse describes Jesus's early childhood. Now consider Luke's evaluation of His adolescence: "And Jesus increased in wisdom and stature, and in favor with God and man" (Luke 2:52). These two verses give a concise but

complete summary of Jesus's moral and spiritual progress. There is no mention of sin.

During a period of life that is considered especially hazardous spiritually, the Lord Jesus remained completely pure. A young believer never has an excuse for sinning. Youth has its temptations, as does every stage of life. Just as Christ remained firm in His resolve to be pure, so must the young Christian today.

Further confirmation occurred at the baptism, the beginning of Christ's public ministry. He stepped into the full light of public attention. What evaluation did God give of His life up to this point? "Thou art my beloved Son; in thee I am well pleased" (Luke 3:22). Would God have been "well pleased" with a life full of sin or one that had any sin at all?

false witness against Jesus, to put him to death; but found none: yea, though many false witnesses came, yet found they none" (Matt. 26:59–60). Pilate examined Him and tried to free Him, saying, "I am innocent of the blood of this just person" (Matt. 27:24). Herod also examined Christ and found Him innocent (Luke 23:15). After Judas had betrayed Jesus, his conscience drove him to suicide. He said to the Jewish leaders, "I have sinned in that I have betrayed the innocent blood" (Matt. 27:4).

> Under the intense scrutiny of the Roman legal system, Jesus was declared innocent. Not even the traitor among the disciples could honestly accuse Him. Ask your students what would happen if their lives were placed under this type of examination. How consistently would their lives prove to be within the will of God? The believer's standard is the sinless Jesus Christ—a demanding standard, but the standard nonetheless.

While Jesus was on the cross, one thief said, "This man hath done nothing amiss" (Luke 23:41). The centurion who watched Him die said, "Truly this was the Son of God" (Matt. 27:54). Jesus died for our sins, not His own. Paul wrote, "For he hath made him to be sin for us, who knew no sin; that we might be made the righteousness of God in him" (2 Cor. 5:21). Peter said, "Who, when he was reviled, reviled not again; when he suffered, he threatened not; but committed himself to him that judgeth righteously: who his own self bare our sins in his own body on the tree, that we, being dead to sins, should live unto righteousness: by whose stripes ye were healed" (1 Pet. 2:23–24). The death of Christ for our sins should motivate us to a holy life.

The record of the Gospels is clear. In the words of the apostle John, "And ye know that he was manifested to take away our sins; and in him is no sin" (1 John 3:5). Christ's life and death were intended to take away our sins—the death by vicarious atonement and the life by powerful example.

Do You Remember?

1. In what two ways did Christ demonstrate holiness? _____
   by dedicating Himself to accomplish His Father's will; by not sinning

2. What three groups of people tried to keep Jesus from doing His Father's will? _____
   His brothers, His disciples, His enemies

3. What are two purposes of Christ's life mentioned in Mark 10:45? _____
   to minister and to give His life a ransom for many

4. What verses tell us how strongly Jesus resisted sin? _____
   Hebrews 12:3–4; Luke 22:44

5. What verse tells about God's provision for us when we sin and need forgiveness? _____
   1 John 1:9

6. How did Peter describe Christ's holiness during His earthly life (1 Pet. 2:22)? _____
   He "did no sin, neither was guile found in his mouth."

24

 ## Special Problems and Topics

• **Could Jesus have sinned?**

Theologians have argued for centuries over whether or not Christ was *posse peccare*—able to sin. Most have concluded that He could not have sinned because His divine nature would have overpowered His human nature. The Scriptures do not address this issue specifically. They do make it clear, however, that Jesus was tempted in every way we are. His experience in temptation makes Him a faithful High Priest. "For we have not an high priest which cannot be touched with the feeling of our infirmities; but was in all points tempted like as we are, yet without sin" (Heb. 4:15).

 ## Extra Activities

Analogy: Use the marriage relationship to illustrate the two aspects of holiness. A man who has a relationship with a woman other than his wife injures his relationship to his wife. Similarly, failure to separate from sin (the negative aspect) injures our relationship to Christ (the positive aspect).

On the other hand, it is not enough to be morally pure in marriage. A good husband must develop and nurture a personal relationship with his wife by talking to her and spending time with her. Similarly, it is not enough to refrain from sin (the negative aspect). The Christian must have a vibrant, vital, personal relationship with Christ (the positive aspect).

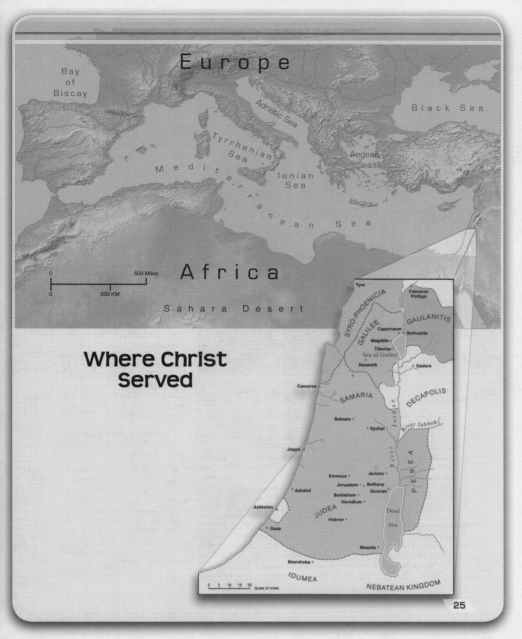

Map 2
Where Christ Served

This is the first of three major maps in the text. Together these maps serve as the primary basis for the map exercises on the CD accompanying this book. This map and the others may be used together as a separate lesson or treated individually at the teacher's discretion.

[Note: Students will need to study or refer to this map in order to complete Map Exercise 1 (on the CD).]

Discussion: Students often struggle with questionable activities, especially in the area of amusements and entertainment. They will usually admit that things such as rock music, liquor, drugs, and pornography are wrong and will hinder their relationship with Christ. But when it comes to things Scripture is not as specific about, their question is "What's wrong with it?" Help your students to realize that this is the wrong attitude. The question should be "What's *right* with it?" Paul tells us that our goal is to "approve things that are excellent" (Phil. 1:10). It is not what is *acceptable* but what is *best* that counts.

Paul uses the analogy of an athlete (1 Cor. 9:26–27). There are certain things that an athlete in training may not do that other people may. The athlete isn't neces-sarily choosing what is right versus what is wrong, but what is *best*. Help your students see that if they are serious about "running the race" for Christ, they must limit themselves to activities that are best, i.e., that will further their goal of holiness.

The Bible says that the way to develop good judgment about what is best is to read the Scriptures. Mature Christians have "their senses exercised to discern both good and evil" (Heb. 5:14). The test of holiness is not whether we are simply refraining from doing wrong but whether we are doing what is best.

Who's who? Students may not be able to positively identify which group each of the three men in the illustration belongs to but may benefit from trying to do so.

The breastplate with twelve stones identifies the man on the left as a priest (see Exod. 28 for a description). The chart indicates that the Sadducees were mostly priests, so students may conclude that this man is probably a Sadducee.

Mark 12:38 says that the scribes loved "long clothing," but both of the other two men are wearing long robes. So this verse doesn't really provide any helpful clues.

The phylacteries and fringes ("borders of their garments") mentioned in Matthew 23:5 were also worn by both Pharisees and scribes but are typically associated with the Pharisees. (Alfred Edersheim wrote in *Sketches of Jewish Social Life*: "While any ordinary Israelite would only put [phylacteries] on at prayer or on solemn occasions, the members of the Pharisaic confraternity wore them all day long.") Since the man in the middle has longer fringes on his robe and is wearing a phylactery, he is most likely a Pharisee, which means the man on the right must be a scribe.

These men represent the three types of religious leaders listed in the table to the right. See if you can identify which group each one belongs to by reading about their clothing in Matthew 23:5, Mark 12:38, and Exodus 28:12, 15–21.

"He came unto his own, and his own received him not" (John 1:11). These words characterize the relationship between Jesus and the Jewish people, particularly the Jewish leadership. Jesus came to bring spiritual deliverance: to deliver people from the penalty of their sins by dying in their place (Mark 10:45).

However, many of the Jews thought He was a political deliverer (Luke 24:21). Most of them would have welcomed the overthrow of Rome, but many of the leaders were leery of such a plan.

They may have feared that a revolution would overthrow their own authority as well as Rome's. They definitely feared Rome's military response to any hint of Jewish rebellion. Indeed, in AD 70 Rome did destroy Jerusalem in response to Jewish rebellion. There is no doubt that many Jews saw Jesus as politically dangerous.

But Jesus was also a religious threat. His authoritative interpretation and application of the Old Testament amazed the Jewish people and silenced the religious leaders. For example, Matthew records the response to Christ's Sermon on the Mount: "The people were astonished at his doctrine: for he taught them as one having authority, and not as the scribes" (Matt. 7:28–29). Christ "put the Sadducees to silence" and the Pharisees as well (Matt. 22:34, 46). Because His teaching contradicted their interpretations of the law and revealed their hypocrisy, they hated Christ and were determined to kill Him. Only His popularity held them back since "they feared the multitude" (Matt. 21:46).

Religious, political, and judicial groups began to cooperate to try to trick Jesus into making statements that they could use against Him. Two religious groups, the Sadducees and the Pharisees, opposed Christ together (Matt. 16:1). The scribes (copyists and teachers of the Law) joined the Pharisees in their opposition (Matt. 12:38). The priests also plotted together against Christ (Matt. 16:21). How interesting that those who were at odds with one another religiously found common ground in their opposition to Christ.

The two leading political groups in Palestine were the Zealots and the Herodians.

The Zealots fanatically opposed Rome. Simon, one of the twelve disciples, came from this faction (Acts 1:13; Luke 6:15). The Herodians, on the other hand, were loyal to Rome and Rome's local rulers, Herod the Great and later Herod Archelaus. They did not want Rome to think of Israel as a place of rebellion.

26

JEWISH RELIGIOUS, POLITICAL, AND JUDICIAL GROUPS MENTIONED IN THE GOSPELS		
TYPE	**GROUP**	**DESCRIPTION**
Political	Herodians	Influential politicians; mostly Sadducean priests who favored the Herods
	Zealots	Revolutionaries committed to the overthrow of the Roman government
Religious	Sadducees	Loyalists to the Law above the rest of the Old Testament; did not believe in the supernatural; mostly priests
	Pharisees	Master interpreters of the oral traditions of the rabbis; placed great emphasis on the strict observance of the Law; viewed themselves as righteous and all others as sinners
	Scribes	Initially, copyists; later, interpreters and teachers of the Law; most were sympathetic to the Pharisees
Judicial	Sanhedrin	Jewish supreme court; consisted of seventy elders, presided over by the high priest; could render decisions in civil and religious cases in Judea

Though the Gospels do not record the Zealots' attitude toward Christ, we do know that the Herodians joined the Pharisees in trying to ensnare Him (Mark 3:6; Matt. 22:15–22).

The supreme judicial body in Israel was the Sanhedrin, or council of elders. This group included approximately seventy priests, scribes, Pharisees, and Sadducees (Matt. 26:59; Acts 23:6). They were the ones who illegally condemned Jesus to death, but their injustice resulted in blessing for us. They did not take His life from Him; He gave it willingly (John 10:17–18).

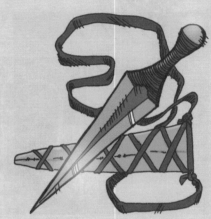

The *sica* (short dagger, usually curved) was often used by members of an extremist group of Zealots to assassinate their opponents.

27

Sanhedrin is a transliteration of the Greek word *sunedrion*. The King James Version always translates this word as "the council." What's the correct pronunciation? Many people say *san HEED run*; others say *san HEAD run*. You may also hear it said *sawn HEAD run* or with the stress on the first syllable as *SAN hid run*. All of these pronunciations are listed as acceptable in various dictionaries. The word also has a variant spelling/pronunciation *Sanhedrim*.

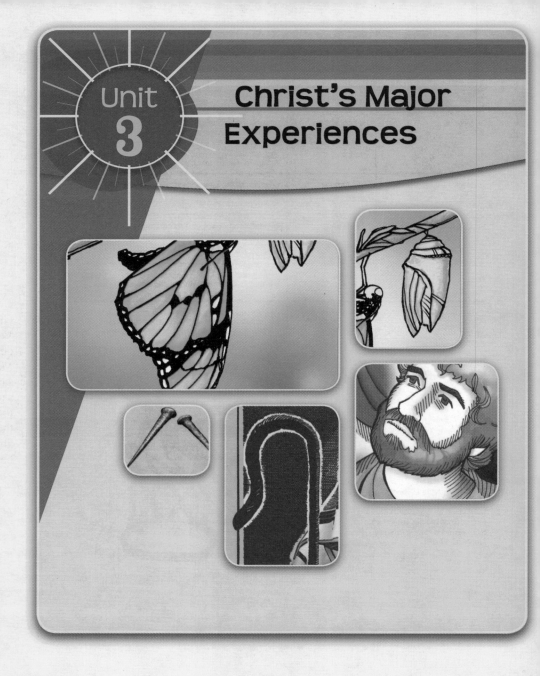

Unit 3
Christ's Major Experiences

Scripture says, "But when the fulness of the time was come, God sent forth his Son" (Gal. 4:4). When the time was right, Christ became a man. On earth, Christ underwent experiences that we should carefully study. The single most significant event in Christ's life was the Crucifixion. The lessons in this unit will help you study the Crucifixion and seven other major events in our Lord's life. Knowing when and where these events took place is important, but understanding the reasons they occurred will strengthen you spiritually and help you become more Christlike in character.

Unit 3
Christ's Major Experiences

This unit focuses on eight crucial events in the life of Christ. Each of these events stands as a turning point in history in our knowledge of God and His will. Lesson 12 focuses on the Crucifixion—the central event in the life of Christ. Without it there would be no salvation for us. This lesson is supplemented by a "Christ's World" feature giving the historical background of crucifixion (pages TE54–55).

You will notice that each of the lessons treats one event in the life of Christ, except for Lesson 9. (Lesson 9 discusses three events that stress the authority of Christ in the believer's life.) Each lesson attempts to show how that particular event should shape the thinking of the Christian.

There are several special features in the student lessons that you may want to utilize in your teaching. A unit overview (page TE38) offers geographical and chronological background information as well as a chart summarizing the biblical applications.

Lesson 8 on the birth of Christ provides a list of the order of events surrounding the birth of Christ. Lesson 12 contains a chart of the seven sayings of Christ on the cross. The CD includes these charts—both the full version and a fill-in-the-blank version.

Map 3
Christ's Major Experiences

This introductory page presents a map that locates each of the events in the unit geographically, a timeline that gives the approximate time of the occurrence of each event, and a chart that lists and describes the events. This page may be taught together with the other major maps in the text ("Where Christ Served" and "Cities Christ Visited") to form a separate lesson on the geography of Christ's life. These maps serve as the primary basis for the map exercises on the CD.

[Note: Students will need to study or refer to this map to complete Map Exercise 2 (on the CD).]

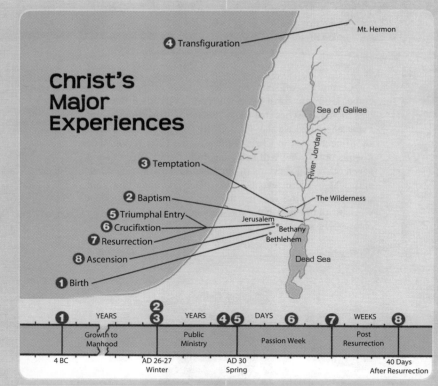

Christ's Major Experiences

④ Transfiguration — Mt. Hermon

Sea of Galilee

River Jordan

③ Temptation

② Baptism

⑤ Triumphal Entry

⑥ Crucifixtion

⑦ Resurrection

⑧ Ascension

① Birth

The Wilderness

Jerusalem

Bethany

Bethlehem

Dead Sea

①	YEARS	②③	YEARS	④⑤	DAYS	⑥	⑦	WEEKS	⑧
	Growth to Manhood		Public Ministry			Passion Week		Post Resurrection	
4 BC		AD 26-27 Winter		AD 30 Spring				40 Days After Resurrection	

LEARNING FROM THE LIFE OF CHRIST

Lesson	Event	Application	Scripture Passages
8	Birth	Trust the Word of God. Appreciate the fact that God became man. Bear reproach as a believer.	Luke 2:1–7
9	Baptism Triumphal Entry Ascension	Respect Christ's authority as (a) Prophet, (b) Priest, and (c) King.	(a) Matt. 3:13–17; Mark 1:9–11; Luke 3:21–23 (b) Matt. 21:1–11, 14–17; Mark 11:1–11; John 12:12–19 (c) Mark 16:19–20; Luke 24:50–53; Acts 1:9–12
10	Temptation	Resist temptations to sin.	Matt. 4:1–11; Mark 1:12–13; Luke 4:1–13
11	Transfiguration	Keep Christ first in your life.	Matt. 17:1–8; Mark 9:2–8; Luke 9:28–36
12	Crucifixion	Trust Christ's death for you.	Matt. 27:33–56; Mark 15:24–42; Luke 23:33–49; John 19:18–37
13	Resurrection	Live for the living Christ.	Matt. 28:1–8; Mark 16:1–8; Luke 24:1–11; John 20:1–10

30

Christ's Birth — L.8

Read: Matthew 1:18–2:23;
Luke 1:5–80; 2:1–38

Memorize: Matthew 1:23

Bible Expressions to Understand

course of Abia (Abijah)—one of the twenty-four segments of the priesthood that served two eight-day periods each year

lot—an object drawn randomly to decide something, such as the duty of a priest during his temple service

dumb—speechless

virgin—a morally pure unmarried woman

dayspring—dawn

espoused—engaged to marry

swaddling clothes—unsewn cloths wrapped around the body of an infant

days of her purification—a six-week period after childbirth, during which a woman and her new child were ceremonially impure

Who was born on June 21, 1982, at 9:03 p.m.? On the day of his birth, cannons were fired, church bells were rung, and choruses were sung. Over two thousand gifts flowed in from all over the world. Though born in a city hospital, he would live in a palace. Why all the celebration? It was the birth of the future king of England, Prince William, son of Charles, the Prince of Wales, and his first wife Princess Diana.

When Jesus was born there wasn't much celebrating—except in heaven. Though He was the King of Kings and Lord of Lords, nobody held a ceremony or threw a party. Born in a stable, He would live in a poor village. Gifts came only from a group of wise men who traveled from the East. Though he had a carpenter for a stepfather and a peasant girl for a mother, this King would rule the universe. His power would not be merely symbolic, as is that of the king of England. He would heal the sick, cast out demons, and raise the dead. He would change the course of nature, save men from their sins, and judge the world. Though everyone will someday forget the birth of Prince William, Christ's birth has never been forgotten and never will be.

Everything about the Lord's birth was unusual. At least seventeen miracles accompanied His birth. Angels spoke to men and women, sang in the heavens, and appeared in dreams. God imparted special information about this birth by His Holy Spirit.

Guided by a miraculous star in the heavens, wise men came to worship Christ. This was no normal birth. All these things signaled the entrance of God, coming as a man to live among humans.

The most unusual thing about the birth of Christ was the nature of the birth itself. Christ was born of a virgin, a morally pure unmarried woman. Isaiah had foretold this event 740 years before. God sent an angel to both Mary and Joseph to explain. The

Though unnoticed by most, the birth of Jesus Christ was the most unusual birth in the history of the world.

31

LESSON 8
Christ's Birth

THEME	The Virgin Birth
SCRIPTURE	Matthew 1:18–2:23; Luke 1:5–80; 2:1–38
MEMORY WORK	Matthew 1:23

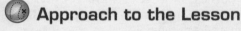 **Approach to the Lesson**

Theme: Christ chose to come into the world through a virgin birth. He did not begin to exist at this point, but He did become human at the instant He was conceived in Mary's womb. What difference does this fact make for practical Christian living? This lesson discusses several practical ramifications of the virgin birth. Remember that not everything in the Bible has to be "practical" to be important. Revelation comes in two forms: truth and duty. Duty is "practiced," but the outward results of truth are not always immediately visible. Nevertheless, truth shapes our thinking and establishes our values. Eventually the effects of truth in our lives will show up in our behavior.

Rationale: Use this lesson to stress the reliability and importance of Scripture. Also emphasize the importance of a proper response to reproach in a Christian's life. Peer pressure has a huge impact on teens, and those who are Christians must understand that they will eventually face rejection if they are true to Christ.

Objectives

KNOWLEDGE (concepts students need to grasp)	the prophecies fulfilled by the virgin birth
	the miraculous nature of the virgin birth
APPLICATION (principles students should put into practice)	If the Scripture is reliable in all it says (and it is), then Christ was born of a virgin.
	Because Christ was born of a virgin, He is more than a man and is worthy of our worship.
	We should be willing to bear reproach as Christ was.
	We can trust the Bible to guide every aspect of our lives.

Background: The passages assigned for this lesson cover four themes: the birth of John the Baptist, the annunciations of the birth of Christ to Mary and to Joseph, the birth itself, and the events immediately following the birth.

Although your students will be reading the accounts in both Matthew and Luke and answering questions about them, your lesson will be structured around three practical applications based on the reality of the virgin birth. References will be made to verses from the assigned passages supporting the development of these applications.

An important teaching aid, a copy of the chart "The Order of Events Surrounding the Birth of Christ" (page 32 in the student text) is found on the CD.

 The Lesson

I. The Reliability of Scripture

The prophecy of a virgin. Matthew explains that the virgin birth was a confirmation of the accuracy of Isaiah's prophecy (Matt. 1:22–23). Isaiah had prophesied to Ahaz, king of Judah, that an Israelite/Syrian invasion would fail and that both Syria and Israel would be destroyed within sixty-five years. God offered to validate this prophecy with a miraculous sign. Ahaz hypocritically said he did not want to tempt the Lord by asking for a sign (Isa. 7:10–12). In reality he didn't believe the Lord and wanted to join Assyria against Israel and Syria. The Lord saw through his hypocrisy and gave a sign anyway, but not a sign that Ahaz understood: the prophecy of the virgin birth of Christ.

The prophecy of an heir. Another prophecy fulfilled by the virgin birth was

Outline

I. The reliability of Scripture
   A. The prophecy of a virgin
   B. The prophecy of an heir
   C. The prophecy of a place
II. The uniqueness of Christ
   A. The uniqueness of the birth
   B. The reasons for the incarnation
III. The necessity of reproach

Isaiah 7 from the Dead Sea Scrolls dated 200 BC
[Dead Sea Scroll (detail), Qumran]

the Lord's promise to David, "And thine house and thy kingdom shall be established for ever before thee: thy throne shall be established for ever" (2 Sam. 7:16). But several generations later, the kingly line (in the person of Jehoiachin or Coniah) was cursed: "Thus saith the Lord, Write ye this man childless, a man that shall not prosper in his days: for no man of his seed shall prosper, sitting upon the throne of David, and ruling any more in Judah" (Jer. 22:30). This curse seems to create a big obstacle to the fulfillment of God's promise to David. The legal right to rule in Judah had been passed down from one male to another, but now that physical link was cursed by God. Joseph, the legal father of Jesus, was of this cursed line.

The solution to this problem is found in the virgin birth. Jesus received the legal right to the throne from His legal father, Joseph, but escaped the curse that a direct physical descent from Joseph would have brought because His mother, Mary, was a descendant of Nathan, a different son of David (Luke 3:31). Through this uncursed line Jesus received His physical right to be king. How else could the Lord Jesus have been the uncursed, legal heir to the throne of David except through the virgin birth and His adoption by Joseph? The fulfillment of Isaiah's prophecy of the virgin birth is the only way the Lord could fulfill His promise to David *and* His curse on Jehoiachin.

The prophecy of a place. The virgin birth of Christ was an aspect of the fulfillment of one other prophecy, the one about the location of Christ's birth. Micah 5:2 predicted, "But thou, Beth-lehem Ephratah, though thou be little among the thousands of Judah, yet out of thee shall he come forth unto me that is to be ruler in Israel; whose goings forth have been from of old, from everlasting." Matthew 2:6 states that Jesus's birth in Bethlehem fulfilled this prophecy.

Luke gives some interesting details about how things unfolded. "And it came

Holy Spirit would cause Mary to conceive and bear a son, the Son of God.

Why is the virgin birth one of the most important truths of the Christian faith? Sometimes when you read the Bible you will come across facts about obscure people, places, and events. If you ask how to apply them to living your life as a Christian, you may have difficulty coming up with a good answer. This seems to be the case, at first, with the virgin birth of Christ. Most of the information in the Bible can fit into one or two basic categories—truth or duty. Duties are actions you must perform to please God. Truths are ideas that affect the way you think about Christ, others, and the world in general. The truths are just as important as the duties: the way you think is as important as the way you act. The way you think about Christ, God's Son, is especially important.

One of the lessons of the virgin birth is that the Bible is reliable—everything it says is true. Matthew says of the virgin birth, "Now all this was done, that it might be fulfilled which was spoken of the Lord by the prophet, saying, Behold, a virgin shall be with child, and shall bring forth a son, and they shall call his name Emmanuel, which being interpreted is, God with us" (Matt. 1:22–23). When the Bible gives a prophecy from God, the record is accurate, and the prophecy will be fulfilled. Of course, the virgin birth is only one of hundreds of biblical prophecies that have already been fulfilled.

Another lesson from the virgin birth is that Christ loved us enough to become one of us. Think of all the things God the Son accomplished by becoming human. How would the problem of sin ever have been solved if Christ had not become a man, died for our sins, and been raised to life to conquer sin and death? If Christ had not lived as a man, we would never have had a perfect example of holiness to follow. If Christ had not lived on earth, we would find it difficult to explain our problems and sorrows to Him in prayer. We would find it hard to believe that He would understand and forgive us. But having been through all the temptations we have experienced, He is sympathetic and will listen in kindness and mercy.

THE ORDER OF EVENTS SURROUNDING THE BIRTH OF CHRIST
1. The birth of John the Baptist is foretold.
2. An angel announces the birth of Christ to Mary.
3. Mary visits Elisabeth, the mother of John the Baptist.
4. John the Baptist is born.
5. Joseph dreams, and an angel explains the birth of Christ.
6. Mary and Joseph go to Bethlehem.
7. CHRIST IS BORN.
8. The angels tell the shepherds about Christ's birth.
9. The shepherds find Christ in the manger.
10. Jesus is presented at the temple.
11. The wise men come to worship Christ.
12. Mary, Joseph, and Jesus flee from Herod into Egypt.
13. Mary, Joseph, and Jesus return and live in Nazareth.

32

to pass in those days, that there went out a decree from Caesar Augustus, that all the world should be taxed" (Luke 2:1). Caesar Augustus ruled the Roman Empire from 27 BC to AD 14. His was a reign of great peace and prosperity for the Romans. When he declared that "all the world" should be taxed, he meant his whole empire. The term translated "taxed" in this passage means "enrolled," as in a census. In other words, all the people in the empire were to return to their hometowns for a census so that the Romans could tax them correctly. Though Joseph was living in Nazareth in Galilee, he and Mary had to go back to "the city of David, which is called Bethlehem; (because he was of the house and lineage of David)" (2:4). The flood of people pouring into Bethlehem for this census explains why

there was no place for Mary and Joseph to stay. They ended up spending the night in a stable, an enclosed area for livestock, where Mary gave birth to Jesus. The wrapping of the baby in rags, called swaddling clothes, indicates the desperate financial condition of this young family.

This amazing set of circumstances had to develop to get a sensible carpenter to travel seventy miles on foot or donkey, with a wife who was about to have a baby, and with no knowledge of where they would stay when they reached their destination. God moved a pagan political ruler to issue an order for a census, which made it necessary for them to make the trip. This was a miracle of God's providence. As a result, Micah's prophecy was fulfilled.

The virgin birth of Christ also teaches the difficult and unpleasant lesson of reproach (shame and disgrace). Mary was a pure and holy young woman. Joseph, the man she was going to marry, was a just and fair man. When it became known that Mary was pregnant, it appeared disgraceful because she was not married. Joseph didn't know what to do. He thought about not marrying her. God then sent an angel to tell Joseph that the Holy Spirit had caused her to conceive the child and the child was God the Son. Mary and Joseph were relieved, but who else would understand? What was a fulfillment of prophecy and a divine blessing for Joseph and Mary was a source of serious misunderstanding for others. No doubt Joseph and Mary suffered shame and humiliation in the eyes of others. Years later, the religious leaders reminded Christ that they considered Him illegitimate (John 8:41).

If you are a Christian, you've experienced a special birth by the Spirit of God. Unsaved people cannot understand that birth and your life as a Christian until they experience it themselves. Christ loves you, and Christians may love you, but to the world you are and always will be a fool. Christ was treated this way when He was in the world, and you should expect no better treatment.

The Virgin Birth: Myth or Miracle?

Christ's entrance into the world was a miracle. No one has ever been born as He was. This was a miracle that began a life of miracles. The lessons from it are important for you today. From the virgin birth you learn that Scripture can be trusted. You also learn that Christ loved us enough to become our example, our Savior, and our friend. The virgin birth also reminds us that being God's child and servant may often result in misunderstanding and embarrassment. That is part of being a Christian

Do You Remember?

1. Where did Mary live? _Nazareth_

2. How long did Mary stay with Elisabeth? _three months_

3. Who issued a decree requiring a census of everyone in the Roman Empire? _____
   Caesar Augustus

4. Who was the Governor of Syria at that time? _Cyrenius_

5. How did the shepherds learn of Jesus's birth? _An angel told them._

6. How many days passed after His birth before Jesus was circumcised? _eight_

7. What sacrifice did Joseph and Mary bring for the birth of their firstborn? _____
   two turtledoves

8. What two godly Israelites in the temple recognized that Jesus was the Messiah? _____
   Simeon and Anna

9. How did the Jewish religious leaders know that the Messiah would be born in Bethlehem? _____
   The prophet Micah had foretold it.

33

The virgin birth of Christ proves the reliability of Scripture. When God says something will happen, it *will* happen as He has said. The practical applications of this truth are abundant. Your students can trust what God says in His Word. Whatever the command or statement of fact, the Word of God is true.

II. The Uniqueness of Christ

The uniqueness of the birth. Christ was unique. Fully God, He became fully man (John 1:1, 14). The virgin birth was the unique means He chose to enter this unique form. Christ, "being in the form of God, thought it not robbery to be equal with God: but made himself of no reputation, and took upon him the form of a servant, and was made in the likeness of men" (Phil. 2:6–7).

The arrival of God the Son into the world as a man did not go unnoticed. Mary and Joseph were not the only ones who knew this was a supernatural event. Elisabeth, Mary's cousin and the mother of John the Baptist, knew that God was entering the world through Mary. When Mary came to visit her, she said, "And whence is this to me, that the mother of my Lord should come to me?" (Luke 1:43) After receiving the announcement from the angel and going to see Jesus, the shepherds realized that they had witnessed a momentous occasion, and they "returned, glorifying and praising God for all the things that they had heard and seen, as it was told unto them" (2:20). When Mary and Joseph brought Jesus to the temple for His dedication, two elderly saints immediately recognized Him as the Christ (Luke 2:28, 38). Later a group of scholars from the East (probably Persia or Babylonia) came seeking Christ and worshiped Him by bowing down and giving gifts to Him (Matt. 2:11). Worship, praise, and spoken testimony at the time of His birth all affirmed that Jesus was God incarnate.

Worship, praise, and testimony are still proper responses to Christ. He is not a fairy-tale character. Stress that those of your students who do not respond to Christ in these ways do not have a right relationship with Him.

The reasons for the incarnation. God the Son had definite reasons for becoming human. This was a means by which God could reveal Himself to man as He never had before and thus receive the praise and honor due Him. That this was one of the purposes of the incarnation is affirmed by the scriptural assertion that Christ is "the image of the invisible God" (Col. 1:15).

Another reason God the Son became human through the virgin birth was to save His people from their sins. When the angel announced the coming birth of Christ to Joseph, he said, "And she shall bring forth a son, and thou shalt call his name Jesus: for he shall save his people from their sins" (Matt. 1:21). If Christ had not become a man, there could have been no sinless life, no substitutionary death for sinners, and no resurrection in victory over sin and the grave (Rom. 5:19).

Christ also became human to set an example of holy living for us. Peter wrote, "For even hereunto were ye called: because Christ also suffered for us, leaving us an example, that ye should follow his steps" (1 Pet. 2:21). God, as man, lived a life according to the perfect standard of the revelation of His will, the Scriptures.

A final reason God became man was to experience temptation and suffering, that He might effectively assist us in our difficulties. "Wherefore in all things it behoved him to be made like unto his brethren, that he might be a merciful and faithful high priest in things pertaining to God, to make reconciliation for the sins of the people. For in that he himself hath suffered being tempted, he is able to succour them that are tempted" (Heb. 2:17–18). Later the same writer says, "For we have not an high priest which cannot be touched with the feeling of our infirmities; but was in all points tempted like as we are, yet without sin" (Heb. 4:15). Thus all the experiences of Christ as a man help Him in helping us.

Without the virgin birth Christ would not have lived as a man and accomplished the things He did. When critics attack the doctrine of the virgin birth, they're really attacking the whole idea of the incarnation, God in the flesh. To eliminate the deity of Christ is the "solution" false teachers use to relieve themselves of the responsibility brought on by the life, teachings, and death of Christ.

III. The Necessity of Reproach

For Mary to be chosen as the mother of the Messiah was a great honor every Jewish woman desired. In the "Magnificat" Mary praised the Lord for His kind dealings with her (Luke 1:46–55). But apparently neither Mary nor Joseph understood Isaiah's prophecy that a virgin must bear the Christ until they had the situation explained to them by angelic messengers. No one else had that benefit. Thus what was a great blessing and miracle was also a source of embarrassment because others did not understand.

The Lord Jesus Himself faced reproach over the virgin birth. During a discussion with Jewish leaders, they said, "We be not born of fornication; we have one Father, even God" (John 8:41). This was probably a reference to the misunderstanding concerning the Lord's birth that had followed Him all those years.

> The world and even other Christians often misunderstand the actions of dedicated believers. To the unsaved, biblical thinking and service to God are foolish, and they treat believers accordingly. Because we are human, this attitude hurts us. This is part of what we are supposed to bear as followers of Christ.

> People of the world will never understand why we love the Bible and worship Christ. We should not expect them to understand, nor should we change our approach to fit what they think is right. Just as the nature of Christ's birth was misunderstood, we must expect the unsaved to misunderstand the nature of our birth. They will not understand it until they experience it themselves.

Special Problems and Topics

• **Was Mary really a virgin or just a young woman?**

Unbelieving scholars argue that the Hebrew word ʽălmâ, translated "virgin" in Isaiah 7:14, simply means "young woman." This is not a logical argument. How would a young woman's bearing a child be a special sign from God? Women bear children all the time. Furthermore, though Hebrew dictionaries state that the word may be used of a young woman, Matthew 1:23 confirms that this prophecy was talking about a virgin. In that verse Matthew (writing under inspiration, of course) uses the Greek word *parthenos*, which means exclusively "virgin," not "young woman." Since the fact that Mary was a virgin is an important point in proving the reliability of Isaiah's prophecy, it is not surprising that unbelievers attack it.

Extra Activities

Discussion: To develop the practical nature of the material in the accounts of Christ's birth, discuss the character of those associated with it.

(a) Shepherds (Luke 2:16)
hurried to worship the Messiah

(b) Wise men (Matt. 2:1, 11)
traveled a long distance to worship Him; offered gifts to Him

(c) Mary and Joseph (Luke 2:21–24)
obeyed the Law

(d) Simeon (Luke 2:25–27)
just; devout; expected the Messiah to come; led by the Spirit

(e) Anna (Luke 2:36–37)
served God constantly in fasting and prayers

Discussion: The world was perfectly prepared for the appearance of Christ. The Bible says, "When the fulness of the time was come, God sent forth his Son" (Gal. 4:4). In what ways were the times "full," i.e., prepared for the coming of Christ?

(a) Roman conquest of the world had prepared the way for unrestricted travel throughout the empire, making it possible for the message of Christianity to spread.

(b) The widespread adoption of the Greek language made it possible to communicate freely the gospel message.

(c) There was peace in the world.

(d) There was an expectant attitude on the part of many Jews. They were looking for the Messiah.

(e) The Roman census caused prophecy to be fulfilled.

LESSON 9
Respecting Christ's Authority

THEME	Christ's Authority Demonstrated
SCRIPTURE	Matthew 3:13–17; 21:1–11; Luke 24:50–53
MEMORY WORK	Matthew 3:17

Approach to the Lesson

Theme: We know little of Jesus's adult life prior to the beginning of His ministry, except what we learn from a simple question (Mark 6:3): "Is not this the carpenter, the son of Mary, the brother of James, and Joses, and of Juda, and Simon? and are not his sisters here with us?" From this verse a few inferences can be drawn. Jesus worked as a builder of household furniture and farm implements. He had brothers and sisters. His mother was apparently widowed (sometime after Jesus was twelve since Joseph is not mentioned after the trip to Jerusalem). We also know that most Israelites looked down on His hometown of Nazareth (John 1:46). The simple record of these unremarkable facts does not inspire a great regard for Christ. If this were all that was recorded of His life, it would have no great significance.

The Gospels, however, give a much fuller record—one that inspires great respect. Certain incidents in Jesus's life underscore His authority. Jesus was ordained by God to be a Prophet, Priest, and King. The incidents in this lesson stress the authority God granted Christ in each of these offices.

Rationale: Students who are believers should view Jesus as their friend, but they should be warned about the serious danger of treating Christ as an equal. The believer must never lose his awe for the power and majesty of Christ. He is to be worshiped with the whole heart. A proper respect for His authority leads to that kind of worship.

Background: Though the incidents in this lesson seem unrelated at first, a single theme unites them: each incident underscores the divinely sanctioned authority of Christ. Christ's baptism was the divine initiation of His ministry as a great prophet, who came to reveal God as no one had before. The triumphal entry underscored

Christ's kingship. The ascension was God's exaltation of Christ to His right hand, where He now ministers for us as a priest. As the anointed Prophet, Priest, and King, Christ has great authority.

The Lesson

I. The Authority of the Prophet (Matt. 3:13–17)

The Son's sinlessness. Christ's sinlessness gave His preaching authority. When Jesus came to the river and presented Himself for baptism, John did not understand why He had come (Matt. 3:13–14). John's response was that he needed to be baptized by Jesus. Considering John's sinfulness and Christ's sinlessness, this response made perfect sense. John's baptism was one of repentance from sin. It was an act by which people demonstrated an inward turning from sin to God. How could Christ need this baptism?

The Lord told John that "it becometh us to fulfill all righteousness" (3:15). Christ saw Himself as responsible to obey in all matters of righteousness, even if in this case the symbol was not necessary to express His inner condition. He thought it essential to identify with John's ministry by submitting to his baptism. For Christ to show agreement with a ministry calling people to repentance was highly appropriate since from that time on He participated in the same ministry. His first sermon was about repentance (4:17).

The Spirit's empowerment. Christ's empowerment by the Holy Spirit gave Him

Objectives

KNOWLEDGE (concepts students need to grasp)	the meaning of John's baptism
	the significance of the dove at Christ's baptism
	the significance of Christ's entering Jerusalem on a donkey
	the part of Christ's work that began at the ascension
APPLICATION (principles students should put into practice)	Our conduct in religious services (e.g., chapel) should reflect our respect for Christ's authority.
	Respect for Christ should show itself in the way we pray.
	Spiritual matters are not appropriate topics for jokes.

Outline

authority. When the Lord was coming up out of the waters of baptism, praying as He came (Luke 3:21), the heavens opened, and the Spirit of God descended on Him in the shape of a dove (Matt. 3:16). All Christ's acts as the Prophet would be done in the power of the Spirit. When He revealed God through miracles, He did it through the power and authority of the Spirit. When He revealed God through the spoken word, He did it through the power of the Spirit. At the synagogue in Nazareth, He read from Isaiah concerning Himself, "The Spirit of the Lord is upon me, because he hath anointed me to preach the gospel to the poor; he hath sent me to heal the brokenhearted, to preach deliverance to the captives, and recovering of sight to the blind, to set at liberty them that are bruised, to preach the acceptable year of the Lord" (Luke 4:18–19; cf. Isa. 61:1–2).

The Spirit's visible descent as a dove is symbolic. The white color of the dove suggests the sinless purity of Christ. The dove is also gentle. Though Christ would be powerful in the exercise of His ministry, He would remain gentle, never abusing His power. He was the perfect balance of power and gentleness in His ministry as the Prophet. This is but one aspect of the remarkable symmetry of Christ's character.

This beginning of Jesus's ministry reveals the basis for His authority. It was based on His sinlessness, His empowerment by the Spirit, and His Father's approval. No prophet ever revealed God as Jesus did. His words and works should be the object of reverent study for every one of your students.

The student text pages for this lesson begin on the next page.

The Father's approval. Christ's ministry had authority because He received the Father's sanction. Immediately after the descent of the dove, there came a voice from heaven saying, "This is my beloved Son, in whom I am well pleased" (Matt. 3:17). In this statement the Father both evaluated the hidden years of Christ's life and offered His approval for the future. Jesus had lived a sinless life during all the years in Nazareth. The cumulative strength of His character, the years of moral perfection, and the promise of the fulfilled will of God in His public ministry brought the benediction and approval of the Father.

II. The Authority of the King (Matt. 21:1–11)

Christ's triumphal entry into Jerusalem occurred at the beginning of the week of His arrest, trial, and Crucifixion. The incident is also recorded in the other three Gospels (Mark 11:1–11; Luke 19:29–44; and John 12:12–19).

During His public ministry, and especially after the feeding of the five thousand, the Lord had faced the problem of those who wanted to make Him a political ruler to overthrow the oppressive Roman government. John records how Christ responded: "When Jesus therefore perceived that they would come and take him by force, to make him a king, he departed again into a mountain himself alone" (John 6:15).

Although the Lord carefully avoided becoming a political ruler, He did present Himself as the true king of Israel in both a spiritual and an actual sense. He was the Lord and king of all those who would submit to Him as Savior. One day in the Millennium, He will rule regenerated Israel from the throne of David. The triumphal entry was the public testimony of Jesus's kingship. He was anticipating His future rule over the nation that in just a few days would reject Him outright by crucifying Him.

The use of the donkey. The manner of the Lord's entrance into Jerusalem underscored His authority as the King. He chose to enter on the back of a young unridden donkey colt and sent two disciples to get the animal (Matt. 21:1–3). Unused animals were viewed as specially suited for spiritual purposes (Num. 19:2; Deut. 21:3; 1 Sam. 6:7). Following Christ's directions, the disciples brought back the colt and its mother, the latter to ensure a calmer ride for Christ on an animal that had never been ridden before. The working out of these seemingly

Bible Expressions to Understand

the foal of an ass—a donkey's colt, usually less than a year old
hosanna—an exclamation of welcome meaning "Save, I pray"
Son of David—a descendant of King David
endued—filled

"The president's coming!"

"To Brookfield?"

Everyone in the small town was surprised at first. *Why would he come here?* they wondered. But soon the whole community got caught up in a spirit of improvement and preparation. Businesses repainted their signs. The mayor had street signs replaced, curbs painted, potholes in the roads repaired, and new flowers and shrubbery planted in the town square.

When the day finally came, a parade marched from the courthouse to the school gymnasium where the president was to speak. The school band led the way, with the president's motorcade following. The platform was jammed with dignitaries. Congressmen, judges, and community leaders were present. There was not an empty seat anywhere. When the president arrived, he was greeted with thunderous applause. His speech was interrupted with applause thirty-five times. No day in Brookfield had ever matched this one.

Small town or large, the reactions that occurred in Brookfield would have happened anywhere the president went. Why? The presence of a powerful person, a person of authority, results in an outpouring of respect and productivity. If this is true, then what about believers' response to the presence of Jesus Christ?

The Lord Jesus Christ is a person of great authority. The passages for this lesson present three incidents that stress the authority of Christ when He lived in this world and the authority He still has today. How should you respond to that authority?

34

small details demonstrates Christ's control of the surrounding circumstances.

The steps the Lord took to acquire the donkey colt were a deliberate move to fulfill the Messianic prophecy of Zechariah 9:9, quoted by Matthew: "Tell ye the daughter of Sion, Behold, thy King cometh unto thee, meek, and sitting upon an ass, and a colt the foal of an ass" (Matt. 21:5). Even though a horse would have been the usual animal for a conquering king to ride into a city, that would not have fulfilled the more specific description of the Messiah given in this Old Testament passage. This method of entrance is also more fitting for Christ. His authority was based first on His submission to the will of God and then on the willingness of others to submit to Him. To enter the city proudly on a spirited horse

simply would not have communicated the meekness that the entrance on the lowly colt did.

The response of the crowd. The actions of the people along the route also underscored Christ's authority as the King. They spread their outer garments on the road for Him to ride over, imitating the ancient method of welcoming a new sovereign (Matt. 21:8–9; cf. 2 Kings 9:13). Carpeting the road with foliage was a further extension of that welcome. The praises of the multitude also emphasized that they viewed Christ as a king. They cried, "Hosanna" (meaning "Save, I pray!") and "Blessed be the King that cometh in the name of the Lord" (Luke 19:38). They called Him the "son of David," suggesting His kingly lineage. They also rejoiced in the coming of

The Lord was about thirty years old when He began His ministry by being baptized. This incident is recorded in Matthew 3:13–17. His baptism showed that He agreed with John's ministry of leading people to turn from sin to God. It also showed God's approval of the coming ministry of Jesus and the great power He would demonstrate in that ministry. The Father's voice from heaven said, "This is my beloved Son, in whom I am well pleased." From that day on, Christ was to be recognized as a prophet, proclaiming God's truth to everyone. When Jesus was coming up out of the water, the Holy Spirit descended from heaven on Him in the form of a dove. All the miracles and preaching that the Lord Jesus did were done in the power of the Holy Spirit. Jesus said this Himself when He preached in Nazareth (Luke 4:17–18).

Many prophets spoke and wrote during the Old Testament era, but none equaled Jesus. He was God in the flesh, and He revealed God perfectly to the human race. He was the greatest, most powerful Prophet who ever lived. Since Jesus had this unique authority, it only makes sense to listen to what He said. To respect and worship Christ is the only right response from a Christian. The words and works of Jesus are nothing to joke about. They are to be lived by, not laughed at.

Jesus was not only the great Prophet but also the great King. Near the end of His ministry, Jesus entered Jerusalem as a king (Matt. 21:1–11). As He rode into the city on a young donkey, the crowds praised Him. They laid palm branches and their coats on the road for Him to ride over. The whole city was curious about this magnificent entrance. This was no ordinary man. This was a king—the King of kings.

Just as crowds showed great respect for the Lord's authority during His entrance into Jerusalem, so should you show great regard for Him as the King of your life. Remember how the people in Brookfield responded to the president's visit? All the improvements were a way of showing respect to the leader. If you knew Christ might come to visit you today, how would you act? What would you change? These are the very things you should change today because the Bible teaches that Christ is with you right now. Only a holy life honors Him.

Christ is also our great Priest. Luke 24:50–53 tells about the Lord's ascension. After His Resurrection, He ascended into heaven and took His place on the throne at the right hand of the Father.

What is He doing there now? Christ performs His priestly ministry for us in heaven today. A priest is a person who talks to God on behalf of people. The New Testament says that Jesus is our High Priest if we have trusted Him as Savior. The writer of Hebrews says, "Seeing then that we have a great high priest, that is passed into the heavens, Jesus the Son of God, let us hold fast our profession" (Heb. 4:14). Christ's prayers for us at the right hand of God assure our success in the Christian life, so we should remain faithful to Him.

No matter how difficult your problems may seem, Jesus understands them and can help you with them. "For we have not an high priest which cannot be touched with the feeling of our infirmities; but was in all points tempted like as we are, yet without sin" (Heb. 4:15).

Because Jesus ascended into heaven, we have a High Priest to help us forever. This is a great encouragement. Our ability to do what we should do and be what we should be does not depend just on our determination and willpower. We have Christ's help. One who has the power and the authority to help us deserves our respect. Jesus is the One Who has that power.

Who Do You Respect?

If the president were to come to your school, you would treat him respectfully. As the leader of our country, he has great authority over you. If your pastor comes to your home or you see him in church, you listen to him because of the authority God has given him to help you as a Christian. God has given your parents power over you. They too deserve your respect and obedience. But no one has more authority over you than Christ. No one deserves more respect from you than He does. He is the great Prophet, the great King, and your great High Priest.

35

---

the kingdom of their father David, heralded by the appearance of Christ (Mark 11:10). These appellations unite to emphasize the authority of Jesus as the King. His entrance into Jerusalem was such an event that it prompted everyone to wonder about the Person being given such a welcome (Matt. 21:10–11).

The crowd's response at the triumphal entry should be the constant response of every child of God. "Blessed be the King that cometh in the name of the Lord" are fitting words for the lips of all Christians. Christ is to be the absolute ruler of our lives. His will should be our will. Respect for the great King of Kings should naturally result in obedience to His commands. The kingship of Jesus is not something of the past. It is a present reality, or at least it should be, for every one of your students.

Just days after this welcome, the crowds—at the encouragement of the Jewish leadership—were calling for Christ's Crucifixion. Those who called for His death may not have been the same people who welcomed Him. However, these Palm Sunday worshipers were guilty of silence when He was tried and crucified later in the week.

III. The Authority of the Priest (Luke 24:50–53)

Mark 16:19 and Acts 1:9–11 present the ascension of Christ. Though the ascension is only briefly described in these passages, Christ predicted it more than once (John 6:62; 7:33), and it is mentioned in eleven other books of the New Testament. The implications of the ascension are profound.

One implication concerns the future. After having charged His disciples to tarry at Jerusalem and wait for the coming of the Holy Spirit, who would empower them for witness, Jesus was lifted up and disappeared into a cloud. Then two angels appeared and told the awestruck disciples—who were staring up into the sky—that Jesus would come again as they had seen Him go (Acts 1:9–11). The ascension of Christ uniquely anticipates His Second Advent as the King of Kings. As He ascended bodily, so will He return.

The other profound implication of the ascension is Christ's perpetual presence with the Father in our behalf. This explains the disciples' reaction after His ascension: "And they worshipped him and returned to Jerusalem with great joy: and were continually in the temple, praising and blessing God" (Luke 24:52–53). As He was ascending, the Lord blessed them, and they had the assurance that He would continue to do so through His ministry at the right hand of the Father, which is the place or position to which Christ ascended: "So then after the Lord had spoken unto them, he was received up into heaven, and sat on the right hand of God" (Mark 16:19).

The Gospels do not fully develop Christ's role as high priest. However, the book of Hebrews picks up the theme and delineates the implications of the ascension with reference to Christ's high-priestly work. Jesus is fully qualified to represent us before the Father because of His experience as a man. "Wherefore in all things it behoved him to be made like unto his brethren, that he might be a merciful and faithful high priest in things pertaining to God, to make reconciliation for the sins of the people. For in that he himself hath suffered being tempted, he is able to succour them that are tempted" (Heb. 2:17–18). The writer later reminds us, "For we have not an high priest which cannot be touched with the feeling of our infirmities; but was in all points tempted like as we are, yet without sin" (4:15). Christ continues as our living Priest, having as-cended on high. "But this man, because he continueth ever, hath an unchangeable priesthood. Wherefore he is able also to save them to the uttermost that come unto God by him, seeing he ever liveth to make intercession for them" (7:24–25).

The Christian's life is one of constant dependence on the ascended, living Christ, who intercedes for us at the right hand of the Father. Our needs are great. Our sins are many. Our weaknesses are profound. Our failings are constant. But Christ our High Priest is ever faithful. Help your students see that their Lord is alive, ministering for them. Encourage them with the truth of His great power and authority to meet their spiritual and material needs.

Summarizing, the writer says, "Now of the things which we have spoken this is the sum: We have such an high priest, who is set on the right hand of the throne of the Majesty in the heavens" (Heb. 8:1). We should all, therefore, "come boldly unto the throne of grace, that we may obtain mercy, and find grace to help in time of need" (4:16).

✳ Extra Activity

Case studies: Using the following case studies, help your students see how they can submit to Christ's authority as their Prophet, Priest, and King.

Case study #1: Marie has just about completed her week at camp. She can't wait to get home to fresh sheets, a clean bathroom, and Mom's good cooking. All week a missionary has been preaching. Life on the mission field as he has described it sounds a lot like camp life all year around. Marie feels a strong urge to submit to the Lord by being willing to go into missions, and at the Friday evening campfire service that feeling is stronger than ever. If Marie submits to the conviction of the Holy Spirit about the mission field, she will be accepting Christ's authority as her _____.
King (He has the right to tell her where to live and what to do with her life.)

Case study #2: Richard has always been frustrated by math. He just doesn't seem to be able to do very well in it. This year has been even more difficult than usual, and he is getting an *F.* At first he tried to be nice to his teacher, but the worse he did, the harder it became to treat her kindly. Eventually he began to complain to his parents about his Christian school. He said he wanted to go to some other school. For the solution to his problems, Richard needs to submit to Christ as his _____.
High Priest (Christ understands Richard's problem. He is able to give him the determination and endurance to face his difficult circumstances. Richard needs to pray for Christ's help.)

Do You Remember?

1. Where did John baptize Jesus? _in the Jordan River_

2. What reason did Jesus give for asking John to baptize Him? ____
   to fulfill all righteousness

3. In what form did the Holy Spirit descend on Jesus at His baptism? _a dove_

4. Why did Jesus ride into Jerusalem on a young donkey? _(Answers may vary.)_
   to fulfill prophecy; to show that He came in peace; to demonstrate humility

5. When observers in Jerusalem asked who it was on the donkey, how did the multitude describe Christ? ____
   "This is Jesus the prophet of Nazareth of Galilee."

6. Where were Jesus and the disciples when He ascended into heaven? ____
   near Bethany outside Jerusalem

7. What did Jesus do for the disciples as He ascended? _He blessed them._

8. How did the disciples respond after Jesus ascended? ____
   They worshiped Him and returned to Jerusalem with great joy.

9. In the days following the ascension, what did the disciples do? ____
   They were continually in the temple, praising and blessing God.

36

Case study #3: Trent has been a Christian since he was five. He was saved one night at home during family devotions. From time to time he has read his Bible regularly, but he has never really become consistent in his study of God's Word. At school his Bible teacher has mentioned how important it is for students his age to discipline themselves to read the Bible regularly. Trent must submit to Christ as his _____.
Prophet (Christ is the great revealer of God. Unless a Christian submits to the revelation of God's Word in Christ, there is no possibility of his ever developing in godliness.)

Read: Luke 4:1–13

Memorize: Luke 4:4

Bible Expressions to Understand

wilderness—an uninhabited area west of Jericho

pinnacle—highest point

Your school's soccer team has endured a long season. Finally the time has come for the district and state championships. The coach has been holding extra practices for several weeks. This week there have been three pep rallies. There are signs all over the school proclaiming that your team is "Number One." Tomorrow the buses will roll out of the school parking lot with everyone cheering at the top of his lungs. This will be one of the greatest times you have ever had at your school—if you get to go. You noticed during math class this afternoon that your stomach started feeling upset.

By the time you arrive home after school, your head is on fire with fever, and you can barely stand up. You spend the rest of the evening and the entire night tossing and turning in bed. Your mother tries to help by bringing cool washcloths for your head.

Nothing seems to help, and by morning you are no better. You go to the doctor and find out you have the flu. You have been sick before, but this time you will miss the championship game. The disappointment is worse than the flu.

The last thing you want at a time like this is a biology lesson explaining why you got sick in the first place. But take a minute to listen to the simple facts. Your body did not have immunity (resistance) to the flu virus that attacked you. Some immunities are inborn; you have them because of inherited characteristics. Others are acquired; your body produces them, or they are injected into your system.

Now think about the passage of Scripture you read for this lesson. Jesus experienced the temptation to sin. He went through this to teach us a valuable lesson concerning our immunity to, or resistance against, sin. When you were born into the family of God by faith in Christ, you inherited some characteristics that help you resist sin. You have a new disposition, or way of thinking, toward God and His Word. You could call this an inborn immunity to sin. You also have the indwelling Holy Spirit to guide you in your choices. The Lord Jesus is always waiting for you to ask for special strength and help against temptation. He has provided you with the Bible, a key to resisting sin. As you memorize its contents, you acquire an immunity to sin that you did not have before.

Our Lord taught these lessons by the example of His temptation. Every time the Devil tempted Him, He quoted Scripture from memory. The Devil responded by stopping one temptation and trying another one until, finally, he gave up for a while.

The Lord's temptation teaches some other important lessons. First, the Devil doesn't give up easily. He attacked Jesus constantly for forty days, trying to trick Him into sinning.

37

Objectives

KNOWLEDGE (concepts students need to grasp)	the three ways Jesus was tempted
	the right way to respond to temptation
	the importance of Christ's experiencing temptation
APPLICATION (principles students should put into practice)	We should be prepared to resist all three of Satan's approaches.
	Consistent Scripture memorization is crucial to resisting temptation.
	Circumstances can strengthen Satan's attack.

temple. Matthew inverts the order of the two. Mark does not discuss the three temptations specifically, but simply presents a two-verse summary of the incident. This lesson follows Luke's account.

 The Lesson

I. The First Forty Days of Temptation (Luke 4:1–2)

A stressful environment, one in which there is constant danger and need, makes sin all the more difficult to resist. After His baptism Jesus went into the wilderness, filled and led by the Holy Spirit. The term used here to describe the filling is the adjectival form of the verb found in Ephesians 5:18, where we are told to be "filled" with the Spirit. The word specifically speaks of a filling that supplies a particular lack or need.

The Spirit of God was in control of the Lord even though He was headed for a season of temptation. Encourage your students to grasp the truth of the help available to us through the Comforter.

Jesus was led by the Spirit as well as filled by Him. He was guided by the Spirit to a particular place at a particular time for a grueling experience. Tradition says that this wilderness was Quarantana, west of Jericho. (See map on page TE38.) Wherever it was, it certainly was a secluded, austere place.

Christ's being filled with the Spirit shows us that without that filling for ourselves during the time of temptation, we are in serious danger of succumbing to sin. With the Spirit present and in control, the Devil will be far less successful in seducing us than if we are empty and open to his solicitations.

LESSON 10
Resisting Sin

THEME	Christ's Temptation
SCRIPTURE	Luke 4:1–13 (Matthew 4:1–11; Mark 1:12–13)
MEMORY WORK	Luke 4:4

 Approach to the Lesson

Theme: The capacity to oppose sin is a major weapon in the Christian's arsenal. Learn to resist temptation, and you will be able to make a positive contribution to the work of Christ.

Rationale: Although the intensity and variety of temptations teenagers face has increased in recent years, the nature of temptation itself has not changed. The method Christ used to defeat Satan still works for believers today. Communicate to your students the excitement of having the solution—a method that works. They need not be defeated.

Background: Jesus's baptism had just occurred. He was beginning His public ministry when the Devil launched this attack.

Luke's account of the temptation is roughly equivalent in length to Matthew's. Both list the temptation to turn the stones into bread first. But Luke then presents the temptation from the mountain, followed by the temptation from the pinnacle of the

Outline

The Lord was threatened by more than the seclusion of the desert. Mark records that He "was with the wild beasts" (1:13). Wild animals are frightening; they are unpredictable and often ferocious. To compound His suffering, He had been fasting for the entire time (Luke 4:2). Abstaining from food for this long would naturally weaken Him physically. Why He fasted for the entire time is not clear. Either food was unavailable, or He wanted to heighten His spiritual perception by avoiding the regular distraction of eating.

> Help your students understand that life in the Spirit does not always lead into comfortable surroundings. The follower of the Lord is to be ready to endure hardness as a good soldier (2 Tim. 2:3). Foreign mission fields are often characterized by this kind of hardness. Inject a missionary story at this point from the life of a missionary such as Hudson Taylor or Adoniram Judson. If you are not familiar with these men, books on their lives and ministries are available at most Christian bookstores or www.bjupress.com.

Certainly the worst part of the forty days was the constant attack of Satan. Luke reports that the Devil's attempts to lure the Lord into sin were constant for the entire period. When Jesus faced the final three temptations, He was facing the climax of Satan's efforts after more than a month of physical deprivation, intimidation, and spiritual attack.

> Long periods of satanic attack are a reality of the Christian experience. Remind your students that their enemy is not weak, nor is he likely to get discouraged in his attempts to destroy them.

II. The Final Attack (Luke 4:3–13)

The temptation to turn stones to bread (4:3–4). After forty days without food, our Lord was hungry. A natural avenue of temptation was this need for food. Jesus had the power to turn the stones to bread. This was not the time for the Lord to prove His

---

One of the possible sites in the Holy Land where Jesus was tempted—The Mount of Temptation

Second, Satan will use timing and circumstances as tools to his advantage. You can expect temptations when things aren't going well at school or when you're physically ill or tired.

The three major temptations Jesus resisted in the wilderness are more subtle than the usual temptations you face. Satan was trying to tempt Jesus to commit sins that might be considered less serious than the open, obvious sins like disobedience to parents or swearing. You can be sure, however, that the sins Jesus resisted were serious ones that you also need to guard against.

The first temptation Satan offered to Jesus sounds innocent. Satan said, "If thou be the Son of God, command this stone that it be made bread" (Luke 4:3). Jesus was hungry because He had been fasting for forty days. Certainly He deserved to have something to eat, but He was willing to depend on God to direct Him concerning what to eat and when. Our Lord is teaching us by His response to Satan that doing the will of God— as it is recorded in the Word of God—is the most important thing in life. To do only what we want to do and when we want to do it is wrong. God wants you to depend on Him when deciding how and when you do things. Just doing the right thing isn't all that matters. If your mother tells you to take out the garbage, but you wait for three days to do it, your timing will ruin your obedience, not to mention the smell of your house.

In the second temptation, Satan tried to get Jesus to accomplish something good by sinning. He told Jesus that if He would worship him, he would give Him authority over all the kingdoms of the world. You are never to do wrong in order to get a chance to do right. Is it right to commit sins with your unsaved friends in order to keep them as friends so that you can witness to them? Of course not. You must live a Christlike life even if it means losing influence with friends.

In the third of the Devil's attacks, he tempted Jesus to ask God to perform a miracle for Him needlessly. Taking Jesus up to a point of the temple high above the valley below, Satan told Him to jump and trust God to protect Him. He tried to deceive Jesus into doing this by misrepresenting Psalm 91:12. You must study the Bible carefully to avoid asking God to do things He never intends to do. You should also understand that the Christian life is one of faithful obedience to the Lord's commands, and not one in which God must constantly be proving His power and love by performing miracles for you. God may help you mi-

> ### Can You Just Say No?
>
> At the time they are born again, God gives His children an inborn capacity to resist sin. He also gives us help in acquiring a greater ability to resist, and He expects us to develop that ability. The ability to say no to invitations to sin is a major weapon in the Christian's arsenal. Learn to resist temptation, and you'll then be able to live a life pleasing to the Lord Jesus Christ and to make a positive contribution to His work.

---

supernatural abilities, however, especially not to the Devil. This was the time to show His utter dependence on the Father for all the necessities of life.

> The most important issue in the lives of your students is that they do the will of God as revealed in His Word. They have the right and the responsibility to work to provide clothing, food, and shelter, but not if the job they choose violates God's will as revealed in the Bible. Furthermore, if that job is an expression of self-dependence, they should not have it. If we are faced with a choice between physical life and obedience to God, we must choose obedience.

Jesus's response to the Devil establishes an order of priorities for any believer who wants to resist temptation of this kind (4:4). Obedience to the Word of God is more important than having physical necessities met, particularly if the meeting of those necessities by self-effort is an act of independence from God (John 4:31–34). Impatience, a violation of God's timing, is simply rejecting dependence on God for a period. It is a sin for a believer to exercise a scripturally established right when he should forego it to demonstrate dependence on the Lord. The Lord had the right and the power to perform a miracle in this setting, but He chose not to. He demonstrated His absolute dependence on God and His will as expressed in written revelation. He could have quoted no more appropriate passage of Scripture than "Man doth not live by bread only, but by every word that proceedeth out of the mouth of the Lord" (Deut. 8:3).

raculously in difficult circumstances, but He is not a genie in a bottle who makes our every wish His command. Sometimes you may want God to do something special for you just to show other people you're special to God. This is the sin of spiritual pride. God resists proud people but gives help and spiritual strength to those who are humble and want to glorify Him.

Do You Remember?

1. Where did the Holy Spirit lead Jesus after His baptism? _into the wilderness_

2. What was the first temptation? _to turn the stones to bread_
   How did Jesus rebuke Satan? _____
   by quoting from God's Word that man shall live by every word of God

3. What was the second temptation? _to worship Satan_
   How did Jesus rebuke Satan? _____
   by quoting from God's Word that we should worship only God

4. What was the third temptation? _to jump from the pinnacle of the temple_
   How did Jesus rebuke Satan? _____
   by quoting from God's Word that we should not tempt God

5. Who assisted Jesus after the temptations? _angels_

39

Behind every command of God is His omnipotence. We need not rely on humanistic schemes to accomplish God's will. For instance, God has commanded your students to preach the gospel to their friends. At the same time they are to live holy, pure lives. They do not have to live like the world to win people to Christ. Their distinctiveness as Christians is what makes their witness powerful. If a teenager goes on living as he did before he was saved and then tries to share the gospel with his unsaved friends, they will not be interested in what he has to say. Unbelievers want to see a difference.

The temptation to rule the world (4:5–8). Having failed to induce disloyalty to the Word of God, the Devil tried again. This time he attempted to get the Lord to use the wrong means to reach a goal He desired. It is God's will for Jesus to rule the world. One day He will rule it in a literal thousand-year reign as He sits on the throne of David (Rev. 20:4). But His rulership will be on His terms, not on the Devil's.

To advance the Devil's cause in any way in our desire to make progress in another area we deem more important is wrong. A student should not steal from his mother to buy a new pair of soccer shoes so that he can make the soccer team and witness to his teammates. Likewise, a student should not cheat on his tests to have high enough grades to be admitted to a Christian college. This would be the same as saying that the Devil's methods are right and useful for reaching spiritual goals. Nothing could be further from the truth. The end never justifies the means.

It is interesting to note the power of Satan as presented here. Since he showed the Lord all the kingdoms of the world in a moment of time, it appears that his powers transcend time and space, but he is neither eternal nor omnipresent. In contrast, the Lord Jesus Christ is both.

What the Devil offered the Lord in this passage was a lie (Luke 4:6). Satan is described as the prince of this world (John 12:31), but he is not the absolute sovereign. The Great Commission clearly reveals that the Lord Jesus already had all authority in heaven and in earth (Matt. 28:18). Why should He stoop to the Devil's request to accomplish what He already had the power to accomplish?

The specific sin the Devil tried to get the Lord Jesus to commit was that of ascribing worth to Satan as the rightful authority over the world and its inhabitants. The Lord would have committed that sin had He worshiped the Devil. He again responded with Scripture, "Thou shalt worship the Lord thy God, and him only shalt thou serve" (Luke 4:8; cf. Deut. 6:13; 10:20). In this response, the Lord implies that to recognize the Devil's attempt to claim authority over any area of life is to do him service, which is a sin.

The temptation to jump from the temple (4:9–13). Finally, the Devil tried to entice Jesus to draw attention to Himself and to manipulate God. This time Satan used Scripture in his effort to entrap the Lord. He quoted Psalm 91:11–12: "He shall give his angels charge over thee, to keep thee: and in their hands they shall bear thee up, lest at any time thou dash thy foot against a stone." The fallacy in Satan's approach was that he misrepresented the promise. Psalm 91 assures the one who loves God that in the dangers of life he will be protected from physical harm. The southern wing of the temple was more than 300 feet above the floor of the Kidron Valley. To go willfully to that high point and jump off, expecting God to perform a miracle, would have been ridiculous. Expecting God to perform a miracle when the motive is spiritual pride or a desire for self-glory is unrealistic. God resists the proud, but gives grace to the humble. Asking God to do this miraculous act would be to tempt Him to evil. Appropriately, the Lord Jesus responded to the Devil's ploy with "Thou shalt not tempt the Lord thy God" (Deut. 6:16).

The inclination to think more highly of ourselves than we ought to think is ever present with us. To go one step further, we generally want others to think better of us than we deserve. Some of the teenagers in your class want answers to prayer so that they can tell people how God answers their prayers. They want to lead people to Christ so that others will think they are effective servants of God. They go to church and act properly in school, not because they fear the Lord, but because they want their teachers and friends to think they are godly. They would like nothing more than for God to perform some special miracle for them so that they could gloat about it in front of others. Your students are now at the age when they need to be warned strongly about this kind of temptation (1 Cor. 10:31; 13:1–3).

Trying to penetrate the mystery of the sinless Lord being tempted to sin is pointless. The reality recorded in Scripture is that He was tempted. We must draw the proper encouragement and instruction from it. Besides being an example for us, the Lord suffered temptation in order to help us in our temptations (Heb. 2:18). We should not think that by going through these temptations the Lord gained some capacity to help us that He would otherwise have lacked. Rather, our knowledge that He has gone through temptation causes us to trust more readily the aid He offers and to seek more fervently His assistance.

Probably the single clearest lesson from the Lord's handling of these temptations is His use of the written Word. He responded with the Scriptures every time the Devil offered a solicitation to evil. This is precisely the idea found in Psalm 119:11: "Thy word have I hid in mine heart, that I might not sin against thee."

Encourage your students to ask you for help in finding verses they can memorize that will help them resist the specific temptations they face.

 Extra Activity

Research: Have your students research the Bible's teachings on specific sins. Each student should find and memorize at least five verses on a particular sin. Show them how to use a concordance, topical Bible, or a Bible software program to find appropriate verses. After about two weeks, have each student state the topic he researched and quote the five verses he has memorized. Give additional points for every extra verse the student learns on the topic.

LESSON 11
Keeping Christ First

Theme	Christ's Transfiguration
Scripture	Luke 9:28–36 (Matthew 17:1–13; Mark 9:1–13)
Memory Work	Luke 9:35

 Approach to the Lesson

Theme: The Lord Jesus is the most important person to the believer. His will and His reputation are what matter above all else. The true disciple considers his own reputation and his service to others as secondary to the overwhelming significance of his love for the Lord. No human authority can take the place of the One Whose name is above every name.

Rationale: Young people tend to worship heroes. Your students have heroes and count them as highly significant. Direct their attention away from mere humans to the only proper hero, the Son of God.

Background: The event in this lesson, called the transfiguration, occurred during the last year of Jesus's public ministry. About a week before, Jesus had informed His disciples of His coming death at the hands of the Jewish leaders. Peter had objected to the idea, earning the stinging rebuke, "Get thee behind me, Satan" (Matt. 16:23). Jesus had then taught the disciples the importance of taking up their crosses daily. In other words, great sacrifice would be demanded of them as disciples; they needed to be ready for it.

There is no record in the Gospels of anything Jesus said or did during the next week. The transfiguration profoundly broke that silence. It communicated a critical lesson to the disciples, namely, that Christ's exalted character places Him before all others in authority and importance and motivates disciples to sacrificial service. On that mountain in northern Palestine, the three disciples saw Christ as they had never seen Him before. From that vision, they gained the inner strength to carry on during the difficult days ahead.

 The Lesson

I. Christ's Preeminence Revealed (Luke 9:28–31)

Christ's preeminence over all others was revealed in a special way in the event called the transfiguration. Jesus took with Him to the mountain His "inner circle" of disciples. Peter and John obviously never forgot this glorious event (John 1:14; 2 Pet. 1:16–18). The apostle James was martyred early and did not leave us any writings. Undoubtedly, however, the event affected him as profoundly as it did Peter and John.

Why did Jesus take only three of His disciples? This seems like favoritism, but we know the Lord would not sin by showing favoritism. In His wisdom, He knew these particular men needed this experience.

> Heighten your students' anticipation of the Lord's future dealings with them. The Lord has special experiences reserved for them that will make them better followers of Him. If they insist on thinking and acting like their ungodly peers, they may miss some special attention from the Lord.

The mountain where this event occurred was probably Mount Hermon, about twenty miles north of Caesarea Philippi. About 9,100 feet high, it is the major peak in that area. While the Lord Jesus prayed there, "the fashion of his countenance was altered" (Luke 9:29). Matthew states that "his face did shine as the sun" and that He "was transfigured before them" (17:2). The term translated "transfigured" is the Greek word from which we derive the word *metamorphosis*. This change was not an altering of the essential nature of Christ, but a revealing of His character as God through the veil of His human flesh. The metamorphosis that Jesus underwent caused a radiance

Objectives

Knowledge (concepts students need to grasp)	the nature of Christ's transfiguration
	the importance of the preeminence of Christ in the Christian life
Application (principles students should put into practice)	We must put Christ first in every area of our lives: family, friends, and school.
	We should not make heroes of the ungodly; idolizing even the godly can diminish our loyalty to Christ.

Outline

(Luke 9:28–36)
I. Christ's preeminence revealed (28–31)
II. Christ's preeminence overlooked (32–33)
III. Christ's preeminence confirmed (34–36)

that shone through His clothing. Mark comments that His clothes were whiter than any fuller (i.e., launderer) could have ever made them (9:3). All three writers describe the radiance as having the brightness of lightning.

> The term used to describe the change Jesus underwent is also used to describe the change that should occur in the lives of believers by faith in Christ (Rom. 12:2; 2 Cor. 3:18). Naturally, your students' outward appearance and conduct will change if they are growing in grace. If there is no regular process of change for the better, perhaps there is no life present at all.

When Jesus was transformed, Moses and Elijah appeared, and they also were glorified (Luke 9:30–31), which is consistent with the teaching of Scripture that all who know Christ as Saviour will be like Him when they see Him (1 John 3:2). This doesn't mean that they will become God, but that they will be more like Him then than they ever were in this life. The two prophets talked with Christ about His death. Literally translated, the word *decease* means "departure." Jesus would depart from this world by way of the cross and in so doing would accomplish salvation for all who believe.

II. Christ's Preeminence Overlooked (Luke 9:32–33)

Peter, James, and John considered Jesus as equal to Moses and Elijah. The three disciples, who had been sleeping, were awakened, probably by the bright light and the conversation. As Moses and Elijah were departing, Peter made an impetuous and misguided suggestion. Placing the Lord on an equal plane with Moses and Elijah, he

> The student text pages for this lesson begin on the next page.

suggested that he and the other disciples build three tabernacles (booths of grass and branches), one for each of the great personages. These two Old Testament men were among the most revered individuals in Jewish history. Moses had led the Israelites out of Egypt, and Elijah had fought the influence of Baal worship. But the problem with Peter's request was that the presence of Christ alone had not been enough to satisfy the three disciples. It had not even been enough to keep them awake.

> Often your students who have grown up in Christian families and gone to Christian schools will be the most insensitive to the presence of Christ and their need to make Him preeminent in their lives. Remind them that great privilege brings great responsibility. Because of the privileges they have enjoyed, they should be the most dedicated believers, not the least.

III. Christ's Preeminence Confirmed (Luke 9:34–36)

To remedy the spiritual dullness in the disciples made evident by Peter's comment, the heavenly Father Himself directly intervened. A cloud appeared and engulfed them all. The disciples were afraid of this obviously supernatural occurrence. Clouds frequently symbolized the presence of God (Exod. 13:21–22; Dan. 7:13; Matt. 24:30; Acts 1:9). When the Father spoke, He settled the question of the absolute preeminence of Jesus. This was His beloved Son. They were to listen to Him and not be enamored by thoughts of glory for themselves or the presence of leading religious figures of the past. Christ and His commands were to be uppermost in their minds.

After that memorable reproof the disciples saw only Jesus (cf. Matt. 17:8). Moses and Elijah were gone. Jesus then warned them not to say anything about the incident until after the Resurrection. Perhaps this instruction was meant to avoid a misplaced emphasis on the future glory to be enjoyed, rather than the present need of sacrifice and service.

> Jesus Christ must be first in the lives of your students. "Christ first" should be their motto in everything they do. If that is to be true, they must recognize that they will have to follow Christ's way, the way of sacrifice and of service to others.

Bible Expressions to Understand

transfiguration—transformation or change in physical appearance
glory—majestic splendor and beauty
Elias—the Old Testament prophet Elijah
Mount Hermon—the highest mountain in northern Palestine
cloud—a visible symbol of the presence of God
decease—death or departure

Have you ever watched a butterfly emerge from a cocoon? It's hard to believe that this beautiful, frail creature was a sluggish caterpillar only a few days before. This rapid, radical change is called metamorphosis. Most human beings don't change this quickly, but people do change as they grow up. You've probably laughed at some old pictures of yourself because you look so different now. The thing that makes those pictures funny is the gradual changes in your appearance that you haven't even noticed. If those changes had taken place overnight, you and everyone else would have noticed them. If you were sitting in your classroom and suddenly grew a foot taller or changed your hair color, you would get quite a reaction.

Is metamorphosis a gradual change or a sudden one?

40

The Bible passage for this lesson talks about a time when the appearance of the Lord Jesus changed miraculously. It was not a gradual change; it occurred suddenly while the Lord was on a mountain (probably Mount Hermon) with His disciples. God caused Christ's appearance to change to show the disciples that Jesus was God even though He usually appeared to them as a normal man.

At the same time, Moses and Elijah appeared with Him. The three of them talked about His coming death. Peter and the other disciples had fallen asleep but were apparently awakened by the brightness of the Lord's appearance and the conversation. After he was fully awake, Peter was so astonished at the presence of the two Old Testament heroes that he suggested building three small booths out of branches and leaves to continue the celebration of their presence.

Peter made a serious mistake by that suggestion. The only one whose presence he should have wanted to celebrate was the Lord. If you're a Christian, the Lord Jesus Christ should be the person you're most interested in. If you'd rather watch a baseball game in which your favorite player is playing than read about the Lord in the Bible, you're making the same mistake Peter made. If you'd rather watch your favorite television star than worship the Lord at church and serve Him, then Christ isn't first in your life. No one and nothing can be more important. Baseball games and television are not always wrong, but in your affections there should be no comparison between them and Christ.

 ## Special Problems and Topics

• Do the Gospel writers disagree about the timing of this event?

Luke states that about *eight* days after Jesus's instruction concerning cross-bearing, Jesus and the three disciples went up the mountain where He was transformed (Luke 9:28). Matthew and Mark say the intervening period was *six* days. Luke's reckoning of the time included days on both ends of the period, which were probably partial days. Matthew and Mark give only the intervening full days. Such differences are common and are not evidence of error.

 ## Extra Activities

Storytelling: The following true story may help you emphasize the theme of this lesson. (Names and details have been changed.)

The church was one of a group of churches that owned a camp. Each summer the youth group spent a week at the camp with teenagers from other churches. It was always a great time—boating, hiking, eating, and making new friends. One summer the camp speaker was Dr. Michael Nesbit, who taught at one of the Christian colleges where some students from the church attended.

When camp week finally rolled around, the whole youth group was excited. The bus trip was great, except for the breakdown

The following questions can help you discern what's most important to you:

- When you are with your friends, what do you talk about?
- When you have some free time after school and on the weekends, what do you do?
- What do you think about most of the time?
- What qualities do you look for in a friend?

God the Father helped Peter and the others realize the primary importance of the Lord Jesus by enveloping them in a cloud and saying, "This is my beloved Son: hear him" (Luke 9:35). The important thing for the disciples was to listen to the Lord Jesus. That's important for us too. We show our love for Christ by obeying His commandments. The wishes of Jesus should determine what we do. What our friends want or think does not matter as much as what Christ wants.

There are some people you should always respect and listen to. You should honor your parents and obey them. Remember, though, that the Lord Jesus is more important than even your parents. He is to be obeyed above all human authority. The police and other governmental authorities are important. We are blessed to have their services. But if they tell

us to do something that Jesus says we should not do, we must obey the Lord.

Your pastor is a man of God. How wonderful it is that the Lord gives us pastors to help us understand the Bible and follow Him. You should respect your pastor, love him, listen to him, and help him any way you can. But your pastor is just a man. Sometimes pastors make mistakes and commit sins. You should continue to be kind and respectful to your pastor even when he makes mistakes or when he sins, but do not let his example cause you to do the wrong thing. Read and study your Bible. Obey the Lord Jesus above all others. Peter made the mistake of thinking too highly of two good men of God and not thinking highly enough of the Lord by comparison.

Are You Letting Jesus Be Number One?

What Christ wants should be what you want. You should be like Him. No other person, no matter how wonderful he may be, is as important as Jesus Christ. Love Him and obey Him above all others. Of course, you should respect other authorities—your parents, your pastor, your government—but above them all must be Christ and His will for your life.

Do You Remember?

1. Where did the transfiguration take place? _____
   on a mountain—probably Mount Hermon

2. What happened to Jesus when He was transfigured? _____
   His appearance changed, and His clothing became white as snow.

3. Who is Elias? _Elijah, the Old Testament prophet_

4. What did Jesus talk about with Moses and Elias? _His coming death_

5. What was the Father's comment? _"This is my beloved Son: hear him."_

6. Who were the other two disciples with Peter on the mountain? _John and James_

7. What did Peter suggest they do when he saw the transfigured Christ, Elias, and Moses? _____
   build three tabernacles, one for each

41

---

that took two hours to fix. That was soon forgotten, though, when they pulled through the entrance of the camp. Cabins were assigned, and activities began.

John was especially enjoying the preaching. He attended a public school and had become a Christian just a few months earlier. Tom Holman, one of the kids in the youth group, had witnessed to him and led him to Christ. They had both been on the wrestling team at school the year before and had become friends.

The wrestling team usually made the state championships because of the tough and effective program Coach Harding had developed. Coach was a great guy, but all that mattered to him was wrestling. He expected the same attitude from the team. He demanded that everyone be at practice every night, including Wednesday night,

which was prayer-meeting night at church. He also expected them to practice on Sunday night. Tom had decided that he just could not have Christ first in his life and be on the team. Coach Harding was angry at Tom and wouldn't even speak to him anymore; in fact, he often ridiculed him in front of the team after he quit. That bothered John, but he never said anything.

The last night at camp, Dr. Nesbit talked about being a productive Christian. He pointed out that no one can be productive unless Christ is first in his life. John thought of next year's wrestling team. He wanted to put Christ first in his life, but what about the team?

He was the best in his weight class and had a good chance at being the state champion.

The struggle in his mind continued through the last part of the sermon. Dr. Nesbit pointed his finger at the audience and said, "You have to make up your mind! Nothing can be before Christ in your life. He must be first. Friends, sports, hobbies, girlfriends, and boyfriends must all be second to Christ. If you will make Christ first, I want you to have the courage to come up where I'm standing and tell everyone here you are making that decision. That takes courage, but you need to show that courage if you really mean business."

John knew what the Lord wanted him to do. He realized that at this point in his life, wrestling was interfering with his personal relationship with Jesus. He couldn't remain on a team that required practice on Sunday and ridiculed Christians who wanted to obey Christ. John knew he had to give Christ priority over everything, including wrestling. He left his seat and walked to the front. He said simply, "I've made up my mind. I can't follow Jesus Christ and wrestle at my school too. Tonight Jesus becomes first in my life."

Make the point with your students that for John to have stayed on the wrestling team would have been wrong. Some might suggest that he could have been a testimony for Christ on the team. But he couldn't effectively do that if his conscience was telling him that he should resign. Christ will give John a better testimony by his being off the team than being on it.

Discussion: Because this lesson contrasts the authority of Christ with authorities the students are normally supposed to obey, be sure to stress their responsibility to obey those authorities under normal circumstances. Discuss the following situations.

(1) Tracy's parents are not Christians. She has been saved through the youth ministry of a local church. She has started to witness to her neighbors, and her parents are objecting. What should she do?

(2) Reza lives in a Middle Eastern country. The government prohibits the public practice of his Christian faith, which includes meeting with other Christians for prayer and hearing the Word of God. Reza is only thirteen. Should he obey the laws of his government and stop attending prayer and preaching meetings?

Crucifixion

Crucifixion was probably derived from the ancient practice of nailing a person's dead body to a town wall or tree or impaling it on a pole to add to the humiliation of the dead and his family. For example, the Philistines nailed the bodies of King Saul and his sons to the wall of Beth-shan to show their contempt for Israel (1 Sam. 31:10–12).

The Persians were the first to use crucifixion as a means of execution. Alexander the Great, who defeated the Persians, popularized crucifixion in the West. He crucified two thousand people after the siege of Tyre.

The Romans began the practice mainly as a punishment for rebellious slaves, to deter further rebellions, but crucifixion soon became a punishment reserved for murderers, thieves, and rebels.

When the Romans put down the slave rebellion of Spartacus in 71 BC, they lined the road from Capua to Rome (about one hundred miles) with six thousand rebels on crosses. When the Romans conquered Jerusalem in AD 70, they crucified five hundred people per day for several months.

The Romans considered crucifixion the most humiliating and gruesome death, too humiliating for a Roman citizen. That fact may explain why tradition says that Paul, a Roman citizen, was beheaded, but Peter and several other apostles were crucified.

A man condemned to die by crucifixion was first scourged with a stick or a *flagellum*. The flagellum was a whip with a short wooden handle and several leather straps, in the tips of which were embedded bits of bone, glass, or iron. Although the purpose of the beating was to increase the agony of the crucifixion, it sometimes was severe enough to cause the victim to die sooner.

After being beaten, the condemned man was forced to carry the horizontal beam of the cross to the crucifixion site, usually located near a busy intersection. Then he was stripped of his clothing and fastened to the horizontal beam by ropes or nails. The horizontal beam was then fastened to the permanent vertical beam. The cross was usually only seven to nine feet tall so the victim was just above the eye level of passersby. Thus they could ridicule him to his face. Sometimes above the victim's head was a plaque bear-ing a description of his crime.

Christ Leaving the Praetorium, Gustave Doré, from the Bob Jones University Collection

42

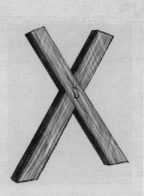  

The Romans used at least three types of crosses for crucifixions. Probably Jesus was executed on a t-shaped cross (rather than the T or the X) since Scripture says a placard stating His "crime" was placed on the cross above His head (Luke 23:38).

If the man was nailed to the cross, the nails were driven through his wrists, where they could support his weight. His ankles were placed side by side and then twisted sideways, and a seven-inch spike was driven through both heels just in front of the Achilles tendons. This caused severe pain and left the victim in an awkward position. The victim was defenseless against flies, wild animals, and extreme heat.

Death eventually came not from loss of blood, but from suffocation. As the victim grew weaker, his legs buckled, placing extreme pressure on the upper body and making it impossible to get a breath. To prolong the process, a peg or seat was added to take some of the pressure off the arms. Death rarely came in less than thirty-six hours. Some of those crucified at the rebellion of Spartacus were still talking to soldiers after three days on a cross.

The corpse of the crucified one was often left to rot on the cross and be picked apart by birds. This presented a vivid picture of Rome's attitude toward lawlessness and thus served as a deterrent to

future crimes. Under Jewish law, however, a family was allowed to bury the victim the same day he was executed. In those cases, therefore, the victim's legs were broken to speed up the death.

Crucifixion was so gruesome that even the Roman orator and politician Cicero wrote, "Let the very name of the cross be far away not only from the body of the Roman citizen, but even from his thoughts, his eyes, and his ears."

The practice was finally outlawed in the fourth century by the Roman emperor Constantine, who called it an insult to Christianity.

43

LESSON 12
Christ's Death for Us

Theme	Christ's Crucifixion
Scripture	Matthew 27:27–56 (Mark 15:16–41; Luke 23:26, 33–49; John 19:16–37)
Memory Work	Isaiah 53:6

Approach to the Lesson

Theme: The death of Christ by the shedding of His blood on the cross is sufficient to pay for the sins of everyone who has ever lived. Every person must respond to what the Lord did by placing his trust in that act to save him from the present power and eternal penalty of sin, which is suffering in hell.

Rationale: The Crucifixion is far more than a historical fact; it is a watershed that determines where a person will spend eternity. Do not let your students approach this lesson casually. All the religious exposure and training in the world will do them no good if they have not placed their trust in Christ's death for salvation.

Background: The Gospel writers spare us the gruesome details of what usually took place during a Roman crucifixion, showing a remarkable dignity and reserve in their treatment of the Lord's death. We should approach it in the same manner. There is no need to be sensational in talking about the details of crucifixion just for the effect on the students. The lesson needs to be approached with humility and reverence. The presentation below follows Matthew's account.

An important teaching aid, a copy of the chart on page 45 of the student text, is found on the CD in both a full version and a fill-in-the-blank version.

Objectives

Knowledge (concepts students need to grasp)	the sequence of events surrounding the Crucifixion of Christ
	the biblical doctrine of the vicarious atonement
Application (principles students should put into practice)	All people need to be saved by trusting in Christ's death for them.
	Only Christ can save.

Bible Expressions to Understand

common hall—the governor's palace or judgment hall
Golgotha—a skull-shaped hill outside Jerusalem
vinegar—sour wine
gall—myrrh mixed in sour wine, used to deaden pain
crucify—to execute by nailing or binding to a cross
Elias—the Old Testament prophet Elijah

How important is the death of Jesus Christ? The New Testament refers to it in about 250 different verses and in all but six books. All these references together equal about half the length of 1 Corinthians. Jesus predicted His own death nineteen times. Nearly every part of the New Testament talks about the death of Christ.

The apostles taught that the death of Christ is important. Paul said, "For I determined not to know any thing among you, save Jesus Christ, and him crucified" (1 Cor. 2:2). Peter, the leader of the apostles, wrote, "For even hereunto were ye called: because Christ also suffered for us, leaving us an example, that ye should follow his steps" (1 Pet. 2:21). These men placed great emphasis on the death of Christ. Why? It was the price that had to be paid to free you from the consequences of your sins—separation from God in this life and eventually separation from Him forever in hell. Only by trusting in Him Who died for your sins can you be released from the punishment that you deserve. Only by trusting in Him can you have a life of fellowship with God.

What happened the day Jesus died? All four Gospels tell us about it. Each writer presents a slightly different viewpoint of the events, but all are accurate. The passage you read for this lesson was Matthew's description. A careful look at what happened is important. You can't trust in something that you don't know anything about.

The day began with the soldiers making fun of Jesus after His predawn trial (Matt. 27:27–32). Pilate delivered Jesus to the Roman soldiers, who began to make arrangements for the Crucifixion.

After taking Jesus into the Pilate's palace, the soldiers stripped Jesus of His robe and put a scarlet robe on Him. While scoffing at His claim to be a king, they wove a crown of thorns and shoved it down on His head. A sturdy reed acted as a scepter in His hand. The soldiers gathered around Jesus and mockingly paid homage to Him. "Hail, King of the Jews!" they yelled.

Not content with this, the soldiers insulted Jesus and spit on Him. They beat Him over the head with the "scepter." After their mockery had reached its limits, the soldiers put His own clothing on Him again and led Him away to Calvary to be crucified. The Romans soon saw that the Lord was not strong enough to carry His own cross all the way through the city. Seeing a man named Simon from Cyrene (a city in northern Africa), the Romans forced him to carry the cross in Jesus's place.

The place where Jesus was crucified looked like a skull, so it was called Calvary or Golgotha, both names meaning "skull." The Lord's hands and feet were nailed to a wooden cross. After He had been lifted up on the cross, wine mixed with a drug was offered to Him to ease His pain. The Lord, however, refused this, knowing that He needed to bear the full suffering.

The soldiers who were responsible for the execution, calloused to such suffering, paid no attention to Jesus's pain. Instead they divided His garments and gambled for them, fulfilling prophecy in doing so (Ps. 22:18). Later, when they had finished gambling, the soldiers sat by the cross and guarded Jesus.

A sign recording Christ's claim to be the King of the Jews was placed on the cross over His head. Two

44

The Lesson

I. Suffering (Matt. 27:27–44)

In the hours before He died, Jesus Christ suffered both physically and spiritually.

The hostility of sinful people toward perfection is vividly portrayed in these situations. Unconverted mankind is wicked, without any part of his nature responding to God. Only the grace of God can change this attitude.

During the trial (27:27–32). Four times during His trial the Lord faced the jeers of unbelievers: before the Sanhedrin (Mark 14:65), before the soldiers of Herod (Luke 23:11), before Pilate (John 19:1–3), and before the soldiers of Pilate (Matt. 27:28–31). The soldiers took Jesus into "the common hall." This phrase, which can be transliterated "Praetorium" (Mark 15:16), refers to the residence of Pilate. The scene probably took place in an open court within the palace.

The soldiers began their mockery by clothing Christ with a scarlet robe. (Mark 15:17 describes it as purple, a color that differs only slightly from scarlet.) They wove a crown of thorns for His head, and a thick, heavy reed was given to Him as a scepter. Then the soldiers mocked Him by offering false homage. Tiring of this, they began to abuse Him physically and spit on Him. The reed was used as a club to beat the crown of thorns down onto His head. The Greek tense indicates that this was a continuous beating.

thieves were also crucified with Him. Passersby, unmoved by His affliction, shouted contemptuously at Him. They called to Him to save Himself if He were the Son of God. Some of the chief priests, the scribes, and the elders also mocked Him. They challenged Him to prove His deity by coming down from the cross.

After several hours the Lord's death drew near (Matt. 27:45–50). The Crucifixion had begun about nine in the morning. At noon a strange darkness descended on all of Palestine and lasted until three in the afternoon. For the first time in His life, Jesus lacked perfect fellowship with His Father. "My God, my God, why hast thou forsaken me?" He cried. The sin of mankind had been laid on Him. The physical sufferings of the Crucifixion paled in comparison to the awfulness of His Father's rejection as He bore the sins of the world.

In Aramaic, Jesus's words were "Eli, Eli, lama sabachthani?" Some who heard His piercing cry thought He was calling for Elijah the prophet to help Him. One ran and filled a sponge with sour wine for Jesus's parched lips. Others contemptuously said, "Let be, let us see whether Elias will come to save Him" (Matt. 27:49).

When His work had been completed, Jesus cried with a loud voice, "It is finished." By an act of His will, the Son of God dismissed His spirit. The atone-

ment was complete! The Son of God had given Himself voluntarily for the sins of the human race.

Finally, Matthew draws our attention to the miracles that surrounded the Lord's death (Matt. 27: 51–56). At the death of His Son, the Father's unseen hands ripped the temple veil from top to bottom, symbolizing that the way into the holy of holies was not closed any longer. Through the blood of the Son, the humblest believer may approach the Father.

In addition, a great earthquake shook the ground, opening many graves. Some of the Old Testament saints rose from the dead and walked around the city in the sight of many Jews. The Roman centurion in charge of the execution was impressed by what he saw. With a trembling spirit, he said, "Truly this was the Son of God."

If you have already trusted in Christ's death on the cross for the pardon of your sins, there is something else you should learn from the Crucifixion. Peter said, "For even hereunto were ye called: because Christ also suffered for us, leaving us an example, that ye should follow his steps" (1 Pet. 2:21). The Lord Jesus gave Himself completely, suffering for our salvation. We are to follow that example. There should be no limit to our devotion to Christ and the spreading of His gospel. We must be willing to suffer for the Word of God and our testimony.

SEVEN STATEMENTS OF CHRIST FROM THE CROSS

	Reference	What Christ Said	What It Teaches About Christ
1	Luke 23:34	"Father, forgive them; for they know not what they do."	He forgave His enemies.
2	Luke 23:43	"To day shalt thou be with me in paradise."	He promised heaven to believers.
3	John 19:26–27	"Woman, behold thy son!" "Behold thy mother!"	He honored His mother.
4	Matthew 27:46	"My God, my God, why hast thou forsaken me?"	He bore our sins.
5	John 19:28	"I thirst."	He was human.
6	John 19:30	"It is finished."	He accomplished our salvation.
7	Luke 23:46	"Father, into thy hands I commend my spirit."	He was the Son of God.

45

Outline

and a heavy mallet, a soldier nailed His wrists to the beam. If the vertical post was not already in the ground, His feet were turned sideways, and a spike was driven first through a piece of wood and then through His heels. (The heel bones of a crucified criminal named Yohanan ben Ha'galgol showed this method of securing the feet to the cross.) The board kept the feet from pulling the spike through the flesh. It is common belief that Jesus was then hung with His feet three to four feet above the ground. (If the vertical post was permanent, his feet were nailed to it after the beam was lifted atop the post.) Probably a small board on the post allowed Him a partial seat and gave some relief from the intense suffering. Some suggest, however, that any such board was sharp, so that sitting on it brought the victim even more pain.

At this point Jesus uttered his first statement from the cross: "Father, forgive them; for they know not what they do" (Luke 23:34).

> Point out to your students that Jesus's attitude was not one of revenge or bitterness, but of love and forgiveness.

As Jesus hung above them, the four soldiers (John 19:23) remained on watch to prevent friends from taking Him down (v. 36). To pass the time, they gambled for His clothing. First it was divided into four parts; then the men drew lots to see who would receive each part. They decided not to tear His seamless robe, so they cast lots separately to see who would keep it (John 19:23–24).

> This is one of the most vivid portraits of hardhearted humanity in the Bible. Man becomes callous to the familiar, whether it be good or evil. Direct the thoughts of your students to the importance of sensitivity to both good and evil. They can maintain this sensitivity only by constant spiritual vigilance. Absorbing the Word of God, seeking God's grace through prayer, and refusing to yield to temptation are all ways to remain sensitive in the inner being.

With the mockery over for the moment, the soldiers put Jesus's clothes back on Him and took Him away to be crucified. As was customary for executions, He was led outside the city walls (cf. Acts 7:58). After all the physical abuse, He was unable to carry His own cross. Simon of Cyrene (a province in northern Africa) was pressed into service to carry the cross. This man was the father of Alexander and Rufus (Mark 15:21). Rufus might be the same man who was later known to the believers in Rome (Rom. 16:13).

On the cross (27:33–44). The hill on which Jesus was crucified had the appearance of a skull. Both names, *Calvary* (Luke 23:33) and *Golgotha*, mean "skull." The former is the Latin name; the latter,

Aramaic. The hill is northeast of the Damascus Gate, about 250 yards from the city.

Crucified (27:33–37). Just before they placed the Lord on the cross, the executioners tried to give Him the customary drink of sour wine ("vinegar") and myrrh ("gall"). Criminals were usually given this drink to numb the body before they were crucified, making it easier to endure the painful ordeal of the cross. Jesus refused the drink, however, not willing to take anything that would keep Him from knowing the wrath of the Father against sin and thus interfere with His atonement.

Scholars are unsure of the exact method of crucifixion. It is commonly held that the horizontal beam was laid on the ground, and He was stretched upon it. Using spikes

Crosses were shaped like an *X*, a *T*, or a *t*. In view of Matthew's statement that the charge against Jesus was set above His head (v. 37), this last shape seems most probable. Pilate's use of the term "King of the Jews" mocked the Jewish leaders. They protested, asking that it be changed to "He said, 'I am King of the Jews,'" but Pilate refused (John 19:21–22).

Ridiculed (27: 38–44). Various observers of this grisly scene, including the priests, mocked Him (vv. 39–43). Even the thieves scoffed at Him. It has been speculated that the two crucified with Jesus were conspirators with Barabbas in his rebellion. If so, then the central cross, on which Jesus died, was likely intended for Barabbas. Only Luke records the repentance of one. Apparently both of them initially mocked Jesus; later, however, one asked for and received forgiveness. This was Jesus's second statement from the cross: "Verily I say unto thee, To day shalt thou be with me in paradise" (Luke 23:43).

Passersby taunted Jesus by twisting His prophecy of the rebuilding of the temple (John 2:19–20). Like the false witnesses, they misquoted the words of Jesus (Mark 15:29). (His actual words were fulfilled in the Resurrection three days later.) At this time Jesus made His third statement from the cross: "Woman, behold thy son!" (John 19:26). Apparently Joseph had died prior to this time, and so Jesus committed His mother to John's care.

The most intense suffering Jesus endured on the cross was the result of bearing the sins of the whole world (1 John 2:2). Christ bore "our sins in his own body on the tree" (1 Pet. 2:24). This is called the vicarious, or substitutionary atonement. Because Christ was bearing our sins, His Father abandoned Him when He was on the cross. Christ willingly endured His Father's wrath against sin. This suffering no doubt far surpassed any of the physical torments. We must always remember that Jesus Christ bore the ultimate punishment so that His followers will never have to.

II. Death (Matt. 27:45–50)

Christ died after six hours on the cross. The Jewish day began at six o'clock in the morning. The "sixth hour" referred to noon. The "ninth hour" was three o'clock in the afternoon. During this time darkness covered all Palestine. At the end of this period, Jesus uttered His fourth saying: *"Eli, Eli, lama sabachthani,"* Aramaic for "My God,

my God, why hast thou forsaken me?" The Son, bearing the sins of the world, experienced the Father's wrath against sin. He Who had known nothing but perfect fellowship with the Father became acutely conscious of the break in that fellowship.

Here is the terrible effect of sin in the life of any person (Matt. 27:45–46). What worse fate could befall anyone than to be cut off from God? He is the source of all wisdom and strength. Warn your students that if they have not trusted Christ as their Savior, they are doomed to a life without God's help and direction. Beyond this life they are doomed to eternal suffering, separated from God in hell. Jesus bore all this separation and suffering for us. Your students must then have faith in Him to be delivered from sin and separation from God.

Some of the bystanders misunderstood Jesus's words and thought that He was calling for the prophet Elijah. Since He was quoting directly from a well-known psalm (Ps. 22:1), their remarks reveal their ignorance of the Scripture. Jesus spoke a fifth time: "I thirst" (John 19:28). A bystander filled a sponge with wine, probably from an onlooker's wineskin. (The Greek word is different from that used in Matthew 27:34; this wine did not have the pain-killing effect of the wine that had been offered previously.) He placed it on the end of a reed and lifted it to Jesus's lips. Others, however, cried for him to stand back so they could see if Elijah would really come.

Then the last two cries came from Jesus's lips. The sixth, "It is finished" (John 19:30), signified the completion of Jesus's

If you have never placed your trust in the Lord as your Savior, He invites you to do that today. The Bible says, "For whosoever shall call upon the name of the Lord shall be saved" (Rom. 10:13). Simply ask the Lord to forgive you for your sins and to help you turn from them. Tell Him you are placing your confidence in what He did on the cross to be saved from your sin. You can pray this honest prayer of faith at home, at school, or any other place.

Are You Trusting in Christ's Death?

Jesus, the Son of God, shed His blood on the cross for the sins of men. His sacrifice was sufficient and acceptable to God. It was the price that had to be paid to free us from the punishment for sin. Each person must trust in the work of Christ on the cross to be saved from sin and its penalty. Christ alone is the source of salvation.

Do You Remember?

1. Where was Jesus taken to be mocked by the soldiers? _____
   Pilate's palace or judgment hall; the common hall

2. Who carried Christ's cross to Calvary? *Simon of Cyrene*

3. Why was the place of crucifixion named "Calvary"? *It looked like a skull.*
   What other name was applied to it? *Golgotha*

4. Why did the passersby shout at Jesus? *to mock Him*

5. Why did the Father forsake His own Son? _____
   Christ took the sins of mankind on Himself, and God could not look upon such sin.

6. What happened to the veil of the temple when Jesus died? _____
   It was torn in two from top to bottom.

7. What other miracles accompanied this event? *An earthquake shook the ground;*
   the sky was dark; people were raised from the dead.

46

work. He had completed His course, facing all temptation without sin and enduring the cross. He then uttered the final cry, "Father, into thy hands I commend my spirit" (Luke 23:46). Having said this, He "gave up the ghost," which literally means He dismissed His spirit, an act of the will that fulfilled His statement earlier to the Pharisees (John 10:18). This same word is used when the disciples "sent away the multitude" (Mark 4:36). Used of death, it is unique to Christ. Though others are said to "give up the ghost," a different word is used in those cases—one better translated "expire." Christ's death was uniquely an act of His will.

Jesus's death occurred at three in the afternoon, the exact time when the priests were sacrificing the paschal lamb in the temple (cf. 1 Cor. 5:7). Shortly afterward, the soldiers came to break the legs of the victims (John 19:31–32). This act interfered with the victims' ability to lift themselves up to obtain relief from the pressure of the body's downward pull. It also made it more difficult to breathe, since the chest was more cramped with the body pulling downward. Thus, death would come more quickly. Since the next day was the Passover feast (a Sabbath), the corpses needed to be taken down so as not to offend the Jews on their feast day. Jesus had already died, however, which surprised the soldiers, since death usually took at least a full day. (Records indicate that some men hung on crosses for as long as nine days before dying.) To verify Jesus's death, a soldier pierced His side with a spear (John 19:34).

III. Authentication (Matt. 27:51–56)

God authenticated Christ's person by sending miracles after His death. The first was the rending of the veil of the temple. The purpose of the veil was to guard the holy of holies from the sight of the priests who served in the holy place. Only the high priest could go into the holy of holies behind the veil, and then only once a year, on the Day of Atonement (Heb. 9:6–7). God supernaturally tore the veil "from the top to the bottom," indicating that a "new and living way" had been opened from heaven to earth for all believers to enter into the very presence of God by the death of Christ (Heb. 10:19–22).

A massive earthquake then shook the area, even causing rocks to split. In many instances the rocks in front of cave tombs were rolled away. Many of the saints were resurrected. Note that this resurrection took place "after his resurrection." Christ was the "firstfruits" from the dead (1 Cor. 15:20, 23). Nothing is said about what happened to these resurrected saints. Some believe that they ascended into heaven at Christ's ascension forty days later (Acts 1:9); others hold that they died again, as did Lazarus.

As these events took place, the centurion at the cross was increasingly impressed that Christ was no ordinary man. Perhaps he had observed how He suffered during the trial. Certainly he had seen His calmness on the cross and had felt the earthquake. He had heard Jesus's last words and had watched Him die. All these events had their impact, and the centurion admitted that Jesus was the Son of God. Early tradition says that the centurion's name was Longinus. He is supposed to have accepted Christ and become a preacher, eventually dying a martyr's death.

> The Crucifixion was a powerful event. So is the teaching of it. Paul said, "The preaching of the cross is to them that perish foolishness; but unto us which are saved it is the power of God" (1 Cor. 1:18). The same effect that tradition says was accomplished in the life of Longinus can be accomplished in the lives of your students if they trust in Christ's death for them.

The account of the Crucifixion closes with a historical note, mentioning the three women who stayed throughout the ordeal and watched the Savior die. Their extreme despair, brought on by this most necessary death, would be matched only by the exhilarating effect of the soon-coming Resurrection.

Special Problems and Topics

• **What did the superscription really say?**

Critics have contended that the variations in the wording of the superscription given by Matthew, Luke, and John prove that the Gospels are inaccurate. This is only one of many cases, however, of the Gospel accounts supplementing one another. Combining the information given by each Gospel writer, the full statement reads: "This is [Matthew and Luke] Jesus [Matthew and John] of Nazareth [John] the King of the Jews [all]."

Extra Activities

Object lesson: Students will be more interested if they can actually see what you are talking about. You may want to buy a large spike from a local hardware store to help the students understand the extent of our Lord's suffering on the cross. Another item of interest would be some large thorns such as those that grow on the locust tree.

Checkup: This is an ideal point at which to check your students' spiritual condition. Ask them to write brief responses to the following questions: (1) Have you trusted in Christ's death on the cross to save you from your sins? (2) If so, when? (3) In three sentences explain in your own words what Jesus accomplished by dying on the cross.

LESSON 13
Living for the Living Christ

Theme	Christ's Resurrection
Scripture	Matthew 27:57–28:20
Memory Work	1 Corinthians 15:17, 20

Approach to the Lesson

Theme: The implications of the Resurrection are profound. Christianity is not merely a system of ethics or a philosophical theory. It is an ongoing relationship with the living Christ. He directs His church through the Scriptures, empowers His church through His Spirit, and offers salvation to all who will turn to Him. A dead Christ could do none of these things.

The Resurrection confirmed that Jesus is God. It ensures canceling of guilt for any who place faith in Him. It also guarantees the believer's resurrection. Through that supernatural event, believers receive the assurance that their mortal bodies will not serve eternally as a tribute to the power of sin. Christ is alive. This is the central truth of the Christian faith.

Rationale: The single greatest need of students in Christian schools, many of them satiated by the gospel, is an appreciation of the living, personal presence of Christ. He is not of the past, like Buddha, or Mohammed, or even Moses. He is of today; He is here; He is alive—more alive, in fact, than you or your students. Drive this concept home.

Background: The first point of the outline will help you develop what the students have read about the Resurrection in the Scriptures. The second is presented in the student lesson in abbreviated form. The last provides a broad overview of the significance of the Resurrection to the Christian Faith.

The Lesson

I. The Proof of the Resurrection (Matthew 27:57–28:20)

The material in this section is paralleled in the other Gospels (Mark 15:42–16:20; Luke 23:50–24:53; John 19:38–20:31). Since Matthew provides a complete overview of the events and a thorough presentation of the proofs for the Resurrection, this lesson follows his account. The others will be referred to when they add clarifying details.

The deliberate burial (27:57–61). The burial of Christ is proof of His Resurrection. Those skeptical about the supernatural element obviously want to make the event something less than a person's coming back from the dead. To do so would make it more explainable. It appears, however, that the Gospel writer anticipated just such an inclination since the burial of Jesus is recorded in detail. A wealthy man named Joseph of Arimathea went to Pilate to ask for the body of Christ. The Scriptures indicate that Joseph was a disciple of Jesus (John 19:38) but in secret, apparently because of his membership in the Sanhedrin (Mark 15:43), the Jewish supreme court. Although he was a member of the Sanhedrin, Joseph had not consented to the condemnation of Jesus (Luke 23:50–51). Pilate granted his request since the centurion in charge had confirmed that Jesus was already dead (Mark 15:44–45).

Joseph's real motive for asking for the body was his relationship with Christ. Outwardly, however, he could have seemed to have other motives. As a member of the Sanhedrin, he would be concerned about the Jewish law's command that a crucified person be taken down from the cross before nightfall (Deut. 21:22–23).

Joseph and Nicodemus brought approximately seventy-five pounds of spices (myrrh and aloes) to be used in the burial

Objectives

KNOWLEDGE (concepts students need to grasp)	the proofs for the Resurrection of Christ given in the Gospel accounts
	the lessons Christ taught in His post-Resurrection appearances
APPLICATION (principles students should put into practice)	Because Christ is alive, we can and should have a personal relationship with Him.
	Christ has both power over death and power to help us live.
	There is no need to be skeptical about the Resurrection.
	The church will be victorious; since Christ is alive, faith in Him will not die.

Outline

I. The proof of the Resurrection (Matt. 27:57–28:20)
  A. The deliberate burial (27:57–61)
  B. The secure tomb (27:62–66)
  C. The angel's message (28:1–7)
  D. The visible Christ (28:8–20)

II. The point of the Resurrection
  A. A physical reality
  B. A different relationship
  C. A new worldwide mission
  D. A precursor of the Second Coming

III. The power of the Resurrection
  A. The foundation of our faith (1 Cor. 15:12–23)
  B. The basis of Christ's ongoing ministry

procedure (John 19:39). These were placed between layers of linen as the body was wrapped. Jesus was then laid in Joseph's newly hewn rock tomb, and a large stone was put in front of the door. Mary Magdalene and Mary the mother of James the Less sat across from the sepulchre in the garden while Joseph completed the burial (Matt. 27:59–61).

Joseph and all the others present saw Christ. They lifted Him, and they wrapped Him in the linen cloth. If Christ had not actually been dead, how could they not have been aware of that fact? They recognized that He was dead, just as the soldiers and centurion did earlier. The record is clear: Christ's Resurrection was not just a "revival" or resuscitation; it was a miracle.

The secure tomb (27:62–66). The security of the tomb is also proof of the Resurrection. The Jewish leaders remembered Jesus's predictions regarding His Resurrection (Matt. 16:21; 17:23; 20:18–19). Concerned that His disciples might steal His body from the tomb and then claim that He had risen, they asked Pilate to "set a watch," i.e., post a guard, at the tomb. Apparently the Jews were so concerned over the possibility of theft that they violated their own Sabbath rules to ensure the tomb's security. Pilate authorized Roman soldiers to guard the tomb and fastened the stone to the walls on either side with an official seal. To violate this security provided by Roman government would have been a serious offense.

There is no record that these soldiers came into conflict with other men trying to rob the tomb. Christ's body simply disappeared. He came out of the tomb without even opening the door. The seal on the

Read: Matthew 27:57–28:20   Memorize: 1 Corinthians 15:17, 20

Bible Expressions to Understand

Joseph of Arimathea—a member of the Sanhedrin and a secret disciple of Jesus

Mary—the mother of James the Less and Joseph

setting a watch—posting a guard

angel of the Lord—in the Old Testament, the Lord Jesus Christ; but here, a messenger of God

What would you think if someone suggested that you make friends with a dead man and that you ask his opinion about where you should live, who should be your friends, and what job you should have? How about telling him that you love him and will do whatever he asks you to do? Wait a minute! Only a crazy person would do that, right? If Jesus Christ is not alive, and if you are a Bible-believing Christian, then you're a "crazy person." But if He's alive, then you're one of the sanest people in the world. It is those who refuse to put their trust in Christ who are misguided.

The Bible teaches that Jesus Christ is alive. After He rose from the grave, He appeared to His disciples ten different times. He was seen by more than five

This is possibly the tomb where Jesus's body was placed following the Crucifixion. When the women came on Sunday morning, what did they find?
[Historic Views of the Holy Land: the 1960s: Photographs of Charles Lee Feinberg, www.bibleplaces.com, 2004]

hundred of His followers at the same time. No one could deny that He had overcome death.

When Jesus appeared to His disciples, He had important instructions and truths to share with them. One of those truths was about His resurrected body. At one appearance, He taught that He wasn't just a spirit being or a ghost (Luke 24:36–43). He showed the disciples His hands and feet. He told them they could touch Him. He ate fish and honeycomb right before their eyes. Why did Christ want them to understand that He had a physical body? He wanted them to know that He would be the Christ they knew forever. Later, the New Testament teaches us that since His body was resurrected, ours will be resurrected too. How could He promise that our bodies would be resurrected if His own hadn't been resurrected?

The Lord also taught that His Resurrection marked a new beginning in His relationship with His followers. When some women saw Jesus near His tomb, they fell down and worshiped Him (Matt. 28:9–10). Jesus accepted their worship. Mary Magdalene, one of the women, held on to His feet. He had to tell her that soon she wouldn't be able to enjoy His physical presence any longer (John 20:11–18). He was going to ascend to heaven to be at the right hand of the Father. His followers would have to learn to believe in Him and follow Him without seeing Him. This is what He taught when He appeared to Thomas and the other disciples not long after the incident with Mary (John 20:26–31).

How would His disciples be able to have such a "sightless" faith? This was a question He answered when He met two disciples on a road leading to Emmaus (Luke 24:13–32). He taught them all about

47

---

directed them, as the angel had, to tell the disciples to go into Galilee to meet Him. He appeared to His disciples and other groups of believers nine more times before His ascension. At one time He was seen by more than five hundred disciples (1 Cor. 15:6). This large number of eyewitnesses is undeniable evidence that His was a true resurrection.

Further confirmation of the truthfulness of the event came from some of the guards at the tomb (Matt. 28:11–15). These men were in danger of losing their lives for what had happened because they had failed in their duty. The body was gone. If they had been able to retrieve it or apprehend whoever stole it, they would have done so. Instead, they rushed to the chief priests and told them what had happened. The priests bribed them to say that the disciples had stolen the body while they slept and promised to keep them out of trouble with the government officials. At the time of Matthew's writing, this lie was still circulating among the Jews. The crafty leaders had done their work well.

The final proof of the truthfulness of Christ's Resurrection was His appearance on the mountain where He had told His disciples to meet Him (28:16–20). Some, however, did not believe it was He. With all the authority of One Who had conquered death, Jesus commanded His disciples to go into all the world to preach the truth concerning Him. Only the living God Himself could presume to give that directive. Many people accepted it and Him without hesitation.

II. The Point of the Resurrection

In eight of Christ's ten post-Resurrection appearances, the Lord gave some instruction, either by word or by example. These teachings can be grouped under four main ideas.

A physical reality. When the Lord first appeared to the disciples as a group (Luke 4:36–48), He showed them that His Resurrection was physical. At the moment of His appearance to them, some of them thought He was a spirit and were afraid. He rebuked them for this, knowing their thoughts. Next He told them to look at His hands and feet. He even invited them to touch Him to see that He was flesh and bone. He then asked for something to eat. They gave Him fish and a piece of honeycomb, and He ate them. Finally, He opened their understanding so that they could comprehend the teaching

---

tomb had not even been broken until the angel miraculously opened it (Matt. 28:2).

The angel's message (28:1–7). A further proof of the Resurrection was the angel's message. Early Sunday morning, when the Sabbath was over, the two Marys came to the tomb with additional spices (Luke 23:56–24:1). They probably felt that the burial had been too hasty and intended to redo it. As the women came, they were concerned about rolling the stone away (Mark 16:3). However, before they got there, an earthquake shook the ground, and an angel rolled the stone away. He then sat on top of the stone and waited for the women to arrive. Understandably, the soldiers fainted at the sight because the angel had a countenance as bright as lightning.

The angel told the two women to look where Jesus's body had been lying. He went on to explain that Jesus was risen and was going to Galilee to meet the disciples. They were to tell the disciples where to meet Him.

If the angel's message wasn't true, then we are faced with the problem of a lying angel. There is such a thing, but this one is called an angel of the Lord. That title precludes the possibility that this was an emissary of the Devil sent to deceive these women.

The visible Christ (28:8–20). Christ's appearance on various occasions to many people is a proof of the Resurrection. As the women were leaving the tomb, Jesus Himself appeared to them. They were overcome and fell down, worshiping Him and holding Him by the feet. The Lord then

of the Old Testament Scriptures about His death and Resurrection. It was their responsibility to preach that message.

This physical Resurrection confirmed the prophecies of the Old Testament. A spiritual resurrection would not have accomplished that, nor would it have accomplished our salvation.

A different relationship. Several of Christ's post-Resurrection appearances indicate that His relationship with His followers was now different. He did not refuse the worship of the women at the tomb (Matt. 28:9). This element of His relationship with His followers remains unchanged. However, when Mary Magdalene wanted to touch Him (John 20:17), He taught her that the former physical presence and visible fellow-ship was over. He would ascend to the Father. His presence with His people would be through the Spirit of God, not a bodily manifestation. This truth demanded a new faith from the disciples—a sightless faith. When Jesus appeared to Thomas and the rest of the disciples, He instructed them on this same point (John 20:26–29). They would have to continue to believe without seeing. This task was made easier by written revelation, the Scriptures—a truth Christ stressed to the two disciples on the road to Emmaus (Luke 24:13–35). He taught them about Himself from Scripture and later revealed Himself to them. In this way He emphasized that the Scriptures contained the information they needed.

> The passage says their hearts burned within them as they walked with Him on the way and heard Him teach. Every believer in this age becomes a disciple with a burning heart as He listens to Jesus speak through the pages of the Bible and as the Spirit illuminates the Word.

A new worldwide mission. During the Lord's appearance to His disciples on the mountain, He commissioned them to go into all the world (Matt. 28:18–20). He said that all authority to command this had been granted to Him. What authority would rest behind such a command if the man who issued it were dead? Christ is not only alive, but He promises His personal presence to all who will obey.

The paths that the disciples took in fulfilling this commission were not identical. Some became pastors, and others didn't. The variety of responsibilities Christ gave His disciples is suggested by the conversation He had with Peter after His Resurrection (John 21:15–22). Peter was restored

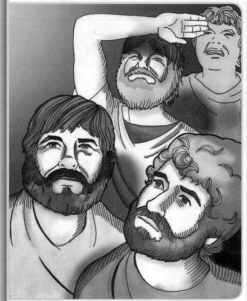

"And while they looked stedfastly toward heaven as he went up, behold, two men stood by them in white apparel; Which also said, Ye men of Galilee, why stand ye gazing up into heaven? this same Jesus, which is taken up from you into heaven, shall so come in like manner as ye have seen him go into heaven" (Acts 1:10–11).

Himself from the Old Testament. As they discussed this experience, they said that their hearts burned within them as they listened to Him teach. The Word of God, made clear by the working of Christ's Spirit in your mind, is the way your faith will stay strong while Christ is in heaven. "So then faith cometh by hearing, and hearing by the word of God" (Rom. 10:17).

The first person Jesus saw after He arose was Mary Magdalene. He told her to tell the disciples to meet Him on a mountain in Galilee. When they saw Him there later, they worshiped Him (Matt. 28:16–20). At that time Jesus taught them that His Resurrection proved He had the authority to command them to go into all the world and preach the gospel. It also proved He could empower them to do this. Since

48

Jesus was alive, He could now assist and direct His followers in spreading the gospel throughout the world.

At another time, when He appeared to just seven disciples, Christ explained to Peter that not every disciple would have the same responsibility in spreading the gospel (John 21:1–25). Peter had failed Christ by denying Him before His Crucifixion, but Christ gave him a job to do. Peter then wanted to know what John was going to do. Jesus warned him not to worry about that. When Peter had compared himself to others before the Crucifixion, he had become proud and failed. Peter was supposed to concern himself with being faithful to the task he had been given to perform for Christ.

The last time Christ saw His disciples on earth was at His ascension (Acts 1:3–11). Just before He ascended, He told them again to go throughout the world, preaching the gospel. Then He suddenly started to go up into heaven. He entered a cloud, and they could not see Him anymore. The disciples were stunned. They had never seen anything like this before.

While they were still looking up, two angels that looked like men appeared. They told the disciples that the way they'd seen Jesus go up into heaven was the way He would come again. This was Christ's last great lesson. He would come again. Just as certainly as Jesus had left them in a physical body, so He would return. The next time, He wouldn't be

The Empty Tomb Makes All the Difference

You don't serve a dead man. The histories of the great religions of the world record the deaths and burial places of their founders. Christianity does the same, with one added feature. It also records that Jesus of Nazareth, God the Son, conquered death by rising again. Since He has done this, He now lives to save people from their sins, help them in life, and eventually take them to heaven to be with Him. If you're a Christian, you should always live as though Christ were alive. There is a simple reason for that: He *is* alive. He prays for you. He loves you more than all others combined. He is your living Lord.

to his role as leader of the disciples. He had denied the Lord, but Christ forgave him. Then Peter wanted to know what John was going to do in the future. Jesus told him not to worry about the responsibilities of others, implying that he should be mainly concerned with meeting his own responsibilities.

A precursor of the Second Coming. At His ascension the Lord reaffirmed the disciples' worldwide mission (Acts 1:8–11). As He ascended into a cloud, the disciples watched in utter amazement. Two angels appeared and told them that Jesus would come again in the same manner that they had seen Him go into heaven. The Resurrection was the first act of the Father's exaltation of the Son; the ascension was the next. The ministry at the Father's right

hand is the one Christ enjoys now, making intercession for us. The final act of exaltation will be the Second Coming. Every believer is to anticipate and to long for His reappearance. What a day that will be when every knee shall bow and every tongue shall confess that Jesus Christ is Lord, to the glory of God (Phil. 2:10–11). The Resurrection makes this final act of exaltation possible.

III.   The Power of the Resurrection

The Resurrection of Christ is central to the rest of the New Testament. Resurrection in general and the Resurrection of Christ specifically are mentioned in 126 different passages, totaling 282 verses. Many of these passages record the significant implications of the Resurrection of Christ.

born as a baby but would rapture the saints, then return to defeat His enemies, and rule the world as a grown man, the Son of God.

The Resurrection offers hope to you. Jesus is alive, and He will rule someday. This world is a sick place, but one day Christ will remove the sickness forever. Sin will be done away with for all eternity. Only a living person could do all this.

The powers of death have done their worst,
But Christ their legions hath dispersed;
Let shouts of holy joy outburst, Hallelujah!

The three sad days have quickly sped,
He rises glorious from the dead;
All glory to our risen Head! Hallelujah!

—Translated by Francis Potts
from a Latin hymn

Do You Remember?

1. Who claimed the body of Jesus from Pilate? _Joseph of Arimathea_

2. Where was the body of Jesus buried? _in Joseph's rock tomb_

3. How was the tomb sealed? _____
   A stone was rolled in front of the entrance.

4. What did the priests do to make sure that no one would steal the body? _____
   They asked Pilate to send soldiers to guard the tomb.

5. What two women were the first to visit the tomb? _____
   Mary Magdalene and Mary the wife of Cleopas

6. Why did the two women visit the tomb? _to anoint Jesus's body_

7. What did they find at the tomb? _____
   an angel who had rolled away the stone

8. What message was given to the women? _____
   that Jesus had risen from the dead

9. To whom did Jesus appear first? _____
   the women, Mary Magdalene specifically (Mark 16:9)

10. How did the priests attempt to cover up what happened? _____
    They bribed the guards to say that while they slept, the disciples stole the body.

11. Where did the Lord appear to His disciples? _in and around Jerusalem and later in Galilee_

12. What commission did He give them just before He ascended? _____
    to carry the gospel into all nations, baptizing and teaching those who believed

49

The foundation of our faith (1 Cor. 15:12–23). Without the Resurrection, all is vain. Paul says that without it his preaching is empty, and the faith of Christians is pointless. He reasons that men will remain in their sins if Christ has not risen and that all those who have died trusting Christ have perished forever. His last assertion is that all who presently trust Christ are miserable fools if Christ has not been raised. *Everything* hinges on the Resurrection.

The Resurrection is the final proof of Christ's deity (Rom. 1:4). Without the Resurrection there can be no salvation for the sinner (Rom. 10:9–10). It is the assurance that a person's guilt is washed away when he comes to Christ in faith (4:25). It guarantees our own physical resurrection (1 Cor. 15:20–23). It is also concrete proof that

Jesus will one day judge people for their sins and reward some for their good works (John 5:22).

That is why Christ's Resurrection is necessary and why faith in that Resurrection is foundational.

The basis of Christ's ongoing ministry. The Resurrection exalted Jesus to the headship of the church, His body (Eph. 1:22–23). He leads it and builds it through His saints and His Spirit. On the basis of His Resurrection, He imparts power to believers and gifts by which we can serve (Eph. 4:8–13). His Resurrection and subsequent ascension made possible His current ministry of intercession for us, which is constant (Rom. 8:34; 1 Tim. 2:5–6). A dead man cannot empower, he cannot lead, and he cannot intercede. Christ performs all

these ministries for us by the power of the Resurrection.

 Extra Activity

Lecture: As a point of interest, read the following two selections from history to your class. These are quotes from sources outside of the Bible and were written within 150 years of Christ, attesting that the Resurrection is true. The Bible itself provides sufficient evidence to prove the Resurrection. These sources do show, however, that belief in the Resurrection is an ancient Christian doctrine and was a fact commonly reported in the first century.

(1) Josephus, a Jewish historian, wrote near the end of the first century in his work *Antiquities* (18.3.3): "Now there was about this time Jesus, a wise man, if it be lawful to call him a man; for he was a doer of wonderful works, a teacher of such men as receive the truth with pleasure. He drew over to him many Jews, and also many of the Greeks. This man was the Christ. And when Pilate had condemned him to the cross, upon his impeachment by the principal men among us, those who had loved from the first did not forsake him, for he appeared to them alive on the third day, the divine prophets having spoken these and thousands of other wonderful things about him. And even now, the race of Christians, so named from him, has not died out." (*Note:* Most scholars think that some parts of this testimony were added later, but the majority agree that Josephus did originally include this reference to Christ and His ministry.)

(2) Ignatius (circa AD 50–115), a leader of the church at Antioch, wrote in his *Epistle to the Trallians*: "He also rose again in three days. . . . On the day of preparation, then, at the third hour, He received the sentence from Pilate, the Father permitting that to happen; at the sixth hour He was crucified; at the ninth hour he gave up the ghost; and before sunset he was buried. During the Sabbath he continued under the earth in the tomb in which Joseph of Arimathaea had laid Him. . . . He really died, and was buried, and rose from the dead."

Unit 4

Christ's Sermon on the Mount

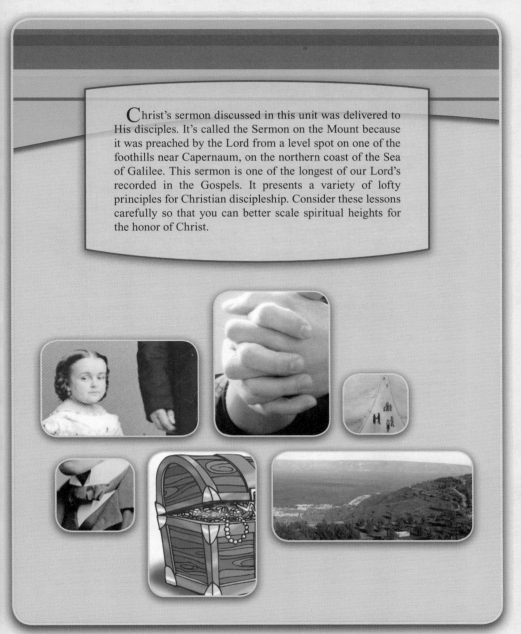

Christ's sermon discussed in this unit was delivered to His disciples. It's called the Sermon on the Mount because it was preached by the Lord from a level spot on one of the foothills near Capernaum, on the northern coast of the Sea of Galilee. This sermon is one of the longest of our Lord's recorded in the Gospels. It presents a variety of lofty principles for Christian discipleship. Consider these lessons carefully so that you can better scale spiritual heights for the honor of Christ.

Christ's Sermon on the Mount

Our Lord preached the Sermon on the Mount specifically to His disciples, not to unbelievers. The sermon contains a series of lofty principles for discipleship that are appropriate for junior high school students as well as Christians in general. The purpose of this unit is to thoroughly discuss the entire sermon.

Each lesson is a discussion of one section of Christ's sermon. The lessons proceed systematically through Matthew 5, 6, and 7. An attempt has been made to explain all the difficult points of the sermon and make appropriate applications to Christian teenagers.

The student text contains two special features in this unit. The first is an essay entitled "The Sea of Galilee" (pages TE82–83). It is included because the Sermon on the Mount was preached near the Sea of Galilee. Following the last lesson of this unit in the student text is the last of three major maps in the text, "Cities Christ Visited" (page TE95).

Lesson 14

Joy

Theme	Joy
Scripture	Matthew 5:1–16
Memory Work	Matthew 5:16

 Approach to the Lesson

Theme: Life has its ups and downs, its good times and its bad. The Christian is by no means spared these normal fluctuations. Unlike the unconverted, however, the Christian can remain constantly pleased with life, delighted with who he is and Whom he serves. This ability is the biblical quality of joy. Joy comes through a right relationship with God and with others.

This attitude is not automatic in the believer. Rather, he arrives at the point of a joyful disposition the same way he cultivates other Christian character traits—through perseverance, deeper understanding of and appreciation for all that God has done in Christ, and the empowering grace of God through the ministry of the Holy Spirit.

Rationale: Your students probably tend to be materialistic and circumstance-oriented. Challenge them to get their satisfaction and stability from their relationships, rather than from things. Turn their attention to others, not themselves.

Background: Jesus preached what is traditionally called the Sermon on the Mount during the first year of His ministry before much opposition had developed and while large crowds were gathering to

Objectives

Knowledge (concepts students need to grasp)	the meaning of each of the qualities Christ used to describe a joy-filled person
	the responsibility of demonstrating these qualities to unsaved people
Application (principles students should put into practice)	Happiness is not found in being the best looking, the smartest, or the most athletic.
	Happiness does not come from getting everything you ask for.
	Abiding happiness comes from having a right relationship with God and others.

Bible Expressions to Understand

savour—flavor or taste
bushel—a container holding 8.5 liters
the Beatitudes—the eight ways Jesus describes the blessed person in the Sermon on the Mount

If you could name one thing that would make you happy, what would it be? A change in the way you look? Money? New clothes? The truth is that if you had your circumstances just the way you wanted them, you wouldn't stay happy very long. Why? Because the key to happiness is what you are inside, not what you have, where you are, who you're with, what you can do, or what you look like.

In the Scripture passage you read for this lesson, Jesus explained to His disciples how a person can experience joy. His formula for joy was not to change a person's circumstances but to change the person through His power. Jesus presented eight qualities or actions that would make a person happy. He began each one with the word *blessed*, which means "happy" or "joyful." Jesus presented these eight items in a special order to show how they are related to each other.

The first four have to do with a personal relationship to God. People who are rightly related to God are characterized by the following:
• They are poor in spirit (5:3).
• They mourn (5:4).
• They are meek (5:5).
• They hunger and thirst for righteousness (5:6).

If you're poor in spirit, you are humble. Humility begins with an admission that you need Christ to save you from sin. A proud, self-reliant person will never turn to the Lord to save him. Once you are saved, your humility will show in the way you treat other people. You won't brag or treat other people as if they were worthless.

Once you've humbled yourself and accepted the Lord as your Savior, then you'll mourn over your sins. You will realize what a spiritually weak person you are and how often you sin against the Lord. The

Lord will comfort you by forgiving your sins and helping you overcome temptation.

Once you recognize your weaknesses and your need for help, you will be meek. This means that you'll submit yourself to the Lord and accept His help in every circumstance. You'll seek His advice in the Bible and His strength in prayer. You'll also follow the directions of the authorities the Lord has put over you, recognizing that He has placed them there to help develop you as a Christian.

As you submit to the Lord, you'll notice that you have a growing desire to know how to live to please Him. The Lord promises that every time you have a desire like this, He will satisfy it through your Bible reading or something that someone else teaches you.

When people are properly related to the Lord as described above, then there are some basic principles they follow in their relationships with others. Jesus listed and briefly developed these four:
• They show mercy (5:7).
• They are pure in heart (5:8).
• They are peacemakers (5:9).
• They accept persecution (5:10–12).

All too often you're confronted with the weaknesses of others. People are rude to you. Sometimes they get angry, lie to you, or steal from you. Jesus says you are to show mercy to these people. That means you aren't to try to get even. You aren't to get angry. You are to forgive them for their sins against you. Another way you can show mercy is to help people who need money, food, or clothing. Perhaps you have a friend who is having a hard time with math or science. You can show mercy to that person by recognizing his difficult position and helping him with his homework after school. If he is having trouble because he hasn't been paying attention, you

52

hear Him. The main ideas of what Jesus taught that day on the hillside in the open air are distilled in Matthew 5–7 and Luke 6:20–49.

Luke 6:17 tells us that this discourse was delivered on a plain. Apparently the Lord began the sermon there and then moved to a higher elevation as the crowd grew. He delivered the sermon to His disciples and was overheard by the multitudes (Matt. 5:1–2). This fact suggests that He intended the contents of the message primarily for believers.

The Lord wants His people to know blessedness. He presents an eight-fold description of a blessed (a happy, or joy-filled) life to help the believer to that end. These qualities present a startling contradiction to the world's conception of hap-

piness. Blessedness begins with a right relationship with God and proceeds from that foundation to a right relationship with others. It is not just a future possibility, but it may be a present reality for all Christians.

 The Lesson

I. A Right Relationship with God (Matt. 5:1–6)

Spiritual poverty (5:3). The first quality necessary for a right relationship with God is poverty of spirit. The Greek term translated "poor" is the strongest possible word with that meaning. It does not describe a person who just barely has his needs met; it is abject poverty, the kind that causes one to beg for the bare essentials. The opposite of this quality is pride, which

might think he's getting what he deserves. However, when a person is merciful, he doesn't act according to what people deserve but according to what they need. Mercy is the only basis for right relationships with others. If you treat others only on the basis of what they deserve and what you like about them, you will not have many friends—if any!

Another way to build right relationships with others is to be pure in heart. In other words, keep your sins confessed and walk close to the Lord. Never say or do anything to hurt someone's feelings. Obey the rules at school for the right reasons—to please the Lord, your parents, and the school officials and to make things run smoothly. If you obey the rules just to stay out of trouble, you are not obeying with a pure heart. Never obey the Lord's commands just to make people think you're a good Christian. Obey the Word of God with a pure heart—for the right reasons. Obey the Lord because you love Him and you want to please Him.

Part of keeping a pure heart is keeping your mind free of sinful thoughts. Don't dwell on what doesn't please the Lord. Many of the programs and commercials on television, for example, shouldn't be watched because they're not pure.

Another important step in relating properly to others is to be a peacemaker. The most important thing a peacemaker does is try to get others to make peace with God. Witnessing is part of being a peacemaker. You must tell your friends the good news of Christ's death for our sin in order for them to gain peace with God. Another thing a peacemaker does is avoid arguing and quarreling. Rather than argue, the peacemaker just stays quiet. He is friendly and tries to get friends to make up when they have had a disagreement.

If people don't like you because you are merciful, pure in heart, and a peacemaker, then you should be happy anyway. The world is full of people who are mean and impure and who fight with God and others. When you're not the way they are, they may not like you because you bother their consciences. They'll be unkind to you in their actions and their words. This is a sign that you're living the way you should. Even the greatest prophets of the Lord were treated this way because people didn't like the way they lived and spoke.

There are several reasons you should be the kind of person Jesus described in this passage. The most

important is that it brings glory to God. Another important reason is that it influences other people for the Lord. The Lord used two illustrations to show us how we are to influence others.

First, you're to be like salt in the world. Salt adds flavor to food. Knowing God gives flavor or purpose to life. When you think about it, life becomes meaningless and confusing without the Lord. Where did you come from? Why are you here? Why must you die? Where are you going? The only satisfying answers to these questions come from knowing the Lord and the teachings of His Word. The Christian brings the message of salt to the lives of others. By his example and words, he offers what will give purpose to those who accept the message. If salt loses its flavor, it is not good for anything; it is worthless. Likewise, if you lose your influence for Christ by sinning, you are really worthless to the Lord in the world.

How do salt and light illustrate the ways we should influence other people?

The second illustration Christ used was light. The world is a dark place spiritually. People don't understand the way God thinks. It's up to the Christian to light the way to the Lord and His salvation. As the Lord explained, it doesn't make sense for you to hide the fact that you are a Christian. Not witnessing for the Lord makes about as much sense as trying to hide a well-lighted city that's located on a hill. You will not be able to hide the fact that you are a Christian. You're different; God has made you that way. Sooner or later it will be obvious to others

53

---

is the father of most other sins. Pride says, "I can make it on my own. Few are as qualified or admirable as I am. I depend on myself. When I am down, I pull myself up by my bootstraps. When I am up, all look to me and admire me." Pride enthrones self and dethrones God, denying the necessity of His grace.

It is natural for young people to try to exalt themselves before their friends. Those who do, however, have failed this most basic test for spiritual blessing.

A person who has not dethroned self and enthroned Christ does not possess the kingdom of heaven. Only when he trusts Christ as his Savior does he inherit the blessing of Christ's presence and power and know the benevolent rule of the Son of God. Poverty of spirit is a prerequisite to

repentance. Only when a person sees how empty of spiritual value he really is will he turn to Christ.

Mourning (5:4). The next step beyond poverty of spirit is spiritual mourning. When the Lord says, "Blessed are they that mourn," He is referring to those who grieve over their sins. They will find comfort in salvation through Christ and continued comfort from Him through confession of sin and forgiveness. The closer a believer walks with God, the more acutely aware of sin he becomes, the more grieved over that sin he is, and the more readily he seeks cleansing.

If a student does not show any remorse over sin, he has a serious spiritual problem. He may not even know Christ as his Savior. Remorse is basic to the Christian spirit.

Meekness (5:5). A person who is poor in spirit and mournful over sin will also be meek. Meekness is submission to God. (Refer to Lesson 4.) It includes acceptance of God's will, unwillingness to assert oneself or to retaliate, and trust in the Lord to guide and sustain no matter what the circumstances. The astounding promise set forth here is that the meek will inherit the earth. Those who have submitted to the Lord in salvation and sanctification will one day rule with Him in glory over a new heaven and new earth. In this life the meek may not know great power and influence, but one day they will know extensive influence as coheirs with Christ.

Spiritual hunger (5:6). A person who has turned from his sins and submitted to Christ will "hunger and thirst after righteousness." One of the best evidences of a person's salvation is an ever-growing desire for the things of God. As the believer's appetite grows, Christ supplies nourishment through His Word, prayer, and fellowship with other believers. The Christian's hunger and thirst for the spiritual won't go unsatisfied; he will be filled.

Those who show no desire for spiritual things show no evidence of salvation. Students in Christian schools often exhibit this problem. Confront it clearly, directly, and forcefully.

II. A Right Relationship with Others (Matt. 5:7–12)

The greatest commandment in the Scripture is to love God. Out of this loving relationship grows a right relationship with others. The last four Beatitudes concern the qualities that contribute to a Christian's relationship with others.

Mercy (5:7). The Lord has looked on all of us in pity and saved us. Not one of us has gotten what he deserves. That is the essence of mercy. Mercy is a fundamental principle by which God governs His conduct toward humans, particularly the saved. Not to show mercy in our dealings with others makes us a contradiction to the fundamental nature and conduct of God. We must not reward others according to their sins if we are to enjoy the continual mercy of the Lord. The Lord takes a dim view of a person who treats others only with strict justice. This Beatitude implies that the unmerciful will receive no mercy.

Purity (5:8). Purity is freedom from sin. This purity is both positional and practical. The believer has the righteousness of Christ imputed to him by faith (positional purity). He must also seek cleansing from the defilement of sin as he lives in this world (practical purity). The Greek term translated "heart" is the richest term in the language to describe the inner person. It refers to the will, intellect, emotions, or conscience, depending on the context. At times, as in this case, the word includes all these aspects and refers to the whole of the inner person, the spiritual nature. The heart is the source of all words and actions. If the heart is pure, so will be all that comes from it. Pollution is almost inevitable in this life; confession of sin is the answer to the problem.

> Stress that personal purity is essential to spiritual success. Many teens think that they can participate in sin and come away unscathed; they cannot.

The reward for the pure in heart is that they will see God. This vision of God is two-fold. First, those who have been made pure through the blood of Christ will see God face-to-face, and "we shall be like him; for we shall see him as he is" (1 John 3:2). This is God's promise to all who know Christ by faith. Second, those who keep a pure heart in the practical sense will know the blessing of fellowship with God today, a sensing of the presence and power of God in their lives. Yet at best this vision of God will be only partial in this life. "For now we see through a glass, darkly; but then face to face: now I know in part; but then shall I know even as also I am known" (1 Cor. 13:12).

Peacemaking (5:9). A peacemaker is one who settles a dispute between warring parties. The Christian peacemaker does

that you're different. Why not tell them about the Lord who has made you a new person instead of being shy and ashamed? Concealing your testimony is also like lighting a lamp in a room and then covering it up. The purpose of the lamp is to give light. What use is it if you cover it after lighting it? Here again you are faced with the fact that you were made a Christian to give people the light of the gospel of Christ. To fail to do that makes your presence in the world pointless.

Jesus's encouragement to you is to be salt and light. Both of these things are good if they are used. Left unused, they are worthless. Follow the Lord's instruction and be a positive influence for the gospel in the world.

Where Does Your Joy Come From?

Joy doesn't come from how you look, what kind of house you live in, or how many friends you have. It comes from having a right relationship with God through Christ. Once you do, you'll turn your attention to the needs of others, first by giving them the gospel and then by helping them when they're in need. This is what makes the Christian joyful.

Do You Remember?

1. According to the dictionary, what does the word *beatitude* mean? _____
   blessedness; happiness

2. How many Beatitudes are there in the Sermon on the Mount? _eight_

3. If a person develops the kind of life described by the Lord in this passage, what will the result be? _joy_

4. What do the first four Beatitudes describe? _____
   how to have a right relationship with God

5. What do the second four beatitudes describe? _____
   how to have a right relationship with people

6. To what two things is a Christian compared? _salt and light_

7. What should we learn from the two illustrations Jesus used to describe the Christian? _____
   Christians are to influence others with the gospel.

54

this primarily by preaching the gospel of peace, which reconciles God to man. The ambassador for Christ confronts people with the cross, the answer to the problem of sin that has caused the breach between man and God (2 Cor. 5:18–21). Speaking of Christ, Paul wrote, "And, having made peace through the blood of his cross, by him to reconcile all things unto himself; by him, I say, whether they be things in earth, or things in heaven" (Col. 1:20).

The believer is also a peacemaker in that he conducts his affairs to ensure tranquility and harmony in his relationships with others. A Christian teacher functions in this capacity when he helps students live in harmony with one another in the classroom.

Few traits distinguish a Christian from a non-Christian as much as peacemaking. Rather than retaliating, holding grudges, and cultivating unrest and bitterness, the Christian pursues forgiveness and restoration of relationships.

Persecution (5:10–12). The thrust of the last Beatitude is that there is joy even in the suffering caused by others. Whether the suffering takes the form of general harassment ("persecuted"), malicious words ("revile"), or slander ("say all manner of evil against you falsely"), there is reward for those who suffer. The condition, however, is that the suffering comes on account of the name of Christ and righteousness.

> Your students must be ready and willing to suffer opposition and rejection because of their stand for Christ.

Suffering should not surprise the saint. Scripture is full of examples of persecution. Elijah (1 Kings 19:2), Hanani (2 Chron. 16:10), Jeremiah (Jer. 37:13–15; 38:4–6), Daniel (Dan. 6:16), and Zechariah (2 Chron. 24:21) are a few examples. It is interesting to note that this Beatitude follows the one concerning peacemaking. Rather than being a blessing to the world, the peacemaker is rejected and persecuted as an irritation.

III. Influencing Others for Righteousness (Matt. 5:13–16)

These verses provide two analogies that illustrate how the Christian exerts his positive influence on others.

Salt (5:13). Salt adds flavor and creates thirst. The believer's life should be so full of joy that unbelievers are attracted to it. Salt is also a preservative. The presence of the believer in the world should prevent "spoilage," the spreading of sin's influence.

The unrefined salt of Palestine was gathered from marshes or deserts. Its impurities caused it to decrystallize, making it worthless. Such salt had to be thrown into the street because if thrown into the fields it would kill the vegetation. If a Christian becomes corrupted by the world, he becomes worthless to both God and others.

Light (5:14–16). Light suggests two things: guidance and illumination. A traveler who sees "a city that is set on an hill" is guided to the city by its lights. Similarly, the believer provides direction to the place of security and rest. When a person lights a lamp in his house, he doesn't cover it up, but he puts it in a place where it will dispel the most darkness. In the same way, the believer should make sure that his good works bring glory to the heavenly Father.

> Now is the time to develop in your students a sense of personal responsibility for those around them. They are to be salt and light in the world, preserving others from the corruption of sin and revealing the light of the gospel for the glory of God.

✳ Extra Activities

Lecture: You might want to use some interesting trivia about salt to "spice" up your lecture:

- If all the water in the ocean evaporated, approximately six million cubic miles of salt would be left.

- The human body contains about four ounces of salt. Without sufficient salt, the muscles won't contract, the blood won't circulate, food won't digest, and the heart won't beat.

- One of the oldest roads in Italy, the Via Salaria (Salt Route), was used to transport salt from Ostia to other parts of Italy.

- The ancient Chinese used coins made of salt, and in Europe some Mediterranean people used cakes of salt as currency. Roman soldiers were sometimes paid in salt. In fact, the word *salary* comes from *sal*, the Latin word for salt.

- Today the United States is both the largest producer and the largest consumer of salt.

- Many common compounds are technically salts: sodium chloride (table salt), sodium bicarbonate (baking soda), and calcium carbonate (limestone).

- According to the Salt Institute, salt has over 14,000 uses, but many of them are no longer common because other products are readily available. For example, salt can be used in place of toothpaste for brushing your teeth, and it's good to gargle with salt water if you have a sore throat. Salt is an excellent cleaning agent, by itself or in combination with other substances.

Object lesson: Place a lighted candle in an obscure place in your classroom, out of the students' sight. You may want to place an opaque, noncombustible container over the candle so that it will not be noticed. (But be sure that the container doesn't cut off the oxygen, causing the candle to go out.) When you are discussing the verses that portray the believer as a candle in a house, turn off the light in the room and uncover the candle. The candle that was previously unnoticeable will immediately become obvious.

Point out that this is precisely to be the role of the Christian. The light of the Christian's testimony should not be hidden from the view of the world. If a Christian is having a testimony in the world as he should, his light (the light of Christ in him) will enlighten those around him.

Class discussion: The subject of joy is presented throughout Scripture. The following outline gives several key points that you can discuss in class.

1. Commanded (Phil. 3:1; 4:4; 1 Thess. 5:16)
2. Fruit of the Spirit (Rom. 15:13; Gal. 5:22)
3. Source
   a. Faith (Phil. 1:25; 1 Pet. 1:8)
   b. Fellowship (Rom. 12:15; 2 Cor. 7:13)
   c. Faithfulness rewarded (Matt. 25:21, 23)
4. Objects
   a. God (Ps. 43:4; Isa. 61:10; Phil. 3:3)
   b. The Word (Ps. 119:14, 111)
   c. Conversion of souls (Acts 15:3; Luke 2:10; 15:10)
   d. Heaven (Rom. 5:2)
5. Permanence (John 16:22)

Lesson 15
The Law

Theme	Appreciating the Old Testament
Scripture	Matthew 5:17–32
Memory Work	Matthew 5:17

 Approach to the Lesson

Theme: Nothing the Lord Jesus ever taught contradicted the Old Testament. He did not come to do away with the law and the prophets but to give a deeper, fuller meaning to what they taught. The Old Testament is God's Word just as much as the New Testament (2 Tim. 3:16–17). We understand from the New Testament that the symbolic, ceremonial laws of the Old Testament pointed to the person and work of Christ and found their fulfillment in His incarnation, death, and Resurrection (Col. 2:13–14). Since those laws have been fulfilled by Christ, we are not required to follow them. However, many of the laws of the Old Testament are moral, teaching us how to be properly related to God and others. We are still responsible to follow those laws.

Rationale: Many students are prejudiced against the Old Testament, particularly because of its genealogies and its "dos and don'ts." Stress the Old Testament's practicality and its fulfillment in the New Testament. For example, note that much of Romans 3, a passage fundamental to salvation, is quoted from the Old Testament. And 1 Corinthians 10 and Hebrews 11 give us practical character lessons from the Old Testament.

Background: This part of the Sermon on the Mount addresses a crucial issue—the believer's relationship to the Old Testament. Even though understanding which Old Testament laws are applicable today is not easy, the Christian has the responsibility to study, know, and obey the moral laws of the Old Testament. He also should consider the many Old Testament examples of personalities and incidents and derive life-directing principles from them. Christ not only confirms these principles but also gives further development of specific Old Testament laws. These laws are of particular practical significance for your students.

 The Lesson

I. The Old Testament's Importance (Matt. 5:17–20)

Christ taught the importance of the Old Testament in the following four ways:

Its fulfillment (5:17). The Lord asserted that He had not come to destroy the law and the prophets but to fulfill them. This is the guiding truth of the whole passage. The difficulty in this verse centers on the word *fulfill*. Some take it to mean that Jesus would personally fulfill all the expectations of the law and prophets in deed and word. He certainly did so, but that interpretation misses the point of the rest of the passage. Christ, as the author of the Old Testament law, expertly fleshed out the fuller significance of the teaching of the Old Testament. The rest of Matthew 5 gives examples of Christ filling out the Old Testament teaching. The term translated "fulfill" is better translated "complete." The teachings of Christ (and the apostles) fill out, or make complete, what was begun by the Old Testament Law (Pentateuch) and Prophets (a Jewish designation for the rest of the Old Testament).

Its reliability (5:18). Jesus next taught that the Old Testament will be preserved to the letter until all its laws and prophecies are proved true. The word here translated *be fulfilled* is a different Greek word from the one used in the previous verse. This term emphasizes "coming to pass." The phrase "till heaven and earth pass" is a proverbial expression meaning "never." Jesus said that the Old Testament will be preserved down

Objectives

Knowledge	the durability of the law of God
(concepts students need to grasp)	the Bible's teaching concerning murder and adultery
	the basis of the New Testament in the Old Testament
Application	We must learn from the examples in the Old Testament.
(principles students should put into practice)	Angry arguing, name-calling, and grudge-holding are serious sins that Jesus equates with murder.
	Lust begins in the mind; consequently, a Christian's mind must be kept free of polluting influences.
	God hates divorce.

Outline

(Matt. 5:17–22)
I. The Old Testament's importance (17–20)
  A. Its fulfillment
  B. Its reliability
  C. Its authority
  D. Its priorities
II. Christ and the Old Testament (21–32)
  A. On murder
  B. On adultery

to the jot and tittle. The *jot* (pronounced "yoth" in Hebrew, to rhyme with *clothe*) is the smallest letter in the Hebrew alphabet. Going a step further, the Lord refers to a *tittle*, which is a part of a Hebrew letter that distinguishes it from another similar letter. He uses an emphatic expression "shall in no wise pass" to communicate the certainty of this promise.

Its authority (5:19). Jesus then took an interesting practical approach concerning the teaching and practice of the law. He said that anyone who breaks the least of the Old Testament commandments and teaches other people to do so is least in the kingdom of heaven. That is a clear stamp of approval on the Old Testament. In contrast, anyone who teaches and practices these laws will be considered great in the kingdom.

Its priorities (5:19–20). Not all laws are equally important; some commandments are less significant than others. A major example of this principle is our Lord's teaching that the greatest commandment is to love God. The second is to "love your neighbor as yourself." All other laws of God are more minor particularizations of these two grand generalizations.

To underscore the importance of careful teaching and observance of the law, Jesus used the Pharisees as an example. Their righteousness consisted of obeying and teaching minute interpretations of the law as handed down by the rabbis. In the process, they lost the Lord's priorities. In a later passage (Matt. 23:23), Jesus condemned them for neglecting the weightier matters of the law in order to focus on minutiae. Their most serious neglect was their failure to love the Lord above all others. Appropriately, Jesus warned that their righteousness would never merit their entrance into heaven. Such entrance depends on a person's relationship to God through Christ.

Read: Matthew 5:17–32 Memorize: Matthew 5:17

Bible Expressions to Understand

jot—the smallest letter of the Hebrew alphabet
tittle—a tiny part of a Hebrew letter
raca—an Aramaic insult meaning "You empty-headed fool!"
Gehenna—the valley of Hinnom, southeast of Jerusalem; a garbage dump; a symbol of hell
farthing—a small Roman coin worth about 1/64 of a day's wage

Laws are important. They help people treat each other fairly. Your parents, for example, have rules (laws) for your home. They help keep the household running smoothly. Your school also has rules. The principal and teachers in your school work to help students obey the rules, making the school run better. The rules help create a better atmosphere for learning, make it easier for you to get along with your classmates while you're at school, and teach you how to live as a Christian. Your community and nation have laws that govern the way you and other citizens live. Those laws are necessary to help all live happy, peaceful lives.

God has given us laws as well; these are found in the Bible. Sometimes they're straightforward statements. Other times the Bible teaches them by examples or stories. Jesus often quoted or referred to the Old Testament laws. His followers, the apostles, did the same.

Jesus taught that the Old Testament laws would never be destroyed. The ceremonial laws concerning Israel's worship pictured the work of Christ in the future for believers. The laws governing Israel's conduct as a nation present principles to learn from today. Jesus taught that it is important both to teach and to obey the laws of God (Matt. 5:19–20). The Pharisees taught the law of God but ignored some of the most important parts. They also did not obey the law as they should have. That is the reason why Jesus often called them hypocrites.

In the Sermon on the Mount, Jesus revealed the true meaning of several Old Testament laws. For example, He explained the commandment not to murder. The Old Testament teaches, "Thou shalt not kill" (Exod. 20:13). It's wrong to maliciously destroy another person's life. On the other hand, God commands that the government end someone's life if he commits certain crimes. On certain occasions, He also commanded His people to go to war in Old Testament times. There are times when taking a human life is the just and right thing to do. However, God has never approved of thoughts, words, or actions that are murderous. Jesus taught that a man can be angry toward another person and be guilty of murder. He also taught that a person can say cruel

55

an angry, hate-filled spirit a person would be "in danger of the council," an allusion to the Jewish supreme court, the Sanhedrin. Jesus used this example to symbolize the justice of God. Again, anyone who calls another "Thou fool" places himself in serious jeopardy before the Lord; he is in danger of hellfire. This refers to the burning of waste and animal carcasses in the valley of Hinnom (southwest of Jerusalem), a place the Lord frequently used to symbolize future eternal judgment. Three times the Lord said that an angry spirit and vicious words make a person as guilty as a murderer.

> It is unlikely that any of your students would kill someone. But it is virtually certain that they speak harshly to or about others, or at least think evil of them. Christ equates this attitude with murder.

Worship will not be accepted until serious contentions or disagreements are solved. Matthew 5:23–24 pictures a Jewish worshiper in the most serious act of worship, bringing a sacrifice to the temple. He gives the sacrifice to the priest and then places his hands on the animal's head, confessing his sins. If he does all this while harboring bitterness, the worship is pointless. Reconciliation with the offended brother must occur before the worship is acceptable.

To emphasize His point, the Lord presented another example (5:25–26). If disagreement and ill will arise between a debtor and a creditor, the debtor should do all he can to settle the matter out of court, even on the road as he goes to court. Roman law demanded that once a case came to court, it could be disposed of only according to the law; there could be no out-of-court settlement. To go to court against a creditor who has a strong case and is full of animosity toward you will bring the worst results. As Jesus said, "Thou shalt by no means come out thence [out of prison], till thou hast paid the uttermost farthing" (5:26). A farthing was a small brass Roman coin worth 1/64 of a *denarius*, which was a day's wage. Even at today's minimum wage (which is inflated by comparison), this amount would be less than a dollar. In other words, the creditor will see to it that he gets the last fraction owed.

On adultery (5:27–32). As in the discussion of murder, the Lord began this discussion by presenting the Old Testament law, specifically the seventh commandment (Exod. 20:14). He then took the law a step

II. Christ and the Old Testament (Matt. 5:21–32)

Two examples of how Christ fleshed out the Old Testament law are found in His teaching on murder and adultery.

On murder (5:21–26). The Lord began His discussion of murder by referring to the sixth commandment (Exod. 20:13), which prohibits only murder, not every kind of killing. This is supported by the Hebrew terminology in the verse and the clear sense of other passages in the Old Testament. A person committing murder was in danger of the judgment of the town

council, which decided criminal cases (Deut. 19:12). The membership of these councils varied in number from three in small towns (those with a population of 150 or fewer) to twenty-three in larger towns.

Before every violent act is a wicked thought and sometimes wicked words. Some of these words and thoughts never bring action, but they are no less wicked. Jesus warned that a person who is angry with another is in as much danger of the judgment as the one who commits murder. This reference to judgment refers to God's tribunal since only God knows people's thoughts.

Harsh words are a natural extension of anger. To say "raca" was to say, "You empty-headed fool!" For using such a strongly derogatory term that demonstrated

further, saying that a man can look at a woman in such a way as to commit adultery with her in his heart. The evil occurs in the man's thoughts, but the guilt is as real as if he had actually committed adultery. Adultery in this case is a reference to illicit sexual relations with a married person. The more general term for sexual sin, *porneia*, which includes fornication, is not used here.

> Sexual lust is a serious problem among teens. Of course, you should deal with the subject in good taste, but you must address it directly. More students will have their effectiveness destroyed by this sin than by any other.

To communicate the importance of avoiding this sin in thought or in practice, the Lord used hyperbole. He recommended plucking out one's eye or cutting off one's hand to avoid sin and judgment. These literary exaggerations effectively communicate the importance of avoiding the sin.

Jesus also raised the issue of divorce in connection with adultery. First, He noted the Old Testament provision for divorce in cases of *uncleaness* (Deut. 24:1). The Greeks and Romans of this time both held a low view of the permanency of marriage. The Jews held two views. The school of Shammai, a noted teacher, allowed divorce only for unfaithfulness. The school of Hillel, another teacher, allowed it for almost any reason. The crux of the issue lay in their interpretation of *uncleanness*. Jesus taught here that marriage is not to be taken lightly; the only basis for divorce is illicit sexual activity. Divorce for any other reason makes remarriage adultery.

things to others, demonstrating his hatred for them, and be just as guilty as if he had murdered them. Not only is a person guilty of a serious crime when he's angry and hateful toward others, but he also completely cancels out any good he might do in worship of the Lord (Matt. 5:22–24). His worship is unacceptable. He must get on right terms with the person he hates and then come to worship.

As a Christian you mustn't allow anger to rule you. There are many negative consequences to such conduct. Worst of all, you're guilty of breaking God's law concerning how you should treat other people. Losing your temper and holding a grudge over a sports event is breaking God's law. Becoming bitter and holding a grudge toward a former boyfriend or girlfriend is breaking God's law. Anger over the rules your mother and father establish for you is breaking God's law. God isn't pleased by such conduct and attitudes.

Jesus also gave additional teaching about the commandment against adultery (Exod. 20:14). Adultery is the sin of sexual involvement with another person's husband or wife, and God forbids it. Jesus taught that it is possible to commit adultery in your mind. By just imagining the sin and desiring it, you've committed it. You're just as guilty as if you had actually committed the act. Jesus taught that an uncontrolled imagination is a dangerous and sinful thing. The Bible teaches that wrong actions begin with wrong thoughts. Corrupt thoughts are sinful. It's especially important for you to control your mind concerning sex. Sexual activity is only for marriage. Dwelling on sexual thoughts outside of marriage is sinful, and it can destroy you.

Jesus used two *hyperboles* to teach how much of an effort you should make to avoid lustful looking (Matt. 5:29–30). A hyperbole is an intentional exaggeration used to make a strong point. Jesus said that a person should slice off his hand and rip out his eye if those body parts inclined him to sin sexually. A man's hand and eye are crucial to a comfortable and productive life. The point He is making is that you should set no limit on your efforts to avoid this sin. Even things that are basically good but may cause sin should be eliminated. You may have friends, pastimes, or places you go that lead you into sin. Get rid of those things! They're not right for you.

Are You Living by the Law?

In your home your parents make the rules. At school the principal makes the rules. In life Jesus Christ makes the rules. Some of His rules are given in the Old Testament. More are given in the New Testament. Jesus didn't come to do away with the Old Testament but to give a deeper, fuller meaning to what it teaches. We understand from the New Testament that the symbolic, ceremonial laws of the Old Testament pointed to the Lord Jesus and were fulfilled in His life, death, and Resurrection. Since those laws have been fulfilled by Christ, we aren't required to follow them. However, many of the laws of the Old Testament are permanent, teaching us how to have right relationships with God and others. God's laws are forever and should be taught and obeyed.

Do You Remember?

1. What's the relationship of the Lord Jesus Christ to the Old Testament? _____
   He came to complete the law of God.

2. What two parts of the Hebrew alphabet are referred to by the Lord in this passage? _____
   the jot and the tittle

3. What two Old Testament commandments did Christ intensify in this passage? _____
   the commandment against murder and the commandment against adultery

4. Whose righteousness must be exceeded in order to enter the kingdom of heaven? _____
   the Pharisees'

5. What effect did Jesus say His coming had on the laws of God? _____
   He came to fulfill the law, not to destroy it.

6. A person who insults someone by calling him a fool is in danger of what? *hell fire*

7. What's always necessary before you worship the Lord? _____
   reconciliation with any fellow believer who has something against you

57

Lecture: Use the following facts to demonstrate the value and prominence of the Old Testament:

- The New Testament quotes the Old Testament about 1,000 times and alludes to it another 1,000 times.
- Christ revealed Himself by preaching from the Old Testament (Luke 24:27).
- All the sermons in Acts (except for the two times when Paul gives his testimony) are based on the Old Testament.
- In Acts 2–3 Peter preached two sermons based on the Old Testament.
- In Acts 7 Stephen gave a beautiful overview of the Old Testament in preaching to the Sanhedrin before his stoning.
- In Acts 8 Philip preached to the Ethiopian eunuch from Isaiah 53.
- The New Testament church was built on Christ revealed in the flesh and the preaching of the cross from the Old Testament.
- The New Testament often quotes the Old Testament to make its point. For example, in 1 Corinthians Paul quoted the Old Testament in 1:19 and 3:19 (Isa. 29:14; Job 5:13) to show the foolishness of human wisdom. He again quoted the Old Testament in 2:9 (Isa. 64:4) to demonstrate God's grace. He quoted Deuteronomy 25:4 in 9:9 to show that the laborer is worthy of his hire. (He also quoted that verse in 1 Timothy 5:18.) He quoted Isaiah 28:11 in 14:21 to explain the purpose of tongues.

 Extra Activities

Writing: Have your students write down what they think of the Old Testament and how it applies to them. Have them do this assignment anonymously so that they will feel free to reveal their true feelings. Reading these essays should help you gear the lecture to their needs. You can also read some of these papers in class to stimulate interest, but be sure to correct any misconceptions they may have expressed.

Analogy: God's expectations for His people in the New Testament are the same as for His people in the Old Testament. The emphasis may be different; that is why Christ said He did not come to destroy the law (change the message) but to fulfill it (add to the emphasis). A good analogy of this principle is the parents' raising of a child. As the child grows older, the parents' goals for the child remain the same, but the method of reaching those goals changes. When the child is young, they place strict rules on him. He has little freedom to do as he wants. All his decisions are made for him. As he matures, the rules become less rigid, but the goals do not change. Rather, the parents begin to emphasize doing right based on a relationship with God and the parents. That is Christ's point in Matthew 5. He is not destroying the law; He is appealing to us to live right on the basis of our relationship to Him, the One Who has fulfilled the law.

Lesson 16
Spiritual Maturity

THEME	Spiritual Maturity
SCRIPTURE	Matthew 5:33–48
MEMORY WORK	Matthew 5:48

Approach to the Lesson

Theme: When someone is mature, he is grown up in his attitudes and actions; he is not childish. A person who can carry on a conversation well, meet new people comfortably, and listen to others thoughtfully is socially mature. One who is mature physically has grown to adulthood in his body. A spiritually mature person, however, has developed a keen sense of right and wrong based on God's law, the Bible, and thinks and does what is right in God's eyes. Generally speaking, he loves God above all others and loves others as he loves himself. He does not think in terms of what is just barely acceptable to God or what he can get away with. Instead he asks, "Which action would bring the *most* glory to God?" The issue is not what is OK to do or say, but what is the *best* thing to do or say. Jesus Christ is both the greatest example of a spiritually mature person and the standard by which every believer evaluates himself.

It might be good to lead a short discussion of the following sentence from the student text: "Dwarfism is an abnormal physical condition, but there's nothing 'wrong' with being a dwarf." Some people consider the terms "dwarf" and "midget" offensive. The important thing

Objectives

KNOWLEDGE (concepts students need to grasp)	the definition of spiritual maturity
	the meaning of the biblical word *perfect*
APPLICATION (principles students should put into practice)	A spiritually mature person is honest and keeps his word.
	A spiritually mature person does not demand his rights but yields them to advance his testimony for Christ.
	A spiritually mature person loves not only those who love him, but also those who abuse him.

Bible Expressions to Understand

swear—promise; vow
yea, yea; nay, nay—*yes, yes,* or *no, no*; an expression of strong positive assurance or denial
smite—hit or strike
coat—a close-fitting inner garment
cloke—a large outer garment like a modern topcoat
twain—two
publican—a Jew who collected taxes for the Roman government

Dwarfs don't appear only in fairy tales. By some estimates, there are about 195,000 worldwide. Dwarfism is a medical condition typically caused by the failure of the pituitary gland to produce a growth hormone. The shortest mature human on record is Gul Mohamed of India. According to the *Guinness Book of Records* website, a physical examination at the Ram Manohar Hospital in New Delhi in 1990 set his official height at only 22.5 inches.

Charles Stratton, AKA General Tom Thumb (on far right), had an adult height of 33 inches. He married Livinia Warren in 1863.

58

Perhaps the most famous dwarf in history was Charles Sherwood Stratton, who was born in Bridgeport, Massachusetts, in 1838. He came to be known as General Tom Thumb, a name given him by P. T. Barnum, the circus king. General Tom Thumb made Barnum millions of dollars as he traveled throughout America and Europe, performing before thousands. A former mayor of New York, Philip Hone, wrote that General Thumb was a "handsome, well-proportioned little gentleman, lively, agreeable, sprightly, and talkative, with no deficiency of intellect. . . . His hand is about the size of a half dollar, and his foot three inches in length." General Tom Thumb died of a stroke at age 45.

Is Anything Stunting Your Spiritual Growth?

Obeying God's law results in spiritual maturity. Maturity is simply growing up. A person who can carry on a conversation well, meet new people comfortably, and listen to others thoughtfully is socially mature. Someone who is mature physically has an adult body. A spiritually mature person has developed a keen sense of right and wrong based on God's law, the Bible, and he thinks and does what is right. He asks, "Which action will bring the most glory to God?" The issue is not what is just OK but what is best. The Lord Jesus Christ is both the greatest example of a spiritually mature person and the standard by which every believer evaluates himself.

for students to realize is that they should accept people for who they are regardless of unchangeable physical traits such as height, sex, and skin color. God's perspective is that inward character is much more important than outward characteristics (1 Sam. 16:7), and that should be our perspective as well.

Rationale: Give your students an outward, mature focus by stressing the importance of treating others fairly and consistently, regardless of the way others treat them.

Background: This section of the Sermon on the Mount continues Christ's "fleshing out" of the Old Testament law that began in the previous section. The last verse of the section is the focal point: "Be ye therefore perfect, even as your Father which is in heaven is perfect." The word

translated "perfect" is *teleios*, which means "complete" or "fully developed," rather than "sinless." Another way to translate the word is "mature."

How is a believer to attain this maturity? The Lord presents truths that one must put to work in his life to be spiritually mature. The ideas are not exhaustive; they are simply examples of the high standards that a Christian must follow if he wants to be spiritually mature.

Two important teaching aids, copies of the charts from pages 59 and 60 of the student text, are found on the CD accompanying this book.

What is it about dwarfs that attracts attention? They don't grow physically as they should, but they do mature mentally and socially. Dwarfism is an abnormal physical condition, but there's nothing wrong with being a dwarf. A dwarf has done nothing wrong that led to his dwarfism. He can be as productive as anyone else. But what about a "spiritual dwarf," a person who has been saved but hasn't grown spiritually? Something is terribly wrong with a person like that. How does a Christian grow up spiritually? In the Sermon on the Mount, Jesus reveals some high standards that we must maintain in order to mature spiritually.

Jesus said that one of these standards is honesty (Matt. 5:33–37). The Lord Jesus said that Christians shouldn't take oaths in everyday conversation. Taking an oath to prove your honesty suggests that normally you're not honest—that if you want people to believe what you say, you have to promise that it's true. You should be known for telling the truth. When your teacher asks you about homework, and you haven't done it, you should tell the truth. If your parents ask where you've been, you should tell the truth. This also means that you keep your word. If you tell one of your friends that you're going to the ball game with him, don't change your mind and go with someone else. If you promise your father that you'll cut the grass by Friday, keep your promise. A mature Christian is straightforward and honest.

The second rule for growing up as a Christian is that you must learn to yield your rights (Matt. 5:38–42). The first example Jesus gave to illustrate this idea was about getting hit. Your natural reaction may be to hit back if someone hits you. It's fine to protect yourself (which may mean getting yourself out of the situation), but don't try to get even. If you get even, you'll probably never be able to develop a friendship with that person and have a spiritual impact on them.

Jesus mentioned another example of giving up rights to something. Suppose someone takes your property away through a lawsuit. What should you do? Let him take it and more. Instead of getting angry or retaliating, you do what you can to

Sure, Ernie ol' pal, I'm GLAD to lend you that dollar . . . and mind you, I'm not expecting ANYTHING in return. But if you DON'T pay me back, I'll have to SELL your watch.

maintain a relationship with that person so that you can help him spiritually.

Next Jesus said that if a person in authority asks you to do something that is unfair or inconvenient, don't get angry and refuse to do it. Do what you are asked and even some extra. That kind of conduct will create a good relationship between you and that person. For instance, if you think your teacher has given you too much homework, don't complain about it to the other students. Do your best. Maintain a good testimony. If your parents give you more chores to do than they give your sister or brother, don't gripe about it. Perhaps it isn't fair, but the only way you'll ever see the situation improve is to be cheerful and obedient. If you rebel, things will only get worse.

The last example Jesus used was about someone who wants to borrow money from you. It's your money. You have the right to refuse to lend it. But

YIELD YOUR RIGHTS		
Situation	**Right Response**	**Wrong Response**
Physical Abuse	Defend yourself, but don't retaliate.	Abuse the abuser in return.
Loss of Property	Protect your property, but don't seek revenge.	Take something that belongs to the offender or otherwise harm him.
Unreasonable Request from Authority	Do what you are asked and more.	Refuse to do what you are asked or do a poor job; complain.
Request to Borrow Money or Property	Lend without expecting to receive anything in return.	Refuse to lend because you do not want to lose money or property.

59

and should not be entered into lightly. Last, Jesus said not even to swear by your head. This means not to take an oath by your life. A person's life is not his to dispose of. God is the One Who decides whether we live or die. We cannot control even minor changes in our bodies, such as when or whether our hair turns grey (without chemicals). So we shouldn't take an oath such as: "Cross my heart and hope to die."

How then is a person to assure another that his word is true? Jesus said, "But let your communication be, Yea, yea; Nay, nay" (Matt. 5:37). That is, be straightforwardly honest, and keep your word. In time everyone will know that your word is trustworthy. They will know that what you say you will do. Anything beyond keeping a simple promise has its source in evil. The whole process of vowing and oath-taking would be unnecessary if everybody always told the truth and kept his word.

Your students must learn the importance of their word. If they say they are going to do something, they must do it. They must always tell the truth. To be a liar is to act like a child of the Devil himself. Jesus said, "Ye are of your father the devil, and the lusts of your father ye will do. He was a murderer from the beginning, and abode not in the truth, because there is no truth in him. When he speaketh a lie, he speaketh of his own: for he is liar, and the father of it" (John 8:44).

Did the Lord forbid taking vows and swearing oaths by these statements? No. Writing under inspiration, the apostle Paul sometimes used strong oaths to add force to his statements (Rom. 1:9; 2 Cor. 1:23; Gal. 1:20). What Jesus forbade is frivolous vow-taking, which results in dishonesty and breaking obligations to God and to others.

II. Sacrificing Your Rights (Matt. 5:38–42)

The Lord quoted Exodus 21:24, which places a limit on retaliation (cf. Lev. 24:20;

⭐ The Lesson

I. Keeping Your Word (Matt. 5:33–37)

Jesus began by discussing taking oaths. The believer must keep his word; he must not make a promise and then break it. He must not take on an obligation and then neglect to fulfill it. The term *perform* in Christ's statement means "to pay in full." When someone makes an oath to the Lord, that obligation becomes a debt to the Lord that he must pay.

Christ was not prohibiting swearing in a court of law. He Himself answered Caiaphas under oath during His trial (Matt. 26:62–64), and the taking of oaths is regulated by the Old Testament (Lev. 19:12; Num. 30:2). But here the Lord encourages people not to make oaths in their everyday communications. Why? Because such oaths may not guarantee the truthfulness or the intent of the one who makes them. This should not be the case, but it often is. A common notion among Jews in the first century was that an oath made with reference to God was more binding than an oath made without such reference. Oaths had come to be virtually meaningless, and so some used this approach to make them more binding. Alluding to Isaiah 66:1 ("The heaven is my throne, and the earth is my footstool"), Jesus said not to swear by heaven or earth because God is Lord over all. Referring to Psalm 48:2, Jesus said not to swear by Jerusalem. Again He asserted that a person so swearing is entering into an obligation to God; such an oath is serious

Deut. 19:21). Jesus suggested a revolutionary approach for responding to wrongs. Instead of retaliating, a person should not resist the evil but should leave the revenge up to the Lord. The Lord used four examples to illustrate His point.

Retaliation is a natural human reflex; Christ commands us not to retaliate. Challenge your students to overcome their natural tendencies as one way of making their Christian testimony effective.

Personal (5:39). The first case is that of physical violence against us. If someone in rage hits you on the cheek, you should turn the other cheek. You are to indicate that no retaliation is coming. Christ's teaching does not forbid self-defense in cases where a person may be seriously injured or lose his life; in fact, good stewardship of life would require self-defense. But self-defense should be simply to prevent further abuse, and not to inflict harm on the attacker. Retaliation for vengeance is specifically forbidden.

Legal (5:40). The second example is a lawsuit. Considering the context, the legal proceeding must be viewed as unjust. Somehow the plaintiff wins and takes your "coat" (a close-fitting, vest-type garment). You are to give the person your "cloak" (outer garment) also. Jewish law supplies the reasoning for this order. The taking of the outer garment was forbidden by law (Exod. 22:26–27). The plaintiff could legally take only the inner garment. But to demonstrate that there would be no retaliation for the injustice, you should willingly give up your outer coat. Jesus was suggesting a radical approach to handling wrongs. One thing is certain: if you respond to mistreatment this way, the opportunity to witness for Christ will still be there. If you retaliate, the opportunity will be lost.

Governmental (5:41). The third example is drawn from the cultural setting. By Roman custom any government official could impress private citizens to carry out state business. Jesus taught that if a Roman soldier were to require a Jew to carry a burden for a mile, he was to respond by carrying it for two miles. There is to be no refusal or vengeful spirit because of the imposition, but submission for testimony's sake. This is the practice from which we derive our cliché "go the extra mile."

Financial (5:42). The last example is an economic one. A person is the steward of the money God has put in his control; it

perhaps you can help someone by lending him something you own. Being generous rather than stingy makes you more like your heavenly Father, who gives freely.

The third high standard for maturity as a believer is to love your enemies (Matt. 5:44–48). Enemies would include any who speak and act against you. Instead of hating these people, you are to say good things about them, treat them with kindness, and pray for them. God treats His enemies this way. He sends rain and sunshine for both the saved and the unsaved. If the only people you treat kindly are your own friends and relatives, you're no different from the unsaved. They naturally love their friends and hate their enemies.

Jesus closed this part of the Sermon on the Mount by saying, "Be ye therefore perfect, even as your Father which is in heaven is perfect." The word *perfect* here does not mean "sinless." It means "mature" or "completely developed." You're to be as much like the Lord as you can be. That's your goal.

LOVING YOUR ENEMIES
Reasons for Loving
• God loves His enemies.
• God rewards those who love their enemies.
• We ought to be different from the unsaved.
Ways of Loving
• Speak well of them.
• Do good to them.
• Pray for them.
Opposites of Loving
• Criticize and complain about your enemies.
• Do things to harm them.
• Never pray for them.

Do You Remember?

1. Why is it wrong for a Christian to take an oath to prove he's honest? *It implies that he is not normally honest. A Christian should always tell the truth and keep his word.*

2. What are the things a person is not to swear by? *heaven, earth, Jerusalem, his own head*

3. Why shouldn't a person who's been physically abused try to get even? *He will lose his opportunity to minister spiritually to his abuser.*

4. What are the four things a person is to do for his enemies? *Love them, bless them, do good to them, and pray for them.*

5. What are two reasons a person is to love his enemies? *(1) So we will be like God Who loves His enemies; (2) reward comes only if we act differently from the typical unsaved person who loves only his friends.*

6. What does the Lord mean when He says, "Be ye therefore perfect, even as your Father which is in heaven is perfect"? *Seek to be a mature Christian, having all the qualities God has that you can possess as a human being.*

60

is his right to control that money, to lend or not to lend when he sees fit. Jesus taught that at times needy people may come to you. They may come at an inconvenient time. They may have created their problem through their own foolishness. Still, you are to be merciful and lend to them. The Old Testament strongly urges helping the needy in this way (Deut.15:7–11; Pss. 37:26; 112:5). Although you have the right to refuse, that right should rarely be exercised.

Remind your students that the principle of stewardship is a counterbalancing truth to frivolous lending. The Lord's standard should not encourage foolishness. A Christian always has the obligation to use wisely the financial means God has put at his disposal. If a person with a legitimate need asks you for money, it is often best to make a gift (either giving

money or purchasing what he needs for him) rather than lending. That way, if he is able and wants to pay you back he can do so. If he doesn't, however, the relationship is still intact.

III. Loving Your Enemies (Matt. 5:43–48)

Christ explained that spiritual maturity is seen in our sincere and wholesale love for people, even—or especially—those who aren't lovable.

How to love them (5:43–44). The Jewish teachers of Jesus's time had combined the scriptural injunction to love your neighbor (Lev. 19:18) with a command God gave the Israelites to have no mercy on the Ammonites and Moabites (Deut. 23:6). In so doing, they created the statement Jesus quoted here. They had derived a general principle of conduct from a limited directive concerning these two groups that had resisted the Israelites' entering the land of Palestine. The Lord confronted this twisting of Scripture with the teaching of loving one's enemies, a position that's more con-sistent with the Old Testament (Exod. 23:4; Ps. 7:4; Prov. 24:17, 29).

In place of revenge, the believer is to bless, do good to, and pray for his enemies. "Getting even" is not the Christian approach. Note that this mistreatment appears to be an ongoing problem, in contrast to the occasional or one-time incidents mentioned in the previous verses.

Why to love them (5:45–48). Next the Lord presented two arguments for loving enemies. First, it is consistent with God's character. By so doing, we become children of our Father. This expression is idiomatic. A "son of peace" (Luke 10:6) is a peaceful man; a "son of consolation" (Acts 4:36) is a consoling man; "children" (literally, "sons") of the Father are ones who are like Him. God is kind to the evil and the unjust by granting them sunlight and rain when needed, just as He does to His children. Our attitude and actions should be the same.

The second argument was that reward comes when we treat our enemies with love. Jesus said that to love only our friends is to be like the publicans. Publicans were minor tax-collecting officials employed by another Jew who had purchased the right to collect taxes for the Roman government. Publicans were unconcerned about popular opinion. They were essentially outcasts from Jewish society because of their occupation. Their love and friendship, therefore, would be extended to a limited circle.

> Teens can usually see that they admire this love of enemies in others, even if they do not require it of themselves. Why don't they do what they admire in others?

The first chapter in Matthew's record of the Sermon on the Mount concludes with the exhortation, "Be ye therefore perfect, even as your Father which is in heaven is perfect." In other words, be mature as a believer. The standard of maturity is God Himself. Every believer should pray for himself and other believers to reach this level of maturity. Paul said he prayed for the Ephesian believers that they "might be filled with all the fulness of God" (Eph. 3:19), i.e., that they would have all the qualities of God that a person can possess.

In theological terminology, these are called the *communicable* attributes of God, since by grace they can be communicated to, or possessed by, humans. This exhortation suggests that the believer has considerable personal responsibility for developing these character qualities.

> Spiritual growth is by God's grace but is not altogether independent of human choice and effort. Your students must realize that time and self-discipline, coupled with a constant dependence on the grace of God, will be necessary to arrive at spiritual maturity.

✳ Extra Activities

Case study: When Ted was in seventh grade, he had lots of friends. His father, the principal, lovingly enforced the rules in his school. The next year, however, Ted's dad became the principal of another school, where the rules had not been enforced. He set out to restore discipline. Many of the boys and girls in Ted's new school were unkind to him because of his father's discipline.

Although a good athlete, he was always picked last for ball teams. Some students were cruel to him. One day he found a sheet of paper on his desk. Almost all of his classmates had signed it. It was a petition saying that they hated Ted. He had done nothing mean or wrong to his classmates. They hated him simply because his father was a strict principal.

Based on the teaching of the Sermon on the Mount, what should Ted do?

a. He should ignore his classmates and be friends with the kids at church.

b. He should write a note to each of the students who signed the petition, telling them that he hates them too.

c. He should find out who thought up the petition and beat him up after school to teach all the other kids a lesson.

d. He should be kind and considerate to his classmates even though they have been cruel to him. He should pray for them to change their attitude.

e. He should tell his father what they have done so he can discipline them.

Case study: Sonya was an Armenian orphan from Iraq. Both of her parents were killed by Saddam Hussein's troops. She was adopted by an American family and came to the United States when she was thirteen. Her adoptive parents were Chris-

tians, and soon Sonya trusted the Lord. She attended the Christian school sponsored by her church. She had few friends at school even though she was a good student and an excellent basketball player.

Marcia was an American girl on the basketball team. Her father had been killed while fighting in Iraq. She did not understand that Sonya's parents were not among the Iraqis who had killed her father. She hated Sonya. One day at basketball practice, Sonya stole the ball from Marcia and scored a basket. Marcia lost her temper, and her hatred came out. She pushed Sonya down and kicked her in the ribs. Sonya was in the hospital for two days and couldn't return to school for a week.

How should Sonya act toward Marcia when she returns to school?

a. Accept her apology if she apologizes but not treat her as a friend anymore.

b. Be nice to her until basketball practice. During practice find an opportunity to push her down and kick her in the ribs.

c. Tell the other players how mean Marcia is.

d. Treat Marcia as a friend and make an opportunity to clear up her confusion about her parents.

Lesson 17
Spiritual Disciplines

Theme	Personal Devotion
Scripture	Matthew 6:1–18
Memory Work	Matthew 6:1

Approach to the Lesson

Theme: It is right for a person to give, pray, and fast if he does these things for the right reasons. All of us are guilty of spiritual pride at one time or another. We actually become proud of our relationship with God, and we want others to know how strong this relationship is. Believers are often tempted to make their relationship with God a public spectacle. They may have mixed motives for giving, praying, and fasting. They want to give glory to God *and* give others a reason to think highly of them. The defense against this temptation is to practice a private life of devotion—not to give, pray, or fast in front of others unless it is unavoidable.

Rationale: Peer pressure is a strange thing. Sometimes it influences young people to be apathetic about spiritual things; sometimes it leads to the opposite. Challenge your students to evaluate their motives. Pride that leads to long, pompous prayers is no different from pride that leads to not praying at all.

Background: This passage continues the Sermon on the Mount. The emphasis of this section is on being private about acts of devotion.

In verses 9–13 the Lord introduces a pattern prayer, which also appears in Luke 11:2–4. Since that prayer will be discussed in Lesson 27, it is not explained here.

The Lesson

I. Giving Privately (Matt. 6:1–4)

This passage begins with an exhortation to take heed. Believers should give careful attention to these instructions because the problem addressed is serious—we must not allow selfish motives in our giving.

At the outset the believer is encouraged not to do his alms in public view. The Greek term for *alms* is a general word for "acts

of righteousness." It does not specifically denote the giving of money, but the context, particularly the next verse, emphasizes that idea. Whatever eternal reward may have been accrued by an act of righteousness is lost if it is done with the motive of gaining glory from others.

The next verse directs attention specifically to giving. The Greek term for *alms* in this verse means to give money to a needy person. It is the word from which we have derived our English term *eleemosynary*, which means "charitable." Believers are told not to "sound a trumpet" before them "as the hypocrites do in the synagogues and in the streets, that they may have glory of men" (6:2). The trumpets should be taken as figurative, representing any action to draw attention to oneself. The Lord Jesus was not giving these instructions without good reason; people in that day were taking steps to draw attention to themselves in giving. The Lord reminds us that such people already "have their reward," the temporary applause or admiration of those who see their good deed. But that is where the reward ends. Jesus calls these people *hypocrites*, from a classical Greek term meaning "actor." The word had taken on negative connotations in Jesus's day. It is significant to point out that Greek actors typically wore masks.

Giving is to be extremely private. The idea of not letting "thy left hand know what thy right hand doeth" cannot be carried out literally; the expression is figurative. If it were possible to be that secretive about our giving, that should be our goal.

Christ promises that the person who practices private giving will be rewarded openly. The time of this reward is indefinite; it may come in the present, in the future, or both. In the present, the Lord honors the person among his peers for his desire

Objectives

Knowledge (concepts students need to grasp)	that giving, praying, and fasting are fundamental acts of devotion for Christians
	that giving, praying, and fasting must have the right motive—the glory of God
Application (principles students should put into practice)	We should be faithful in giving, but we should not discuss our giving with others.
	We should not pray in public just to be heard by others.

Outline

[Matt. 6:1–18]
- I. Giving privately [1–4]
- II. Praying privately [5–15]
  - A. The motives for prayer
  - B. The form of prayer
  - C. The precedent for prayer
- III. Fasting privately [16–18]

to honor only Him. And at the judgment, the believer will be rewarded for eternity.

II. Praying Privately (Matt. 6:5–15)

The Lord's teaching about prayer includes a warning against selfish motives, but it also warns of other common pitfalls in prayer: an improper view of God and improper relationships with other people.

The motives for prayer (6:5–6). The hypocrites are mentioned again: "They love to pray standing in the synagogues and in the corners of the streets, that they may be seen of men." The synagogues and corners were public places where the hypocrites' acts would be seen by many. Again the Lord says, "They have their reward," meaning the honor of other people. The implication is that they will get no honor from God.

In contrast, the believer is told to go to the most private place in his house in order to communicate with God alone. That place is called a "closet," meaning a storeroom or any private part of the house, not just the tiny place for storage of clothes or other items, as we think of a closet today. Again the Lord promises an open reward for those who pray privately.

The form of prayer (6:7–13). Closely associated with the problem of praying in public is the practice of repeating empty prayers. False religions used this practice in the first century as they still do today. The followers thought they would be heard better if they repeatedly voiced the same prayer. But the Lord points out that prayer is not intended to inform God of what we need because He already knows (cf. Isa. 65:24). The purpose of prayer is to express our desires to God. Thus, empty and often-repeated form prayers are useless.

Nevertheless, having a pattern to follow in prayer is a good approach (Matt. 6:9–13). Our minds wander easily. A pattern helps keep us from getting distracted. Also, we may become too limited in our praying, and following the Lord's pattern broadens our concerns.

Spiritual Disciplines — L.17

Bible Expressions to Understand

alms—money given to help the poor
synagogue—Jewish religious meeting place where Jews heard the Old Testament taught and worshiped God
closet—storeroom or private room in a house
vain—empty, meaningless
anoint—pour liquid on, usually oil

What would you think of living a life of total dedication to the Lord and not being rewarded at all in heaven for it? Suppose you gave a million dollars to the Lord's work, prayed three hours every day, and fasted twice a week but then heard the Lord say at the judgment, "I'm sorry. None of what you have done will count for eternal reward."

You might think, *That could never happen.* Yes, it could! In fact, it probably will happen to someone you know. It might even happen to you. How could things go so wrong spiritually? A person gives up the things of the world to live for Christ but with no effect for eternity. Yes, he is saved, but . . . nothing else. Why?

The answer is simple. That person gets rewarded for what he has done. His reward is the admiration of others. Any person can fall prey to this subtle device of Satan—choosing to do good things but doing them to be seen and honored by other people.

In the Sermon on the Mount, the Lord Jesus taught that there are three actions that we may be particularly tempted to perform for the wrong reason: giving, praying, and fasting. Giving money to the Lord's work is the right thing to do. If you do chores around the house for which you get an allowance or earn money at a job, you should give some of it to the Lord regularly. But according to what the Lord Jesus said, you should be careful about who knows. Others should not know how often you give or how

much you give. Jesus said that if it were possible, your left hand should not know what your right hand is doing when you're giving. In other words, you should do it privately so that no one else knows. The Lord promised that those who give this way will be rewarded openly. That reward will come when we meet Him in heaven.

Praying is another practice you have to be careful about. Often, volunteering to pray in front of the youth group or your class at school is a way to get attention and make people think highly of you. Jesus said that your prayers should be a private matter. If

61

The general application of this lesson, which you should stress throughout, is that if your students are more spiritual in public than in private, they have a fundamental spiritual problem.

When properly done, fasting is a private practice. Other people should not know when we fast. The believer is to look refreshed, with hair clean and combed ("anointed") and face washed. Secret fasting will bring an open reward from the Lord.

While fasting is not explicitly commanded for Christians, Jesus taught that His followers would practice fasting after His death (Matt. 9:15). In the early church certain religious holidays (Easter, for example) were observed with fasts. With the rise of Roman Catholicism, fasting degenerated into ritualism. Most Protestant churches do not require fasting; however, it is recognized as a spiritual discipline that allows the believer to focus his prayers and worship on the Lord and to remove distractions when seeking God's guidance. Jesus warned against fasting for show and gave guidance for proper fasting in this passage; He associated prayer with fasting in Mark 9:29. Several examples of fasting are mentioned in the New Testament: Jesus (Matt. 4:2), Anna (Luke 2:37), Paul (Acts 9:9; 2 Cor. 6:5; 11:27), Cornelius (Acts 10:30), and leaders of the Antioch church (Acts 13:3).

The precedent for prayer (6:14–15).
Immediately following the model prayer, the Lord briefly discusses forgiveness. This topic may seem at first like an interpolation, but careful examination will reveal why it belongs here. The Lord has listed as one of the standard petitions in prayer the requesting of forgiveness, but there is a condition attached to the granting of that request—we must forgive others for the sins they commit against us. At stake is our continual fellowship with the Lord. Our bitterness and unwillingness to forgive keep the Lord from cleansing us from our sins when we come to Him in prayer. Such a breach between the believer and the Lord precludes effective prayer altogether. This is why the Lord strongly emphasizes this point here.

III. Fasting Privately (Matt. 6:16–18)

Finally, the Lord warned against fasting with improper motives. Hypocrites come under the Lord's rebuke again in this section. When fasting, they were in the habit of putting on a sad expression and then "disfiguring" their faces, even smearing ashes on their faces during times of great personal and national duress. This was a common practice in oriental nations of the first century, but those who were doing this were called hypocrites. Apparently they were not really serious about this act of personal devotion. Jesus again warns, "They have their reward."

your teacher asks for testimonies about answered prayers, be sure you tell about those answers for the right reason—to bring glory to God. Don't use your answers to prayer to convince other people that you are an especially spiritual person.

If you are called on to pray in public, be sure you follow Jesus's instructions to avoid vain repetition. Pray about things that are important to you, your friends, and your family. Don't just repeat things you have heard other people pray; tell God about what is really on your mind, things you really need to say to Him. Jesus taught that even people who are not saved sometimes pray the same thing over and over, thinking that God will hear them because they are praying so much.

Jesus reminded His disciples that asking God for forgiveness when we have not forgiven other people is pointless. You must never hold a grudge, hoping that you can get even with someone for a wrong that he has done to you. That will hurt you as well as him. It will hurt you because God will not respond to your prayers.

Another practice Jesus talked about is fasting, or not eating for a period of time. Some people fast because they think it's healthy for the body. The Lord Jesus fasted, and so did His disciples. They fasted for spiritual reasons. They went without food at times so that they would have time to pray and think about the Word of God. Perhaps the reason this practice is not very common today is that people aren't concerned enough about their relationship to God to go without eating for a while.

Like prayer and giving, fasting should be a private matter. If you decide to fast, you shouldn't tell your friends or go around looking as though you're starving. Although it is a worthwhile spiritual discipline, fasting doesn't necessarily make a person especially godly. In fact, if you do it so that other people will admire your spiritual devotion, it proves just the opposite. The Lord does not reward that kind of fasting.

Why Do You Do Things for God?

Christianity is a relationship with God. When you give, or pray, or fast, you should do it to please God, not so that other people will see and admire you. If you act "spiritual" only in front of others, you are a hypocrite, perhaps not a Christian at all. You will be rewarded at the judgment not just for the things you have done, but according to the reason you did those things. The only proper reason is to bring glory to God by being obedient to Him.

62

Do You Remember?

1. What reward is given to someone who gives to charity or fasts in a way that draws attention to himself? *the praise of others*

2. What kind of giving is blessed by God? *private giving*

3. Where did the Pharisees love to pray? *standing in the synagogues and on street corners*

4. What kind of fasting is blessed by God? *private fasting*

5. What is the condition the Lord puts on the forgiveness that He is willing to grant us? *We must forgive others for their offenses.*

6. What is vain repetition in prayer? *empty, meaningless, repeated phrases*

7. What makes a person a hypocrite when he prays, fasts, or gives? *doing it to be seen by other people*

63

✳ Extra Activities

Survey: Poll your students anonymously concerning their devotion to the Lord.

1. I give financially to Christian ministries.
   a. weekly
   b. monthly
   c. occasionally
   d. seldom or never

2. I commune with the Lord in prayer.
   a. daily in personal devotions
   b. occasionally at church
   c. only when I'm called on to pray at church or school
   d. rarely or never

3. I fast for spiritual purposes.
   a. frequently
   b. occasionally
   c. never

Calculate percentages on the basis of the responses and share the composite results with your students.

Quiz: Have your students answer the following questions from their Bibles and lecture notes.

1. What key word is used six times in this passage? *secret*

2. What are the three private spiritual disciplines the believer may perform? *giving, praying, fasting*

3. What reward can a person expect if he does Christian acts of devotion in public to be seen by others? *honor from people, but no honor from God*

4. What act of devotion by the Jews was accompanied by a sad countenance and the rubbing of ashes on the face? *fasting*

5. In contrast to the vain repetitions of the heathen in prayer, what should be the practice of the Christian? *expressing sincere desires, following the pattern for prayer Jesus provided*

The Sea of Galilee

The Sea of Galilee was the geographical focal point of most of Christ's ministry. Around this freshwater lake (seven miles wide, thirteen miles long), Christ performed ten of His thirty-five documented miracles—He fed the five thousand, healed the demoniacs, walked on the water, and calmed the storm.

Along these shores He called six of His disciples, and on a hill overlooking the lake He preached the Sermon on the Mount. He used the lake and its surrounding fields in many of His parables, including those of the sower, the wheat and tares, and the dragnet.

Jesus visited many of the twelve cities located on the lake. Once He even preached from a boat to a crowd on the shore. It was along these shores that He appeared to His disciples after His Resurrection.

Its importance to the life of Christ is indisputable.

The Sea of Galilee covers only sixty-four square miles in northern Israel, at the north end of the Jordan Valley. It is fed by the Jordan River and several clear springs. Rising from its shore are several mountains ranging from two thousand to four thousand feet in height. On its eastern side are the famous Golan Heights, which divide Israel and Syria today. The deepest part of the lake is 160 feet deep. In the Old Testament the lake was called the Sea of Chinnereth (meaning "harp") because of its shape. Along its southern shores are several hot springs, which Roman officials used as vacation resorts.

Several important cities of commerce were located near the lake. Tarichea, not mentioned in the

Gospels, was a busy fishing city. Its name means "preserving" or "pickling," and its salted fish were famous throughout the Roman Empire. Tiberias, the largest town on the lake in Christ's day is still the region's most important city today. It was built by Herod Antipas, who beheaded John the Baptist and tried Jesus before His Crucifixion.) Because of its heavily Gentile population, Tiberias was not liked by the Jews.

Jesus and His disciples apparently avoided Tiberias, spending most of their time along the northern shore of the lake. The city of Bethsaida was the hometown of Peter, Andrew, and Philip. Bethsaida means "home of fishing," reflecting the occupation of the disciples who lived there. Capernaum was a commercial center and a customs collection point. It was here that

64

Christ found Matthew collecting taxes and called him to be a disciple.

One of the hazards of this small but beautiful sea is that it is subject to terrible winter storms, which seem to arise out of nowhere due to the high mountains surrounding the lake. When cool air from the mountains sweeps down over the water, the difference in air temperature causes violent storms that can threaten the lives of those in boats (Matt. 8:24; 14:24).

The region around the Sea of Galilee continues to grow in population today. Besides being the principal reservoir in the nation's water supply system, the lake is still a center of fishing and agriculture. The surrounding area produces most of Israel's wheat, barley, figs, and grapes. Cotton, alfalfa, dates, and bananas are also produced here. The lake itself contains twenty-two varieties of fish, including catfish and sardines, and the annual catch is about two thousand tons.

Regardless of the economic or political significance this locale may attain, it will always be remembered as the place where Jesus walked. In the words of an ancient rabbi, "Jehovah has created seven seas, but the Sea of Galilee is His delight."

65

Lesson 18
Spiritual Priorities

THEME	Putting Christ First
SCRIPTURE	Matthew 6:19–34
MEMORY WORK	Matthew 6:33

 ## Approach to the Lesson

Theme: To set priorities is to establish an order of importance. The Lord taught that a person should be more concerned about getting a reward in heaven than money or material wealth in this life. He also taught that worrying about physical necessities instead of being concerned about God's will is wrong. Though we live in the world, we cannot allow ourselves to be overcome by material concerns. People's souls are more important to God than anything about the material world. They should be more important to us too.

Rationale: Encourage your students to analyze their priorities. After they have recognized what really matters to them, encourage them to reevaluate those priorities from a biblical perspective.

Background: After contrasting the value of a private life of devotion with that of a public, hypocritical show of love for God (Lesson 17), Jesus emphasized another contrast. Rather than making material things the great priority in life, we should focus on the spiritual. This passage has several parallels in Luke's Gospel.

Sermon on the Mount	The Gospel of Luke
Matthew 6:19–21	Luke 12:32–36
Matthew 6:22–23	Luke 11:34–36
Matthew 6:24	Luke 16:13
Matthew 6:25–34	Luke 12:22–31

The Lord indicated two ways people make the material more important than the spiritual. They do this by aggressively pursuing the accumulation of material wealth and by continually worrying about their material needs, such as food and clothing.

Bible Expressions to Understand

heart—the inner person or soul, which thinks, feels, desires, and decides
mammon—money
cubit—about eighteen inches
single—(referring to the eye) healthy, having clear vision
evil—(referring to the eye) unhealthy, having faulty vision

By the time he was sixteen years old, C. T. Studd of England was already an expert cricket player. (Cricket is a British sport similar to baseball.) Three years later he was captain of his team at Eton College, and he soon became world famous. He had accepted Christ, but for several years he did not live for the Lord.

While attending Cambridge University in England, he heard D. L. Moody preach and dedicated his life to the Savior. He spent hours trying to convert his teammates to the Lord. He later went to China as a missionary and worked with the famous British missionary Hudson Taylor.

While in China, Studd inherited about half a million dollars, but he decided to give the entire inheritance away, investing it in Christian ministries. Later he was forced to go back to England because of failing health. Eventually he went to Africa,

English missionary C. T. Studd (1860–1931) faithfully served the Lord in China, India, and Africa. His motto was "If Jesus Christ is God and died for me, then no sacrifice can be too great for me to make for Him."

66

even though the doctors said that he probably wouldn't live long if he went. His only answer was that he had been looking for a chance to die for Jesus. "Faithful unto death," he accepted God's direction and labored another twenty years before the Lord took him home to heaven.

What lesson can we learn from the life of C. T. Studd? He had decided what would be most important in his life, and that determined how he made all other decisions. Nothing was more important to him than serving Christ. When he became wealthy, he didn't stop his ministry for Christ in China and return to England to manage his fortune. He gave his money to Christian causes and stayed in China. The Lord doesn't lead every believer to give away a fortune, but that's what Studd thought God wanted him to do. Obeying the will of God was more important to him than anything else. Every believer should decide that spreading the gospel and living a holy life are more important than wealth or financial security.

You set priorities every day without giving it much thought. The homework that has to be done for tomorrow is more important tonight than the things that have to be done for next week. Studying for a fifty-point test is more important than studying for a ten-point quiz. You even set priorities in your friendships. Time spent with some of your friends is more important to you than time spent with other friends. The responsibilities your parents give you should take priority over the responsibilities others give you.

In the passage of Scripture you read for this lesson, Jesus said that a believer must have the right priorities. What's important to God must be

Objectives

KNOWLEDGE (concepts students need to grasp)	the difference between earthly treasure and heavenly treasure
	the meaning of the phrase *take no thought for your life*
	the way to seek first the kingdom of God and His righteousness
APPLICATION (principles students should put into practice)	We should value heavenly treasure more than earthly possessions or activities.
	We should not worry about our material needs.

⭐ The Lesson

I. Spiritual Treasure (Matt. 6:19–24)

Jesus first explained why a person should find satisfaction in spiritual treasure rather than trying to get more and more material things.

Permanence. Spiritual treasure should be a priority because it is permanent. Earthly treasure can be lost, as when clothes are ruined by moths. Verse 19 refers to the moth larva that feeds on cloth, destroying the garment. People should not emphasize building a large wardrobe to enhance their personal appearance because it can be lost so easily. Neither should we emphasize accumulating material objects of wood and metal. These things degenerate; rust corrupts, and all

important to him. The Lord knew that two things could cause a Christian to get confused about what's important: the desire for material wealth and concern about the basic necessities of life.

The Lord first talked about trying to store up large sums of money and material goods (Matt. 6:19–24). He warned that material wealth is not permanent. Clothing and other items are often destroyed by moths or other insects. They also wear out. Thieves can steal your wealth. At best, such wealth lasts only during this life. You cannot take it with you into eternity. Since this is true, storing up treasure in heaven is a better idea than storing up treasure on earth.

How does a person store up treasure in heaven? By doing what C. T. Studd did. He invested his time and money in helping Christians and reaching other people with the gospel.

Another reason for storing up treasure in heaven is that what you value most tends to control you. The Lord used two illustrations to teach this idea. The first was from the human body (6:22–23). Your eyes are like a lamp for the rest of your body. Without them you cannot see. If your eyes are bad, your whole body is in darkness. If your eyes are good, your body has light and will not stumble.

If your heart focuses on matters that concern God and not on material wealth, it's a good heart— a good lamp to light your way. You'll make the right decisions and do the right things. If it's focused on both spiritual treasure and material wealth, you have double vision. You'll make wrong decisions and do the wrong things. You'll stumble and fall into sin.

The second illustration Jesus gave was drawn from everyday life in the first century.

In that time many people were slaves. Christ taught that a slave cannot serve two masters. He'll either love one and hate the other, or he'll be loyal to one and despise the other. People are inclined to place their love and loyalty with one employer. Confusion comes when a person tries to work for two employers. Christ then said, "Ye cannot serve God and mammon" (6:24). Your love and loyalties must be decided. Are you after spiritual treasure or material treasure? As Christ said, "For where your treasure is, there will your heart be also" (6:21).

The second major thing Jesus knew could confuse a person about priorities is worry about the basic necessities of life (6:25–34). The Lord began discussing this idea by presenting a series of reasons why you shouldn't worry about things like food and clothing. Most people in the United States worry little about such things. We have been blessed by being born in a place where opportunities to earn a living are plentiful. However, sometimes difficult times come. Money is short, and the need for food and clothing is great. Then the Lord Jesus says our priorities must still be the spread of the gospel and personal holiness.

The first of the five reasons Jesus gave is that life consists of more than food and clothes for the body. We're not just physical beings. The body is not the most important part of a person. Your relationship with God should be top priority. The second reason Jesus gave was that God takes care of animals as insignificant as birds. Certainly you can trust Him to take care of you.

Third, worrying about life's necessities will not solve the problem anyway. Worry never extended a

67

objects of wood and metal are ruined by the passage of time. Material items may also be stolen. All such things are at best temporary, subject to destruction and loss. Spiritual treasure is not this way. Obedience to God's commands brings rewards that will never be lost.

How many of the things your students most want or admire will still be here in a thousand years? Their answer to this question will indicate the validity of their priorities.

Control. Another reason to place greater value on the spiritual is the controlling power of what we value most. Jesus said, "For where your treasure is, there will your heart be also" (6:21). *Heart* here does not mean the physical organ in the body. The term is used consistently

throughout both Testaments to refer to the inner person. Depending on the context, it may represent any functions of the nonmaterial aspects of human beings—our emotions, intellect, conscience, capacity to make decisions, or desires. This passage says that one who places great value on material wealth will be delighted by wealth, think about it, make decisions on the basis of it, and ceaselessly desire more of it. Such a person has his priorities confused.

To illustrate this truth, Jesus presented a brief analogy from human anatomy. The eye is the light of the body. If a person's eye is "single" (i.e., healthy), his whole body will be full of light. Without a healthy eye, a person is in darkness. "The light that is in thee" refers to the heart, more specifically the capacity for spiritual discernment. If a

person's will is in darkness or confusion because of a divided focus on the material and spiritual, his decision-making ability is greatly hindered. He will make the wrong choices and do the wrong things.

Jesus summarizes this point through another illustration—the relationship between servant and master. A person cannot serve two masters. The natural inclination is to be single-minded; he will prefer one master over the other. No one can be servant to both God and material wealth.

II. Spiritual Necessities (Matt. 6:25–34)

Jesus also explained that there are many reasons not to worry about material necessities. When Jesus said, "Take no thought for your life," He meant "do not worry or be full of anxiety about material necessities." *Thinking* about material needs is a normal responsibility, but *worrying* about them is a sin.

The first reason Jesus gave is that life consists of more than the material. Food and clothing are not everything. Second, we have a heavenly Father. God feeds the birds, and Christians certainly are more important to Him than birds. Third, worry does not help; it won't add a single cubit to a person's stature. Since a cubit is unit of length measurement, the word translated "stature" is probably better translated here "length of life" or "lifetime." The point of this exquisite, intentionally mixed metaphor is that God is in control of our lives; a person cannot add a single inch to his physical life by worrying about it.

Fourth, worry is illogical. To make this point Jesus used an example from nature, the lily of the field. The type of lily is not specified, but Palestine has a violet-colored lily that would be an appropriate reference, considering His allusion to Solomon's royal garments. In any case, the lily does not spin to make clothing for itself. It does not labor to earn money. God simply provides. Jesus said that even Solomon, the great king, was not clothed in a manner comparable to the lily's beauty. (See 1 Kings

Outline

(Matt. 6:19–34)
I. Spiritual treasure (19–24)
  A. Permanence
  B. Control
II. Spiritual necessities (25–34)

10:4–7, 21–23 for a description of the opulence of Solomon's court.) If God goes to this extent to adorn the grass of the field, which is cut down and burned, will He not take care of us?

A person who questions God's ability and willingness to provide has little faith. When he worries about material necessities, he is acting just like the unsaved, who have no God to provide for them. Scripture commands us not to be conformed to the world (Rom. 12:1–2), but when we worry, we are conforming ourselves exactly to the world's approach.

Christ gives a great promise to those who make God's cause (the kingdom of God) and personal holiness (His righteousness) their highest priorities. The Lord says He will take responsibility for that person's material needs, but He also gives an important guideline for the fulfillment of this promise. Simply put, do not borrow trouble from tomorrow. Though every person should plan ahead, this planning should be positive and constructive.

> Fretting about potential difficulties is fruitless. Mishaps and trials are inevitable. Enjoy God's blessing and presence today. When difficulty comes, cast your care on Him. God's grace is sufficient for the believer, as long as he faces difficulties as they come, but if he borrows trouble from tomorrow, he will not be able to cope.

✴ Extra Activities

Discussion: What are some of the rewards or treasures believers can lay up for themselves in heaven, and what does the Bible teach about these rewards? Display the following Scripture references, and have your students look them up to discover answers. Keep in mind that the word *crown* is often used to designate a reward.

Matthew 10:41–42 *prophet's reward for those who treat a prophet properly*

Matthew 25:14–30 *varying ability and opportunity but the same reward if faithful*

Luke 19:12–27 *ability and opportunity varying, but reward based on faithfulness*

1 Corinthians 3:8, 14 *everyone rewarded according to the quality of his work for the Lord*

1 Corinthians 9:25 *Christians labor for an incorruptible crown*

---

person's life by one moment or caused a person to grow a single inch. Fourth, Jesus said that if God bothers to make the fields beautiful by putting lilies there that grow one day and die the next, certainly He'll see to it that you have the clothes you need. Fifth, if you worry about the necessities of life, you're acting just like unsaved people, who have no heavenly Father Who cares for them. For all these reasons Jesus said, "Therefore take no thought, saying, What shall we eat? or, What shall we drink? or, Wherewithal shall we be clothed?" (6:31) To "take no thought" means not to worry about these things.

The Lord gave a promise to those who make living for Him the most important thing. He said, "But seek ye first the kingdom of God, and his righteousness; and all these things shall be added unto you" (6:33). If you take care of God's concerns, He will take care of yours.

Jesus warned that thinking about what might happen tomorrow is a major threat to receiving the benefits of this promise. Enjoy God's blessings and provision today. Trust Him for tomorrow's necessities when tomorrow comes. Pray, work hard, think ahead in a constructive way, and then be grateful to God for His provision today and in the future.

What's Top Priority in Your Life?

To set priorities means to establish an order of importance. The Lord Jesus taught that a person should be more concerned about getting a reward in heaven than money or material wealth in this life. He also taught that to worry about physical necessities instead of being concerned about God's work is wrong. Though we live in the world, we cannot allow ourselves to be overcome with material concerns. What God thinks is important is what we should think is important. The glory of God and people's souls are more important to God than anything in the physical world. They should be most important to us too.

Do You Remember?

1. What often happens to earthly treasures? _____
   They may be ruined by insects or rust, or they may be stolen.

2. What type of treasure should a believer store up for himself? *heavenly treasure*

3. What member of the body is like a right heart? *a good eye or a single eye*

4. What example from everyday life did Jesus use to teach that a person cannot serve both God and material wealth? *the master/slave relationship*

5. What does the Scripture mean when it says, "Take no thought for your life"? _____
   Do not worry or be filled with anxiety.

6. What two things from nature did Jesus use to teach that we shouldn't worry about life's necessities? *birds and lilies*

7. What illustration did the Lord use to stress the powerlessness of worry? _____
   Worry won't add a cubit to your stature.

8. When a Christian worries about the necessities of life, what sort of person is he acting like?
   an unsaved person

68

---

1 Thessalonians 2:19 *those the believer ministered to are his crown of rejoicing at the Lord's coming*

2 Timothy 4:8 *believers receive a crown of righteousness from the Lord*

James 1:12 *believers receive a crown of life from God*

1 Peter 5:4 *faithful shepherds receive a crown of glory that doesn't fade away*

2 John 8 *the believer should take care not to lose the full reward*

Revelation 2:10 *believers receive a crown of life from the Lord*

Revelation 3:11 *hold fast so that no reward is lost*

Revelation 22:12 *the Lord has His reward with Him at His coming*

Research: Have your students look up *worry*, *anxiety*, and *stress* in dictionaries and encyclopedias. Have them research the physical results of anxiety in medical journals or on the Internet. Then have them summarize their findings in a page or two.

Discernment in Relationships

Read: Matthew 7:1–12   Memorize: Matthew 7:12

Bible Expressions to Understand

mete—measure, deal out
mote—a speck of dust or straw
beam—a large piece of lumber
rend—tear violently

Jim Smith got caught shoplifting. Mr. Allen, the store owner, had him taken to court, and now the trial is nearly over. Having heard the testimony of several witnesses, the judge has carefully reviewed all the evidence. Before he can announce his verdict though, a man bursts into the courtroom, walks to the front, and steps up behind the bench. It's Mr. Johnson, the owner of a local bank. Everybody knows that he's been embezzling funds for years but has never been brought to justice. He picks up the judge's gavel, bangs it loudly, and announces, "Jim Smith is a thief; he's guilty as charged!"

You may be thinking, *That's outrageous!* You're right, but what if Mr. Allen had gotten up and said the same thing? Neither one of them has the legal authority to hand down a verdict. Surely it was worse for Mr. Johnson to pass judgment on Jim since he's guilty of the same crime. But wait a minute. Do you ever criticize other people for sins that you haven't dealt with in your own life?

The Lord Jesus began this section of the Sermon on the Mount (Matt. 7) by saying, "Judge not." Did He mean that it is never right for anyone to judge another person under any circumstances? Judges play a vital role in our legal system, but they are either elected or appointed. No one can assume that position by his own authority. Besides that, judges are supposed to decide cases on the basis of what the law says, not according to their own prejudices or preferences. So part of what Jesus was teaching is that in your everyday

relationships you must not take on a role you're not authorized to perform.

As the verses that follow indicate, Jesus was also talking about attitudes. He gave a rule that applies to all our relationships: Don't judge others unless you want to be held to the same standard (7:2). A judgmental attitude involves putting yourself in a position of deciding whether people are right or wrong, good or bad, based on your own opinion. Someone who has this attitude is quick to point out others' faults and mistakes in order to make himself look good.

If there's one thing I can't stand, it's a liar!

69

Lesson 19
Discernment in Relationships

THEME	Discernment in Relationships
SCRIPTURE	Matthew 7:1–12
MEMORY WORK	Matthew 7:12

Approach to the Lesson

Theme: Discernment is an aspect of spiritual wisdom that enables us to see others from God's perspective rather than through the lens of our own egotism. Discernment involves making proper distinctions based on biblical principles, whereas a judgmental attitude treats people differently based on selfish motives.

Rationale: Teens are quick to criticize and put others down (often based on externals such as clothes, hairstyle, or possessions). Show them how discernment can help them build better relationships. Encourage them to see the biblical rationale behind treating others the same way they would like to be treated.

Background: In the previous section of the Sermon on the Mount (Matt. 6), Jesus focused on material things (not being a slave to money, not storing up treasure on earth, and not worrying about physical needs). At the beginning of this section (Matt. 7), He turned a corner and began considering

Objectives

KNOWLEDGE (concepts students need to grasp)	the difference between discernment and a judgmental spirit
	the scriptural reason for following the golden rule
APPLICATION (principles students should put into practice)	We must seek to be discerning rather than critical of others.
	We should persist in prayer, trusting the Lord to give us what's best.
	We are to treat others the way we want to be treated.

another aspect of life—our relationships. These verses may at first appear to be an unrelated series of sayings. On closer examination, however, we see the principle of discernment running like a strong cord through the entire section. Discernment allows us to appreciate the good in others while not being naïve about their weaknesses (1 Thess. 5:14–15).

The Lesson

I. In All Your Relationships (Matt. 7:1–2)

Your role. When the Lord said, "Judge not, that ye be not judged," He was not prohibiting all judging. Lots of people—not only judges in the judicial system—have a responsibility to judge. Authorities such as teachers, parents, employers, police officers, and pastors often have to make judgments about those under their care or supervision. Whether it's assigning a grade, evaluating someone's work performance, or confronting someone about a wrong, this duty should be carried out with the right attitude. And anyone not authorized to judge should refrain from taking on that role (James 4:12).

What Jesus was condemning was a bitter, hostile, fault-finding spirit. The severity with which a person unjustly criticizes others is the standard of severity by which he can expect to be judged (7:2). Notice that the judge is not named. The context suggests that God is the judge, but He may execute that judgment through others. We could become victims of this wrong spirit through other people. People are far less merciful and sympathetic to someone who always sees the faults of others. Both phrases "with what judgment ye judge" and "with what measure ye mete" mean essentially the same thing. The second phrase emphasizes the *amount* of

Outline

censorious judgment, while the first focuses on the *intensity* of the judgment.

Your responsibility. While it is not our role to judge everyone, we do have a responsibility to not treat people with a judgmental attitude. The opposite of a judgmental spirit is a spirit of discernment that objectively evaluates another person's attitudes and actions according to scriptural principles. The discerning believer wants all his relationships to honor the Lord, so he seeks to build others up rather than tearing them down. His awareness of his own sins and failures causes him to strive to forgive as he has been forgiven by the Lord (Eph. 4:32).

> You may want to supplement this point with the material under "Special Problems and Topics" on page TE90.

According to Scripture, there is one person you are always responsible to judge, and that's yourself. Paul said, "For if we would judge ourselves, we should not be judged" (1 Cor. 11:31). Clearly, each believer is responsible to scrutinize carefully his circumstances, practices, and attitudes, to see if they are pleasing to God. Scripture talks about "them that are of full age, even those who by reason of use have their senses exercised to discern both good and evil" (Heb. 5:14).

II. In Your Relationships with Believers (Matt. 7:3–5)

Not hypercritical in your attitude. We tend to have more patience with unsaved people than with our fellow Christians because we expect believers to always do what's right. When they don't, it's natural

In contrast, a person who exercises discernment doesn't seek to criticize but to objectively evaluate other people's actions or attitudes based on what the Bible says. His primary concern is what's good for others, and his goal is to edify (help, build up, encourage) believers or to evangelize (witness to, present the gospel to) unbelievers.

If there is something wrong with the way someone talks or acts, and you are convinced you should say something about it, discernment means that you first check your own attitude and actions to make sure that you don't have the same problem. Jesus used a humorous illustration (Matt. 7:3–5) to describe the person who thinks he should correct the wrong in someone else's life but fails to see his own weaknesses. He told about someone who could see a speck of dust or straw in another person's eye but could not see the log in his own. Anyone with a log in his eye knows that it's there, and he couldn't possibly see well enough to detect a speck in someone else's eye.

Another area where you need to have discernment is in your relationships with unbelievers (Matt. 7:6). Jesus used striking examples to make this point. He said that you are not to give that which is holy to dogs or throw your pearls to swine. The dogs and the swine Jesus was talking about are both wild animals and represent people who have no regard for God's truth, which is holy and of great value like pearls (Matt. 7:6).

Are You a Discerning Disciple?

Spiritual discernment is the opposite of a judgmental attitude. Having a proper, Bible-based perspective toward himself and others enables a person of discernment to be honorable and considerate in his dealings with people. He doesn't proudly try to correct the weaknesses in others that he knows he has himself. He discerns when not to keep witnessing to someone who considers the truth of God's Word worthless. In his relationship with God, the discerning Christian is persistent in praying and depending on the Lord. Discernment in relationships leads a person to treat others the way he would like them to treat him.

You should be a bold witness for the Lord Jesus Christ. A Christian should never refuse the leading of the Holy Spirit to witness to someone. But if that person rejects the truth again and again, you must exercise discernment to know when you've reached the point when your efforts should be directed elsewhere. Jesus warned that sometimes persisting in ministry to people who do not want it may result in unnecessary persecution just as hungry wild boars, which obviously can't appreciate fine pearls, may suddenly attack.

Next, Jesus applied the principle of discernment to our relationship with the heavenly Father. His comments about prayer (Matt. 7:7–11) teach us two truths about how we relate to God.

First, prayer takes effort. This doesn't mean that praying the same thing over and over will make God hear us. (Jesus already dealt with that misconception in Matthew 6:7.) We need to persist in prayer because the process of asking, seeking, and knocking requires a level of communication (back and forth) with the Father that changes us by giving us the ability to perceive what He is doing. We won't keep praying unless we discern that it's worthwhile to do so even when answers seem to be a long time in coming.

Second, we must discern what it means to be dependent on God. We can ask for what we think we need and trust that He will not give us anything that's not good for us any more than a loving parent would give a hungry child something not fit to eat.

To sum up these instructions about discernment in relationships, the Lord Jesus presented the principle of treating others the way you would want to be treated (Matt. 7:12). People all over the world and in every period of history have seen the value of this concept; that's why it has been called the golden rule. You have no difficulty discerning how you would like others to treat you, so use that as a guide for your conduct.

for us to become extremely critical. This kind of self-righteous nit-picking can easily wreck a spiritual friendship, disrupt the harmony of a marriage, or destroy the unity and effectiveness of an entire congregation.

Not hypocritical in your actions. Ironically, the hypercritical person is often blind to his own shortcomings. Christ's imagery is humorous. The idea of seeing a mote (a small piece of dust or straw) in a brother's eye emphasizes how hypercritical this person has become. Someone would have to be examining it very closely to notice something like that. In contrast, failure to notice the "beam" (a large piece of lumber) is impossible. The insensitive, hypercritical person not only notices the problems in the lives of others but also tries to remedy them

even though his own problems are much worse. (See Rom. 2:1–3.)

The Lord calls such people hypocritical. One definition of a hypocrite is an individual who says one thing but does another. Perhaps the most glaring example of this in recent history is the popular television evangelist who preached against adultery and fornication yet went out at night to be with prostitutes. But this sin usually isn't so blatant. Consider the teenager who exhorts her friend to stop gossiping but has a habit of sharing confidential "prayer requests" freely as a covert means of criticizing others.

Even though a person may be insensitive to his own faults, he is usually not com-pletely unaware that he has them. But the fact that he still has them means he

Do You Remember?

1. Why is it unwise to be overly critical of others? _____
   We will be judged in the same way we judge others.

2. What does Jesus call a person who condemns someone else for doing the same thing that he himself practices? *a hypocrite*

3. What two animals are used to describe the worthless character of those who refuse the truth of God's Word? *dogs and swine*

4. How is the truth of God's Word described? _____
   as something holy and like pearls (valuable)

5. How does Jesus use the parent-child relationship to illustrate God's willingness to answer prayer? _____
   Just as a father tries to give good gifts to his children, so God wants to bless us.

6. What two items does Jesus use to emphasize that God will not give what is harmful or worthless in answer to our prayers? *a stone and a serpent*

7. What is the summary of the law and the prophets Jesus presented concerning our relationships with other people? _____
   Do unto others as you would have them do unto you.

71

---

probably can't help someone else get rid of the same flaws.

III. In Your Relationships with Unbelievers (Matt. 7:6)

The believer must be discerning about how he presents the Word of God to others. Jesus was illustrating two important concepts here. The first is that truth of the gospel is something very special. It is both holy (set apart for God's extraordinary purposes) and precious (of great value, like expensive gemstones). Secondly, Jesus used two similar metaphors to teach that some people are not able or willing to receive the deeper truths of the Christian faith. Giving what is holy to dogs and throwing pearls in front of swine both represent giving something valuable to those who do not value it and

who may even become vicious toward the giver.

Students may think that the idea of reaching a point where you stop witnessing to someone is inconsistent with the love and concern we should have for lost people. However, point out to them that even the Lord limits His outreach to individuals in accordance with their lack of response. He set a deadline for people to repent in Noah's day, and those who didn't repent perished in the Flood (Gen. 6:3).

This was, in part, Jesus's rationale for teaching in parables (Matt. 13:10–17). He concealed the truth from those who wanted only to criticize. He expended His effort in preaching and teaching the Word of God to those who would profit from it.

Often further instruction from God's Word is not what a person needs; what he needs is to respond to what he already knows about God's Word. Rebellion against the truth, often typical of young people, is rarely remedied by more knowledge. Strong exhortation, discipline, and prayer are the solutions to that problem.

IV. In Your Relationship with God (Matt. 7:7–11)

Jesus changed the subject from witnessing to prayer, but the underlying theme is still discernment. If we discern what God is really like and how He wants to relate to us, it will make two differences in the way we approach prayer.

The parallel verses from the Gospel of Luke are covered in more detail and from a slightly different perspective in Lesson 27.

Diligence in prayer. For one thing, we will realize that prayer is hard work. This is not to suggest that by praying better, longer, or harder we are more likely to get answers. That would be tantamount to the "vain repetitions" of the heathen, which Jesus rejected earlier in the sermon (Matt. 6:7). But genuine prayer requires effort. We don't just "ask," and then we're done. We are also to "seek," which means to diligently and thoroughly search for something hidden. Finally, taking things to an even higher level, we must "knock." This implies doing what it takes to gain access to the one behind the door. The kind of ongoing two-way communication with God that takes place in the process of praying this way changes the one who's praying. He comes to understand better what the Father wants and learns to want that more than his own will.

Dependence on the Father. The other thing we need to learn here is that our heavenly Father is far wiser and more compassionate than any earthly parent could ever be. We can trust God to give us what is best for us and not something as worthless as a rock or as harmful as a snake.

Some students may struggle with asking for God's guidance concerning their future vocation because they're afraid that God may call them to the ministry or to missions. Help them see that such a fear is incompatible with what the Bible teaches us about the nature of God.

V. In Your Relationships with All People (Matt. 7:12)

What to do. This section on discernment in relationships is summarized effectively by Christ's statement of what has been called the golden rule. Similar principles are found in every world religion, reflecting a virtually universal agreement that this statement expresses the way everyone should live. Despite the familiarity of the maxim, very few people—even Christians—know what the rest of verse 12 says without looking it up. Yet without the second part ("for this is the law and the prophets"), the golden rule is little more than a nice idea.

Why to do it. Our understanding of it as an ethical guideline must be rooted in the fact that this principle reveals the way our Creator (the one true God revealed in Scripture) has designed us to relate to our fellow human beings. We must live by the golden rule in submission to God, not out of enlightened self-interest ("I'll treat you right so you'll treat me right"). Otherwise, the rule ultimately fails because it is dependent on fallible human morality rather than on the character of God Himself. You can't yank the golden rule out of the context of the whole of Scripture and expect it to work—except superficially.

The golden rule encapsulates all the requirements of the law concerning our relationship to our neighbors. The beauty of many of Christ's statements is their succinctness and applicability in every situation. When faced with a decision, a Christian can ask, "What would I want the other person to do to me if our roles were reversed?" The answer is then usually obvious.

> Most young people find it difficult to put themselves in somebody else's shoes. Memorizing the golden rule and working through several hypothetical situations in class will help them implement it.

Special Problems and Topics

• **May a Christian ever judge others?**

When it is not your position to judge, you should avoid being critical of other believers, especially in matters of personal conviction where no clear-cut distinction is made in the Word. Paul dealt with this type of situation in the church at Rome. He admonished: "Let us not therefore judge one another any more" (Rom. 14:13).

However, if it is a responsibility that your position entails, you will have to make judgments about others. Examples of this in the New Testament include Paul's rebuking Peter for his hypocritical behavior in Antioch (Gal. 2:11–14) and John's condemnation of Diotrephes for his attitude and actions (3 John 9–10).

It is appropriate to judge someone when there is a clear violation of Scripture. We may not like what another person does simply because he goes against one of our prejudices or preferences. This is not grounds for criticism or judging. In dealing with the situation in the church at Corinth, Paul says that he has already judged the man involved in fornication and then instructs the church leaders to judge him (1 Cor. 5:3–13). He goes on to talk about the fact that Christians should allow their church leaders to judge between them when there is a conflict rather than taking such matters to the secular courts (1 Cor. 6:1–7).

When it is necessary to make such judgments, it should be done with the proper attitude, or it may lead to unnecessary conflicts and become a source of bitterness among Christians.

• **What guidelines should you follow in judging others?**

First, judging should be done in love. Christians are to be marked by their love (John 13:34–35). No believer should ever criticize another except in a kind, loving spirit. We should always be willing to forgive (Matt. 6:14).

Second, judging should be helpful. We do not criticize another believer just to tear him down. We should be positive, attempting to help him correct a problem. The goal is not to drive him away but to win him over (Matt. 18:15), so we should attempt to "restore" our brother (Gal. 6:1). Scripture commands us to "consider one another to provoke unto love and to good works" (Heb. 10:24).

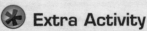 **Extra Activity**

Research: Have your students search the Scriptures to find one biblical person who did or did not practice the golden rule. Have several of them present their examples in class. You can assign this project on the day you lecture and then review it during the first part of the class period one or two days later.

Lesson 20

Discernment About Ideas

Theme	Discernment About False Teaching
Scripture	Matthew 7:13–29
Memory Work	Matthew 7:13–14

Approach to the Lesson

Theme: There are two kinds of people in the world—those who follow truth and those who follow falsehood. Falsehood may be found in a religious system, a political philosophy, or a general disregard for God. Where there is the real, there will be the counterfeit. And where there are preachers of God's truth, not far away will be proclaimers of falsehood.

No believer can afford to be spiritually naïve. Deceivers want to lure believers and unbelievers alike down the road to destruction. The only defense is to know the truth.

Rationale: Encourage your students to prepare themselves for assault by cultists and other false teachers. Defeat these false teachers by depriving them of their breeding ground—young people who feel unwanted and unloved.

Background: The Lord closes His great Sermon on the Mount with a realistic warning that a person must enter spiritual life the right way and then continue on the narrow path. We must be discerning and base our lives on the truth of God's Word, the Bible.

★ The Lesson

I. The Contrast (Matt. 7:13–14)

Jesus exhorted His listeners to enter at the "strait" gate. The term *strait* is an archaic English word that means "narrow." Entrance into spiritual life is restricted; there is only one way (John 14:6). In contrast, the unbiblical attempts are many, "for wide is the gate . . . that leadeth to destruction." The word *destruction* means "utter ruin" or "suffering," specifically hell; it does not mean "annihilation."

It is striking that so many people choose this way. Multitudes march down a wide road to their doom. The appeal of this broad way is the flexibility it allows for the expression of sinful will. There are few restraints. No one is asked to alter his personality or preferences. Self-love reigns supreme, but this supposed freedom is really a subtle form of enslavement. Sin finds its root in self-love and manifests itself most clearly in a person who is committed to doing only what he wants to do when he wants to do it. Most whose lives are governed by self-love rarely realize that they are slaves to their own selfishness and thus are not free at all.

> Stress that popularity with the world and Christianity do not mix. True Christians are in the minority and always will be, this side of the Millennium. Your students must not hope that the world at large will find their Christian testimony acceptable.

In one sense, a life led in obedience to God's commands is narrow, like the way of salvation. An individual who seeks to walk with God must keep his sinful nature in check by following the precepts of God's Word. At first glance the words "narrow is the way, which leadeth unto life" seem to suggest that we must lead a certain kind of life to gain salvation. However, this interpretation would mean salvation comes by human effort. Rather, the point is that once a person has entered spiritual life by faith in Christ, he must lead a life of obedience to enjoy spiritual life in the fullest sense.

Comparatively few find the narrow gate and way. The passage does not say "few there be that *enter* it," but rather "few there be that *find* it." By neglect and oversight men travel on to destruction. Carelessness with their own souls is the reason so many

Objectives

Knowledge (concepts students need to grasp)	the characteristics of the truth as opposed to those of falsehood
	the characteristics and destiny of a false prophet
	the characteristics of a discerning person
Application (principles students should put into practice)	We should know the truth well enough to resist false teaching.
	We should belong to a church that preaches the truth.
	We should expose false teachers when we have the opportunity.

Outline

enter the wide gate. People simply do not take their spiritual destiny seriously. They do not seek God as they should. Scripture says, "There is none that understandeth, there is none that seeketh after God" (Rom. 3:11) even though God promises, "Ye shall seek me, and find me, when ye shall search for me with all your heart" (Jer. 29:13). This is the reason that believers must take the gospel to lost men and women.

II. The Warning (Matt. 7:15–23)

Neglect is not the only reason people do not enter the narrow gate. Many are misled by false teachers, who preach alternatives to the true way—Christ. These false teachers are deceptive. They pose as real believers but come dressed in "sheep's clothing." Their character, however, is that of ravening wolves. The word *ravening* means "violent" or "greedy." These false teachers are out to fleece the sheep to get whatever they can—whether financially or in some other way.

Identifying false teachers (7:16–20). You can discern who false teachers are by what their lives produce. Jesus used the example of plants common in Palestine. When He asked about gathering grapes from thorn bushes or figs from thistles, He was not expecting a positive answer. *Thorns* (bramble bushes) are damaging to any crop. The designation can represent many kinds of thorn bushes but most probably refers here to a plant called *Onionis spinosa*. *Thistles* refers to a prickly weed that still grows in Palestine.

Working from these examples, the Lord then generalized to arrive at a governing principle—every good tree bears good fruit.

> The student text pages for this lesson begin on the next page.

The term *good* emphasizes positive usefulness. On the other hand, every corrupt tree bears evil fruit. The term *corrupt* means "unfit for use, worthless, or of poor quality." This tree bears fruit that is evil in its results. It may look all right; but when eaten, it will bring sickness and death.

Is it possible for any tree to bear fruit uncharacteristic of its nature? No. This statement does not imply that a saved person can never sin (1 John 1:8) or that an unsaved person cannot do some good things. But the general trend of a person's life is revealing. Jesus taught that false teachers will bring spiritual sickness and death. True teachers will bring salvation and life.

The destiny of false teachers is sure. Jesus said, "Every tree that bringeth not forth good fruit is hewn down, and cast into the fire" (7:19). He reiterated the principle by which these teachers can be judged: "Wherefore by their fruits ye shall know them" (7:20). Their teachings are what must be examined carefully. Are they consistent with the truth of God's Word or not? "O generation of vipers, how can ye, being evil, speak good things? for out of the abundance of the heart the mouth speaketh" (Matt. 12:34). If a man is a teacher but unregenerate, he will not teach the truth correctly, nor will his actions be consistent with the teaching of Scripture.

Refuting false teachers (7:21–23). What claims do false teachers use to prove they are right with God? The first is that of earnest profession: "Not every one that saith unto me, Lord, Lord, shall enter into the kingdom of heaven." The repeated word *Lord* shows that this is an earnest profession, but not everyone who seems earnest is a Christian.

> Your students must honestly face the evidence of their faith, and you should not hesitate to raise this issue with your students. Are they really saved (2 Cor. 13:5)? Do their lives prove it?

To enter heaven requires more than profession. A person's life must reflect the genuineness of his faith (Titus 1:16). Jesus once asked, "And why call ye me Lord, Lord, and do not the things which I say?" (Luke 6:46). Note that Jesus did not teach salvation by works, but rather that saving faith evidences itself by works (James 2:17–18).

The next two arguments used by false teachers (Matt. 7:22) may be grouped under the heading of miracles. Some false teachers will prophesy or foretell the fu-

Bible Expressions to Understand

ravening—violent, greedy
devils—demons (part of the host of angels that fell with Satan at the time of his rebellion)
wonderful works—miraculous acts
scribes—experts in the Old Testament law and Jewish tradition
strait—narrow

What do wolves and poisonous trees have in common? Jesus used both of them to describe false teachers.

The gray wolf has a sharp sense of smell, keen eyesight, good hearing, and razor-sharp teeth. While not as strong and fast as some predators, the wolf has gained a reputation for cunning and amazing endurance. Able to run all night at fifteen to twenty miles per hour, wolves hunt in packs and show amazing cooperation in downing their prey.

Though usually sportsmanlike in tracking other wild animals, wolves seem to turn savage around domesticated animals. They become crazed by the passive, nonresisting conduct of sheep or cattle and

A wolf's jaws can crush the bones of its prey with fifteen hundred pounds of pressure per square inch (psi), compared to a German shepherd's biting pressure of 750 psi.

72

will kill far more than they need for food. One wolf in southern Arizona is known to have killed an average of one or two calves every week for eight years. On some occasions it slaughtered fifty sheep in one night.

A wolf in sheep's clothing (Matt. 7:15) is a vivid way to describe a false teacher since he hates Christians and is extremely cunning. He will gladly sacrifice the sheep to get what he wants.

Even though we enjoy eating the fruit that grows on trees, some varieties are poisonous. Did you know that the shell of a cashew nut is extremely poisonous until roasted? The fumes that come from cooking the nuts can be highly irritating or even deadly. Delicious fruit comes from the mango tree, but many people react violently to its sap, the skin of its fruit, or even the smell of its blossoms. Californians warn visitors about the arrow tree that grows there. Legend has it that it's so toxic that a person who falls asleep under it may wake up blind.

Some stories about the powers of trees and their fruit are merely legends, but some are true. When Jesus said that a false teacher is like a poisonous tree, He was making a point well-illustrated in nature (Matt. 7:16–20).

In the last section of the Sermon on the Mount, the Lord Jesus is encouraging believers to be wise and discerning concerning truth and falsehood. As a follower of Christ, you must not be *naïve*—lacking perception or judgment. A naïve person doesn't use common sense.

ture, claiming to give a special revelation from God. False teachers may possess some uncanny abilities. They may even have the power to cast out demons or do *wonderful works*, which means "works of power," used interchangeably in the New Testament with other words designating the miraculous. If a man can heal people, solve their emotional problems, and ease family difficulties, is he a true man of God? Not necessarily. What does he teach about the Lord Jesus Christ, the way of salvation, and eternity? Do his teachings correlate with Scripture? These questions are the standard by which false teachers must be evaluated (7:23).

III. The Challenge (Matt. 7:24–29)

Following His severe warning about false teachers, the Lord Jesus introduced a parable. His aim was to challenge His hearers to choose truth rather than falsehood. The one who listens to the Lord's teachings and patterns his life after them is a wise person, like the man who built his house on a stone foundation. When the storms of life come, he will not lose his stability and sense of direction. On the other hand, the individual who rejects the Lord's sayings and goes his own way is like the man who builds his house on the sand. Any storm will wash away the foundation.

Those who listened to the Sermon on the Mount were astounded by the way Jesus taught (7:28–29). Among the scribes the

You should expect to hear false teachers offering a way to be saved other than Jesus's way. They'll be crafty and subtle and even pose as real Christian teachers. They'll talk about the Lord Jesus, the Bible, and salvation while all the time assigning meanings to their words that do not agree with what the Bible teaches.

Every person is faced with the choice of which way he will go (Matt. 7:13–14). Either he'll choose the broad way that leads to destruction, or he'll choose the narrow way that leads to life. The broad way refers to the way of false teachers and the ungodly. The narrow way is salvation through Christ. Jesus said, "I am the way, the truth, and the life: no man cometh unto the Father, but by me" (John 14:6). You can be sure that for every good teacher of the Bible who shows people the true way of salvation through Christ, there will be others who lead people astray into the broad way of destruction.

False teachers are deceptive. Often the only way to tell that they're not true teachers of the gospel is to evaluate their teachings and their actions. This is what Jesus calls their "fruit" (7:20).

This passage also teaches that there are two contrasting destinies, one for the true teacher and another for the false (7:21–23). The teacher of truth can expect salvation and reward. The one who teaches falsehood can expect to be driven from the presence of God to spend eternity in hell. False teachers may have a seemingly earnest belief in Christ, but it's not the Christ of the Bible. They may even cast out demons, give prophecies, and perform miracles, but that doesn't prove that they're saved or that they're true teachers of the Word of God.

Jesus closed His instruction with a parable (7:24–27). A person who follows the teachings of Christ is like a man who builds his house on a solid foundation. No matter what comes, he'll be able to cope with it, just as a house built on a rock will not be washed away in a storm. Someone who follows the instruction of false teachers is like a house built on the sand. A storm will come, wash away the foundation of sand, and destroy the house.

Following the sermon, Matthew adds a comment about how the people responded to the teachings of Christ (7:28–29). No one ever taught as Jesus taught. The tone of His voice alone communicated that what He said was true. He was and always will be the greatest example of what a true teacher ought to be.

Learn to Discern

There are two kinds of people in the world: those who follow the truth of Christ and those who follow falsehood in its many forms. Falsehood may be in the form of a religious system, a political philosophy, or just a general disregard for God. Where there is the real, there will be the counterfeit. Where you have the truth of God, there you will also find the lies of the Devil. Where men preach God's truth, not far away will be proclaimers of falsehood.

You cannot afford to be spiritually naïve. Deceivers aim to lure believers and unbelievers alike down the pathway to destruction. They will talk of being born again, though not by the Spirit of God. They will speak of Jesus, though he is not the Jesus of the Bible. They will claim the Bible as their only rule for faith and practice, and then follow the teachings of their leaders as if they were of equal authority. Be wise about truth and falsehood.

73

Special Problems and Topics

• Who can cast out demons?

When the Jewish leaders accused Jesus of casting out demons by Satan's power, He argued that Satan would never give anyone such power. Did Christ contradict Himself, then, in Matthew 7:22? Will people in the last days cast out demons with Satan's power? Did Christ deceive the Jewish leaders with His argument? Certainly not. He did not say that those referred to in verse 22 acted under the power of Satan. Apparently they indeed used God's power. Throughout the Scripture God worked through evil men (e.g., Isa. 45:1). Judas apparently cast out demons in Jesus's name and power but went to hell anyway (Luke 9:1; Acts 1:25). A person may well know something of the power of God without being saved. That is the situation of those in this passage.

characteristic method of teaching was simply to quote well-known teachers of the past. Jesus did none of that. He spoke on His own authority (cf. "but I say unto you," 5:22, 28, 32, 34, 39, 44). What He said and the way He said it left a lasting impression.

This attitude of authority should always be true of those who preach the Word of God. The teacher of God's Word comes with a message that has divine authority behind it. He offers not just human opinions, but the revealed message of God.

✳ Extra Activities

Research: Divide the class into small groups and assign them one cult or false religion to research. (See suggested list below.) They should focus on the religion's teachings concerning Christ, the Bible, and salvation. Have the groups check the Internet, visit a library, or interview a pastor to gather information.

a. Church of Jesus Christ of Latter Day Saints (Mormons)

b. Church of Christ

c. Seventh-day Adventists

d. The Holy Spirit Association for the Unification of World Christianity ("Moonies")

e. Jehovah's Witnesses

f. Roman Catholicism

g. Judaism

h. Islam

i. Buddhism

Each group should make an oral presentation or turn in a written report of their findings.

Be sure to follow up this assignment with a brief but thorough explanation of what the Bible teaches on each of the three doctrinal points they researched.

Testimony: Have a Christian who has come out of a nonbiblical but religious background visit your class and give a testimony about his previous involvement in false religion. Ask him to focus on the three items you have stressed to your students: Christ, salvation, and the Bible.

Do You Remember?

1. How many go in through the narrow gate? _few_

2. How many choose the wide gate? _many_

3. What animal is used to describe the character of false teachers? _the wolf_

4. How can we recognize false teaching? _by comparing it with the teaching of Scripture_

5. What mistake did the people in Matthew 7:21–23 make? _They thought that an earnest profession of faith or miraculous acts were enough to ensure their salvation._

6. What kind of foundation is compared to obeying God's commands? _a foundation made of stone_

7. What kind of foundation is compared to ignoring the commands of God? _a foundation of sand_

74

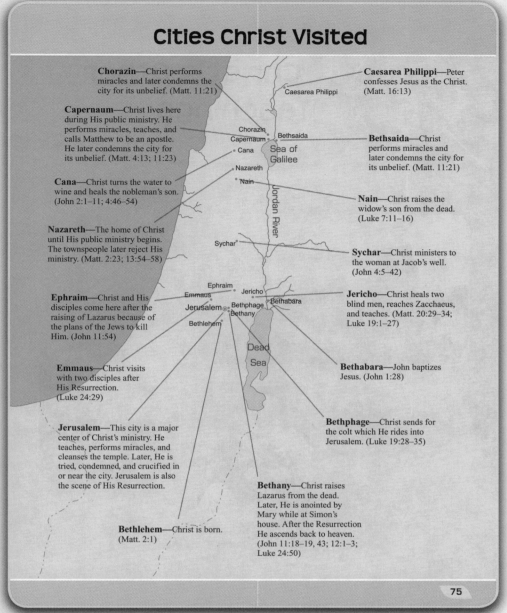

Cities Christ Visited

Chorazin—Christ performs miracles and later condemns the city for its unbelief. (Matt. 11:21)

Capernaum—Christ lives here during His public ministry. He performs miracles, teaches, and calls Matthew to be an apostle. He later condemns the city for its unbelief. (Matt. 4:13; 11:23)

Cana—Christ turns the water to wine and heals the nobleman's son. (John 2:1–11; 4:46–54)

Nazareth—The home of Christ until His public ministry begins. The townspeople later reject His ministry. (Matt. 2:23; 13:54–58)

Ephraim—Christ and His disciples come here after the raising of Lazarus because of the plans of the Jews to kill Him. (John 11:54)

Emmaus—Christ visits with two disciples after His Resurrection. (Luke 24:29)

Jerusalem—This city is a major center of Christ's ministry. He teaches, performs miracles, and cleanses the temple. Later, He is tried, condemned, and crucified in or near the city. Jerusalem is also the scene of His Resurrection.

Bethlehem—Christ is born. (Matt. 2:1)

Caesarea Philippi—Peter confesses Jesus as the Christ. (Matt. 16:13)

Bethsaida—Christ performs miracles and later condemns the city for its unbelief. (Matt. 11:21)

Nain—Christ raises the widow's son from the dead. (Luke 7:11–16)

Sychar—Christ ministers to the woman at Jacob's well. (John 4:5–42)

Jericho—Christ heals two blind men, reaches Zacchaeus, and teaches. (Matt. 20:29–34; Luke 19:1–27)

Bethabara—John baptizes Jesus. (John 1:28)

Bethphage—Christ sends for the colt which He rides into Jerusalem. (Luke 19:28–35)

Bethany—Christ raises Lazarus from the dead. Later, He is anointed by Mary while at Simon's house. After the Resurrection He ascends back to heaven. (John 11:18–19, 43; 12:1–3; Luke 24:50)

Map labels: Caesarea Philippi, Chorazin, Capernaum, Bethsaida, Cana, Sea of Galilee, Nazareth, Nain, Jordan River, Sychar, Ephraim, Emmaus, Jericho, Jerusalem, Bethphage, Bethany, Bethabara, Bethlehem, Dead Sea

75

Map 4
Cities Christ Visited

This map may be discussed separately or taken together with the two other major maps ("Where Christ Served" [page TE33] and "Christ's Major Experiences" [page TE38]) to form a separate lesson on the geography of Christ's life. "Cities Christ Visited" pinpoints only those towns in Palestine that the Gospels say Christ visited. The Gospels reveal that Christ ministered in the vicinity of other communities but did not enter them.

There is some question about two locations included on the map. Some ancient manuscripts of the New Testament refer to Bethabara, where John baptized, as Bethany. Also, archaeologists have not positively identified the site of first-century Bethphage. It is mentioned in several Talmudic references, sometimes as a separate village and at other times as part of Jerusalem.

[Note: Students will need to study or refer to this map in order to complete Map Exercises 2 and 4 (on the CD).]

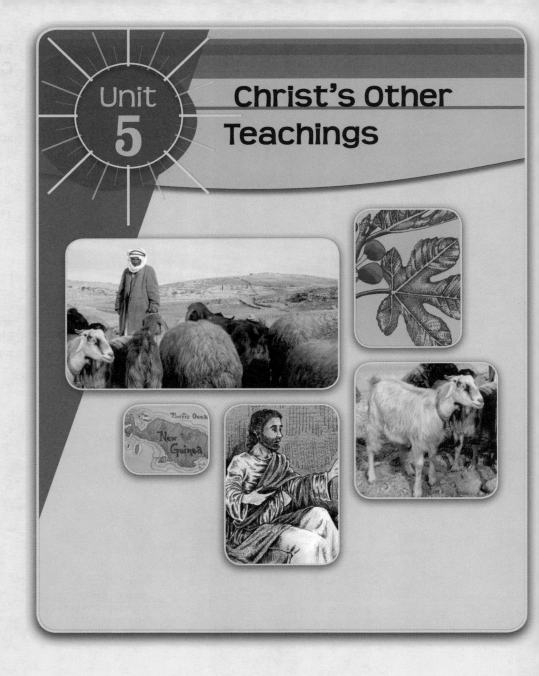

Unit 5

Christ's Other Teachings

Jesus was a master teacher. He often preached outdoors to large crowds of people. He frequently engaged His disciples in discussion as they walked along the dusty roads of Palestine. At times He taught small groups in the homes of those He knew, and on some occasions He preached in Jewish synagogues.

Wherever Jesus taught and preached, the people listened. He knew that what He said was true, and this caused Him to preach with great authority (Matt. 7:29). Mark comments, "And the common people heard him gladly" (Mark 12:37). Once the enemies of Christ reported to their leaders, "Never man spake like this man" (John 7:46).

One reason Jesus was such an effective communicator is that He used stories about everyday situations (a wedding), object lessons involving familiar items and animals (the lost coin and the lost sheep), and analogies based on natural phenomena (the wind). His teachings are simple enough to be understood by children yet deep enough to fascinate scholars. They are just as relevant today as they were thousands of years ago.

Unit 5
Christ's Other Teachings

This unit discusses some of Christ's teachings besides those in the Sermon on the Mount. Christ sometimes taught only His disciples, and other times He addressed the multitudes. Material given to both groups is included here. The unit is selective, giving attention to material particularly appropriate for the junior high student.

Jesus was a proclaimer of good news. He preached in diverse circumstances and to many different kinds of people. Christ is the model for all teachers and preachers, and His lessons and sermons are the words of life for all people.

Each lesson in this unit takes one of two basic approaches to the material. Most of the lessons are discussions of a single passage of Scripture. You will notice that the length of these passages varies significantly. This is due to an attempt to stay within the limits set by the Gospel writer in discussing a topic rather than imposing an artificial limit. A second approach to the biblical material is taken in two of the lessons. Lesson 23 is a topical discussion of Christ's teaching concerning eternal punishment. Likewise, Lesson 28 is a topical discussion of the ministry of the Holy Spirit as presented in the Gospels.

Lesson 21

The New Birth

THEME	Salvation
SCRIPTURE	John 3:1–21
MEMORY WORK	John 3:6–7

 Approach to the Lesson

Theme: Birth is the beginning of life. When a baby is born physically, it begins its life in the world. When a person is born spiritually, he is beginning a life in Christ. In spiritual birth the Holy Spirit makes an individual a child of God and implants in him a new holy disposition. Spiritual birth, or *regeneration* as it is called elsewhere in the New Testament (Titus 3:5), is only one aspect of salvation; others include Redemption, justification, propitiation, and conversion.

Rationale: This lesson provides an opportunity for you to put positive pressure on your students concerning their salvation. Many of them may have grown up in Christian homes and in Christian schools but show little evidence of real spiritual life. If the evidence is not there, then there is cause for serious concern.

Notice that this passage about spiritual birth is a true-life situation. The Lord was not merely chatting about this topic coolly and dispassionately. His heart burned with zeal and love for Nicodemus as He gently reasoned with him about his need for spiritual birth. You need both an understanding of Christ's words and the filling of the Holy Spirit to present this lesson effectively.

Objectives

KNOWLEDGE (concepts students need to grasp)	that spiritual birth has always been necessary for eternal life, even before and during Christ's ministry
	that the New Testament terms *born again* and *regenerated* are synonymous
APPLICATION (principles students should put into practice)	We all need to be saved.
	Trusting Christ should be our response to God's love in sending His Son.
	Trusting Christ should result in a transformed life.

Bible Expressions to Understand

Sanhedrin—the Jewish supreme court
rabbi—a teacher of the Jewish religion
master of Israel—a teacher of Jewish law and traditions

James Chalmers was born in a small town in Scotland in 1841. He didn't do well in school and spent most of his teen years "sowing wild oats." One man, Pastor Meikle, had a godly influence on him. James didn't respond to the truth, though, until one Sunday while listening to a preacher from Ireland. He became deeply convicted about his sin. The next day Pastor Meikle led him to Christ. James was a changed person.

James immediately began telling others about his conversion. He applied to the London Missionary Society, was accepted, and went to college to train for the mission field. He was appointed to an island in the South Pacific where he served for ten years. Eager to pioneer a new work, he received permission to move on to New Guinea in 1877.

New Guinea, one of the largest islands in the world, sits across from the northern tip of Australia. Largely unexplored, it was inhabited by cannibals at the time Chalmers arrived. The risks were high, but as a man changed by the power of God, Chalmers had uncommon boldness. For thirty-five years he preached, calmed tribal violence, and built churches. Finally, on an extremely dangerous mission to a ferocious tribe, he was clubbed to death, beheaded, and eaten.

What had begun as the unimpressive life of a mischievous boy became a model life of Christian fervor, courage, and personal sacrifice for the glory of Christ. When James Chalmers was born again, he became a new man and left an impact on Christian missions that will be remembered for centuries.

Though quite rebellious as a teenager, James Chalmers was transformed by being born again and became a fearless and effective pioneer missionary. Today the western half of the island of New Guinea is Irian Jaya (part of Indonesia) and the eastern half is Papua New Guinea (an independent nation).

78

Background: The new birth is central to our Lord's teaching on salvation. This passage is the fullest discussion on spiritual birth in the Bible.

 The Lesson

I. The Need for Spiritual Birth (John 3:1–3)

All people need spiritual birth, regardless of their personal status. Nicodemus was a Pharisee. The Pharisees were zealous for the law and even for the oral traditions taught by rabbis of the past. Although some of the Pharisees were hypocrites (Matt. 23), others were sincere. Nicodemus was also "a ruler of the Jews," a member of the Sanhedrin. This body ruled over the religious affairs of the Jews. It is first mentioned in

records from the reign of the Syrian Antiochus the Great about 200 BC. At the time of Christ it consisted of seventy men, who came from the leading families in Judaism. Priests, Pharisees, and Sadducees were included in the group. Nicodemus was undoubtedly respected for both his seriousness as a Jew and his authority, but he was a man in need of spiritual birth.

The circumstances of Nicodemus's coming to Christ reveal the need he sensed in his heart. He came at night, for which various motives have been suggested. Perhaps he had no opportunity during the day. Or he may have wanted an uninterrupted conversation. The most likely motive is that he feared criticism. As "a master of Israel" (John 3:10), a leading teacher of the law, coming as a student to Christ took humil-

Spiritual birth is what made the difference in his life. It's what will make the difference in any person's life. Unless you're born again, you won't love God and hate sin.

In the passage you read for this lesson, the Lord was explaining spiritual birth to Nicodemus. Nicodemus was puzzled by this teaching, assuming that Jesus was talking about a second physical birth. Jesus corrected him by telling him that the physical and the spiritual aren't the same.

Although Nicodemus was one of the foremost teachers of Israel, he didn't understand the most basic of spiritual truths, the truth of the new birth. Jesus reasoned that Nicodemus ought to accept what He said since He, as the Son of God, had been in heaven and knew that what He was saying was true.

As a Pharisee, Nicodemus was well-versed in the law and the prophets, but he had trouble grasping what Jesus meant by being "born again."

In addition to talking about being born a second time, Jesus illustrated the meaning of salvation by referring to the bronze serpent Moses had made when Israel was in the wilderness. Just as it was lifted up for Israel to see, so Jesus Christ was to be lifted up on the cross. All who believe in Him will be saved.

What are some of the truths we can learn from this conversation? First, just knowing about God and religion isn't enough. Understanding how a person

is born again isn't enough. You must experience spiritual birth yourself for it to matter. Consider the case of Nicodemus. This man was one of the best teachers of the Old Testament law in all of Israel. He knew many things about God and His Word. He was a serious, religious person. Other people recognized this and gave him a position of leadership in the Sanhedrin, but all this wasn't enough; Nicodemus hadn't experienced spiritual birth. Jesus interrupted his questions by telling him, "Except a man be born again, he cannot see the kingdom of God" (John 3:3). If you're not saved, the problem is not what you don't know, but rather what you haven't experienced. You need to experience spiritual birth.

A second truth is that faith in Christ is what brings spiritual birth. People must trust in what Christ has done on the cross in dying for their sins. If a person doesn't believe, he's already condemned by his sins (John 3:18).

Another point Jesus emphasized to Nicodemus is that people are sinners by nature and prove that they deserve judgment by their evil words and deeds. People love sin and hate the truth of Christ's salvation because they're sinners by nature (John 3:19–20). They don't want to be told that their way of life is not pleasing to God. They don't want to hear about God and what He likes and dislikes. It is a miracle that anyone is ever saved. God is merciful to work in hearts by His Spirit to bring people to believe in Christ. He's also merciful in that at the moment a person trusts Christ, he's born again. He becomes a new person with a new attitude that helps him love God and pursue righteousness.

Born Once, Die Twice— Born Twice, Die Once

Birth is the beginning of new life. When you were born physically, you began a new life in this world. When a person is born spiritually, he is beginning a new life in Christ. The Holy Spirit makes a person a child of God and puts in him a new desire for holiness and love for God. You can experience spiritual birth by placing faith in Christ as your Savior from sin. When you do, you'll become a new person. God will change your desires and help you live a life of victory over sin as well as delivering you from spiritual death.

79

ity and a willingness to risk his reputation. Nicodemus had concluded that Jesus was a teacher sent from God because of the miracles he had seen Him perform (John 2:23), and this conclusion prompted him to come.

These first two verses portray a man in spiritual crisis. He had a deep sense of personal spiritual need. His political and religious success had not satisfied him, and he concluded that he must go to Christ. Like Nicodemus, all people, regardless of their personal status, need spiritual birth.

Verse 3 contains the first use of the phrase *born again*. The word translated "again" is translated "from above" in verse 31. The word can have either meaning, depending on the context. Either is appropriate for verse 3.

What does it mean to enter the kingdom of God? The kingdom of God is the dominion over which God rules, which is not just heaven. It encompasses all creation but refers specifically to individuals' spiritual submission. A person enters the kingdom of God when he becomes a willing servant over whom God rules. No one has that relationship with God without the new birth.

II. The Characteristics of Spiritual Birth (3:4–13)

Nicodemus's question reveals that he had a major problem in understanding the nature of the new birth. He thought Christ was talking about a second physical birth, which he knew was impossible. Jesus then explained several characteristics of the new

Outline

birth. First, He taught that it was an inner birth caused by the Holy Spirit. To clarify, the Lord then plainly stated that the two births, physical and spiritual, were completely different. A person's family background, physical appearance, or stature has nothing to do with being born again.

The meaninglessness of social position was an important idea to stress to Nicodemus since he was probably from an influential family; it is important to stress today because of the great value placed on physical attractiveness and family position in our culture.

To explain that spiritual birth is not physically discernible, Jesus used an illustration from nature. The wind blows the way it blows without anyone knowing where it comes from or where it is going (3:8). The Spirit of God works similarly. He works as He wills, and like the blowing of the wind, which causes the leaves to rustle, His work is perceived only by the effect it brings—a change from unholiness to holiness, from self-centeredness to Christ-centeredness.

Christ then told Nicodemus that spiritual birth was taught in the Old Testament. Jesus told him that he should have understood these truths already (3:9–10). The basis of Christ's rebuke was the fact that Nicodemus was a renowned teacher of the law and that regeneration was taught in the Old Testament: "And the Lord thy God will circumcise thine heart . . . to love the Lord thy God with all thine heart, and with all thy soul, that thou mayest live" (Deut. 30:6; cf. Rom 2:27–28). This is not the only Old Testament reference to spiritual birth. Both Jeremiah and Ezekiel taught it (Jer. 4:4; Ezek. 36:25–27).

Nicodemus should have known about spiritual birth intellectually. He needed to know about it experientially. Christ underscored this fact by using the words *knowest not* in His question (3:10).

The same question is appropriate for your students. They've known about spiritual birth for years; they must also know it by experience.

Jesus then asserted that His status as a teacher from God, which Nicodemus had already affirmed, demanded that he accept and personally appropriate the idea of spiritual birth (3:11–13). If Nicodemus was having problems understanding earthly-oriented truths, such as regeneration, how would he ever understand more complex truths about God? Christ's presence with the Father before His incarnation made His knowledge precise and His reasoning irrefutable. For Nicodemus to refuse this truth was unreasonable, even rebellious.

III. The Source of Spiritual Birth (3:14–21)

As a capstone to the discussion, John records that trust in Christ is the means to spiritual birth. Knowing how the process works is really not the issue. The issue is personal faith in Christ the Savior, which will bring spiritual birth. Just as Moses told the Israelites in the wilderness to look in faith at the metal serpent on the pole to free them from the scourge of the vipers (Num. 21:5–9), so we must look in faith to Christ, who suffered on the cross for our sins to save us from judgment. The serpent on the pole was the image of the danger that was threatening Israel. Christ on the cross became sin for us, the literal embodiment of that which threatens men with spiritual death (cf. 2 Cor. 5:21).

Faith in Christ should be our response to God's great love in sending His Son to die for our sins. He bestowed this benefit on humanity totally apart from anything desirable in human beings. His sending of Christ for the salvation of sinners was never intended to be an act of judgment; it was an act of mercy (John 3:17). However, the cross stands at a crossroads. If a person rejects Christ's work on the cross, he is condemned. God's greatest act of mercy thus becomes His greatest act of judgment.

That judgment is not only future; it is a present reality. The wrath of God abides presently on everyone who does not know Christ. This wrath is fully justified by the wicked lifestyle of men (3:18–20). Even though the law of God is written in their hearts (Rom. 2:14–15), and even though the world is full of Bibles and Christians, people continue in darkness. They do not come to the light because they love darkness; they do not want anyone to tell them that their life is wrong. They are self-willed, headstrong in iniquity. There is a marked contrast between these people and the sub-missive, holy Christian who seeks God's will and way (3:20–21), as well as a marked contrast in their destinies.

Impress on your students their need for salvation. Also impress on them that their holiness of life (or lack thereof) indicates their true spiritual condition. "Whosoever is born of God doth not commit sin [does not continually practice sin]" (1 John 3:9). Trusting Christ should result in a changed life.

Do You Remember?

1. When did Nicodemus come to Jesus to question Him? _at night_

2. Why did Nicodemus believe that Jesus was "from God"? _____
   because of the miracles He had performed

3. What did Nicodemus think Jesus meant by being "born again"? _physical birth_

4. What force of the physical world did Jesus use as an illustration? _the wind_

5. What kind of teacher did Jesus say Nicodemus was? _a master of Israel_

6. Why could Jesus speak so confidently of spiritual things? _____
   He came from heaven and was an eyewitness to their truth.

7. What Old Testament incident did Jesus use to illustrate His Crucifixion? _____
   Moses lifting up the serpent in the wilderness

8. What action is necessary to avoid being condemned? _____
   to believe; to accept Christ by faith

80

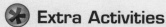

Special Problems and Topics

• What does it mean to be "born of water"?

This phrase has been the subject of considerable discussion. What is the "water"? (1) Some suggest that it is a reference to a pregnant woman's water breaking prior to her giving birth. In that case "born of water and of the spirit" might be interpreted "born both physically and spiritually." (2) Others suggest that the phrase should read, "Except a man be born of water, even the Spirit." This interpretation is consistent with Greek grammar and with the symbolism of the New Testament. Using the cleansing effect of water to illustrate the work of the Spirit in regeneration lines up with Titus 3:5, which states, "Not by works of righteousness which we have done, but according to his mercy he saved us, by the washing of regeneration, and renewing of the Holy Ghost." (See also Ezek. 36:25.) (3) Another suggestion is that "water" refers to baptism as the symbolic act that shows inward faith. (4) A fourth proposal is that it refers to rain falling from heaven. The word would then allude to the idea of being born "from above," as discussed earlier. All these explanations are tenable, but the second is probably the best.

• Was Nicodemus saved?

Evidently so. Later on in this Gospel we see him taking Christ's side before the Sanhedrin (John 7:50–51). He also assisted Joseph of Arimathea in preparing Jesus's body for burial (John 19:39). Tradition says that after Nicodemus was baptized by Peter, the Jews removed him from his position on the Sanhedrin and forced him to leave Jerusalem. After Jesus's burial nothing is definitely known of Nicodemus.

Extra Activities

Lesson opener: Write the following eight words on the board: *Born once, die twice. Born twice, die once.* Ask students which of Christ's teachings these phrases summarize.

Object lesson: When discussing the blowing of the wind, use a fan or get your students to look out the window. Ask them if they see the wind. They may say that they do. Correct them, telling them they see only the *effects* of the wind, not the wind itself. Make the application that it is important for others to see the effects of regeneration in our lives.

Analogy: Emphasize the parallels between the serpent on the pole saving the Israelites when they looked in faith, and Christ on the cross saving us when we look in faith. Stress that the exact manner in which the children of Israel were saved by looking at the serpent is not explained in the passage. The "how" was not important. It was obviously a miracle and God's work. The same is true of the cross. If a person becomes obsessed with understanding *how* Christ's death on the cross saves people from sin, he may never take the necessary step of saving faith.

Discussion: How was the bronze snake a type of Christ? Throughout the Bible the serpent symbolizes evil or Satan (Gen. 3:1; Pss. 58:4; 140:3; 2 Cor. 11:3; Rev. 12:9). Jesus Christ, on the cross, became sin for us (2 Cor. 5:21). Moses raised the brazen serpent high enough for everyone to see; likewise, Christ was lifted up on the cross (John 12:32).

Testimonies: Give your students opportunity to talk about their own salvation experiences. This may encourage an unsaved student in your class to trust Christ. Many of your students may be struggling with assurance of salvation. If they trust Christ, God will save them. He will make them new beings and give them new desires. If they have no desire for the Scriptures, holy living, prayer, and fellowship with believers, they may not be regenerate. Warn them that they are under condemnation if they are not.

Lesson 22
The World

Theme	The Christian and the World
Scripture	John 17:1–26
Memory Work	I John 2:15–17

 Approach to the Lesson

Theme: The term *world* has various meanings in the Bible. It is used of the planet Earth as well as its inhabitants. It is also used, with ethical connotations, to describe human culture with God left out. This is the meaning of the term in this passage. The believer is *in* the world but not *of* the world. He does not love what sinful people love, and his love for God marks him as apart from the world. He has a mission to take the gospel to the world. This is the only hope of freeing the world from the lust of the flesh, the lust of the eyes, and the pride of life. The people of the world may hate him for his witness, but he loves them.

Rationale: Bring before your students two key concepts: Christ's personal care for them and their obligation to prefer Him to the world. Teens experience strong pressure from the world, and you need to counterbalance that pressure.

Background: John 17 has been described as the "holy of holies" of the New Testament. Christ was in the presence of the Father, making intercession for His followers. As our High Priest, the Lord was seeking the Father's blessing on us. Today He intercedes directly at the right hand of the Father for us. Here we have a glimpse ahead of time of what He is doing for us now.

The material in John 14–17 is unique to John's Gospel. Matthew 26:36–46, Mark 14:32–42, and Luke 22:39–46 all record Jesus's prayer in the garden; John alone records the prayer John 17, apparently spoken in the upper room or on the way to the garden.

Often this prayer is outlined according to the ones Christ was praying for: (1) Himself (17:1–5), (2) the disciples (17:6–19), and (3) Christians in general (17:20–26). Although this approach is valid, the prayer can be better organized thematically, as it is here.

 The Lesson

I. Glorify Christ in the World (John 17:1–5)

Christ's motivation was His desire that God be glorified in the world. The word *glorification* is derived from a word family that focuses on the idea of thinking. To glorify someone is to cause others to perceive his good qualities and give him praise or a deserved position of honor. The Lord mentioned two reasons that the Father sought to have Himself glorified through His Son. The first was Christ's authority to grant salvation. As Christ grants eternal life, He grants an experiential knowledge of God (17:2–3). When people have the knowledge of God in their hearts, they bring praise and honor to Him.

> With this example Jesus gave guidance to believers today. Even though our lives may not be filled with sin, we still need to reaffirm our consecration to the Lord continually. Since we do not want to drift away from this attitude, we must consecrate ourselves afresh regularly and submit ourselves to the Father's will continually.

The second reason Christ asked the Father to glorify Himself through the Son was the coming completion of His work (17:4–5). The work of the cross is spoken of here as already accomplished because of its certainty. What had to occur for God to proceed? Nothing—everything was all set. God would soon reveal Christ to the hearts of people in all His divine glory and thus bring glory to Himself. That occurred through Christ's death, burial, Resurrection, and ascension. The capstone was the consequent preaching of the apostles and other early believers. God the Father and the Son do not receive the glory due them from humans unless the gospel is preached in the world.

Objectives

Knowledge (concepts students need to grasp)	the term *world* as it is used in the Bible
	the concept of *glory* in Scripture
Application (principles students should put into practice)	We must be separate from the world's sinful lifestyle.
	We must be faithful in reaching the world with the gospel.
	We should grow in grace, even though the world does not.

Outline

(John 17:1–26)
I. Glorify Christ in the world (1–5).
II. Be separate from the world (6–17).
   A. Positional separation
   B. Practical separation
   C. Results of separation
   D. Means of separation
III. Reach out to the world (18–23).
IV. Keep growing while in the world (24–26).

The apostles glorified the Lord Jesus by their faith and works. Your students must follow their example (John 17:10).

II. Be Separate from the World (17:6–17)

Next the Lord prayed about the sanctification of His followers. Sanctification is twofold: it is separation *from* sin and separation *to* God for holy purposes.

Positional separation. The basis of the believer's separation is his position in Christ (17:6–10). The Father had given the disciples to Christ, and He had shown the Father's name to them. The name of the Father represents His whole person or character. Through His careful teaching, the Lord had revealed the character of the Father. The disciples had accepted this revelation. The words the Father had given Him were the crucial factor in revealing the Father.

> Revelation is always the best teacher. Experience is second to it. The disciples' experiences with Christ were secondary to the revelation He had given them through His words about the Father.

The disciples' position in Christ resulted not only in revelation of the Father, but also in special prayer by Christ. Christ carries on a ministry of intercession for the disciples and for us that the world does not enjoy.

Practical separation. Since the disciples were separated from the world unto the Lord positionally, the Lord wanted them to remain separated practically (17:11–12). This would be a special challenge since He would soon ascend to heaven Himself. The disciples' inclination would be to scatter and slip back into their former lifestyles. He prayed that they would continue in unity of purpose. He reasoned that He had performed His duty by keeping the disciples safe from the world and losing none except Judas. (Judas was lost, how-

Read: John 17:1–26   Memorize: 1 John 2:15–17

Bible Expressions to Understand

hour—the time of the Crucifixion of Christ
eternal life—salvation through Christ and a relationship with Him forever
son of perdition—Judas Iscariot
the evil—the evil one; Satan

Question: What is a product of both Christ's genius and the Devil's design? What is the believer told both to love and to hate?

Answer: The world.

Planet Earth is often spoken of as "the world," but what else can the term *world* refer to?

We use the word *world* to describe the planet on which we live. The Bible uses the same word to describe life without God and people who are in rebellion to God. How are believers to be related to the world? Christ answered that question in His prayer just before His death.

Christ's prayer teaches us that Christians should be separated from the world. This doesn't mean that you somehow have to leave planet Earth. It means that you are not to be involved in the evil in the world. You're to be a holy person. You don't belong to sin and Satan anymore. You're owned by Christ if you've accepted Him as your Savior.

What can you do to remain pure and holy in this world? Jesus gave the answer in His prayer. He said, "Sanctify them [make them holy] through thy truth: thy word is truth" (John 17:17). You can read and obey the Bible. The Bible is the book that warns about sin. The New Testament alone mentions more than ninety sins the Christian should avoid. The Bible also teaches about the good things a Christian should do. It teaches about what Christ is like and therefore what you should be like. It isn't just a book of facts. It's a book that teaches you how to live apart from sin for the glory of God. The Bible is a manual for living.

Why doesn't God just take Christians out of the world once they are saved? Why does He leave them here to be tempted? One reason is that the world needs the gospel. Christ came into the world to save

81

through which the power of God could flow into their lives (Acts 20:32).

Separation is still the means by which the Lord causes us to be holy. The Word of God is a purifying agent in the believer's life. Emphasize the importance of daily devotions and Bible study.

III. Reach Out to the World (17:18–23)

One purpose of sanctification is the glory of God. Holiness brings honor to Him. Another goal is the evangelization of the world. By being holy the believer offers the world a contrast.

As Christ was sent into the world to reach it with the truth, the Christian is also sent. Christ set Himself apart to suffer the worst of deaths for the salvation of mankind. This sacrifice also set an example to Christians of service to others. Christ's death was the ultimate living out of His repeated instruction to His followers to take up their crosses and follow Him.

Christ knew that faithful service would bring results. Many would believe on the Lord. Christ prayed for these future followers, that they would be one with the original disciples in the purpose of spreading the gospel. The result of this unity would be that many more would come to Christ.

Humble service is the way to reach people ("that the world may know" [17:23]). The glory the Father had given Jesus was a glory of service and sacrifice. This was the same glory the disciples were to have as Christ dwelt in them. This glory would keep the future followers of Jesus unified and cause the world to listen to their message.

IV. Keep Growing While in the World (17:24–26)

Christ wants Christians to have a full knowledge of His divine glory. While believers are in the world, they will never have a complete grasp of Christ's magnificent character. The Lord looks forward to when believers will be with Him and fully appreciate Him. This will be the greatest joy of heaven—to know Christ better.

Most of us have known someone who left a great impression on us. Usually this person was of outstanding character or accomplishment. He inspired us and motivated us to great heights. Think of what it will be like to know Christ Himself. Consider the heights to which our desires and abilities will soar as we are empowered by Him to serve for endless ages.

ever, because of his own choice to reject the Lord and follow his sinful inclinations to destruction as the "son of perdition." As is often the case in Scripture, his wicked works proved to be a fulfillment of prophecy (Pss. 41:9; 109:4–13). Now the Father needed to give the disciples help in remaining separate from the world.

Results of separation. The product of practical separation is joy in this life (17:13). The Lord had already expressed His desire that the disciples know joy in their service for Him. He had said, "I am come that they might have life, and that they might have it more abundantly" (10:10). Just before His prayer the Lord had told them, "These things have I spoken unto you, that my joy might remain in you, and that your joy might be full" (15:11). One of "these things" the

Lord had talked to them about was obedience to His commands. This was to be one of the ways to continued holiness and joy.

Holiness and separation are not restrictive obstacles to joy, as many Christian teens perceive them to be. Indeed, there can be no lasting joy without them.

Means of separation. The Lord then emphasized the centrality of the Word of God in maintaining a separated life (17:14–17). Since the world hated Christ, it hated the disciples too. The solution to this problem is not removal from the world, but preservation from evil. The invaluable tool in accomplishing this preservation is the Word of God. The written revelation would tell the disciples what was expected of them, and it would serve as a channel

The knowledge of God that the Christian has in this life makes him different from the world. Christ revealed God to His disciples, and they understood the character and purposes of God as manifested through Jesus. This set them apart from the world because the world does not seek to know God. "There is none that understandeth, there is none that seeketh after God" (Rom. 3:11). Only the new birth changes this inclination.

The disciples' knowledge of God was not static but kept increasing. Jesus had revealed God to them, and He committed Himself to continuing the process: "And I have declared unto them thy name, and will declare it" (17:26). This growing knowledge would be not merely a growing body of factual knowledge, but a richer, fuller experience of God's working in their lives through the instruction of the Word and the illumination of the Spirit.

Paul understood the words of Jesus in this prayer and wanted to see them fulfilled in his life (Phil. 3:7–8). This desire should be the goal of every believer. You can help your students understand this by using the example of their admiration of some important person. They strive to be like him and accomplish what he accomplished. This is the effect Christ should have on us.

sinners, people who are in the world. He preached and performed miracles for this purpose. Most important, He died for this purpose. Like Christ, you're to reach the people of the world, who are lost in sin, with the good news. The good news for the world is that Jesus saves people from sin and condemnation.

Do you know anyone who needs to hear the good news—your neighbor, a close friend, or a relative? Whoever it may be, that's the person the Lord Jesus wants you to take the gospel to. If you obediently spread the gospel, someone will be saved because of it. If that person is obedient and gives the gospel to someone else, then others will be saved. This way the good news of Christ can spread throughout the whole world.

Sometimes the Lord picks a person to go as a missionary to another country, to another culture, or to another area of our own country. Many great missionaries have decided to be missionaries when they were only in junior or senior high school. You aren't too young to make that decision.

Listen to your pastor carefully, read your Bible faithfully, and pray that God will help you know whether He wants you to be a missionary.

Jesus also taught through His prayer that He wants Christians to grow in their knowledge of God. Would it make any difference to you if you got to meet a famous baseball player or Olympic champion? What about a world-famous musician or scientist? Let's suppose you became close friends with such a person. Do you think you would be interested in what he does and in being like him? You would. That is the way we are. People we admire and know well are people we try to be like. This is why we need to get to know the Lord Jesus better.

Just imagine what it will be like when we get to heaven! We'll know Christ better than we ever will in this life. He's looking forward to that time, and we should be too. That should be an encouragement while we're living for Him in the world.

Until we get to heaven, how can we get to know God better? Of course, the Bible teaches us about the Lord Jesus and God. But many people know the facts the Bible contains but never establish a relationship with God. What is the secret of knowing Christ intimately and becoming His close friend and follower?

The secret is that we must be saved from our sins by trusting Christ's work on the cross. He took the penalty for our sins, and if we trust what He did for us, He promises that we will become God's children. At the moment we are saved, the Lord allows the Holy Spirit to come and live in us to help us understand what the Bible says about Him and His will. The Holy Spirit also helps us obey the Lord. This is how we can keep getting to know Christ better and better right up until the day we see Him face-to-face.

Out of This World?

The term *world* has different meanings in the Bible. It's used to refer to the planet Earth. It's used to describe all the people who live on the earth. It's also used to describe people who do not love God.

How are you to think and act while living on a planet full of people who don't love God as you do? Keep yourself pure from the sins of the world. Give the world, those who don't love God, the good news about Christ. Work hard at growing to know God better even though the world doesn't want to know Him. You're the light of the world. Help them know Him and love Him as you do.

Do You Remember?

1. What important truth can we learn from what Jesus prayed in John 17? _____
   how Christians are to be separated from the world

2. According to John 17:4–5, why was Christ seeking to be glorified with the Father? _____
   because He had finished the work God had given Him to do

3. According to verse 8, how do believers know that the Son has been sent by the Father? _____
   because of the words He said, which God had given Him

4. Who was "the son of perdition"? _Judas Iscariot_

5. What blessing is based on the fact that the Son has committed believers to the Father? _____
   joy

6. Who is "the evil [one]"? _Satan_

7. Name one means of sanctification mentioned in John 17. _the Word of God (17:17)_

8. Why is John 17:20 a particular blessing to believers today? _____
   Jesus prayed for all future believers, not just His current disciples.

83

 Extra Activities

Discussion: The memory passage for this lesson (1 John 2:15–17) summarizes the Christian's view of the world. This outline may help you develop the ideas in these verses:

I. Controlling nature of love (15)
   A. If the world is loved, then God is not.
   B. If God is loved, then the world is not.

II. Attractions of the world (16)
   A. Lust of the flesh: physical desires
   B. Lust of the eyes: intellectual desires
   C. Pride of life: desire for power and prestige

III. Contrasting destinies (17)
   A. The world and its lusts pass away.
   B. He who does God's will abides forever.

Case studies: These stories may help your students understand the danger of the world's attractions:

Case 1—Mr. and Mrs. Rimstottler liked their church because their pastor's sermons were good. However, he often planned evangelistic services and witnessing campaigns on weekends. Some people attended these special services, but not the Rimstottlers. They had a travel trailer that they took to the beach or mountains every weekend. To them it was bad enough to have to come back for church on Sundays; special meetings were out of the question.

Which of the "lusts of the world" did the Rimstottlers allow to control them?
The lust of the flesh. They wanted physical relaxation and pleasant surroundings more than service.

Case 2—Tim Farber grew faster than most of his friends. By eighth grade he was already six feet three inches tall. By ninth grade he was almost two inches taller. The basketball coach saw potential in him for college and pro basketball, so he worked hard with him. The Farbers were Christians, however, and they wanted Tim to serve the Lord. But he could not get national attention playing basketball if he went to a Christian college. Finally, his parents let him go to the state university. There he forgot the Lord and His work. His one goal in life became professional basketball and the fame and money it would bring. He eventually became one of the first-draft picks for the pros and earned a big salary playing for a well-known team.

Which "lust of the world" did Tim allow to control him?
The pride of life. He wanted fame and the power that money brings.

Lesson 23
Eternal Punishment

THEME	Hell
SCRIPTURE	Luke 16:19–31
MEMORY WORK	Luke 16:23

Approach to the Lesson

Theme: Jesus taught that those who die in their sins will suffer eternal punishment. The truth of eternal punishment should be a source of terror for the unbeliever and of motivation for the Christian. Those who rebel against God's authority deserve punishment. God is not sadistic; He is just. All sin must be rectified.

Rationale: Hell is an extremely serious subject. Do not make light of it, and do not allow your students to make jokes about it. Furthermore, you should present it as a burden. Since God takes no pleasure in the death of the wicked (Ezek. 18:32; 33:11), neither should we.

Background: All of the New Testament teaching on hell is in the Gospels except for the material in Revelation 20 concerning the lake of fire. The fact that Jesus directly taught on the subject or alluded to it as often as He did is significant.

We all must have a right view of God's justice. God is loving and merciful, but He is also just. Mercy travels long on the road, looking for those who will accept it in the person of Christ. But the time comes when mercy no longer beckons. Justice takes over and summons all to the judgment, where they will receive a sentence in proportion to the wrong they have done.

Outline

I. Who sends people to hell?
II. Who is in hell?
   A. The neglectful
   B. The hypocrites
   C. The hateful
   D. All sinners
III. What is hell like?
   A. Everlasting
   B. Graded
   C. Painful
IV. What does God do to warn people about hell?

Bible Expressions to Understand

Abraham's bosom—the place of dead saints; paradise
hell—the place of torment

Hell isn't the product of creative religious imaginations. It's a place God says actually exists. In the Bible, particularly the Gospels, it's described in detail. That description doesn't fit the common ideas of life after death. Some think hell is the place where the Devil lives with all his friends. Others think it is an eternal party where evil people go and have a good time together forever. Still others would say there's no life after death—that if there is a hell, it's just the hard times in this life.

Jesus taught specifically about hell on several occasions. One time He told a story about a rich man who died and went to hell. In life, the rich man was well provided for with fine clothes, plenty of food, and everything else he wanted. There was also a beggar, Lazarus, who lived off scraps of food from the rich man's table. Both the rich man and Lazarus died. In death, their roles were reversed, with Lazarus enjoying the blessings of paradise while the rich man suffered the torments of hell.

The beggar Lazarus (not Jesus's friend from Bethany) was the only character in any of Christ's parables given a name. The rich man in the story is sometimes called Dives (from the Latin word for "rich").

84

There in the fires of judgment, the rich man was able to look across a "great gulf" (literally a huge chasm) into paradise. Seeing Lazarus enjoying the company of Abraham, he cried out to Abraham for mercy. "Send Lazarus," he said, as he pleaded for just a single drop of water to cool his tongue from the heat of the fire. Abraham replied that he couldn't do that, however, because of the vast expanse between paradise and hell.

Realizing that there was no more hope, the rich man pleaded with Abraham to send Lazarus to his father's house to warn his five brothers about the place of torment. Again Abraham refused, explaining that the brothers already had a witness—the words of Moses and the prophets. The rich man continued to plead, reasoning that the testimony of a messenger from the dead would have a greater impact on them. But Abraham explained that one who rejects the Word of God will also reject other forms of testimony.

What can we learn about hell from this story? First, the people listening to Jesus were probably surprised that the poor man was in heaven and the rich man in hell because they thought of wealth as a

---

Answering the questions in the outline will help you present accurately and thoroughly the subject of eternal punishment as found in Christ's teaching. The lesson covers several scattered passages.

The Lesson

I. Who Sends People to Hell?

Christ's answer to this question is recorded in Matthew 10:28 and Luke 12:5. Christ is the One Who determines who will enter the place of eternal punishment. Note that both body and soul will be cast into hell. This may seem strange since bodies are usually buried. However, Jesus also taught that all will be resurrected (John 5:28–29). The resurrection of the ungodly takes place just before the Great White Throne Judgment. They receive justice and are cast into the lake of fire (Rev. 20:13–15).

We tend to conform our lives to the expectations of others. We fear their opinions. We sometimes fear the physical harm that may come from following Christ. Jesus warned against this fear. Instead we are to fear the One Who can cast body and soul into hell.

II. Who Is in Hell?

The Lord answered this question in John 3:18—"He that believeth on him is not condemned: but he that believeth not is condemned already, because he hath not believed in the name of the only begotten Son of God." Originally hell was prepared for the Devil and his angels (Matt. 25:41), but everybody who refuses to trust in Christ will be there also.

sign of God's favor (Mark 10:25–26). However, these two men weren't where they were because of their financial condition before they died. The poor man was in heaven because he had trusted Christ as his Savior. The rich man was in hell because he hadn't trusted Christ. Since he had no relationship with Christ, he had lived a wicked, compassionless life. This was clear from his attitude toward Lazarus.

Second, this story teaches that hell is a terrible place. The rich man was tormented constantly by thirst and fire. He wanted help from Lazarus, but he couldn't get it. The same impassable separation between heaven and hell that made it impossible for Lazarus to cross over also ensured that the rich man could never escape from hell. He was imprisoned forever.

The third lesson is that we can avoid going to hell. When the rich man realized that he would never be released from the place, he asked Abraham to send Lazarus to alert his brothers. Abraham's answer was that they had Moses and the prophets (the Old Testament) to learn what they needed to know to escape hell. A person coming back from the dead to warn them wouldn't do any good if they were unwilling to believe God's Word.

The Bible has the answers about eternal life. A person shouldn't expect God to work miracles to convince him of the reality of heaven and hell. If God's Word isn't enough, nothing will ever be enough to convince him. When the Bible teaches that sin separates us from God, we must believe it. When the Scripture says a person's sin will condemn him to hell, we must trust it. When the Word of God instructs us to trust Christ's death on the cross to save us from our sin, we must believe it and repent in faith. If we choose not to believe the Bible, all hope of being saved from hell is lost.

Believe It or Not, Hell Is Real

Jesus clearly taught that those who die in their sins will suffer eternal punishment in hell. The truth of hell should be a source of terror for the unbeliever and a motivating factor for the Christian. The Christian who knows this truth must share the good news of salvation.

God's not cruel; He's just. He offers all men salvation, and no one goes to hell who doesn't deserve it.

Do You Remember?

1. What was the rich man wearing that showed his wealth? _purple and fine linen_

2. What was the poor man's name? _Lazarus_

3. What happened to the rich man when he died? What happened to the beggar? _The rich man was buried and went to hell; the beggar went to heaven._

4. What caused the rich man's torment in hell? _fire or flame (thirst)_

5. Who did the rich man see far away in paradise? _Abraham and Lazarus_

6. Why couldn't Abraham send help to the rich man? _because of the great gulf fixed between heaven and hell_

7. What was the rich man's second request? _that Abraham would send Lazarus to warn his five brothers so they would not go to hell_

8. Why wouldn't Abraham do what the rich man requested? _because the brothers already had Moses and the prophets (God's Word) to persuade them to avoid hell_

85

The neglectful. Those who neglect spiritual opportunities will be punished. The inhabitants of Capernaum fit into this category. While in Galilee, Jesus had His base of operation in this community; yet most people there rejected Him. Jesus said it would be more tolerable for Sodom in the day of judgment than it would be for that town (Matt. 11:23; Luke 10:15). Both the parable of the wedding feast and the parable of the talents present characters who had great opportunity, neglected it, and were cast into outer darkness, where there was weeping and gnashing of teeth (Matt. 22:13; 25:30).

Since they have heard the gospel, your students have greater responsibility than others. If they reject it, they will face great judgment as Capernaum will.

The hypocrites. Three times Jesus explicitly stated that hypocrites will have a place in hell (Matt. 23:13, 15; 24:51). Two of the three remarks were directed at the Pharisees. A pretended religious profession is offensive to God; to know the truth and secretly not accept it is treacherous. A hypocrite has advanced to a serious level of sin, a level that is perilous because of the slim likelihood that he will repent.

Hypocrisy is very common in Christian schools. Stress that God singles it out for special judgment—even greater, for example, than murder.

The hateful. A life characterized by hatred also brings eternal punishment. Jesus said, "But whosoever shall say, Thou fool, shall be in danger of hell fire" (Matt. 5:22). If a man hates his brother, he probably

Objectives

KNOWLEDGE (concepts students need to grasp)	the characteristics of hell presented in Christ's teachings
	the qualities and actions of those who will experience eternal punishment
APPLICATION (principles students should put into practice)	We must be saved from hell.
	We must witness to the lost.
	We should be thankful to the Lord for delivering us from hell.

knows little or nothing of the love of God himself. If he doesn't know God's love, then he is a candidate for eternal punishment.

All sinners. Jesus's pattern for treating this subject is important. He makes a general statement about the basic failure of those who are condemned to eternal punishment, and then He lists several specific kinds of sinners who will experience it. The specific classes He mentions do not include every kind of sinner because that kind of comprehensiveness is unnecessary. The Lord gives adequate examples from which to draw the right conclusions. If an individual rejects Christ and lives in sin, he will suffer eternal punishment.

III. What Is Hell Like?

To think of hell only in general terms is a mistake. The Lord intends for us to know what it is like specifically. The greater our knowledge of this place, the greater our incentive to escape it ourselves and to help others do the same. Hell is a place where sinners will suffer everlastingly, though not every sinner will receive the same degree of punishment.

Everlasting. Once a person enters hell, he faces everlasting punishment (Matt. 18:8; 25:41, 46). Hell is a prison from which there is no escape. In Christ's story of the rich man in hell, Abraham said to the rich man, "And beside all this, between us and you there is a great gulf fixed: so that they which would pass from hence to you cannot; neither can they pass to us, that would come from thence" (Luke 16:26). This kind of punishment may seem merciless, but it helps us understand the seriousness of this life. The problem of sin can be resolved in only one of two ways: having faith in Christ's death and Resurrection or suffering an eternity of punishment.

Graded. Not everyone will receive the same punishment in hell. We have already mentioned that the unbelievers who lived in Capernaum will be punished more severely than those who lived in Sodom. Jesus addressed this issue explicitly when He said, "And that servant, which knew his lord's will, and prepared not himself, neither did according to his will, shall be beaten with many stripes. But he that knew not, and did commit things worthy of stripes, shall be beaten with few stripes. For unto whomsoever much is given, of him shall be much required: and to whom men have committed much, of him they will ask the more" (Luke 12:47–48).

Painful. The suffering awaiting the unconverted is terrible to consider. They will know the pain of burning and the stress of great thirst (Luke 16:24). They will express their anguish by weeping and grinding their teeth (13:28). They will be in outer darkness, a place of extreme loneliness (Matt. 8:12) and corruption, where maggots infest their wounded flesh (Mark 9:46, 48). All the while they will be longing for paradise, which they can see but cannot reach (Luke 13:28; 16:23, 26).

On and on this cycle of torment and hopelessness goes. The fire is not quenched, the worm never dies, heaven is never nearer, and despair never ceases. Knowing the nature of hell as He did, Jesus used radical illustrations to describe the lengths to which a person should go to escape it. Gouge out your eye or slice off your hand or foot to avoid going to hell (Matt. 5:29–30; 18:8–9; Mark 9:43–48). Jesus was not suggesting that amputation could save one from hell. He was warning us to take whatever steps are necessary to get right with God and avoid that awful place.

IV. What Does God Do to Warn People About Hell?

You would think that the most convincing way to warn people about hell would be to have someone return from it, tell about the place, and explain the way of salvation. This suggestion was made by the rich man in hell (Luke 16:27–28). Jesus said that the message would not be convincing. If someone refuses to believe the Bible on the subject, there is no hope for him (16:29–31). Not even a person returning from the dead could convince the unbeliever.

God entrusts His Word to His people and expects them to carry the message about hell and salvation to the world. Jesus promised His people, "I will build my church; and the gates of hell shall not prevail against it" (Matt. 16:18). In Greek the thrust of this statement is that the gates of hell will not hold up against the church's attack. The church will be successful in rescuing people from hell, even those who for all practical purposes are in its confines already because of unbelief.

✸ Extra Activity

Pretest: Give an ungraded quiz before your students begin to study this topic. Ask the following questions to find out how much they know about hell and to encourage them to learn more.

a. What is the main reason people must be eternally punished in hell?
    sin and rejecting Christ

b. Where is hell?
    In the Bible it is figuratively described as being down (e.g., Ps. 55:15). The actual location is unknown.

c. Do people spend eternity in hell, suffering in their physical bodies?
    yes, after the Great White Throne Judgment

d. Can a person in hell see heaven?
    Yes; this is part of what causes extreme anguish in hell.

e. Would a God who loves people let them go to hell?
    Yes. It is a destiny people accept by choosing their sin rather than the Savior. God is just and must punish sin.

Lesson 24
Materialism

Theme	Materialism
Scripture	John 6:1–71
Memory Work	John 6:35

 ## Approach to the Lesson

Theme: All people yearn for the kind of contentment in which needs are met, desires fulfilled, and appetites gratified. Yet few know how to find it. Most look to externals—consumable goods, sensual gratification, food, and wealth. But they soon hit a wall of disappointment because the temporal cannot satisfy.

God's Word gives insights into contentment. "Better is little with the fear of the Lord than great treasure and trouble therewith" (Prov. 15:16). "I have learned, in whatsoever state I am, therewith to be content" (Phil. 4:11). "But godliness with contentment is great gain. For we brought nothing into this world, and it is certain we can carry nothing out. And having food and raiment let us be therewith content" (1 Tim. 6:6–8). "Let your conversation be without covetousness; and be content with such things as ye have: for he hath said, I will never leave thee, nor forsake thee" (Heb. 13:5).

Contentment is in God alone. Worldly things and pleasures cannot bring satisfaction. They are powerless to meet our most basic needs.

Rationale: Challenge your students not to seek satisfaction in material things. Materialism usually begins to get a foothold during adolescence, and it should be crushed early.

Have your students focus on their own hearts. Where are their priorities? Would they rather have new clothes or the firm assurance that everything is right between them and God? We must never focus on the outside; we must always look within.

Background: In this passage Christ fed 5,000 men and probably at least that many women and children, using only five loaves and two fish. Naturally the crowd responded. They wanted more from this teacher who could supply their physical needs. Jesus used this opportunity to point them to the real source of satisfaction: Himself.

 ## The Lesson

Young children are naturally immature, temporal-minded creatures. They yearn for contentment, but in unacceptable ways. For example, they may become enamored with a glittering, sharp object and yet be unaware that the knife is harmful. They may want to play on a hearth, not recognizing the danger of fire. They may reach out for brightly colored pills even though the medicine could kill them.

Children's antics are well known to young people and adults. We do our best to keep alert, to be on the lookout for dangers, to protect our young friends as best we can. Yet we fail to realize that we are a lot like them. We sometimes seek satisfaction in counterproductive ways.

I. Our Need—Spiritual Contentment (John 6:26–27)

Christ attacked the limited perspective of the Galileans who followed Him for material gain. Many of them hoped that He would become their king, helping them throw off the Roman yoke and establishing a utopian state. But ultimately, material comforts are of little value. Thus Christ declared, "Labour not for the meat which perisheth, but for that meat which endureth unto everlasting life" (6:27). Christ wasn't criticizing everyday work. Scripture approves of an industrious worker (2 Thess. 3:10; Prov. 10:5; 12:11). Yet Jesus did condemn the heart that views earthly success as its top priority.

> We, like Israel, do not need and should not expect an earthly utopia in this age. The most pressing need for our world is neither sociopolitical reform nor equity for all peoples. Although we should be concerned for the poor, we must not forget that we have a more important mission—the salvation of those who don't know Christ. Full stomachs can go to hell just as quickly as empty ones. Liberated peoples will face God's judgment

Objectives

KNOWLEDGE (concepts students need to grasp)	our ultimate need for spiritual contentment
	Christ alone as our source of spiritual contentment
APPLICATION (principles students should put into practice)	We must not seek for satisfaction in possessions.
	We must live for Christ to experience true satisfaction.

Outline

> (John 6:26–58)
> I. Our need—spiritual contentment (26–27)
> II. God's answer—Christ (32–58)
>   A. The incarnate Son of God (32–36)
>   B. The perfect sacrifice for sin (51–58)
>   C. The only object of faith (53)

just as surely as enslaved ones. Youth is often idealistic, willing to crusade for a cause, but you must warn your students that it is not enough to crusade for political, social, or economic reform. Christ could have fulfilled these needs in an instant, but He recognized that more important matters were at stake.

Scripture emphasizes the folly of living for earthly treasures. First, the Bible teaches that wealth can be taken away in an instant. An accident, a theft, a bad business deal, and wealth is gone forever. Certainly everyone is but a heartbeat from death, at which time the rich and the poor are in the same situation. Wealth cannot gain a person entrance into heaven. The righteous Lazarus, though poor, found favor with God. The rich man, though he possessed the treasures of this life, found himself sadly lacking in what really mattered (Luke 16). (Note also Job 1:21; Prov. 23:5; 27:24.)

> Your students may already have a problem with materialism. This is hardly surprising since our culture worships material prosperity. A beautiful house, an expensive car, and stylish clothes are widely accepted marks of success. Most people are striving to find acceptance, to gain respect, and to make names for themselves. Encourage your students to reject this worldly philosophy.

Second, the desire for wealth usually leads to spiritual destruction. It opens a person up to "temptations," "snares," and "foolish and hurtful lusts" (1 Tim. 6:9). *Temptations* are enticements to sin. They dangle before the unwary, leading them into ruin. *Snares* are traps. Looking harmless to the casual observer, they spring into action, destroying their prey.

> The student text pages for this lesson begin on the next page.

Lot is an obvious scriptural example of this principle. Preferring the "greener grass" of the plain of Jordan (Gen. 13:10), he ended up being almost destroyed in Sodom (Gen. 19). Many have followed in his footsteps. In seeking contentment in earthly treasures, they find nothing but ruin. Our true needs are spiritual, not material or financial. Our true desires cannot be satisfied by physical things.

II. God's Answer—Christ (John 6:32–58)

Christ is the answer to man's most basic needs. As He dealt with the Galileans, He identified Himself as the "Bread of Life." Unlike physical bread, which is perishable and can give but brief physical sustenance, Christ brings satisfaction to the hungry soul. He alone can cleanse the sinful heart. Christ's discourse teaches three key concepts that all point to this major truth.

The incarnate Son of God (6:32–36). Christ describes Himself as the bread that came down from heaven (6:33), a title that has several implications:

First, it implies that man has a hunger that earthly food cannot satisfy. Man may focus on the material and try to find contentment in the physical, but in his soul he cries out for something more. In the dark hours of the night he wonders, *Does God exist? Is there life after death? Am I prepared to face eternity?*

> Perhaps this hunger is the main motivation for drinking, drug abuse, and thrill-seeking. These are merely attempts to drown out this spiritual need. Do your students complain about restless nights? Do they hate to slow down and think? Are they running from that inner hunger?

Second, Christ alone can satisfy this inner hunger. We are powerless to help ourselves because we are depraved and controlled by sin (Jer. 17:9; Rom. 3:10, 23). But the "bread of heaven" is "very God" and "very man," truly human and truly divine (John 1:1, 14; 20:28; Titus 2:13). As God, He could live a perfectly sinless life and satisfy the demands of a holy God. As man, He could take our place, paying the price for our sin on the cross.

The perfect sacrifice for sin (6:51–58). The Lord would give His flesh and His blood for the sake of humanity. There can be no doubt that in this passage Christ pointed to the cross, where His flesh would be broken and His blood spilled. The blood of bulls and goats could not take away our

L.24 — Materialism

Bible Expressions to Understand

furlong—about an eighth of a mile
pennyworth—a denarius, about a day's wage for the average worker
sign—a display of divine power, designed to teach a lesson
quicken—make alive

Richard Cory

Whenever Richard Cory went downtown,
We people on the pavement looked at him:
He was a gentleman from sole to crown,
Clean favored, and imperially slim.

And he was always quietly arrayed,
And he was always human when he talked;
But still he fluttered pulses when he said,
"Good morning," and he glittered when he walked.

And he was rich—yes, richer than a king—
And admirably schooled in every grace;
In fine, we thought that he was everything
To make us wish that we were in his place.

So on we worked, and waited for the light,
And went without the meat, and cursed the bread,
And Richard Cory, one calm summer night,
Went home and put a bullet through his head.
—Edwin Arlington Robinson

Did the ending of this poem shock you? If so, you're not alone. Ever since Edwin Arlington Robinson wrote "Richard Cory" in 1897, it has bothered a lot of people. Yet it illustrates an important truth: Wealth cannot bring contentment to a person.

You live in a materialistic age—an age in which people think that primarily money and possessions bring happiness. Lots of people spend their lives in search of wealth and fame. To many, satisfaction is driving a new car, having a big-screen HDTV, taking expensive vacations, and wearing the latest fashions. Magazine and television advertisements glamorize the privileged few, the rich and famous, who have it all.

What are your goals? Do you want to amass a personal fortune? Do you live for material success? Most of your friends and neighbors do. Most people throughout history have made material goods their top priority. As a result they have lived unhappy, discontented lives. You should think twice before deciding to follow their example.

The people of Palestine in Jesus's day weren't all that different from people today. John 6 opens with a notable miracle. From five loaves of barley bread and two small fish, Christ fed a huge crowd of Galileans. His act of kindness filled their hungry stomachs, but it also revealed their cold, barren hearts. Thrilled with a free meal, they claimed Jesus as Messiah and tried to make Him king. They got excited about the potential of a bountiful food supply

Those who ate the bread and fish Jesus provided supernaturally were satisfied only for a while. The next morning they were back, hoping for another miracle to satisfy their physical hunger.

sin (Heb. 10:4). But Christ's blood was sufficient to wash us clean (Isa. 53:4–6; Rom. 5:8; 2 Cor. 5:21).

The price He paid for man's sin was overwhelming, but the result is hope for all mankind; we can find eternal life through Christ. Physical bread brings temporary sustenance, but the Bread of Heaven brings eternal life.

> We live in a works-oriented society, and many professing Christians depend on works to satisfy God. Your students must recognize that church attendance, tithing, visitation, and abstinence from sin will not save them. Christ alone is the answer to their need (John 14:6; 1 John 5:11–12).

The only object of faith (6:53). The Lord teaches that He must be the focal point of our lives. We must have a close,

living, personal relationship with Him—so close that Christ metaphorically compared it to eating His flesh and drinking His blood. (It may be significant that the words for *eat* and *drink* are in the aorist tense in the Greek. Often the aorist tense signifies a "once-for-all" action. Certainly after salvation we are in a "once-for-all" relationship with Christ.)

This metaphor may trouble some students. Explain that Christ simply desires us to have a part with Him, to be part of Him by seeking His fellowship. In order to be a part of Him, we must turn to Him in faith and accept His sacrifice. Unfortunately, most people, like the Galileans of Christ's day, refuse to turn to Him in faith.

The Galileans refused for two reasons. First, they did not respect Christ's person (6:41–42). They viewed Him as the human

that they didn't have to work for, but they failed to recognize the true mission of Jesus Christ.

Israel's Messiah was not a miracle-working hero. Christ came not to bring political, military, and economic success to Israel. He came to bring salvation to all who would believe—to "save his people from their sins" (Matt. 1:21). Christ was aware of His mission and proclaimed it to those who would listen. "For the Son of man is come to seek and to save that which was lost" (Luke 19:10).

After feeding the people, Christ condemned their shallow materialism. "Labour not for the meat which perisheth, but for that meat which endureth unto everlasting life" (John 6:27). Full stomachs ultimately don't satisfy. Material goods cannot save. "For riches certainly make themselves wings; they fly away as an eagle toward heaven" (Prov. 23:5). Only the Bread of Heaven can bring eternal satisfaction. Only Christ can meet our spiritual needs.

> ### "For what shall it profit a man, if he shall gain the whole world, and lose his own soul?"
> ### (Mark 8:36)

Christ declared, "I am the living bread which came down from heaven: if any man eat of this bread, he shall live for ever: and the bread that I will give is my flesh, which I will give for the life of the world" (John 6:51). With these words Christ pointed to His death on the cross. His blood alone can cleanse our sins. His blood alone can heal our sinful souls.

Do you know the crucified Lord? Have you tasted the Bread of Heaven? Unless you accept His sacrifice through faith, looking to Him as your only hope, you'll never find contentment for your soul. Where are your priorities—on material goods or spiritual truths? The world or the Word? Where do you search for contentment—in worldly luxuries or in the Son of God? Those who desire to save their

lives will lose them (Matt. 16:25). You cannot get away with loving the world over loving God. A day of judgment is coming when every deed and thought will be judged. Those who ignore Christ to pursue friendship with the world will suffer great loss.

Obsession with Possessions

We all search for contentment; we want our needs met, our desires fulfilled, and our appetites gratified. Yet we often search in the wrong places. Externals cannot satisfy. Material possessions bring no lasting contentment.

God's Word declares, "But godliness with contentment is great gain. For we brought nothing into this world, and it is certain we can carry nothing out. And having food and raiment, let us be therewith content" (1 Tim. 6:6-8). The message is clear. Worldly possessions are powerless to meet our most important needs. Only Christ can help the troubled soul.

87

---

son of human parents and thus unworthy of special consideration. Second, they despised Christ's plan of salvation (6:52). They refused to see the import of Christ's words. Instead they focused on the act of eating flesh and drinking blood, both of which were repulsive and prohibited by God's law (Gen. 9:4).

Modern man still rebels against God's plan of salvation, and for the same two reasons. Many today deny the deity of Christ. They view Him as a man—a good man, perhaps, but only a man nonetheless. Others balk at the preaching of the cross. They see no need to accept a bloody religion, a religion that focuses on the blood of Christ. Yet we need not fear the heckling of unbelievers (Rom. 1:16; 1 Cor. 1:21–24).

The Lord alone must receive the glory for man's salvation, "that no flesh should glory in his presence. . . . That, according as it is written, He that glorieth, let him glory in the Lord" (1 Cor. 1:29, 31). But in humble, penitent faith we can find satisfaction of our most basic need—contentment of the soul.

Special Problems and Topics

• What does manna have to do with the Messiah?

At first glance it seems strange that the Galileans should seek manna from Christ (John 6:30–31). Yet careful study of contemporary ideas solves the problem. It was commonly accepted among first-century Jews that the Messiah would begin to supply manna to God's people again. The apocryphal book 2 Baruch says, "It shall come to pass . . . that the treasury of manna shall again descend from on high, and they will eat of it in those years" (29:8).

• How are God's sovereignty and man's responsibility related?

Christ's discourse illustrates the inexplicable relationship between divine sovereignty and human responsibility.

Jesus clearly states God's part in the salvation process: "No man can come to me, except the Father which hath sent me draw him: and I will raise him up at the last day" (John 6:44). But He also stresses man's duty to come to Christ: "And this is the will of him that sent me, that every one which seeth the Son, and believeth on him, may have everlasting life: and I will raise him up at the last day" (6:40).

From a human perspective it is impossible to reconcile these truths. We must simply believe God's Word. God is sovereign and elects some to salvation. Man is responsible and must believe God's message. In eternity we will understand just how these truths fit together.

✳ Extra Activities

Essay: Assign a one-page essay on the topic "What Must I Do to Be Saved?" Have your students set forth the plan of salvation as they understand it. Look these essays over carefully. You may recognize some severe weaknesses. If so, you should stress the appropriate parts of this lesson carefully and arrange to talk with those whose understanding of salvation seems weak.

Witnessing: You may wish to take your class witnessing with you, one by one. Your students will gain valuable insights into dealing with unsaved people. They will also recognize the antagonism that many have toward the gospel. People have not changed; they use the same excuses as the Galileans of Jesus's day. Your students may be quite surprised to observe this.

Research: Ask the students if they know what *affluenza* is. They won't find the word in the dictionary, but an Internet search for the term will yield a dozen or more websites. Have them visit some of them and write short reports about why even nonbelievers are concerned about our society's obsession with material things.

Do You Remember?

1. What important truth does the poem "Richard Cory" illustrate? _____
   Material prosperity does not satisfy. Externals cannot bring contentment to the soul.

2. What's the result of making worldly goods your top priority? _____
   an unhappy, discontented life

3. What miracle opens John 6? What did this miracle reveal about the Galileans? _____
   the feeding of the 5,000; the materialism in their hearts

4. Why did the Galileans want to make Christ king? _____
   They wanted a never-ending free food supply.

5. What was Christ's true mission, which the Galileans failed to recognize? _____
   to bring salvation to all who would believe

6. What can cleanse your sin? *the blood of Christ* _____

7. How can we find contentment? _____
   accept Christ's sacrifice through faith, looking to Him as our only hope

88

Conduct Reveals Character — L.25

Read: Matthew 12:22–50   Memorize: Matthew 12:34–35

Bible Expressions to Understand

Beelzebub—literally, "lord of the dwelling" (of demons); Satan
blasphemy—speaking evil of God
viper—a poisonous snake
dry places—areas not suitable for living
garnished—decorated; put in order

Benedict Arnold was born in colonial America in 1741. As a teenager, he loved the excitement of military conflict and ran away from home twice to fight in the French and Indian War. During the Revolutionary War he became known for his bravery and outstanding leadership ability. He led successful attacks against the enemy, defended American positions, and was wounded twice. His successes brought him promotions to brigadier general and then to major general.

Though he had a brilliant career, Arnold became bitter when others were promoted before him. His

Even before he betrayed his country, Benedict Arnold had been involved in smuggling and other unethical dealings, such as using U.S. government wagons for his personal business.

bitterness led him to betray the American cause. He planned to help the British capture West Point, a fort over which he had command.

The British major who was carrying the message of his plan to the British generals was captured and revealed Arnold's plan. Arnold found out what had happened and escaped to the British, who paid him ten thousand pounds for his loss of property and made him a brigadier general in the British army. Arnold later moved to England, where he died in 1801 after suffering from depression and a nervous disorder.

Benedict Arnold is one of the most famous traitors in history. He did what he did because he had become bitter. He had always been driven by ambition and pride. Finally, what he had become drove him to betray his country.

The sad case of Benedict Arnold teaches that a person's conduct reveals his character. Jesus taught this principle: what a person thinks determines what he will do. Those who are saved and growing in the Christian faith will do the right things. Those who are unsaved will do and say the wrong things often enough that it will be clear they don't know Christ.

In the passage for this lesson, Jesus taught that His own conduct revealed His character (Matt. 12:22–23). Since He was the sinless Son of God, His actions and words were always good. After Jesus healed a man possessed by a demon, all the people were amazed at His good deed. The Pharisees and the scribes began to accuse Him of doing the miracle through the power of evil. They claimed that what He had done in the power of the Holy Spirit wasn't from the Holy Spirit at all. They were questioning His character.

89

Objectives

KNOWLEDGE (concepts students need to grasp)	the identity of Beelzebub
	the nature of the unpardonable sin
	the meaning of the word *blasphemy*
	the role of the people of Nineveh and the queen of the south in the future judgment
	the relationship of Christ to His family at this point in His ministry
APPLICATION (principles students should put into practice)	Our conversation must reflect Christian character.
	Our actions demonstrate the sincerity of our faith.
	We must not count on good conduct to substitute for Christian character.

the religious establishment. The teachings covered in this lesson were given around the midpoint of Christ's public ministry. As His popularity increased, so did the opposition, which ultimately culminated in the Crucifixion. Often such opposition gave our Lord a platform for instruction. This is one example of how He used hostile reactions as a teaching opportunity.

At first glance this passage appears disjointed, but a closer look reveals otherwise. Those listening to the Lord were asking questions or objecting, and at each turn the Lord was bringing them back to the idea that conduct reveals character, whether bad or good.

⭐ The Lesson

I. Christ's Conduct Revealed His Character (Matt. 12:22–32)

Christ's opposition to Satan (12:22–29). The healing of a demon-possessed man brought two contrasting responses. The people who witnessed the miracle were amazed. The Pharisees, sensing Christ's growing popularity, leveled a ludicrous accusation—that He was working through the power of Beelzebub, the prince of demons. This name, though variously explained, likely means "lord of the dwelling" (i.e., the dwelling place of the demons). The lord of that place is Satan. The Pharisees' accusation was that Jesus worked as Satan's subordinate.

Rather than reacting to a personal insult, Jesus refuted the accusation with

---

Lesson 25
Conduct Reveals Character

THEME	The Importance of Conduct
SCRIPTURE	Matthew 12:22–50
MEMORY WORK	Matthew 12:34–35

ⓧ Approach to the Lesson

Theme: The way a person thinks about God, others, and himself will eventually become clear by the way he acts. If a student's conversation is in bad taste or even

vulgar, it reflects the condition of his heart. If a student dresses in a worldly manner, he does so because he loves the world. If a student is always quick to follow fads, he is strongly influenced by his peers. If he does not do his homework, he does not think his homework is important. What he thinks influences what he does.

It is true that people look on the outward appearance, while God looks on the heart. But it is also true that a person's actions are evidence of his spiritual condition.

Rationale: Do not allow this lesson to become an opportunity for students to criticize one another. Stress their need to judge *themselves*. What does their own behavior say about their character?

Background: Christ's ministry had barely begun when opposition came from

Outline

logic. He showed that His conduct (casting out demons) proved His character—that He was against demons. Using a kingdom, city, and household as examples, Jesus reasoned that if those who are supposed to be loyal to each other are divided, they will fall. Since this is true, Jesus then asked how Satan's kingdom could survive if he were fighting against himself. The obvious answer was that it couldn't. His goal certainly is not to destroy his own influence over people, as the Pharisees were illogically suggesting.

The Lord strengthened His argument by showing the Pharisees their inconsistency. If they were willing to give God the credit for exorcisms done by men they sanctioned, what right had they to say Christ's exorcisms were done in the power of the Devil? Their inconsistency revealed their dishonesty. Those the Pharisees approved of would serve as adequate judges of their hypocrisy (12:27).

Since Christ cast out demons in the power of the Spirit of God, the Pharisees should have recognized Him as the promised Messiah that every good Jew waited for. The kingdom of God had arrived in the person of the King (12:28).

Taking one last step to devastate the logic of the Pharisees, the Lord offered an example and a pointed conclusion from it (12:29). No man could walk into the house of a powerful criminal and take the criminal's ill-gotten gain without restraining him first. What is implied is that Satan is the criminal. He has taken many lives into spiritual bondage through the influence of his demons. He would never willingly give up what he had fought to win. When Jesus healed the man the demons had made blind and dumb, He proved His power to subdue

The Lord quickly proved that their thinking was foolish. He challenged them to explain why Satan would want to deliver a man from the control of a demon. Their reasoning didn't make sense. It showed that they were determined not to believe in Jesus, no matter what He did to prove that He was the Son of God.

Jesus explained that a person characterized by this type of unbelief could never be forgiven. A person who says that what the Holy Spirit does is done by the Devil will never accept the message of the Spirit, that is, the message that he can be saved from sin only by trusting Christ. If he will not accept that message, there is no hope that he will ever be forgiven.

How did the men Jesus was talking to get to this point? They had become hardened through hearing God's Word without believing it and living by it. They were hypocrites who acted religious but were really living for reasons other than the glory of God.

All who read the Bible should understand, as these men failed to, that the things Jesus did prove that He is good and that He is God. His conduct revealed His character.

Jesus also taught that your words and actions will be used to judge you (Matt. 12:33–37). Since your actions reveal what you are inside, then this is the way that you'll be judged. Just as a good tree bears good fruit and a bad tree bears bad fruit, Christians honor God by their conduct, and the unsaved don't. The Lord taught that your words are especially revealing of your character. What do your words say about your love for God and others? Complaining, lying, slandering, cursing, and telling dirty jokes don't show your love for God or other people. Conversation dominated by these things raises serious questions about your relationship with the Lord.

The Lord Jesus added an important explanation to these lessons (12:38–50). Even though right conduct reveals right character most of the time, it's possible for people to pretend. Good outward conduct can never replace being a child of God by faith in Christ. The scribes and the Pharisees told Jesus that all they wanted was to see a miracle that would really convince them of His character. They were not telling the truth; He had just performed a miracle. They were only pretending to be interested. Jesus told them that they didn't deserve a miracle. He explained that the miracle of His coming Resurrection would be proof enough to convince them of who He really was—their God and their Savior.

Pretending to be interested in Christ is a dangerous thing. If you don't have true Christian character that comes from genuine faith in Christ, then trust Him now. Bible reading, praying, going to church, and listening to sermons will do you no good if you aren't truly a Christian. If you've been pretending to be a Christian for some time, admit it. You should stop pretending and accept Christ as your Savior now.

The Jews of Jesus's day were very moral people. Many of them tried to avoid committing sins against others and God. Jesus warned them that good living is not enough. He told a story about a man who was freed from a demon and tried to live a good life. When the demon came back, the man had no power to resist him. A person who obeys God's law but doesn't know God is in a hopeless condition. He needs to repent of his sins and trust Christ. No one can do enough good or obey enough of God's law to pay for his own sins. Only Christ can save.

"Even so every good tree bringeth forth good fruit; but a corrupt tree bringeth forth evil fruit" (Matt. 7:17).

90

Satan and to wrench from Satan's grasp a person enslaved by evil.

The Pharisees' opposition to Christ (12:30–32). Summarizing, Jesus turned from refuting the Pharisees to directly accusing them. He asserted that someone who does nothing to assist Him in His work is as bad as an opponent. For further illustration, we could say that he who does not contribute to the harvest may as well be destroying the crop. Since a passive attitude must be considered antagonism, where did that leave the Pharisees, who were actively opposing him?

To actively oppose the work of the Holy Spirit is dangerous indeed. But the breadth of God's forgiveness is remarkable. All kinds of sin and blasphemy fall within the boundaries of what God is willing to for-give. Even those who at times unwittingly opposed the Lord Jesus could be forgiven. However, anyone vigorously slandering work obviously done in the power of the Holy Spirit is guilty of the sin of blasphemy and can have no hope of forgiveness. The Spirit of God is the One Who brings conviction. Anyone ascribing His works to Satan will never respond to conviction.

Your students should understand that perceiving who has and who has not committed the unpardonable sin is impossible for anyone who lacks omniscience. Only God knows who has committed it. Therefore, the believer should always persist in praying for and witnessing to the unsaved, even if he thinks his efforts are to no avail. Believer have often been surprised by the sudden conversion of a person who seemed to be one of the church's worst enemies.

The final thing Jesus warned against in this passage is the wrong idea that having right family relationships is more important than being a faithful Christian. Being kind to your brothers and sisters is important. Obeying your parents is good. But you may be the best son or daughter or the best sister or brother and still be lost. You must have a right relationship with Christ. Even if your family opposes Christ, the Lord must still come first. You must obey Him and love Him above all others. If family members who are not Christians reject you, remember that other Christians are spiritual brothers and sisters to you.

What You Do Speaks Louder than What You Say

What you think about God, others, and yourself will become clear by the way you act. The things you do may not always reveal what you are, but they usually will. Christ's conduct revealed His character. He taught that an unsaved person's words and actions will be so consistent with his character that God will judge him by those things. What does your conduct say about your relationship with Christ? The way you wear your hair, the way you dress, the way you talk, and the way you act toward those in authority over you indicate how you think. God will help you reveal Christian character if you really have it.

Do You Remember?

1. What effects of demon possession were evident in the man that Christ healed? _____
   He was blind and mute.

2. By whose authority did the scribes and Pharisees say Jesus cast out the demon? _____
   Beelzebub, the prince of demons

3. What four things mentioned in this passage cannot be divided against themselves and stand? _____
   a kingdom, a city, a house, and Satan

4. What must happen before a strong man's house can be robbed? _____
   The strong man must be bound.

5. By whose power did Jesus claim to be casting out demons? *the Holy Spirit's*

6. What sin can never be forgiven? *blasphemy against the Holy Spirit*

7. What will each person have to give account of in the day of judgment? *every idle word*

8. Who did Jesus say would rise up in judgment against the men of His generation? _____
   the queen of the south and the people of Nineveh

9. Who caused the queen of the south and the men of Nineveh to turn to the Lord? _____
   Solomon shared wisdom with the queen of the south, and Jonah preached to the people of Nineveh.

10. Who did Christ say were His mother and brothers? _____
    His disciples; those who do the Father's will

91

Blasphemy against the Holy Spirit is often and appropriately called the unpardonable sin. It is not a sin that a Christian can commit. There is no sin that a Christian can commit that cannot be forgiven by the Father, who sent His Son to die for the believer's sins.

II. Our Conduct Will Be Our Judge (Matt. 12:33–42)

After proving that His conduct was evidence of His character, the Lord proceeded to show that the Pharisees' conduct evidenced their character as well. He began by establishing this principle of nature: A healthy, well-cultivated tree bears good fruit, but a sick, poorly-cultivated tree bears bad fruit. Just as fruit is a sure sign of the health of a tree, a person's conduct will reflect his spiritual condition and his character.

The Pharisees' evil words (12:33–37). Moving beyond the general principle, the Lord asserted that foolish, wicked words could be expected from the Pharisees since their hearts were wicked. No matter how hard someone tries, his words will ultimately reveal the way he is inside. This is so consistently true that the Lord will use a person's idle conversation as evidence at the judgment.

The context indicates that this evidence will judge the unsaved. A Christian is not consigned to eternal punishment, or any punishment, on the basis of his words and actions. His judgment was taken by Christ on the cross. On the basis of the imputed righteousness of Christ, the believer is assured of eternal life.

The believer should be careful about his words. James writes that the control of the tongue is a sure sign of the maturity of a believer's faith (3:2). A believer should expect chastening from God if he consistently sins with his words.

The Pharisees' evil wishes (12:38–42). In response to Christ's strong rebuke, some Pharisees and scribes asked Him to give them a sign that He was truly the Anointed One of God. This hypocritical request covered the scribes' and Pharisees' insincerity. Jesus had just performed a remarkable miracle, which they had rejected outright. Why should He perform more miracles for people whose hearts were hardened against the truth of His character and work? Jesus called them a wicked and adulterous generation, stripping them of their pretense, and told them that the only sign they would receive was the sign of the prophet Jonah. Just as Jonah was three days and three nights inside the big fish, so the Lord would be three days and three nights in the grave before His Resurrection. The Pharisees' need was repentance and faith in the resurrected Christ, not more miracles.

To emphasize His point, the Lord reminded the Pharisees of two examples in the Old Testament—the inhabitants of Nineveh, who repented when Jonah preached, and the queen of the south (the queen of Sheba), who came to hear the teaching of Solomon. The message of God from mere humans was enough to bring a response from these people. Certainly that message from the Son of God should be enough for the Pharisees. Jesus warned that the repentance of these characters from the Old Testament would be evidence against them at the judgment.

These verses need not be construed to mean that the Ninevites and the queen of the south will actually speak at the Great White Throne Judgment. The scriptural record of their repentance will cry out against the unrepentant generation of Jesus's day. Jesus's message was that a hypocritical claim to religious interest was no substitute for true Christian character through regeneration and sanctification.

III. Conduct Cannot Replace Christian Character (Matt. 12:43–50)

Failure of reformation (12:43–45). Alluding to His miracle, the Lord taught the uselessness of moral self-improvement as compared to the possession of Christian character. This is important because people may appear to behave well, but their character is actually reprehensible in the sight of God. Empty adherence to laws was not enough to please God. This was the great error of Jesus's generation.

This emphasis on good moral conduct is also the great error of many of the families from which your students come. They are good, moral people who do not know Christ as their Savior from sin and judgment.

The Lord used the hypothetical example of a man freed from demon possession, an obvious reference to His miracle. After leaving the man, the demon wandered, trying but failing to find a new person to indwell. He returned to the man he originally indwelt, to find the man's life clean and orderly, *decorated* ("garnished") with good conduct. The cleanliness could not prevent the re-entrance of the demon. He even took seven other demons with him to indwell the man, and the man was worse off than he had been in the first place. The man's deliverance and consequent moral reformation were not enough to free him from spiritual bondage. Reforming oneself can never take the place of regeneration and sanctification.

Failure of relationship (12:46–50). While Jesus was still speaking, His mother and brothers came to speak to Him. Their appearance provided an opportunity for Jesus to make a final point about alternatives to Christian character. Not even His own blood relatives could count on that relationship to take the place of Christian character. This incident implies that Jesus's family was not sympathetic to His mission, though later they became so.

These subtle ploys are the same that those who do not know the Lord have always used. Some of your students may fit the pattern. Warn them about false piety—pretending to be rightly related to God when they are not. Encourage them to see past the humanly good things in the lives of unsaved friends and neighbors and to see in these people a need for Christ. A Christian's sense of obligation to the lost can disappear if he does not look past the outward appearances that others present.

Jesus asserted that His disciples were closer to Him than His own family. Those who do the will of God are Christ's true family. Christ was not rejecting His natural

Jewish life has traditionally been punctuated by many festive activities and holy days. To Gentiles these celebrations may seem somewhat confusing. But to understand the earthly ministry of Jesus Christ, you need to understand Jewish culture, including the holy days. Several holy days—the Passover, the Feast of Unleavened Bread, Pentecost, the Feast of Tabernacles, and the Feast of Dedication—are directly mentioned or alluded to in the Gospel accounts. Other holy days—the Feast of Firstfruits, the Feast of Trumpets (Rosh Hashanah), the Day of Atonement, Purim, and Jubilee—are not directly mentioned in connection with Christ's earthly ministry. The chart on the next page explains the significance of the holy days mentioned in the Gospels.

The most important holy day to the Jews was their weekly holy day, the Sabbath. The word *sabbath* means "rest." When God rested on the seventh day of the Creation week, He established the biblical pattern for a "day of rest" for His creation. The Sabbath was instituted later as a requirement for Israel (Exod. 20:8; 31:13, 17). The weekly Sabbath, the seventh day (Saturday), was to be devoted to the Lord. No work was to be done (Exod. 20:10). Breaking the Sabbath was a serious offense (Num. 15:32–36; Neh. 13:15–22).

During the four centuries between the Old and New Testaments, Jewish rabbis expanded the Sabbath laws. Their interpretations and applications were imposed on the people of Israel. By the time of Christ, these extrabiblical rules held the people in bondage. Their applications went beyond the Bible but were considered just as binding as the Bible. The Jewish rabbis lost the spirit and intent of God's laws by focusing on their own specific interpretations. Jesus came into constant conflict with them, particularly over their Sabbath rules. He accused them by quoting the prophet Isaiah, "But in vain they do worship me, teaching for doctrines the commandments of men" (Matt. 15:9).

It appears that Jesus purposely provoked the Jewish leaders by His activities on the Sabbath in order to show that they had gone beyond the Bible in their strictness. He defended His disciples for plucking and eating grain on the Sabbath (Matt. 12:1–8). On the Sabbath he healed a man with a withered hand (Matt. 12:10–13), a man with dropsy (Luke 14:1–6), a blind man (John 9:1–41), and an infirm man (John 5:1–18), which caused another conflict because the man "unlawfully" carried his bed at Christ's command.

The Pharisees were so bent on keeping Sabbath laws that even the wonderful restoration to health was disdained, but Jesus argued, "The sabbath was made for man, and not man for the sabbath" (Mark 2:27).

The shofar, made from the horn of a ram or ibex, was not a musical instrument used to accompany singing, but was blown by the priest during a festival to signal when the people were to worship.

family; He was merely showing that the basis for acceptance into the family of God is salvation and that His working in Christians after salvation allows them to develop the Christian character for which there is no substitute. Being part of a physical family or racial group never entitles anyone to a special relationship to God. The Jews of Christ's time were convinced that being descendants of Abraham qualified them for special privileges (John 8:39). They failed to understand that a true child of Abraham was a person who had trusted in the Lord by faith, as had Abraham.

Though upright conduct should be characteristic of a true Christian, it is no substitute for salvation. The Jewish leaders may have shown an outward interest in religion, sought to reform themselves morally, and had a great family heritage, but all this was to no avail without faith in Christ and consequent regeneration.

ANNUAL HOLY DAYS MENTIONED IN THE GOSPELS			
Holy Days	**Relation to Christ's Life**	**Purpose**	**Old Testament Basis**
Passover (April)	Three Passovers are mentioned in Christ's ministry (John 2:13; 6:4;11:55). Both temple cleansings were at Passover time. The Passion week occurred during the week of Passover. A large portion of John's Gospel is set during Passover (John 12–20).	To commemorate the Exodus from Egypt (also symbolic of Christ's sacrifice as mentioned in 1 Cor. 5:7)	Exod. 12:1–20 Lev. 23:5–8
Feast of Unleavened Bread (April)	The Last Supper was during the Feast of Unleavened Bread (Matt. 26:17; Mark 14:1; Luke 22:1), which was eaten on the evening of the day on which the Passover week began. Because Jews were required to attend the Feast of Unleavened Bread and Passover, many Jews were in Jerusalem at the time of Christ's death and Resurrection.	To commemorate the Exodus from Egypt, to recall the hastiness of the departure (i.e., no time for the bread to be leavened and rise)	Exod. 12:15–20
Feast of Weeks or Pentecost (June)	Before His ascension, Christ commanded His disciples, "Tarry ye in the city of Jerusalem, until ye be endued with power from on high" (Luke 24:49). After about ten days, the Holy Spirit came down on Pentecost (Acts 2:1–47). The word *pentecost* means "fifty" in Greek (i.e., fifty days after Passover). The many Jews in Jerusalem for Pentecost heard Peter's initial preaching of the gospel.	To mark the end of the harvest; to recognize God as the giver of the harvest	Lev. 23:15–21
Feast of Tabernacles or Booths (October)	The events in John 7 (and possibly John 8:3–11) took place during this feast. On the last day of the feast, Jesus boldly presented Himself to the Jews.	To commemorate the wilderness wanderings by living in booths around Jerusalem	Lev. 23:33–44
Hanukkah or Feast of Dedication (December)	John 10:22 records Christ's words given at this time in Jerusalem. Hanukkah is also known as the Feast of Lights because the Jews celebrate by lighting lamps and candles in their homes.	To commemorate the cleansing of the temple by the Jews in 165 BC after it had been defiled by a Seleucid king; a celebration of Jewish determination and survival	(No Old Testament basis, since it started during the period between the Old and New Testaments)

93

Burr was born into a highly respected family in New England. His father was the president of the college that is now Princeton University. His grandfather was Jonathan Edwards, the famous American preacher and theologian.

With this background, Burr went to college and became a successful lawyer, eventually serving as attorney general of New York. Later he was elected to the United States Senate and the vice-presidency. In 1804 he ran for the governorship of New York but lost due to the opposition of the powerful New York politician Alexander Hamilton (the man whose image is on the U.S. ten-dollar bill). Hamilton insulted Burr during the campaign, so Burr challenged him to a duel and killed him.

Burr then planned to found his own empire, stretching from the Ohio River to Mexico. His plans were found out, and he was tried for treason. He was not convicted, but he was never trusted again. Burr left the United States and traveled in Europe. When he returned, he suffered through the deaths of his grandson and daughter. At the age of seventy-seven he married again, only to be divorced on the day of his death. Aaron Burr's proud, ambitious character led to foolish actions that ruined his life.

✳ Extra Activities

Questions and answers: A good way to stimulate interest as you introduce this lesson is to ask questions that your students have difficulty answering but that you will answer in the lesson.

a. Can a person be possessed by more than one demon at a time?
Yes, Christ's parable in Matt. 12:43–45 speaks of seven demons possessing one man.

b. Can an unsaved person commit a sin for which he can never be forgiven?
yes, the sin of blasphemy against the Holy Spirit

c. What Old Testament incident is a picture of the death, burial, and Resurrection of Christ?
Jonah being swallowed by the fish for three days and nights

d. How can the kingdom of God come to a person today?
in the person of the Lord Jesus Christ (Matt. 12:28)

Storytelling: Use the following story to teach that conduct reveals character.

Aaron Burr was a famous American. He fought in the War for Independence and became vice president of the United States under Thomas Jefferson. Although he was a successful politician, his life was tragically ruined because of his bad character.

Lesson 26
Christ's Care

THEME	Christ's Care
SCRIPTURE	John 10:1–42
MEMORY WORK	John 10:10–11

 ## Approach to the Lesson

Theme: God has been good to all people. He sends rain on the just and the unjust. He provides food for everybody, gives them families, and watches out for their welfare. Theologians call this equal treatment "common grace." It reflects the nature of God. Its purpose is expressed in Romans 2:4—"Or despisest thou the riches of his goodness and forbearance and long-suffering; not knowing that the goodness of God leadeth thee to repentance?" People who have experienced the ways God takes care of them should turn to Christ as their Savior.

Christians enjoy the special care of Christ. This care goes far beyond common grace. As their Shepherd, the Lord protects, guides, and nourishes believers. He will never fail in these responsibilities.

Rationale: Many of your students may come from broken homes and need reassurance that someone cares about them. Even those who come from intact families may feel unloved, while others simply feel excluded by their classmates. All these should find the truths in this lesson encouraging.

Objectives

KNOWLEDGE (concepts students need to grasp)	the first-century practice of shepherding, from which the analogy of Christ's care is taken
	the unity of the Father and the Son
APPLICATION (principles students should put into practice)	We must accept Christ's care by being saved and by seeking Him for grace.
	We should let Christ be our guide, the One we look to in prayer during times of decision.
	Christ's care for us is constant, in spite of our weaknesses and failures.

Bible Expressions to Understand

verily—truly
door—opening into a sheepfold
porter—doorkeeper
hireling—one who is hired or paid wages to work
blasphemy—speaking evil of God

Our Lord's teaching about His care for us is based on the common Palestinian experience of shepherding. But the sight of sheep grazing on a hillside under the care of a concerned shepherd is unfamiliar to many Christians today. We may understand dairy farming or cattle ranching, but usually not sheep raising. A shepherd in the Middle East is close to his sheep; he loves them and cares for them. He leads them to pastures where they can find food. The sheep know their shepherd, and when he calls them or whistles to them, they follow him.

John 10 discusses Christ's care for believers. He calls Himself the "door of the sheep" as well as the "good shepherd." His sheep are people who are saved. They continually follow their Shepherd. Elsewhere in Scripture (Heb. 13:20; 1 Pet. 5:3–4) Jesus is called "that great shepherd of the sheep" and "the chief Shepherd," while believers are referred to as "the flock." As you study this lesson, ask yourself some questions: Am I really in Christ's flock? Does my life truly show that I am listening to His voice and following Him? Am I confident in my Shepherd's care?

What is a sheepfold? Today farmers and ranchers almost always use barbed wire to keep their cattle fenced in, but in Bible times there were no barbed-wire fences. There was very little wood for fencing, but one natural resource was abundant—rocks. So the fences were built of stone. The stone walls formed an enclosure into which the sheep were herded at night to be protected from wild animals. The only entrance was an opening a few feet wide at one end of the sheepfold. The shepherd would sit or lie down across that entrance. To get to the sheep, a wild animal or robber would have to either disturb the shepherd or climb over the wall.

Background: The two major discourses in John 10 did not occur at the same time. The first (10:1–21) was presented in approximately October or November of AD 29, along with the discourses in chapters 7–9. The second (10:22–42) was presented about two months later. John recorded them together because the topics are similar—the Lord's care for His people.

 ### The Lesson

The Lord used an illustration of a shepherd and a sheepfold to serve as the basis for His instruction. The sheepfold was usually a large area under the open sky enclosed by stone walls. In the larger folds a doorkeeper, or porter, watched the single entrance. Only the shepherd was allowed to enter through the door. Anyone entering another way was automatically viewed as a thief or a robber. The term *thief* suggests a sneak thief. The term *robber* implies that the thief would have no aversion to violence if it served his ends.

The intimacy between an oriental shepherd and his sheep was remarkable. The shepherd had a name for each of his sheep, and the sheep would follow him because they recognized his voice. The sheep would run from someone who was not their shepherd if he tried to lead them. Using this brief description of the relationship of sheep to their shepherd, the Lord Jesus began to discuss His care for His people.

The imagery of the Shepherd's care for His sheep speaks volumes to the believer about the Lord's care for him. Our God is holy. He is transcendent, or above

Anyone who tried to enter the fold except through the opening was immediately considered "a thief and a robber."

As the Shepherd, Christ is also the Door into the sheepfold. No one can come into Christ's flock without first believing in Him. Any attempt to come into the flock another way is pointless. But people try anyway. The Jews of Christ's day rejected Him. They wanted to be thought of as part of God's flock, but they weren't. Today false teachers abound. Sometimes they teach that there's another way to God besides Christ. They teach falsely that "we're all God's children" or that "all religions lead us to God" (John 8:44; 14:6). They say that salvation means being delivered from a poor self-image or that you can be saved by doing good works. Cultists, such as the Jehovah's Witnesses and Mormons, present an incomplete Christ tacked on to their heresies in order to appear Christian to their would-be converts. In all this confusion do not be disturbed. Jesus Christ is the only Shepherd, and He is the only Door. Listen only to His Word.

Let's go back to the hillside, where the sheep innocently graze beneath the deep blue sky. Imagine that suddenly a wolf darts into the flock. Immediately the shepherd and his hired hands are alert to trouble. The wolf seizes a small lamb. The men have only their clubs. Will they attack the wolf at close range, risking their own lives, or will they let it have its prey? While the hired hands hesitate, the shepherd races toward the wolf. He clubs it again and again until it drops the lamb and runs away, limping and yelping. The shepherd takes the lamb into his

There are many parallels between the way a shepherd leads and protects a flock of sheep and the way Christ relates to His followers. How many can you list?

arms to soothe it and examine the wounds. As he looks up from the lamb's now blood-stained wool, the hired hands approach. The shepherd looks at them with scorn for their failure to help. But what would you expect? Only their jobs were at stake—they are only hirelings. The shepherd had much more at stake—these sheep are his own!

A good shepherd will care for his sheep. He feeds and leads, as the "Shepherd Psalm" (Ps. 23), poetically points out. A good shepherd follows David's example of protecting the sheep from attackers (1 Sam. 17:34–35). A good shepherd will also search for a lost sheep (Luke 15:4). Christ in every way fulfills this model. He doesn't flee from danger but gives His life for the sheep (John 10:11–18). He voluntarily gave His life for us. What a demonstration of His love and care! What assurance this gives us that our living Shepherd will "never leave . . . nor forsake" us (Heb. 13:5). He Who went to such an extent to save us will surely go to any extent to care for us.

You'll face some challenges in the days ahead. Your parents have provided your needs so far, but soon you'll be on your own. You'll be buying your own food and clothing. You'll be making your own decisions and living with the results. You'll have to get a job and hang on to it. You'll have to protect your own family from harm. It may sound exciting, and it should; but how are you going to do it?

Christ will take care of you. Stay close to Him! He's interested in your well-being. He wants to fulfill His purpose for your life. He'll help you all along

95

His people. We should worship Him and fear Him. But He is always present with us. The Lord Jesus, wanting our fellowship, promises to sustain us by His grace as we commune with Him.

I. Acceptance of Christ's Care (John 10:7–10)

Christians gain great benefits by accepting Christ's care and protection.

Its beginning. Jesus describes Himself as the Door of the sheepfold. He is the way a sheep enters into protection. If anyone enters the fold through the Door, he will be saved. Then he can find pasture. Christ's care begins at the moment of salvation.

Its benefits. A believer under Christ's protection is safe from thieves and robbers and the harm they do. The thieves and robbers represent false teachers. This is likely

an allusion to the incident in John 9, when the Pharisees rejected Christ even after He had proved His deity by healing a man born blind.

One of the greatest single threats to anyone's spiritual well-being is false teaching. A person who otherwise might have realized his need of Christ often becomes convinced he does not need the Lord's salvation because of the misleading words of some deceiver. The instruction is particularly dangerous because it comes in the guise of religious truth. The false premise that "since it is religion, it is true" often leads many into believing false teachers.

Christ said, "I am come that they might have life, and that they might have it more abundantly" (10:10). What is this abundant life? When a person is saved, his outward

circumstances do not necessarily change. His family will stay the same, and his job will probably not change. However, the man *himself* changes. His life improves in proportion to his ability to respond properly to the pressures on him. Running from circumstances has never been the answer to problems. A change of environment may help, but it will not solve all the problems. Christ's gift of abundant life is the answer. This will determine the capacity to rejoice in adversity, to excel in hard times, to see the opportunity in opposition, and to reflect the glory of Christ to others. One who has an abundant life is an overcomer in the spiritual realm. (The book of Revelation uses this idea repeatedly, e.g., "He that overcometh shall inherit all things" [21:7].)

Christ's life, teaching, death, burial, Resurrection, and ministry at the right hand of the Father are all for the purpose of glorifying the Father and making it possible for us to glorify God and in the process enjoy an abundant life. The believer must draw constantly on the grace of Christ to know the abundance of forgiveness, strength, and guidance that only He can give.

If you want to have abundant life and be an overcomer, develop the habit of seeking God in prayer all the time. "Pray without ceasing" (1 Thess. 5:17).

II. Extent of Christ's Care (John 10:11–21)

The care which Christians enjoy is limitless and includes all believers.

Its limits. Christ's self-sacrifice verifies that there are no limits to His willingness to care for His sheep. He repeatedly asserted that He would lay down His life for the sheep (10:11, 15, 17–18). Paul had a similar thought about God the Father: "He that spared not his own Son, but delivered him up for us all, how shall he not with him also freely give us all things?" (Rom. 8:32)

(John 10:7–42)
I. Acceptance of Christ's care (7–10)
   A. Its beginning
   B. Its benefits
II. Extent of Christ's care (11–21)
   A. Its limits
   B. Its inclusiveness
III. Permanence of Christ's care (22–42)

If Christ has already given His life for believers, what would cause Him to hold back His care in any degree?

Christ expressed the same idea negatively in the example of the hireling. A hireling was one who cared for the sheep strictly for money and was unwilling to take risks to protect and provide for them. His level of commitment was significantly less than the shepherd's. Jesus asserted that He was not a hireling but a true shepherd. Again, He was probably alluding to false teachers.

Not only are there no limits to the steps Christ will take to take care of His people, but what He does do will be perfect. The Lord stated, "I am the good shepherd, and know my sheep, and am known of mine" (10:14). Before our salvation the Lord made us and cared for us in common grace. He has had plenty of experience with us, and He knows us perfectly. As His knowledge is complete, so is His care. His sheep can testify that He never fails.

The basis of this limitless care is Christ's knowledge of the Father. Jesus said, "As the Father knoweth me, even so know I the Father: and I lay down my life for the sheep" (10:15). Christ's complete dedication to taking care of Christians is merely a reflection of the character of the heavenly Father in Christ. He knows what the Father wants, and He intends to do the Father's will and be the "express image" of the Father (Heb. 1:3). Just as it is the nature of the Father to care for the saints, so it is the nature of Christ.

Because of Christ's conformity to the will and nature of God, a great bond of love exists between the Father and the Son. Part of the will of God for Christ was His death and His Resurrection (10:17–18). The Resurrection is a logical truth to mention when discussing the ongoing care of Christ for His sheep. A dead shepherd cannot do much protecting, providing, or guiding.

Its inclusiveness. One passing statement by Christ gives us an answer to the question of who's included. He said, "And other sheep I have, which are not of this fold: them also I must bring, and they shall hear my voice; and there shall be one fold, and one shepherd" (10:16). Christ's vision was not limited to His disciples, or even to His nation. The Great Commission tells in specific terms the extent to which Christ extends His tireless care—to all those in the world who will believe.

the way—in every phase of your life. He'll help you achieve His goals for you, and He'll meet your needs. If you wander from the path, He'll be there to pull you back. If you're in danger, He'll protect you. He's the Good Shepherd.

You may ask, "For how long will He take care of me?" You are secure forever in your Shepherd's care. Christ said, "And I give unto them eternal life; and they shall never perish, neither shall any man pluck them out of my hand. My Father, which gave them me, is greater than all; and no man is able to pluck them out of my Father's hand" (John 10:28–29).

Have you ever gone to an amusement park, football stadium, or another crowded place and worried that you would get separated from the person you came with? Some Christians feel just like that even though they've been saved. They fear that the Lord is going to leave them. They may even imagine that

He has left them. But it's all in their imagination, or perhaps Satan is planting seeds of doubt. Scripture promises that Christ "will never leave thee, nor forsake thee" (Heb. 13:5).

Christ's care for you is evident in His receiving, protecting, and keeping you. He receives you into the fold by His sacrificial death on the cross. He protects you from spiritual harm by fighting off enemies. He keeps you in the fold securely. You never have to wonder if God cares because "He that spared not his own Son, but delivered him up for us all, how shall he not with him also freely give us all things?" (Rom. 8:32)

Do You Remember?

1. When someone tried to climb over the stone wall of the sheepfold rather than entering through the door, what was he considered? _____
   a thief and a robber

2. What does John 10:4 say about how sheep respond to the Shepherd's voice? _____
   The sheep follow Him because they know His voice.

3. What did Jesus mean when He said He was the "door of the sheep" (10:7–9)? _____
   He is the only way into the flock; a person has to be saved through Christ to be in God's flock.

4. Which verse points out that Christ's death was voluntary? *John 10:18* _____

5. What person is the good shepherd contrasted with? *the hireling* _____

6. What two other passages mentioned in the lesson call Christ a shepherd? _____
   great shepherd (Heb.13:20); chief Shepherd (1 Pet. 5:4)

7. In what three ways is Christ's care for us demonstrated? _____
   He receives us, protects us, and keeps us.

96

The Jewish leaders had great difficulty with Christ's words. They debated among themselves how they should respond. They should have seen themselves as part of the group that Christ was willing to shepherd, but for the most part they did not.

III. Permanence of Christ's Care (John 10:22–42)

Jesus's deity means that His care for us will never cease.

While at the Feast of Dedication in December, Jesus entered the temple and was confronted by the leaders of the Jews. They wanted to know if He was the Christ. He reproved them for refusing to believe despite His many works. They had the evidence they needed; their problem was a matter of the will. They refused to believe

and manifest that belief by works because they were not Christ's sheep. Those who are prove it by obeying His commands (10:26–27). The verbs for *hearing* and *following* in Greek are in the present tense, suggesting a continual hearing and following, a pattern of life. This pattern comes from saving faith in Christ.

These verses provide a serious reminder about the emptiness of profession without works. A profession of faith in Christ is not enough to substantiate your faith before others. Good works must flow from a regenerated heart. Scripture teaches, "For we are his workmanship, created in Christ Jesus unto good works, which God hath before ordained that we should walk in them" (Eph. 2:10). Ours is an age of empty profession. Works do not save a person, but they do give evidence that a person is saved. The lack of works raises serious questions about a person's spirituality and even his salvation.

The believer's works show that he is under Christ's care. But what is the assurance that this care is permanent? Christ's oneness with the Father guarantees permanent care for the Christian (10:28–30). Eternal life comes to all who have exercised saving faith. None who have ever received eternal life can perish. They are safe in Christ's hand. This provision of safety is not only the work of Christ; but also of the Father, Who holds the believer in His hand (10:29). The Father and the Son are one in this endeavor of eternal preservation of the believer. Jesus was not saying that the Father and He were the same person in the Godhead but that they had the same purpose. No one can ever thwart the purpose of God to preserve His people from condemnation.

When the Lord claimed unity with the Father in purpose and character, the Jews were ready to stone him. Apparently they had picked up rocks somewhere else and brought them into Solomon's porch in the temple. These people had decided not to wait for due process of their own law but to become judges and executioners on the spot.

> The deity of Christ has always been a watershed doctrine for false teachers. They will not agree that Jesus really is God. No one who professes Christ as Savior but believes only in a human Jesus is really saved. Mention to your students that whenever they are witnessing to someone who has been influenced by a cult, they can simplify the discussion by focusing on the doctrine of Christ. Cults usually have many strange teachings, but the central problem is what the cult teaches about Him.

The Lord replied with utter courage, asking them for what good work they were going to kill Him. When they answered that Jesus had made Himself God, He replied with Psalm 82:6, in which Israel's judges are called gods because of the authority they had from God. He reasoned that if they were called gods, it certainly was not blasphemous for Him to call Himself the Son of God (10:34–36). He asserted that the Old Testament Scriptures could not be broken or incorrect.

Our Lord's argument did not end there, however. He went on to say that He, of all people, had the right to claim He was the Son of God because He was set apart by God and sent into the world. Further, His works had proved He was sent from the Father, that He was in the Father, and that the Father was in Him. Again they tried to take Him, but He escaped and crossed the Jordan River into the area where John had first preached. Many came to Him and believed, remembering all that John the Baptist had preached about Him (10:36–42).

Extra Activities

Discussion: If a professing Christian becomes a member of a cult such as the Jehovah's Witnesses, is he truly saved?

In most cases he is not. John 10:4–5 points out that the sheep "know his voice" and that "a stranger will they not follow, but will flee from him." (See also 1 John 2:19.) This means that a professing Christian who leaves the truth and follows the darkness of a cult is probably not saved. He may have "professed Christ," but he did not "possess Christ." It is conceivable that a born-again person might be caught up in a cult simply because he is ignorant of what the Bible teaches. However, when the truth of the Bible is presented to him, he will respond because he will recognize the voice of the Master in its pages.

An interesting verse is Titus 1:16— "They profess that they know God; but in works they deny him." Which speaks louder, the life or the mouth? Scripture is clear that a person who lives continually in sin and does not respond to the voice of the Good Shepherd is not saved (Matt. 7:21–23; Luke 6:46; 1 Cor. 6:9–10; 1 John 3:6, 9). At the same time, Scripture gives great as-surance to those who know Christ and obey His Word that their souls are secure in the hands of the Good Shepherd (John 10; Romans 8:38–39).

Lecture: The deity of Christ is the cardinal doctrine of Christianity because Christianity is Christ. This lesson emphasizes that Christ claims to be one with the Father. Use the following passages to show your students that Christ is God.

In John 20:28–29 Christ accepts Thomas's proclamation, "My Lord and my God." Paul tells us in Titus 2:13 of the "appearing of the great God and our Saviour [literally, 'our great God and Savior'] Jesus Christ." In Hebrews 1:8, God the Father refers to His Son as "God." John 1 speaks of Christ as God coming in the flesh.

Lesson 27
Prayer

THEME	Prayer
SCRIPTURE	Luke 11:1–13
MEMORY WORK	Luke 11:9–10

 Approach to the Lesson

Theme: Communicating with God is essential for a Christian's growth in grace and fruitfulness. Prayer offers the believer an opportunity for private praise, petition, and faith-filled persistence. The loving Father inclines His ear toward His children. No request surpasses His powers. He is always just yet merciful, kind but firm. He desires the best for His children and will use blessings or trials to strengthen them. "Every good gift and every perfect gift is from above" (James 1:17).

Rationale: No area of the Christian life is more sorely neglected, in young people and in adults, than prayer. Keep this lesson practical; constantly remind your students that they should be putting these truths to work daily.

Background: Throughout His ministry, the Lord encouraged His disciples to pray. Prayer was a major topic in His teaching. In the Sermon on the Mount, in the parable of the unjust judge, and in many other teachings, He developed the specifics of the doctrine of prayer. The single most concentrated passage of instruction on prayer in the Gospels is Luke 11:1–13. Nearly everything Jesus taught elsewhere about prayer is compactly presented here.

 The Lesson

I. A Pattern for Prayer (Luke 11:1–4)

The "Lord's Prayer" provides the themes our prayers ought to return to time and time again. The opening verse gives the reason Jesus presented this pattern for prayer. One of the disciples requested instruction because the disciples had seen Jesus praying, and they had heard about John the Baptist's teaching his disciples how to pray.

Example is the strongest human means of exciting interest. If we are not con-

cerned enough to be involved personally and directly in a Christian activity, how can we expect our students to be?

Who to pray to. The pattern for prayer begins by directly addressing God as "our Father which art in heaven." This underscores the importance of the One we are praying to. Only Christians can legitimately call God their Father. A closeness of fellowship is assumed in this opening address. Such intimacy, however, is not incompatible with reverence. Our Father is in heaven. He is our superior. He is not our equal in His authority or His person. All of us naturally speak differently to people we respect because of their position or character. The same should be true in our prayers.

Being too casual in prayer is wrong. God is not our good buddy. He is our heavenly Father with Whom we have intimate fellowship, but He is to be respected and worshipped. Many of your students do not understand the concept of reverence. In their thinking, everyone should be treated alike. Friends, parents, teachers, and pastors all are spoken to the same way. This attitude may manifest itself even in their prayers. Help your students understand that one of the ways to show respect for others is the way we talk to them. This is also true in our relationship with God. (Lev. 19:32; Rom. 13:7; Heb. 12:28–29.)

What to pray for. The first three petitions, which all contain the pronoun *thy,* are God-focused. The other four petitions are man-focused and contain the pronoun *us.*

God's goals. To pray that God's name would be hallowed (11:2) is to pray that others will view God as holy. Helping people have the right perspective of God is part of our responsibility. When a pro-

fessing Christian lives a sinful life, others may think that the person's God expects no more of him and overlooks his sin. It is tragic for the world to think of God as an old man in a white robe, overlooking every injustice and smiling at every act of barbarism. To pray "hallowed be thy name" is to consecrate ourselves to holy living and to express the hope that other believers will live that way also.

The next two statements should be studied together. Praying for God's kingdom to come is a request that has both a present and a future dimension. The present dimension means we pray for successful evangelism and the edification of believers. The only way for God's kingdom to be evident in the present is for individuals to be born again and to grow in their submission to Christ in every area of their lives. Sanctification is the gradual extension of the rule of God in a person's life until his whole being is in complete subjection to Christ. The future dimension of this request is a prayer for the physical reign of Christ on the earth and for eternity. This desire will be fulfilled during the Millennium and in the eternal state. It is appropriate for the believer to have a forward look, a longing for the better future. One of the ways to gain that perspective is to regularly pray to that end.

A desire to see God's will done on earth as it is in heaven is another request about Christ's dominion. God's will is done in heaven immediately, joyfully, and without a hint of unsubmissiveness. We should pray that the Lord will grant to His people that same spirit of obedience. This request expresses Christians' submission to their Master. Without faith it is impossible to please God. To please the Lord, we must have utter confidence in Him, and we must express that confidence in prayer.

Our needs. The next request (11:3) establishes one of our responsibilities toward material things. God has promised to provide for us materially. He has told us that

Objectives

KNOWLEDGE (concepts students need to grasp)	the essential elements of the Lord's pattern for prayer
	the importance of persistence in prayer
	God's basic attitude in responding to prayer
APPLICATION (principles students should put into practice)	We should follow a pattern in prayer.
	We should persist in prayer.
	We should be reverent in prayer, never addressing God as our equal.
	We should expect answers to prayer on God's terms.

Prayer · L.27

Read: Luke 11:1–13

Memorize: Luke 11:9–10

Bible Expressions to Understand

hallowed—holy; sacred
indebted—owe; be obligated to
importunity—urgent, repeated asking

The small Ohio town had always been home to Jay. Moving to the city three hours away seemed like going to a different world. New friends, a new school, and new problems awaited. Jay's father had sold his business and gone to work for another company. It was a good move for the family, but it led to an unhappy chapter in Jay's life.

The first year away from Chestnut Street and Eastside School wasn't too bad. It was when Jay got into junior high school that the problems started. One day Jay and his friend Steve decided to make a bomb out of gunpowder from some caps, adhesive tape, tissue paper, and a fuse from a firecracker that they had purchased at a neighborhood store. Neither had experience in such things, but they succeeded in putting together what was really nothing more than a large firecracker.

The school building seemed to be a good place to test their workmanship. No one would be in the first-floor restroom, and the echo from the explosion would be heard all over the school. It was. Since this happened before school shootings and terrorism became so commonplace, it was treated as a prank rather than a crime. The principal vowed to expel the culprit. Even though he was terrified by the prospect of being expelled, Jay confessed the next day.

That incident blew over, but others soon followed. Shoplifting, smoking, drinking, and gambling filled the after-school hours. Jay's parents were concerned. His mother faithfully prayed year after year that her son would trust the Lord as his Savior. It seemed that her prayers were not being answered. Not content to pray only that Jay would be saved, she also prayed that the Lord would call him to the ministry.

One night at a Christian camp, Jay listened to other boys his age talk about their love and devotion for Christ. Miraculously, the light of the message of

Jay was obviously headed down the wrong road. What happened to turn him around?

salvation shone into his heart, and he called on the Lord to save him. A year later he enrolled in a Christian college and began training for the ministry. He later went on to serve the Lord as a preacher and teacher in a Christian college, training other young men for the ministry.

This story, which is true except for the names, shows that prayer does make a difference. Prayer can change your parents, your brother, your sister, your friends, and even you. Jesus knew the importance of prayer; He taught His disciples how to pray. One of His longest teachings on prayer is recorded in the passage you read for this lesson.

The first thing He taught was the value of following a pattern when you pray. He gave what is often called the Lord's Prayer or the Model Prayer as an example. That prayer has seven petitions:

(1) Hallowed be thy name.

(2) Thy kingdom come.

we are to work and, in this passage, to pray for our daily bread. *Bread* is used here to represent the things necessary for life. There is a conservatism about this request. It does not read, "Give us day by day our daily wants." One of the great challenges for the believer is to carefully distinguish between what he wants and what he needs. This is not a simple task; there is no easy formula that settles the issue. Faithful prayer seems to be at least a part of the way to avoid extravagance. Making foolish and self-indulgent requests should be inconceivable. Following this pattern also regularly reminds the believer Whom he depends on for his sustenance.

The remaining petitions (11:4) all concern the problem of sin. The first deals with sins already committed. Confession to God

brings cleansing (1 John 1:9). God is ready to forgive. However, that forgiveness depends on the forgiveness we grant others for the offenses they commit against us. This idea is more fully developed in the Sermon on the Mount (Matt. 6:14–15), but it is concisely expressed here.

Next comes a request for protection from future temptation. On the surface, the form of the request seems to suggest that God is in the habit of leading us into temptation. He is not. God cannot be tempted, nor does He tempt anyone (James 1:13). What then does this request mean? It means that we want God, by His grace, to keep us from the enticements of Satan. This is a recognition of our weak human condition. God responds to this humility by granting the request.

The final petition (for deliverance from the evil one) states the same idea positively, asking the Father to rescue us when Satan's assaults do come. We can have confidence that He will keep us from circumstances in which we could not stand against sin (1 Cor. 10:13). Preparation for the attacks of Satan is wise Christian living. This prayer looks beyond the superficial and sees the world as it really is; it appeals to God to help us overcome a world of sin.

II. Persistence in Prayer (Luke 11:5–10)

It is one thing to pray once. It is another thing to keep on praying, especially when you pray for the same thing repeatedly. The Lord's example teaches us that we are right to do this. He tells of a man who has a friend from out of town come to visit him, arriving late at night. The traveler is weary and hungry. The host has no food to give the visitor, so he goes to another friend, asking for three loaves of bread. When awakened from his sleep, the man does not want to help because of the lateness of the hour. The strong bonds of friendship alone are not enough to get the awakened man to respond. However, the importunity of the one requesting gets the desired response. To *importune* is to request help urgently and repeatedly. There is power in importunity. Persistence pays off.

The Lord directly encouraged His disciples to persist in prayer. Jesus describes three scenes to communicate this message. The first is the picture of a man repeatedly asking for something. The second is of a person diligently searching until he finds what he is looking for. The third is of a man knocking on a door until someone finally answers. All the verbs in Luke 11:9 are in the present tense in Greek. This means that the action is continual. The happy conclusion to the asking is receiving. The result of the seeking is finding. The climax to the knocking is having the door opened. What an encouraging end to a long process! Eventually a clear answer will come.

III. The Response to Prayer (Luke 11:11–13)

What can a Christian expect in answer to his prayers? God will answer them, but He has standards by which He governs His answers. One of these is usefulness. If a son asks for bread, the father will not give him a stone. When someone is hungry, a stone is useless. Only food will take care of hunger.

The Lord is also careful never to give us what would harm us. If a son asks for a fish or an egg to eat, a good father would never give him a serpent or a scorpion. Of course, no one in his right mind would ask for a serpent or a scorpion. However, a person could unknowingly or foolishly ask God for something dangerous. The Lord condescends to our need. He will not grant those foolish and dangerous requests.

Finally, Jesus noted that no one can be wiser or more generous than God in responding to requests. It is natural for a father to give his children what is useful and safe. How can we expect anything less of God? The Lord will grant even His very presence by His Spirit when He indwells the believer. Romans 8:9 clearly teaches that He indwells the believer at salvation: "Now if any man have not the Spirit of Christ, he is none of his."

Having the Spirit present in us and our sensing that presence are two different things. We are commanded to be filled with the Spirit (Eph. 5:18). We are to be controlled by Him in every particular. When we submit to His directives in Scripture, we come to know Christ by experience. The great aim of the believer's life is to know Christ in this way. Paul wrote of this aim, "That I may know him, and the power of his resurrection, and the fellowship of his sufferings, being made conformable unto his death" (Phil. 3:10).

A major focus of a believer's prayer life should be to know Christ by experience. Knowing about Christ is not enough. Some of your students do not know Christ by experience in salvation. Others know nothing of Him by experience beyond the point of salvation. A Christian life without the frequent experience of the presence of Christ through His Spirit will quickly become a dry, boring ritual.

(3) Thy will be done.
(4) Give us this day our daily bread.
(5) Forgive us our sins.
(6) Lead us not into temptation.
(7) Deliver us from evil.

These seven petitions make a good outline to follow when we pray. Everything a Christian needs to pray for can fit under one of these requests. The Lord expects us to ask for things specifically, not just to repeat the words of this pattern prayer. But the pattern can help us organize our thoughts.

Notice, too, that Jesus began this prayer by addressing the heavenly Father. Prayer is important because of Who you're talking to, not because you're the one talking. There's no prayer request too small or too difficult to take to God. When you pray with a right attitude, He always hears.

Jesus then told a story of a man who went to a friend's house in the middle of the night to ask him for bread. The friend refused at first because it was so late, but the man kept pleading with him. Finally the friend gave him what he needed. Jesus said that the man gave him the bread because he wouldn't

"Knock, and it shall be opened unto you" (Matt. 7:7).

Our Father which art in heaven,

Hallowed be thy name.

Thy kingdom come.

Thy will be done in earth,

as it is in heaven.

Give us this day our daily bread.

And forgive us our debts,

as we forgive our debtors.

And lead us not into temptation,

but deliver us from evil:

For thine is the kingdom,

and the power, and the glory, for ever.

Amen.

(Matt. 6: 9–13)

quit asking. His persistent asking was more powerful than the difficulties that had to be overcome.

We shouldn't give up after we start praying for something. We're to keep praying until we receive an answer. That may be a long time, but we're still supposed to keep praying.

When was the last time you received an answer to prayer? How long ago was it answered? How long did you pray about it? What is the longest you've ever prayed over a particular request? Your answers to these questions indicate whether your prayer life is healthy.

Conversing with the Lord

Communicating with God is essential if you want to grow as a Christian and be used by God. Prayer provides you an opportunity to praise the Lord for the good things He has done for you. It's also an opportunity to ask for things you need. You can prove to God that you are serious about the things you are asking for by not giving up too soon. Remember, when you ask God for something over and over again, you're not telling Him about something He doesn't know. You're showing Him you believe what He says about persistence.

98

God always responds the right way to prayers. He gives people only what is right for them. Sometimes people don't ask for the right things. We make mistakes, and we don't know everything. The most important thing to pray for is the influence of the Lord in and through our lives. This is what the Bible means when it says that the Lord will give us the Holy Spirit when we ask Him. The Lord will be close and powerful when we ask Him to be close to us. "Draw nigh to God, and he will draw nigh to you" (James 4:8).

Do You Remember?

1. What was the first thing Jesus did after the disciples asked to be taught how to pray? _____
   presented a pattern prayer for them to follow

2. According to that pattern, who is prayer to be addressed to? *the heavenly Father*

3. What are the seven petitions in the Lord's pattern prayer?
   a. *Hallowed be thy name.*
   b. *Thy kingdom come.*
   c. *Thy will be done.*
   d. *Give us our daily bread.*
   e. *Forgive us our sins.*
   f. *Lead us not into temptation.*
   g. *Deliver us from evil.*

4. What condition must a believer meet before God will forgive his sins? _____
   The believer must forgive others.

5. Why did the man give his friend the loaves he asked for? _____
   the friend's importunity, or persistence; he kept on asking

6. What are the action words used to describe the persistent prayer of a Christian? _____
   ask, seek, knock

7. What does the fact that a father gives his son bread and not a stone teach about prayer? _____
   God gives only what is right in answer to prayer.

8. What's the most important answer God gives to prayer? *the Holy Spirit*

99

✳ Extra Activities

Testimonies: Several days before you present this lesson, ask students privately how God has answered prayer for them recently. Select three students to write out their testimonies and read them to the class.

Scripture search: Have students look up the following verses in class, read them aloud, and then give their conclusions based on the passages.

- *When to pray*—Ps. 86:3; 88:1; Luke 18:1; 1 Thess. 5:17

- *Where to pray*—Matt. 6:5–6; Luke 6:12; Acts 10:9; 12:12; 16:13, 25; 1 Tim. 2:8

- *What to pray for*—Matt. 6:11; 15:36; 21:22; Phil. 1:9–11; Col. 1:9–11; 1 Tim. 2:1–2; Rev. 22:20

- *How to pray*—2 Chron. 7:14; Luke 18:1–8; Rom. 8:26–27; Heb. 11:6; James 1:6

- *How sin hinders prayer*—Ps. 66:18; Mark 11:25; James 4:3; 1 Pet. 3:7

Summarize their ideas on the board.

Lesson 28
The Spirit's Ministry

THEME	The Work of the Holy Spirit
SCRIPTURE	John 16:7–15
MEMORY WORK	John 16:13

Approach to the Lesson

Theme: Before Christ ascended, He taught His disciples that He would not leave them without someone to help them in their ministry. He promised to send the Holy Spirit to empower them for witnessing and to instruct them in His truth. He taught them that the Spirit would live in them and help them whatever happened. All those promises apply to the believer today. At the moment of salvation, the Holy Spirit takes up residence in the believer's body and performs the ministries that Jesus said He would.

Rationale: Help your students realize that if they are saved, a real person—as real as their classmates—is living inside them. He is always with them, and He helps them do things they could not do otherwise. What things? Refer them to the main points of the outline.

Background: The Holy Spirit is God (Acts 5:32). He is sent by the Father and the Son into the heart of every believer. Jesus said, "But when the Comforter is come, whom I will send unto you from the Father, even the Spirit of truth, which proceedeth from the Father, he shall testify of me" (John 15:26). The indwelling of the Spirit of God is a sure sign that a person is a be-

Objectives

KNOWLEDGE (concepts students need to grasp)	the ministries of the Spirit to the believer
	the Spirit's relationship to the Father and the Son
APPLICATION (principles students should put into practice)	We should ask the Spirit to give us boldness to witness for Christ.
	We should pray for the Holy Spirit to help us as we study the Bible.
	We should yield to the Spirit as He speaks to us through the Bible.

Bible Expressions to Understand

expedient—appropriate; profitable; helpful
reprove—convict the conscience
the world—the unsaved
righteousness—God's standard, attainable only through Christ
judgment—justice resulting in punishment or reward
the Comforter—the Holy Spirit; the One Who is present to help

When was the last time you saw the wind? Think carefully. There's only one correct answer to that question: You have never seen the wind. You've seen only its effects. You've seen it blow the tree-tops, and you've felt it on your face.

Wind can turn into a tornado. Tornadoes occur more often in North America than in any other continent. Approximately one thousand tornadoes occur each year in the United States, resulting in about eighty deaths. The winds whirl at up to three hundred miles per hour. The forces created by a tornado are so intense that whole buildings collapse and are blown away.

The Bible uses the wind as an illustration of the Holy Spirit. However, the Holy Spirit doesn't use His power destructively. He changes people into children of God when they exercise faith in Christ. He cannot be seen as He works in human hearts, but the effects of His work can. This is what Scripture means when it says, "The wind bloweth where it listeth [wishes], and thou hearest the sound thereof, but canst not tell whence it cometh, and whither it goeth: so is every one that is born of the Spirit" (John 3:8).

If you've trusted Christ as your Savior, the effects will be evident in the way you live. You'll love God,

Even though tornadoes can be seen and photographed, what you see is actually not the wind itself but the whirling cloud and the debris it picks up.

100

---

liever. Romans 8:9 teaches, "Now if any man have not the Spirit of Christ, he is none of his." What are the ministries the Spirit performs for the believer? Jesus answered that question thoroughly in His teaching recorded in the Gospels.

The Lesson

I. The Spirit Regenerates (John 3:1–21)

Christ's interview with Nicodemus teaches this truth. Jesus told Nicodemus that he had to be born again to enter the kingdom of God. Review briefly the material from Lesson 21.

Make several important points about the Spirit's work of regeneration. First, your students are not part of God's family just because their parents are Chris-

tians. The new birth is brought by the Spirit of God, apart from natural birth or family relationships. Second, if they have been born of the Spirit (regenerated), there will be a change in them. If there isn't, then they are probably not regenerated. Some of your students probably have never really trusted Christ from a heart of faith. Third, just like Nicodemus, they can be religious and not experience the new birth. They must be born again by the Spirit to enter the kingdom of God.

II. The Spirit Empowers for Witness (John 16:7–11)

Christians are in the world to help bring others to Christ. Through them the Spirit reproves the world of sin, righteousness, and judgment. When the believer witnesses, the Spirit uses his words to convict the sinner's conscience of the fact of sin, the need for

His Word, and His people. You'll pray to Him and tell those who do not know Him how they can be saved. If you have no desire to do any of these things, it's possible that you've not really trusted Christ as your Savior.

Jesus promised that when He left, He and the heavenly Father would send the Holy Spirit to dwell in each person who had believed in Christ. He said He would send "the Spirit of truth; whom the world cannot receive, because it seeth him not, neither knoweth him: but ye know him; for he dwelleth with you, and shall be in you" (John 14:17). Jesus called the Holy Spirit the Comforter (John 16:7) because of the constant help He would be to believers.

The work of the Holy Spirit in the world is three-fold (John 16:8–11). First, He makes people conscious of their sins—primarily the sin of rejecting the Son of God. Jesus said, "And when he [the Holy Spirit] is come, he will reprove the world of sin . . . because they believe not on me" (John 16:8–9). Second, the Holy Spirit helps people understand God's standard of right, something they can attain only through Christ. This is why the Scriptures say, "And when he is come, he will reprove the world . . . of righteousness, because I go to my Father, and ye see me no more" (John 16:8, 10). Third, He confronts men and women with the reality of judgment. Satan has already been condemned for his rebellion against God. Everyone else who rebels against God and rejects Christ will be condemned too. Jesus emphasized this idea when He said, "And when he is come, he will reprove the world . . . of judgment, because the prince of this world is judged" (John 16:8, 11).

Although the Holy Spirit works directly in the hearts of people, He also works through the testimony of believers. Your testimony can be used by the Spirit to convict others of their sin and rebellion. Witnessing for Christ is a big task, but you shouldn't be afraid. Paul wrote, "For God hath not given us the spirit of fear; but of power, and of love, and of a sound mind" (2 Tim. 1:7).

In addition to witnessing, learning to love God more through His Word is something the Holy Spirit will help you do. The Bible can be understood by every Christian. Sometimes, however, pastors and teachers can help us understand difficult passages. The Holy Spirit uses these people and even works in our minds to reveal God's truth to us. Jesus said, "Howbeit when he, the Spirit of truth, is come, he will guide you into all truth" (John 16:13). This process is called illumination. Paul explained it when he said, "But as it is written, Eye hath not seen, nor ear heard, neither have entered into the heart of man, the things which God hath prepared for them that love him. But God hath revealed them unto us by his Spirit: for the Spirit searcheth all things, yea, the deep things of God" (1 Cor. 2:9–10). The "deep things of God" are the biblical concepts the Holy Spirit helps us understand.

"Do not pray for more of the Holy Spirit. The Holy Spirit is the Third Person of the Trinity and is not in pieces. Every child of God has all of Him, but does He have all of us?"
—F. B. Meyer

Many have said that any emphasis on the Holy Spirit is an overemphasis since the Spirit came to glorify Christ and the Spirit would not "speak of himself" (John 16:13–14). No doubt the Spirit did come to glorify Christ. However, to say He won't speak *of* Himself doesn't mean He won't speak *about* Himself. He most certainly has spoken about Himself. The New Testament has more than three hundred references to Him. Rather, the statement means He won't speak *from* Himself. In other words, He will speak from God the Father just as Christ did when He was on earth (John 8:28).

So is it wrong to emphasize the Holy Spirit? Absolutely not. To emphasize the Spirit is to

101

I. The Spirit regenerates (John 3:1–21).
II. The Spirit empowers for witness (John 16:7–11).
III. The Spirit instructs in the Truth (John 14:26).

The empowering by the Spirit is a fulfillment of Jesus's promise. He said, "And, behold, I send the promise of my Father upon you: but tarry ye in the city of Jerusalem, until ye be endued with power from on high" (Luke 24:49). The event that began the Spirit's special empowering for witness was Pentecost. The Spirit of God entered into those who had believed, and He has done the same ever since to every person who believes.

III. The Spirit Instructs in the Truth (John 14:26)

Jesus said, "But the Comforter, which is the Holy Ghost, whom the Father will send in my name, he shall teach you all things, and bring all things to your remembrance, whatsoever I have said unto you." This verse plainly asserts that the Spirit teaches believers.

There are two applications of this passage. One is to the disciples present at the time. They would receive special help from the Spirit in remembering and understanding the significance of what Jesus had said. This would be essential as they later wrote the books of the New Testament. The second application is to believers today. They will receive light from the Holy Spirit to understand the Truth and remember it at important times of ministry and meditation. The same idea is underscored by John 16:13—"Howbeit when he, the Spirit of truth, is come, he will guide you into all truth: for he shall not speak of himself; but whatsoever he shall hear, that shall he speak: and he will shew you things to come."

All this instruction comes by means of the authoritative written Word of God. Jesus said, "It is the spirit that quickeneth; the flesh profiteth nothing: the words that I speak unto you, they are spirit, and they are life" (John 6:63).

The central point of the Spirit's work of instruction is to increase the believer's knowledge of Christ. Scripture says, "But when the Comforter is come, whom I will send unto you from the Father, even the

righteousness, and the inescapable truth that he will answer for his conduct before God. Some will repent because of this conviction, and others will not. But the conviction will be real and powerful.

Sometimes the Lord calls believers to witness in trying circumstances or under persecution. He promises that His Spirit will especially help the believer be bold and will give him the right words to say (Matt. 10:20; Mark 13:11; Luke 12:12; 21:14).

After being saved by drinking the "living water," the new Christian becomes like a spring of water, a source of refreshment to many. Jesus said, "He that believeth on me, as the scripture hath said, out of his belly shall flow rivers of living water" (John 7:38; see also 4:10, 13). Once a person has

been born of the Spirit, he naturally begins serving others and helping them spiritually.

Witnessing for Christ is an awesome responsibility. The world is full of people needing Christ. Many oppose the message. Governments persecute Christians. Liberal, so-called Christians view the witnessing Christian as a throwback to a more primitive day. They think the message of the gospel is no longer enough for the needs of the world and thus resent the one who preaches it. With this opposition, not to mention his own fears and the enormity of the task before him, the Christian can find great comfort in the promise of the Spirit's power for witness. There is no lack of power for witnessing, only a lack of those who will accept the power and do the work.

Spirit of truth, which proceedeth from the Father, he shall testify of me" (John 15:26). "He shall glorify me: for he shall receive of mine, and shall shew it unto you" (John 16:14). The Spirit always seeks to bring the believer into a deeper understanding of Christ and his responsibility to Him.

Vital doctrinal sections of the Bible emphasize the significance of the Spirit of God (Rom. 8:1–17; 1 Cor. 12:3–13; 2 Cor. 3:3–18; Gal. 5:16–26). It's the presence of the Spirit in believers that is the main distinction between the way God dealt with Old Testament believers and the way He deals with New Testament believers. Old Testament believers were not "by one Spirit . . . baptized into one body" (1 Cor. 12:13). In 2 Corinthians 3:6–8 Paul makes it clear that the ministry of the New Testament is a "ministry of the Spirit."

✳ Extra Activities

Quiz: The following quiz will help your students see their need to know more about what Jesus said concerning the Holy Spirit in the Gospel of John.

a. In what chapter of the Gospel of John did Jesus say the Holy Spirit is like wind?
John 3

b. In what chapter did He say the Holy Spirit is like a river?
John 7

c. In what chapter did He describe the Holy Spirit as a reprover?
John 16

d. In what chapter did He say the Holy Spirit would dwell in Christians?
John 14

e. In what chapter did He describe the Holy Spirit as a teacher?
John 14

Survey: Have your students respond anonymously to the following survey. These statements focus on often misunderstood ideas about the Holy Spirit, so expect many incorrect answers.

True or *False*:

a. The Holy Spirit is God.
True

b. The Holy Spirit begins to dwell in a person when he dedicates his life to Christ after he is saved.
False

---

emphasize God. It is wrongheaded to make a distinction between emphasizing Christ and emphasizing the Spirit. When the Spirit gets glory, Christ gets glory.

The question in modern times isn't which of the members of the Godhead to emphasize. The question is whether what we typically do really glorifies God. We hear a lot today about "proper" or "Spirit-filled" worship, but the New Testament exhorts believers to commit themselves to serving God (all three Persons) "acceptably with reverence and godly fear" (Heb. 12:28).

God's Wind

The Holy Spirit causes a person to be born into the family of God when he puts his faith in Christ. At that moment, the Spirit takes up residence in the believer. If you're a believer in Christ, the Holy Spirit lives in your body. You're His temple. The Holy Spirit takes the responsibility to empower you to witness for Christ. He also helps you understand the Bible. Most important, while you study the Bible, He'll help you learn more about the Lord Jesus Christ.

Do You Remember?

1. Why was it necessary for Jesus to leave the apostles? _____
   so the Comforter could come

2. Who sent the Holy Spirit? *Jesus Christ and the heavenly Father*

3. What is the Spirit's ministry to the world? *to reprove people*

4. What three things will the Spirit reprove the world of? _____
   sin, righteousness, and judgment

5. Into what will the Spirit guide believers? *all truth*

6. Who does the Spirit always glorify? *Jesus Christ*

102

---

c. The Holy Spirit helps a Christian once he is saved, but He is not involved in the Christian's salvation.
False

d. The Holy Spirit began influencing people after Jesus's Resurrection. Before then, He was not working among Christians.
False

e. The Holy Spirit has influence only on Christians.
False

Faithfulness to Christ

Read: John 15:1–16:4

Memorize: John 15:5

Bible Expressions to Understand

husbandman—farmer; gardener
purgeth—prunes or cuts back; cleanses
abide—remain; continue
Spirit of truth—the Holy Spirit

Polycarp was a leader in the church in the second century AD. He sat under the preaching of the apostle John during the last years of John's life. He entered the ministry and eventually became leader of the church in Smyrna, a city in what is now Turkey. He was a devoted pastor and friend of the people of God.

One day, about AD 110, the church at Smyrna received a distinguished visitor, Ignatius, the aged pastor from Antioch. This wasn't a happy occasion, however. Ignatius was under arrest for being a Christian. Roman soldiers were taking him to Rome, where he would be thrown into an arena and killed by wild animals. After leaving Smyrna, Ignatius wrote letters back to the church and to Polycarp, thanking them for their comfort. Ignatius urged Polycarp to be strong for Christ. "Stand thou firm, as an anvil when it is smitten," wrote Ignatius. "It is the part of a great athlete to receive blows and be victorious. But especially must we for God's sake endure all things."

Some forty years later, Polycarp had his opportunity to "stand firm." Persecution of Christians broke out in Smyrna. The Roman authorities were upset because Christians wouldn't take an oath of loyalty to Caesar. The oath required everyone to swear, "Caesar is lord," and Christians wouldn't claim any lord but the Lord Jesus Christ. The Romans began calling Christians "atheists" because they denied the Roman gods!

Polycarp was arrested and taken to the city stadium. There a huge crowd had gathered to watch the slaughter of the Christians. The Roman ruler of the city tried to get Polycarp to take the oath. "Have respect to thine age," he said to Polycarp. "Repent and say, 'Away with the atheists [Christians].'"

Polycarp looked out at the crowd of pagans, pointed toward them, and said, "Away with the atheists."

The ruler ignored this gesture and said, "Swear the oath, and I will release thee; revile the Christ."

Polycarp shook his head and replied, "Fourscore and six years have I been His servant, and He hath done me no wrong. How then can I blaspheme my King, who saved me?"

Polycarp was seized and tied to a stake. The executioners piled wood around him and then set fire to it. As the flames climbed higher around him, Polycarp prayed for the Lord to receive him. He was faithful to Christ unto death.

Faithfulness to our friends, our family, and other Christians is important, but faithfulness to Jesus Christ is the most important of all. You must keep

While Polycarp was waiting for his executioners to light the fire that would burn him to death, he prayed: "Lord God Almighty, . . . I bless You that You have thought me worthy of this day and hour, to be numbered among the martyrs and share in the cup of Christ."

103

Objectives

KNOWLEDGE (concepts students need to grasp)	the symbolic meaning of the vine and branches
	the requirements and benefits of friendship with Christ
	the idea of "the world" from a biblical perspective
	the relationship of faithfulness to fruitfulness
APPLICATION (principles students should put into practice)	We must be faithful to Christ to be fruitful.
	We must be faithful to Christ to develop a close friendship with Him.
	If we are faithful to Christ, we can expect opposition from the world.

as receive. Remind them that faithfulness is evident in practical ways, such as regular attendance at church, consistent study of God's Word, and persistent witness. Faithfulness is intensely practical. It touches virtually every part of our lives.

Background: The passage for this lesson is found only in the Gospel of John. The group had just finished the Passover feast, and Jesus had instituted a new ritual in which they all drank of the "fruit of the vine" (Matt. 26:29). This could have stimulated the discourse on the vine and its branches, but more likely the path they followed after leaving the city on their way to the Garden of Gethsemane (John 14:31) provided the illustration. Vineyards on the hillsides would have served as an object lesson through which the Lord could teach these truths.

The Lesson

I. Faithfulness and Fruitfulness (John 15:1–8)

Jesus began His discussion of faithfulness with an allegory. He described Himself as a grapevine, professed believers as branches, and God the Father as the gardener who tends the vine. The fruit represents the faithfulness of the believer working itself out in concrete actions. The only way we can bear fruit faithfully is if we have the care of the gardener and the sustenance of the vine.

The care of the gardener (15:1–3). You can't bear fruit faithfully without God's continual care. Note first that the Father treats the fruitful believer and the fruitless

---

Lesson 29
Faithfulness to Christ

THEME	Faithfulness
SCRIPTURE	John 15:1–16:4
MEMORY WORK	John 15:5

Approach to the Lesson

Theme: When a person trusts Christ as Savior, a new life begins. That new life centers on a new relationship with a person—Jesus Christ. Having placed his faith in Christ for salvation, the believer should continue trusting Christ to deliver him from sin and to lead him in the right way. Remaining steadfast in our confidence in Christ is a natural result of being born again. This steadfast confidence, or continuing trust, is called faithfulness. Without determined faithfulness, the believer's contribution to the body of Christ will dwindle, his love for Christ will shrink, and his interest in the world will increase. A Christian must go on with Christ.

Rationale: Underlying the idea of faithfulness is that of personal responsibility. Because of current trends, your students probably know much more about their rights—real or imagined—than about their responsibilities. Challenge them to determine to stand faithful—to give as well

Outline

believer differently. "Every branch in me that beareth not fruit he taketh away" (15:2). Although this could be a reference to pruning, in which branches are cut back to be made more productive, the Greek term is often translated "lifts up." Grapevines were allowed to grow along the ground to keep moisture in the ground in the dry climate of Palestine. When the blossoms started to flower, however, they needed to be lifted up on stones or sticks so they could germinate. God takes responsibility for putting every believer where he can be fruitful.

> Young people often question their circumstances: "Why did this happen? Why am I like this?" Remind them that the Father has put them where they will be most productive. As a farmer would not leave his plants in a position where they could not bear fruit, so God will not leave us barren.

The passage continues, "and every branch that beareth fruit, he purgeth it, that it may bring forth more fruit" (15:2). This is cleansing to increase production. The gardener followed a meticulous process of picking insects off the vine and washing the leaves by hand. If the plants were left unattended, the dirt and insects would prevent them from yielding their potential. Likewise, the Lord takes great care in cleansing us. Every believer has been cleansed in regeneration through the Word of God. Peter wrote, "Being born again, not of corruptible seed, but of incorruptible, by the word of God, which liveth and abideth for ever" (1 Pet. 1:23). The cleansing process continues as the believer responds to the written revelation of God, the Bible. Paul writes, "That he might sanctify and cleanse it [the church] with the washing of water by the word" (Eph. 5:26). The psalmist asks, "Wherewithal shall a young man cleanse

---

In the Christian life, what's the connection between fruitfulness and faithfulness?

trusting Him after He saves you from your sins. You must love Him even if others don't. You must obey His commands no matter what the risks and dangers.

The passage you read for this lesson teaches some valuable lessons about faithfulness to Christ. Jesus began His teaching on faithfulness by using the illustration of a vineyard. He said that He is the vine, Christians are the branches, and the Father is the gardener. He taught that a person who's faithful to Him will be fruitful or productive as a Christian.

Productive Christians are those who are becoming more like Christ in their character, doing good works for others, and bringing others to Christ as their Savior. The Lord helps productive Christians become even more productive by cleansing them through His Word. If a Christian isn't bearing fruit spiritually, then the Lord will work with him to get him to improve. If a believer stops bearing fruit, the Lord may even take him home to heaven.

A faithful Christian has the right to ask God to help him. God shows that He is a good God by answering the prayers of His people.

Another valuable lesson is that faithful Christians enjoy a close friendship with Christ. God loves all Christians, but faithful believers have some special privileges. The way a believer proves his love for Christ is by obeying His commands. If you love Christ this deeply, Jesus will show you things from the Bible that other people won't understand. Christ does this through the Holy Spirit and by your diligent study of His Word.

The Lord is the One Who started the friendship you have with Him by saving you from your sins. He wants it to be a good friendship. He's willing to

104

hear and answer your prayers so it can be. Good friends talk to each other. You probably have some friends who are closer to you than others. They tell you things about themselves and their families that they don't tell most other people. They spend more time talking to you than to their other friends. This is the type of friend Christ wants to be—the closest friend of all.

If you're a close friend of Christ, His enemies will be your enemies. This is the last valuable lesson about faithfulness that Jesus taught in this passage. When the Lord was in this world, many people hated Him. He told them the truth about their sins and about God. They didn't want to hear the truth. As a Christian, a faithful friend of Christ, you'll do the same thing. Unsaved people will not want you to do this. At times, some will dislike it so much that they'll wish you were dead. The New Testament says we are to love our enemies. Even when people hate us this way, we're to care for them by giving them the gospel. Without the gospel they have no hope. Their minds are darkened and enslaved by Satan. The only thing that can give them light and freedom is the good news that Jesus Christ died for their sins.

Hatred isn't easy to live with. If someone hates you, it makes you sad, especially when he hates you because you're faithful to Christ. Christ promised to send the Holy Spirit to help you be brave and joyful even when people hate you because you're a Christian. The Spirit of God will help you witness to others of the love of God shown in Christ by His dying on the cross.

Continuing to Produce Spiritual Fruit

Once you're saved, you must become a faithful follower of the Lord Jesus Christ. You should continue to read your Bible, pray, work at being a better person, and do good works for others. If you're a faithful friend of Christ, you'll love His friends and continually go to church with them, encourage them, and pray for them. Faithfulness is continuing to do right in the sight of the Lord, no matter how difficult the circumstances may be. A faithful Christian never gives up. He never gets bored with being a Christian. He follows Christ until one day he enters heaven to be with his greatest friend forever.

---

his way? by taking heed thereto according to thy word" (Ps. 119:9).

The importance of the vine (15:4–8). You can't bear fruit faithfully without Christ's continual sustenance. Just as a branch cannot bear fruit apart from the vine, neither can the believer hope to be productive apart from Christ. Any time a believer is not depending on the Lord, the result will be fruitlessness. For a true believer, this will be a temporary lapse, and the Lord will deal with him (15:2). If it is an ongoing condition, it means the person is not truly a believer and is therefore incapable of bearing fruit: "If a man abide not in me, he is cast forth as a branch, and is withered; and men gather them, and cast them into the fire, and they are burned" (15:6). Be careful not to interpret this verse as meaning that those

who are truly saved can lose their salvation. It is not just fruitlessness Jesus is speaking of here but spiritual deadness due to a person's lack of saving faith in Him.

The two practical aids to remaining faithful to the Lord Jesus Christ and thus being fruitful are the Word of God and prayer. Faithfulness to Christ is impossible without an understanding of His desires as recorded in the Word of God. As Christ stated, "Ye abide in me, and my words abide in you" (15:7), which is to say that a believer is faithful to Christ by faithfulness to revelation. The natural result of understanding Christ's will is seeking His grace to perform His will and praying for His personal intervention in our affairs. These practical steps of searching the Scriptures

---

Do You Remember?

1. What will happen to Christians who do not bear fruit? <u>God will chasten them.</u>

2. What must a Christian do before he can bear fruit? _____
   <u>be in fellowship with Christ; abide in Christ</u>

3. What privilege is given to obedient Christians? <u>prayer</u>

4. Who has the assurance that he will continue to experience God's love? _____
   <u>the Christian who is obedient to Christ's commands</u>

5. Why did Jesus teach these things to His disciples? _____
   <u>so they could experience the joy of their faith</u>

6. What is the greatest example of love? _____
   <u>when someone gives his life for another person</u>

7. Why have believers been chosen by the Lord? <u>to bring forth fruit</u>

8. Why should believers expect persecution from the world? _____
   <u>because the world persecuted Christ</u>

9. Why do people in the world hate Christ? <u>because Christ shows them their sin</u>

10. What promise did Jesus make concerning future guidance of believers? _____
    <u>He would send them the Holy Spirit, the Comforter, to guide them and
    help them witness.</u>

105

and praying ultimately bring fruitfulness and glory to God (15:8).

II. Faithfulness and Friendship (John 15:9–17)

Faithful obedience to God results in various benefits that can be summed up as friendship with God.

Friendship with God results in joy (15:9–11). Obedience to Christ's commands is the practical step to friendship with Him. Christ has taken the initiative to establish a relationship with us. His reasoned choice to give of Himself for our good parallels the relationship He has with the Father. To maintain intimacy, as the Father and Son do, the believer must obey Christ's commands, even as Christ has obeyed the commands of the Father. The result will be an abiding sense of spiritual contentment called joy. Joy is a condition of the inner being. A joyful person is satisfied that his life is pleasing to God and that he is doing all he can to live in communion with Christ. Of course, a believer does not experience the most complete sense of this joy on earth, but he can have more of it than a disobedient Christian.

Friendship with God results in love (15:12–14). Friendship with God cannot be enjoyed without obeying His command to love. To summarize His commands, Christ said we are to love one another as He has loved us. Elsewhere He stated that love for our neighbor is the second greatest command, the first being to love the Lord our God (Matt. 22:36–39). This love of others is to be of the same quality as Christ's love for us. To stress the extent to which we should go in the ser-vice of others, Jesus said that the greatest love a person could have for another is demonstrated by laying down his life for him.

To conclude, the Lord asserted that to be His friend, the believer must obey Him. The Greek term for *friend* suggests a close relationship of mutual affection and attraction. Disregarding Christ's commands will cause the believer to sense that he is alienated from Christ. The sin nature troubles the saint enough already. Failure to obey Christ's commands compounds the problem and steals joy.

> We don't worship an idea, a place, or a system of ethics, but a Person. As affections can cool and distance can develop in our relationships with other people, our relationship with Christ can be similarly affected. One way we can avoid this cooling is through obedience.

Friendship with God results in understanding the Word (15:15). One of the great benefits of a relationship with Christ is illumination. For those who seek to do His commands to the fullest, Christ reveals His will through His Word. All Christians equally *possess* the Bible, but not all equally *understand* the Bible.

The Bible cannot be understood by mere intellectual attainment; it is understood through the illumination of the Spirit. Paul wrote, "Eye hath not seen, nor ear heard, neither have entered into the heart of man, the things which God hath prepared for them that love him. But God hath revealed them unto us by his Spirit: for the Spirit searcheth all things, yea, the deep things of God" (1 Cor. 2:9–10). And the writer of Hebrews says, "For every one that useth milk is unskilful in the word of righteousness: for he is a babe. But strong meat belongeth to them that are of full age, even those who by reason of use have their senses exercised to discern both good and evil" (Heb. 5:13–14).

Both these passages suggest a progress in wanting spiritual knowledge from the Word of God. In the earlier verse the Spirit grants this greater knowledge. In the other verse the believer's own maturity, caused by his determination to apply the Scriptures to his experience, brings the greater knowledge. These two elements are not mutually exclusive. Here we have the divine and human elements of illumination. The obedient, fervent Christian is granted special assistance from Christ to understand the Word of God.

Friendship with God results in answered prayers (15:16–17). Another great benefit of a relationship with Christ is His response to our prayers. Christ has initiated this friendship and has every intention of being generous. He wants us to bear fruit and wants our fruit to remain. Based on our purity and obedience, Christ will respond to our prayers, making us productive. When we bear the fruit of character development, good works, and soulwinning, Christ is honored.

III. Faithfulness and Opposition (John 15:18–16:4)

Though opposition is certain, God helps us to remain faithful in it.

Certainty of opposition (15:18–25). Christ presented two specific reasons for opposition from the world, or unsaved people, in their ungodly approach to life. The first reason is the Christian's unwillingness to go along with the world's ungodliness. The faithful Christian sees problems with the world's attitude and conduct and will not take part. Since the world does not understand God's standards, it distrusts this lack of cooperation. To the unsaved person, a believer is a "stick in the mud" who does not like anyone. Thus the unconverted feel justified in hating Christians and openly opposing them.

A second reason for opposition is the Christian's positive witness for the righteous God (15:20–25). The world views God as a weak, spineless character Who overlooks every imaginable crime and act of wickedness in the name of love. This god is certainly not the God of the Bible. But the believer testifies about a holy God, just as Christ did; he tells of a God Who has all power and to Whom all men are answerable. The Lord Jesus did the same with the miracles He performed in the power of the Spirit of God.

How does the world respond? It hates the believer, just as it hated Christ. Why? The world wants a God it can control, not One Who controls it. The unsaved want a genie in a bottle, acting at their beck and call. They do not want a God to Whom they must submit. Furthermore, they reason that the Christian has no right to tell them what God is like. They are just as wise as he is. And so, just as they hated Christ, they hate the believer without reason. They hate him because he tells them the truth, and they do not like the truth about themselves and about God. They would rather go on living in a fairy-tale world, traveling down the broad road to destruction.

> We cannot be bitter toward these people. They are slaves to sin and victims of the great deceiver. Their minds are darkened. Even though they hate us, we must give them the light of the gospel of Christ. It is their only hope.

Help in opposition (15:26–6:4). Opposition is a hard burden to bear. Thus the Father and the Son have sent the Spirit to help us. He is called the Comforter. He could also be called our Helper or Encourager. In the face of intimidation, He will help us bear witness. He will help us remain strong and not go astray. The resistance of the world may be fierce. The unsaved sometimes even kill Christians, thinking they are rendering a favor to everyone. None of these facts should surprise the believer because the Lord predicted that this would happen. In a subtle way even this prediction should be an encouragement to us. Yes, the hatred is difficult to face, but in predicting it the Lord again proved His absolute control and knowledge of all things.

> Your students may be unfamiliar with opposition from the world. Their environment has probably been largely friendly. Christian parents, Christian friends, a good church, and a Christian school have all provided a pleasant atmosphere in which to grow up. However, they need to be prepared for reality. In some cases they may not have experienced opposition because they have not lived for Christ. They are just like the world, and the world loves its own. If your students find themselves comfortable with the unsaved and their lifestyle, they need to take a hard look at their own level of faithfulness to Christ.

✳ Extra Activity

Object lesson: If possible, obtain part of a grapevine to illustrate the first part of the lesson to your class. The wood of a grapevine is almost useless apart from its natural function of bearing grapes. Because of its softness, it cannot be used for building. Its coarse fiber and lack of stiffness render it useless even as a peg for hanging something on. As a fuel it burns too rapidly and gives off only a little heat.

Lesson 30
Discipleship

THEME	Discipleship
SCRIPTURE	Matthew 10:32–39
MEMORY WORK	Matthew 16:24

Approach to the Lesson

Theme: A disciple is a learner or pupil. A disciple of the Lord is a student in the school of the Master Teacher. The disciple-teacher relationship implies several things. First, it implies a need for instruction in living, a fundamental recognition that we do not have all the answers. Second, it implies a willing submission to the Teacher. This submission demonstrates itself in careful listening and ready obedience. Last, this relationship implies a bond of loyalty and admiration. The student is quick to defend the words of the Master Teacher and adamant in refusing to consider contradictory instruction in the name of open-mindedness. Having found the One with the words of life, the student remains faithfully by His side for eternity.

Rationale: This lesson may be the greatest personal challenge for you this year. Your students will learn of their relationship to the Master Teacher by comparing (or contrasting) it with a relationship they can see—namely, your relationship with them.

Background: Jesus chose twelve men to be His constant followers and to receive intensive instruction for the founding of His body, the church. These men were called *disciples*, which means "learners" or "pupils." They were also called *apostles* ("sent ones") since they were sent to the lost of Israel and then to the whole world to preach the gospel. The names of the twelve are listed in four passages in the New Testament: Matthew 10:2–4; Mark 3:16–19; Luke 6:14–16; and Acts 1:13 (which doesn't include Judas Iscariot). In all the listings Peter is first. There were only twelve apostle-disciples, but anyone who trusts Christ and follows Him is a disciple.

The Gospels record Jesus's teachings on the requirements for being one of His disciples as well as the obstacles to that relationship. These teachings are summarized in three commands: deny yourself, take up your cross, and follow Christ. These commands appear in six passages in the Gospels (Matt. 10:32–39; 16:24–28; Mark 8:34–38; 10:21; Luke 9:23–27; 14:25–33). For clarity, this lesson follows the order of the first passage and adds material from the others as they provide additional insight.

⭐ The Lesson

I. The Disciple's Reproach (Matt. 10:32–33)

The context of this passage is a warning about those who will threaten and persecute believers. The first response to these occasions is to be afraid and not speak out for Christ. However, the Lord forcefully condemned being ashamed of Him from a motive of self-preservation. He said that if a person confesses Him before others, then He will confess that one before His Father in heaven. In contrast, if a person denies Him before others, He will deny him before His Father.

Jesus was not suggesting that a person could be a child of God and lose his salvation because of his fear of persecution. If a person is so faithless that he denies Christ and refuses to return to Him in repentance, then he was not a believer in the first place (1 John 2:23). A willingness to bear reproach for Christ is a sure indication that a person loves Christ more than the opinion and approval of men.

> Your students have probably not faced physical danger for Christ. Yet they allow fear of persecution to keep them from

Objectives

KNOWLEDGE (concepts students need to grasp)	the derivation and meaning of the term *disciple*
	the names and roles of the twelve disciples in the founding of the church
	the obstacles to discipleship presented in the Gospels
APPLICATION (principles students should put into practice)	We must be willing to bear reproach for Christ.
	If the instructions of parental or governmental authorities conflict with what Christ has commanded, we should obey Him first.
	We may have to sacrifice financial gain and prestige to make spiritual progress.

Outline

(Matt. 10:32–39)
I.   The disciple's reproach (32–33)
II. The disciple's priorities (34–37)
III. The disciple's sacrifices (38–39)

witnessing. If they cave in under such small pressure, what will they do in the face of real danger?

A Christian disciple is also not to be ashamed of the Bible. Jesus said, "For whosoever shall be ashamed of me and of my words, of him shall the Son of man be ashamed, when he shall come in his own glory, and in his Father's, and of the holy angels" (Luke 9:26). The Bible reveals the mind of Christ. Its miracles, parables, historical details, and scientific claims must be accepted. If an individual is ashamed of the Bible, he is ashamed of Christ.

II. The Disciple's Priorities (Matt. 10:34–37)

Jesus came not to bring peace but a sword. Because of Christ, interpersonal relationships will change. Specifically, family members will not always be in favor of your profession of Christ. Few things are as unsettling as mothers, fa-thers, sisters, brothers, and in-laws who object to your faithfulness to Christ. Would it be better to stop being a fervent believer? No. If some of those who oppose you are your relatives, so be it. Christ must be feared and obeyed above all others, including those closest to us.

A Christian must love his family even if they reject his faith. If, on the other hand, they love him, he still must carefully order his priorities. It is possible for a Christian to place his love for his family above his love for his Lord. Even though it is natural to love one's mother, father, daughters, and sons, they can become stumbling blocks. If selfish affection for close relatives keeps the Christian from going where Christ wants

The student text pages for this lesson begin on the next page.

him and doing what He wants him to do, then that affection is not true biblical love. Love for Christ should be so great that affection for all others seems like hate (Luke 14:25–27).

III. The Disciple's Sacrifices (Matt. 10:38–39)

The believer must deny himself, take up his cross daily (Luke 9:23), and follow Christ. To take up a cross daily is to die to our own ambitions and preferences. To follow Christ is the positive reaction that comes naturally after the death of self. Our goals and preferences are replaced by Christ's. In short, this sacrifice is essential to being a true disciple and experiencing reward. When Jesus said, "And he that taketh not his cross, and followeth after me, is not worthy of me," He meant that if we do not leave selfish desires behind, we will never know the exhilaration of fulfilling the will of God.

To develop this idea, Jesus asked, "For what is a man profited, if he shall gain the whole world, and lose his own soul? or what shall a man give in exchange for his soul?" (Matt. 16:26). In the view of the world, success is measured by how much prestige, power, and wealth you attain. A disciple must set these worldly goals aside and seek instead to be honored by the Lord, to know His spiritual power, and to store treasure in heaven. Spiritual goals sound empty to the worldly man or woman, but not to the disciple. These spiritual attainments are real; the goals of the world will ultimately become meaningless.

> If spiritual goals sound empty to your students, they have reason to question their relationship with Christ.

The sacrifices the Christian is called on to make are great. Recognizing the seriousness of these sacrifices, the Lord likened the choice of becoming a disciple to beginning a major building project or entering into a war (Luke 14:26–33). There must be enough money, supplies, and manpower to finish the tower before the building is begun. There must be enough troops to attack another force before the battle begins. Embarrassment and even devastation can result from a hasty decision about discipleship. Becoming a pupil of Christ is costly. Entered into lightly and without adequate thought, the relationship will not last.

Bible Expressions to Understand

variance—disagreement; dissension
cross—Roman method of execution; used figuratively as the Christian's responsibility of self-denial

Perhaps you have never thought of yourself as a disciple of the Lord Jesus Christ, but you should. If you've trusted Christ as your Savior, then He's also your teacher. You're His student (that's what *disciple* really means) for the rest of your life. Jesus teaches His followers how to live for Him in this world in a way that reflects His glory and brings others to salvation.

Jesus taught that there are major barriers or obstacles to being a disciple in His school. If you don't overcome these barriers, then you won't be a successful pupil.

One barrier is fearing what people may think or do to you for being a Christian. You should be more concerned about the opinion of the Lord Jesus Christ than the opinions of others. If you're more concerned about His opinion, then you'll listen to Him and obey Him—come what may. You must never be ashamed of your Savior in front of friends who don't know Him. Rather, you should boldly tell them how to be saved. If you have friends you haven't told about Christ because you're too embarrassed, then you should correct that sin.

The Bible says that you shouldn't be ashamed of Christ or of His words. If you're a disciple, is it right to be ashamed of other disciples, that is, other members of the church? Of course not. Laughing at and making fun of older Christians in your church is not

When eating in a public place, are you embarrassed for others to see you pray before the meal?

106

---

pleasing to Christ. If you love Christ, you must love His people and willingly identify with them. We all have some friends who are closer to us than others, but we are to be friends of all faithful believers.

Those who don't know Christ often think the miracles of the Bible and the standards in the Bible are strange and silly. You cannot allow their attitudes to make you embarrassed or afraid to speak about the Lord. Disobeying Christ by not living by the standards of the Bible is the same as denying Christ before others.

Jesus said that if a person denies Him before others, then He will deny that person before His Father in heaven. Jesus is saying that if you're so ashamed of Him that you deny Him and won't repent of it, then you're not really a Christian; you don't love Him, and He has no choice but to deny you entrance into heaven.

Another area that is often a challenge for disciples is family relationships. Sometimes a person comes to Christ but the members of his family remain unsaved. You may be in that situation or know someone who is. It's hard for non-Christians to understand why a person who becomes a disciple changes so many things in his life. They especially don't understand why the new disciple loves Jesus so much and always wants to go to church and read the Bible. They often resent the efforts of the new disciple to witness to them.

The reactions of these unsaved family members may be unpleasant and even cruel. Mothers and fathers sometimes throw their children out of the house, forbid them to go to church, or punish them in other ways. A teenager who has unsaved family members must be particularly careful. It is never right to be rebellious or disrespectful to your parents even if they are mean and wrong in their demands.

Some day you may face a situation in which you have to disobey your parents in order to be obedient to Christ. If that time comes, obey Christ and accept the consequences. But remember, no matter what those consequences may be, you have an obligation to honor and obey your parents in every way possible. Never argue with your parents. Calmly explain to them what your obligations to Christ are, and let them make their decisions. If you're a new Christian and find yourself in these circumstances, always get the advice of a pastor or another mature Christian.

In contrast, maybe you have parents who are saved. That is a wonderful thing. You should be thankful to God for His goodness to you in giving you Christian parents. Usually, Christian families are loving families. How could that ever be a problem? Only if a disciple loves his family so much that he won't do what Christ asks him to do. For example, let's suppose that God calls you to go thousands of miles from home to be a missionary to people of a different culture and a strange language, where nobody knows or cares about you. Facing circumstances like those can make a person decide to stay home close to his family. If God has called you to go to the mission field, thoughts of the love and security of your family and your home shouldn't keep you from going.

The last great obstacle to following Christ is our desire to be successful in the world's way. It's all too natural to want to have respect, influence, and plenty of money. Within limits, none of these things are sinful. Out of balance, they will ruin your life. If a single one of these things keeps you from obeying Christ, then it is a sin. Seldom do Bible-believing Christians enjoy the respect and admiration of non-Christians. It should never be our goal to seek that respect or admiration. Often Christian work offers little money. You must decide before you enter Christian work that you will be happy with little, or else you will never be happy. Decide now to find your happiness in the only real worthwhile thing—a life of following Christ.

Overcoming Barriers to Following Christ

A disciple is a learner or pupil. If you have decided to be a disciple of Christ, then you have made yourself a student in the school of the Master Teacher. He'll teach you how to live to glorify Him and bring others to salvation. Obstacles will crop up, but you can overcome them. Fear, family pressures, and the desire for worldly success must never stop you from following Christ.

107

✳ Extra Activities

Memory work: Using an overhead transparency or the board, teach the memory verse for this lesson to the class. Display the entire verse, and read it aloud several times with the class. Then cover part of the words or use a transparency that has only the first letter of each word. Repeat the verse aloud several times. Remove all aids and repeat it aloud. Using this teaching method will introduce some variety into the learning of the memory verses.

Scripture search: Create six columns on the board. Head each column with one of the major discipleship passages: Matthew 10:32–39; 16:24–28; Mark 8:34–38; 10:21; Luke 9:23–27; 14:25–33. Have six students go to the board to write down the elements of each passage. One by one have each student read the passages, pointing out the different obstacles and responsibilities presented for disciples. Coach the students through the passages. The benefit of this exercise will be to get the students to see the recurring ideas as well as the points that come up only once.

Do You Remember?

1. What did Jesus say He would do if people confessed Him before others? _____
   confess them before His Father in heaven

2. What did Jesus say He would do if people denied Him before others? _____
   deny them before the Father

3. What did Jesus say He came to send to the earth? _not peace, but a sword_

4. What did Jesus teach concerning the relationship between a disciple and his family? _____
   Family members can be a hindrance to discipleship because they can oppose
   the disciple or draw his affection away from Christ.

5. What must a person take up if he is going to be a disciple of the Lord? _his cross_

6. What must a person lose in order to find it? _his life_

7. What must a disciple do in addition to taking up his cross? _follow after Christ_

Repentance — L.31

Read: Matthew 19:16–30 Memorize: Matthew 19:26

Bible Expressions to Understand

eye of a needle—the small opening in a sewing needle
Master—teacher
the regeneration—the millennial kingdom

Jesus was the Master of personal evangelism. Not only did He preach to multitudes, perform amazing miracles, and bring relieving healing, but He also endeavored to win others to Himself through personal interaction. His personal soulwinning conversations include His talks with Nicodemus, the woman at the well, and the rich young ruler. Let's take a closer look at the last example. In this confrontation, Christ taught a major principle—the principle of repentance.

The wealthy young man was sincere and probably well respected in the community, but he had one big problem. He wouldn't admit that he—like all sinners who need to repent—was spiritually bankrupt. (See Matt. 5:3.)

A sincere young man approached Jesus with the most important question a person can ever ask. "Good Master, what good thing shall I do, that I may have eternal life?" Knowing that we have eternal life is more important than having money, power, or prestige. This young man who had everything, even apparently a good upbringing, still felt a hollowness in his soul. He hadn't settled the question, "Where will I spend eternity?"

Have you ever settled that issue? You can have a good family background, live a moral life, have everything this world offers, and yet still be empty inside. If you're living with the fear of going to hell, consider the importance of what this lesson deals with—repentance.

Repentance is a change of mind. That begins with a change in the way you think about Christ. Jesus challenged the young man about his concept of Him. He called Jesus good, but he had failed to call Him God. Jesus responded, "Why callest thou me good? There is none good but one, that is God." Christ is certainly good, but He's more than that; He's God. Christ repeatedly asserted that He was God. The Jews understood His claim of deity and killed Him for it (Matt. 26:63–66). If He claimed to be God and wasn't, then He wasn't good. Knowingly making a false claim to be God would have made Him a liar.

Many people believe that Christ was a good teacher, while others rank Him among the religious prophets or sons of the gods. Yet these evaluations fail to give Him His rightful place as the only Son of the only true God. These people fail to recognize that He's God in a human body. Any belief that falls short of giving Christ His true identity as God will also fall short of eternal life. To be saved, people

109

Lesson 31
Repentance

THEME	Repentance
SCRIPTURE	Matthew 19:16–30
MEMORY WORK	Matthew 19:26

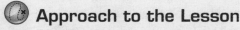

Approach to the Lesson

Theme: Conversion comprises two elements: faith and repentance. Saving faith is a personal choice to trust Christ's work on the cross. Repentance is a change of thinking, feeling, and acting with reference to sin. When a person repents, he realizes the seriousness of his sin. He feels sorrow or regret over his sin. His understanding and sorrow lead him to turn from his sin to Christ for salvation.

This first act of repentance is the beginning of constant repentance that follows in the Christian's life. As the believer sees sin in his life, he repents and gives himself more fully to the Lord. Without this process, the believer does not progress in holiness.

Rationale: Your students have often heard the truth that works cannot gain salvation. Many, however, pervert this doctrine to conclude that works are irrelevant to the Christian. They fail to see that a change in behavior, though not the *cause* of salvation, is an *evidence* of it (Eph. 2:8–10; James 2:26). Remind your students that a lack of

---

Objectives

KNOWLEDGE (concepts students need to grasp)	what Jesus meant when He asked the rich young ruler, "Why callest thou me good?"
	what Jesus meant when He told the young man to keep the commandments to gain eternal life
	what Jesus meant when He told the young man to sell all he had and give to the poor
APPLICATION (principles students should put into practice)	To repent, we must view Christ and ourselves correctly. We must turn from our sins and accept Christ as the only Savior.
	To repent, we must forsake self-righteousness and any entrenched sins.
	We should pray and trust God for the gift of true, heartfelt, and continual repentance.
	Repentance is a continuing process in the Christian life.

change in their lives is evidence of a lack of salvation.

Background: The interview between Christ and the rich young ruler appears in three Gospels (Matt. 19:16–30; Mark 10:17–31; Luke 18:18–30). The specific identity of the man is not known. It appears that he was sincere in his question.

The crux of the man's problem was repentance. He would not forsake self-dependence and specific sins in his life in order to put his faith in Christ. Although he did not respond properly to Christ, his response and the instruction Christ gave through the incident are valuable in sharing the centrality of repentance to true Christianity. This lesson summarizes the most important elements of repentance.

⭐ The Lesson

I. Thinking Correctly About Christ and Ourselves (Matt. 19:16–17)

Seeing Christ as merely a good man is not adequate for salvation. When the man approached Christ, he called Him *good master*. The term in Greek means "teacher." The man recognized Christ as a superior teacher by using this designation of respect. He respected Christ's authority and ability. He was young, rich, and powerful himself (Luke 18:18); as a "ruler," he was apparently a member of the Sanhedrin. But to

Outline

view Christ as just a man of authority and ability was not enough.

This man's wrong conception of Christ led him to think he could perform some action to attain eternal life. No amount of *doing* would get him an inch closer to eternal life. If he had understood Christ's role as Savior, he never would have asked this question.

The Lord asked the young man a surprising question to point out his error. "Why callest thou me good? there is none good but one, that is, God" (19:17). Jesus was not denying His own goodness. He was leading the man into revealing his limited understanding of Christ.

The suggestion that he should keep the commandments to earn eternal life was honest. If a person could keep the commandments perfectly, he could have eternal life. No one can do that, however, because of our sinful nature. Only Christ's death on the cross gives the believer eternal life. Through God's grace he can then obey God's commands in the power of a regenerated life, through the strength of the Spirit of God. By His question the Lord gave the man the opportunity to say that he understood these things. He did not. Instead he revealed his complete misconception of his own nature, the character of Christ, and the way to eternal life.

Christ challenged the young man in order to expose his faulty thinking about the Son of God. A person cannot be led to repentance unless the soulwinner understands his problem. One of the great challenges of being a Christian teacher is discerning the spiritual condition of your students. Without that important step, ministering to them will be difficult, if not impossible.

II. Forsaking Specific Sin (Matt. 19:18–22)

Self-righteousness keeps people from seeing themselves as sinners and thus keeps them from trusting Christ as their Savior. The young ruler was self-righteous because

must change their minds about Who Christ is; they must repent!

Repentance also includes a change of mind about sin. The young ruler asked what he could do to have eternal life. Actually, he asked the wrong question since people can do nothing that will earn them salvation. He was posing the same question many people ask, and he was sincere. But he wasn't prepared to do what Jesus told him. Knowing the young man's heart, Jesus simply replied, "Keep the commandments." (Perfect knowledge of another person's thoughts and motives is an advantage Christ had in witnessing that we don't have.)

This young man was moral in his own eyes and probably was better than the average person. He expected Jesus to tell him the specific commandments to obey. Jesus mentioned five of the Ten Commandments as well as the statement that summarizes the second half of the law: "Thou shalt love thy neighbour as thyself" (Lev. 19:18). The young man replied, "All these things have I kept from my youth up: what lack I yet?" Then Jesus put his finger on the man's major sin. "Go and sell that thou hast, and give to the poor." In His list, Jesus had purposely left out the final commandment, "Thou shalt not covet." The young man, unwilling to give up his riches and recognizing his own covetous heart, "went away sorrowful." The Lord skillfully showed him his need to repent of sin.

> "If you have sinned, do not lie down without repentance; for the [lack] of repentance after one has sinned makes the heart yet harder and harder."
> —John Bunyan

Before anyone can be saved, he must also change his mind about his own sinfulness. The average person looks favorably on his lifestyle, thinking, *I'm not all that bad. In fact, I'm a pretty good person. I don't need a Savior to take care of my sin.*

Most people view the Ten Commandments just as the rich young ruler did—as stairsteps to heaven. They view the law as a way to gain eternal life. But God's Word reveals that the purpose of the law is just the opposite. It reveals the impossibility of gaining eternal life through self-effort. Paul says,

"Now we know that what things soever the law saith, it saith to them who are under the law: that every mouth may be stopped, and all the world may become guilty before God. Therefore by the deeds of the law there shall no flesh be justified in his sight: for by the law is the knowledge of sin" (Rom. 3:19–20).

No one keeps the law perfectly. All of us fail. Even if a person could keep all but one point of the law, he would still be just as guilty before God. James 2:10 says, "For whosoever shall keep the whole law, and yet offend in one point, he is guilty of all."

To be saved, you must humbly admit before God that you're thoroughly sinful and unable to lift one finger to help yourself. The only thing we as sinners can do is to recognize that Jesus Christ, God's Son, died as a perfect sacrifice for our sins. By choosing to believe that, the sinner stakes his eternal destiny on the finished work of Christ on the cross. When he does that, the spiritual reality that "whosoever believeth in [Jesus] should not perish, but have everlasting life" (John 3:16) is applied to him. What a wonderful promise!

Repentance involves God working in a person's heart. The disciples were amazed at the requirement of repentance placed on the rich young ruler. "Who then can be saved?" they asked. Jesus assured them, "With men this is impossible; but with God all things are possible" (Matt. 19:26). In our own strength it is impossible for us to admit our own sinfulness. It is impossible for us to turn from our sin to the Savior through willpower. God must work in our hearts for us to be saved.

God does work in hearts. Acts 11:18 states, "Then hath God also to the Gentiles granted repentance unto life." The ministry of the Holy Spirit is to convict people of their sin and reveal to them the righteousness of Christ and His future judgment on sin (John 16:7–11). God "will have all men to be saved, and to come unto the knowledge of the truth" (1 Tim. 2:4). When God sends preachers to declare salvation and sends His Holy Spirit to stir hearts to faith, He's actively bringing people to Christ. Has He done this for you? Do you now feel God working repentance in your heart? Turn to Christ today.

Ultimately, repentance leads to reward. Peter asked Jesus, "Behold, we have forsaken all, and followed thee, what shall we have therefore?" Christ

he misunderstood God's standards and his own failure to keep them. The young man asked Christ which commands he should obey to gain eternal life. Jesus listed five of the six laws on the second table of the Decalogue. He also quoted the generalization of those laws, "Thou shalt love thy neighbor as thyself" (Lev. 19:18). The laws Jesus listed deal with our relationships with other people. These are often the laws people think they are best able to keep. The young man's response shows that he felt this way. He asserted that he had kept all these laws from the time he was a child. No one who understands the law of God or himself would make such a statement. Only because he misunderstood the law and himself did he feel confident about his ability to keep it.

In spite of his pharisaical attitude, the young man still sensed that something was lacking. He said, "All these things have I kept from my youth up: what lack I yet?" (19:20). Anyone who thinks he is self-sufficient will eventually end up with a sense of his own inadequacy before God. This feeling can create an opportunity for those attempting to minister spiritually to others.

In addition to the young man's general self-righteousness, he had a specific sin problem. When he asked Jesus what he lacked, the Lord then focused on the one commandment from the second table of the Decalogue He had not listed earlier—the prohibition against covetousness.

The Lord said, "If thou wilt be perfect, go and sell that thou hast, and give to the

assured the disciples that their willingness to repent and follow Him wouldn't go unrewarded. Rewards will come in this life and in the next. While Peter's question seems to be based on a wrong motive for service, it's a question many people have. Our motive for service shouldn't be what we get out of it, but we can be sure that Jesus will never disappoint us. Have you ever noticed that the happiest, most fulfilled people in the world are believers in the Lord Jesus Christ? Those whose lives are genuinely submissive demonstrate a peace and joy that all the money in the world cannot buy.

A Change of Mind

Repentance is a change of mind toward sin and the Savior. It's a gift from God as He works in the heart to stir people to believe on Christ. Faith and repentance are inseparably linked (Acts 20:21). You can't believe on Christ without first admitting you are a sinner. If you don't know Christ as your personal Savior, turn away from your sin and turn to Him now. The rewards are eternal!

Do You Remember?

1. What adjective did the rich young ruler use to describe Christ? _good_

2. How did the young man think a person gets eternal life? _by doing something_

3. What sin was he particularly guilty of? _covetousness_

4. How do we know this? _He went away sorrowful when Christ told him to sell his goods and give to the poor._

5. Define repentance. _a change of mind toward sin and the Savior; turning away from sin_

6. Who asked a question about the rewards for following Christ? _Peter_

7. Which verse in the Matthew 19 passage speaks of the possibility of repentance? _v. 26 ("With men this is impossible; but with God all things are possible.")_

111

poor, and thou shalt have treasure in heaven: and come and follow me" (19:21). This test was designed specifically for a person who put personal possessions before God. Jesus was not saying that anyone who wants to be saved must sell everything and give to the poor. He was saying that this man had to confront his sin and turn from it. Having made his material wealth the god of his life, he needed to turn from that god to the God of heaven. This is repentance. The young man was also told to follow Christ. Simple reformation is not enough.

When someone comes to Christ, he does not have to be pure. That is impossible. What is required is that he turn from iniquity to the Savior. Sometimes that means renouncing a specific major sin, as it did in this case. Sadly, this young man would not renounce his first loyalty.

Approaching typical teenagers' specific sin problems is an important step in bringing your students to repentance.

III. Allowing God to Work (Matt. 19:23–26)

Without the supernatural working of God, no one can be saved.

The Lord emphasized the difficulty that the rich have in entering the kingdom of heaven. The terms *kingdom of heaven, kingdom of God,* and *salvation* are used interchangeably here. When a person submits to Christ by repentance and faith, he becomes part of His kingdom. The Lord stressed His point by using two objects common to the disciples' experience—a camel and a needle. The camel was the largest domesticated animal in the Middle East.

The needle was one of the smallest household implements. The picture Christ gave is comical. Imagine a huge beast going through an opening the size of a needle's eye. Christ was stressing the impossibility of a rich person being saved without turning from trust in his riches. The disciples obviously got the point. That's why they asked, "Who then can be saved?" Among the Jews of that time it was commonly thought that the wealthy were the most likely candidates for getting into heaven because they could give more alms. If it was impossible for them to enter, the disciples thought, then how much more so for the ordinary people.

Repentance is always difficult. Any sin (even a "small" one) can hinder the well-meaning seeker. But saving faith is always accompanied by repentance. Without God it is impossible to repent (19:26). The Spirit of God must convict a person of sin and draw him to Christ. The seeker should be encouraged by the fact that God's power is responsible for his salvation.

Remember, it is God who works in us the desire and the ability to do His will (Phil. 2:13). If you fear you haven't truly repented, first pray that God would be merciful and work it into you. Then trust Him for the results as you strive to live for Him.

IV. Receiving Rewards (Matt. 19:27–30)

Those who are saved will receive great reward in the kingdom of heaven.

Peter and the other disciples were listening to Christ's conversation with the wealthy young man. Realizing its implications, Peter asked what reward the disciples would receive for forsaking all to follow Christ. Jesus promised them an unparalleled reward. The twelve would be given the responsibility of governing the twelve tribes of Israel in the millennial reign of Christ, or the *regeneration,* as it is called in this verse. (The term is referring to the renewal of the earth, not personal regeneration.) For the disciples to be promised this reward is a great blessing since they were going to be persecuted by the Jewish leaders during Christ's life and after His death.

Material reward. Great reward is promised to all who repent of their sins and follow Christ. All that is forsaken for Christ will be returned a hundredfold. Houses, brothers, sisters, father, mother, wife, children, and lands forsaken will be returned many times over. Any sacrifices the believer makes in his life will be compensated for. What is startling is that he can expect this compensation now as well as in the future. Mark's Gospel records Jesus as saying about this same list of things, "But he shall receive a hundredfold now in this time" (Mark 10:30). The things a follower of Christ may have to give up can be divided into two categories: family and property. The great blessing of family is fellowship and consequent absence of loneliness. If family members reject the believer because of his newfound faith, the Lord will bring others into his life who will be like family to him.

The disciple, however, should not forsake God-given responsibilities. No one should abandon his family arbitrarily to serve the Lord. Scripture clearly teaches family responsibility (1 Tim. 5:8). If the service of Christ demands financial sacrifices, the Lord will compensate, but Mark notes that these things will be received along with persecution (Mark 10:30). This world is a mixed blessing.

> Help your students see that though this life may have its rewards, it will have its persecutions as well if they follow Christ. Your students should be willing to forsake all for Christ, as the twelve did and many have done since.

The believer's reward is in both this life and the life to come. A time is coming when all persecutions will cease and sacrifices will be over. This passage clearly teaches that there is a life for the saints beyond this world. It will be enjoyed in fullest measure.

Positional reward. The Lord closed His comments on this topic with the statement, "But many that are first shall be last; and the last shall be first." Those who are first or most highly revered in this world will not be so in the next. Christ's standard of judgment is righteousness. Against that standard even the rich and powerful people of the world fall woefully short. Those who are viewed as last in this world will then be most greatly honored. Christians, thought of as foolish and out of touch with society's mainstream, will become the focal point of Christ's attention and reward (1 Cor. 1:26–28; 4:9–13).

> Warn your students about being too concerned about honor from the world. The world loves and honors its own, not the followers of Christ. If the world loves and honors them too much, some question about their godliness arises. Encourage your students to do what they do to honor Christ. With pure motives they can look forward to reward in His presence.

Even among Christians, some are honored in this life and others are not. In the future, believers' motives will be known, and those who are truly worthy will be honored. Those names and faces familiar during this age may not be the great Christians after all. By contrast, those who were unknown, who served God in some out-of-the-way place, may be honored as the greatest.

✳ Extra Activity

Analogies: (1) A good analogy to illustrate our reluctance to repent is the ancient method of catching a monkey. Hunters would find a gourd with a small opening and place some food inside it. When the monkey came, he would squeeze his hand into the gourd and grab the food. Because his hand was in a fist, he could not get it out. When the men came out of their hiding places to catch the monkey, he would refuse to let go of the food and therefore was caught. His own greed was his undoing. In a similar way, the rich young ruler refused to give up the world and therefore lost all. "What shall it profit a man, if he shall gain the whole world, and lose his own soul?" (Mark 8:36)

(2) A good analogy of faith, the partner of repentance in salvation, is the law of gravity. Ask your students if they have ever seen gravity. They have faith in gravity even though they cannot see it. None of them jump off ten-story buildings. They are cautious around high places. Their actions prove their faith. Another example is people who smoke. Every pack of cigarettes carries a warning about the harmful effects of cigarette smoking. Yet people go right on smoking. Why? Because they do not really believe that it will harm them. They know that smoking can cause cancer, but they do not truly believe that it will affect them. If they had *faith* in that warning, they would quit. Real faith produces action.

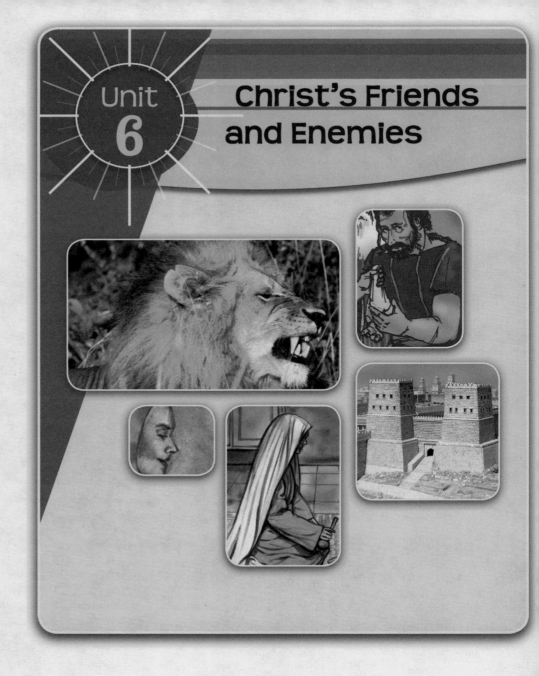

Unit 6

Christ's Friends and Enemies

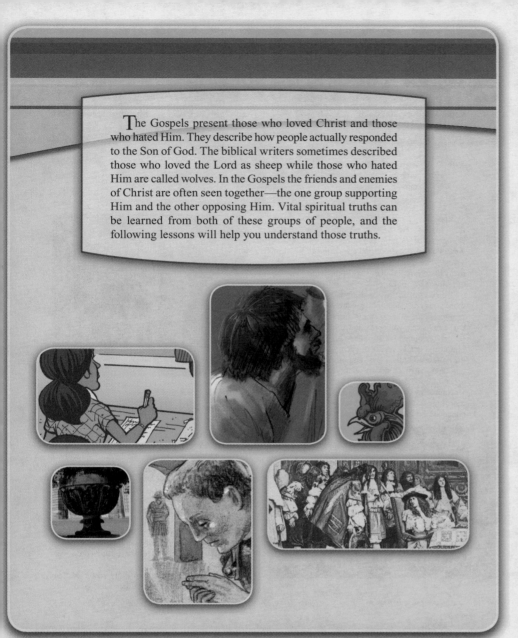

The Gospels present those who loved Christ and those who hated Him. They describe how people actually responded to the Son of God. The biblical writers sometimes described those who loved the Lord as sheep while those who hated Him are called wolves. In the Gospels the friends and enemies of Christ are often seen together—the one group supporting Him and the other opposing Him. Vital spiritual truths can be learned from both of these groups of people, and the following lessons will help you understand those truths.

Christ's Friends and Enemies

This unit focuses on the biographical material in the Gospels. The purpose of the unit is to show your students how the lives of those who interacted with Christ during His time on earth instruct us about good and bad character.

The lessons in this unit take a variety of approaches to the biblical material. Each lesson is either an exposition of a single passage or a topical treatment of several passages in which the personalities under discussion are mentioned. Some lessons zero in on a single personality mentioned in the Gospels while some discuss two people. Still others examine groups (Lessons 35–37 and 40).

The unit includes several special features you may want to utilize in your teaching. The student text provides an essay entitled "Herod the Builder" to present information that is not found in Lesson 37 on the Herod family. There are also several maps and charts in the student text that are also found in the CD accompanying this book. These include a chart listing the twelve disciples (Lesson 32), the family tree of the Herod family along with a map of the division of Herod's kingdom among his sons (Lesson 37), and an overview chart of the unit (following Lesson 40). The chart on pride for use with Lesson 39 is found on page TE177 and on the CD (but not in the student text).

Lesson 32
Leading by Serving

THEME	Servanthood
SCRIPTURE	Matthew 20:20–28; Mark 10:35–45
MEMORY WORK	Mark 10:44

Approach to the Lesson

Theme: Many people want to have power and prestige, but God is looking for people who will lead by example—the example of service. The extent to which a person goes to serve others is the extent to which that person can lead others in the way of our Lord. Jesus said, "For even the Son of man came not to be ministered unto, but to minister, and to give his life a ransom for many" (Mark 10:45).

Rationale: Young people love to be popular. They usually try to gain popularity, however, by showing off or placing themselves in situations that bring them attention—either positive or negative. Challenge them to consider themselves servants. Only then can they truly lead.

Background: Few instances in the Gospels show the flawed humanity of the disciples as glaringly as the incident discussed in this lesson. James and John sought superior positions of authority for themselves in the future kingdom.

Another passage bears some resemblance to this event, but it involved all the disciples, not only James and John. That event, recorded in Luke 22:24–30, occurred during the last week of the Lord's earthly

Objectives

KNOWLEDGE (concepts students need to grasp)	the contrast between worldly leadership and Christian leadership
	the extent to which we should seek to serve others
	that popularity is not the same as leadership
APPLICATION (principles students should put into practice)	We can be leaders by serving even if others do not recognize us as leaders.
	We should constantly seek new areas of service.

Bible Expressions to Understand

exercise lordship/dominion—bring under one's power; subdue
exercise authority—use power
ransom—a price paid for sin and its consequences

Louis XIV (1638–1715) was king of France longer than anyone else. In fact, no other king in all of Europe ruled as long as he did. He became king when he was only four and reigned until his death seventy-two years later. He was so powerful that many historians call the years of his reign "The Age of Louis XIV" in Europe.

Everything he did was designed to make himself more powerful. He built a great palace at Versailles to impress the other rulers of Europe. It was nearly half a mile long and contained hundreds of lavishly decorated rooms. He also made his nobles live with him at the palace a part of each year. While there, they attended balls, plays, and other kinds of entertainment. Most of the time, though, they flocked around Louis, doing little tasks to make him happy. One noble would hand him his shirt to put on in the morning, and another would take him a cup of hot chocolate before he went to bed each night. These

The official residence of French kings from 1682 to 1790, the Palace of Versailles was originally built as a hunting lodge, but Louis XIV expanded both the building and the elaborate gardens surrounding it.

were not very noble tasks, but they made Louis feel important. He even chose the sun as the symbol of his reign. He thought that as the planets revolved around the sun, so everyone else in Europe revolved around him.

Besides being self-centered, Louis was cruel. He persecuted the Protestant Christians of France because they weren't Catholics. He made them house uncouth French soldiers in their homes. He took children from Protestant families and had them reared as Catholics. He even took away the Protestants' freedom to worship. Some 250,000 Christians fled France to find a place where they could worship God freely.

Louis XIV was richer and more powerful than any other man during his lifetime. Yet according to

King Louis XIV's favorite thing was hearing his generals, government officials, and aides flatter him. The sad thing was he believed their lies.

114

ministry. The conversation with James and John took place about a month before that. In light of the other ten disciples' response to the self-seeking request of James, John, and their mother, one wonders how these ten could have fallen prey to the same temptation just days later. Such is human nature: quick to condemn yet quick to commit the same sin it has condemned. The Lord quickly set John and James straight on the issue of leadership.

This lesson follows Mark's account. An important teaching aid for this lesson (a copy of the chart from page 115 of the student text) is found on the CD accompanying this book.

The Lesson

I. Not About Getting Honor (Mark 10:35–37)

James and John's desire for honored positions is a negative example, showing that we should not seek honor and glory for ourselves. James and John sent their mother to ask Jesus the question. Matthew gives additional insight into their approach. He says that they came "worshipping him, and desiring a certain thing of him" (Matt. 20:20). While recognizing the Lord's character and position, they failed to recognize the true spirit of His leadership and the type of leadership He wanted them to have.

The request they made was shocking. They wanted the greatest positions of

biblical principles he was a poor leader. He used his position as king to increase his own power and prestige, not to serve other people. Jesus teaches that a Christian leader is a servant. He looks for ways to help other people physically and spiritually. He doesn't use a position of leadership to increase his personal power and prestige.

THE TWELVE DISCIPLES		
Name	Surname or Nickname	Other Facts
Simon	Peter (Cephas)	son of Jona; Andrew's brother
Andrew		Peter's brother
James	Boanerges ("Sons of Thunder")	older son of Zebedee
John		younger son of Zebedee
Philip		not Philip the Evangelist of Acts 8
Bartholomew	Nathanael	
Thomas	Didymus	a twin brother?
Matthew	Levi	son of Alpheus; a tax collector
James	the Less	also son of Alpheus; possibly Matthew's brother
Thaddeus	Judas or Lebbeus	
Simon	Zelotes; the Canaanite	a Zealot (member of a radical political party)
Judas	Iscariot	son of Simon; betrayed Jesus

The story you read for this lesson is about two brothers, James and John, the sons of Zebedee. These men were two of the first disciples Jesus had. James ended up being killed by Herod shortly after Christ's Resurrection. John went on to serve the Lord faithfully for many years and eventually wrote a Gospel, three epistles, and Revelation. He wrote Revelation while he was in exile for being a Christian.

Even though these two men loved God and served Him, they—like all of us—committed some serious sins. One of those sins is recorded in the passage you read for this lesson. We need to learn an important lesson from their mistake.

James and John wanted Jesus to promise them that they would have the two most important positions of honor in His future kingdom. Jesus told them that He couldn't promise that. He wasn't the One Who would assign those positions—His Father would. The problem behind the request was their failure to understand the true nature of spiritual leadership, which is all about service to others rather than power and prestige. Jesus spent His life leading people to God by His example and His words. Through His service countless numbers were saved. Through His death, the final act of service, the whole world can be saved.

Have you ever wanted to have an important position of responsibility? Your teacher probably gives certain students special jobs to perform. Your coach chooses a captain for the basketball team. Somebody picks the cheerleaders. Only a few get chosen for the lead roles in the school play. Why do you want to have such positions? Jesus teaches that the only valid reason for seeking opportunities like these is to serve other people. Somehow you must make a

115

responsibility and honor in the future kingdom. Looking beyond their present lowly occupation as disciple-servants, they were hoping for something better.

II. Likely to Involve Suffering (Mark 10:38–40)

Jesus's response corrected the misunderstanding James and John had about leadership. Jesus told them that they did not know what they were asking and then asked two questions to teach them that great suffering comes with spiritual leadership. First, He asked if they could drink of the same cup He would drink, meaning that they would have to live a life filled with sacrificial serving (Phil. 2:17) and suffering (1 Pet. 4:12–13). To this they responded positively.

"All that will live godly in Christ Jesus shall suffer persecution" [2 Tim. 3:12]. All who want to follow the Lord must walk a path of sacrifice and service to others. Take some time to develop for your students a realistic view of the Christian life in this world. They are not guaranteed health and wealth if they serve the Lord. This description may not sound inviting, but it may keep them from having misconceptions about what it means to follow Christ.

Then He asked them if they were prepared to be baptized with the same baptism with which He would be baptized. By using the present tense in Greek, Jesus described Himself as being baptized continuously with this baptism. He wanted to know if they were willing to be continuously identified with Him in reproach, sacrifice, and service. Again the disciples responded

(Mark 10:35–45)
Leadership is
I. Not about getting honor (35–37)
II. Likely to involve suffering (38–40)
III. Not for the selfishly ambitious (41)
IV. Accomplished by serving (42–45)

positively. Our Lord conceded that they were right; they would, in fact, remain faithful to Him even though their later faithfulness was due to God's grace and had nothing to do with the carnal self-dependence that motivated their request on this occasion.

Scripture reveals that both of these men did live out this prophecy. James was faithful until his martyrdom by Herod (Acts 12:2), and John suffered in the salt mines on the isle of Patmos, where he wrote the book of Revelation (Rev. 1:9).

Encourage your Christian students to be honest in their witnessing. Often in presenting the positive features of our faith to non-Christians, we give a lopsided view of the Faith. There are great benefits in the Christian life, but there are great demands as well.

Christ said that the positions of honor and authority on His left hand and on His right hand were not His to give. He did not dismiss the idea that there would be such positions during His millennial reign; He simply said the responsibility of filling those positions belongs to the Father.

Subordination in the Trinity does not imply inequality. The three persons of the Godhead have agreed among Themselves to perform certain roles in the plan of salvation. The Son agreed to a role subordinate to the Father. Yet the three are equal, as infinite God.

Even as the Son has agreed to subordinate Himself to His equal (Phil. 2:6–8; 1 Cor. 15:28), and even to His inferiors (e.g., Matt. 17:24–27), so we must often be in submission to our peers and even to those we might consider inferiors. We do not "lower" ourselves when we submit, any more than Christ lowered Himself by voluntarily submitting to the Father.

III. Not for the Selfishly Ambitious (Mark 10:41)

The response of the other disciples shows that they were all selfishly ambitious.

The other ten were incensed by the request of James and John. Our Lord did not side with them in their response, nor did He rebuke them. The selfishness these two demonstrated wasn't likely to improve their relationship with their fellow disciples, but they had been willing to take that risk. Ambitious self-centeredness does not please the Lord or others. A manifestation of pride disqualifies a person from grace or power to serve the Lord. When those around us observe pride in our character, their confidence in and appreciation for us quickly diminish. Consequently, our ministry to others is decreased.

IV. Accomplished by Serving (Mark 10:42–45)

Jesus explained that leadership in His kingdom is the opposite of leadership in the world. The essence of worldly leadership is power and prestige. The secular leader enjoys being known as one of the "great ones." He loves to "exercise lordship," or to show his authority at every opportunity. Nothing could be further from Christ's conception of leadership. Certainly leaders have authority in the church, and we are commanded to "obey them that have rule over" us (Heb. 13:17). Often God will use someone in authority over us to guide us into His will. However, the Christian should not become a leader just to get this authority.

Many students struggle with the problem of pride. They want to be thought of highly by their peers and will do almost anything to win their praise. Some already think highly of themselves and take every opportunity to convince others of how special they are. Teach your students the value of staying in the background and not putting themselves forward to be seen by all (James 4:10).

What then is the correct Christian perspective on leadership? Jesus simply stated that service was the whole issue. In His eyes, if an individual was to be great, a leader of others, he must be a servant. Great service to others is great leadership. Positions of honor and responsibility should be sought only for the opportunities of service they provide. To seek an office for glory or authority is wrong.

We can derive from Mark 10:35–45 that it is not wrong to strive to become qualified for a position of authority if our motive is greater service for Christ. Self-improvement seems to result naturally in greater opportunity and service. En-

courage your students to develop their abilities and talents so they can be used greatly in the service of the Lord.

Jesus ended His instruction by using Himself as an example. He viewed His life as a ransom paid to set men free from sin. He did not come to subjugate others. The whole point of His life on earth was spiritual service to others. He set an example that we are to follow—an example of selfless service, night and day, that has never been equaled. Peter wrote, "Christ also suffered for us, leaving us an example, that ye should follow his steps" (1 Pet. 2:21).

If this was an appropriate way for Jesus to spend His life, it is an appropriate way for us to spend ours. As a teacher you cannot give too much emphasis to the effect of Christ's life in the world. His

death and Resurrection are the hinge point of human history, but His life is also extremely significant.

Special Problems and Topics

• Who did the asking?

Mark attributes the request for leadership to James and John themselves (Mark 10:37), but Matthew says it was their mother (Matt. 20:21). There is no contradiction; all three were in agreement. Having the mother make the request took a bit of the sharp edge off the egocentrism of the petition.

---

leadership position a way to serve others. If you can't do that, then you shouldn't seek the position. Wanting it so that other people will like you, think you're important, or have to do what you say is wrong. God is looking for servants, not big shots.

The way you become a servant is to start serving. How can you serve others? Here's a way to begin. Choose three acts of service (one from each of the following lists) that you are not presently performing. Begin doing one of those three things this week. Add the second one next week. Add the third one the week after next.

Home
- Wash the dishes once a week.
- Cut the grass.
- Take out the trash.
- Clean the bathroom.
- Wash the car.
- Clean the garage.
- Babysit your little brother or sister.
- Do the laundry once a week.
- Vacuum the carpet.
- Do yard work for an elderly neighbor.

School
- Wash the school van or bus.
- Sweep the halls.
- Clean the boards.
- Participate in a fund-raising activity.
- Clean up the gym after a ball game.
- Help another student with homework.

Church
- Do errands for your pastor.
- Trim the shrubs on the church property.
- Sweep the sidewalks around the church.
- Clean the restrooms.
- Work in the nursery.
- Go on visitation.
- Help in vacation Bible school.

Servant Leadership

True Christian leaders are those who set an example of Christlikeness by serving others. A true leader doesn't seek to be important or to boss other people around. He doesn't care if he's ever recognized for his efforts. He never brags about himself or tries to look better than others. He's a servant of God by serving people.

Do You Remember?

1. Which two disciples asked for important positions in Christ's future kingdom? _____
   James and John, the sons of Zebedee

2. How did the other ten disciples react to their request? _____
   They were angry with James and John.

3. What are the two things that rulers over Gentiles exercise? _____
   dominion (or lordship) and authority

4. What two actions did Jesus use to describe the similarities between His life and the lives of James and John? _____
   being baptized with the same baptism and drinking from the same cup

5. If a person wants to be a great Christian, what must he do? *serve others* _____

116

✳ Extra Activities

Survey: Challenge your students to take seriously the project suggested on page 116 of their textbook. Within one week of teaching this lesson, take an anonymous survey of the class. Suggested questions:

(1) Which act of service did you choose for this week?

(2) Have you done it yet? If so, what were the results?

(3) What act of service do you plan to do next week?

Express appreciation for those who have done something, and encourage those who haven't that it's not too late to begin.

Give the same survey again a week later.

Symposium: Invite three area pastors (senior, associate, or youth) to speak for ten minutes each on the qualities and behavior of a Christian leader. After all three are finished, ask each to give a brief explanation (two to three minutes) of how he decided to enter the Christian ministry and what he had to do to prepare.

Writing: Have each of your students write a one-page summary of the life of a leader in church history. They will need to research on the Internet or check books out of their church and school library for this report. Suggest that they ask their pastor for the name of a famous missionary, pastor, or Christian teacher to write about. The character qualities that made this person an effective leader should be the focus of the report rather than the biographical details of his life.

Ask the students to list evidences of whether this person did or did not follow Christ's example of servant leadership.

Lesson 33
Boldness

THEME	John the Baptist
SCRIPTURE	Matthew 14:1–12 [Matthew 3:1–12; 11:7–15; John 1:19–34]
MEMORY WORK	John 1:29

⊙ Approach to the Lesson

Theme: Showing boldness—a courageous, daring spirit and contempt for danger— in our service for Christ is pleasing to God. The Lord has not given us a spirit of fear. He has given us a spirit of love, power, and a sound mind (2 Tim. 1:7). Like a lion that's unafraid of other animals, the believer should courageously do God's will. Risking physical harm, slander, and failure, the bold believer is strong and aggressive in his pursuit of God and His glory.

Rationale: Encourage a spirit of boldness but discourage foolhardiness. Young people may have difficulty distinguishing between the two. Stress that they must know the Bible and what it expects of them before they can tell whether their boldness is appropriate.

Background: All four Gospels supply information about the life and ministry of John the Baptist. It is largely restricted to the first few chapters in each Gospel. The life of this man, who apparently never performed any miracles, began with a miraculous birth. His mother, Elisabeth, cousin to Mary the mother of Jesus (Luke 1:36), was advanced in years and barren. While John's father, Zacharias, was serving as a priest in the temple, the angel Gabriel appeared to him and told him that his wife would conceive a son and that his name should be called John (1:7–23). Filled with the Holy Spirit "from his mother's womb" (1:15), John spent most of his adolescence and early manhood in the Judean wilderness (1:80). Some speculate that he may have lived with the Essenes, a conservative Jewish sect that had withdrawn from corrupt Jewish culture and lived in the area.

One thing noticeable in virtually every biblical reference to John's life is his boldness. The man was utterly fearless in the face of opposition to the truth he preached and the ministry he performed. This lesson is designed to show how this quality is demonstrated through his life.

 ## The Lesson

I. Boldness Against Hypocrisy (Matt. 3:1–12)

With exemplary boldness, John warned the religious hypocrites that they would be judged and punished.

The first portrait of John presented in the New Testament is an austere one. He preached in the wilderness of Judea, urging the people to repent. The motivation for that repentance was that the kingdom of heaven was "at hand," meaning that the long-awaited Messiah was coming soon. John is described as the fulfillment of a prophecy that spoke of one shouting in the wilderness, "Prepare ye the way of the Lord, make his paths straight" (Matt. 3:3; cf. Isa. 40:3). His clothing was rugged (a camel-hair tunic and a leather belt) and his diet was simple (locusts and honey).

Why did John follow such an austere lifestyle? Probably he wanted it to be a contrast to the way the religious leaders of that day lived. Many of them were in religious service merely for money. John made a strong statement against that practice by the way he lived. His sincerity and the power of his message were recognized by crowds who came to him from Jerusalem, Judea, and the region all around the Jordan River. Many repented and were baptized (Matt. 3:1–6).

Not surprisingly, John's fame attracted the attention of the religious leadership. The Pharisees and Sadducees, fat with the best food and dressed in Jerusalem's finest, came to observe his ministry. He publicly called them snakes, telling them to repent. He told them to bear fruit that was consistent with repentance. By this he meant they should come to Christ with truly penitent hearts, not in a hypocritical, pious attitude. They had mistakenly concluded that being the physical descendants of Abraham was adequate to gain favor with God (Matt. 3:7–9; cf. Rom. 2:25–29). This wrong conclusion led them to live hypocritical lives.

John warned that the Lord was coming. On those who repented would be bestowed the presence of the Holy Spirit; on those who did not, judgment. John used two images to illustrate this judgment. One was of a man ready to cut down a fruitless tree with an axe. The other was of a man sweeping up the chaff from his threshing floor and then burning it. A time of judgment was approaching for the hypocritical religious leadership of Israel. Failure to repent meant certain judgment (Matt. 3:10–12). God is always merciful; for nearly forty years after Israel's leaders killed Jesus, they had an opportunity to repent and avert judgment. But finally the time came. Jerusalem was razed by the Roman general Titus in AD 70. About 1.1 million people were killed, and the rest were deported to the far reaches of the empire.

> Boldness is appropriate when dealing with sin that has advanced to the stage of hypocrisy. This problem exists with many young people who profess Christianity. When they become smug and apathetic toward true faith, they need to be boldly confronted.

II. Boldness Against Moral Corruption (Matt. 14:1–12)

[Of the four passages covered here this is the only one of the four students are assigned to read. It parallels Mark 6:14–29 and Luke 9:7–9. Mark is especially helpful in explaining this lesson, since he adds several details not found in the other Gospels. In teaching this section, keep in mind that students often confuse the Herods. Herod Antipas, who murdered John the Baptist, was the son of Herod the Great. Two other sons of Herod the Great had the same name, Herod Philip. One was the tetrarch of northern Palestine east of the Jordan. The other Philip, mentioned in this passage, held no formal administrative position under Rome. The Herods will be discussed more thoroughly in Lesson 37. For now, you can refer the students to the Herod family tree on page 130 in their books.]

John the Baptist preached publicly against the king's immoral marriage to his brother's wife.

Apparently Herod Antipas had John arrested as he ministered near Aenon (John 3:23). Herod, already alarmed at John's increasing influence among the people, was angered further by John's criticism of his recent marriage. He had divorced his wife to marry the wife of his brother, Herod Philip. John had denounced the marriage as a violation of Jewish laws against incest (Lev. 18:16; 20:21). John's arrest had actually resulted from the enmity of Herodias, Antipas's new wife (Matt. 14:3; Mark 6:19). Herod himself had protected John because of his fear of the common people.

> His own boldness and Herodias's cruelty cost John his life. Would it have been better if John had not said anything about the moral practices of the political leadership? No; it was right for him to say what he did. Political leaders have a grave responsibility before God. They must set the right example morally. The Bible tells us to pray for our political leaders, and John's example instructs us to reprove them when they live in wickedness. Christians serve as the conscience of any nation in which they reside. To remain silent when leadership commits open sin is cowardice. As such, it is a violation of the spirit of Christianity because God has not given us a spirit of fear.

In a moment of weakness during his birthday celebration, Herod promised his stepdaughter anything she asked because she had pleased him by dancing. Her mother, Herodias, instructed her to ask for John's head. Herod was grieved by the request, but he carried it out. Because of Herodias's revengeful spirit and Herod's weakness, John the Baptist was beheaded. After his execution, John's disciples buried his body (Matt. 14:6–12).

Objectives

KNOWLEDGE (concepts students need to grasp)	the historic change that the ministry of John the Baptist signaled
	John's familial relationship with Jesus
	the office and role John filled
	the circumstances under which John demonstrated boldness
APPLICATION (principles students should put into practice)	We should be bold against religious hypocrisy.
	We should be bold against moral corruption.
	We should be bold in sharing the gospel.

Boldness — L.33

Read: Matthew 14:1–12   Memorize: John 1:29

Bible Expressions to Understand

tetrarch—governor of one-fourth of a country
Herodias—wife of Herod Antipas
charger—a large dish or platter

It was a moonless night, so the five-hundred-pound tawny beast was practically invisible as he made his way silently through the African jungle. The darkness was no problem for the lion. Though colorblind, lions can see clearly with only an eighth as much light as the human eye needs. Guided by his keen sense of smell, the lion approached the camp where about fifty railroad workers (all from India) slept in canvas tents. It was 1901, and these workmen had come to Kenya to construct the new rail line from Mombasa to Lake Victoria.

The men had no weapons, but, having heard of lion attacks at other camps, they had built a crude fence of thornbushes around their camp. The fire had died down to embers, and the lone sentry was snoring by the time the lion approached the fence. Putting his paw on the thorny barrier, he could tell it wasn't sturdy. He found an opening between the branches and easily pushed himself through.

The odors were stronger now, but a particular scent drew him to one of the tents. Ignoring the watchman, he boldly crossed the small clearing. He stopped outside the tent flap and listened. Hearing only breathing, he slipped quietly inside and stepped over two sleeping men to get to his prey. No one in the tent even knew the lion was there until he bit down on the victim's skull, crushing the bones as if they were thin plastic.

The man died instantly. His awakened coworkers yelled in terror as the lion pulled the body out of the tent. The lion stopped a short distance from the tent and began to eat, not even bothering to drag the corpse into the forest as he had at other camps. He obviously felt no fear.

The lion has long been a symbol of courage. Its strength and boldness made it a favorite animal in the arenas of Rome. In just forty years the Romans

The average male African lion is nine feet in length (including his tail) and stands three feet tall at the shoulder. Typically weighing 350 to 400 pounds, he can leap more than ten yards horizontally.

brought fifty thousand lions to Rome for bloody fights between man and beast. Normally lions do not attack people, but they do not fear other animals. They have been observed attacking a full-grown hippopotamus, taking on a vicious crocodile, and tearing a giant python in half. Scripture speaks of the lion as unusually bold: "The righteous are bold as a lion" (Prov. 28:1).

Scripture presents John the Baptist as an outstanding model of boldness. He seemed to be fearless. John was a relative of the Lord Jesus, born six months before Him and filled with the Holy Spirit from the time of his birth. He had a special task in

117

John with a reed. Reeds were a common sight along Palestine's riverbanks. The reed plant, *Arundo domax*, grows up to twelve feet tall. It is slender and has a blossom on the top. When the wind gusts, it will lie almost flat along the water but will quickly resume its position when the wind dies down. John was not like a reed; he was unmovable in his convictions.

Neither did John seek favor with the rulers of the land. The Talmud records cases in which Jews had abandoned their usual somber dress for the bright, flamboyant dress of the king's court, in hopes that Herod would grant them favors. John never did this; instead he boldly reproved the ruler's sin.

Jesus emphasized that the people had not gone to see a vacillator; they had gone to see a bold prophet. But He went on to indicate that John was more than a prophet. He was unique, the one who fulfilled the Old Testament prophecy that the Messiah would be preceded by one who would prepare His way (Mal. 3:1).

Jesus anticipated the Jews' argument that Moses or Abraham took priority over John. He delivered an unmistakable tribute to John's position. He then taught that John's bold ministry marked the beginning of a new era in God's working in human affairs (Matt. 11:11–15). From that point on, those who accepted the Lord's teaching could consider John equivalent to Elijah in his work, turning the hearts of Israel to the Lord (Mal. 4:5–6; Luke 1:16–17). Christ concluded with the solemn exhortation, "He that hath ears to hear, let him hear" (Matt. 11:15).

III. Boldness About Jesus (John 1:19–34)

John boldly proclaimed Jesus even though it meant diminishing his own influence. When the Jews, particularly the priests and Levites of the Pharisaic sect, asked John who he was, he was quick to tell them who he was not. He was not the Christ, the Anointed One of God, to save men from sin. He was not a reincarnation of Elijah (John 1:21), who was expected to return before the Messiah. He also was not the Prophet that Moses had foretold (Deut. 18:15). John was the one preparing the way for the Lord Who was to come, and he stressed his own inferiority when compared with Him (John 1:19–27).

The day after this conversation, John saw the Lord twice and on both occasions announced, "Behold the Lamb of God" (John 1:29, 36). The first time, he identified Christ as the Lamb of God "which taketh away the sin of the world." He was clearly assigning to Jesus the role of Savior. When he first made this statement, the audience was probably a multitude; the second time it was at least two of his disciples, who then left him and followed Jesus. John showed no hesitation in proclaiming this message even though the Jews were challenging his ministry and his own disciples were leaving him.

IV. Boldness Commended by Jesus (Matt. 11:7–15)

Jesus commended John for his resolute and uncompromising prophetic ministry. This passage has been called John's "funeral oration." Jesus began by contrasting

Special Problems and Topics

• **How did the Pharisees misunderstand Messianic prophecies?**

By their questioning of John (John 1:19–21), the Pharisees demonstrated a serious misunderstanding of the Scriptures. The Old Testament uses several designations for the One who would come: Messiah (Dan. 9:25–26), the Servant of the Lord (Isa. 42:1), and the Prophet (Deut. 18:15), among others. In varying degrees the Jews failed to identify these offices or titles as belonging to a single Person. John's separate answers to the Pharisees should not be construed as implying that their interpretation was right. Peter would later make it clear that the Prophet Moses spoke of was indeed the Messiah (Acts 3:22–26).

• How did John the Baptist point to the deity of Christ?

An evidence for Christ's absolute deity that is often overlooked is found in John 1:23–29. There John equates the Messiah, Jesus, with "the Lord," Whose way he is preparing. This reference quotes Isaiah 40:3, where the word translated "the Lord" is the Tetragrammaton *YHWH*, or Jehovah. Jehovah's Witnesses, who distinguish between Jesus and Jehovah, have no satisfactory response to this use of the name YHWH for Jesus.

• Who is "least in the kingdom of heaven"?

When Jesus commended John by saying no one greater had arisen, He immediately contrasted John's position with that of the one "that is least in the kingdom of heaven" (Matt. 11:11). This passage has long puzzled students of Scripture. The early church understood this statement to refer to Jesus Himself, interpreting it, "He that is lesser [in age and public approval] is greater in God's kingdom."

More recently it has been taken in a dispensational sense, designating those who have followed John in the kingdom. While John was familiar with the holiness of God and the promise of a coming King, he was not a witness to the sacrifice of Christ at Calvary; thus he did not know the full expression of God's love for mankind. Because John was an Old Testament saint, he did not have the privileges of Christianity, such as the constant presence of the Holy Spirit and the completed revelation of God's Word.

• How can "the violent" enter the kingdom "by force"?

The words *violent* and *force* (Matt. 11:12) should not be taken negatively. The point is that to enter the kingdom, a person must overcome opposition. The world has opposed Christ and His message throughout the centuries. The convert must overcome the world system in order to trust the Savior. *Violent* and *force* describe the bold character and activity of the believer in concrete terms. Rather than passively fitting into the world, the convert must actively put it aside when he comes to the Lord (Luke 14:26).

the plan of God. He was the one who prepared the hearts of the people of Israel to follow Christ. His life and ministry fulfilled Malachi's prophecy: "Behold, I will send you Elijah the prophet before the coming of the great and dreadful day of the Lord: and he shall turn the heart of the fathers to the children, and the heart of the children to their fathers, lest I come and smite the earth with a curse" (Mal. 4:5–6).

John encouraged people to repent of their sins and be baptized to show that they'd trusted God. Once Jesus began His ministry, John directed his disciples and everyone else to follow Christ, not him. He said, "Behold the Lamb of God, which taketh away the sin of the world" (John 1:29). He was a humble but bold servant.

One time, some hypocritical religious leaders came to listen to John preach. He called them snakes and boldly told them to repent of their hypocrisy. Not afraid of what others did or thought, he spoke the truth fearlessly.

Jesus asked the crowd about John (Matt. 11:7), "What went ye out into the wilderness to see? A reed shaken with the wind?" He answered His own question by explaining that John was a prophet. "Among those that are born of women there is not a greater prophet than John the Baptist" (Luke 7:28).

118

John's boldness cost him his life. Herod Antipas had imprisoned him when he criticized Herod's marriage to his half brother's wife, Herodias. Herod wanted to put John to death, but fear of the people kept him from it. Later, however, at a feast celebrating Herod's birthday, he rashly promised to give Herodias's daughter whatever she wanted as a reward for her dance. Having been instructed by her mother, she asked for the head of John the Baptist.

Herod was a powerful political official, a man who had the power of life and death over John. However, John rebuked him for his sin. John had discovered and put an important truth into practice in his life: he didn't have to keep on living, but he did have to obey God. For him to sit back in cowardly silence while this leader set a sinful example would've been wrong. He couldn't be silent just to protect himself. He spoke out, was imprisoned, and died. Would it have been better for John to preserve his life in order to continue his ministry? John didn't think so, and neither did Jesus.

Jesus said that John was no reed shaken by the wind (Matt. 11:7). He wasn't like a tall stalk of marsh grass that bent in a breeze. He wouldn't give in to religious or political pressure. He wouldn't even cave in to the fear of losing his own life. John acted in a manner that pleased God, and not men. No wonder Jesus said that no one who lived before John was greater than he (Matt. 11:11). He was fearless of all but God. He was concerned about God's opinion of his conduct and his words, and no one else's. This man was greater than Abraham, Moses, and Joseph. He was greater than David, Solomon, and Hezekiah. He was greater than Isaiah, Jeremiah, and Ezekiel. His boldness will always be a model for Christians.

Bold as a Lion

You should show a courageous, daring spirit and contempt for danger in your service for Christ. This is pleasing to God. The Lord hasn't given you a spirit of fear (2 Tim. 1:7). Like a lion that's not afraid of any other animal, you should courageously do God's will. Risking physical harm, slander, and failure, the bold believer will be strong and aggressive in his pursuit of God and His glory.

Do You Remember?

1. Why did Herod think Jesus was John the Baptist resurrected from the dead? _____
   because Jesus was doing miracles and preaching the same message John had preached

2. Why did Herod imprison John the Baptist? _____
   for criticizing Herod's unlawful marriage to Herodias, his half brother's wife

3. What was the people's opinion of John? _____
   They thought he was a prophet.

4. What had kept Herod from putting John to death at first? *fear of the people*

5. Why did Herod promise to reward Herodias's daughter? _____
   Her dance pleased him.

6. Who had instructed Herodias's daughter to ask for John's death? *Herodias*

7. Why did Herod go ahead and execute John even though he didn't want to? _____
   because he had made a promise in front of his dinner guests

119

Extra Activities

Personal evaluation: Timidity or shyness can be a great hindrance to your students in their walk with Christ. Some are inclined to have this problem because of their natural disposition. An honest self-evaluation would probably help them see how to apply this lesson. You may want to use the following questions, asking students to respond with *never, sometimes, often,* or *always.*

(1) When my friends are doing wrong things that adults don't know about, I correct them.

(2) When my friends break the rules at school, I speak to them and the teacher about it.

(3) When my siblings disobey my parents, I confront them about it.

(4) When I am around someone who does not know Christ, I witness.

[A form for this self-evaluation can be found on the CD.]

Writing: Have each student write a one-page report about another person in Scripture who demonstrated boldness. On the day they submit these reports, select several students to read theirs aloud to the class. Some of the students will cite other character qualities from the examples they use. Make suggestions to help them clearly define the trait of boldness.

Lesson 34
Worship

THEME	Mary of Bethany
SCRIPTURE	John 12:1–11 (Matthew 26:6–13; Mark 14:3–9)
MEMORY WORK	Matthew 26:10–11

 ## Approach to the Lesson

Theme: Actions that show our humble devotion to Christ—our deepest love for Him—are valuable to Him. Service given as an act of worship is the best kind of work. However, service rendered in the Lord's name without any thought of Him is displeasing. An act of true worship may be an hour of sitting quietly in prayer and meditation. It may involve giving a sacrificial gift. Or it may be a period of vigorous activity. But the worshiper will always have Christ foremost in his mind with His glory being the chief goal.

Worship is not confined to a church building. Christ may be worshiped anywhere at any time in keeping with the standards of God's Word (John 4:23–24). This truth does not relieve Christians of the obligation to meet with other believers for worship, but it does permit a broader understanding of worship. Anything done for the glory of Christ is worship.

Rationale: Sometimes teens have difficulty distinguishing motive from action. They often think that merely "doing what they're told" is enough. Stress the importance of a proper motive in Christian service.

Objectives

KNOWLEDGE (concepts students need to grasp)	what prompted Mary's act of worship
	how valuable Mary's gift was to Jesus
	what impact Mary's worship has had throughout church history
APPLICATION (principles students should put into practice)	Becoming active in a youth group or church does not mean that we are devoted to Christ.
	When we go to church services, we must do it to glorify Christ for it to be true worship.
	Sacrifice as part of the act of worship of Christ is appropriate for every believer, young people included.

Bible Expressions to Understand

ointment of spikenard—a perfumed oil made from nard, a plant that grows in northern India; imported in sealed alabaster jars

three hundred pence—three hundred denarii; nearly a year's wages

bag—a simple leather or cloth pouch in which the disciples kept the group's money

alabaster box—a long-necked flask used as a container for perfumed oil and other liquids

How do you think people in your neighborhood would react if your brother, who died last week, had been raised from the dead and was coming to supper at a friend's house? Suppose the friend had recently been miraculously healed from a terrible disease. That would be a supper everyone would want to attend. An incident like this occurred just a few days before Jesus was crucified.

Earlier Jesus had said of Mary as she sat as His feet and heard His words: "Mary hath chosen that good part, which shall not be taken away from her" (Luke 10:42).

120

Six days before the Passover, the Jewish celebration of deliverance from Egypt, Jesus went to Jerusalem. He traveled through Jericho, where he visited Zacchaeus and healed a blind man named Bartimaeus. Finally He arrived at Bethany, just a short distance from Jerusalem. There He visited in the home of Simon the leper at a supper prepared by some of His best friends.

Although Scripture doesn't say, Jesus had probably healed Simon of his leprosy, and this supper might have been a united effort by Simon and the family of Lazarus to honor Jesus. While others rejoiced to sit at the table with Jesus and share in His fellowship, Mary, who had sat at His feet before, felt compelled by love to take this opportunity to demonstrate her devotion.

As she looked at Jesus, she must have thought, *This is my Lord and King. He is going to die soon because that's what He has told us. The others don't believe that He will die, but I do. I must show Him how much I love Him!*

She remembered that she had a pound of precious anointing oil much like expensive perfumes available today. It would take a full year's labor to purchase that much. She might have been keeping it for a long time, perhaps planning to use it on some special occasion. Now maybe she thought, *I want to give Him my best. I want to give Him the most expensive thing I have, to show Him that I love Him and believe in Him.* She broke the alabaster

Background: The Scripture reading for this lesson subtly refers to an earlier incident in the life of the two sisters, Mary and Martha, recorded in Luke 10:38–42. Jesus was visiting the home of Mary, Martha, and Lazarus in Bethany just three months before His death. Martha was serving her guest and family, while Mary sat near Jesus and listened to Him teach. Martha became irritated that her sister was not helping her and approached the Lord about her sister's "neglect." Jesus corrected Martha, telling her that all her anxiety and scurrying about was not necessary, but that which Mary was doing was.

The problem with Martha's activity was not what she was doing, but the spirit in which she was performing her tasks. She was distracted from Christ. Mary was not; she was assigning great worth to the words of Jesus. This is the essence of worship. In the John 12 passage, Mary is worshiping again while Martha serves in distraction.

The dinner at which Mary performed her singular act of worship was given in honor of Jesus. Although Martha served, the supper was in the home of Simon the leper, who may have been a relative of Mary and Martha (Matt. 26:6). This supper was held about one week before the Crucifixion. Jesus had evidently healed Simon, and this supper was a joint effort on the part of Simon and the family of Lazarus to honor Him. Lazarus had recently been raised from the dead, so he was quite an attraction on this occasion. He was no doubt totally dedicated to Jesus because of what He had done for him.

vase and poured its contents on Jesus's head and feet in a gracious act of personal devotion.

Have you ever given something to Christ that was valuable or important to you? This is a way you can worship Christ and show Him how much you love Him. What you give may not be a material object. It may be your time or, most important, yourself. Giving yourself to Christ in service is the greatest gift you can give Him.

Be careful, though, not to become like Martha, Mary's sister. At a similar dinner on another occasion, she was so busy preparing and serving the meal, she didn't take time to worship Christ. You can become too busy doing things with your Christian friends at your Christian school. They may be good things, but if you stop focusing on Jesus and His Word, you're too busy. Slow down. Take time to read God's Word and pray. Listen to what Jesus has to say, and express your love to Him. Sometime the Lord may want you to perform some special act of worship like Mary. You must be close enough to Him to know when that time is.

When Mary broke open the vase of expensive perfume, Judas, the one who would soon betray Jesus, didn't approve of her action. "Why wasn't this ointment sold for three hundred pence and given to the poor?" was his irreverent question. The poor? Had Jesus ever been indifferent to the needs of the poor? No. Had Mary? Not as far as we can tell. Was this the only possible use for this ointment—to trade for money to give to the poor? Judas didn't understand that one who worshiped and adored the Lord as Mary did wasn't one who would forget the needs of those around her.

Judas's real motivation wasn't to help the poor anyway. "This he said, not that he cared for the poor; but because he was a thief, and had the bag, and bare what was put therein" (John 12:6). Jesus and the disciples had appointed Judas as their treasurer for what meager sums of money they had. But as a covetous man, Judas felt that Mary was wasting her treasure on Jesus. He saw only the loss of some wealth that he could have gained.

Mark's account of this incident (Mark 14:3–9) tells us that Judas made his critical remark after the other disciples had complained about what they thought was Mary's wastefulness. The other disciples were not thieves, but they did have a problem recognizing the purpose of Mary's gift. They thought it was extravagant. The mistake they made was to underestimate the value of the Lord. Worship is based on the idea that the person being worshiped is worthy. Small, insignificant acts of worship tell unbelievers that Jesus is small, insignificant, and unworthy. Bold worship like Mary's speaks highly of Jesus's character and the worshiper's relationship to Him. What does your worship of Christ say about Him? The way you live should show every person who knows you that you think Jesus is worthy of your best. This is the way to inspire others to appreciate the Lord Jesus. Challenge them by your example of sacrificial worship through giving and serving.

The Savior understood what was going on in the hearts of both Judas and Mary. So He said, "Let her alone: against the day of my burying hath she kept this. For the poor always ye have with you; but me ye have not always" (John 12:7–8). Jesus, the One Who sacrificed Himself for sinners, would not stand in the way of Mary's loving heart if she wanted to show devotion to Him. Jesus knew that such love and sacrifice would have its reward.

Worthy Worship

When you do things to show your deepest love and devotion to the Lord Jesus, you're worshiping Him. Work that is done as an act of worship is the only kind of work a Christian should do. Work, however, can distract you from Christ Himself. You can serve in the name of Jesus Christ without a thought given to Him or a prayer uttered to Him to get His direction in that work. An act of true worship may be an hour sitting quietly in prayer and meditation. You can worship by giving a sacrificial gift, as Mary did. You can even worship the Lord by doing your best for Christ in school and at church. Whatever you do, worship must be uppermost in your mind, and Christ's glory must be your chief goal.

121

cerned for the poor (who could have benefited from some of the money acquired by selling the perfume), he denounced her act as frivolous. He really had other reasons for his complaint. Judas was a thief and had charge of the disciples' funds. If the perfume had been sold, he could have stolen the money. Much to his dismay, he lost that opportunity.

In every generation those who are devoted to God are thought extravagant in their display of love, and they are condemned for it. The lukewarm believer cannot understand the disciple with the burning heart, and he never will unless he experiences God's cleansing as Isaiah did (6:6–7).

What a contrast between Judas and Mary this scene presents. Mary is the worshiper; Judas is the thief. Mary is loyal; Judas is a traitor. It takes great light to bring out the shadows. The light of Mary's devotion reveals the shadow of Judas for what it really is—dark and deceptive.

The contrast between Mary and the other disciples is not as stark, but it is evident. The disciples obviously could not conceive of an act of devotion like Mary's; it was beyond them.

III. Worship Is Appreciated (John 12:7–8)

Jesus sharply rebuked Judas and the other disciples for their stingy attitude. Mary had decided to use this perfume that she had been saving. Jesus knew that she was anointing Him before His death and deeply appreciated her gift. His appreciation was so deep that He prophesied that her act of devotion and love would be remembered throughout history (Matt. 26:13). His prophecy has come to pass through the preservation of the incident in the inspired record, the Word of God.

Since one act memorialized this woman forever, is it possible that the same could be true of us? Our devotion can and should be just as pure and our zeal just as great as Mary's.

 ## The Lesson

I. Worship May Be Costly (John 12:1–3)

Mary's act of worship was remarkable. In an overflowing act of love and gratitude, she poured perfume worth a year's wages on Jesus's feet and head as an expression of personal devotion to Him. Taking a small vessel of costly perfume, made from the fragrant nard plant, she broke it open and administered it to the head and feet of the Lord. Then in a humble act of adoration, she wiped His feet with her hair, the aroma of the perfume filling the house. It is possible that this perfume was purchased earlier as an extravagant self-indulgence before Mary was a believer. Or it may have been purchased for anointing one of her relatives for burial.

Be careful not to mistake false worship for true worship. Church attendance, being active in the youth group, emotional singing—these and other outward actions are often equated with true worship. But all of them can be done selfishly. A good sign of whether you really love and worship God is a willingness to give up something you value highly for Him like May did. David said, "Neither will I offer burnt offerings unto the Lord my God of that which doth cost me nothing" (2 Sam. 24:24).

II. Worship May Be Condemned (John 12:4–6)

Judas Iscariot, noting the objections raised by several of the other disciples (Matt. 26:8), took the opportunity to express hypocritically his own concern over the supposed waste. Pretending to be con-

In response to Judas's pettiness, Jesus said that there are some gifts given directly to Him for His glory that should not be given for meeting the needs of the poor. His rationale has long been cited by conservative Christians as a polemic against the social gospel. And it is true that the poor will always be with us; no amount of human ingenuity will ever eliminate the problem of hunger and material need. This fact does not relieve the believer from his responsibility to the poor (e.g., James 1:27), but it does establish a set of priorities. Christ comes before everything and everyone else. Family, friends, the poor, and even the spiritually destitute take second place to Christ. Responsibility in each of these spheres is not always mutually exclusive of our responsibility to Christ, but there are times when it may be. Only those who walk close to Him will know when those times are. Mary knew because she had learned to abide in Christ.

> Attending church services, participating in church programs, and heartfelt praise are all important, but we must be sure we do them for the right reason—the glory of God (1 Cor. 10:31).

IV. Worship May Be Opposed (John 12:9–11)

The religious leaders of the day opposed Jesus and His followers because Jesus's power undermined their authority. Many of the Jews began to gather when they heard that Jesus was at Simon's home. His presence was not their only motive for gathering; they had heard that Lazarus, the man who had been raised from the dead, was also there. The chief priests were deeply troubled over the testimony of Christ's power as demonstrated by His raising Lazarus. How could they deny His power and His deity when a man He had brought back from the grave was alive, sitting and eating at a dinner? Convinced that something must be done, they plotted to kill Lazarus, but church tradition indicates that he lived an additional thirty years, dying at age sixty. (See Lesson 46.)

Many of the common people were withdrawing their loyalty from the chief priests and stale Judaism and were trusting Christ. Naturally this was a great concern to the religious establishment, but why were the chief priests so concerned about the people? Certainly they did not care about the spiritual well-being of the people. But they *were* concerned about the possibility

of losing money. People who forsook Judaism would stop giving to the temple treasury. The love of money is the root of all kinds of evil (1 Tim. 6:10).

✳ Extra Activities

Question and answer: To stimulate classroom interaction, intersperse the following questions in your lesson.

a. What is true worship?
   Anything done for the glory of Christ may be worship.

b. Who were Mary's sister and brother? Where else are they mentioned in the Bible?
   Martha and Lazarus; in Luke 10:38–42 and John 11:1–45

c. What was the significance of the gift Mary gave Jesus?
   its value (a year's wages) and its purpose (to express great devotion)

Writing: Have your students do a simple one-page report on the definition of *worship*. They will want to check several dictionaries and the encyclopedia. Church hymnals might be checked for hymns indexed under *worship*. They may also interview a pastor, search the Internet, and check the library for relevant resources. Have them use their reports to respond to the question "What is true worship?" This should get your class discussion started successfully.

Do You Remember?

1. When did the anointing of Jesus take place? _six days before the Passover_

2. Where in Bethany did this supper take place? _at Simon the leper's house_

3. Why were so many Jewish leaders present on this occasion? _because they wanted to see Lazarus, who had been raised from the dead_

4. Why did Judas complain about what Mary did? _He wasn't concerned about worshiping Jesus and would have liked to get his hands on such a large amount of money._

5. What did Mary see by faith that others did not? _that Jesus was going to die soon_

6. How much was the ointment worth? _three hundred pence—almost a year's wages_

7. What did the ointment represent to Mary (Mark 14:8)? _the best she had to give_

Impartiality

Read: Matthew 4:18–22; Mark 2:13–17; 3:13–21; John 1:35–51

Memorize: James 3:17

Bible Expressions to Understand

receipt of custom—the tax collector's office
scribe—an expert in Jewish law
Boanerges—a nickname meaning "Sons of Thunder"
Canaanite—member of a radical political group; Zealot
guile—deceit or treachery

The famous American author Mark Twain wrote a book called *The Prince and the Pauper*. Though the story is fictional, it illustrates an important truth. It tells how a prince, Edward, trades places with a poor man named Tom. Edward wants to be free of his responsibilities, and Tom wants to live in wealth. They soon find, however, that both princes and paupers have problems. For example, since no one knows that Edward is really a prince, they treat him rudely and even cruelly.

Eventually the two switch back to their original positions. Edward sums up the lessons of the story by saying, "I have learned the value of mercy. And you shall be a better subject, for you have learned to understand the burdens of your king."

The prince had learned that people treat you differently when you're an ordinary citizen rather than royalty. This is called partiality. Favoritism toward others because of their wealth or fame is a sin. Christ demonstrated, and the Bible teaches, that showing favoritism can cause serious problems. If you're willing to associate with obedient Christians, you'll be a great asset to Christ and His work.

Christ does want you to be partial, in a way—toward Christians rather than toward unsaved people. You should love unsaved people and try to reach them with the gospel, of course. When it comes to friendships, though, you should choose obedient Christians.

How can you avoid playing favorites in order to be most useful in God's work? Christ had many friends and followers. How did He treat them? Jesus never played favorites on the basis of a person's background. In the view of many Jews, Matthew (also called Levi), a tax collector who became one of Christ's disciples, had been disloyal to his country. He had decided to work for "the enemy" (the Romans) by collecting taxes for them. In the process, he'd stolen from his fellow Jews by overtaxing them. On the other hand, Simon the Zealot, another disciple, had been a member of a group of political radicals. He was fiercely loyal to his country. He would even kill Roman soldiers if he got a chance.

Even though they came from opposite ends of the political spectrum, they both responded affirmatively to Christ's call to follow Him, and He accepted each of them. He was impartial. As far as Jesus was concerned, what was in the past was in the past. As far as we can tell from the New Testament, Jesus didn't prefer either of them. They had similar powers (to heal and cast out demons) and responsibility (to preach) along with the rest of the twelve (Mark 3:14–15).

> "Of a truth I perceive that God is no respecter of persons [does not show favoritism]: But in every nation he that feareth him, and worketh righteousness, is accepted with him."
> —Peter (Acts 10:34–35)

It didn't seem to matter to Jesus what a man's job was before he became a disciple or where he came from. Many of the disciples were fishermen. All but one came from Galilee, the northern part of Palestine; the one exception, Judas, may have been from

123

Lesson 35
Impartiality

THEME	Christ's Choice of Friends
SCRIPTURE	Matthew 4:18–22; Mark 2:13–17; 3:13–21; John 1:35–51
MEMORY WORK	James 3:17

Approach to the Lesson

Theme: The Lord set no personal limits on who could follow Him. The total absence of favoritism, self-interest, or indulgence of His likes and dislikes is one of the striking things about His choice of friends. He had the great capacity to see spiritual potential in people with widely diverse backgrounds and varied relationships. He befriended a political radical and a traitorous tax collector. A formerly demon-possessed woman and a disciple of John the Baptist were among His closest associates. Men and women alike were His faithful servants.

By His life Christ showed that in order to be what He intended it to be the church should never be restricted by social class, race, or vocation. This broad-minded approach, coupled with the great need of sinners, has made Christianity the one truly universal religion. All other religions are restricted by geography, nationality, or race. The single great restriction laid down by

Objectives

KNOWLEDGE (concepts students need to grasp)	the great diversity among the close followers of Christ during His ministry
	the familial relationships between some of Christ's disciples
	the inner circle of Christ's disciples: Peter, James, and John
APPLICATION (principles students should put into practice)	We have spiritual potential regardless of our background.
	Our family members are potential fellow servants in the Lord's work.
	Both men and women are important in service for Christ.
	Impartiality does not restrict us from having special friends or ministries to particular groups of people.

the Head of the church was spiritual: a person must deny himself, take up his cross, and follow Christ. He must turn from his sins and trust Christ as Savior. This is the narrow road that leads to life.

Rationale: This lesson's instruction could serve to remove a cliquish spirit among your students. They should not exclude others from friendship merely because of personal likes and dislikes.

Background: No fewer than fifty-four different people are mentioned by name in the Gospels. Many were close friends of Christ. But this number does not begin to cover the many in the unnamed multitudes that He preached to and helped. The Gospels are in part a handbook on human relations. By examining the way the Lord worked with people, believers can learn much about loving, serving, and living with others in the body.

The other lessons in this unit focus on various individuals in the Gospels who teach some important lessons by their lives. This lesson is much broader; it deals generally with the many relationships Christ had with His followers, revealing how impartiality governed His approach to them. The Lord is the greatest example of the teaching of James 3:17: "But the wisdom that is from above is first pure, then peaceable, gentle, and easy to be intreated, full of mercy and good fruits, without partiality, and without hypocrisy."

Outline

 ## The Lesson

I. Unity in Diversity

People from diverse political, vocational, geographical, and spiritual backgrounds are all valuable and can serve together in the kingdom.

Political diversity. Those of differing political persuasions can serve Christ together. Christ operated on this principle in choosing His disciples. Levi the publican, called Matthew, was viewed as a traitor by his fellow Jews. He had been a minor tax collector for the oppressive Roman government, which is precisely what he was doing in Capernaum the day Jesus called him to be one of His disciples (Matt. 9:9). Worse yet, he was successful. This idea is suggested by the banquet he held at his home, attended by many publicans and sinners (Mark 2:14–15). The result of his call to be a disciple was the end of his tax collecting. This allowed the Jews to whom he was to minister to regard him much more favorably.

Now consider Simon the Zealot, who is called a *Canaanite* (Matt. 10:4; Mark 3:18). This word is an English transliteration of the Aramaic word that means "zealous one." (It's not related to the geographical term *Canaan.*) He is also referred to as Simon Zelotes (Luke 6:15; Acts 1:13). The Greek word *zēlōtēs* means "zealous one" as well. From these names it appears that Simon belonged to the Jewish sect called the Zealots before his call to discipleship. Josephus records that the rebellion against the taxation of Augustus (Luke 2:1), led by the Zealot leader Judas the Galilean (Acts 5:37), marked the beginning of Jewish conflicts with the Roman Empire (*Antiquities,* VIII, 8.8). Eventually those conflicts led to the destruction of the temple in AD 70.

There can be no greater political contrast than that between Matthew and Simon, the one a traitor and the other a Jewish nationalist. Yet they became one in Christ, members of a close-knit group of twelve disciples who were Christ's special assis-

Judea, the southern part. It didn't matter to Christ. All He wanted was willing, obedient servants who loved God above everything else.

You'll meet Christians who are not from your country or your culture. You should treat them with as much kindness and concern as you do those who share your background. You've probably met Christians from different parts of the country or perhaps just from a nearby town or school. If they enroll at your school or attend your church, make them feel at home. Befriend them. Don't show partiality toward your old friends by excluding the newcomers from conversation and activities.

Christ didn't even show favoritism toward His friends who had a better religious background than others. Andrew, one of the twelve disciples, was a disciple of John the Baptist before he became a follower of Christ. On the other hand, Mary Magdalene, one of the women who ministered to Christ and the disciples, had been possessed by seven demons before she was saved. She witnessed the Crucifixion and was the first person to see the resurrected Christ. Andrew had a strong background spiritually; Mary didn't. Christ showed no favoritism. If you meet a Christian who doesn't know as much about the Bible as you do, be kind to him. Don't make fun of his ignorance.

Christ didn't choose His friends because their families agreed with His work. In some cases, the families of Christ's followers also followed Him. Andrew brought his brother Simon Peter to Christ. James and John, the sons of Zebedee, followed Jesus. Their mother, Salome, also became a follower of the Lord and helped with His ministry in Galilee. Mary, the mother of James the Less, followed the Lord. Though these families had several members serving the Lord, Jesus did not show favoritism toward them. He had many followers who were the only ones from their families. These were as special to Him as the family groups that served Him. The New Testament doesn't indicate that Jesus gave any special privileges to his four younger half-brothers.

The fact that a family has many members in a church doesn't mean they should get special treatment. This isn't Christ's way. You should be loyal to your family and thankful if they're serving the

Lord, but your family's godliness is no replacement for your own godliness. That's what Christ is concerned about.

Did Jesus prefer His followers to be men or women? Neither. But didn't Jesus choose twelve men to be his closest disciples? Yes, He did. The New Testament does restrict church leadership to men, but that doesn't mean that women are in any way inferior. Neither does it mean that women are restricted in their responsibility to serve the Lord. During His ministry the Lord had help from many women. Joanna, Susanna, Mary Magdalene, Martha, and her sister Mary are just a few who served the Lord faithfully. Church history is full of accounts of women who made great contributions to the work of Christ as teachers, missionaries, wives, mothers, and even martyrs. If you're a young woman, you should make it your goal to make a similar contribution.

Did Christ have any "best friends" during His time on earth? At times He gave special attention to certain disciples. He particularly seemed to enjoy

> ### Don't Play Favorites
>
> The Lord set no limits on who could be His followers. The total absence of favoritism is one of Christ's striking qualities. He saw spiritual potential in people from widely diverse backgrounds. This approach, begun by the Son of God and empowered by His Spirit, has made Christianity a universal faith—not restricted by geography, nationality, race, or sex.
>
> Your treatment of others should reflect the same impartiality. Limit your friendships only on the basis of a person's love for Christ. Never treat a person better than others because he dresses better, has more money, or is more intelligent. Look for what is good in every Christian you know. Build relationships to encourage others in their walk with Christ. This is true impartiality.

tants and founding members of the church. Separately neither of these men held admirable political positions. Neither was wise in his conduct. Yet Christ still chose them. The presence of these two men together was a reminder to all Jews that Christ could bring harmony where discord had existed. It also proved that nothing they had done before was a hindrance to their becoming followers of Christ. Christ was politically impartial in those He chose to follow Him.

Vocational diversity. By His impartiality Christ also proved that those with diverse occupational backgrounds can serve together. The vocations of several disciples are not clearly stated. The Gospels do relate, however, that several were fishermen. This group included James and John, Peter and Andrew, as well as possibly Thomas,

Nathanael, and two other disciples (Matt. 4:18–22; John 21:1–2). Fishing was active outdoor work. Contrast these men with Matthew, who had a desk job. What were the other disciples? Perhaps they were farmers or merchants. The Gospels don't say, but we know for certain that Christ didn't choose them on the basis of their occupations.

Christ saw an advantage in the diversity of these men. Unity in diversity was one key to the strength in this circle of close disciples. This unity could occur only because Christ was impartial. Your students have not yet entered their adult occupations, but they can learn an important rule from the occupational diversity of the disciples. Not all your students' friends need to enjoy the same things. They should be impartial to the interests of others. A person is not odd simply

the company of Mary, Martha, and Lazarus in Bethany. He gave special instruction to Philip, Andrew, and Thomas. He allowed Peter, James, and John to experience some things the other disciples didn't. Do these facts mean that Jesus did show favoritism to some after all?

There were good reasons that Christ gave special attention to some people at times. In some cases the disciples needed instruction in areas in which they were weak. In other cases the Lord had chosen some men to be leaders who needed some experience the other disciples didn't need. Christ was just in what He did, always doing what He knew in the long run would be good for all His followers and the glory of God.

Do You Remember?

1. Beside what body of water were four fisherman called to become Christ's disciples? *the Sea of Galilee*

2. Whose sons were James and John? *Zebedee's*

3. How soon after Christ's call did James and John respond to His invitation to be His disciples? *immediately*

4. In whose home did Jesus eat a meal where many publicans and sinners were in attendance? *Matthew's*

5. What was Matthew's other name? *Levi*

6. Where was Matthew when he was called to be a disciple? *sitting at the receipt of custom*

7. What nickname did Jesus give James and John? *Boanerges, the sons of thunder*

8. What powers and responsibilities were granted to the twelve disciples? *preach, heal sicknesses, and cast out demons (Mark 3:14–15)*

9. What did Christ's friends do when they heard of the great crowds He was attracting? *They came to get Him because they thought He was beside Himself.*

10. Who did Jesus describe as an Israelite in whom there was no guile? *Nathanael*

125

This is an unhealthy partiality that should not be true of Christians. It may be natural for us all to prefer familiar friends, but we must be willing to expand our circle of friends. This willingness is essential to the progress of the church.

Spiritual diversity. The Lord clearly demonstrated that people from spiritually diverse backgrounds can serve together in His work. Mary Magdalene was one of the faithful women of Galilee who contributed her time and substance to Christ's ministry (Luke 8:1–3). She had suffered from a severe case of demon possession before Jesus healed her. Mark notes, "Now when Jesus was risen early the first day of the week, he appeared first to Mary Magdalene, out of whom he had cast seven devils" (16:9). This was a great honor afforded a woman who had previously been in such poor spiritual condition.

In contrast, Andrew had been a disciple of John the Baptist. The fact that he was John's disciple suggests high level of interest in spiritual matters. The day after Christ's baptism, he and another disciple of John heard John say, "Behold the Lamb of God" (John 1:36–40). Immediately Andrew left John and followed Christ. Andrew's heart was already prepared spiritually for the appearing of Christ. He was anxious for His coming and followed Him as soon as he was introduced to Him. Mary's background and Andrew's background were extremely different, but Christ did not show partiality.

II. The Irrelevance of Family

People from diverse family lineages may work together for the Lord. Several brothers were among the disciples. James and John, both sons of Zebedee, served the Lord together (Matt. 4:21). Andrew, the disciple of John the Baptist, brought his brother Peter to the Lord (John 1:40–42). Peter became the leader of the twelve (Matt. 16:18) and wrote two epistles in the New Testament.

The Gospels record that among the larger group of disciples were faithful women of Galilee. One was Salome, the wife of Zebedee and mother of James and John (Matt. 27:55–56; Mark 15:40). Another was Mary, the mother of James the Less and Joses (Matt. 27:56; Mark 15:40). This Mary was also the wife of Alphaeus (Matt. 10:3). Matthew's father was also named Alphaeus (Mark 2:14). In two of the four listings of the disciples, Matthew immediately

---

because he has a hobby different from what most enjoy. Having friends with varied interests is a way for your students to broaden their horizons.

Geographical diversity. Christ also taught that those from geographically diverse backgrounds can serve together. The record of foreign missionary enterprises repeatedly attests to this fact. There also seems to be a hint at this concept in the selection of the disciples. All but one were apparently from Galilee, the northern region of Palestine. If *Iscariot* is a place name, as most agree it is, then Judas was from Kerioth in Judea, the southern part of Palestine. Palestine was a small land in the time of Christ, but as is true in most countries, geographical prejudice was not lacking. Consider the attitude of Nathanael when Philip told him that Jesus of Nazareth was the Messiah; he asked if anything good could come out of Nazareth (John 1:46). This demonstrates a negative attitude toward that community. Further, those living in Judea generally viewed everyone in Galilee as crude frontier settlers. From all evidence, Judas, a Judean, had no conflict with his fellow disciples over his geographic background. He even enjoyed a degree of confidence from them as their treasurer. Although he eventually betrayed Christ, the fact that he was a Judean and Jesus was a Galilean does not seem to have contributed to the rift between them.

When new students move in from other schools, your students will tend not to gravitate toward them. Their thinking usually is that the new kids are "outsiders."

precedes James, the son of Alphaeus (Matt. 10:3; Acts 1:13). The close proximity of the names in these lists and a father with the same name suggest that Matthew and James the Less may have been brothers. These family relationships indicate that the Lord saw family ties as possibly advantageous to service.

Many of the disciples have nothing mentioned about their families, but they were not any less effective in their service. Family ties are irrelevant to usefulness. A person's family may or may not agree with his ministry. Just six months before His death, our Lord's own brothers questioned His ministry (John 7:1–5). They did not believe in Him. After His death and Resurrection, that changed. "These all continued with one accord in prayer and supplication, with the women, and Mary the mother of Jesus, and with his brethren" (Acts 1:14). This meeting was held about seven months after their earlier expression of unbelief. Now they believed. James, Christ's half brother, became the leader of the church at Jerusalem (Acts 15:13; 21:18; Gal. 2:9, 12) and wrote the epistle that bears his name (James 1:1). The Lord's brother Judas authored the short New Testament epistle of Jude (Jude 1). There is no record of the contribution the other brothers made to the work, but we can assume from Acts 1:14 that they were believers.

The fact that Christ's mother and brothers served Him must have made Him glad, but it was irrelevant to the accomplishment of the task that the Father had set before Him. The New Testament does not record that Jesus was ever partial in His treatment of His brothers. However, as the faithful oldest son of a widowed mother, He did see to it that Mary would be taken care of after His death (John 19:27).

> Some of your students have families who love Christ and encourage them in things of the Lord. They should be thankful and yet careful that their loving families never distract them from service to Christ. Other students have families who are neutral or antagonistic toward the gospel. Perhaps, the only reason they are allowed to go to a Christian school is to get better academic training. Try to be an encouragement to them. They should remember Psalm 27:10: "When my father and my mother forsake me, then the Lord will take me up."

III. The Irrelevance of Gender

People of both genders are valuable and can serve together in the kingdom. Consider the example of Mary of Bethany. As we saw in Lesson 34, nothing mattered to her more than worshiping the Lord. She showed this by the costly gift she gave Christ, which was worth a year's wages (John 12:1–3). The Lord had performed an astounding miracle in raising her brother Lazarus from the dead, and she wanted to express her gratitude. Men and women alike should pattern themselves after Mary in her worship.

Women should also serve in necessary and vital roles in Christian ministries. The Gospels record that Mary Magdalene, Mary the mother of James the Less, Joanna, Susanna, and Salome were all part of the group of Galilean women who gave funds to Christ and His disciples (Matt. 27:55–56; Luke 8:2–3). These women provided an invaluable service. Without them the preaching and healing ministries of the disciples would have been constantly interrupted.

Except for Susanna, the women mentioned above prepared the spices with which they planned to anoint the body of Jesus after the Sabbath (Mark 16:1; Luke 23:55–56; 24:10). They did this after they had observed the burial of Christ (Luke 23:50–56). Even in the hour of death, the women were there to minister.

> Great ministries await your female students as missionaries, Christian school teachers, and godly wives and mothers. They can serve just as these women did. Christ shows no favoritism on the basis of sex.

After His Resurrection the Lord appeared first to a woman, Mary Magdalene (Mark 16:9). This Mary, Joanna, Mary the mother of James the Less, and Salome all received a special message concerning the resurrected Christ from an angel when they visited the tomb to anoint Jesus's body (Matt. 28:1–7; Mark 16:1; Luke 24:10; John 20:11–18). They were the ones who told the other disciples that Jesus was alive.

> The Lord has not restricted the right of Christian women to tell the message of the Resurrection. It is their responsibility, just as it is the responsibility of Christian men. Girls should be as bold in their witness for Christ as boys are.

IV. Impartiality and Special Relationships

The Lord Himself is impartial; He will give special help to any of His children who need it. Christians may need special instruction at times. This is not a sign of favoritism, but merely a necessity. In an effort to teach both Andrew and Philip, the Lord asked Philip how they were going to feed the multitude who had been listening to Christ's preaching (John 6:5). Christ knew that Philip needed to learn a lesson about the power of the Lord. Andrew offered the boy's five loaves and two fish. Christ fed the multitude with them. He dealt personally and directly with these two disciples because they needed some special instruction about His power.

After Christ's death and Resurrection, Thomas was not with the disciples the first time the Lord appeared to them. From the record of Scripture, it seems that Christ later reappeared to the disciples solely to reestablish Thomas's faith (John 20:24–31).

Peter, who had denied the Lord, and six other disciples spoke to Him beside the Sea of Galilee after the Resurrection (John 21:1–19). During that meeting Jesus reinstated Peter as the shepherd of the flock. This was a great act of kindness to a man who had been shattered by his own cowardice.

Whenever one of His followers needed special help, the Lord Jesus gave it. This was not partiality, but kind and sensible concern.

> Encourage your students to be sensitive to their friends' special needs. Everyone is different, and teens need to work at being sensitive to the varying needs of different people.

The Lord singled out three of His disciples—Peter, James, and John—for instruction because He planned leadership roles for them. Choosing leaders is not an act of favoritism; it's a matter of making necessary distinctions. These three men had been present at the transfiguration of Christ—the moment of His greatest exaltation—and in Gethsemane, the time of His greatest personal agony before the cross (Matt. 17:1–2; 26:36–37). The other disciples were not allowed these experiences. Later Peter preached at Pentecost and also opened the door of salvation to the Gentiles (Acts 2:14; 10:44–45). James became the first martyr (Acts 12:2), and John received unequaled revelation and became a leader in the first-century church

(Rev. 1:1). In His wisdom Christ gave these men special experiences. He did not do this out of favoritism, but out of the necessity of preparing them for their future ministries.

Christ was impartial in His choosing of disciples. Personal background, family ties, and gender did not affect His choice of followers or the relationship He had with them. At times He gave special attention to a disciple, but always with good cause. Christ was in all respects "without partiality." So should we be.

Extra Activities

Writing: Assign a character from the Gospels to each of your students. Have them look up all the Bible references for their character and then have them write a descriptive report about the major events and qualities in that person's life. Have them read their reports in class. (The numbers in parentheses represent the number of people with that name in the Gospels.)

Andrew
Anna
Cleopas
Elisabeth
James (son of Zebedee)
Joanna
John (son of Zebedee)
Joseph (3)

Judas (2)
Nicodemus
Martha
Mary (4)
Matthew
Salome (mother of James and John)

Simon (6, excluding Peter)
Philip (one of the twelve)
Susanna
Thomas

Question and answer: After the lesson ask your students the following questions.

1. What does Christ's association with Matthew and Simon the Zealot show?
   Christ did not show partiality on the basis of political background.

2. What does Christ's friendship with Andrew and Mary Magdalene prove?
   Christ did not especially favor those with a strong spiritual background.

3. Which of Christ's followers were members of the same families?
   James, John, and Salome; Andrew and Peter; possibly Matthew and James the Less

4. Who were the first people to see the risen Christ, and what does this fact suggest?
   The women of Galilee, Mary Magdalene being the first; Christ held women in high esteem.

5. What occupation was most common among the disciples?
   fishing

6. Which disciple was from a different region geographically, and what idea can we derive from this fact?
   Judas Iscariot, from Kerioth near Hebron in Judea; Christ was not partial toward people of a single geographical area.

Lesson 36
Hypocrisy

THEME	The Scribes and Pharisees
SCRIPTURE	Matthew 23:1–36
MEMORY WORK	Matthew 23:11–12

 Approach to the Lesson

Theme: Simply pretending to have Christian beliefs and virtues is a sin. Our English word *hypocrisy* is derived from the ancient Greek term for "actor." A hypocrite is one who acts in a way that deceives those around him, causing them to think he is something he really is not. A hypocrite is conscious of his deception. He knows he is trying to fool people, and he does so because he thinks it is to his advantage. He fails to realize that hypocrisy is to his disadvantage spiritually. The Lord forcefully condemned those who pretended to be spiritual but were not.

Rationale: We can usually spot hypocrisy easily in others, but not so easily in ourselves. Your students don't really need to be told what hypocrisy is; they need to be challenged not to tolerate it in their own lives.

Background: Most of the material in this lesson is unique to Matthew's Gospel. The first portion is partially repeated in Mark 12:38–40 and Luke 20:45–47. Likewise, the second portion is partially repeated in Luke 11:39–52, but it is set in a different context there.

Objectives

KNOWLEDGE (concepts students need to grasp)	the origins and purposes of the scribes and the Pharisees
	Christ's description and eightfold denunciation of the scribes and Pharisees
APPLICATION (principles students should put into practice)	We should not take positions of spiritual leadership to be seen or to be respected.
	We should not perform Christian actions, such as praying and witnessing, to impress others.
	We should evaluate our hearts and repent of any hypocrisy.

Bible Expressions to Understand

phylacteries—strips of parchment with Scripture written on them that were rolled, placed in a box, and strapped to the forehead or left arm during prayer

borders of their garments—tassels of blue and white thread at the corners of the outer robe, a symbol of the law

rabbi—("my master") a title of honor commonly applied to teachers of the Jewish Law

Zacharias—the last prophet to be killed (His death is recorded in 2 Chronicles 24:20–22, the last book of the Hebrew Bible.)

Julie's parents divorced when she was in elementary school. Her grandparents raised her as their child. They didn't spoil her, but they did give her love and attention and a Christian education. She attended a Christian school and seemed interested in the Bible and in living for Christ.

When Julie reached high school, everyone admired her. She was attractive, had a pleasing personality, and studied hard. Her friends elected her to positions of responsibility in student organizations. Her teachers honored her in her senior year with the Christian leadership award.

After graduation Julie talked her grandfather into letting her rent an apartment in the city two hours away, near the state university she was going to attend.

126

She'd been awarded a four-year scholarship to the school, and she saw that as her opportunity to break away from the restrictions of the past.

As the first year of school progressed, Julie became more and more interested in the world's way of having fun. Parties, weekends at the beach, and after-the-game celebrations at the local bars became a regular part of her life. Julie didn't care who knew about her activities or what they thought. She had left Christianity behind once and for all.

What happened to Julie? Did she just suddenly decide she didn't like being a Christian? Not at all. She had thought about graduation and the freedom it would bring long before it came. She'd never really believed what she'd been taught, but she acted like she did to make everybody happy.

Julie was a pretender—a hypocrite. Our English word *hypocrite* is derived from the ancient Greek term for an actor. In those days actors always wore masks. A hypocrite is an actor, one who tries to deceive those around him, causing them to think he is what he really is not. For a while it was to Julie's advantage to act like a Christian and even pose as a leader among Christian friends. Jesus had strong words for people like her.

Following a question-and-answer session with the Jewish religious leaders, Jesus spoke to the crowds about the scribes and Pharisees. Eight times he called them hypocrites. Five times he said they were spiritually blind. This wasn't true of every scribe and every Pharisee, but it was true of the ones Jesus was talking about. He reminded His hearers that these men were their religious leaders, interpreting

The scribes were experts in the Law of Moses (the Torah) and traced their lineage back to Ezra. Most of them were Pharisees, but they were a distinct party. They functioned as preservers of the law, both written and oral tradition (originating from their interpretation of the written Law and holding precedence over it). They were teachers of the Law and demanded greater reverence from their students than the latter were to give to their own parents. They also served as judges in the Sanhedrin (Matt. 16:21; 26:3). One of their most enduring contributions to Jewish culture was the origination of the synagogue service. Most of the scribes opposed Christ (Matt. 21:15), though some believed (8:19).

The name *Pharisee* first appears in documents from the period of the Hasmo-

naean kings, roughly two centuries before Christ. The name probably means "the separated ones." The group split during this period, with the minority withdrawing from public life and waiting for God's future supernatural intervention while the majority sought to control Israel's religion through political means. The Pharisees were always a minority, numbering just over six thousand during the time of the Herods. They stressed rigid adherence to the oral traditions of the Jewish teachers in personal life as well as temple worship. They were also known for their belief in the immortality of the soul, the resurrection, and the overruling sovereignty of God. After the death of Herod the Great, the Pharisees concluded that political means would never accomplish spiritual ends and

the Mosaic commandments and applying them to everyday situations. Yet their own works didn't measure up to their teachings. They had caused others to bear heavy spiritual burdens while they wouldn't lift a finger to help. Instead, they concentrated on ritualistic religious ceremonies. They wore showy *phylacteries* (small leather cases that contained verses from the Law) on their foreheads and wrists. Their garments caught everyone's attention, and they always tried to get the best seats at feasts or in the synagogues. They loved for people to publicly greet them as "rabbi."

Jesus paused to teach a positive lesson to His own disciples. Instead of seeking after self-glorifying titles, they were to realize that only one person, the Messiah, deserved such preeminence. They were all brothers and equal before the Lord. Similarly, instead of exalting one another with the title "father," they were to recognize the only Father, God in heaven. The title "master" shouldn't be given among Christians since only Christ is our Master. Rather than exalting themselves, God's children should seek positions of service. Those who exalt themselves will be humbled; those who humble themselves God will exalt.

Jesus then pronounced a somber series of eight woes on the scribes and Pharisees, each woe directed toward a particular sin. He began by denouncing their shutting other people out of the kingdom of heaven. The teachings of the Pharisees had kept many from understanding the truth of God. Jesus then denounced them for their covetousness. Even while they were making long, eloquent prayers, they were defrauding widows of their possessions. The third woe condemned them for their wicked proselytizing, putting great effort into luring others to buy into their misguided teachings.

In the fourth woe, Christ denounced the moral blindness of the scribes and Pharisees. They taught that an oath sworn by the temple was meaningless and could be broken. But an oath sworn by the gold of the temple was binding. Likewise, an oath taken on the altar of the temple could be broken. An oath taken on the sacrifice being offered on the altar, however, couldn't be broken. Christ called them "fools" and told them that they were spiritually blind.

The scribes and Pharisees were meticulous in their tithing practices, but they often neglected the more important issues of justice, mercy, and faithfulness. Christ denounced them for this in His fifth woe, telling them that they were straining at gnats but swallowing camels whole; that is, they were being picky in their religious practices while permitting great sins to go unchecked.

The Pharisees were focused on the external details of religious observances rather than a genuine, intimate relationship with God.

Christ next condemned the scribes and Pharisees for their ritualistic practices of making sure that cups and saucers used in serving food were ceremonially clean while failing to cleanse themselves from inner sin. He then condemned them for maintaining an outward appearance of righteousness while inwardly their hearts and minds were filled with iniquity.

127

petitioned for direct Roman rule. They also opposed the revolt that eventually resulted in the destruction of Jerusalem by the Roman general Titus. By the second century AD the Sadducees and Zealots had disappeared, and Pharisaic teaching became synonymous with Judaism.

Had the motives of the scribes and Pharisees been genuine and their lives consistent with what they taught, Jesus would not have condemned them as He did. We may assume that some of these people were sincere, but from Jesus's remarks we know that many were not. His condemnation has forever branded the scribes and Pharisees as the epitome of religious hypocrisy.

⭐ The Lesson

I. Hypocritical Attitudes Exposed (Matt. 23:1–12)

Wrong authority (23:1–4). The rabbis exalted their tradition as their final authority instead of Scripture. Jesus described the scribes and Pharisees as sitting in the seat of Moses to refer to their position of judging and interpreting the Law. The scribes particularly carried this responsibility. Jesus counseled the multitude to obey their teachings that were based on the Law. However, He warned, "Do not ye after their works: for they say and do not" (Matt. 23:3). That means not to follow the hypocritical example of the rabbis. It seems startling today, but the rabbis placed tradition above the Law. Their system of interpretation had led

them to devise an intricate, detailed code. It was a "heavy burden" to the people, one they could not possibly keep. For example, in its discussion of Sabbath rules, the Talmud states, "One shall not search for vermin or read before a lamplight." It was also forbidden to make more than two stitches if sewing on the Sabbath or to write more than two characters. The rabbis could not keep the law either, but they excused themselves by working out technical codes in their own traditions for their benefit. For instance, the sixth commandment established that people should honor their parents. The rabbis created one of their own laws which relieved them of the responsibility to pay for their parents' care if they gave money to the temple. Therefore if they could say, "It is Corban," or a gift (Mark 7:9–13), they would be free. This convolution of the Law shows the wicked, hypocritical hearts of the rabbis.

Wrong motives (23:5–6). Jesus next described the scribes and Pharisees as doing everything in order to be seen of men. Not a single act sprang from pure motive of service to God and others. In some instances they were guilty of broadening their phylacteries—leather boxes worn on either the forehead or the left wrist. In them were several sections of the Law (Exod. 13:1–16; Deut. 6:4–9; 11:13–21). This practice followed from a literal interpretation of certain verses (Exod. 13:9, 16; Deut. 6:8; 11:18). Although the size of the phylactery was supposed to be uniform, some rabbis enlarged the width of the bands that fastened the leather box to the body, thus calling attention to their observance of the Law.

These men also wore tassels on the hems of their robes. As directed by Scripture

(Num. 15:38–39), the Jews had tassels of blue and white thread, a symbol of the Law, at the corners of their outer robe, but the scribes and Pharisees enlarged these, again calling attention to themselves. What they failed to understand was that, although a person's clothing may bring into question his discretion and morality or may by its tastefulness and beauty bring glory to God, the inner person is most important. No garment should ever be worn to make the false statement, "I think I am holy, and I want you to think so too."

Obeying school dress codes will not bring a student into a proper relationship with God, nor will it fool anyone into thinking he is more spiritually minded than he really is. As an illustration of a person's heart, clothing is important; but it cannot substitute for inner righteousness.

Wrong ambitions (23:7–12). The Pharisees tried to obtain the chief places at feasts and the synagogue and demanded that titles be applied to them in public as a mark of respect. Jesus does not condemn proper honor for position or accomplishment; however, He does denounce the self-seeking attitude that encourages empty plaudits. Edersheim's *Life of Christ* relates several rabbinic stories to illustrate how proud the Pharisees were. One story was about a rabbi who was an expert on purity. One day, so the story goes, God and the heavenly angels were debating about purity, and God ended the rabbi's life just so he could come to heaven and decide a point of disagreement between them. All the other problems with the story aside, the rabbi is painted as such an expert that he could even give guidance to God. Supposedly God decreed a full week of mourning after that rabbi's death because of his greatness.

The word *rabbi* means "my master." It was commonly applied to great teachers of Jewish law. Jesus stated, however, that it was not to be given to any man since there is only one Master, the Messiah. Neither were people to address anyone as *father* in a religious sense, which was also a practice of the scribes and Pharisees. This usage was based on Elisha's exclamation to Elijah: "My father, my father" (2 Kings 2:12). Christ pointed out that we have one Father, God in heaven. (Of course, Christ was not referring to earthly fathers.) The Roman Catholic Church attempts to get around this prohibition by stating that the term is to be used only with the recognition that

In the last woe, Christ denounced them for hypocritically honoring the Old Testament prophets. They boasted that they wouldn't have killed them as their ancestors had. The Lord pointed out that they were the children of their fathers, with the same evil character traits. They would do just as their fathers had done. They, too, would be held guilty for their crimes. God would be just in pouring out His judgment on Jerusalem to punish their sins.

Taking Off the Mask

Pretending to have Christian beliefs, feelings, and virtues is a sin. If you're a hypocrite, you know you're trying to deceive people. You may choose to be a hypocrite because people admire you for your supposed Christian testimony and you like being admired. It's possible for a genuine believer to be a hypocrite, but trying to make others think you're more spiritual than you really are is hypocrisy. You should repent of this deception and make an honest effort to grow in grace. And if you're an unbeliever, you need to realize that pretending to be a Christian won't fool God.

Do You Remember?

1. What does it mean to sit in the seat of Moses? _____
   to interpret Moses's commandments and apply them to everyday situations

2. How did the Pharisees "bind heavy burdens" on people? *Their interpretation of the laws was a very intricate, burdensome system and impossible to keep.*

3. What sinful attitude does Christ rebuke in Matthew 23:5–7? *pride*

4. What's God's requirement for one who would be exalted? *He must humble himself.*

5. How did the scribes and Pharisees keep people out of the kingdom of heaven? _____
   Their teachings kept many from understanding the truth of God.

6. How did the scribes and Pharisees avoid keeping their oaths? _____
   They devised technicalities to allow them to make nonbinding oaths.

7. What does it mean to "strain at a gnat, and swallow a camel"? _____
   to be picky in religious practices but ignore big sins

8. How were the Pharisees like "whited sepulchres"? *They maintained an outward appearance of righteousness, but inwardly they were filled with iniquity.*

128

the priest is a "father in Christ," that is, in union with and subordinate to the Lord and to the Father. However, to use the word in this manner is still a violation of the command that the term not be used by the followers of Christ. Likewise, they are not to use the title *master* (literally, "leader"), as the Pharisees did (cf. Rom. 2:19–20). Again, the Messiah is the only leader.

Jesus concludes His reproof of these practices by a public pronouncement of what He had already privately taught the apostles (Matt. 20:26–27). Jesus Himself was the best example of His maxim: "But he that is greatest among you shall be your servant" (Matt. 23:11). Hebrews 12:2 tells us that the Lord Jesus, "the author and finisher of our faith," suffered shame willingly for our good in His death on the cross.

II. Hypocritical Actions Judged (Matt. 23:13–36)

After His graphic description of the attitudes of the scribes and Pharisees, Christ recounted a series of eight "woes" pronounced on them for their hypocritical actions. With each woe comes further description of their lifestyle.

Selfish hindrances (23:13). In the first woe Jesus pronounced judgment on them for their sin of hindering others from entering the kingdom of heaven. The Gospels give us two examples of their attempts to keep others from the truth: accusing Jesus of serving Satan (Matt. 9:34) and excommunicating followers of Christ from the synagogue (John 9:22, 34). The scribes and Pharisees rejected the truth themselves and were afraid of losing their influence over the people, so they tried to keep them from accepting the truth.

False piety (23:14). Christ's second denunciation was of their long prayers in public. They performed these prayers to draw attention to their supposed piety (Matt. 6:5). Even while they were proclaiming their devotion to God, however, they were scheming to take away the property of widows (cf. Exod. 22:22; Deut. 24:17). Christ promised judgment for their actions.

Deceptive leadership (23:15). In His third denunciation Jesus noted their great efforts to convert other Jews to their sect. He did not condemn them for proselytizing, but only for their efforts to turn their converts into "children of hell" like themselves. By convincing others that all they needed was to follow the Jewish ritual, they turned people aside from the truth.

Moral blindness (23:16–22). The fourth woe illustrates how blind to right and wrong the scribes and Pharisees had become. One illustration of the extent to which they had bought into the philosophy that the end justifies the means is the way they used oaths to get out of their responsibility to honor their parents (Matt. 15:4–6). They had also devised technicalities to allow them to make nonbinding oaths. They distinguished between the temple and the gold of the temple, or the altar and the sacrifice on the altar. Christ said that the temple was of more importance than mere ornamentation on it. Likewise, the altar sanctified the sacrifice (Exod. 29:37) and was therefore more important. The Pharisees and scribes, however, held that one swearing by the temple or altar was not bound by the oath. Only one who took an oath on the gold of the temple or the sacrifice on the altar was "a debtor" or "guilty" (Matt. 23:16, 18; in both places, the same word, *opheilo*, is used, indicating one who is bound to keep the oath).

Again Christ pointed out that one who swears by heaven swears by all that is in heaven, including the throne of God. This viewpoint contradicted the Pharisees, who taught that such a general oath was not binding.

Misplaced priorities (23:23–24). Fifth, Jesus condemned the Pharisees' failure to practice the major requirements of God—justice, mercy, and faithfulness (Hosea 12:6; Mic. 6:8). The Pharisees were proud of their attention to detail in tithing. The Law commanded the tithe for corn, wine, and oil (Deut. 14:23). The Pharisees, however, tithed even the smallest products from the soil, including the seeds, stalks, and leaves of the plant. Jesus didn't condemn their meticulous practice of tithing, but their weakness in more important spiritual matters. In verse 24, "strain at [literally 'out'] a gnat" is an example of hyperbole, a deliberate exaggeration for the sake of making a point. Here He criticized them for overattention to the smallest ritualistic detail while readily accepting the gross sins of injustice, lack of mercy, and infidelity to God.

Dead ritualism (23:25–26). The sixth woe is directed at ritualism. The Jews carried out elaborate cleansing rituals (Matt. 15:1–2; Mark 7:1–5) while tolerating inward filth. They had extended the laws regarding cleansing into detailed regulations. For instance, a hollow clay vessel could become unclean only on the inside. A flat clay plate without a rim could not become unclean at all. Jesus condemned this preoccupation with material items while the inward sins were overlooked.

Hidden uncleanness (23:27–28). The seventh woe is a polemic against the hidden defilement of the scribes and Pharisees. According to custom, about the middle of the month Adar (equivalent to the last half of February and the first half of March) the Jews whitewashed tombs and other burial places in preparation for the Passover. This made burial places conspicuous, so that no one would defile himself by touching or walking on one (Num. 19:16). Jesus compared the scribes and Pharisees to these sepulchres, outwardly beautiful but inwardly rotten.

Pretended honor (23:29–36). In the final woe Christ denounced the murderous attitude of the Jewish religious leaders. They boasted that they were different from their fathers. Had they been alive in earlier times, they claimed, they would have honored the prophets instead of murdering them as their fathers had. Jesus pointed out, however, that their own words identified them as children of their fathers (and thus, by implication, having the same nature as their fathers). The fact that they were persecuting Jesus and His followers proved His point. When He exhorted them to complete the work started by their fathers, He was challenging them to quit pretending and go ahead and carry out their evil plans.

Jesus's concluding words were particularly stinging as He prophesied that judgment would come on these men for their wickedness. He told them they would persecute and martyr His messengers, thereby bringing on themselves the same guilt incurred through the murders of the Old Testament messengers of God, from Abel (the first to be slain) to Zacharias (the last to be slain), whose death is recorded in the last book of the Hebrew Scriptures (2 Chron. 24:20–22).

Do you preform religious functions to draw attention to yourself? Do you focus on less important matters and ignore love and justice? Do you take comfort in outward customs but tolerate sin in your heart? Do you think of yourself as spiritual and take pride in being "better" than others? If so, you have a profound spiritual disease that needs radical treatment so that the Pharisees' woes don't become yours. Evaluate your heart and repent of any hypocrisy.

✳ Extra Activities

Object lessons: To introduce the lesson, bring a piece of quartz with flecks of iron pyrite ("fool's gold") in it, if possible. Pass it around the class. Point out that things are not always what they appear to be as illustrated by the familiar saying, "All that glitters is not gold." The fact that an individual is active in "religious work" does not necessarily mean that he is spiritual. The Pharisees and scribes of Jesus's day were in this position: religious but unspiritual.

Another approach that requires a little preparation is to switch labels on cans of vegetables. Discuss what a label indicates. Your students will have all sorts of suggestions—content, weight, nutritional value, and so forth. Ask the class to describe the contents of each can from its label. Then open each can and pour its contents into a bowl to show that they were fooled by a false label. Using this starting point, lead into a discussion of misleading labels used by people in religious work.

Lesson 37
Cruelty

THEME	The Herods
SCRIPTURE	Matthew 2:1–23
MEMORY WORK	Matthew 2:1–2

Approach to the Lesson

Theme: Unnecessarily inflicting pain and suffering on others is a sin. Pain and suffering may be caused by words or by actions, and they may be inflicted physically, mentally, or emotionally. If a Christian is cruel, he is not kind. If he is not kind, he has failed to manifest the fundamental disposition of Christ toward others, which is love. Love is kind; it is not cruel (1 Cor. 13:4). As the greatest of Christian virtues, love is broad and many-faceted. Kindness is one of those facets. For us to fail in kindness by being cruel distorts people's view of Christ.

Rationale: The amount of cruelty that goes on in junior high school is astonishing. Your students are not Herods, of course, and most of the girls probably get no joy out of pulling legs off grasshoppers. But the same girls, as well as boys, have no scruples about saying or doing cruel things to their classmates. Bring the relevance of this lesson home to them.

Background: Teachers and students alike can become confused when studying the Herod dynasty. Several members of this family appear in the Gospels and the book of Acts. Because they all appear in governmental positions and are mainly ruthless and wicked, they tend to blend together in the reader's thinking. To clarify the relationships, a family tree of the Herods who appear in the New Testament is included on page 130 of the student text and also on the CD.

Herod the Great, king of the Jews, ruled Judea from 40 to 4 BC. He is the first Herod referred to in the New Testament (Matt. 2:1–13) and the founder of the Herodian dynasty. The slaughter in Bethlehem was typical of his style of governing. He suspected everyone who might have the slightest interest in his throne, and that suspicion often led to murder. He killed many of the relatives of one of his ten wives, Mariamne,

because he was suspicious of their political designs. Ultimately he murdered Mariamne, her mother Alexandria, and his two sons by her, Alexander and Aristobulus, for the same reason. As the map on page 130 of the student book shows, he bequeathed his kingdom to three of his four remaining sons: Archelaus, who ruled Judea and Samaria (Matt. 2:22); Antipas, often called Herod the Tetrarch, who ruled Galilee and Perea (Matt. 14:1–12; Mark 6:14–29; Luke 3:1, 19–20; 9:7–9; 23:7–12); and Philip, who reigned over the northeastern territories (Luke 3:1). All these decisions were ratified by Caesar Augustus.

What further complicates the genealogy of this family is the intermarriage of its members. Two of Herod the Great's sons had the same name, Philip. One had no political position; the other was given a third of his father's kingdom, as already mentioned. Aristobulus, one of Mariamne's murdered sons, had four children. Two of these, Agrippa I and Herodias, play a role in the history of Christ's ministry and the early church. Herodias first married her uncle, the nonpolitical Philip. Then she divorced him and married another uncle, Antipas, who beheaded John the Baptist after he criticized their marriage (Matt. 14:1–12; Mark 6:14–29). Antipas also tried Jesus and sent Him back to Pilate (Luke 23:7–12). The other significant descendant of Aristobulus, Agrippa I, became king over Palestine (AD 37–44) martyred James, and imprisoned Peter (Acts 12:1–3, 20–23). He had three children: Agrippa II, before whom Paul spoke (Acts 25:13–26; 26:32); Bernice (Acts 25:13; 26:30); and Drusilla, the wife of Felix, Roman procurator of Judea, to whom Paul preached (Acts 24:24).

Objectives

KNOWLEDGE (concepts students need to grasp)	the relationships among the Herods in the New Testament
	the role of each of the Herods as recorded in the Gospels
APPLICATION (principles students should put into practice)	We should guard ourselves against any natural tendency toward cruelty.
	We should avoid making cutting remarks, establishing cliques, playing games that glorify mindless violence, or inflicting bodily pain and suffering.
	We should not imitate the cruel actions of others.

Outline

I. Suspicion can lead to cruelty (Matt. 2:1–18).
II. Example can lead to cruelty (Matt. 2:19–23).
III. Bitterness can lead to cruelty (Matt. 14:1–12).

The members of the Herod family mentioned in the Gospels figure directly in the drama of Christ's earthly ministry. Together they present a graphic illustration of cruelty.

The Lesson

I. Suspicion Can Lead to Cruelty (Matt. 2:1–18)

This passage begins with the birth of Jesus and the subsequent supernatural guidance given to the wise men (Greek *magoi*, men trained in medicine, science, or philosophy) from the East. Herod was deeply troubled that these men came looking for the "king of the Jews," who had just been born. He was obsessively suspicious. This birth meant a threat to his throne and his dynasty. Feigning an interest in the child in order to worship Him, Herod called all the chief priests and scribes together, found out where the Christ (Messiah) was to be born, and then told the wise men to search for Him so that he could come and worship.

The wise men departed, found the Lord, and worshiped Him. Then they were miraculously warned through a dream not to return to Herod and inform him of Jesus's whereabouts. Apparently Herod was so devious that they did not suspect his wicked motives. After their departure an angel appeared to Joseph to warn him that Herod would seek to destroy Jesus and that he should take his family and flee into Egypt. They stayed in Egypt until the death of Herod the Great, thus fulfilling Hosea 11:1 ("When Israel was a child, then I loved him, and called my son out of Egypt.") Twice the Lord miraculously warned men to avoid Herod because of his savagery.

Herod was so enraged by the wise men's failure to return that he sent soldiers to Bethlehem to kill all the male children two years old and younger, thereby fulfilling the prophecy of Jeremiah 31:15—"A voice was heard in Ramah, lamentation, and bitter weeping; [Rachel] weeping for her children refused to be comforted for her

Cruelty | L.37

Read: Matthew 2:1–23   Memorize: Matthew 2:1–2

Bible Expressions to Understand

Rama—a community about ten miles north of Bethlehem
Archelaus—son of Herod the Great; oppressive ruler of Judea and Samaria after his father's death
Antipas—ruler of Galilee and Perea
tetrarch—governor of one-fourth of a country

Down through history many kings, emperors, and dictators have gained a reputation for cruelty. For example, Pedro I, a Spanish king who ruled over the regions of Castille and Leon from 1350 to 1369, became known as Pedro el Cruel (Peter the Cruel). He threw his wife, whom he deserted for another woman, into prison and later had her murdered. He ruthlessly suppressed those who rebelled against his rule and committed a number of murders in order to protect his throne, which his half brother took over when Pedro was killed in a duel at age 35.

In what way were Peter the Cruel (above) and Herod the Great alike? Consider both their public acts as well as their private lives in making the comparison.

The Old Testament records the cruelty of many pagan kings. God instructed Ezekiel to pronounce judgment even on the kings of Israel for ruling "with force and with cruelty" instead of seeking to meet the needs of the people (Ezek. 34:1–4). Later, during the lifetime of Jesus, the Herods were a family of rulers that were infamous for being cruel.

The first Herod in the New Testament was Herod the Great. He murdered many of his own family members in seeking to keep his throne. He was the murderer of harmless infants in Bethlehem. He wanted no competition from the newborn "King of the Jews" the wise men had told him about. Only the angel's warning to Joseph saved the life of the baby Jesus.

Sometimes cruelty shows itself in physical abuse and even murder, as in Herod's case, but even less extreme actions can be physically cruel. Intentionally injuring another player in an athletic game is cruel. Practical jokes and teasing that cause someone pain are cruel. Physical cruelty is always wrong. It is a sin.

Archelaus, the son of Herod the Great, is the second Herod recorded in the Gospels. Ruling in Samaria and Judea for ten years after his father died, he had the worst reputation of all his father's sons. The Roman emperor Augustus finally banished Archelaus for being so cruel. When Mary and Joseph returned from Egypt, they heard that Archelaus was ruling in Judea, where Bethlehem was. Fearing his cruelty, they went back to Nazareth because it was outside his jurisdiction (Matt. 2:22–23).

129

oppressively from 4 BC to AD 6 and has the worst reputation of all the sons of Herod. This fact reflects on the cruelty of Herod the Great; he gave the biggest and best portion of the kingdom to the cruelest son.

"Like father, like son," says the familiar adage. Archelaus's reputation as a beast was established by the time Joseph returned to Israel. Undoubtedly children often learn how to be cruel at home. Archelaus's tyranny endured until his removal from the throne and banishment by Augustus.

After the death of Herod the Great, an angel appeared to Joseph and told him to take Mary and Jesus back into Israel. Hearing that cruel Archelaus was ruling in Judea, Joseph was afraid to return to Bethlehem. God warned him in a dream to go into Galilee, and the family residence was reestablished in Nazareth, resulting in another fulfillment of prophecy.

III. Bitterness Can Lead to Cruelty (Matt. 14:1–12)

Herodias's bitterness at John the Baptist's bold preaching led to John's beheading. A cruel husband-and-wife team, Herod Antipas and Herodias were partners in crime against John the Baptist (Mark 6:14–29; Luke 9:7–9). John denounced them for their immoral marriage because Herodias had divorced her husband Philip and married his brother Antipas. Herodias was so embittered by John's criticism that she plotted to kill him. Herod imprisoned John but refrained from killing him because he feared an uprising among the people, who considered John a prophet. However, at a birthday celebration Herodias's daughter enticed Antipas by a dance, and the king promised her whatever she asked. Following the instructions of her mother, she requested the head of John the Baptist on a dish. Not wanting to lose face, Herod commanded the deed to be done. The head was brought to the daughter, who in turn brought it to her mother. (See previous discussion of this incident in Lesson 33.)

How do young people demonstrate cruelty? They make sarcastic and cutting remarks about others. They establish cliques, implying that those not in their group are inferior. They inflict bodily pain and suffering on others. Student should avoid these sins and strive to live by Christ's golden rule: "Whatsoever ye would that men should do to you, do ye even so to them: for this is the law and the prophets" (Matt. 7:12).

---

children, because they were not." Jeremiah used the figure of Rachel (the grandmother of Ephraim and Manasseh, two tribes that settled northern Palestine) weeping as the Assyrians slaughtered her descendants in 722 BC. Matthew has applied this poetic word-picture to the inhabitants of Bethlehem, where Rachel was buried (Gen. 35:19). Even in Ramah, about ten miles to the north, the cry of sorrow is heard. Although some estimates of the number killed in the slaughter by Herod range as high as fourteen thousand, a more realistic estimate is twenty to thirty children. Bethlehem was only a small town, and it is unlikely that thousands of children were killed.

Your students might never think of murdering someone, but at times they can be merciless in the way they treat their

peers. Suspicion of the motives of others may lead to sin. Emphasize that their sins are certainly different in degree but that the spirit of cruelty is present in both cases.

This passage describes Satan's first attempt to kill Jesus (cf. Rev. 12:4). Satan's instrument was Herod. Consider what a brutal monster this man was; his suspicion led him to barbaric acts. He had no regard for the hearts of these mothers and fathers, not to mention the screams of the children.

II. Example Can Lead to Cruelty (Matt. 2:19–23)

Herod the Great's example apparently had a profound effect on his son, Archelaus. After the death of his father, Archelaus became ruler of Judea and Samaria. He ruled

Special Problems and Topics

• What was the star the wise men saw?

Several explanations of the star of Bethlehem have been suggested. However, all natural explanations fall ludicrously short. It is simply not credible that a comet, a nova, or a planetary conjunction could lead someone from Jerusalem to a particular house five miles away in Bethlehem. Whatever it was, the star was low enough to indicate a specific location. Furthermore, the star was evidently visible only to the wise men since it did not bring crowds of people to the house. Perhaps it was similar to the Old Testament "pillar of fire" (Exod. 13:21), by which the presence of God led the Israelites.

Contrary to tradition and certain Christmas carols ("Westward leading, still proceeding . . ."), the Bible does not say that the star led the wise men from the East to Jerusalem. It says that they saw the star in the East (Matt. 2:2), but not that they had been *following* it. If they had, there seems to be no reason for their great rejoicing on leaving Herod's presence. Apparently they weren't expecting the star to appear since they evidently had made their way to Jerusalem without its guidance. Mesopotamian tradition mentioned a Judean king, so the star's appearance in the East would have logically prompted them to travel to Jerusalem. From there the star reappeared to lead them south to Bethlehem.

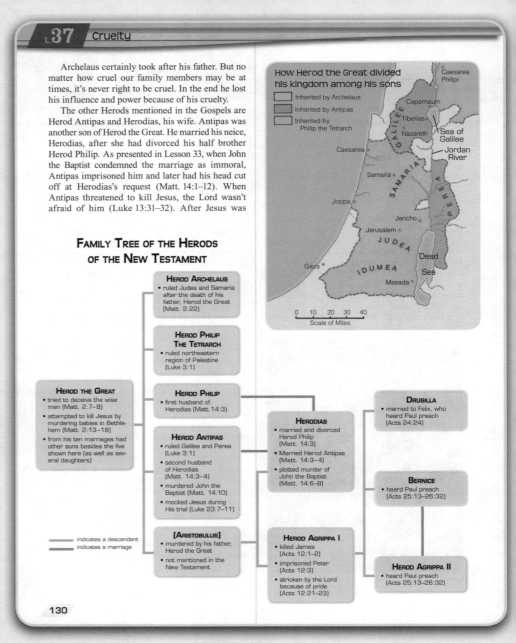

Archelaus certainly took after his father. But no matter how cruel our family members may be at times, it's never right to be cruel. In the end he lost his influence and power because of his cruelty.

The other Herods mentioned in the Gospels are Herod Antipas and Herodias, his wife. Antipas was another son of Herod the Great. He married his neice, Herodias, after she had divorced his half brother Herod Philip. As presented in Lesson 33, when John the Baptist condemned the marriage as immoral, Antipas imprisoned him and later had his head cut off at Herodias's request (Matt. 14:1–12). When Antipas threatened to kill Jesus, the Lord wasn't afraid of him (Luke 13:31–32). After Jesus was

How Herod the Great divided his kingdom among his sons

130

Map 5
The Division of Herod the Great's Kingdom

Not long before Herod the Great died in 4 BC, he had his sons Aristobulus and Antipater executed and decreed that Antipas was to rule Galilee and Perea as a tetrarch, Philip was to rule the Golan Heights area as a tetrarch, and Archelaus was to rule Judea, Idumea, and Samaria as ethnarch ("national leader").

[Note: Students will need to study or refer to this map in order to complete Map Exercise 3 (on the CD).]

arrested, Pilate sent him to Antipas (Luke 23:7–11), who questioned Him at great length, but Jesus refused even to answer him. After the questioning, Antipas and his soldiers mocked Jesus by dressing him in a fancy robe and laughing at Him.

Christ was the Son of God, giving Himself for the sins of the world. He was dying even for the soldiers who mocked Him. Perhaps their jeers hurt Him more than the blows on His back and the nails in His hands.

Have your classmates ever made fun of you? If so, then you know how cruel words can be. Such cruelty is as much a sin as physical cruelty. You should guard your tongue, keeping it from cruelty.

Even if what you would like to say is true, it's not always right to say it. The principle you must follow is kindness, which is consideration for the feelings of others.

Only a Fool Likes Being Cruel

Causing others pain and suffering is a sin. You can cause pain or suffering by words as well as actions; you may be cruel to a person's body or to his soul. If you're a Christian and are cruel, then you've failed to show the basic attitude of Christ toward others, which is love. Love is kind, not cruel. Love is the greatest of Christian virtues.

Do You Remember?

1. Who came to Herod the Great and asked to see the newborn king of the Jews? _____
   wise men from the East

2. What was Herod's reaction to their request? *He was greatly troubled and called the*
   Jewish leaders together to find out where the Messiah was to be born.

3. What did Herod plan to do when he found Jesus? *kill Him*

4. How did God warn Joseph of Herod's threat? _____
   An angel appeared to him in a dream.

5. What wicked act did Herod order? *He ordered all the boy babies in Bethlehem two years*
   old and under to be killed.

6. How did Joseph know it was safe to return to Palestine? _____
   The Lord revealed it to him in a dream.

7. Why did Joseph not return to Judea? _____
   Herod's wicked son Archelaus was ruler there.

8. Which sons of Herod the Great are mentioned in Scripture? _____
   Archelaus, Antipas, Philip the tetrarch, Herod Philip

9. Who was Aristobulus and what happened to him? _____
   another son of Herod the Great; murdered by his father

131

Extra Activities

Herod family tree: The chart of the Herods on page 130 is fundamental to the teaching of the lesson. After a brief introduction, have the students turn to the chart in their books or a handout you've made by printing the chart from the CD. Use the background information at the beginning of this lesson to supplement the genealogy. As you go through the genealogy, point out the acts of wickedness by each individual.

Quiz: After discussing the material, give this brief true/false quiz.

1. Herod the Great was the founder of the Herodian dynasty.
   True

2. Herod Antipas killed the babies in Bethlehem.
   False; Herod the Great did.

3. Herodias first married Herod Antipas and then Herod Philip.
   False; she first married Philip.

4. Archelaus was the Herod that Joseph feared when he returned to Israel from Egypt.
   True

5. Philip, the husband of Herodias, ruled over the northeastern territories of Palestine.
   False; the Philip who married Herodias had no political position.

About the photos: The pictures on these pages of Sebaste (Samaria), Masada, and Caesarea are obviously of ruins. However, your students may wonder if the fortress Antonia and Herod's temple still exist. The picture at the top of this page and the one at the bottom of the next page are photographs of an extensive scale model of Jerusalem that was constructed in the 1960s on the grounds of the Holyland Hotel in Jerusalem. The model is intended to be a historically accurate representation of the city in AD 66, shortly before it was ransacked by the Romans. It is built on a 1:50 scale, using authentic construction materials.

Herod the Great was the king of Judea under Roman rule when Christ was born. To keep both the Romans and the Jews happy, he spent a lot of his time building things and naming them after famous people. To please the Jews, he rebuilt part of the wall of Jerusalem, but for the Romans he built a fortress inside the city called the Tower of Antonia. It was named after Mark Antony, a close friend of Julius Caesar and a powerful Roman ruler.

Herod also rebuilt the city of Samaria, including Ahab's palace, and then renamed it Sebaste (the Greek name for Caesar Augustus). He built many towers and pillars and named them after his wives and friends. He built a theater in Jerusalem and an amphitheater outside Jerusalem's walls. He also built himself a palace in the city, equipped with banquet halls and fancy bedchambers, which were adorned with rare stones and gold. The grounds were

Adjacent to the temple, the Antonia fortress also served as the official Jerusalem residence of the Roman procurator as well as the barracks of the Roman garrison (600 soldiers) headquartered there.

decorated with beautiful gardens, complete with pools and canals.

Although those who love Christ will always remember Herod as a cruel man who massacred the babies of Bethlehem, history credits him with being one of the greatest builders of all time. His most famous building projects were a fortress, a seaside city, and the Jerusalem temple.

Masada

Masada was a fortress built on a rock plateau that rises thirteen hundred feet from the desert floor near the Dead Sea. It included a three-tiered palace on the side of the plateau, complete with aqueducts to bring water for drinking and for elaborate public baths. Herod built this palace as a refuge from an expected invasion from Egypt. After the Romans conquered Jerusalem in AD 70, the

One street in the Herodian city of Sebaste was lined with six hundred stone columns.

132

Masada, which means "fortress" in Hebrew," is the most visited archeological site in modern Israel.

Zealots, a group of radical Jews, took refuge in Masada and held off the Roman army for two years. When the Romans finally broke through the wall of the palace, they found that the 960 people inside had committed suicide.

Caesarea

Herod built the whole city of Caesarea from the ground up. Located on the Mediterranean coast between the sites of the modern cities of Haifa and Tel Aviv, it was Israel's finest seaport in that era. First, he constructed a two-hundred-foot-wide breakwater to protect the harbor and its ships from strong currents. Besides streets and houses, he built over one hundred vaults to store cargo. In the middle of the city, he built a temple to Caesar Augustus, for whom the city was named. By the sea he built a large amphitheater, which is still in use today. He had fresh water brought in by aqueducts from Mount Carmel, thirteen miles away.

Caesarea eventually became the Roman capital of Israel. It was the home of the Roman governors Felix and Festus, and it is where Herod's grandson Agrippa I died, eaten by worms (Acts 12:21–23).

The Temple

Solomon's magnificent temple was destroyed during the Babylonian invasion in 586 BC. The Jewish governor Zerubbabel built another after the Babylonian captivity, but the new temple was not as large and splendid as Solomon's. Herod decided that he would rebuild it. Because the temple was to be in use during the construction and because Gentiles

In Herod's day, the harbor at Caesarea was considered one of the most modern seaports in the world. Near the port, Herod constructed arched storehouses, some of which are still standing.

weren't allowed into it, Herod trained the priests to be masons and carpenters so they could remodel the inside.

Herod's temple was the temple Jesus knew. There He was brought for His dedication. There He listened to the teachers of the Law at age twelve. From there He twice drove out the moneychangers, and there He taught and healed during His earthly ministry.

Most historians think Herod undertook the temple project to appease the Jews for having broken some Jewish laws and for being so friendly with Rome. Others believe he simply wanted a monument to his own glory. Whatever his motive, the temple was his biggest and most glorious building project. It took eighty-four years to complete. Then in AD 70, just six years after its completion, the Roman army under the general Titus marched into Jerusalem and destroyed the city, including the temple. It has never been rebuilt.

To greatly extend the base of the temple, Herod built a high retaining wall constructed of huge limestone blocks (some as big as twenty-five by thirty feet). The western portion of this wall, now called the Wailing Wall, is all that remains of the original structure.

133

Lesson 38
Double-Mindedness

Theme	Judas Iscariot
Scripture	Matthew 10:1–15; 26:1–5, 14–16, 47–56; 27:3–10
Memory Work	James 1:8

Approach to the Lesson

Theme: To be double-minded is to have two conflicting purposes. A spiritually double-minded person wants to serve both Christ and the Devil. He divides both his loyalties and his energies. In time he must choose whom he will follow. If he does not, he will experience emotional and intellectual effects that are damaging or even devastating. As James says, "A doubleminded man is unstable in all his ways" (1:8).

Rationale: Many teens are "Christians" not because they have decided to be, but because they're running with a "Christian" crowd. Emphasize that they must make a choice. In the long run, drifting with a good crowd is not much better than drifting with a bad one; a double-minded person will eventually come to ruin.

Background: The life of Judas is one of the most dramatic and pathetic in the New Testament. Virtually every passage that mentions his name adds a qualifying phrase such as "the one who betrayed Jesus."

Several men named Judas are mentioned in the New Testament, and certainly the qualifying phrase is to keep us from confusing Judas Iscariot with the others. However, it also reminds us of the legacy

Objectives

Knowledge (concepts students need to grasp)	that the prophecies about Judas did not force him to sin
	the priority God gives to developing Christlike character in us
Application (principles students should put into practice)	With great privilege comes great responsibility.
	Any disobedience to the Lord for gaining popularity, recognition, or pleasure shows a heart like Judas's.
	Disloyalty to close friends, family, and the Lord is despicable.

Bible Expressions to Understand

covenanted—made an agreement; contracted
staves—(plural of *staff*) rods or poles
repented—felt sorry
Jeremy the prophet—Jeremiah
potter's field—the field of blood
Aceldama—(Aramaic for "field of blood") name given to the field the chief priests purchased with Judas's money

What do these three things have in common?

- a type of tree in Palestine
- a goat that leads sheep
- a person who betrays a friend

They are all called "Judas."

The Judas tree got its name from a legend that Judas hanged himself on that kind of tree. It has reddish flowers resembling drops of blood that grow right out of the trunk. Tradition says that the tree weeps blood for Judas each spring.

A Judas goat is an old goat that is trained to lead unsuspecting sheep into the pens where they are to be slaughtered.

For an animal and a man to have the same name is unusual. But both the Judas goat and a person who is a "Judas" are guilty of betraying others. The tradition of calling a traitor "Judas" comes from Judas Iscariot, one of the twelve disciples of Jesus.

The New Testament mentions several other men named Judas, but Judas Iscariot is the one most people think of when they hear the name Judas. Almost every time he's mentioned in the Bible, he's described as the one who betrayed Jesus. That's why people who betray their friends are called "Judases" today. Judas worked closely with Christ for about three years, yet he made a deal with the religious leaders who hated Christ so they could catch Him and kill Him. Why did Judas commit this terrible act?

The Gospels suggest several reasons for Judas's betrayal. His biggest problem, though, was that he

134

was double-minded. He wouldn't make up his mind to love God more than himself. Sometimes he wanted to, and sometimes he didn't. He was a frustrated man.

What reasons did Judas have for being single-minded in his love for Christ? He was given a position of great honor as a disciple. He had the power to heal people, cast out demons, and even raise the dead. He was a preacher taught by Jesus Himself. He went throughout the land of Palestine, preaching to the Jews. Though he had all these privileges, he was unsaved. He hadn't put his faith in Christ.

Judas even had a special position of responsibility among the disciples. He was the treasurer; he kept all the money the group used in their ministry. He was the one who took money to the poor. He bought the disciples' supplies. Although he had this additional authority, he abused it by stealing some of the money he was appointed to guard. The trust Christ and the disciples placed in him didn't make him love Christ with all his heart. Instead, he used this situation as an opportunity to satisfy himself.

If you were born into a Christian family, belong to a good church, and have a Christian school to attend, you're a privileged person, as Judas was. These are reasons you should love Christ with all your heart. They don't make you better than others, any more than Judas was better than others. On the contrary, they make your weaknesses and sins even worse.

Why was Judas double-minded? It was because of sin. He apparently struggled with covetousness. He wanted to have as much money as he could get. He couldn't seem to be satisfied without getting

of disloyalty he left. He was a traitor; he sold out his best friend, the Son of God, for a pittance.

When Judas's life is viewed as a whole, an array of contradictions immediately surface. He was a disciple and a thief. He was numbered among the twelve, but in the end that didn't matter. He was a friend of Christ but became His enemy. A man cannot go on living two lives, as Judas was trying to do. He had two seriously conflicting purposes. That conflict had to be resolved.

The goal of this lesson is to put the pieces of Judas's life together and come up with a composite of his problem. By analyzing the man this way, your students will be warned to avoid his mistake and eventual fate.

★ The Lesson

I. Deterrents to Double-Mindedness

Christians should be single-minded because of all the spiritual privileges they have been blessed with. Judas had every reason to be single-minded. He had the privilege of being one of the twelve apostles. He enjoyed a remarkable position. Scripture teaches that the church is built on the foundation of the apostles and the prophets (Eph. 2:19–20). This means that Judas had the opportunity to be a foundational member of the church. Had he not fallen, his name would have been inscribed on one of the foundational layers of the New Jerusalem, commemorating forever his contribution to the work of God (Rev.

more material things. This wasn't the way a disciple should have acted. A disciple wants to see people saved. He's to live a holy life and not focus on material things. Judas never learned the lesson of being content. As the disciples' treasurer, he had ample opportunity to satisfy his greed by stealing from the common funds. He even asked the chief priests for money when he offered to help them trap Jesus. Money wasn't the only reason he betrayed Christ, but it did enter into the decision.

If you're going to serve Christ with your whole heart, you must decide not to make decisions based on what you can get out of something. If you start focusing on money and other temporary rewards, you'll become double-minded. Look for ways you can do the most for Christ regardless of what you will get out of it.

"A double minded man is unstable in all his ways" (James 1:8).

Judas was proud as well as greedy. He was willing to see Christ glorified as long as he got glory out of it too. He wanted others to think that he was important. He didn't like to be criticized even if he deserved it. When Jesus rebuked him for complaining about Mary's gift, he got angry and went to the Jewish leaders to arrange to betray Christ. His pride was hurt because he'd been reproved in front of the other disciples. His pride made him double-minded because he was more concerned about his reputation than he was about Christ's.

Another sin that made Judas double-minded was disloyalty. Judas never made up his mind that he would follow Christ no matter what. He always kept

Dangers of a Double Mind

To be double-minded is to have two conflicting purposes. If you're double-minded, you want to serve both Christ and the Devil. You're divided in your loyalties, your energies, and your actions. Double-mindedness isn't a natural or healthy condition. Eventually the double-minded person must choose whom he'll follow. If he doesn't, he'll experience devastating consequences.

According to Exodus 21:32, what is the significance of the amount of money Judas Iscariot received for betraying Jesus?

in the back of his mind the possibility of abandoning Christ. When he decided the time was right, he sided with the enemies of Christ and betrayed Him. Anyone who'll abandon his friends isn't a genuine friend in the first place. A true friend is one who decides that he'll be devoted to another person with all his heart. He isn't double-minded.

What was the final result of Judas's double-mindedness? He committed suicide. After Judas had betrayed Jesus, some things happened that Judas didn't expect. He never thought they would kill Jesus. But after a hurried trial, the Jewish supreme court condemned Jesus to die. Judas rushed back to the Jewish leaders and admitted that Jesus was innocent. He even tried to give back the money they'd given him, but they weren't going to change their minds.

By now Judas's conscience had driven him to the breaking point. Instead of finding the Lord and the

135

Judas had remarkable spiritual privileges: He had great positions of responsibility in the work of the Lord, and he had the continual fellowship of Christ and the other disciples. He had many reasons to give himself wholeheartedly to Christ. But he did not yield himself. He was a divided man.

II. Desires of Double-Mindedness

Assigning a single motive for Judas's betrayal of Christ is virtually impossible. Many sinful desires gnawed at him, all putting him at cross purposes with Christ.

Covetousness. Judas desired things; he was not satisfied with what he had. For him, life consisted in the abundance of the stuff he could accumulate. When the Lord commissioned the disciples, He told them, "Provide neither gold, nor silver, nor brass in your purses, nor scrip for your journey, neither two coats, neither shoes, nor yet staves: for the workman is worthy of his meat" (Matt. 10:9–10). From the outset the Lord taught these men material contentment and the danger of covetousness. The Pharisees had this problem (Luke 16:14), and since the Lord regularly came into conflict with this group, He frequently addressed the subject.

But Judas absorbed little or none of Jesus's teaching on this point. Once he objected to an expensive gift Mary gave Christ, using the pretense of wanting to sell the gift and give the money to the poor (John 12:5–6). The perfume Mary placed on the feet and head of the Lord was expensive, costing a year's wages. Mark records that several other disciples also objected to what Mary had done (14:4–5). Apparently Judas was the ringleader in expressing this discontent.

Sometimes desire for money leads us to do things we wouldn't do otherwise. But covetousness is more than lust for money. If your students would disobey the Lord for any kind of gain—popularity,

---

21:14). Had he remained faithful, he would have helped rule the twelve tribes of Israel during the Millennium (Matt. 19:28).

Judas had great power as a disciple during Christ's ministry. When Jesus sent Judas and the others out to minister to the lost sheep of Israel, He said, "And as ye go, preach, saying, The kingdom of heaven is at hand. Heal the sick, cleanse the lepers, raise the dead, cast out devils: freely ye have received, freely give" (Matt. 10:7–8). These men received astounding powers. Furthermore, they were to expect complete material and monetary provision from those they ministered to. Judas was part of the band that received this commission. He participated in these powers and privileges.

Not everyone with miraculous power is godly. We must evaluate religionists by

the Scripture, not by what they can or cannot do.

Judas also held the privileged position of treasurer for the disciples (John 12:6; 13:29). This does not necessarily mean that the disciples did not keep money individually. However, funds for assisting the poor and similar projects were kept and dispersed by Judas. When a persons holds financial responsibility in any organization, he has additional authority. This probably was the case with Judas.

With privilege comes responsibility. Judas's "achievements" do not make us admire him more; rather they make his heart condition seem even worse. Your students cannot count on recognition or positions of leadership to make them better; such achievements may well make them worse by depriving them of any excuse.

recognition, pleasure—they have the same problem Judas did.

The Lord rebuked them for their attitude and told them that what Mary had done would go down in history as a great act of devotion, never to be forgotten (Mark 14:9). That prophecy has been fulfilled. Judas, though, could not accept Christ's rebuke. Both Matthew (26:14) and Mark (14:10) record that Judas immediately approached the Jewish leaders for the purpose of betraying Christ. With wounded pride pushing him and the chance to make money pulling him, he sold out the Lord for thirty pieces of silver. All the synoptic Gospels record that he made the arrangement for money (Matt. 26:15; Mark 14:11; Luke 22:5).

Pride. Another subtle but certain sin Judas demonstrated was pride. His act of betrayal was vindictive; he did not make that decision solely for financial gain. Jesus had just rebuked him for misunderstanding the value of Mary's act of devotion (Matt. 26:10–13; John 12:7–8). That was the last rebuke he would take. The rash act was not the response of a man who has been crossed only once. He was fed up with the reproofs of the Lord because of his wicked heart. "Correction is grievous unto him that forsaketh the way: and he that hateth reproof shall die" (Prov. 15:10). No better words could describe Judas.

> We all are prone to do wrong to others as a form of vengeance against insults or other perceived injuries to our pride. Because this tendency is nearly universal, we usually fail to recognize the depth of its wickedness.

It is interesting to note that Judas was a man of authority among the disciples and yet was not included in the inner circle (Peter, James, and John). This situation was probably a source of irritation to him. Not to be preferred as a close confidant is an insult to a man who thinks himself wiser than others. At the last meal with Jesus, Peter and John were made aware of what Judas was about to do while all the other disciples remained in confusion (John 13:22–26). This must have inflamed Judas's indignation beyond control.

Another thing this proud man doubtless found humiliating was his failure in deception and intrigue. Jesus knew that he would betray Him. He predicted it over and over. Nothing Judas tried fooled Jesus; he could not outwit the Master (John 13:27). Again, this circumstance would frustrate a

other disciples and admitting his wrong, he took extreme steps. He threw the money down onto the temple floor, rushed out, and hanged himself. The rope he hanged himself with came loose or broke, and he fell down a steep place onto some rocks, cutting himself open.

What a horrible way to die! What drove Judas to this insane act? He couldn't cope with his double-mindedness. One minute he thought and performed evil. The next, he was filled with remorse. This man needed the new birth. That's the only thing that would have resolved his torturous conflict.

Do You Remember?

1. Why did the priests decide to wait until after the Passover to arrest Jesus? _____
   because there would be fewer people around and a riot would not be as likely

2. How much money did Judas receive for betraying Jesus? _____
   thirty pieces of silver

3. Why was Judas's offer to betray Jesus helpful to the priests? _____
   They could then arrest Him when it was convenient for them.

4. Where did the Jews find Jesus? *in the garden of Gethsemane*

5. Why do you think Judas chose a kiss as the sign of his betrayal? _____
   Answers will vary but will probably include the idea that by giving Jesus a kiss of friendship Judas hoped to deceive Him about his part in the betrayal.

6. What led Judas to return the thirty pieces of silver to the priests? _____
   He regretted his action against Jesus and felt guilty.

7. How did Judas die? *He tried to hang himself and fell down a cliff.*

8. What did the priests purchase with the money from Judas? _____
   a field for burying "strangers" (indigents)

136

man who viewed himself as particularly alert and crafty.

Disloyalty. Judas's only loyalty was to himself. His interests won out every time.

Predicted. As early as a year before His Crucifixion, Jesus said, "Have not I chosen you twelve, and one of you is a devil?" (John 6:70–71) John explains that Jesus was saying this about Judas, who betrayed Him. Again, shortly after the transfiguration, Jesus said, "The Son of man shall be betrayed into the hands of men: and they shall kill him, and the third day he shall be raised again" (Matt. 17:22–23). At the last supper Jesus predicted this betrayal (John 13:18, 26).

These predictions reflect David's words: "Yea, mine own familiar friend, in whom I trusted, which did eat of my bread, hath lifted up his heel against me" (Ps. 41:9). Peter quoted from the Psalms to demonstrate that Judas's betrayal was a fulfillment of prophecy: "For it is written in the book of Psalms, Let his habitation be desolate, and let no man dwell therein" (Acts 1:20, quoting Ps. 69:25; 109:8). Did these prophecies bind Judas to a certain doom? Was he forced into treachery? This is not the teaching of Scripture. Judas unwittingly chose to be the fulfillment of those passages. He did not have to betray Christ.

Calculated. Another dimension of Judas's disloyalty is evident in his cold, detailed calculations to betray Christ. Because the Jewish leaders feared the crowds, Judas "sought opportunity to betray him unto them in the absence of the multitude" (Luke 22:6). He decided Gethsemane was the ideal spot because he "knew the place: for Jesus ofttimes resorted thither with his disciples" (John 18:2).

To guarantee his success, Judas brought a large number of armed men with him. John describes the group as a "band" (18:3), which technically means one-third of a Roman cohort, so there may have been as many as two hundred men. By merely speaking and causing the soldiers to fall to the ground, the Lord showed that He would not be taken unless He chose to allow it (John 18:6).

Satanic. It was Satan who hatched this insidious, treasonous plot. Luke writes that Satan "entered" Judas and caused him to act disloyally (Luke 22:3). John says that the devil had "put [it] into the heart of Judas Iscariot" and later "entered into him" (John 13:2, 27). The Scriptural evidence suggests that Satan gave Judas the idea to betray Christ and then actually possessed him while he did it. The idea of satanic possession is a point about which commentators disagree, but the plot was definitely from Satan. Satan is the author of disloyalty.

Micah wrote, "He hath shewed thee, O man, what is good; and what doth the Lord require of thee, but to do justly, and to love mercy, and to walk humbly with thy God?" (Mic. 6:8) The Hebrew word translated "mercy" in this passage could be translated "loving loyalty." God encourages loyalty; the Devil discourages it. Loyalty is an indispensable element in any lasting relationship. Without it people soon find fault with each other and split up, for the root of disloyalty is self-love, whereas the basis of loyalty is a love for God and others above oneself. Judas was simply more concerned about himself and his goals than he was the Lord's. He was unregenerate. He was, in Jesus's words, a "son of perdition" (John 17:12), doomed to damnation because of his sinful nature and conduct, which proved that he was unsaved.

III. Dangers of Double-Mindedness

When Judas realized that his betrayal would cost the Lord His life, his conscience troubled him. In the Gospels only Matthew 27:3–10 records what transpired with him after Christ's arrest.

Judas felt great remorse over his sin. He tried to give the money back to the chief priests and elders, admitting that he had betrayed innocent blood. The leaders scorned his concern as none of their business.

With no satisfaction from the leaders, he resolved the deep conflict in his soul the wrong way. He could have gone to Christ, repented directly to Him, and told Pontius Pilate that Christ was innocent. Apparently, however, in his weakness he couldn't bear the thought of the humiliation and the possible suffering. In desperation he threw the silver down in the temple and went out and hanged himself. Peter later said that Judas, in the process of hanging himself, fell and ruptured his intestines (Acts 1:18).

The elders' response to the money on the temple floor is an apt picture of the distorted religious thinking of these people. Since the money was a bribe to bring someone to death, they believed that they should not put the money into the temple treasury. Instead, they bought a piece of property called the potter's field, in which to bury foreigners. At the time of Matthew's writing, the field had come to be known as "the field of blood" because of the circumstances surrounding its purchase. This purchase was a fulfillment of prophecy: "And they took the thirty pieces of silver, the price of him that was valued, whom they of the children of Israel did value; and gave them for the potter's field, as the Lord appointed me" (Matt. 27:9–10; referring Jer. 32:9–10 and Zech. 11:12–13).

Judas, a man with great opportunity, ended tragically. He was a tortured man—tortured by his own divided heart, which he would not give to Christ.

Special Problems and Topics

• Did Matthew cite the wrong prophet?

According to Matthew 27:9, the prophecy about the potter's field was from Jeremiah; yet it is apparently from Zechariah. Was Matthew mistaken? No. The quotation is largely from Zechariah 11:12–13, but Matthew has combined with it certain elements from Jeremiah 32:6–10. The most important of these elements is the purchase of a field, which is Matthew's primary point. Thus he ascribes the quotation to Jeremiah on the basis of its primary teaching.

Extra Activities

Discussion: The Bible records several cases of suicide or suicidal thinking. Since this is a prevalent problem among American teenagers, it is a subject worth talking about from a scriptural point of view. Have your students look up each of the following passages about a suicide or suicidal thinking. Have them cite who was involved and the sin that contributed to that person's desire to commit further sin by ending his own life.

Numbers 11:10–15—Moses (frustration)
Judges 9:50–56—Abimelech (pride)
Judges 16:28–31—Samson (revenge)
1 Samuel 31:4—Saul (pride)
1 Samuel 31:5—Saul's armor-bearer (fear)
2 Samuel 17:23—Ahithophel (humiliation)
1 Kings 16:18—Zimri (fear)
1 Kings 19:1–4—Elijah (fear)
Acts 16:27–28—Philippian jailer (fear)

Discuss the following passages in the New Testament to establish clearly that suicide is a sin: Romans 14:7–9; 1 Corinthians 6:19–20; Ephesians 5:27.

Scripture search: Have your students read the following passages to get a thorough overview of Judas's life.

Call and ministry: Matthew 10:1–4; Mark 3:13–19; Luke 6:13–16; John 12:1–11

Early prediction of betrayal: John 6:70–71; Matthew 17:22; John 13:1–30

Betrayal: Matthew 26:14–16, 47–50; Mark 14:10–52; Luke 22:2–53; John 18:1–12

Replacement by Matthias: Acts 1:15–26

Lesson 39
Pride

THEME	Peter
SCRIPTURE	Matthew 26:30–75 (Mark 14:26–72; Luke 22:38–65; John 18:1–27)
MEMORY WORK	Matthew 26:41

 Approach to the Lesson

Theme: A Christian should not have too high an opinion of himself. Few things offend God more; He resists the proud (James 4:6). Since the proud are convinced that they can make it on their own, He refuses to impart spiritual power to them. The inevitable result is that the proud believer will fall when Satan attacks.

Rationale: Our culture places great emphasis on self-sufficiency and confidence. Counteract this emphasis by showing the inevitability of failure for the one who refuses to acknowledge his own weaknesses.

Background: One of the arguments for the inspiration of the Bible is the way it honestly portrays the best of God's men. The greatest heroes of the Faith sinned. Abraham had great faith but at times was a coward. Moses was a man of great compassion with the people of Israel; yet at times he was violent in his temper. David was a man after God's own heart, but again the Bible openly recounts how he became an adulterer and murderer.

Peter's life illustrates the same principle. He was the leader and spokesman of the disciples, and Jesus predicted that he and the other apostles would be the founding members of the church. But for all this man's strengths, there were counterbalancing weaknesses. He was impulsive and at times brazenly proud. His pride was glaringly manifested just before the arrest and trial of Jesus. The events that followed provide a framework for discussing the results of spiritual pride.

An important teaching aid, the "Christian Character Response Chart" (a chart on pride that is not included in the student text) is found on the CD accompanying this book.

 The Lesson

I. Foolish Boasting (Matt. 26:31–35)

Peter's pride caused him to boast that he would never deny Christ even if everyone else did. After the disciples had celebrated the Passover with the Lord, they went out to the Mount of Olives. On the way, Jesus warned them that they would be a part of the fulfillment of an Old Testament prophecy (Zech. 13:7), which speaks of the smiting of a shepherd and the consequent scattering of his sheep. The Lord was the Shepherd, and the sheep were the disciples. In preparation for the reversal of this scattering, the Lord told His disciples that He would meet them in Galilee.

Then Peter made his foolish declaration. To say he would not flee when the Lord was taken was foolish for two reasons. First, the Lord had already said it would happen. Second, Peter exalted himself above everyone else, suggesting that he had some great personal ability to resist this sin. He could have expressed a humble desire to be faithful to the Lord and could have admitted his total dependence on the grace of Christ, but he did not. Instead he used the situation as an opportunity to build himself up before the others.

The Lord explained to Peter how wrong he was. He told Peter that he would deny Him not just once, but three times before the cock crowed. Peter vehemently responded that this would never happen. Interstingly, Peter's further boasting began to affect the other disciples. The rest chimed in that they would never deny the Lord either. Pride and self-dependence are infectious. A poor example can do more damage than evil deeds done privately or a thousand wicked thoughts.

Objectives

KNOWLEDGE (concepts students need to grasp)	the sequence of events that led up to Peter's denial of Christ
	the results of pride in the believer's life
APPLICATION (principles students should put into practice)	Pride will cause others to be proud.
	Pride contributes to prayerlessness.
	Pride causes rash actions.
	Pride leads to cowardice.

Outline

(Matt. 26:31–75)
Results of pride
I. Foolish boasting (31–35)
II. Functional prayerlessness (36–46)
III. False confidence (47–55)
IV. Failure under pressure (56–75)

II. Functional Prayerlessness (Matt. 26:36–46)

The disciples' pride allowed them to fall asleep when they should have been praying. The Mount of Olives is a ridge a little more than a mile long, running north and south to the east of Jerusalem. The garden where Jesus took His disciples to pray was at the foot of this ridge. The name Gethsemane means "oil press," a reference to the valuable oil pressed from the olive trees that grew there. Jesus often went there for prayer and communion with His Father (Luke 22:39). This became the scene of the Lord's traumatic struggle.

Eight of the disciples were left at the entrance to the garden; only Peter and the "sons of Zebedee," James and John, accompanied Jesus. (Judas, of course, was not with the others.) These three seem to have formed an inner group within the apostles. On several occasions they shared experiences with Jesus apart from the others, such as the raising of Jairus's daughter (Luke 8:51) and the transfiguration (Matt. 17:1). Jesus called on them to watch and pray with Him in this time of great pressure.

Jesus proceeded a little farther into the garden, leaving the three disciples to pray together while He prayed alone. When He returned, He found them all asleep and He gently rebuked Peter for not being alert. Peter was singled out because he was the leader and spokesman for the disciples. He was also probably singled out because of his recent boast. Jesus warned them that they must watch and pray that they might be able to endure the coming trial. He went away to pray a second time. Returning, He found them sleeping again but went back and prayed a third time.

The disciples didn't have the urgency in prayer that they should have had. Peter particularly must have felt no need to be overly concerned about seeking God's help for the coming trial. A man who thinks he needs no special help will not

Read: Matthew 26:30–75   **Memorize:** Matthew 26:41

Bible Expressions to Understand

be offended—fall away
staves—(plural of *staff*) rods or poles
legion—a division of the Roman army consisting of 5,400 men
Caiaphas—Jewish high priest; son-in-law of Annas
bewrayeth—betrays; reveals or makes known one's character
Sanhedrin—the Jewish supreme court
Annas—former high priest; probably president of the Sanhedrin

Todd had attended his church since he was in elementary school. He was a leader in his youth group. Everyone looked up to him as a good Christian. He had a reputation for being a bold witness for Christ and living a good Christian life. Because of his good looks and his athletic ability, he was well liked by the other students at the large public high school he went to. In fact, after a while Todd came to the point that he began to think of himself as a pretty strong Christian, ready to take on anything for Christ. He imagined himself winning great battles for God—or even dying as a martyr!

He didn't anticipate, however, what would happen in biology class one day when the teacher began to talk about evolution and Creation. Mr. Gossage was a friendly man, but he didn't like the Bible. He said, "Now, intelligent people know that evolution explains how we all got here. Anybody who believes that God created human life is just holding on to what he was taught in Sunday school as a child." Mr. Gossage continued, "I certainly hope there is no one foolish enough in my class to believe those fairy tales from the Bible. If you think the Bible is true, stand up and tell us why."

By this time almost everyone in the class was snickering. They all knew that Todd was a Christian and that he believed the Bible. His youth pastor had held after-school Bible studies on campus. Todd sometimes gave a testimony at these meetings.

Tammy sat near Todd. She was a Christian too, but she was so shy she never spoke to anyone. Renee also belonged to Todd's youth group, but she acted like all the other kids, and no one expected her to say anything. Todd knew he ought to stand, but what would the others in the class think? Wouldn't he look like some sort of fanatic? Mr. Gossage paused, waiting for someone to respond. Todd's heart was beating so hard it seemed about to come out of his chest. How could he say anything? Mr. Gossage would make him look ridiculous in front of the whole class.

Then Mr. Gossage said, "Well, since there are no super saints in the crowd, let me tell you why evolution is true and the Bible isn't." Todd didn't hear much that Mr. Gossage said after that. He was

137

feel inclined to seek it. Pride certainly contributed to their prayerlessness on this occasion. Prayer is a humble act. It recognizes a greater person, a higher authority as possessing the power and answers for life. Self is dethroned in prayer.

There is a time for prayer. But that time may pass, and it may become too late to seek the strength and help needed (Matt. 26:45-46). When the Lord returned from His third session of prayer, the time of petition had ended; the betrayal had been done, and the soldiers were on the way to take Him.

III. False Confidence (Matt. 26:47–55)

Peter's pride led him to defend the Lord at the wrong time and in the wrong way.

Peter's self-confident reaction was important enough to be recorded in all four Gospels. John 18:10 identifies Peter as the one who struck off the ear of Malchus, a servant of the high priest. Luke 22:51 tells us that Jesus healed Malchus's ear by a touch of His hand.

Peter was completely out of step with what was going on. Jesus quickly gave him three pointed reasons for not conducting himself the way he had. First, violent conduct will bring more violent conduct. If Peter had continued to resist physically, he would have been killed. Armed resistance against spiritual persecution is usually, if not always, wrong. Second, the Lord did not need Peter's protection. He could have called on twelve legions of angels to help Him if He had desired. A legion of

Roman soldiers was six thousand men. Twelve legions is an imposing number of angels. Third, if Jesus had not been taken and crucified, the plan of God would not have been fulfilled. What was occurring had been prophesied, and it needed to be fulfilled, not prevented.

After He had pointed out the cowardice of those who came to arrest Him late at night, they took Him, and the disciples fled for fear of being arrested themselves. Peter ran away because he was not prepared for this spiritual challenge. He had been proud and had not prayed. He was weak, and the process of failure had begun.

> The natural result of self-reliance is failure. We are not strong enough to overcome life's challenges, regardless of what our pride tells us. Pride is a losing proposition.

IV. Failure Under Pressure (Matt. 26:56–76)

Peter's pride caused him to deny the Lord when his life was at stake. Before taking Jesus to Caiaphas and the Sanhedrin, the mob brought Him before Annas for a brief preliminary hearing, which only John records (18:13). Annas was an unusual personality. He had been high priest for seven years but had been removed by the Roman authorities. Four of his sons and Caiaphas, his son-in-law, succeeded him. Because of his experience in leading the council, Annas retained a lot of power over the Jewish system. Some believe that he was president of the Sanhedrin at this time. This would explain why Jesus was taken first to him before going to Caiaphas's house to stand before the Sanhedrin.

The Sanhedrin was composed of three groups: elders, chief priests, and scribes. The chief priests, usually twenty-four in number because of the twenty-four temple orders (1 Chron. 24:18–19), included the high priest. The most famed from among the scribes and scholars were also included. The Sanhedrin thus represented the Jewish nation politically, religiously, and intellectually.

The second hint of Peter's weakness is seen here—he followed "afar off" instead of openly identifying with his Lord. He followed the crowd to the "high priest's palace," which probably refers to the courtyard of the high priest. Peter remained outside the courtyard until another disciple (probably John), who had previously entered, arranged for him to enter too (John 18:15–16).

During the illegal trial of Jesus, Peter waited, watched, and denied. While he was waiting in the courtyard, a young woman approached him. She remarked that he "also" was a follower of Jesus. The woman was the one who had acted as doorkeeper a few moments earlier when John had gone to the door to bring Peter inside (John 18:17). This fact explains the word *also*. She knew that Peter was one of the men who had followed the Lord. However, in fear Peter publicly denied her assertion. Following this denial the cock crowed for the first time (Mark 14:68).

Peter retreated to the "porch," away from the fire where he had been warming himself. As he went, another woman accused him of being one who had accompanied Jesus of Nazareth. Peter forcefully denied knowing Jesus, taking an oath to lend credence to his words. The word *oath* here does not indicate cursing; rather, it denotes a solemn pledge, much the same as a legal oath.

About an hour later (Luke 22:59) a kinsman of Malchus, whose ear Peter had cut off (John 18:26), saw Peter. He charged him with being a follower of the Lord, pointing out that his Galilean accent (Matt. 26:73; Mark 14:70; Luke 22:59) "bewrayed" (or "betrayed") him. Peter then reached his lowest point, cursing and swearing in order to show that he did not know Jesus. Immediately the rooster crowed for the second time (Mark 14:72).

Pride goes before a fall. Peter was not ready in his spirit for the trial that came because he was so self-confident. He boasted, misled others, and then pathetically failed his Lord. Such a fall is often the only cure for the vicelike grip of pride. Self must be shown in all its weakness if it is ever to be left behind. How much better to get a clear view of self from the mirror of the Word of God and avoid the pain and scarring of a fall like Peter's.

Jesus then turned to look at Peter (Luke 22:61). Seeing the Lord and hearing the crowing, Peter suddenly remembered his boastful pledge (Matthew 26:75). Under deep conviction for his failure, he went out to weep bitterly. Medieval church tradition states that for the rest of his life Peter could not hear a rooster crow without falling on his knees and bursting into tears.

humiliated and felt guilty that he'd been ashamed of the Lord and His Word. Now Tammy and Renee would probably never stand up for the Lord. And what about the Bible studies? Who would attend now? And Todd had thought that he was so strong spiritually!

The bell rang. The walk home after school was a sad one. Todd had been proud of his knowledge and his ability. He'd been overconfident and hadn't sought the Lord's strength in prayer. When he got home, he went straight to his room, knelt beside his bed, and asked the Lord to forgive him for his sin of pride and his failure in class.

What if you'd been in Todd's place? Could you speak for the Lord when you fear others will ridicule you? No matter how strong you think you are, you must pray for God's strength to be strong in such situations. If you're proud and overconfident, you'll fail and deny the Lord.

As one of Jesus's first disciples, Peter became the leader and spokesman for the others. He became a bold leader of the church at its beginning, preaching a powerful sermon at Pentecost that resulted in several thousand people being saved. Later he wrote two letters that became books in the New Testament. The Gospel of Mark is probably based on information that Mark got from Peter about the life of our Lord. Peter accomplished a lot for the Savior.

But there was a time when Peter failed the Lord. He failed because he trusted in his own strength rather than relying on the Lord. This incident happened just before Jesus was crucified. Jesus had told His disciples that they would all flee when He was arrested. Peter was quick to say that he wouldn't. Jesus then told him that he would deny Him three times before a rooster crowed the next morning. When the other disciples saw how bold and confident Peter was, they too said they wouldn't flee and deny the Lord. Peter's fleshly confidence was catching, like a disease, and the other disciples caught it. If you brag around your friends, some won't like you, and others will imitate you. Both results are bad.

Shortly after Peter's boastful remarks, Judas arrived with soldiers to take Jesus away. Peter tried to defend Jesus with a sword. He cut off the ear of a servant of the high priest, but Jesus healed the man's ear and told Peter to put away the sword. Peter had reacted in a courageous way, but it was the wrong reaction. He was trying to handle the situation in his own strength. Since he couldn't use his sword, Peter ran away with the rest of the disciples. Remember, this is the man who was full of self-confidence just hours before.

Pride Goes Before a Fall

Every Christian is weak. If you depend on your own intelligence, personal appearance, abilities, and personality to do the work of the Lord, you'll fail. Pride will make you prayerless because you'll think you don't need God's help to live as a Christian. It will cause you to say and do things you shouldn't because you'll think you can control your life and the lives of others. God is offended by people who think they're important. He doesn't give proud people help in living for Him; He resists the proud but gives grace to the humble.

After that bitter moment, do you suppose Peter ever heard a rooster crow without thinking of how he denied his Lord?

138

While Jesus was on trial, Peter waited outside. Three times people said he was one of Jesus's disciples. He was such a coward that he denied it each time. The last time, he cursed to convince the people he wasn't a disciple. When he did, the rooster crowed just as Jesus had said it would. At that moment, Jesus turned and looked out into the courtyard at Peter.

Peter immediately realized what he'd done. Leaving that place, he went out and wept bitterly because of his failure. He had something serious to weep about. He had denied the Lord because he was self-confident, depending on his own boldness and physical strength instead of on God's power.

Do You Remember?

1. What prediction did Jesus make about Peter? _that Peter would deny Him three times that night before the rooster crowed_

2. How did the disciples react to this prediction? _All of them agreed with Peter that they would not deny the Lord._

3. What did the disciples do while Jesus prayed? _They slept._

4. How did Jesus face his betrayer and the mob? _He calmly went to meet them._

5. How did Peter rashly react to those who came to arrest Jesus? _He cut off the right ear of one of the high priest's servants._

6. Who was Malchus (John 18:10, 26)? _the high priest's servant whose ear was cut off_

7. How many of the disciples abandoned Jesus? _all of them except John (John 18:15)_

8. What was the reason for Peter's denial? _trusting in his own strength; pride_

9. What are two ways we deny the Lord in our daily lives? _by not speaking to others about Him and by not living for Him_

139

Christian Character Response Chart

	Inferiority	Pride	Humility
Performance	"I can't do anything well."	"No one does things as well as I do."	"The things that I do well I do well by the grace of God."
Appearance	"I hate the way I look."	"I'm better looking than most people."	"God created me, and I joyfully accept the way He made me."
Friendships	"Nobody likes me."	"Everybody likes me."	The Lord has been good to give me the friends that I have."
Intelligence	"Everyone is smarter than I am."	"Nobody knows as much about things as I do."	"My mind is a gift from God, and I intend to use it for His glory."

✳ Extra Activities

Visual aid: As you begin the lesson, it may be helpful to orient the students to the sequence of events you will be discussing. List the various incidents chronologically on an overhead transparency or on the board to put these events in time-order perspective

Discussion: Make a handout of the Christian Character Response Chart below (also found on the CD accompanying this book), copy it on the board, or make a transparency of it.

If you put it on the board, leave the "Humility" column blank. Discuss the responses in the "Inferiority" and "Pride" columns, and then elicit from the students what a Christlike response would be. Write their best answers or those suggested below in the "Humility" column. You can use this same approach if you make a handout from the fill-in-the-blank version of the chart on the CD.

If you make a transparency, cover all the response columns when you first display the chart. Discuss how a person who feels inferior might think about the various aspects of his personality. Then uncover the "Inferiority" column. Next talk about what the proud person thinks of himself and show those responses. Ask what a person with a Christlike attitude would say in each case before revealing the "Humility" column.

Lesson 40
Compromising

THEME	Compromise in Christ's Trials
SCRIPTURE	John 18:12–19:22
MEMORY WORK	John 18:37–38

 ## Approach to the Lesson

Theme: God gives every person a conscience—that aspect of the human spirit that urges one to do right and to shun wrong. When an individual violates his conscience, it condemns him as guilty. An unsaved person's conscience functions on a basic understanding of the law of God placed in the heart by God Himself (Rom. 2:15). The law written in the heart then becomes either more clearly understood through salvation or confused by the perversions of human culture. An unsaved person may defile or permanently impair his conscience by sinful acts and thoughts (Titus 1:15). He may even sear or desensitize it to the point that he is unable to discern right from wrong (1 Tim. 4:2). The believer has a conscience cleansed and renewed by the Holy Spirit in regeneration (Heb. 9:14). He also has the Word of God, which teaches him how God thinks. By the Lord's grace the Christian is able to discern between good and evil more clearly as he matures spiritually. He also gains more power from the Lord to respond properly to his conscience. The sin of compromising becomes less frequent as a result.

Objectives

KNOWLEDGE (concepts students need to grasp)	the role of Pilate in the trial and death of Christ
	the role of the chief priests and the Sanhedrin in the trial and death of Christ
	the roles of the disciples and the mob in the death of Christ
APPLICATION (principles students should put into practice)	Compromising for fear of losing power or influence (leadership and popularity) is a sin.
	Compromising for fear of reproach will weaken us spiritually and damage our testimony.

Bible Expressions to Understand

Annas—former Jewish high priest
Caiaphas—Jewish high priest; head of the Jewish supreme court
Pilate—Roman governor of Judea at the time of the trial of Christ
hall of judgment—the Praetorium; Roman governor's official residence
Barabbas—a murderer and political revolutionary; released instead of Christ

Listen to the details of the most important series of trials in history. The accused was brought before three different courts. The first court consisted of seventy justices. No evidence or clear testimony was presented against the supposed criminal. The witnesses against him contradicted themselves. The trial was held in the middle of the night in direct violation of the law. The death sentence was passed within hours even though the law said that such a sentence couldn't be handed down the same day as the trial.

The justices hurried the prisoner to the second court, the highest in the land. The judge of this court listened to the other justices give their evidence against the man. They had none. He found the man innocent but sent him to the third court, which found him innocent as well and sent him back.

The guilty verdict was unjust from two perspectives: the accused had done nothing wrong, and the trials were not conducted according to the law.

140

The judges of the first court were angry. Though the man was innocent, they wanted him dead. They kept accusing the man, and none of his friends came forward to defend him. Finally, the judge of the highest court gave in and condemned the man to die. The innocent victim was taken away and executed.

These were, of course, the trials of the Lord Jesus Christ. The first court was the Jewish supreme court, the Sanhedrin. The highest court was Pilate's, and the third court was Herod's. Both Pilate and Herod found Jesus innocent, but Pilate condemned Him to death anyway.

The Jewish judges, Pilate, Herod, and Christ's silent friends all committed the same sin—they compromised by giving in and doing what they knew wasn't right. They had different motives for committing this sin, but the end result was the same: Jesus was condemned and crucified.

The Jewish judges envied Christ. Many of the people loved Christ's preaching and miracles. They listened to Him and believed His words. When Jesus began to call attention to the leaders' sins, they hated Him for it and decided to kill Him. These were supposed to be the spiritual leaders of the Jews. They were really thieves and liars. They loved their power, and they weren't going to let anyone take it away. Rather than murdering Christ in cold blood, they plotted to commit a "legal" murder—to condemn Christ falsely as a criminal and have Him executed. They eventually succeeded. These leaders knew the law of God, but they broke it to keep their power. They compromised with evil.

Rationale: Teens often do not stand against pressure to do wrong, especially if that pressure comes from peers. However, they usually have active consciences. You can use that conscience as a partner in encouraging them to do right even if it costs them something.

Background: Many of the men directly involved in the trials and death of Christ present a sad portrait of moral and spiritual compromise. They didn't do what they knew to be right in the hour of crisis. This lesson considers several of them. Pilate, the high priest, and the Sanhedrin are major characters. Lesser but significant participants include Joseph of Arimathea and Nicodemus. The disciples, both individually and corporately, are mentioned. And of course the multitude must not be overlooked. Many of them rejoiced at the words of Jesus (which caused the Jewish leaders to fear losing their power), but they were strangely silent as Jesus was condemned and crucified. What is the unifying element? They all simply failed to do right. They violated their consciences and the law.

An important teaching aid, a copy of the chart from page 143 of the student text, is found on the CD accompanying this Teacher's Edition.

 ## The Lesson

Note: In the first three paragraphs of the lesson in the student text, the pronouns referring to Christ are purposely not capitalized to keep readers guessing as to the identity of the man on trial.

"When Pilate saw that he could prevail nothing, but that rather a tumult was made, he took water, and washed his hands before the multitude, saying, I am innocent of the blood of this just person: see ye to it" (Matt. 27:24).

Pilate was the Roman governor of Judea. The Jews had some power, but the Romans had the final say in political matters. If someone was to die, the Roman leader had to give the go-ahead. When the Jewish rulers came to Pilate, they wanted him to pass judgment on Christ on the basis of their decision without hearing the evidence for himself. Pilate wouldn't agree. After listening to their accusations and examining Christ, he was convinced that Jesus was innocent. To get rid of the case, he sent Jesus to Herod, ruler of another political jurisdiction. Herod also examined Jesus, but Jesus refused even to respond to his questions because He knew how wicked Herod was. Herod also found Jesus innocent and returned Him to Pilate. Now even more convinced than before that Jesus was innocent, Pilate wanted to let Him go.

Pilate offered to beat Christ and then release Him. The Jewish leaders, however, would not be satisfied with the scourging. They wanted death. Pilate tried to release Jesus, but fearing that the Jewish leaders would send a bad report to the Roman emperor, he eventually sent Jesus away to be crucified. Pilate gave in because he was afraid of losing his power and influence. He knew he was doing the wrong thing, but he compromised anyway.

Where were Christ's friends during this trial? They were all guilty of cowardly silence. Two of the men on the Jewish court, the Sanhedrin, knew Christ. Nicodemus and Joseph of Arimathea were members of the court. Nicodemus had come to Jesus at night and asked about being born again. Joseph of Arimathea was actually a secret disciple of Jesus. He wouldn't tell anyone because he was afraid of the other Jewish leaders. Both of these men buried Jesus after His death. What could they have done to prevent His death if they had tried? That is difficult to say, but the Gospels record nothing about any efforts to save Jesus from the wrong that was being committed against Him. They were probably afraid of the embarrassment of being associated with Jesus. They were also probably afraid of the possible physical harm that might come to them. They compromised because of fear.

The Fear of Man Is a Snare

God has given you a conscience—a part of your soul that urges you to do right and avoid sin. When you violate your conscience by doing wrong, it tells you that you are guilty. If you fail to stand up for Christ when you should, you'll feel guilty. You *should* feel guilty because you've sinned. Being silent as a Christian when you should be bold and speak out for the Lord is a sin. Even if you are afraid of what will happen if you speak out, you must. If some of your friends don't want to be your friends anymore because you're a bold Christian, then let them go. If your family or others make fun of you or threaten you because you're faithful to Christ, you should still stand courageously. Regardless of the consequences, never compromise by failing to do what you know to be right.

141

the Jews had to work together. In civil as well as religious matters, the Sanhedrin had considerable authority. It could mete out judgment on almost all crimes except those demanding capital punishment. In those cases the procurator had to approve the punishment, often after a retrial before the Roman official. To build rapport, a Roman governor sometimes simply accepted the Sanhedrin's decision and approved the punishment.

First hearing. After the Sanhedrin had found Jesus guilty of blasphemy, they took Him to Pilate for the death sentence. (The fullest presentation of Christ's appearance before Pilate is recorded in John 18:28–19:22, part of the reading passage for this lesson.) Pilate asked what accusation they were bringing (John 18:29). The Jews responded vaguely, hoping that he would simply grant the sentence without a retrial. This approval would keep them from having to fabricate more accusations against Him since blasphemy was not a crime punishable by Roman law. But Pilate refused to grant a sentence without a retrial. He was taking the opportunity to remind these proud Jews of their subjugation to Rome. At this point the animosity was high.

The Jews next offered a threefold accusation against Jesus (Luke 23:2). They said that He was guilty of insurrection, that He caused people not to pay taxes to the Roman government, and that He claimed to be king of the Jews. Pilate then took Jesus inside the judgment hall and asked Him if He had claimed to be king of the Jews (John 18:33). During their brief conversation the Lord explained that His kingdom was not of this world. It was a kingdom of truth, and all those who received the truth would become part of His kingdom. Pilate cynically replied, "What

I. Fear of Loss

Pilate. Pontius Pilate was the fifth Roman procurator of Judea, replacing Valerius Gratus in AD 26. He ruled until AD 36. There were two kinds of Roman provinces: senatorial and imperial. Senatorial provinces were governed by a proconsul chosen by the Roman senate with the approval of the emperor. Imperial provinces were under the direct control of the emperor and were ruled by procurators. Judea was a relatively small imperial province, and thus Pilate was directly answerable to Tiberius Caesar, the emperor.

Trouble with the Jews. Tiberius was subject to shifts in mood. Pilate, therefore, was in a delicate position. If he made one poor decision, he could be deposed, particularly if that move were personally offensive to Tiberius. Pilate got off to a bad start with the Jews when he ordered Roman soldiers in a parade to carry emblems that the Jews considered idolatrous. Even worse, the parade was on the Day of Atonement. At first Pilate threatened to kill anyone who objected. When the Jews continued their opposition, he backed down.

Pilate compounded his problems by appropriating money from the temple treasury to build an aqueduct to Jerusalem. Many of the Jews who rioted to protest Pilate's actions were killed by his soldiers. The Jews may have been referring to this incident in Luke 13:1.

Pilate showed himself insensitive to the religion of the Jews. He brought much of their opposition on himself. Regardless of their disdain for each other, Pilate and

is truth?" (John 18:38) In that statement he betrayed himself because it revealed his philosophy of life. For him there were no absolutes, no truth or falsehood—only what had to be done to stay ahead. Compromise was part of his approach to life. Unwittingly, Pilate answered his own question a little later when he said of Christ, "Behold the man!" Christ Himself is truth.

The Jews had charged that Jesus was stirring up sedition in both Galilee and Judea. Pilate accepted these words as the escape he was looking for. He sent Jesus to Herod Antipas, who governed Galilee. Herod and his soldiers mocked the Lord, putting a royal robe on Him. Finding no crime worthy of death, Herod sent Jesus back to Pilate. The diversion had not accomplished anything in Christ's trial, but it did heal the breach between Herod and Pilate (Luke 23:5–12).

Second hearing. When Jesus had been returned, Pilate told the Jewish leaders that neither he nor Herod had found any fault in Him. He said that he would scourge Christ and release Him, according to the custom of releasing one prisoner at the Passover (Luke 23:14–17; John 18:39). But the high priests stirred up the people to cry out for Barabbas. To satisfy them, Pilate symbolically washed his hands of the situation (Matt. 27:20–24) and released Barabbas, an insurrectionist and murderer (Mark 15:7, 15).

Finally the Jews gave their real reason for wanting Christ crucified. It was because He had claimed that He was the Son of God. At that statement Pilate became afraid (John 19:7–8). This superstitious Roman had already received a message from his wife about a dream she had had (Matt. 27:19). Now the Jews asserted that Jesus claimed to be the Son of God. The Romans had legends about gods who appeared as men. He must have wondered what would happen if he perpetrated a crime against such a man.

Pilate went back inside the judgment hall and asked Jesus where He was from. Jesus, however, did not answer. Exasperated by His refusal to respond, Pilate threatened Christ with his power to have Him crucified. Jesus responded that Pilate had no power except what God allowed him to have. From that point on, Pilate tried to release Jesus, but the Jews said that he was not Caesar's friend if he allowed such a man to live. Jesus had claimed that He was a

The twelve disciples didn't do much better than Nicodemus and Joseph. They ran when the guards arrested Jesus. John alone had the courage to go with Jesus to the trial before the Sanhedrin. Peter followed at a distance but later denied Jesus out of fear. The rest of the twelve were nowhere to be found. Only John was at the Crucifixion. Some women who followed Jesus were there also, but that was all. The first time Jesus appeared to the disciples as a group after His Resurrection, they were gathered together in a room secretly because of their fear of the Jewish leaders. They were unwilling to risk being bold followers. They were afraid to do right and let it be known that they were Christ's friends. They, too, compromised because of fear.

Do You Remember?

1. Who was Christ taken to first after His arrest? _Annas_

2. Who recommended that Jesus be killed? _Caiaphas, the high priest_

3. Why did the Jews not want to go into Pilate's judgment hall? _____
   They did not want to be defiled and therefore prohibited from eating the Passover.

4. When Pilate asked what accusation the Jewish leaders had against Christ, how did they respond? _____
   They said they would not have brought Jesus to him if He were not a malefactor.

5. Why did the Jewish leaders bring Christ to Pilate? _____
   The Jews did not have the power to sentence Christ to death.

6. For what purpose did Jesus say He came into the world? _____
   to bear witness to the truth

7. Who asked, "What is truth?" _Pilate_

8. What did Pilate conclude after examining Christ? _that He was innocent_

9. What was the custom in Judea at the time of the Passover concerning prisoners? _____
   One was released by the Roman authorities as a kind gesture.

10. According to Jesus, who granted Pilate his authority to rule? _God_

142

king. If Pilate let Him go, they would report it to the emperor (John 19:9–12).

Collapse. The pressure on Pilate was great. His record had not been good. He took Jesus before the people and asked, "Shall I crucify your King?" To this the leaders replied, "We have no king but Caesar" (John 19:15). This utterly hypocritical remark was the end. Pilate commanded that Jesus be crucified, but his disgust with the trial remained. He refused to change the wording of the sign on the cross (John 19:19–22), and he granted the watch at the tomb with disgust (Matt. 27:65).

Pilate believed that Jesus was innocent. Three times he announced that conviction to the Jewish leaders (Luke 23:4, 20, 22). He became convinced that Jesus deserved to be free and tried to release Him. But his beliefs did not matter in the end; the Jews threatened to report him to Caesar, and losing his power was more than he was willing to risk for the man from Nazareth. Pilate knew in his conscience that Jesus did not deserve death, but he consented to it. He compromised to keep his influence.

The situation is really not different when a student sells out what he knows to be right to remain popular. Your students who conduct their affairs on the basis of what seems to be right at the time, instead of what God says in His Word, will find that the popularity they fought so hard to preserve will count for nothing. If they do not have trouble in this life because of that approach, they certainly will in eternity.

Pilate's end. It is ironic that not long after Christ's Resurrection, Pilate slaugh-

Lessons Learned from the Friends and Enemies of Christ

LESSON	PEOPLE	TEACHING
32	James and John, the sons of Zebedee	Lead by serving.
33	John the Baptist	Demonstrate boldness.
34	Mary and Martha	Worship Christ.
35	Friends of Christ	Show impartiality in your choice of Christian friends.
36	Scribes and Pharisees	Practice honesty and not hypocrisy.
37	The Herods	Show kindness and not cruelty.
38	Judas Iscariot	Be single-minded and not double-minded.
39	Peter	Be humble and not proud.
40	Witnesses of the trials and death of Christ	Never compromise right.

143

tered a group of Samaritans who had gone to Mount Gerazim to search for some items of gold that Moses had supposedly left there. Because they were armed, he thought that they were going to cause a rebellion, and he wiped them out. The outrage over this act was so great that he was removed from office and called back to Rome in AD 36 to stand trial before Caesar. But Tiberius died on March 16, AD 37, before the trial. No one knows for certain what happened to Pilate. A common tradition says that he was later exiled to Gaul (modern France), where he eventually committed suicide.

The Jewish leaders. The high priests and the Sanhedrin also compromised because of their fear of losing power. Luke reports that both Annas and Caiaphas were high priests when John the Baptist began his ministry (Luke 3:2). Annas was high priest from AD 6 to AD 15. He was appointed by Quirinius, the governor of Syria, and deposed by Valerius Gratus, the man Pilate replaced as procurator of Judea in AD 26. Although Annas technically never held the office of high priest after that time, his son-in-law Caiaphas, four of his sons, and one of his grandsons did. In a sense he was the high priest emeritus for years after he left the position officially.

Their hatred for Christ. Six months before His death the Lord prophesied that the chief priests and rulers would bring about His death (Matt. 16:21). About a month prior to His death, He repeated the same prediction (Matt. 20:18–19). The most serious confrontation between Jesus

and the high priests came at the two cleansings of the temple. The high priest's family owned most of the business in the temple. When Christ drove the men out and overthrew the tables, He was hurting them where it counted—in the pocketbook.

The day after the second cleansing, Jesus returned, and the chief priests and elders confronted Him again, asking by what authority He was doing what He was doing (Matt. 21:23). When Jesus asked them by what authority John the Baptist had carried out his ministry, they did not answer. He then told two parables denouncing their hypocritical conduct. They understood the parables but did not arrest Christ then because they feared the people, many of whom viewed Jesus as a prophet (Matt. 21:24–46). The next day the high priests, scribes, and elders met and began plotting to kill Christ (26:3–4). Caiaphas unwittingly prophesied that one man should die for the nation (John 11:49–52). They found their opportunity when Judas offered to betray Him (Matt. 26:14).

Their abuse of their office. After Christ was arrested, He was first taken to Annas's home, where the former high priest questioned Him about His teaching and His disciples (John 18:13–23). Christ was then sent to Caiaphas and the Sanhedrin (Matt. 26:57–68).

This assembly was held illegally in the middle of the night. The leaders tried to get false witnesses to condemn Christ, but they could not find any. Finally, two men said that they had heard Christ talking about destroying the temple and rebuilding it in three days. To this accusation Jesus did not bother to respond. Then the high priest Caiaphas asked Him if He was the Son of God. Christ boldly stated that He was. Everything the Lord had done to this point had proved that He was, but the high priest tore his clothes, as a sign of hearing supposed blasphemy. Relieved, he declared that they did not need any more witnesses, since they concluded that they had heard blasphemy from Christ Himself. They all agreed that He was guilty. They then spit on Christ and beat Him (Matt. 26:59–67). Early the next morning the Sanhedrin met again to agree officially on the verdict to validate their actions of the previous night. (Of course, the proceedings had been conducted at night to keep the multitude from objecting.) Next they took Christ to Pilate (27:1–2). These leaders accused the Lord before Pilate, then before Herod, and then before Pilate again. Later they mocked Him while He hung on the cross (27:41–43). They acquired a guard for the tomb to prevent any efforts to feign a resurrection. When the Resurrection did occur, they bribed the soldiers to lie about it (28:11–15). The dishonesty, greed, brutality, and envy of these supposed religious leaders is sickening. They were determined to keep their power. It did not matter that the law of God, which they were supposed to represent, was being violated repeatedly. They gladly compromised to maintain their power.

II. Fear of Persecution

Reproach and physical harm are the two main forms of persecution. Often this double-edged sword of persecution has tested the devotion of Christians. These tests came to many who were involved in the circumstances surrounding Christ's trials and death.

The secret disciples. Joseph of Arimathea was a member of the Sanhedrin (Mark 15:43) as was Nicodemus, who had come to Christ at night and received instruction on spiritual birth (John 3:1–21). Later, six months before Jesus's death, Nicodemus defended Him before the Sanhedrin, encouraging them to conduct themselves according to the Law (7:50–52). Their response was one of scorn. Nicodemus is not mentioned again in the Gospels until the burial of Jesus, when he helped Joseph (19:39). It is not conclusive from Scripture whether he was a disciple of Christ, but it appears that he was.

What Nicodemus did *not* do is what is disturbing. He knew in advance of the plans to kill Christ. The morning Jesus was sent to Pilate, the Sanhedrin met to decide what to do (Mark 15:1). No comment is made about Nicodemus's objecting to the decision. The vote to seek the death sentence for Christ did not have to be unanimous; a two-thirds majority was adequate. Perhaps Nicodemus did object, or perhaps he was not present.

Joseph of Arimathea was a secret disciple of Jesus because he feared the authorities (John 19:38). He prepared Jesus's body for burial and placed it in his own tomb (19:38–42; Matt. 27:59–60). Joseph had not consented to the death of Christ with the Sanhedrin (Luke 23:50–51), but he was sinfully timid. He should have renounced his membership in the Sanhedrin

or defended Christ before Pilate and Herod. Where was he?

> Both Nicodemus and Joseph were silent out of fear of reproach and possible physical harm. A true Christian has to suffer reproach or danger. Bearing reproach and being willing to suffer physical harm are part of taking the name of Christ.

The twelve. The disciples, too, gave a pathetic portrait of cowardice in the face of reproach and possible physical suffering. When Jesus was arrested in the Garden of Gethsemane, Peter attempted a defense by cutting off the ear of the high priest's servant (John 18:10). Shortly after, all the disciples fled (Mark 14:50). Peter followed from far behind but later denied the Lord in fear. Only one disciple, probably John, was courageous enough to enter the residence of the high priest for the trial (John 18:15). The rest were nowhere to be found. At the Crucifixion only John and the women followers of Christ were present (19:25–27). Where were the rest?

Some light on this point comes from John 20:19—"Then the same day at evening, being the first day of the week, when the doors were shut where the disciples were assembled for fear of the Jews, came Jesus and stood in the midst, and saith unto them, Peace be unto you." They had fled out of fear.

> These men should have been as bold during Christ's trials and death as they were after the ascension and Pentecost, but they weren't. Your students, too, serve the living Christ. They must not compromise (fail to give a bold testimony) because of a fear of reproach or physical harm.

The multitude. The crowds had praised Jesus. They had adored Him on the day He rode into Jerusalem (Matt. 21:8–9). Even the children sang His praises in the temple (21:15). And when the Jewish leaders wanted to take Him, they feared to do so because of the affection of the multitude, who viewed Him as a prophet (21:46). But once Christ was taken and tried, the only multitudes were those who cried out for the release of Barabbas and the death of Jesus (27:20, 25). When Jesus hung on the cross, others mocked (27:39–40). None of those who had believed or been healed came to His defense; they all stood in guilty silence because they feared reproach and physical harm. They compromised to save themselves.

Paul's face turned red with embarrassment and anger. "Who are you to judge? If you were in my place, you would have done the same thing!" Paul stormed away.

That night Danny stopped by Paul's house after supper. "Paul, I know you got mad this afternoon, but what I said was right, and you know it. Either you turn yourself in tomorrow or I'll have to. You don't deserve a grade you didn't earn honestly."

"Some friend you are, Danny. After all these years we've been friends, how could you do a thing like that?" Paul fumed. "Get out of my house," he shouted. "I guess you were never really my friend anyway."

Three days later Paul still had not said a word to Mrs. Ricter about cheating. Danny knew what he had to do. That afternoon, he went to speak to her.

"Mrs. Ricter, I don't like to have to talk to you about this, but you need to know that Paul cheated on his test. I saw him copying answers from Roxanne."

"Are you sure about this, Danny?" asked Mrs. Ricter.

"Paul admitted it to me the other night when I was at his house," Danny replied.

Mrs. Ricter checked Roxanne's and Paul's tests the next day. The cheating was obvious. Paul received an *F* for cheating and was taken off the soccer team. Paul and Danny were no longer friends, and Paul refused to speak to Danny.

1. Because of Paul's difficult situation, was it all right for him to cheat?
   No; cheating is always wrong regardless of the circumstances.

2. Would it have been better if Danny had just ignored Paul's cheating and let the Lord work in his heart?
   No; Danny had the biblical responsibility of reproof in this situation.

3. How would you evaluate Paul's response to Danny?
   He did not respond properly. He should have admitted his wrong and turned himself in.

Unit 7

Christ's Miracles

The first miracle Jesus performed was at a wedding in Cana of Galilee. To the embarrassment of the bride and groom, they ran out of wine at the wedding feast. Seeing their problem, Jesus had the servants fill six pots with water. He then turned the water in the pots into the best wine. This demonstration of power by Christ was only the first of numerous miracles. Thirty-five specific miracles of Jesus are recorded in the Gospels. The Gospels also tell us that, at times, Jesus healed multitudes of people. Jesus used His miracles to prove that He was God, strengthen the faith of believers, and teach important lessons about living for Him.

Unit 7
Christ's Miracles

The purpose of this unit is to introduce your students to the miracles of Christ. The goal is for the students to understand not only what miracles Jesus performed but also why He performed them. In addition to proving His divinity and helping people in need, Christ had a didactic purpose for most of His supernatural works. Christ's miracles gave Him an opportunity to teach certain ideas that He wanted to communicate.

The first three lessons in this unit (41–43) discuss several miracles, each lesson focusing on a common theme found in the miracles. The last three lessons of the unit (44–46) each discuss a single miracle. Lessons 44 and 45 provide charts which list other miracles of Christ that are similar to the ones emphasized in the lessons. You will find that the charts provided with the lessons (and of course the Scripture reading) are essential to teach these lessons effectively.

This unit offers several charts of Christ's miracles as special features in the student text. The first and most important is the "Master Chart of Christ's Miracles." This is a vital teaching aid since it summarizes all the miracles discussed in the unit. It is also an important reference tool since the numbers assigned to the miracles on this chart are often used when a miracle is discussed within a lesson. Lessons 42–45 contain more specialized charts discussing specific categories of miracles. All of these other charts use the same numbering system as the master chart. All of the charts in this unit are also included on the CD (both the full chart and a fill-in-the-blank version).

Master Chart of Christ's Miracles

Physical Illness and Death

1. Nobleman's son at Cana healed of a severe fever	John 4:46–54
2. Blind man at Bethsaida received sight	Mark 8:22–26
3. Man born blind received sight	John 9:1–41
4. Lazarus raised from death	John 11:1–45
5. Jairus's daughter raised from death	Matthew 9:18–19, 23–26; Mark 5: 22–24, 35–43; Luke 8:41–42, 49–56
6. Paralytic at Bethesda healed	John 5:1–18
7. Woman healed of twelve years of bleeding	Matthew 9:20–22; Mark 5:25–34; Luke 8:43–48
8. Paralytic at Capernaum healed	Matthew 9:1–8; Mark 2:1–12; Luke 5:17–26
9. Leper at Gennesaret healed	Matthew 8:1–4; Mark 1:40–45; Luke 5:12–15
10. Peter's wife's mother healed of a severe fever	Matthew 8:14–17; Mark 1:29–31; Luke 4:38–39
11. Man with withered hand healed	Matthew 12:9–14; Mark 3:1–6; Luke 6:6–11
12. Two blind men at Capernaum received sight	Matthew 9:27–31
13. Deaf-mute in Decapolis healed	Mark 7:31–37
14. Bartimaeus and another blind man received sight	Matthew 20:29–34; Mark 10:46–52; Luke 18:35–43
15. Centurion's servant with paralysis healed	Matthew 8:5–13; Luke 7:1–10
16. Widow's son at Nain raised from death	Luke 7:11–16
17. Man with dropsy healed	Luke 14:1–4
18. Ten men with leprosy healed	Luke 17:11–19
19. Severed ear of Malchus, servant of the high priest, healed	Luke 22:49–51; John 18:10–11

146

Weather and the Laws of Physics	
20. Storm stilled on the Sea of Galilee	Matthew 8:23–27; Mark 4:35–44; Luke 8:22–25
21. Jesus and Peter walked on the Sea of Galilee	Matthew 14:22–33; Mark 6:45–52; John 6:16–21

Plant and Animal Life	
22. Tax money found in a fish's mouth	Matthew 17:24–27
23. First astounding catch of fish	Luke 5:1–11
24. Astounding catch of 153 fish	John 21:1–14
25. Withering of a fig tree	Matthew 21:17–22; Mark 11:12–14, 20–25

Food and Drink	
26. Water changed into wine	John 2:1–11
27. Two loaves and five fish fed more than five thousand	Matthew 14:15–21; Mark 6:35–44; Luke 9:12–17; John 6:5–15
28. Seven loaves and a few fish fed more than four thousand	Matthew 15:32–39; Mark 8:1–9

Demon Possession	
29. Two men from Gadara delivered	Matthew 8:28–34; Mark 5:1–20; Luke 8:26–39
30. Epileptic boy delivered	Matthew 17:14–20; Mark 9:14–20; Luke 9:37–43
31. Blind and dumb man delivered	Matthew 12:22; Luke 11:14
32. Dumb man delivered	Matthew 9:32–34
33. Syro-Phoenician girl delivered	Matthew 15:21–28; Mark 7:24–30
34. Man in the synagogue delivered	Mark 1:23–27; Luke 4:33–36
35. Woman crippled for eighteen years delivered	Luke 13:10–17

Lesson 41
The Deity of Christ

THEME	Deity of Christ
SCRIPTURE	Matthew 8:16–17; 11:1–6; 15:29–31
MEMORY WORK	John 20:30–31

 ## Approach to the Lesson

Theme: Christ performed many miracles; thirty-five are recorded in the Gospels. A miracle is the direct operation of divine power that results in an effect contrary to the ordinary course of nature or human life. By His miracles Christ showed His authority over nature, physical illness, death, evil spiritual beings, and even sin. This diversity is astounding. It establishes the validity of His power. These miraculous acts were not the result of sleight of hand or crafty deception. Many people witnessed them.

The performing of a miracle does not prove that a person is God. But when someone demonstrates the consistent, all-encompassing authority Christ did through genuine miracles, it is significant. The number, variety, and power of Jesus's miracles prove beyond question that He is God.

Rationale: Many students have difficulty understanding the practical application of doctrines such as the deity of Christ. If Christ is not God, He has no more claim on them than Buddha, Mohammed, or today's most popular athlete. But if Jesus is God, then He is the source of everything they need every day of their lives. This single doctrine literally makes all the difference in their day-to-day lives.

Objectives

KNOWLEDGE (concepts students need to grasp)	what constitutes a miracle
	the four ways Christ used miracles to prove He is God
	the relationship between Christ's deity and the importance of His teachings, His death, and His Resurrection
APPLICATION (principles students should put into practice)	We should obey Christ wholeheartedly because He is God.
	We must not allow false teachers to fool us into thinking they represent Christ.

Bible Expressions to Understand

possessed by devils—controlled by evil fallen angels under the direction of Satan
miracle—a supernatural act by which God alters the laws of nature, the activities of evil spiritual beings, or the conduct and physical wellbeing of people

Have you ever heard of the Thundering Legion? A legion was a group of about 5,400 soldiers in the Roman army. An early Christian writer named Tertullian recorded the popular legend of the Thundering Legion.

The Old Testament teaches that God controls the weather. "The Lord hath his way in the whirlwind and in the storm, and the clouds are the dust of his feet" (Nah. 1:3).

148

In AD 176, the Roman army was fighting the Germans. The Romans found themselves surrounded by mountains, where the Germans were hiding. A severe drought had shortened the water supply, and all the soldiers were suffering from extreme thirst. In desperation a Roman commander told the emperor that one of the legions in the army was made up largely of Christians, who believed that God could work a miracle in behalf of the Roman army. The emperor encouraged the Christians in that legion to pray, and they did so. Soon after they finished, a great thunderstorm began. Hailstones drove the Germans from their mountain strongholds and put them at the mercy of the Romans, while rain replenished the army's water supplies. The emperor declared that the legion should be called the Thundering Legion.

God works miracles. The Bible and church history testify to that fact. Nature speaks to us of the great power and intelligence of God, but sometimes God does something out of the ordinary. He causes a miracle—a supernatural demonstration of divine power that supersedes the laws of nature and changes the lives of people (John 6:14).

No other time or place saw miracles like those in Palestine in the first century during the time Jesus Christ lived on the earth. The Gospels record thirty-five specific miracles that Jesus performed. They also teach that He did many other miracles that aren't recorded. Why did Jesus perform so many miracles? First, He wanted to help people. Second, He wanted to teach people how to live for Him. He used miracles as object lessons. Third, He wanted to prove that He's God.

Background: This lesson shows how Christ's miracles prove He is God. The nature of the miracles the Lord performed and the manner in which He performed them present overwhelming evidence of His deity. Only God could have done the things He did, as often as He did, in the way He did them, and under such different circumstances.

Numbers in parentheses in the lesson represent entries in the "Master Chart of Christ's Miracles" found on pages 146–47 of the student text and on the CD.

 ## The Lesson

I. Christ's Authority over Sin

In all the recorded miracles of Christ, only once did the subject of forgiveness of sins come up. That one occasion, however, has great significance. When the Lord restored the paralytic at Capernaum (#8), He said, "Son, be of good cheer; thy sins be forgiven thee" (Matt. 9:2). The scribes who heard Him thought, "Why doth this man thus speak blasphemies? who can forgive sins but God only?" (Mark 2:7) The Lord knew what they were thinking and asked, "Why reason ye these things in your hearts? Whether is it easier to say to the sick of the palsy, Thy sins be forgiven thee; or to say, Arise, and take up thy bed, and walk?"

Do the miracles that Jesus performed really prove that He's God? If they do, then you should believe He's God—the Creator of all things, the Sustainer of the universe, your Savior from sin, and the Lord of your life. If they don't, then Jesus was a master deceiver and doesn't deserve to be followed or served. The Bible teaches that Jesus was without sin. He never tried to deceive anyone. He clearly stated several times that He's God, and His miracles prove that fact.

"Who but God can forgive sins?" was the question some men asked once when Jesus was about to heal a paralyzed man. They thought that Jesus was sinning by claiming the power to forgive sins. Jesus answered their question with another: which is easier to do, to heal a man of paralysis, or to forgive his sins? Christ then healed the man to prove that He had the power to forgive sins. No one has that power but God. If Jesus said He had the power and proved it, then He is God.

Having "suffered many things" at the hands of various doctors, the woman finally received healing from the Great Physician (Mark 5:25–29).

What Do Jesus's Miracles Prove?

Christ performed many miracles, thirty-five of which are recorded in the Gospels. By His miracles Christ showed His authority over sin, nature, physical illness and death, and evil spiritual beings. The variety of the miracles He performed is astounding. These miracles were not the result of sleight of hand or deception. Many people witnessed them, and He did them in many different places. Although performing a miracle doesn't automatically prove someone is God, the consistent, all-controlling authority of Christ is much stronger evidence. The number, variety, and power of Jesus's miracles prove beyond question that He's God. Jesus was not just a good man, a great teacher, or the founder of one of the world's great religions. He was all of these things, but much more.

If you're a Christian, you have Christ as your Friend and Savior. He'll help you live as you should, make the right decisions, and be what you ought to be. If He has the power to do miracles, He certainly has the power to help you.

Now for a second question: does anyone but God have the power to control nature? No. Then what about what Jesus did? The Gospels tell us that at least nine times He showed His control over nature. He controlled the weather and the laws of physics (Master Chart #20–28). He told plants and animals what to do. He could make food and drink. He told the wind to stop blowing. He walked on water. He told fish to swim into fishermen's nets. He spoke to a tree, and it withered because of the power of His words. Twice He fed thousands of people starting with almost no food. If Jesus Christ could control nature, then He must be God since only God has that power.

What about physical life and health? Who controls that? God alone does. Did you know that Jesus healed massive crowds of people of all kinds of illnesses? The Gospels record that He cured at least ten kinds of illnesses. He even raised three people from the dead (Master Chart #1–19). He didn't heal people by putting them into hospitals and treating them with medicines. He just spoke or touched them, and they were healed. One woman, who had been bleeding for twelve years, came up to Him in a crowd and touched His clothes, thinking that she

149

(Mark 2:8–9) He then healed the man to prove that He had the power to forgive sins.

By this miracle Christ established that His power to heal revealed His power to forgive sins. Therefore, every time Jesus healed a person, He was asserting His ability to forgive sins and heal them spiritually. The Gospels record nineteen specific miracles of healing and seven of exorcism; several other passages record times of general healing (Matt. 4:23–24; 9:35; 12:15; Luke 4:40–41; see also John 21:25).

The scribes said, "Who can forgive sins but God only?" Their attitude toward Christ was wrong, but their theological understanding was correct. Only God can forgive sins. If Christ could heal all sorts of physical maladies supernaturally, He could also forgive sins. And if God alone has that power, then Christ is God.

II. Christ's Authority over Nature

Man has been able to control the forces of nature in minor ways. By long and arduous processes humans have learned to control the flow of rivers. By careful breeding we can increase livestock production. Crop rotation, irrigation, and insecticides help enhance food production. Scientists are even succeeding at genetic engineering. But such changes are accomplished by natural processes involving time and a significant expenditure of energy. God controls nature supernaturally. He can alter what we call laws of nature instantaneously to accom-

plish His ends. Christ frequently demonstrated this supernatural control of nature.

Food and drink. Christ supernaturally produced food and drink. While teaching more than five thousand men plus women and children, Jesus took five loaves of bread and two fish and fed the whole crowd and had food to spare (#27). He used seven loaves of bread and a few little fish to feed four thousand men with their wives and children (#28). While at a wedding feast in Cana, He turned approximately 120 gallons of water into high-quality wine (#26).

Weather and laws of physics. Christ also demonstrated the ability to control weather and the laws of physics. While Jesus was with His disciples in a boat on the Sea of Galilee, a severe windstorm arose, creating threatening waves. By a simple command the Lord stopped the storm and saved the lives of the disciples (#20). On another occasion, just after the feeding of the five thousand, the disciples began to cross the Sea of Galilee while Christ remained behind to pray. Later He went to them by walking on the water (#21). Then Peter, by faith, did the same thing at Christ's command and by His power. After Jesus entered the boat, the sea became instantly calm. The final miraculous element in this incident is recorded in John's Gospel. By Christ's power the ship came instantly to its destination, overruling time and space (6:21). In these two incidents Christ demonstrated that He is God.

Plant and animal life. Christ also had the power to change the habits of animal life and alter the life cycle of plants. Three times He gave directions to fish. Once He did it to provide money for the temple tax (#22). A particular fish had once swallowed just the right amount of money. Peter, at Christ's direction, caught the fish and paid the tax. Two other times the disciples were not having success fishing, so Jesus directed them to cast their nets in a slightly different place, after which they came up with a large catch (#23–24). And during the week before Christ's Crucifixion, He was walking by a fig tree from which He wanted to pluck some fruit (#25). Because it was not bearing, He pronounced judgment on it. The next morning the tree was dried up from the roots. Christ's command had caused the tree to wither.

Christ's authority over nature was comprehensive. He showed His ability to control the production of food and drink, weather, the laws of physics, animal life, and plant life. Who but God could do these things?

III. Christ's Authority over Physical Life and Health

That we have since found cures for many of the diseases Christ healed does not lessen the significance of His miracles. His healings are significant not only because of the severity and variety of the diseases cured, but the manner in which He cured them. He did not cure by a process or treatment resulting in gradual recovery; He cured instantly and supernaturally. The maladies Christ healed can be classified in ten categories. (See the chart "Miracles of Healing" on page 160 of the student text and on the CD.) The Gospels list nineteen specific healing incidents, plus seven exorcisms, totaling twenty-six of the thirty-five recorded miracles of Christ. No other person has ever demonstrated the same power to cure diseases Christ did. He is in a class by Himself, a fact that strongly suggests that He is God.

The most remarkable of these categories is the reversal of death, the capstone of the healing miracles. Humanly speaking, death is irreversible. Yet Christ raised the only son of the widow of Nain (#16), and He raised Lazarus of Bethany four days after his death (#4). A third possibility is the daughter of Jairus, a ruler of the synagogue at Capernaum (#5). The girl was either dead or comatose so that everyone thought she was dead. Christ returned her to health in a moment.

Does raising someone from the dead prove that the healer is God? We know that Elijah raised a widow's son from the dead by the power of the Lord (1 Kings 17:17–23). Of course, Elijah was not God. The book of Acts also records miracles of resurrection performed by Peter (Dorcas, Acts 9:36–41) and Paul (Eutychus, Acts 20:9–12) by the power of Christ. These men were not God. But all the miracles of resurrection recorded in the Bible were performed

would be cured. She was healed instantly because of her faith in the Lord's power. Christ caused blind people to see, deaf people to hear, and paralyzed people to walk. He placed a man's severed ear back on his head. Over and over Christ performed such miracles. He had complete control over physical life and health. God alone has that kind of control.

Who can control the unseen world besides God? The Bible teaches that there's a world that none of us sees. This is a world full of angels, both evil and good. These aren't fairy-tale characters; they're real. Jesus helped many people who were being hurt by evil spirits or demons. The New Testament tells of seven times when Jesus helped such people (Master Chart #29–35). The demons knew the power Christ had, and they respected it. Repeatedly Christ commanded them, and they obeyed. Often they overcame the power of men to resist them, but they could not resist Christ's power. God alone can control these creatures that are more powerful than man. Christ demonstrated this power. He is God.

Do You Remember?

1. How many miracles of Christ are recorded in the Gospels? _thirty-five_

2. What do we call evil angels? _demons_

3. Why did Jesus perform miracles? _____
   to help people; to teach them how to live for Him; to prove that He is God

4. What did Jesus do to prove He had the power to forgive sins? _____
   He healed a paralyzed man.

5. How many times do the Gospels record specific instances of Christ controlling nature?
   nine

6. How many people did Jesus raise from the dead? _at least three_

7. What do Christ's miracles say about His power to help us today? _Answers will vary but_
   should include the idea that everything is subject to His control.

150

by Christ Himself, by His power, or in the name of Jehovah. (The only possible exception is the resurrection of the Beast recorded in Rev. 13:3.) Jesus asserted in John 8:58 that He is Jehovah. Therefore, virtually all of the miracles of resurrection in the Bible are either directly or indirectly attributable to Christ. And Christ's Resurrection proves that He can control His own life and death. All men who have had even a vague conception of God have recognized Him as the controller of life and the One Who determines the moment of death. A reasonable person must conclude that Jesus is God, based on biblical evidence.

IV. Christ's Authority over Evil Beings

The Bible teaches that there are two classes of angels: good and evil. The evil angels are further divided into two groups. Some were immediately chained in hell upon their fall with Satan from their original innocent state: "And the angels which kept not their first estate, but left their own habitation, he hath reserved in everlasting chains under darkness unto the judgment of the great day" (Jude 6; cf. 2 Pet. 2:4). Other fallen angels are servants of Satan in his wicked schemes to spiritually and physically oppress human beings. We call these angels demons. These angels expect the same end as those who have gone before them into hell. When confronted by Christ, one of the two demoniacs of Gadara said, "What have we to do with thee, Jesus, thou Son of God? art thou come hither to torment us before the time?" (Matt. 8:29)

The New Testament records seven times that Jesus delivered people from demon possession. (See the chart "Miracles of Deliverance from Demons" on page 163 of the student text and on the CD.) Probably a more accurate way to describe some of the people in the New Testament is to say they were influenced or controlled by demons. They may or may not have been possessed (indwelt). As the chart reveals, the effects of demonization are horrible, ranging from physical maladies to insanity.

Christ's contacts with demons reveal not only that He had power to free a person from demon control and oppression, but also that demons fear Christ's authority and recognize His exceptional character. Of the seven incidents, four include the issue of Christ's character and power (#29, 31, 32, 34). In two of these four, the demons themselves addressed Christ with names that showed they understood Who He was (#29, 34). One of them called Him "the Holy One of God" (Mark 1:24), and another called Him "the Son of God" (Matt. 8:29). In the remaining two cases (#31–32), the Pharisees argued that Jesus cast out demons by the power of the prince of demons. On one of these occasions (#31), Christ refuted their position with a parable, asserting that He did what He did by the power of the Holy Spirit. He said, "But if I cast out devils by the Spirit of God, then the kingdom of God is come unto you" (Matt. 12:28). By this statement Christ claimed that He was the manifestation of God in His ruling power and that the listeners should submit to Him as God and Savior. In essence He was saying that every deliverance from demons was a demonstration of His deity.

Christ's authority over sin, nature, human life, and evil spiritual beings proves that He is God. Christ had several reasons for performing miracles, but a major reason was to prove His deity.

Your students need to be absolutely convinced that Jesus is God. If He is not, then He is a liar, all His claims about Himself are false, and His teachings are suspect. Certainly if Jesus is not God, the whole idea of salvation through Him is a farce. If Christ is not God, why do we worship Him? Why should we obey Him? Why should we follow the Bible as the guide for life, particularly if it is full of fabrications? The deity of Christ is the foundational truth of Christianity. Jesus was not just a good man, an outstanding teacher, and founder of one of the world's great religions. He is the Almighty God, the Creator and Sustainer of all life, and the Lord and Savior of the human race. Every one of your students should humbly submit to His authority. They should do whatever He commands. They should give their whole lives to Him because He alone is worthy of loyalty and devotion.

✳ Extra Activities

Reading: Using the "Master Chart of Christ's Miracles," have your students read one account of each of the miracles of Christ. Combined, these passages will equal about two long chapters of Scripture. The students will read firsthand of the wonderful works of our Lord.

Writing: Have each student write an essay on one of Christ's miracles, focusing on what the miracle teaches about living for Christ or about the Lord Himself.

Quiz: Have your students study the "Master Chart of Christ's Miracles." Do not have them memorize the list but tell them to learn the categories and to be familiar with the different problems Christ's miracles solved. Use the following true-false quiz as an evaluation.

_____T_____ 1. The New Testament records thirty-five specific miracles Christ performed.

_____T_____ 2. Christ's miracles prove that He is God.

_____F_____ 3. Jesus never healed a demon-possessed girl.

_____T_____ 4. Demon possession caused a woman to be crippled for eighteen years.

_____T_____ 5. Peter's walking on the water showed that Jesus controls the laws of physics.

_____F_____ 6. Jesus raised only one person from the dead.

_____T_____ 7. Christ cured several people of blindness.

_____T_____ 8. Christ's miracles show that He controls plant and animal life.

_____T_____ 9. Christ once helped the disciples catch 153 fish.

Lesson 42
Living by Faith

THEME	Miracles Teaching Faith
SCRIPTURE	Matthew 8:5–13; 15:21–28; Mark 9:14–29
MEMORY WORK	Hebrews 11:6

Approach to the Lesson

Theme: Faith is an unwavering confidence in Christ and His power to save. Some synonyms for *faith* are *trust*, *belief*, *confidence*, and *reliance upon*. The Bible teaches, "But without faith it is impossible to please him: for he that cometh to God must believe that he is, and that he is a rewarder of them that diligently seek him" (Heb. 11:6).

The Christian must not have just a vague faith; he must have faith in Christ. Faith alone is ineffective if the one being trusted is unreliable. The believer should live day by day with a constant sense that Christ is alive, is looking after his affairs, and can be called on to help in any difficult situation. Faith is the practice of looking to the eternal Christ, Who cares for our every concern and will help us bear every burden. Through His miracles Jesus taught important lessons about exercising faith in Him.

Rationale: Your students probably think they know all about the Bible. They probably need to apply what they know more than they need to know additional facts. Challenge them to appropriate personal faith in Christ to believe that He will meet their needs every day.

Background: Nineteen of Christ's miracles give instruction on faith. The chart "Miracles That Teach About Faith" (found on page 152 of the student text and on the CD accompanying this book) provides you and your students with a "bird's-eye view" of these miracles and what they teach.

As in the other lessons on miracles, the number in parentheses is the number the miracle has been assigned on the "Master Chart of Christ's Miracles" (found on pages 146–47 of the student text and on the CD). The Scripture passages in which the miracles appear are listed there.

The Lesson

I. Faith Must Grow

Three times the Lord condemned weak faith in His disciples: when He stilled the storm on the Sea of Galilee (#20), when Peter walked on the water (#21), and when the disciples failed to heal the demon-possessed boy (#30). "O ye of little faith," He said to His disciples on the Sea of Galilee (Matt. 8:26). The Lord was grieved whenever His disciples showed a lack of confidence in Him. Similarly He warned Jairus (#5) to avoid allowing his faith to be mixed with fear or doubt (Luke 8:50).

> Weak faith does not please the Lord. He expects total confidence in His ability to aid us in any situation.

Jesus never simply condemned weakness in His disciples; He always took steps to correct the weakness. He used His miracles to build the disciples' faith. This was true of His first recorded miracle (#26). John says, "This beginning of miracles did Jesus in Cana of Galilee, and manifested forth his glory; and his disciples believed on him" (John 2:11). The miracle was designed to build the faith of His new disciples. Later, just a month before His death, He was still working on building up their faith. Lazarus had died, and his sisters were full of sorrow. Jesus came, but not just to console them. Before He crossed the Jordan River from Perea, He said, "And I am glad for your sakes that I was not there, to the intent ye may believe; nevertheless let us go unto him" (John 11:15). He knew that the miracle He was about to perform (#4) would strengthen their faith in Him. On arriving, Jesus reasoned with Martha about

Objectives

KNOWLEDGE (concepts students need to grasp)	which of Christ's miracles teach about faith
	that Christ used miracles from every category on the "Master Chart of Christ's Miracles" to teach about faith
APPLICATION (principles students should put into practice)	Christians must be committed to seeing their faith grow through prayer, the Word, and Christian experience.
	Christians should desire great faith, believing without seeing.
	Strong faith is a constant, persevering reliance on Christ in every situation.

Outline

> I. Faith must grow.
> II. What is faith?
> III. How is faith shown?

believing in His power to raise her brother. At first she did not understand. But just before He raised Lazarus, He said to her, "Said I not unto thee, that, if thou wouldest believe, thou shouldest see the glory of God?" (11:40)

Saving faith is trust in Christ as the only Savior from sin and judgment. Three times the Gospels record that a miracle resulted in saving faith. The man born blind gained spiritual sight as well as physical (#3). After Jesus identified Himself as the Son of God, the man declared, "Lord, I believe," (John 9:38) and then worshiped Christ. The demoniac of Gadara went everywhere in Decapolis preaching about the Lord Jesus after he was both freed from his oppressor and saved from his sin (#29). When one leper of the ten that were healed returned to Christ to give glory to God, Christ told him to go his way because his faith had made him whole (#18). The passage gives the impression that the man experienced more than just physical healing.

> Of course, your students' faith cannot be built up until they have first exercised saving faith. Then they must realize that their faith is small and needs developing. It is encouraging to see that the Lord actually plans experiences that build the faith of His disciples. As His disciples, we should pray the same way the demon-possessed boy's father did when he cried out to the Lord, "Lord, I believe; help thou mine unbelief" [Mark 9:24].

II. What Is Faith?

Christ appeared to His disciples several times after His Resurrection. Once He appeared just to speak to Thomas. Thomas had said that he would not believe that the Lord was resurrected until he actually put his finger in Christ's wounds. When Jesus saw him, He said, "Reach hither thy finger, and behold my hands; and reach hither thy hand, and thrust it into my side: and be not faithless, but believing" (John 20:27). In response Thomas said, "My Lord and my God" (20:28). Then Jesus said, "Thomas, because thou hast seen me, thou hast believed: blessed are they that have not seen, and yet have believed" (20:29). This appearance isn't one of the miracles; it is

Living by Faith

Read: Matthew 8:5–13; 15:21–28;
Mark 9:14–29

Memorize: Hebrews 11:6

Bible Expressions to Understand

centurion—a Roman army officer who usually led a company of one hundred men
grievously vexed—severely troubled
deaf and dumb spirit—a demon that afflicts a person with an inability to hear and speak

As part of a New England pastor's family, Adoniram Judson grew up receiving careful instruction in the things of the Lord. He heard the prayers and the preaching. He had the Bible read to him and read it himself. He learned quickly and soon became known, even as a young boy, for his intelligence. After graduating from high school, he went to what was soon to become Brown University in Rhode Island. There he made friends who changed his views and brought him into disagreement with his family. One of his friends was Jacob Eames, who opposed Christianity and soon influenced Adoniram to think the same way.

In 1832, Judson wrote a letter of advice to some missionary candidates: "Come out for life, and not for a limited term. Do not fancy that you have a true missionary spirit, while you are intending all along to leave the heathen soon after acquiring their language. Leave them! For what? To spend the rest of your days in enjoying the ease and plenty of your native land?"

Adoniram graduated with highest honors. He left college with a good education, but no faith in Christ. Before he was twenty, he had started a school and written two books, one about English and the other about math. He then decided to "see the world" and began to travel.

While returning from a disappointing trip to New York City, he stopped for the night at a country inn. The only room left was next to a man who was sick and about to die. All night, as Adoniram heard the man suffering, he thought about death and eternity. He was frightened but reasoned away his fears.

The next morning, when leaving, he asked the innkeeper how the man was. He replied, "He is dead." Stunned, Adoniram asked his name. "Jacob Eames, from the college in Providence, Rhode Island." Jacob Eames, the one who had convinced him not to believe in Christ, had died in a room next to his in an obscure country inn! Had this been a coincidence? Adoniram didn't think so. He returned to his parents' home deeply troubled about his own spiritual condition.

Within two months, after careful thought and prayer, he trusted Christ as his Savior. That act of faith was the beginning of a life of trusting Christ.

Adoniram Judson believed Christ's words in the Great Commission, "Go ye therefore, and teach all nations, baptizing them in the name of the Father, and of the Son, and of the Holy Ghost: teaching them to observe all things whatsoever I have commanded you: and, lo, I am with you alway, even unto the end of the world" (Matt. 28:19–20). He became one of the first foreign missionaries from America. He went to Burma,

151

mentioned here because of the lesson Jesus taught. People who believe without seeing are blessed. They are to be admired and recognized as special. Faith, then, is believing without seeing.

It is no wonder that Christ responded as He did to the centurion whose servant was ill (#15). The servant was being tortured by an extremely painful paralysis and was at the point of death. When Christ offered to come and heal him, the officer responded, "Lord, I am not worthy that thou shouldest come under my roof: but speak the word only, and my servant shall be healed. For I am a man under authority, having soldiers under me: and I say to this man, Go, and he goeth; and to another, Come, and he cometh; and to my servant, Do this, and he doeth it" (Matt. 8:8–9).

Jesus marveled at the man's faith, saying, "I have not found so great faith, no, not in Israel" (8:10). What was so great about this man's faith? He believed in the power of the word of Christ. He knew Jesus had the authority to back up His words. He understood that Jesus's authority transcends space, time, and all physical illness. He expressed that confidence even without seeing. His servant was healed, and the centurion received one of the most remarkable commendations in the New Testament.

Faith that believes only when it sees is a lesser faith. The Lord said this Himself when He healed the nobleman's son (#1). The nobleman had traveled to Cana because he had heard that Jesus was there. He thought that perhaps Christ could help

him. The Lord said to him and the Galileans present, "Except ye [plural] see signs and wonders, ye will not believe" (John 4:48), generalizing about the way most people believe, i.e., seeing is believing. Then Jesus gave the nobleman a test by telling him to go home because his son was healed. The man chose to believe what Jesus said (without seeing it) and found out later that his son had indeed been healed at the exact time Jesus spoke those words.

The secret to believing without seeing is to grasp the authority of Christ. If your students understand the scope of His power, they will have less difficulty believing that He will do what He says. This is why the Bible says, "So then faith cometh by hearing, and hearing by the word of God" (Rom. 10:17). The Word of God shows many examples of what Christ can do. It explains the character of Christ and describes His great power in order to increase our confidence, our trust, our reliance on Him. The best faith is one that believes Christ's promises. It is pure confidence in the stated word of Christ before seeing the promise worked out in experience.

III. How Is Faith Shown?

Faith is demonstrated by perseverance—staying with a purpose and persisting in a goal or a belief. Faith that perseveres will not stop trusting Christ's ability or willingness to help. It looks past the obstacles and continues to ask until the Lord responds. The Lord honors persevering faith. This is clear from His miracles. He responded to people who were determined to get their problems solved.

The woman with the hemorrhage had tried to get her problem solved for twelve years (#7). She had spent almost all her money on doctors who couldn't help her. One day she saw Jesus at a distance, in the middle of a thick crowd. Fighting her way through, she reached out and touched the hem of Christ's garment, believing she would be healed—and she was. She refused to give up, despite previous disappointment. She had faith in Christ's power.

Think of the obstacles various people overcame to have Christ perform a miracle for them. Some were opposed by others when seeking help from Christ. The mother of a Syro-Phoenician girl came to Jesus to get help for her demon-possessed daughter (#33), but the disciples did not want Christ to help her because she was not a Jew. Surprisingly, Jesus agreed with them in principle, saying, "It is not meet to take the children's bread, and to cast it to dogs" (Matt. 15:26). Jesus viewed the Jews as His first priority in His ministry of preaching and healing.

This priority is consistent with the approach Jesus took with His apostles after His Resurrection: Peter was the apostle to the Jews; Paul was the apostle to the Gentiles. The setting of priorities is necessary because we cannot be everywhere ministering to everyone all the time. We must decide to whom we will minister primarily. But when the Lord saw this woman's persistence, He temporarily changed His priorities. He said, "O woman, great is thy faith: be it unto thee even as thou wilt." (15:28). Even when the disciples were against her and the Lord had stated His priorities, this woman pursued Him in faith, and He responded.

When Christ was passing through Jericho, two blind men called after Him for help (#14). One of them was Bartimaeus. The Scriptures say, "And the multitude rebuked them, because they should hold their peace: but they cried the more, saying, Have mercy on us, O Lord, thou Son of David" (Matt. 20:31). The crowd did not want them to be a nuisance to Christ. But the Lord stopped and asked them what they wanted. They told Him, and He healed them. Despite opposition, they persisted in their belief that Christ could help them, and He did.

In our culture, where for most people things come easily, your students need to learn perseverance. They need to keep believing, despite apparent failure and opposition, until their prayers are answered. God isn't being difficult when He refuses to answer immediately. He's teaching them perseverance, a character quality that will stand them in good stead for eternity.

Miracles That Teach About Faith

Major Lesson	Miracle	Master Chart #
FAITH MUST GROW FROM WEAKNESS TO STRENGTH	Storm stilled on the Sea of Galilee	20
	Peter and Jesus walked on the Sea of Galilee	21
	Epileptic boy delivered from demon	30
	Jairus's daughter raised from death	5
	Water changed into wine	26
	Lazarus raised from death	4
	Man born blind received sight	3
	Gadarene men delivered from demon	29
FAITH IS BELIEVING WITHOUT SEEING	Centurion's paralyzed servant healed	15
	Nobleman's son healed of severe fever	1
FAITH IS MANIFESTED BY PERSEVERING CONFIDENCE	Woman with twelve years of bleeding healed	7
	Syro-Phoenician girl delivered from demon	33
	Bartimaeus and another blind man received sight	14
	Paralytic at Capernaum healed	8
	Leper at Gennesaret healed	9
	Ten lepers healed	18
	Blind man at Bethsaida received sight	2
	Deaf-mute in Decapolis healed	13

where he worked for years before gaining his first convert. Over his nearly forty years in Burma, he translated the entire Bible from Hebrew and Greek into the Burmese language. In spite of the deaths of his first wife, his second wife, and several of his children, he continued to trust the Lord.

The lesson of Judson's life is faith. Judson trusted Christ to save him and guide him. You need faith not only to be saved, but also to continue to live a life that pleases the Lord. To have faith in Christ is to trust Him, to rely on Him, or to place confidence in Him.

Christ taught His disciples about faith all during His ministry. He used miracles to teach important ideas about faith. At least eighteen of His thirty-five recorded miracles teach something about faith. Each of the Scripture passages you read for this lesson teaches a major idea about faith that Christ wanted His disciples to learn.

First, faith must grow from weakness to strength. Christ used several miracles to teach this idea; one was the miracle for the boy with the demon. (See Master Chart, #30.) The boy's father brought him to Jesus. The child was suffering from terrible seizures—falling down, grinding his teeth, foaming at the mouth, and becoming rigid. At times he would fall into fire or water. The father came directly to Christ after the disciples had failed to heal his son.

When Jesus heard that they had failed, he said, "O faithless generation, how long shall I be with you? how long shall I suffer you? bring him unto me" (Mark 9:19). He condemned the weakness of their faith. He then told the father, "If thou canst believe, all things are possible to him that believeth" (9:23). The father immediately replied with tears, "Lord, I believe; help thou mine unbelief" (9:24). When the disciples asked why they couldn't drive the demon out, Jesus told them it was because of their lack of faith (Matt. 17:20).

Both the father and the disciples had a problem with their faith. Their confidence in the Lord wasn't what it should have been. At least the father had enough perception to recognize his problem; the disciples needed special instruction to understand theirs. The Lord used this occasion to help His disciples build their faith. He will bring incidents into your life to build your faith, too, if you're His follower.

Another lesson is that believing without seeing is great faith. A faith that believes only when it sees is weak. A centurion, an officer over a hundred Roman soldiers, demonstrated great faith when he came to Christ about his servant, who was seriously ill with extremely painful paralysis. (See Master Chart, #15.) Jesus said, "I will come and heal him" (Matt. 8:7). The man responded by saying that it was not necessary for Jesus to come to his house; if He'd just speak the word, that would be sufficient.

Why did Jesus commend the Roman centurion?

He believed in the power of Christ's spoken word alone to heal his servant. To this Jesus replied, "I have not found so great faith, no, not in Israel" (8:10).

What was great about this man's faith? He didn't believe that Christ's presence or touch was necessary to heal his servant. Christ didn't have to do anything to convince this man of His ability; he believed without seeing. He believed before the miracle occurred. It's not difficult to believe that something has happened when you've seen it happen. But belief in Christ's promises is great faith.

A third lesson is that we prove our faith by persevering confidence—by not giving up on the Lord's

153

⊛ Extra Activity

Research: Have your students read one account of each of the miracles of faith. They can find the passages by looking on the chart on page 152 and comparing it with the one on pages 146–47. (Although they will be reading about nineteen different miracles, the number of verses they will be reading is relatively small.) Have them focus on the faith statement in each of the passages.

This lesson is a great opportunity to have your students tell about answers to prayer they and their families have experienced. This approach will help them to see that faith is a working principle in the lives of believers today.

power or willingness to help. No matter what the obstacles may be, we continue to trust Him, expecting Him to help. This is the way the Syro-Phoenecian woman acted. (See Master Chart, #33.) Her daughter was being tortured by a demon. The disciples were against Christ's helping her because she was a Gentile. Jesus agreed that His primary work was with Jewish people. Christ had priorities. He came to die for all, but His preaching and healing ministry was primarily for the Jews. Yet He was willing to make an exception for this woman. She was persistent. She wouldn't give up. Even when the disciples opposed it, she begged the Lord to help her daughter. Christ couldn't disregard this demonstration of great faith in His power and willingness to help. He said, "O woman, great is thy faith: be it unto thee even as thou wilt" (Matt. 15:28). At that exact hour her daughter was delivered from the demon.

Don't Trust Your Faith—Trust Christ

Faith is an unwavering confidence in Christ—His power to save you from your sins and to work in your behalf. Some synonyms for *faith* are *trust*, *belief*, *confidence*, and *reliance*. When a person has faith in Christ, he trusts Him, believes in Him, and relies on Him. The Bible teaches, "But without faith it is impossible to please him: for he that cometh to God must believe that he is, and that he is the rewarder of them that diligently seek him" (Heb. 11:6).

A Christian must not merely have faith; he must have faith in Christ. Faith alone is pointless if the one you trust is unreliable. To live a life of faith means that you live day by day with a constant understanding that Christ is alive, is looking after you, and can be called on to help in any situation.

Do You Remember?

1. What three lessons did Christ teach about faith through His miracles? _____
   Faith must grow from weakness to strength; faith is believing without seeing;
   faith is manifested by persevering confidence.

2. What were the effects of the demon's influence on the boy that Jesus healed? _seizures_
   resulting in dangerous falls, grinding of teeth, foaming at the mouth, and rigidity

3. What was the job of the man who came to Christ to get help for his servant
   with paralysis? _He was a centurion._

4. Why did the Syro-Phoenecian woman come to Jesus? _____
   because her daughter was possessed by a demon

5. Why did Christ refuse to heal the woman's daughter at first? _____
   His primary responsibility was to help Jewish people.

6. What was the disciples' attitude toward the woman? _____
   They did not want her to bother Jesus.

7. What are some synonyms for *faith*? _trust, belief, confidence, reliance_

154

Right Relationships — L.43

Read: Luke 5:1–11; 7:11–16;
14:1–4, 22:49–51

Memorize: Luke 5:10b–11

Bible Expressions to Understand

Lake of Gennesaret—the Sea of Galilee
draught of fishes—catch of fish
Nain—a city of Galilee, about ten miles south of Nazareth
bier—a coffin or a stand on which a corpse is carried
dropsy—abnormal accumulation of fluid in the body
suffer ye thus far—"that is enough"

Compare the mink and the otter. They both have beautiful coats and are often hunted by man. They're both members of the weasel family, having sleek bodies with short legs. They're both wanderers. They eat a similar diet—mostly crayfish, frogs, and fish.

Yet in one way they aren't at all alike. They don't have the same disposition. The mink is always hostile. Often it will kill its own kind and even its own offspring. It'll slaughter a hen house full of chickens for the savage delight of it. Bred and raised in captivity for its pelt, the mink is as vicious in the barn as in the woods. It will quickly bite the hand that feeds it.

By contrast, the otter is very friendly and incurably playful. Naturalists have seen otters frolicking in a stream or a pond for hours. When raised in captivity, the otter will make friends with all other kinds of animals, dogs included. A loving pet, it gets along well with humans and other animals alike.

Some people are like the mink, and others are like the otter. "Mink people" can't get along with others. They are often fighting, rebelling, or arguing. Others, like the otter, build and maintain right relationships.

The Lord Jesus Christ used miracles to instruct His followers about the importance of building such relationships. Having a right relationship with God is the most important thing in the world. Having right relationships with other people follows close behind as the second greatest priority in life. What are some rules that Christ gave to help us succeed?

First, Christ taught us to avoid unnecessary conflicts. The incident in the Garden of Gethsemane was one dramatic illustration of this truth (Master

Minks and otters look a lot alike, but they're different in one crucial aspect. Are you more like an otter or a mink?

155

Lesson 43
Right Relationships

THEME	Miracles That Teach About Relationships
SCRIPTURE	Luke 5:1–11; 7:11–16; 14:1–4; 22:49–51
MEMORY WORK	Luke 5:10b–11

Approach to the Lesson

Theme: A right relationship with God is the highest priority for believers. We are to love the Lord with all our heart, soul, mind, and strength. The second most important commandment is to love our neighbor as ourselves. That is a broad, sweeping command. Our relationships with others vary greatly. Though we are to love all people, not all are equal in their relationships with us. We do not have the same relationship with our relatives that we have with our friends. We do not usually have the same relationships with our friends that we have with our employees and employers. Loving all people doesn't mean we treat everyone alike. It does mean we treat everyone as the Bible says we are supposed to treat them.

By performing miracles Christ taught some important truths about having right relationships. He used His miracles as object lessons on right relationships. Often He began or concluded instruction on relationships by performing a miracle.

Objectives

KNOWLEDGE (concepts students need to grasp)	that Christ used many of His miracles as object lessons to teach us how to treat others
	that Christ used miracles of every type to teach about right relationships
APPLICATION (principles students should put into practice)	We must avoid financial and physical conflicts to have right relationships.
	We must be fishers of men to have right relationships.
	We must be more concerned about helping people than about appearing outwardly religious.
	We must show compassion toward those in need.

Rationale: Your students are probably in a transition stage between acting out of self-interest and acting from the result of peer pressure. This is an ideal time to stress the importance of building right relationships. Stress that this lesson gives them some practical points on having the right kind of relationships.

Background: The chart "Miracles That Teach Right Relationships" (found on page 157 of the student text and on the CD accompanying this book) gives a convenient summary of the miracles presented and discussed in this lesson. This chart shows how each miracle contributes to instruction in one of the major types of relationships.

Again, numbers in parentheses refer to the "Master Chart of Christ's Miracles" (pages 146–47 of the student text). The Scripture passages where the miracles are presented can be found on that chart.

The Lesson

I. Avoiding Conflicts

Two miracles teach about avoiding conflicts.

Conflicts with authorities. The miracle of the tax money in the fish's mouth (#22) teaches us to avoid conflict with those in authority. Those who collected taxes for the temple asked Peter if he and Jesus paid their taxes. Peter responded that they did. The Lord instructed Peter to go to the Sea of Galilee, throw in a hook, and catch a fish, which would have the appropriate amount of money in its mouth.

Outline

In an age that emphasizes personal rights, you should help your students see that Christ's business is more important than our rights. Sometimes we must voluntarily set aside our rights for the good of the cause (e.g., 1 Cor. 6:7).

Before Peter went, Christ asked him a question about His responsibility to pay the tax. He asked whether kings normally collect taxes from their own sons or from their other subjects. When Peter responded that they tax others, Jesus asserted that the royal family would be free of the tax. The point of His argument is that He was not really responsible to pay the tax since it was for His Father's temple. But then He told Peter to pay the tax anyway (Matt. 17:25–27). To offend the authorities over a small matter would have been unwise.

The greater principle is to avoid offending authorities unless they order us to disobey Scripture (Acts 5:29). Offending parents, employers, or spiritual leaders is unwise. Even if the authority figure is in the wrong, or as is often the case, only makes a request he has no right to make, we should obey anyway, as Christ did in the payment of the tax.

Physical conflicts. The second miracle teaches us to avoid physical conflict. The restoring of Malchus's ear (#19) offers a straightforward warning that those who are violent can expect to suffer for it. After Judas's betrayal of Christ, the soldiers of the high priest came to take Him away. Peter rose up in Christ's defense and cut off the ear of Malchus, one of the servants of the high priest. Jesus said, "Suffer ye thus far," which means, "That's enough" (Luke 22:51). He then healed the ear. The Lord commanded Peter, "Put up again thy sword into his place: for all they that take the sword shall perish with the sword" (Matt. 26:52).

Those who are physically abusive—hitting, shoving, and tripping others—can expect the same treatment. The temptation to fight usually comes to those who are bigger than their peers. If

Chart, #19). Judas came with armed servants from the high priest to take Jesus. He kissed Jesus on the cheek to identify Him to the soldiers. As they were about to take Him, Peter drew a sword and cut off the right ear of Malchus, a slave of the high priest. Jesus said to Peter, "Put up again thy sword into his place: for all they that take the sword shall perish with the sword" (Matt. 26:52). Jesus then healed the servant's ear, thus averting an armed conflict between the disciples and the servants of the high priest.

Christ avoided this conflict. Sometimes our conflicts may be conflicts of words, which is commonly called arguing. At other times the conflict may strictly be a matter of attitude; we may be unwilling to talk with someone or be kind to him. We should especially avoid conflict with those in authority. Your parents, teachers, employers, youth pastor, and pastor deserve your respect.

A second lesson about right relationships is that we must care enough about other people to give them the gospel—even if we're tired and it's inconvenient.

Peter and the others were reluctant to put out their nets again for two reasons. Not only were they exhausted from having worked all night, but they also knew that the fish that frequent the shallows during darkness would now have gone back to the depths beyond the reach of the nets. But they obeyed and were rewarded with a miracle.

156

Jesus used two similar miracles (one when He called some disciples and one after His Resurrection) to reinforce this truth. On the first occasion, Jesus had been teaching a multitude of people from Peter's boat, which was anchored a little offshore. After He'd finished teaching, He asked Peter to move the boat out into the deep water to put down nets to fish. Peter objected; he had fished all through the previous night without catching anything. But he did as Christ asked. To his surprise, he caught many fish (Master Chart, #23). He called for James and John to come and help him, and they filled their boats, almost sinking them. These hard-working fishermen were amazed. Jesus said to Peter, "Fear not; from henceforth thou shalt catch men" (Luke 5:10). From that moment on those three men were Christ's disciples.

Every believer is to be a "fisher of men." Catching people for Christ should be your goal. Just as fishing was hard work for the disciples, reaching others with the gospel will be hard work for you. Faithfulness, knowledge of the Bible, and enthusiasm are necessary for the task. Christ will be by your side, assisting you in every effort.

Jesus commanded His followers just before He ascended into heaven, "Go ye therefore, and teach all nations, baptizing them in the name of the Father, and of the Son, and of the Holy Ghost: teaching them to observe all things whatsoever I have commanded you: and lo, I am with you alway, even unto the end of the world" (Matt. 28:19–20).

A third lesson is that loving people is more important than being only outwardly religious. Christ performed five miracles teaching this truth. One was the healing of the man with dropsy, which you read for this lesson (Master Chart, #17). Christ healed this man in the home of an important religious leader. Just before He did, He asked, "Is it lawful to heal on the sabbath day?" (Luke 14:3) No one said

someone decides to be a bully, he'd better watch out. Somebody is sure to "bully" him back.

II. Reaching Others with the Gospel

Two almost identical miracles emphasize the importance of witnessing. The first preceded the call of Peter, James, and John to be disciples (#23). Jesus was preaching by the Sea of Galilee, and the crowds were so big that He got into Peter's empty fishing boat. Jesus asked him to push out into the water so He could teach from there. After He finished teaching, He told Peter to go into deeper water and cast his nets for fish. Peter objected, saying they had been fishing all night without success, but he did as the Lord directed. The catch turned out to be

so large that the nets began to break. Peter called to James and John for help, and the three of them filled the two boats to the point of sinking. Peter was awestruck by this miracle, as were the other two men. Then Jesus said to Peter, "Fear not; from henceforth thou shalt catch men" (Luke 5:10). From that moment on, the three left their fishing and followed Christ.

Why was Christ's miracle impressive enough to prompt three grown men to leave their livelihood and follow Him as His students? They recognized this as a miracle because they knew how difficult it was to catch fish, yet there was no difficulty for Christ. They became what He said they would become—fishers of men. A follower of Christ is an individual who is out to

Miracles That Teach Right Relationships

Relationship Principle	Miracle Jesus Performed	Master Chart #
AVOIDING CONFLICTS	Tax money in a fish's mouth	22
	Malchus's ear restored	19
REACHING OTHERS WITH THE GOSPEL	First catch of fish	23
	Catch of 153 fish	24
PUTTING HUMAN NEEDS BEFORE OUTWARD RELIGION	Man born blind received sight	3
	Paralytic at Bethesda healed	6
	Man with withered hand healed	11
	Woman crippled for eighteen years healed	35
	Man with dropsy healed	17
HAVING COMPASSION LEADS TO ACTION	Five thousand taught and fed	27
	Four thousand taught and fed	28
	Peter's wife's mother healed	10
	Widow's son at Nain raised from death	16
	Leper at Gennesaret healed	9
	Lazarus raised from death	4

anything. Christ then healed the man. He then asked, "Which of you shall have an ass or an ox fallen into a pit, and will not straightway pull him out on the sabbath day?" (Luke 14:5) Jesus knew that they all would. If they would help an animal, why shouldn't He help a man on the Sabbath? The others couldn't respond to Him because they knew He was right.

The religious leaders of Jesus's day had made obeying the laws of the Sabbath the major test of a person's love for God. The Lord had never intended the keeping of the law to become more important than love for God and others. One of the Ten Commandments says that men should keep the Sabbath holy. It was to be a special day. However, it was foolish not to help a suffering person on that day for fear of breaking some human rules.

What lessons can you learn from this incident? First, the Lord wants you to show your love for God by helping other people spiritually and physically. Just being involved in religious services or attending a Christian school is not enough. You must love God from the heart and prove it by loving others. Second, be careful about making up rules that you

157

catch other people for Christ. He will be successful as he follows the Lord.

The second miraculous catch of fish (#24) occurred after Christ's Resurrection. Six of the disciples were following Peter, who had decided to go fishing. They fished all night but caught nothing. In the morning they were still out fishing when Christ called to them from the shore, telling them to cast their nets on the other side of the boat. As a result, they caught 153 fish. Peter and the other disciples knew immediately that it was the Lord even though they had not recognized Him before. When they reached the shore, they found that the Lord had cooked some fish for them to eat. After they ate, the Lord recommissioned Peter, in spite of his earlier shameful denial, to leadership of the disciples and of the church

that was soon to be born. The scene reminds us of the first miraculous catch and the commission to catch men. All three of the disciples present the first time witnessed this second miracle. Here, at the end of His earthly ministry, Christ reaffirmed that spreading the gospel is the duty He expects all His disciples to perform.

III. Loving People vs. Outward Religiosity

The Lord often addressed the issue of Jewish teaching concerning the Sabbath. Observance of the Sabbath was a good thing, but it had been taken to extremes. The Pharisees and scribes valued the Sabbath more than the needs of spiritually and physically desperate people. Christ was not pleased with this attitude.

Once, after the disciples picked some grain in a field on the Sabbath to satisfy their hunger, Christ said, "The sabbath was made for man, and not man for the sabbath: therefore the Son of man is Lord also of the sabbath" (Mark 2:27–28). By this statement He forever settled the issue of what was most important on the Sabbath—the meeting of human needs. He also asserted His authority over that day and His right to prompt people to do what He pleases on that day. The real issue was much greater than just the Sabbath; it was the importance of serving and loving others.

Healing on the Sabbath. Five times the Lord used miracles to make this point. One was the healing of the paralyzed man at the pool of Bethesda (#6). The man had been in that condition for thirty-eight years. Like many people he believed that getting into special pools of water at the right time would heal him. But he was so weak that every time he tried to get down into the pool, someone else would shove him aside and get there first. Seeing his prolonged and pathetic condition, the Lord healed him. By the simple command, "Rise, take up thy bed, and walk" (John 5:8), He healed this man who had suffered all his adult life.

The religious leaders, however, objected to the healed man carrying his pallet on the Sabbath because tradition forbade it. Since Jesus was the one who had told the man to carry his pallet, He was held responsible for the supposed transgression. The leaders' reaction was extreme and ridiculous. Scripture says, "And therefore did the Jews persecute Jesus, and sought to slay him, because he had done these things on the sabbath day" (5:16).

Notice a similar reaction from the Pharisees after the Lord miraculously granted sight on the Sabbath to a man who was born blind (#3). "Therefore said some of the Pharisees, This man is not of God, because he keepeth not the sabbath day" (John 9:16). Among the Pharisees, the keeping of the Sabbath had become the acid test of a person's love for God. When Jesus healed a woman who had been crippled for eighteen years (#35), the ruler of the synagogue said, "There are six days in which men ought to work: in them therefore come and be healed, and not on the sabbath day" (Luke 13:14).

Teaching about the Sabbath. Twice the Lord directly challenged the prevailing attitude about the Sabbath. When He was about to heal the man with a withered hand

(#11), He asked the Jewish leaders, "I will ask you one thing; Is it lawful on the sabbath days to do good, or to do evil? to save life, or to destroy it?" (Luke 6:9) Jesus then healed him. The Lord was clearly displeased with this emphasis on religious activity at the expense of loving people and helping them. Once, when He went to eat in the home of an important Pharisee, a man suffering with dropsy was present (#17). Christ confronted the issue boldly. He asked those present, "Is it lawful to heal on the sabbath day?" (Luke 14:3) They did not say anything. Jesus then healed the man and asked them if they would pull an ox or donkey out of a ditch on the Sabbath. Again they refused to answer.

Why did the Lord create opportunities to deal with this problem so often? Outward religious activities were never intended to be the measure of a person's love for God. The attitude of the heart is most important. Every chance He got, the Lord showed that obedience to the second greatest command—loving your neighbor as yourself—supersedes empty acts of religious worship. The Jews had made the foolish mistake of thinking that keeping the rules was all there was to being godly. But spiritual life is not that simple or impersonal.

How then does God respond to church attendance when the heart is not in it? He is unimpressed and in fact displeased. What about attendance at a Christian school? Does this impress Christ? Not in the least, unless it is done with a heart of devotion to Christ. Even pastoring a church, leading a youth group, or teaching in a Christian school are pointless unless the person has a heart to serve the Lord and help others. These passages make clear the truth that love for God and love for others always have priority over mere religious form.

IV. Showing Compassion to People in Need

When Jesus saw people in need, He did something about it. No doubt the Lord was moved with compassion for every person He saw in an unhealthy or difficult condition—physically or spiritually. At times, however, Scripture specifically records Christ's sympathetic reaction as if to emphasize the importance of that spirit.

As Jesus looked on the five thousand whom He would feed miraculously (#27), the Bible says He "was moved with compassion toward them, because they were as sheep not having a shepherd" (Mark 6:34).

think will make you a better Christian than your friends. Being a good Christian is much more than keeping rules—it's having a close, loving relationship with God Himself. A person who loves God loves others and likes to spend time talking to God in prayer and having God speak to him through the Bible.

The final lesson Christ taught about right relationships was that you should show sympathy toward people in need. Christ demonstrated this attitude over and over during His ministry. When He was near the community of Nain, he met a funeral procession. The only son of a widow had died. She was weeping over her loss. The Lord Jesus was moved with compassion for the woman. He then did something to help; He went to where the young man was lying and raised him from the dead (Master Chart, #16). You won't be able to do that, but you can help when someone's in trouble. Perhaps you can help someone with his homework or with some chores. Write him a card, or call him on the phone. If he's sick, visit him and cheer him up. Showing compassion is the important thing. Don't just feel sympathy; show it.

The Right Way to Relate

A right relationship with God is the highest priority for every Christian. You're to love the Lord your God with all your heart, soul, mind, and strength. Second, you must love your neighbor as you love yourself. That's a difficult command. It doesn't mean that you treat everyone alike. It does mean, though, that you're to treat each person as the Bible says to.

Through the miracles He did, Christ taught that avoiding conflicts, spreading the gospel, meeting needs, and showing compassion were necessary to having right relationships with others.

Do You Remember?

1. What is the most important relationship a Christian has? _____
   his relationship to God

2. What truth did the healing of Malchus demonstrate? _____
   We should avoid unnecessary conflicts.

3. Who helps us when we give out the gospel? *Christ/the Holy Spirit* _____

4. Why did the religious leaders object when Christ healed the man with dropsy? _____
   because their human rules prohibited healing on the Sabbath

5. What did Christ do when He felt sorry for the widow of Nain? _____
   raised her son from the dead

158

When more than four thousand gathered to hear Him teach (#28), He said, "I have compassion on the multitude, because they have now been with me three days, and have nothing to eat" (8:2). The result was that He fed them all even though He started with hardly any food.

Again, just outside Nain, Jesus met a funeral procession (#16). The young man who had died was the only son of a widow. The heart of the Savior could not bear the sight of the grieving mother. "And when the Lord saw her, he had compassion on her, and said unto her, Weep not" (Luke 7:13). The Lord ended the funeral by raising the widow's son. Why? He was moved with compassion.

The leper near Gennesaret came beseeching the Lord to heal him (#9). "And Jesus, moved with compassion, put forth his hand, and touched him, and saith unto him, I will; be thou clean" (Mark 1:41). When Peter's wife's mother was severely ill with fever, Jesus entered the house and without a moment's hesitation had mercy on her and healed her (#10).

The shortest but most powerful verse on the compassion of Christ is found in John 11, which describes Christ's coming to the tomb of Lazarus (#4). Many of the friends of Mary and Martha were weeping. Scripture records, "Jesus wept" (John 11:35). Why? Out of compassion for Mary, Martha, and their friends, and no doubt for His good friend Lazarus, who had died. The occasion did not end in sorrow. When moved with compassion, the Lord took action. Lazarus was raised.

An important pattern emerges in the miracles that show Christ's compassion. Christ's sympathy always resulted in action. He did something to alleviate the sorrow or the suffering. He did not stand idly by.

When a believer sees suffering and need, that's the time to act. He should not wait until the motivation dies and his compassion cools. He must act while the impulse is fresh, following through on the holy inclination and letting it result in holy work.

Extra Activities

Discussion: As you work your way through the main ideas in this lecture, have your students use the "Master Chart of Christ's Miracles" to locate each of the miracles you refer to. (Summarize the longer passages.) Have them read aloud an account of the miracle in class. This will be effective in getting your students to see from the biblical text the ideas that you are presenting.

Case study: Bob and his parents are leaving for Sunday evening church when the phone rings. It is Mrs. Russell, their widowed neighbor who is unsaved. She says she is ill and needs some medicine to be picked up at the drugstore immediately. Bob's father leads the singing at church and cannot be late. What should they do?

(1) Ask Mrs. Russell if she can wait until after church.

(2) Tell her they're on their way to church, but give her the names of other neighbors who might be able to help.

(3) Send Bob to the drugstore even though he'll miss church.

(4) Invite her to church, promising to pick up the medicine on the way back.

Lesson 44
Gratitude

Theme	The Healing of the Ten Lepers
Scripture	Luke 17:11–19
Memory Work	1 Thessalonians 5:18

 Approach to the Lesson

Theme: Gratitude is appreciation or thankfulness for kindnesses done for us. We know from the Bible that it is the will of God for us to have an attitude of gratefulness and to express it. Insensitivity in this regard is an attitude foreign to the true Christian spirit.

Rationale: Gratitude is a mark of maturity. Children, because they are self-centered, don't realize that others don't have to do things for them. Your students are eager to be considered adults. Challenge them to earn that status by demonstrating this adult characteristic.

Background: Among the Gospel writers, Luke alone records the incident of the ten lepers. Christ's final journey to Jerusalem took several months because of the ministry He performed along the way. The healing of the lepers occurred as He was about to enter a town whose location we do not know.

An important teaching aid, a copy of the chart from page 160 of the student text, is found on the CD.

 The Lesson

I. Gratitude as a Response to Kindness (Luke 17:11–14)

Christ was halted by the cry of ten lepers—nine Jews and one Samaritan. (Jews and Samaritans were normally enemies, but these lepers were drawn together by their common affliction.) Jews considered leprosy the most dreaded disease. Although rabbinical writings list home remedies for nearly every common ailment, nowhere is there a remedy for leprosy. The leper was to wear torn clothing, keep an uncovered head, have a beard and mustache, cry "unclean, unclean," and live outside any walled city (Lev. 13:45–46). All these things proclaimed openly that he had an incurable, fatal disease.

The rabbis had added further restrictions to the scriptural ones: the leper was not allowed to talk with anyone except another leper; he could enter a synagogue for worship, but he was required to enter first, leave last, and sit only in a special section so that he would not contact anyone not a leper; he could not enter a home; he had to stay at least four cubits (about six feet) away from non-lepers, and when the wind was blowing, he had to remain at least a hundred cubits away. One rabbi would not eat an egg if it had been purchased on a street where a leper was walking; another boasted that he threw stones at lepers to keep them away; others hid themselves or ran away from lepers. Because a leper was to show continual mourning over his disease, rabbinical teaching forbade him ever to wash his face. If he broke any of these rules, he could be punished with thirty-nine stripes.

Rabbis believed that diseases had moral causes, saying, "No death without sin, and no pain without transgression." Leprosy was regarded as a punishment for great sin, especially uncontrolled speech. Next to defilement caused by contact with a dead person, rabbis considered defilement from leprosy to be the worst form.

Leprosy actually results from a bacterial infection. It is contagious, though not usually through casual contact. Missionaries have worked among lepers for years without contracting the disease themselves. In its most common form it slowly anesthetizes the affected parts of the body. In the more extreme form the extremities (the fingers, toes, nose, and ears) drop off after being eaten away.

These lepers were socially ostracized. Their lives were pathetic. Is it any wonder that they came to the Lord for a cure from this seemingly incurable disease? Although

Objectives

Knowledge (concepts students need to grasp)	the connection between the instruction that begins the passage and the miracle that follows
	the meaning and importance of gratitude
Application (principles students should put into practice)	We should be grateful for kindnesses done.
	God notes gratitude and misses it when it is not expressed.

Outline

(Luke 17:11–19)
Gratitude is . . .
I. A response to kindness (11–14)
II. Rarely expressed (15–17)
III. An evidence of salvation (18–19)

He is often called "Rabbi" in the New Testament, even by His disciples, Jesus was not a typical rabbi. He never demonstrated the cruelty other rabbis did. He responded in kindness by healing great afflictions. His kindness to them when no one else was kind should have evoked gratitude in them.

II. Gratitude Rarely Expressed (Luke 17:15–17)

Notice that the ten lepers were told to go to the priests before they were cleansed, demonstrating their faith in Christ's word. Such action was prescribed in the Old Testament (Lev. 14:1–32) to certify that a person no longer had the disease. Scripture says these men were healed as they went. They had faith that Christ would perform a miracle for them. They must have had a good reason for this trust; perhaps they had previously heard about Christ's miraculous deeds or even witnessed them themselves.

Note that a person can believe that God can do miracles and even experience miracles, all without being saved. The nine lepers were delivered from leprosy but probably not from their sin. How would you know for sure if you have been saved from sin? Consider the Samaritan's example. If you have prayed for Christ to work the miracle of salvation for you, has the result been a changed life that gives glory to God?

The Bible reveals four primary periods of miraculous intervention in the affairs of men: (1) the time of Moses and Joshua, (2) the time of Elijah and Elisha, (3) the first century, including Christ's ministry and the ministry of the apostles, and (4) the future ministry of the two witnesses during the Tribulation. Together the first three periods cover about 200 years of the 3,500 since the birth of Moses—less than 6 percent. We can conclude from this that the miraculous is not the norm for God's dealings with humans. He can do the miraculous whenever He wishes, of course, but ordinarily He does not, aside from the miracles of salvation and sanctification.

When the Lord asked about the other nine lepers, He was pointedly stressing that He thought all ten should express gratitude.

Gratitude — L.44

Read: Luke 17:11–19   Memorize: 1 Thessalonians 5:18

Bible Expressions to Understand

leprosy—a general term designating various forms of skin disease; here, an incurable disease that numbs and destroys the skin, producing fever, crippling effects, and, ultimately, death

Samaritan—a person from Samaria, held in low regard by the Jews

A jackal is a doglike animal that lives in Africa. In studying the habits of the silver-backed jackal in Africa, scientists discovered a fascinating characteristic. The female bears litters of several cubs. After growing up, the cubs leave and establish their own areas. But often one young jackal of a litter returns to help the parents raise another litter. In such cases the young of the next litter are much more likely to survive.

Is the one that returns expressing gratitude to its parents? It's difficult to say what causes the return, but it's interesting to note that only one returns and performs this self-sacrificing duty. This illustration from the animal world seems strikingly similar to an incident that occurred during Christ's ministry.

On Jesus's last journey to Jerusalem, He passed through the regions of Samaria and Galilee. Near one village He met a group of ten lepers. These men, outcasts because of their affliction, were huddled

Silver-backed jackals (also known as black-backed jackals) mate for life. The one cub that remains with the parents to help in rearing the next litter will guard the younger cubs from predators and assist the parents in hunting for food.

together outside the village, in accordance with the Old Testament command to remain where they wouldn't contact others (Lev. 13:45–46). As a group they cried out to Jesus for mercy. It's clear from their actions that the fame of Jesus had spread throughout the land.

Jesus responded to their plea. Showing compassion to them, He directed them to fulfill the Old Testament law by going to the priest for the cleansing ritual (Lev. 14:1–32). Jesus was giving them a test. If they would obey Him and go to the priest, they would be healed. But if they hadn't obeyed, nothing would've changed. The men started off to find their village priest, and as they went they realized they'd been healed.

Nine of the men were Jews; one was a Samaritan, a natural enemy of the Jews. But when this man discovered that his disease was gone, he turned back and found Jesus again. Like the silver-backed jackal, he was the only one to return. Jesus asked what had happened to the nine Jews, who also had been healed. Why had only this one Samaritan returned to give thanks? Jesus encouraged the Samaritan, "Arise, go thy way: thy faith hath made thee whole."

Gratitude is a distinctive quality. People who have it stand out from the crowd. Not many people are thankful for what others do for them or for what God does for them. When things have always gone well for you, it's easy to take things for granted. But think about all the good you enjoy because of other people. You were probably hungry this morning. You went to the refrigerator and got some breakfast. One or perhaps both of your parents work all day every day so that you can eat good meals. Then there are your teachers, even the ones you don't particularly

159

As the memory verse states, "In every thing give thanks: for this is the will of God in Christ Jesus concerning you" (1 Thess. 5:18). A thankless heart is a spiritually underdeveloped heart. Just as in the case of the ten lepers, most people's hearts are underdeveloped and thus expressions of gratitude are rare.

III. Gratitude as an Evidence of Salvation (Luke 17:18–19)

Only the Samaritan returned to give Jesus thanks. Jesus saw in this a picture of man's usual reaction to God's goodness (Rom. 2:4–5). The Samaritan returned, glorifying God with a loud voice. He gave the Lord the honor due His name for the work He had done. The humility and sincerity shown by this man are exemplary.

This was no casual demonstration of gratitude. He let it be known just how grateful he was.

Our Lord went on to note that the man least likely to give thanks returned. The nine Jews, all of whom had known the blessings of the Law and the working of God in their nation for centuries, didn't come back.

Not only did this Samaritan praise God, but he returned to give thanks to the One through Whom the miracle had come. We owe thanks to others whom God uses to be an encouragement and help to us. Ingratitude is common among junior high students. Encourage your students to consider whether they appreciate the gospel of Jesus Christ. Is salvation showing itself in their lives by continual rejoicing and thanksgiving? Make the point that if their lives are characterized by

sullenness or discontent, then they probably don't appreciate the riches God gives in the gospel. At best they are inconsistent Christians.

Jesus said to the Samaritan, "Arise, go thy way: thy faith hath made thee whole" (17:19). These words probably speak of a spiritual healing that he received along with his physical healing. This man had been healed physically, but Jesus is saying he was also healed spiritually. He had saving faith. No person is truly whole until he has been saved from sin by faith in Christ. God's goodness to unsaved people is designed to lead them to repentance, as it did in this case. No doubt the gratitude the cured leper displayed was an evidence of the internal heart change he had experienced.

Many of your students have known incredible blessings as young people. Christian parents, a Christian school to attend, and a church where the Word of God is proclaimed are but a few of the blessings they have enjoyed. Challenge them to repent of ingratitude and to show their gratitude to God and to those who have made these blessings possible for them.

Miracles of Healing

Category	Description of Malady	Number of Times	Master Chart #
1. Fever	body temperature distinctly high; may rise to 108° as body fights disease; death may result	Two	1, 10
2. Blindness	two kinds (from birth or acquired later from various causes)	Four	2, 3, 12, 14
3. Leprosy	begins with white spots on skin leading to swellings, destruction of nerve endings, and loss of limbs	Two	9, 18
4. Paralysis	often caused by muscular dystrophy or polio meningitis; causes of biblical cases unknown	Four	6, 8, 11, 15
5. Deaf-mute	loss of hearing resulting in difficulty in speech	One	13
6. Hemorrhage	excessive bleeding	One	7
7. Dropsy	abnormal accumulation of fluid in the body tissues or cavities	One	17
8. Severed body part	ear cut off	One	19
9. Demon possession	the indwelling and/or influence of demons resulting in a variety of physical symptoms (seizures, insanity, extreme pain, blindness, deafness)	Seven	29, 30, 31, 32, 33, 34, 35
10. Death	cessation of all vital signs	Three	4, 5, 16

like. They've worked hard to prepare lessons and activities so that you'll find class interesting and learn something of value for the future. What about your pastor, your coach, and your Lord? The list could go on and on. Do you regularly express your gratitude to God in prayer? How often do you find yourself saying "thank you" or writing a thank-you note to those who help you?

Evaluate the level of your gratitude by honestly answering the following questions:

160

The sad thing is that it's not our natural inclination to be grateful to God or to others. Your responses to the questions may reveal that you're not grossly ungrateful. Remember, though, that gratitude is a positive, distinctive quality. If you're neutral, you don't show gratitude. It's one thing not to complain. It's another thing altogether to express your thanks to God and others for the many kindnesses they show you.

1. How many times in the last two weeks have your parents had to tell you to stop complaining?

2. When you talk with your friends, do you talk more about the things you wish you had or the things you already have?

3. When you talk about your teachers, do you usually talk about things you like or things you don't?

4. If you had a choice, would you go to a different school?

The Gratitude Attitude

Thankfulness comes easier for people who see things as they really are. They understand and appreciate all that they've received from God. Insensitivity to the gifts God constantly bestows ought to be foreign to Christians because they've received so much from the gracious hand of God. People who "rejoice evermore" and "in every thing give thanks" are demonstrating Christlike character. Those who don't are guilty of being self-focused. Make it your goal to learn more about God and to cultivate gratitude for all the wonderful blessings He's given.

Do You Remember?

1. How many lepers did Christ heal in Luke 17:11–19? How many returned to give thanks?
   ten; one

2. Why were the men huddled together outside the village? _____
   They were social outcasts because of their leprosy.

3. Why did Jesus tell them to go to the priest? _____
   to fulfill the law and demonstrate faith

4. What test did Jesus give the lepers? _____
   It was a test of obedience. If they went to the priest, they would be healed.

5. What ethnicity was the one who turned back to thank Jesus? *Samaritan*

161

Extra Activities

Singing: Since gratitude is the thrust of this lesson, you may want to begin your class with a song of praise to the Lord. "Praise Him! Praise Him!" by Fanny Crosby is a good one. To end the class, the first two stanzas of "Revive Us Again" are appropriate.

Testimonies: Immediately after the opening song, have a student give a testimony of praise to the Lord. Do the same just before the closing hymn.

Scripture search: Using the following outline, assign a Scripture passage to each student. Put the three major points of the outline on the board or overhead projector. As the students read the verses they have looked up, develop the outline fully for them. This will give them a broader perspective on the subject of gratitude in the Bible.

I. Commands to give thanks (Ps. 50:23; Phil. 4:4; 1 Thess. 5:16, 18)

II. Methods of giving thanks
   A. Emotion (Pss. 33:21; 103:1; Luke 1:46–47)
   B. Speech (Pss. 34:1; 40:10; 51:15)
   C. Song (Ps. 40:3; Eph. 5:19; Col. 3:16)
   D. Public praise (Exod. 15:1, 20–21; Matt. 26:30; Acts 16:25)

III. Motives for giving thanks
   A. Majesty of God (1 Chron. 29:11–13; Ps. 104:1)
   B. Holiness of God (Ps. 30:4; Isa. 6:3)
   C. Mercy of God (Ps. 89:1)
   D. Works of God (Pss. 103:1–5; 105:2)
      1. Goodness (Ps. 40:5; Eph. 1:3)
      2. Salvation (Ps. 5:11; 1 Pet. 1:3; Rev. 5:12)
      3. Assistance (Ps. 116:6; Jude 24–25)
      4. Establishing the kingdom (Ps. 98:7–9)

Lesson 45
Spiritual Deliverance

Theme	Deliverance from Demons
Scripture	Mark 5:1–20 (Matthew 8:28–34; Luke 8:26–40)
Memory Work	Mark 5:19

Approach to the Lesson

Theme: The power of Christ is the only hope for those in spiritual bondage. Satan, through the power of sin or by direct control, enslaves humans to his will. Only the redeeming power of Christ can end that enslavement.

Rationale: Encourage your students to respect, but not fear, Satan's power. We cannot defeat him on our own, but he cannot defeat us if we face him in the power of Christ.

Background: No story in the New Testament presents man in a more pathetic condition than the story of the two demoniacs of Gadara. These men were completely controlled by demons (Matt. 8:28). Mark and Luke recount the deliverance of only one, apparently because of the dominant place the one had in the incident. What happened to the other is unknown.

This incident makes it clear that demons are not mythological. They are real spiritual beings who seek to enslave individuals. Conservative theologians generally hold that there are two classes of fallen angels: those who were immediately consigned to hell (Jude 6) and those who wage war against the saints (Eph. 6:12).

Objectives

Knowledge (concepts students need to grasp)	that the demoniac's worshiping Christ proves His deity
	that Christ has absolute power over demons
Application (principles students should put into practice)	A testimony of Christ's power to deliver from spiritual bondage is an effective approach in witnessing.
	Christ's presence is more important than material prosperity.
	The Christian should never fear demons since Christ has authority over them.

Bible Expressions to Understand

Gadarenes—people who lived near Gadara, a village near the southeast coast of the Sea of Galilee

tombs—burial places carved out of rocky hillsides

unclean spirit—demon; fallen angel

fetter—ankle chain used to restrain a person

chains—metal restraints used around the upper parts of a prisoner's body

adjure—entreat; beg

Decapolis—a region of Palestine southeast of the Sea of Galilee

Since you were a little child you have heard people talk about ghosts, goblins, and other wicked, invisible creatures of the night. If you believe such stories, you probably expect to meet one of these beings every time you're alone at night outside or even in your own bedroom. Everyone has a story about some unexplainable incident in the basement, at Grandmother's house, or in Uncle Jerry's old barn out in the country. People often tell these stories at a slumber party or on a campout. Aside from all such foolishness, there are important questions to ask about the unseen world: Do demons exist? If they do, what does the Lord Jesus Christ say about them? Answers can be found in the biblical account of an incident near a town called Gadara.

Getting out of the boat after crossing the Sea of Galilee, Jesus saw a terrifying man charging toward Him (Mark 5:1–2). The man was possessed by unclean spirits. He'd apparently been living in the local cemetery. People had tried to control him by chaining him but to no avail. With superhuman strength, the man broke the chains and continued to roam the area night and day, cutting himself with

Why did the demons immediately destroy the swine? Perhaps they were angry at being cast out, or maybe they did it to create problems for Jesus.

stones and screaming. Instead of attacking Jesus, however, he fell down and worshiped Him. The man called Jesus "the Son of the most high God." The demons who possessed the man begged Jesus not to torment them. Jesus commanded the demons to come out of the man. They did, going into a nearby herd of pigs and driving them over a cliff to drown in the lake.

The people who were feeding the pigs were terrified. They ran throughout the area, telling everyone what had happened. A crowd came out to see what was going on. To their surprise, they found the man who'd been possessed sitting quietly by Jesus with his clothes on and appearing normal. They were frightened and asked Jesus to leave the region.

The man who had been delivered from the demons wanted to stay with Christ and serve Him. Jesus explained to him that the best thing he could do was to return to his friends and tell them what He'd done for him. The man not only went to his home but also went through the ten towns in that region to tell everyone what had happened.

162

Although demons attack Christians and even indwell and control the unsaved at times, we need not fear them. They are powerful, but Christ is more powerful (1 John 4:4). As Jesus said to the seventy, we should not become preoccupied with the battle that rages in the unseen realm or by our power over demons through Christ (Luke 10:17–20). We should have our hearts focused on Redemption through Christ. Our names are written in heaven, and the names of others may be there as well through God's grace because of our influence.

It is not wise to become overly interested in the subject of demons. Every Christian should know what the Bible has to say about them, but we should also avoid an unhealthy, morbid curiosity. When you teach this lesson, you will naturally want to avoid creating a "ghost story" atmosphere. Emphasize the power of Christ and the terribleness of sin and its bondage.

An important teaching aid, a copy of the chart from page 163 of the student text, is found on the CD.

The Lesson

I. Results of Spiritual Bondage (Mark 5:1–5)

Spiritual bondage can result in various devastating personal problems.

After crossing the Sea of Galilee, during which time He miraculously ended a storm, Jesus landed on the southeastern shore in the country of the Gadarenes. Matthew 8:28 calls the area the country of the Gergesenes. Ruins and extrabiblical

There are several important lessons to learn from this incident. First, demons do exist and do gain control of people. How does this happen? That's difficult to say, but one thing is clear: this man and all the other demon-possessed people in the New Testament were not Christians when the demons took control of them. When a person is a Christian, the Holy Spirit lives within him. The Holy Spirit won't allow a demon to share His home.

The second lesson is that Jesus is more powerful than demons. The demons knew that Jesus was God and had the power and authority to punish them. They obeyed Him when He commanded them to come out of the man. They had no choice; they had to do what He said. Since Jesus is our Good Shepherd, we should never fear demons. He is more powerful and will protect us. "Greater is he that is in you, than he that is in the world" (1 John 4:4).

Miracles of Deliverance from Demons

Victims	Symptoms	Results of Healing	Master Chart #
Man in Gadara	Violence, insanity, demon-controlled speech, nakedness	Man is clothed and gains self-control and sanity; whole region hears of the Lord's greatness.	29
Boy near Mount Hermon	Inability to speak, seizures	Boy instantly cured and returned to father; disciples rebuked for their lack of faith.	30
M an in Galilee	Blindness, no speech	Man receives sight and speech; people amazed; Pharisees accuse Christ of healing by the power of Satan.	31
Man in Capernaum	Inability to speak	Man begins to speak; people amazed; Pharisees accuse Christ of healing by the power of Satan.	32
Girl in Tyre area	Severe pain/anguish	Girl instantly cured.	33
Man in Capernaum	Demon-controlled speech	Man instantly cured; people amazed; news of Christ's power spreads quickly through Galilee.	34
Woman in Perea	Deformity (bent over and unable to stand up straight)	Woman instantly cured and offers praise to God; synagogue ruler rebukes Christ for healing on the Sabbath.	35

163

records give evidence of two cities in the area, Gergasa and Gadara, accounting for the different names. On getting out of the boat, Jesus was met by two demon-possessed men. The one on whom Mark's passage focuses was clearly indwelt by an unclean (defiled) spirit and was living as a social outcast in the tombs. No normal person would choose to live in such an environment.

People in the district had tried to restrain the man by using chains and fetters. (Fetters are ankle locks attached to chains.) Demonstrating supernatural strength, the man broke out of these restraints. No one could control him because he was like a wild animal.

As if this picture were not grim enough, the description continues. This poor man

did not sleep as do normal people. Night and day he screamed out and cut himself with sharp stones. Note that demon influence created a desire for self-destruction. This narrative does not prove that every person who commits suicide is demon-possessed, but anyone who does so certainly is conforming to the will of Satan. For a person to attempt to harm himself or take his own life is far from God's ideal of peace and productivity in life.

II. Causes of Spiritual Bondage (Mark 5:6–13)

Though spiritual bondage can have other causes, this man's condition was caused by demons. He ran to Christ, falling at His feet and bowing down as if in worship. The evil spirits recognized Christ's

Outline

authority over them even though they did not love Him or obey willingly. They feared the Lord (5:7; cf. James 2:19). They were terrified of being confined to hell like their counterparts, who were already imprisoned there, waiting the final judgment. When the Son of God entered this area, the demons indwelling this man recognized that they had only one hope—to beg for a temporary reprieve. Fleeing was impossible. The remark "What have I to do with thee, Jesus, thou Son of the most high God?" is a protest showing that these demons were not submitted to Christ. The phrase sounds disrespectful in English, but it wasn't. It could be paraphrased, "Why me? Why have you singled me out for this punishment?"

The Lord Jesus commanded the unclean spirit to come out of the man; then He asked the spirit what its name was. It replied, "My name is Legion: for we are many" (5:9). A Roman legion had between three thousand and six thousand soldiers. This comment provides us with information on several points. First, more than one demon can possess a person at the same time. Here one demon served as spokesman for the rest. Second, demons seek embodiment even if it means cohabiting with other demons.

When commanded to leave the man, they offered no protest to that order specifically but requested that they be allowed to stay in the region. A possible explanation for this request is based on Daniel 10:5–21. An angel appeared to Daniel in a vision and explained that he was opposed by the prince of the kingdom of Persia, who prevented him from coming earlier. Another spirit is called the prince of Grecia. Both of these fallen angels are described by geographical territories. Perhaps the demons indwelling this man were assigned to this region and did not want to be driven from their post.

This is the condition to which Satan reduces people. He would gladly have us all become like servile animals, groveling at his feet.

The demons asked to be sent into a herd of swine grazing nearby. The swine, crazed by the demons' presence, ran straight over a cliff into the Sea of Galilee and were drowned. Did the Lord command the demons to go into the swine? If he had, He would be indirectly responsible for the economic loss incurred by their drowning. But Jesus did not command them to do that; He ordered them to leave the man. What they did from that point on was their responsibility. They were intent on doing harm to the inhabitants of the area, including this considerable economic loss. God should not be blamed for their inhabiting the swine, any more than for their inhabiting the man in the first place. They might also have been trying to cause problems for Jesus.

III. Responses to Deliverance (Mark 5:14–20)

Wrong response (5:14–17). The first response to deliverance came from the unbelievers in the area. Those who had been feeding the swine ran in fear to the people in the town and surrounding area and told them what had happened. A mob approached Jesus and saw the man who had been demon-possessed sitting there, fully clothed and in his right mind. They were afraid because they knew something supernatural had transpired, but they could not understand it. Their unfortunate conclusion was that it would be good for Jesus to leave the area. Consider the facts: Here was a man who had been tormented by demons, a public nuisance, and even a threat to community safety. Now he is normal, even serene. The Person Who caused the change is in their midst, and the crowd wants Him to leave. They preferred the demons over Christ. This is a strange twist of human reasoning. Probably the death of the swine was at the root of this request. At least when the demoniac was raving, they were not suffering economically. Now they had suffered a significant financial loss. They rejected the One Who could have been the greatest blessing spiritually and economically.

Right response (5:18–20). In stark contrast to the callous response of the local folk, the delivered man did not want to be out of the Lord's presence. This is the response of any person delivered from spiritual bondage. People who claim to have been delivered and have no desire to be in

The third lesson concerns Satan. The conduct of the demons gives us a glimpse of the true nature of Satan. At heart he's a savage beast. He would like to reduce every person to a sick, wounded animal, just as he did this man. If he allowed that to happen to all who were unsaved, though, no one would want to follow his way. To deceive people, Satan lets some people live comfortable lives, making them think they are free to do as they please. If it weren't for the saving grace of Christ, all of us would end up in a condition much worse than that of the man in this lesson.

God's Light vs. Spiritual Darkness

Demons are real. They are servants of Satan, and their job is to control people and bring them into spiritual slavery. They are powerful and can do their jobs well. But they cannot control a Christian because the Holy Spirit lives in him. However, a Christian can be hindered and troubled by sin.

The power of Jesus Christ is the only deliverance from spiritual bondage of whatever kind. No amount of determination or change of circumstances will bring freedom. Jesus alone can grant it, and He'll grant it to all who call on Him.

Do You Remember?

1. Where did Christ deliver the demon-possessed man? _____
   in the country of the Gadarenes; near Decapolis

2. How had people in the area tried to restrain the man? _____
   They had chained him hand and foot.

3. What unusual things had the man done before Jesus delivered him? _____
   He had lived in the tombs, had broken his chains, had screamed day and night, and had cut himself with stones.

4. How did the man respond to Jesus when He came ashore? _____
   He ran to Christ and worshiped Him.

5. What was the first request the demons made of Christ? _____
   that Christ would not torment them

6. What was the demons' name? *Legion* _____

7. Where did the demons go after they left the man? _____
   into a herd of about two thousand pigs

8. How did the people in the area react to Jesus's miracle? _____
   They were afraid and asked Jesus to leave the area.

9. What did Jesus tell the delivered man to do? *to tell others what Jesus had done for him*

10. Where did the man tell about what Jesus did for him? *the Decapolis/the ten towns*

164

the presence of the Lord and His people have probably never truly been delivered from sin. Jesus encouraged this man to stay and testify of the great miracle that had occurred. Jesus had compassion on him when the compassion of others was of no avail.

No person is ever so low that the compassion and power of Christ cannot make him different. The one who appears entirely without hope is the one who will prove to be the greatest example of the grace of God. Help your students understand that there is hope for the drug addict, the alcoholic, the gambler, the worst of sinners (Matt. 9:12–13). Jesus is in the business of changing people no one else can change. We find instant rehabilitation in this passage.

This man became an effective evangelist, going throughout the Decapolis (an area that was about thirty-five miles long by ten miles wide), telling of the great thing the Lord had done. Everyone marveled at the change. He had probably gained a reputation while in his demonized condition. People knew about the wild man near the coast. Now here he was, sane, clothed, and preaching the gospel. What a testimony to the power of Christ!

✳ Extra Activities

Case studies: Present two case studies to add to the clarity and interest level of your lesson. The first should be of a man or even a teen who was once enslaved to drugs or alcohol and then delivered. The second should be a recounting of a modern-day demonization and subsequent deliverance. Missionary biographies sometimes include such material, and works on demons and demonology may also provide some help. The purpose of presenting two case studies is to show that regardless of whether a person is enslaved by sin or directly by Satan and his angels, he must be delivered by the power of Christ. Again, be careful not to fixate on demon possession.

Quiz: Give your students the following quiz before your lecture.

1. Do demons exist today?
   yes

2. If they do exist, where did they come from?
   They are fallen angels.

3. Can a Christian ever be demon-possessed?
   No; this would be impossible because of the indwelling of the Holy Spirit.

4. Have demons ever had certain geographical areas that they are responsible for?
   yes (Dan. 10)

5. Should a Christian be afraid of demons?
   No, but he should acknowledge their power.

Discussion: Using the chart on page 163 of the student text, discuss additional lessons that could be learned from the other times Jesus delivered demon-possessed people.

Lesson 46
Relying on the Life-Giver

THEME	Resurrection of Lazarus
SCRIPTURE	John 11:1–57
MEMORY WORK	John 11:25–26*a*

 Approach to the Lesson

Theme: Christ is the source and sustainer of all life, both physical and spiritual (Col. 1:16–17). However, physical illness and death may come to His followers. It is sometimes His will to heal a person for His glory, but He is not obligated to do so. At the resurrection of the just, the Lord will win the final victory over physical illness and death (1 Cor. 15:54–55). Currently His will is to see every person raised to spiritual life by faith in His work on the cross.

Rationale: Some of your students are probably already facing sickness and death in their families or among their friends. Their most common response is to ask, "Why?" Emphasize that all our lives—even the low points—are designed for God's glory. Rather than seeking an easy way out, they should look for God's working in these difficulties (2 Cor. 1:3–5).

Background: Just two months before His own death and Resurrection, Jesus performed one of the most astounding miracles of His ministry: He raised to life a man who had been dead for four days. The man was a close personal friend, as were his sisters. This family lived in Bethany, about two miles east of Jerusalem. Not many weeks earlier, the Lord had been in Bethany and Jerusalem.

He had incensed the religious leadership by His teachings, but He had escaped from their attempts to kill Him. He had crossed over the Jordan River to Perea until He heard about the death of Lazarus. News of this death precipitated a bold trip back into Judea to Bethany, within range of the religious leaders who wanted to eliminate Him.

 The Lesson

I. Christ Allows Sickness and Death for the Glory of God (11:1–16)

Mary and Martha sent the news that their brother Lazarus was sick. As Jesus's good friends, they felt at ease requesting His aid. Even though the Lord is God, He was truly man (John 1:11, 14) and had normal human relationships. Hearing of the illness, Jesus said that the sickness was not "unto death, but for the glory of God" (11:4). His words cannot be taken to mean that Lazarus would never die because he did die—twice. But Jesus saw beyond death to the greater glory of God. He waited two days after receiving the news of the situation and then proposed to the disciples that they go back to the home of Lazarus. This waiting period was part of Christ's plan for the miracle He was about to perform.

The disciples protested because of the recent danger they had encountered in the area. Jesus responded that as long as someone walks in the light of day, there will be no stumbling. Since He was walking in the light of obedience to God's will, He had nothing to fear.

Jesus then told His disciples that Lazarus was dead. Part of His purpose in performing this miracle was to build their faith. He was not talking about their belief in Him for salvation, but about the development of their faith as believers. To these statements Thomas characteristically responded that they should follow Him into Judea and die with him. He missed what the Lord was saying about the strengthening of their faith. He was loyal to the Lord, but he did not understand Christ's power as God. Thomas continued to wrestle with

Objectives

KNOWLEDGE (concepts students need to grasp)	the doctrine of the resurrection of all believers
	that physical illness may be for the glory of God
APPLICATION (principles students should put into practice)	Christians should pray in faith for healing.
	The Christian should look to God for healing, realizing that He may use a physician or medicine to accomplish it.
	God may use the illness and death of a saint to bring spiritual life to a sinner.

Outline

(John 11:1–57)

I. Christ allows sickness and death for the glory of God (1–16)
II. Christ is the source of victory over death (17–32)
III. Christ is moved by the tragedy of death (33–35)
IV. Christ can overcome death (36–44)
V. Christ brings saving faith by His power over death (45–57)

this problem even after Jesus was raised from the dead.

The Lord planned experiences for His disciples to strengthen their trust in Him. Following the Lord by faith resulted in greater, stronger faith. He also brings experiences into our lives as present-day disciples to strengthen our faith.

II. Christ Is the Source of Victory over Death (11:17–32)

Before Jesus arrived at the house, Martha heard that He was coming and ran to meet Him. One of the first things she said was that if Jesus had been present before Lazarus's death, Lazarus would not have died. Martha's faith in Jesus's ability to heal her brother was strong, but she was unsure about Him raising Lazarus from the dead. When Jesus told her that her brother would rise, Martha agreed that he would rise at the last day. She didn't know what was about to happen, but she did demonstrate some understanding of the future.

Jesus then described Himself as the Resurrection and the Life. Humans do die physically, yet that death will be overcome at the resurrection through Christ (1 Cor. 15:54–57). Once a person is born again, he will never die spiritually. Martha understood the spiritual intent of Jesus's words. She made one of the clearest confessions about the identity of Jesus in the New Testament: "I believe that thou art the Christ, the Son of God, which should come into the world" (11:27).

While Jesus was still a distance from their home, Martha left Him and ran and told her sister that He had come. Mary ran to meet Him, fell down at His feet, wept, and repeated Martha's words, saying that if He had been there, her brother would not have died. Mary's worshipful attitude is typical of her (Luke 10:38–42).

Read: John 11:1–57   Memorize: John 11:25–26a

Bible Expressions to Understand

Bethany—a town two miles east of Jerusalem; home of Mary, Martha, and Lazarus
twelve hours in a day—the Jewish day (from 6 a.m. to 6 p.m.)
sleep—a figurative expression for death
Didymus—a Greek name meaning "twin"
grave—a natural cave or a tomb carved out of a hillside
furlong—about the length of two football fields
graveclothes—strips of linen cloth wrapped around a corpse
napkin—a small piece of cloth placed over the face in burial
Ephraim—a small town twenty miles northeast of Jerusalem

Jesus performed some astounding miracles to prove that He was God, the giver and the sustainer of both physical and spiritual life. One of these was the raising of His friend Lazarus from the grave (Master Chart, #4). Through this miracle Jesus wanted to strengthen the faith of His disciples and lead others to believe in Him as their Savior (John 11:15, 45).

Lazarus's sickness seemed unexplainable to Mary and Martha. Why would Jesus permit Lazarus to become so ill when He was able to heal him? Even though Jesus was across the Jordan River in Perea, distance was no problem to the Master. Hadn't He healed both the nobleman's son (Master Chart, #1) and the centurion's servant (#15) from a distance?

If Jesus really loved the family at Bethany, why did He still wait around—not just an hour or two but two whole days? Why did He deliberately avoid healing Lazarus? He looked on Lazarus's death as a kind of "sleep," from which he would be awakened to begin life again. His delay had given the impression that He didn't care, but that wasn't the case. Jesus was never indifferent to human problems. When He saw the family and the mourners crying, His heart was moved, too. He wept, not with the hopeless wailing of the relatives, but with compassion for His friends. Because He loved the family at Bethany and because Lazarus was His friend, He wouldn't leave him in the grave.

Jesus had a different view of the illness than the sisters did. He looked beyond the immediate situation

There was no doubt that Lazarus was really dead. He had already been in the tomb for four days when Jesus raised him.

165

III. Christ Is Moved by the Tragedy of Death (11:33–35)

Seeing Mary and the other mourners weeping, the Lord was deeply troubled. This sorrow was more than His benevolent spirit could bear. He asked where Lazarus had been buried; they showed Him, and He wept (11:35). Observers noted the deep love that the Lord had for Lazarus. They also speculated about why the Lord had not come and healed Lazarus.

Certainly this scene gives the believer a glimpse of the depth of human emotion in our Lord. He was not unfeeling, but rather tender and concerned about the grief that others felt. He is a pattern for all Christians. We must rejoice with those who rejoice and weep with those who weep (Rom. 12:15).

IV. Christ Can Overcome Death (11:36–44)

Even before Lazarus died, Jesus had intended to raise him. He commanded that the stone be removed from the mouth of the tomb of Lazarus in spite of Martha's protest that after four days the body would be decomposing. He told Martha to remember that if she would now believe, she would see the glory of God.

Then Jesus addressed the Father and thanked Him for hearing His request. He knew that the Father would hear His request because of His relationship to the Father as the Son and for the purpose of moving the observers to faith in Christ as Savior. Note the combination of ideas in this miracle. The faith of Mary and Martha was involved. Yet the intercession of Jesus and the responsiveness of the Father were essential. Usually these elements are necessary to the working of any miracle. Human faith, the working of the Son of God, and the approval and grace of God the Father overturn the normal course of human events and result in the miraculous.

Standing at the mouth of the cave where Lazarus was buried, Jesus commanded Lazarus to come out. Lazarus was supernaturally raised from a prone position and propelled alive, but unable to walk, to the opening of the tomb. Bound from head to toe with linen burial cloths, Lazarus had to have his burial cloths unwrapped by those nearby.

In full view of numerous witnesses, Christ miraculously restored to life a man who had been four days in the grave; Christ is victor over death.

V. Christ Brings Saving Faith by His Power over Death (11:45–57)

The reactions to this miracle were varied. According to John 12:10, the priests plotted to kill Lazarus to eliminate this evidence of Jesus's miraculous powers. There is no record that they were successful. A tradition recorded by Epiphanius, bishop of Salamis in Cyprus (c. 314–403), says that Lazarus lived for thirty years more, dying when he was sixty.

Our lives are safe in Christ's care. If the Lord doesn't come back first, we will all die someday. Staying alive is not important; serving Christ until our certain death should be our priority.

Some who witnessed or heard about the raising of Lazarus believed on Jesus immediately. This miracle was adequate proof of His deity for them. The reaction of the Jewish leadership, however, was to try to protect their selfish interests. Rather than viewing this act as a clear indication of Christ's deity and their need to turn to Him (John 20:31), they decided to kill Him. Their rationale was that there would be such a turning of the people to Jesus that the upheaval would displace them as leaders. This reaction reflects their accurate understanding of Roman policy. The Romans tried to abide by the wishes of their subjugated peoples on local political leadership. However, they felt threatened by any leader who became too popular. They would hold the priests responsible for the influence Jesus had gained and would possibly take serious steps against the existing political structure.

Caiaphas, the high priest, prophesied that one man should be sacrificed so that the whole nation would be spared. He prophesied that the One Who should die "should gather together in one the children of God that were scattered abroad" (11:52). Of course, there was no spiritual understanding behind these prophetic remarks; they were merely political. The spiritual truth, however, is profound.

> People are under God's control even if they do not believe in Him. We need not fear God's enemies when they threaten us with harm. Whatever the outcome, God's will and the greatest good will be done.

After the council had decided that Jesus should die, the leadership was intent on accomplishing that goal. Forced to curtail His public movements among the Jews, Jesus went to Ephraim, a small city about twenty miles northeast of Jerusalem. Passover was to begin soon, and the leaders expected that Jesus might come to Jerusalem for that. Jesus had ventured into dangerous territory just long enough to accomplish what the Father wanted and then withdrew to a safer area. He demonstrated no presumption, but absolute harmony with a plan that was not of human origin.

and saw God's purpose. Though He shared in the sorrow of those who were suffering, He didn't despair.

Jesus was capable of raising Lazarus with no help at all. However, He deliberately made Martha exercise her faith in Him, which she declared by saying, "I know that he shall rise again in the resurrection at the last day. . . . I believe that thou art the Christ, the Son of God, which should come into the world" (John 11:24, 27). To open a tomb where a human body was decaying would be both futile and offensive. It seemed foolish. Yet Jesus required Martha to place such firm trust in Him that she had to obey even an apparently pointless command (11:39). Jesus may take us through difficult and unpleasant experiences to teach us to trust Him, just as He did Martha.

At Christ's dramatic words, "Lazarus, come forth," the dead man stood bound at the entrance to the tomb. This restoration of life to a dead man proved that Jesus spoke the truth when He said, "I am the resurrection and the life" (John 11:25).

Instead of worshiping Jesus, some of the observers reported His words and the miracle to the Jewish leaders. The Pharisees weren't pleased that a man had been restored to life. Instead, they were annoyed that Jesus had upset their thinking and had stirred up the crowds again. They reasoned that if Jesus gained too much popularity, the Romans (who were jealous of political rivals) would hold the Jewish priests responsible.

This rebellious attitude of unbelief was carried to its logical conclusion by Caiaphas, the high priest. He asserted that it would be better to sacrifice Jesus, one person, than to risk the annihilation of the entire nation of Israel. Little did Caiaphas know that Jesus was indeed going to die for the whole nation so that Jews and Gentiles alike might receive forgiveness of their sins.

The raising of Lazarus from the dead confirmed the disciples and the family at Bethany in their faith in Christ. It also made His opponents more determined than ever to kill Him.

Resurrection Power

The Lord Jesus is the source and sustainer of your physical and spiritual life. Sometimes He may miraculously heal a person of a physical illness for His glory. You may know someone who has been healed, or perhaps you've even been healed yourself. However, this isn't the normal thing Jesus does or is obligated to do. There's a day in the future when Jesus will eliminate all illness and death forever. For now, Jesus's main concern is that everyone be raised to spiritual life by faith in His work on the cross.

166

Do You Remember?

1. How far from Jerusalem was Bethany? _two miles_

2. Where was Jesus when He received the message from Mary and Martha? _____
   across the Jordan River in Perea

3. Why did Jesus delay His coming? _____
   so He would have the opportunity to do a miracle in raising Lazarus from the dead

4. How did Jesus refer to Lazarus's death? _He said Lazarus was sleeping._

5. Why did Jesus command that the stone be taken away from the grave? _____
   so that Martha could exercise her faith

6. Why did Jesus pray to the Father before raising Lazarus? _____
   so that those who were there would recognize that He was the Son of God

7. What were the two reactions to Jesus because of this miracle? _____
   Some worshiped; others were displeased.

8. What prophecy did Caiaphas give regarding Jesus? _____
   that Jesus would die for the entire nation of Israel

167

✳ Extra Activities

Memory work: Make an overhead transparency of the memory verse for this lesson. Display the entire verse, and read it aloud with the class several times. Then substitute another transparency that has only a few words or only the first letter of each word. Repeat the verse aloud several times. Remove all aids and repeat it aloud. Using this teaching method will inject some variety into the learning of the memory verse.

Discussion: Use the following topics and Scripture passages to discuss the resurrection of believers.

a. The time of the resurrection (1 Thess. 4:16)

b. The resurrected body (1 Cor. 15:42–48, 52; 2 Cor. 5:1–5; Phil. 3:21)

c. An encouragement to serve for Christ (Phil. 3:11)

d. The present experience of "resurrection" as newness of life (Rom. 6:13; Eph. 2:6; Phil. 3:10; Col. 2:12)

Unit 8

Christ's Parables

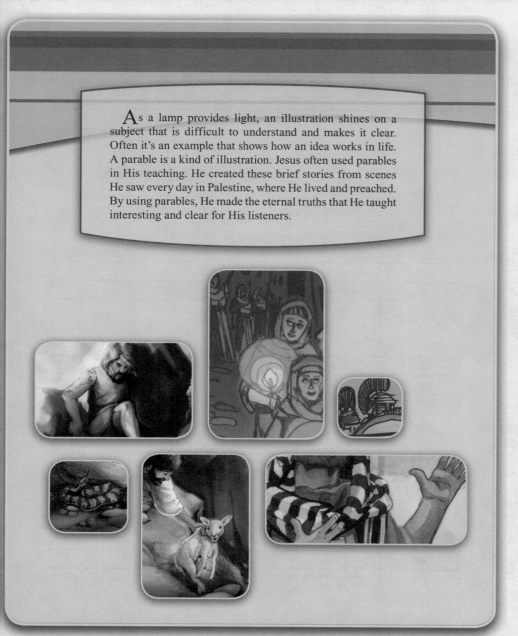

As a lamp provides light, an illustration shines on a subject that is difficult to understand and makes it clear. Often it's an example that shows how an idea works in life. A parable is a kind of illustration. Jesus often used parables in His teaching. He created these brief stories from scenes He saw every day in Palestine, where He lived and preached. By using parables, He made the eternal truths that He taught interesting and clear for His listeners.

Christ's Parables

The purpose of this unit is to introduce the student to Christ's major parables. The student should gain an appreciation of how important this teaching method was in the ministry of Christ. Junior highers should also be helped spiritually by the profound ideas that Christ taught through this approach.

Seven of the eleven lessons in this unit discuss one parable each. Lesson 48 treats seven parables; Lesson 51, three; Lesson 54, three; Lesson 55, five parables. Consistent with the approach followed throughout the text, the multi-parable lessons are centered on a common theme. You may need additional time to teach these multi-parable lessons.

Since Christ's parables were developed from scenes He witnessed in first-century Israel, a special essay entitled "Israel Past and Present" is included in this unit on pages 186–87 of the student text. This essay will help your students understand the similarities that exist between modern-day Israel and the Israel of Jesus's time.

Lesson 57 includes a chart that compares the parable of the pounds with the parable of the talents. The charts which appear in the student text may also be found on the CD accompanying the Teacher's Edition.

This summary chart of all the parables discussed in the lessons lists the main teaching of each parable, the Scripture passage in which it is found, and the lesson in which that parable is discussed. This may assist you with in-class review and will help your students prepare for a test over the unit. The CD includes the full chart as well as a fill-in-the-blank version.

PARABLES JESUS TOLD

Lesson	Teaching	Parable	Scripture Passages
47	Responding to the Word of God	Sower and seed	Matt. 13:3–8, 18–23; Mark 4:3–20; Luke 8:4–15
48	The growth of the kingdom	Wheat and tares	Matt. 13:24–30, 36–43
		Dragnet	Matt. 13:47–50
		Mustard seed	Matt. 13:31–32; Mark 4:30–32; Luke 13:18–19
		Leaven	Matt. 13:33; Luke 13:20–21
		Hidden treasure	Matt. 13:44
		Pearl of great price	Matt. 13:45–46
		Householder	Matt. 13:52
49	Managing money	Unjust steward	Luke 16:1–13
50	Covetousness	Rich fool	Luke 12:16–21
51	Seeking the lost	Lost sheep	Luke 15:4–7
		Lost coin	Luke 15:8–10
		Lost son	Luke 15:11–32
52	Loving others	Good Samaritan	Luke 10:30–37
53	Forgiving others	Unmerciful servant	Matt. 18:23–35
54	Humility	Workers in the vineyard	Matt. 20:1–16
		Lowest seat at the feast	Luke 14:7–11
		Pharisee and publican	Luke 18:9–14
55	Being ready for His coming	Master returning from a wedding	Luke 12:35–38
		Goodman and thief	Matt. 24:43–44; Luke 12:39–40
		Wise servants and wicked servants	Matt. 24:45–51; Luke 12:42–48
		Ten virgins	Matt. 25:1–13
		Faithful porter	Mark 13:34–37
56	Expecting a reward	Pounds	Luke 19:11–27
57	Faithfulness until He comes	Talents	Matt. 25:14–30

170

Responding to the Word of God

Read: Matthew 13:3–8, 18–23 Memorize: Matthew 13:23

Bible Expressions to Understand

way side—a travel-hardened path

stony places—areas where the soil is only a few inches deep, with a limestone slab underneath

anon—immediately

James, Melanie, Rich, and Tricia entered the auditorium and sat down on the back row just as Pastor Dave, the youth pastor, announced the first hymn for the evening service. When the singing was over and the offering had been taken, Pastor Roberts began his evening message. James and Melanie began writing notes back and forth to pass the time. Both of them were from Christian homes, and each had made a public decision to be saved while at camp last summer. They had seemed sincere when they went forward at the campfire service. Melanie had even given a testimony in front of everybody. But after school started again in the fall, James began hanging out with the same people he had gotten into trouble with the year before. Even though it was a Christian school, they made fun of James for acting religious during class devotions in homeroom. Then James started smoking.

Melanie sometimes felt guilty for even sitting with James at church, but she liked him a lot, and she tried to overlook his weak points. Melanie had really thought she was serious when she had made her profession of faith in Christ at camp, but she was beginning to wonder now. She wanted to live for the Lord, but she never seemed to have time to read her Bible. After homework and television every night, there wasn't much time left. Saturdays were the time Pastor Dave always planned youth evangelistic activities, but that was the only day she had to work at her family's restaurant and make extra money to buy the clothes she wanted.

Rich liked Pastor Dave a lot. He had been especially nice since Rich's mom and dad had gotten divorced last year. He liked the kids at church and his Christian school too. Preaching was boring, though. He could never really follow Pastor Roberts's

Just as some soils are not fertile enough for growing crops, some people's hearts are not open to the truth of God's Word.

171

Lesson 47

Responding to the Word of God

Theme	The Parable of the Sower
Scripture	Matthew 13:3–8, 18–23 (Mark 4:3–8, 14–20; Luke 8:4–8, 11–15)
Memory Work	Matthew 13:23

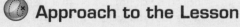

Approach to the Lesson

Theme: The ideal for every believer is total responsiveness to God's Word. Our attitude should be, "Whatever God says, I will believe; whatever God commands, I will do; and whatever God desires, I will be." This produces maximum spiritual growth and productivity for the glory of God.

Rationale: Your students may not realize that their responses to the gospel are not automatic. Their choice to live for Christ is not your responsibility or their parents' or their pastor's. It is theirs. By contrasting the outcomes in this parable, stress the difference their choices can make.

Background: The Lord gave this instruction during the second year of His public ministry, near the Sea of Galilee. This time period has been called "the year of public favor" since His ministry was largely unopposed by the religious authorities. Those who heard Him during this time

Objectives

Knowledge (concepts students need to grasp)	the meaning of the phrase *the kingdom of heaven*
	the scriptural teaching that there are varying responses to the Word of God
Application (principles students should put into practice)	We should be sure our hearts are not hard, shallow, or pre-occupied with the wrong things.
	We should avoid some things to ensure our maximum productivity as believers responding to the Word.

noted that He spoke with authority, boldness, power, and graciousness. The theme of His preaching was the kingdom of God (the kingdom of heaven).

The parable of the sower begins a series of parables describing the kingdom of heaven. This phrase denotes God's rule in the past, present, and future. Consequently it introduces comments (1) about Christ's ministry ("the kingdom of heaven is at hand") in the sense that the King is present and deserves spiritual recognition; (2) about the church age, during which Christ rules in the hearts of men, beginning at salvation (the parables of the sower, wheat and tares, dragnet, and others); and (3) about the future, when He will rule the entire earth from an earthly throne (the parables of the pounds and the talents). Matthew 19:23–24 shows that the phrases *kingdom of God* and *kingdom of heaven* both refer to salvation. The kingdom parables teach us how to live as subjects in His kingdom as well as what to expect in the future kingdom.

Christ presents the parable and its explanation separately. The simplest way to teach the parable is to read it to the class and then explain it verse by verse.

The Lesson

I. The Hardened Heart

The wayside is a path of hard-packed soil that runs between fields. There is no way a seed could penetrate that kind of soil; the seed remains on top. This pictures the person who hears the Word and does not understand it. It does not penetrate, and the Devil can snatch it away. All three of the synoptic Gospels record this parable, but each calls the Devil by a different name. Matthew 13:19 calls him "the wicked one," stressing his evil character. Mark 4:15 calls

Outline

him "Satan," which means adversary or opposer, stressing the Devil's role as the rebel against God. Luke 8:12 labels him "the Devil," a name that emphasizes his role as a slanderer. Satan opposes the advancement of Christ's kingdom by causing men to misunderstand the true character of God and the gospel, so that they reject the truth.

> Help the students understand that by living an ungodly life they can cause people to fail to see the benefit of knowing God through the gospel of Christ. We must do all we can to prevent the snatching away of the Word from people's hearts.

The Word is called "the word of the kingdom," emphasizing the central role it plays in getting men and women to receive Christ and become part of His kingdom. Knowing the Word's importance, the Devil snatches it away when it is not understood. The Greek verb translated "catcheth away" is derived from a word for a mythological beast, half human and half bird, that was known for swooping down suddenly and carrying its prey away. The same term is used to describe our being caught away in an instant at the Rapture. The "word of the kingdom" is suddenly taken away from the "hearts" of these people. The term *heart* represents the inner, spiritual person.

II. The Shallow Heart

In Palestine the depth of the soil is restricted in many places by large slabs of limestone a few inches below the surface. This shallow soil doesn't allow plants to send roots down far enough to acquire the water necessary to survive and grow. The scorching sun dries up the moisture in the soil, and the plant withers and dies. This example represents the person who hears the Word and "anon" (immediately) receives the message but with no depth of thought, no real repentance and faith. What is especially disturbing about this person is the seeming genuineness of his profession. He appears to be sincere. Later, because of

sermons. What was worse, he didn't *want* to understand them. His parents were Christians, supposedly, but they didn't live by what the pastor taught. James, his best friend, wasn't a bit different after "getting saved," so why should he bother trusting Christ?

Tricia had been standing in the lobby telling James, Melanie, and Rich about the youth group's plan to go to a nearby park and witness that Saturday when they had heard Pastor Dave's voice and had quickly gone in and sat down. Tricia had trusted Christ at camp two summers before. Her dad, a deacon in their church, had helped her work out a Bible study program and answered her questions about the Bible. Around Christmastime, Rita Young, a missionary to Togo, West Africa, had stayed in their home and talked to her a long time about what it was like to be a missionary. Tricia liked Miss Young.

Pastor Roberts was preaching about the church at Laodicea in the book of Revelation that night. As he began his sermon, Tricia got out her notebook and pen. Her mom had told her it was a good idea to write down the main ideas of the pastor's sermon and decide at the end of every service how she could grow in her life for Christ based on what she had heard. She'd been doing that for about a year now, and it had made a noticeable difference in her attitude toward the preaching and toward the needs of other people too. She'd gotten the courage to witness

---

What Is Your Heart's Response?

Once you have read this lesson and the parable of the sower, you need to respond to this truth. Jesus said, "I am the vine, ye are the branches: He that abideth in me, and I in him, the same bringeth forth much fruit" (John 15:5). Christ died for your sins on the cross, was raised from the dead, and is alive, waiting for you to respond to Him by turning from your sins and making Him the One Who directs your life. Then you must stay close to Him by listening to His Word and obeying its commands. Your personality will develop into what the Lord Jesus wants, you'll help other Christians live for Jesus Christ, and you'll win others to the Lord Jesus Christ.

172

---

to Debbie, the girl next door who went to a public school, and she was helping Mrs. Simpson, an elderly widow in their church, clean her house once a week.

James, Melanie, Rich, and Tricia are each examples of responses to the Word of God presented in Christ's parable of the sower. The seed in the parable is the Word of God. The hard-packed wayside soil represents people who hear the gospel but don't understand it. Satan is then able to turn them away from the truth. The shallow stony ground symbolizes people who receive the gospel emotionally but quickly turn away from their profession when opposition comes into their lives. The carnal believer, with worldly cares and riches choking out fruit from his Christian life, is depicted by the thorn-infested ground. Finally, the fruitful believer is represented, with varying amounts of fruit produced by his dedicated life.

Can you match the four teens with the kinds of soil in the parable of the sower?

1. James	c	a. good, fertile soil
2. Melanie	d	b. hard-packed soil
3. Rich	b	c. shallow soil
4. Tricia	a	d. thorn-infested soil

---

pressures and persecution brought on by trying to live according to the Word of God, this person falls away (Luke 8:13). He stops putting into practice the truths of the Bible and fellowshipping with believers.

Was he saved before he fell away? The passage describes him as having no root, which indicates he wasn't. These verses contrast a deep, permanent profession with a shallow, temporary one. John gives us insight into this problem when he states, "They went out from us, but they were not of us: for if they had been of us, they would no doubt have continued with us: but they went out, that they might be made manifest that they were not all of us" (1 John 2:19).

> Encourage your students to consider their decisions for the Lord very carefully, particularly their decision of salvation.

Younger people sometimes make spur-of-the-moment professions with their friends at camps, youth revivals, and other special teen gatherings. Encourage your students to make up their minds to stick with their profession for the Lord, regardless of the ridicule of their friends and the waning of their initial excitement.

III. The Thorn-Infested Heart

There is some disagreement about what the third type of soil in the parable represents. Since the passage does not explicitly say whether this person is saved or lost, it is best not to be dogmatic on that issue. The factors that make him unfruitful are the cares of this world, the deceitfulness of riches, the desire for other things (Mark 4:19), and the pleasures of this life (Luke

Do You Remember?

1. What is the seed in the parable of the sower? _____
   the Word of God; the message of the gospel

2. What are the four kinds of soil presented in the parable? _____
   hard-packed, shallow or stony, thorn-infested, good or fertile

3. What kind of person does the shallow soil represent? _____
   one who makes only an emotional decision

4. Does all "good soil" produce the same amount of fruit? *no*_____

5. What are some of the "thorns" that limit the influence of the Word of God
   in a person's life? *care of this world, deceitfulness of riches*_____

6. Who takes the Word of God away from the hardened heart? *Satan*_____

173

8:14). All three versions of the parable present the cares of this life as detrimental to a fruitful Christian life. The term translated *cares* could be rendered "worries" or "anxieties." These anxieties are associated with living in this age.

Students are often preoccupied with their peers' opinions, their clothes, their hairstyles, and their success or failure in temporal activities such as athletics and cheerleading. Instead, they should be preoccupied with their relationship to Christ through His Word.

Mark 4:19 refers to the "lusts of other things" that compete with the Word of God. The phrase could be rendered "the desires for other things." Your students are at the age when they experience strong desires to become an authority in some area. They will build collections, develop athletic skills, memorize the details of the achievements of professional athletes, musicians, and actors. Challenge your students to give foremost attention to becoming authorities in the truths of Scripture and living for Christ.

The deceitfulness of riches is another impediment to fruitfulness. In our culture the influence of materialism starts early. Children watch television commercials telling them that having a new bike, doll, or game will make them happy. Teenagers are persuaded by television and their friends that wearing the newest fashions, owning the best sports equipment, or having money to spend on the most recent fad is the way to have a satisfying life. With good reason, riches are described as deceitful.

Luke 8:14 presents the "pleasures of this life" as causing unfruitfulness. This is the time to begin teaching your students the importance of setting priorities. Fun is not number one! Learning, working, and reaching spiritual goals bring lasting satisfaction. Encourage your students to seize the opportunity before them to be all they can be for the Lord.

In summary, note that the person described in this part of the parable hears the Bible and knows its teachings. Your students, too, have had the Bible taught to them by their pastors and Bible teachers in school. They must be careful not to have a "thorny heart" response to the Word, but rather be fruitful, eliminating all influences that would hinder their progress.

IV. The Good Heart

This soil represents the person who receives the Word and bears fruit with endurance. Mark 4:20 gives the degrees of fruitfulness in ascending order, Matthew 13:23 in descending order; Luke 8:15 presents no degrees of fruitfulness. Luke says only that the fruit comes through patience. This is the patience of the overcomer, a brave patience, or endurance. Through temptation, pressure, sickness, and persecution, the Christian with the "good heart" obeys the Word of God. His character is developed, and the lives of others are changed through his influence.

A Christian who is responsive to the Word of God may be productive, very productive, or extremely productive. The degree of productivity depends on his brave patience, his determination to do and be what God desires, no matter what the cost. Without the grace of God—the Lord's daily strengthening—he will not demonstrate this courageous determination. The prospect of being a hundredfold Christian should motivate the believer to great dependence on the Lord, Who is his strength. Starting early in life with this courageous determination is part of the secret to being useful and productive.

✳ Extra Activity

Question and answer: As you discuss each kind of soil in this parable, list it with its characteristics on the board or an overhead. When you finish explaining each type of soil, ask the class to identify which character in their student lesson exemplifies it.

Lesson 48

The Growth of the Kingdom

Theme	The Kingdom Parables
Scripture	Matthew 13:24–52
Memory Work	Matthew 13:52

Approach to the Lesson

Theme: Jesus does not leave us without information about how His kingdom will grow. In the years since His ascension, His kingdom has grown into a universal organism, found in every nation. This growth is consistent with what Jesus taught in the kingdom parables. The growth of the kingdom (1) involves some who are not genuine believers, (2) results from conversions, and (3) is facilitated by faithful preaching.

Rationale: Encourage your students to evaluate their faith and their dedication to Christ's kingdom. Faith and dedication are central to a Christian's purpose in life; students should not treat these matters casually.

Background: In the autumn of Christ's second year of public ministry, near the Sea of Galilee, Jesus taught the series of eight parables that have come to be known as the kingdom parables. They appear in Mark 4:1–20, 30–32 and Luke 8:4–15;

Objectives

Knowledge (concepts students need to grasp)	the perspective each kingdom parable gives regarding the growth of the kingdom in this age
	the symbolic significance of the details in each parable
Application (principles students should put into practice)	We should not try to figure out who is really saved since a false profession cannot always be detected.
	We should pray for believers in other countries.
	Although the kingdom is universal, it grows as individuals are added one by one through our witness.
	The influence of the kingdom gradually increases over time.

Bible Expressions to Understand

kingdom of heaven—Christ's rulership, spiritually or on earth in the future
tares—bearded darnel, a poisonous wheat-like grass
leaven—an ingredient in dough that produces fermentation and rising
scribe—an expert in the Law of God

Once while teaching by the Sea of Galilee, Jesus presented eight parables about the kingdom of heaven. When He talked about the kingdom of heaven, He was referring to the way He would govern those who know Him, from His ascension until the final judgment. Jesus knew that it was important for us to understand what things would be like in His kingdom as time went by.

Christ's first parable was about the sower and four types of ground, which we studied in Lesson 47. The main point of that parable was that the kingdom of heaven grows when people respond to the gospel. The other seven parables in this chapter teach other important truths about the kingdom.

Fishermen in Jesus's day sometimes used a dragnet, which had floats on the upper edge and weights on the lower edge (to keep it close to the bottom). The net was let down from a boat and then hauled in by men on the shore.

174

Two of the parables teach that there will always be false believers—people who associate with real believers and outwardly become part of Christ's kingdom. The first of these parables, the parable of the wheat and the tares, is drawn from country life. Tares, poisonous plants that look like wheat, often grew in wheat fields in Israel. The farmer couldn't tell the difference between the plants until the grains formed. The wheat grains were much fuller and heavier than the grains of the tares. Not until harvest could the tares be removed without harming the wheat. The wheat represents the true members of Christ's kingdom. The tares are the children of the Devil, false members. Though the Devil can put people among God's people who pretend to be Christians and are not, his ploy will not work. The judgment will come, and the tares will be removed.

The second of these two parables is the parable of the net. It's based on the practices of fishermen. When men fished with nets in Israel, they couldn't choose the kind of fish they would catch. After drawing the catch to shore, they'd separate the worthless fish from those that were good to sell. Similarly, as the gospel spreads throughout the world, many will make a profession but not really believe. There's no way to separate the true from the false until the end of the era, when the Lord, who knows the hearts of all people, can do the judging.

The second pair of parables—the mustard seed and the leaven—teaches about the small beginning of the kingdom and its growing influence through the years. It has grown like the mustard plant, which begins as a small seed and becomes a tree in which birds can build their nests. The kingdom began in a small country, Israel, and has grown out to every part of the world.

13:18–21, but the most thorough presentation is in Matthew 13:3–52. Taken together, these parables provide a comprehensive picture of the growth and influence of the kingdom.

The first of these, the parable of the sower, was treated in Lesson 47. It is significant that this series begins with a discussion of response to the Word. Without God's Word there would be no standard against which to measure true profession. There would be no gospel of salvation, no belief, and thus no kingdom. It is no wonder that the psalmist says, "Thou hast magnified thy word above all thy name" (Ps. 138:2).

The remaining seven parables may be organized as three pairs, with one concluding parable on scribes in the kingdom. This classification is warranted by the similarity of the material in each set. Rather than following the chronological arrangement of the material as it is presented in Matthew 13, this lesson follows the logical pairing of ideas.

The Lesson

I. False Profession

Two of the kingdom parables discuss the reality of false professors in the kingdom. As the kingdom grows, some will say they believe even though they do not.

The wheat and the tares (Matt. 13:24–30, 36–43). Jesus first told this story to the crowd and later explained it to His disciples privately. The one who is sowing good seed is the Son. The children of God are

The parable of the leaven pictures a woman putting a small quantity of leaven (yeast) in dough to cause it to ferment and to rise. A small quantity spreads all throughout the batch of dough. The leaven of the gospel has spread throughout the world after beginning in a small group of disciples. The gospel and therefore the kingdom of Christ continue to spread.

The next pair of kingdom parables—the treasure and the pearl—teach how individuals enter the kingdom of Christ. Some are like the man who found the treasure in the field. The man wasn't out looking for the treasure; he just happened to find it. Some people may not seem interested in the gospel, but we should still do what we can to reach them.

Others are like the man looking for the pearl. They are seriously looking, considering various philosophies and religious systems. When they hear the truth of the gospel, they'll recognize its value and abandon all the others. The fact that someone is a member of a particular church or religious group shouldn't discourage us from witnessing to him; it's often a sign that he is looking for the truth.

The last kingdom parable concerns the scribe of the kingdom, an expert on the Law of God. He's said to be like a man who manages a large estate. He uses the wealth of the estate for the benefit of others, bringing out items of value, both new and old. Likewise, a preacher should offer instruction of value to others. Some truths you hear are a review. At other times your teacher or your pastor will instruct you about things you didn't know before, expanding your understanding of God's truth.

Does God's Expansion Plan Include You?

Christ's kingdom started out small, but it has grown. Over the years it's expanded to include people from every nation. These people have entered the kingdom by faith in Jesus Christ, God the Son. Some have made false professions and will be found out at the judgment. The kingdom will continue to grow as people hear the gospel and repent. Whether they hear the gospel or not depends in part on the faithful witness of Christians like you.

Do You Remember?

1. In the parable of the wheat and the tares, what does the good seed represent? Who sows it? _believers; Jesus_

2. What do the tares represent? Who sows them? _unbelievers; Satan_

3. What happens to the tares? _They are allowed to grow up with the wheat and are thrown into the fire at harvest time._

   What happens to the wheat? _It grows up with the tares but is separated at harvest and put into the master's barn._

4. How is the kingdom of heaven like a mustard seed? _Although it is small when planted, it will be very large when fully grown._

5. How is the parable of the treasure like the parable of the pearl? _Both tell how a person enters the kingdom._

6. Explain the parable of the net. _Just as a dragnet catches both good fish and bad, so there will be both professing and genuine Christians. One day, however, the genuine will be separated from the false, just as the good fish are separated from the bad._

175

---

the good seed that He sows. The tares represent the children of the Devil. Tares, or bearded darnel, are a poisonous grass indistinguishable from wheat while the two are growing into blade. At harvest time the grains at the top of the darnel are smaller and fewer. The wheat stalk, weighed down with its grain, bends over while the darnel stands taller. Only then can the farmer easily distinguish the two. When eaten, darnel can produce nausea, convulsions, diarrhea, and even death. The Devil sows these "tares" in the world. The wheat and the tares grow side by side until the harvest, which will take place at the end of the world. (*Age* is a stricter translation of the Greek word in this case.) Jesus sends the angels, who are the reapers, to gather up the wicked, who are then judged by the Lord.

The time of this judgment is difficult to pinpoint. Probably the safest identification is the Great White Throne Judgment, just before the eternal state. The wicked are cast into the furnace of fire, which is equivalent to the lake of fire (Rev. 20:14). The result is the exaltation of the righteous in the kingdom of their Father. This is a glorious picture of our eternal state. The wicked are separated from the righteous forever. No shadow of evil is present. The gold has been refined to utter purity, and the reflection is blinding. We will shine like the sun.

The Devil infiltrates and damages the church through his children, who sometimes look saintly. But an end to that infiltration is coming.

The net (Matt. 13: 47–51). A similar picture is presented in the next parable.

The fishing net in the parable is a dragnet, which has floats on the upper edge and lead weights on the lower edge to keep it close to the bottom. These nets were used in shallow, sandy-bottomed areas. The net was sometimes taken out from shore by a boat and then pulled in by someone on the shore. Obviously, the fishermen had no choice about the kind of fish that would be caught in the net. Some were good for market, and some were not. The fishermen separated the good from the bad and threw the bad away. Again, the angels are those who separate the righteous from the wicked, the good from the bad. The wicked are thrown into the furnace of fire.

Reference to the fishing process is not unusual in the New Testament since Jesus said He would make His disciples fishers of men (Mark 1:17). The spreading of the gospel will result in false and true believers being gathered in. As the kingdom grows, many of its professing members will be genuine, and many will not.

The truth of these parables keeps believers from becoming overly disturbed by unbelievers in the kingdom. The fact that there will be unbelievers simply substantiates the truth of the Word of God. If the Lord senses the need for purging His kingdom before the judgment, He certainly can bring about persecution that will accomplish that end.

II. Growth of the Kingdom

The mustard seed (Matt. 13:31–32). The seed of the mustard plant, *Sinapis nigra*, is extremely small. Many rabbis used the metaphor "small as a mustard seed." The mustard plant, however, grows to the size of a small tree (six to twelve feet tall) in the rich soil of the Jordan Valley. In comparison with other shrubs, it is "a tree" that provides food and a resting place for birds. The birds in the parable probably represent the peoples of the world (Ezek. 17:23; 31:6), meaning that individuals from all over the world will find shelter in the gospel. The gospel began its influence in an area limited geographically and even racially, but this influence has since grown to great proportions in both respects. From small beginnings has come a great body of believers.

The leaven (Matt. 13:33–35). This parable has caused a difference of opinion among Bible interpreters. Some have seen the yeast as representing the influence of the gospel even though nowhere else in Scripture does leaven represent good. In fact, it uniformly symbolizes evil (Matt. 16:6; 1 Cor. 5:6–8; Gal. 5:9). In specific cases of symbolism, however, an object, plant, or animal may represent something different from context to context. Since this parable forms a pair with the mustard seed, and since growth is the point, it is strongly possible that the leaven represents the spreading of the kingdom's influence and growth just as a small quantity of yeast spreads throughout dough.

If the concept of evil, generally attached to leaven, is included in the explanation, then the parable is teaching the spreading of evil throughout the kingdom. Certainly sin has always been present in the kingdom, but to conclude that it will increase in its pervasiveness nearer the end of the age is not necessary. In the church and in the world, the believer and false professor live side by side for now.

III. The Worth of the Gospel

The treasure (Matt. 13:44). The meaning of this parable hinges on what the treasure represents. It is best to see the treasure as salvation. In life people often seemingly stumble onto the gospel by accident, like the man who went to look at the field and found the treasure in it. The drastic action the man took to obtain the treasure is a good picture of true repentance. Everything else that he had was no longer worth keeping; he sold it all to get that field and the treasure. No one is ever saved by accident, but the way some come to the truth does appear that way at times. They are not looking for the truth; but when they hear it, they respond and are converted.

The pearl (Matt. 13:45–46). The next parable illustrates a contrasting way people come to Christ. In this case a man was looking for high-quality pearls; when he found a valuable one, he sold all he had and bought it. The man was searching for pearls by design. The pearl is best understood as representing Christ. He is the One of inherent value. He alone is worth searching for and giving up all for.

> Regardless of the way we discover the gospel, it is worth everything. Whether your students have grown up in Christian homes or have just recently been exposed to scriptural truth, they must devote themselves wholeheartedly to it.

In summary, some people find Christ when they are not looking for Him, whereas others find Him as a conclusion to a long search for the truth. Either way, people enter the kingdom and contribute to its growth one by one.

IV. Effective Teaching

The final kingdom parable describes the "scribe of the kingdom" (Matt. 13:52–53). A scribe is an expert in the Scripture—today the pastor-teacher or evangelist. The scribe is likened to a householder, the one who controls all the resources of the household. He brings out valuable items (that have been stored) for trading, purchasing, and giving for the needs of others.

This is the role of the pastor-teacher. He must bring forth ideas of value from the Word of God for the hearts of his hearers. Some of the ideas will be new, freshly presented, and keenly insightful. Others will be old truths, familiar and stabilizing. He will preach the examples and illustrations of the Old Testament, and he will explain the doctrines of the New. His ministry will be varied and interesting. What he offers will be of value, a respectable contribution in the marketplace of ideas.

The kingdom thrives or languishes, depending on the quality of the presentation of the Word of God. Weak preaching makes for weak churches. Strong preaching, responded to by fervent hearts, sets churches on the march to victory.

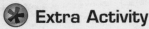

Extra Activity

Writing: Have your students write a two-page report on the different church groups represented in your community. Bring a telephone book to class and assign students to each kind of church. (Though each student will do his own paper, there may not be enough churches for each student to have a different one.) You can make this especially interesting if you give the three major church groups in the area to the three best students in your class. They will provide good material for class discussion. Your students will need to do research on the Internet, gather information in the library, or interview the pastors of these churches (with your approval, of course). Choose the best of the two-page reports the students have prepared, and have these students present their reports in class.

Benefits of this project include the opportunity to point out the conservative beginnings of many churches that now are extremely liberal. Help your students see that not all those who call themselves Christian are genuine followers of Christ. The good churches in the community will help your students see how the kingdom is growing as Jesus said it would.

Lesson 49
Managing Money

THEME	The Unjust Steward
SCRIPTURE	Luke 16:1–15
MEMORY WORK	Luke 16:10

 ## Approach to the Lesson

Theme: The Word of God teaches that a person should manage his money rightly, using it for necessities and the work of Christ. A person who is faithful with his money will have great spiritual opportunities. A person who is unfaithful will have few or no opportunities for spiritual service.

Rationale: Your students probably see money only as something of benefit to them. Teach them that their money is not theirs; it is a resource entrusted to them to be used in God's service.

Background: Just three months before His death, while in Perea, Jesus instructed His disciples about managing their money for the glory of God. He began His instruction with what is usually called the parable of the unjust steward. This parable is unusual in that the steward was clearly dishonest. Yet the Lord told His disciples that they should be similarly shrewd with their money in God's service. Jesus was not commending the man's dishonesty, only his shrewdness in financial management. This was the only case in which Jesus used a bad person to illustrate a good quality. You will probably want to make this clear to your students before you begin.

The Lesson

I. Using Money to Build Eternal Friendships (Luke 16:1–9)

In the beginning of this parable, the rich man accuses his steward of poor management. Notice that he did not accuse him of dishonesty. Someone else had drawn the rich man's attention to the steward's inefficiency. The steward was given the opportunity to prove he had not been inefficient. If he could not, then he would lose his position. How had the steward been inefficient? There were large debts owed his lord, which he had apparently done nothing about. Any efficient manager

would see to it that debts were paid. Perhaps this was his problem. In any case, the steward knew he hadn't managed his master's finances properly and that he needed to prepare for the future.

The steward was dishonest in the way he solved his problem. He had grown accustomed to making a good income without doing manual labor. He was not strong enough to do physical work and was too proud to be a beggar. So he committed himself to a swindling scheme. He clearly made the wrong choice. He cheated his employer in order to ingratiate himself to every one of his lord's debtors. The amounts the steward discounted the debts are staggering. For example, a hundred measures of oil is about 850 gallons. The amount forgiven was 425 gallons of olive oil. A hundred measures of wheat is about 1,100 bushels. The amount forgiven was roughly 825 bushels. He apparently offered similar deals to *all* those who owed his master something.

It wasn't long before the rich man discovered what the steward had done. What is surprising is the way he reacted; he must have been extremely rich to handle the situation as he did. He commended the steward for his shrewd actions. Perhaps it was because the steward had learned these "tricks of the trade" from the rich man himself.

Jesus then drew an application for Christians. "For the children of this world are in their generation wiser than the children of light" (Luke 16:8). This man had been shrewd with the money at his disposal. He had made a number of friends or at least had obligated many people to himself. We should be just as shrewd with our money by managing it for spiritual causes. Our Lord said, "Make to yourselves friends of

Objectives

KNOWLEDGE (concepts students need to grasp)	Scripture sometimes uses bad examples to teach good qualities
	the definition of *unrighteous mammon*
APPLICATION (principles students should put into practice)	When money manages us instead of our managing money, then money is our god.
	Proper use of material wealth can result in people being saved.
	How a person manages his material wealth determines the degree of his spiritual wealth.

Outline

the mammon of unrighteousness; that, when ye fail, they may receive you into everlasting habitations" (16:9). By this He meant that we are to make spiritual friends by means of the material wealth at our disposal. The word *mammon* means "wealth" in Greek. This mammon is called unrighteous because unrighteousness is often connected with the getting of money. Money is not good in itself; it is only good when used properly. Until it comes into the hands of a righteous person, it is likely to be misused.

The friends we make by means of material wealth may be waiting for us in heaven when we die. This is the meaning of the statement, "When ye fail, they may receive you into everlasting habitations" (16:9). Those we bring to Christ by using our money for evangelism become our spiritual brothers and sisters. This parable establishes the importance of giving to missions and evangelism.

This is a responsibility every Christian must take seriously. Even your students are not too young to start their missionary giving. They are also not too young to buy gospel tracts to distribute. Using their money to pay a friend's way to a youth activity would be another way of fulfilling this directive.

II. Viewing Money as a Test (Luke 16:10–12)

In addition to seeing money as a means of evangelism, Jesus taught that the use of money is a test. If a person is faithful with money, then the Lord knows He can trust him with greater spiritual responsibility. If he is unfaithful with money, then the opposite is true. Going a step further, Jesus directs our attention to eternity: if we have

> The student text pages for this lesson begin on the next page.

not been faithful in this life of stewardship, then the Lord will limit our inheritance in heaven. Our rewards will not be as large as they could have been.

III. Putting Money in Its Place (Luke 16:13–15)

One of the great temptations in managing money is to let it manage us. Money can become a god. People are naturally inclined to devote themselves wholeheartedly to one thing. If our devotion begins to center on money, our devotion to Christ will become secondary. We will love the one and hate the other, or vice-versa. There simply is not room for wholehearted devotion to two things: "Ye cannot serve God and mammon" (16:13).

Thus money must be secondary. In this life money may offer the opportunity to acquire possessions. It may provide a measure of influence or power. These ideas must not sway us. We must rest contentedly with the possessions God provides. We must hunger only for the spiritual influence that comes through the presence of Christ in a holy life.

The Pharisees opposed what Jesus was saying. They were covetous and did not like the priorities He established. They probably accused Him of being impractical and unrealistic in a material world.

This is usually the way covetous people justify their perspective. They say, "Well, we have to eat, have a home, and have clothes on our back!" Nobody would argue with that, but a covetous person may be hiding behind those remarks. He is never satisfied with the necessities of life; he must always have more.

Our culture testifies to the intense craving of Americans for possessions. Your students are already being infected with this spirit. A warning to them is highly appropriate. They don't have to be adults to get caught in this trap.

Bible Expressions to Understand

steward—one who manages another person's household or business
mammon—riches; material wealth
everlasting habitations—heaven

In 1844, Henry John Heinz was born near Pittsburgh, Pennsylvania, into a close-knit Christian family. As a young man, Heinz worked on the family farm. He frequently took his produce to stores in town to sell it. One day Heinz had the idea of selling products bottled or canned so that they could be moved over longer distances and kept fresh until they were needed. He started by selling bottled horseradish and soon began to offer pickles, ketchup, mustard, and many other products, including his famous steak sauce. Eventually the H. J. Heinz Company took as its motto "57 Varieties" because of the number of items it produced.

While still a young businessman, Heinz made an important decision. His church, wanting to pay off a debt, asked five members to donate a certain amount of money. Heinz believed that God wanted him to promise the money, but he didn't have it. Finally, Heinz decided to trust God and promise the money anyway. Soon afterward, his business improved and he was able to fulfill the pledge. From this experience, H. J. Heinz learned to put God first in his business. For the rest of his life, Heinz used his wealth to serve God. He gave especially to Sunday school work, and when he died, Heinz left $300,000 for the training of Sunday school teachers. In his will Heinz wrote, "I desire to set forth, at the very beginning of this Will, as the most important Item in it, a confession of my faith in Jesus Christ as my Savior."

H. J. Heinz lived by the principles the Lord Jesus taught in the parable of the unjust steward. A wealthy man called in his steward because he'd found out that the steward had "wasted his goods." When the steward saw that he was about to lose his job, he was desperate because he didn't want to do manual labor or become a beggar. He called in his master's debtors and reduced their debts to win their friendship,

The food company H. J. Heinz started is today a $2.5 billion international corporation and sells several thousand different products (not just fifty-seven). Mr. Heinz liked to say, "To do a common thing uncommonly well brings success."

176

Jesus saw through the Pharisees' attitude. They rationalized their preoccupation with money, but God knew their hearts. Their selfish focus was an abomination to Him. The solution was repentance, not whitewashing. No wonder Jesus once called these men "whited sepulchres" (Matt. 23:27). Rather than let their conviction turn into repentance, they became angry with Christ for His words.

planning to go to them after he lost his job. When the master found out what he'd done, he praised him for his wise act. Although the master lost a great deal of income, he realized that the steward had planned shrewdly.

Jesus used this story to teach three lessons. First, we should use what money we have to win people to Christ. We're stewards of the opportunities God has given us. One day our lives will end. When they do, will we meet people who are in heaven because they were saved as a result of our giving? The dishonest steward had enough discernment to make friends by the use of money, so he would have someone to help him when his stewardship was over. Jesus wasn't telling us to be dishonest but to be wise and manage our money well so that people would become our friends in the Lord.

Second, Jesus taught that the way we use our money determines both our opportunity and our reward. Christ said, "If therefore ye have not been faithful in the unrighteous mammon, who will commit to your trust the true riches?" (Luke 16:11). The true riches spoken of in this statement represent spiritual responsibility. If we can't be trusted, our opportunities to serve the Lord will be limited. "And if ye have not been faithful in that which is another man's, who shall give you that which is your own?" (16:12). We receive what is our own when we receive our inheritance in heaven—eternal rewards. These benefits will be ours to enjoy because we are children of God and have followed Christ faithfully in this life. Our rewards will be in proportion to our faithfulness.

Third, Jesus taught the proper place of money. Money is a powerful thing. A person can become so concerned about material wealth that everything else becomes secondary. When this happens, money has become his god. The Lord won't let this situation go on for long. He'll correct these wrong priorities. The Lord always knows whether money is the most important thing to us. We cannot hide that fact from God.

Do You Have a Money Management Problem?

The Word of God teaches that you should manage your money the right way—wisely using it for necessities and for the work of Christ. Using money to reach others with the gospel is what Christ desires. A person who's faithful with his finances will have great spiritual opportunities and rewards. Your money should never manage you; you should manage it for the glory of God.

Do You Remember?

1. Why was the steward in danger of losing his position? _____
   because he was accused of wasting his master's goods

2. How did he act wisely? _____
   He reduced the debts of his master's debtors in order to win their friendship.

3. How many of the master's debtors had their debts reduced? *all of them*

4. What is the great principle of faithfulness stated in Luke 16:10? _____
   He that is faithful in that which is least is faithful also in much.

5. What happens to those who are faithful in the small responsibilities that God gives them? *They are given greater responsibilities and opportunities.*

177

✳ Extra Activities

Giving: Select a missionary on deputation. Explain the purpose of deputation to your students (to raise prayer and financial support). Then introduce the missionary you have chosen. Have one student make a container in which offerings can be deposited. These offerings may be collected periodically at your discretion. At the end of the semester or school year, have a student write the missionary a letter to be signed by the class and sent with the gift. If possible, have the missionary come and present his work to the class.

Speaker: Have a pastor or the administrator of your school speak to the class about the importance of careful financial management in Christian ministries. Encourage him to bring copies of the budget of his church or school so the students gain an understanding of the need for financial planning in Christian ministries.

Lesson 50
Covetousness

THEME	The Rich Fool
SCRIPTURE	Luke 12:13–21
MEMORY WORK	Luke 12:15

Approach to the Lesson

Theme: A person with an insatiable and uncontrolled desire for material things is covetous. His life is governed by the idea that life consists of the things that he possesses. No Christian should allow this attitude to characterize his life. A believer should demand of himself that he be content with the things he has and seek only what he needs. Trusting in the grace of God, he can say, "I am satisfied with what I have and with the riches of the Spirit in Christ."

Rationale: Review Lesson 24 and again emphasize the sinfulness of an inordinate devotion to possessions. But note that covetousness goes beyond mere materialism; it includes a desire for anything outside of God's will.

Background: Covetousness is condemned in the Ten Commandments and repeatedly throughout the Old Testament. It is a regular theme of the New Testament writers and is addressed at least four times in the life and teachings of Jesus. This passage presents Christ's most direct teaching on the subject.

Objectives

KNOWLEDGE (concepts students need to grasp)	the term *covetousness*
	the circumstances in which covetousness may be a problem
APPLICATION (principles students should put into practice)	We should not continually want a larger income, new clothes, or greater leisure.
	We should not constantly work to acquire more money while neglecting other responsibilities.

L.50 Covetousness

Read: Luke 12:13–21   Memorize: Luke 12:15

Bible Expression to Understand

bestow—collect or gather up

Have you ever heard the expression "the almighty dollar"? Since *almighty* means "having absolute power," this adjective cannot accurately be applied to anyone or anything other than God Himself, but the phrase is a good indication of the way some people view money. What do you think about money? What's good and bad about it? How should you earn it? How should you spend it? How much do you need? How much should you give to your church and other Christian organizations?

The most crucial question is whether money will become your god. That may sound like a strange issue to raise, but it isn't. Every person has to settle it. If all the decisions you make in life are determined by money, then money is your god; and if money is your god, then you're what the Bible calls covetous.

Jesus talked about covetousness several times during His ministry. For example, when a man asked Jesus to persuade his brother to give him part of an inheritance, Jesus responded by telling the parable of the rich fool.

The first thing to learn from this parable is that a person can have all the money he wants or needs and still be covetous (Luke 12:17–18). The farmer was both rich and greedy.

The conclusion he came to after having a good crop wasn't that he should share part of his increase with others but that he should build bigger barns for himself. A person can be poor and greedy, moderately prosperous and greedy, or rich and greedy. Covetousness isn't a sin of those in a particular economic condition.

The rich man's strategy of building bigger barns so he could hang on to all his wealth turned out to be tragically shortsighted. What are some ways covetousness motivates people today to build "bigger barns"?

178

⭐ The Lesson

I. Injured Relationships (Luke 12:13–14)

Soon after the Lord's discussion of the blasphemy against the Holy Spirit, a listener approached Him about his brother's failure to share an inheritance with him. Christ refused to be drawn into this family squabble, choosing rather to address the spiritual problem of both brothers. That problem was covetousness. This approach is instructive. The Lord could have worked out this particular dispute with arbitration, but the long-term problem would have remained. Jesus performed spiritual surgery on the cancer of covetousness that afflicted this man. Confrontation (getting the man to face his own spiritual condition) was the answer. Though not used in this passage, the Greek word for *reprove* or *admonish* appears seventeen times in the New Testament. It is clearly a Christian responsibility. Six times the Bible commands it.

Loving confrontation for the purpose of long-term correction is God's will for the believer. Encourage your students to obey the Lord by following His example. Covetousness can crop up at any time. For example, the passing of a loved one is a sad time, but the focus may suddenly shift when the will is discussed. At the dividing of an inheritance, people often become greedy, but a Christian should demonstrate love and consideration for others. Remind students that maintaining and building their Christian testimony is far more important than material gain through inheritance. Fighting and bickering with relatives over such matters is not Christlike.

The second lesson is that a covetous person is out to accumulate far more than he needs so that he can spend money on virtually anything he wants. The statement of the rich man "Take thine ease, eat, drink, and be merry" sums up his attitude. He intended to indulge himself. All his wealth was a way for him to stop working. Life would be one long vacation. He also intended to eat and drink. That sounds reasonable. Everyone has to eat and drink, but his desires went beyond normal eating and drinking. This, in fact, would become one of his primary pastimes. Banqueting and partying would become a major part of his life. To complete his activities, he would "be merry," providing entertainment for himself and his friends.

A desire for ease, lavish foods, and constant entertainment is the reason many people seek money. Covetous people want more when they already have enough. Measure yourself against the attitude of this man. If you hate work and can never get enough free time, you have an excessive desire for what you don't need. You're lazy and covetous. If you can never watch enough videos, play enough computer games, talk long enough to your friends, or buy enough clothes, you're covetous.

The spirit behind covetousness is a dissatisfaction that comes from comparing your circumstances to someone else's. That leads to a desire to have more, which is covetousness. This in turn results in actually getting more and more of what you want and hoarding it. If the greed cannot be satisfied, then there's frustration, which usually finds expression in complaining. To state the case simply, covetousness makes a mess of everything.

The third lesson from the rich fool is that there is no point in coveting. If you covet and get what you want, you still won't be satisfied. You'll live your life in dissatisfaction until one day God stops the whole process and asks you to give an account of your life. What will you have to show for all those years of wanting, getting, and worshiping the almighty dollar? Absolutely nothing. In contrast, the person who's content and generous is spiritually wealthy. Be this kind of person.

Is Your "Wanter" Out of Control?

Is it wrong to want things? No. So how do you know when you're coveting? You'll know when you're preoccupied with getting more. You'll know when you have little gratitude for all the blessings God has already given you. You'll know when you leave God out of your purchases and your decisions about how to use your money. These are all signs that your heart is fixated on "stuff" in the world and not on God. "Love the Lord thy God with all thy heart." "In all thy ways acknowledge Him." "In everything give thanks."

179

II. Inaccurate Views of Life (Luke 12:15)

Jesus said to take heed and beware. The Lord underscored His warning twice at the outset. Why does He show this intense concern? Covetousness is one of those thorny plants that can easily spring up and choke out the effect of the Word of God in the life of a person. Obsession with material things is certainly a "care of this world" (Matt. 13:22). This problem can deteriorate into an all-consuming drive if a person is not on his guard. The attitude that says, "I must have more," may easily infiltrate the heart that says, "I am satisfied." This attitude can take over because it is easy for us to think of the material things in life as what will really satisfy. This world and all it offers are only temporary, so our focus should be on eternal spiritual realities (Col. 3:1).

Jesus doesn't condemn the reasonable acquiring of what we need and may appropriately desire; it is the tyranny of things that He warns against. The material must never be our master.

III. Inadequate Preparation for Eternity (Luke 12:16–21)

The parable first presents the prosperity of the covetous rich man. The man was a wealthy farmer whose land produced well for him. This came through the grace of God. The wealthy man's skill as a farmer may have had a lot to do with the prosperity he was enjoying, but God was gracious to him. No farmer prospers without the right weather and good soil, and these matters are God's business. Because he was out of storage space, the man began to consider what to do. He concluded that he would need to build larger barns. This demonstrates sound judgment. What else could the man do for the immediate future?

The problem began as the man pondered his wealth. His prosperity did not motivate him toward thanksgiving to God or generosity to the needy. Instead he determined that the purpose of his wealth was to allow him to be free of work, to have abundant provision, and to enjoy entertainment. The man's statement shows that he viewed life in terms of material prosperity. He had wealth, so everything would be all right. He was incredibly shortsighted.

Consider in detail the wrong conclusions this man drew from his prosperity. He concluded first that a result of his prosperity would be freedom from work. Work is God's will; it is necessary. People must be stewards of their time. For an individual to waste his life in leisure is far from God's ideal. A person who won't work doesn't deserve to eat (2 Thess. 3:10).

The second wrong conclusion looks harmless on the surface. To eat and drink certainly sounds legitimate. But the statement implies sumptuous banqueting as a way to while away the hours.

The third wrong conclusion is that wealth was intended to provide endless entertainment. (Nowadays, a second home on the lake, a big-screen TV, a yearly three-week cruise, and frequent shopping sprees have become the preoccupation of some.) The man in the parable was more concerned about his amusements than he was about being productive.

No wonder God called the rich man a fool. He had not given a moment's thought to God, life beyond this life, or the needs of others. He failed to consider that he would take nothing material with him from this life. He hadn't made any provision for the life of his soul. Others would acquire all his wealth.

This passage begins with a man asking the Lord to settle a dispute over inheritance

Outline

(Luke 12:13–21)
Covetousness results in . . .
I. Injured relationships (13–14)
II. Inaccurate views of life (15)
III. Inadequate preparation for eternity (16–21)

and ends with the Lord telling the rich fool that all his wealth will be an inheritance for others. It's that way with all personal wealth. But God assures us that we can choose to be rich toward Him in this life. People can use their wealth properly; they don't have to be covetous and foolish.

Encourage your students to set God's cause as a financial priority. Part of their allowance and any other money they earn should be used to advance the kingdom of God. Giving at church or helping a needy family is being rich toward God.

✳ Extra Activities

Discussion: The following series of questions will help you spark a class discussion about covetousness. Most of your students will not have given this subject any thought, but the seeds of covetousness are sown during the teen years. They need to be uprooted, so that seeds of contentment can be planted in their place.

a. Why are people supposed to work?
God commands it.

b. What are the basic needs God has promised to provide for His people?
food and clothing (Matt. 6:26–33; 1 Tim. 6:6–8)

c. Is it all right to spend money on entertainment?
Yes, but entertainment should not be a major expense.

d. How should a teenager use his money?
in order of priority: (1) giving, (2) saving, (3) expenses, (4) entertainment

e. When is it right to buy something new?
It is right when what you presently own is worn out or no longer appropriate. Whether something is appropriate may be determined by the following questions:
(1) Does what I own cause me to look my best, reflecting honor on the Lord?
(2) Does what I own draw unnecessary attention to itself?
(3) Does what I own allow me to perform to the best of my abilities?

Do You Remember?

1. What did the man in Luke 12:13 ask Jesus to do? _____
   He asked Jesus to speak with his brother about dividing an inheritance.

2. How did Jesus respond to the man's request? _____
   He refused to speak to the man's brother and told a parable instead.

3. What kind of financial circumstances was the farmer in when he became covetous? _____
   He was rich.

4. What did the farmer intend to do after he had filled his new barns? _____
   take it easy, eat and drink, and be merry

5. What did God call the farmer? *a fool*

6. What had the farmer failed to consider? _____
   the temporary nature of material possessions

7. How can a person be rich toward God? _____
   by being thankful and content

180

(4) Does what I own look right only for older or younger people?
(5) Will what I want to buy cause others to view me as wasteful and extravagant?

Scripture search: Looking up and summarizing the main ideas of the following passages should help your students see the danger of covetousness.

a. Prohibited (Luke 12:15; Eph. 5:3)
b. Turns a person from salvation (1 Cor. 6:10)
c. Considered idolatry (Col. 3:5)
d. Root of other sins (1 Tim. 6:9–10)
  (1) Lying (2 Kings 5:20–27; Acts 5:1–10)
  (2) Theft (Josh. 7:21)
  (3) Domestic troubles (Prov. 15:27)
  (4) Murder (1 Kings 21:1–13)

  (5) Betrayal (Matt. 26:14–16)
  (6) Lack of trust in God (Heb. 13:5)
e. Distracts from true riches
  (1) Grace (Eph. 1:7; 2:7)
  (2) Glory (Rom. 9:23; Eph. 1:18; Phil. 4:19)

Seeking the Lost — 51

Bible Expressions to Understand

publican—a Jew who collected taxes for the Roman government
sinner—a person who did not follow the Jewish law or traditions
pieces of silver—Greek coins, each worth about a day's wages
riotous living—uncontrolled, wasteful activities
fain—to desire

Your school probably has a lost-and-found department. If you're like most people, you have gone there once in a while. Probably you've been disappointed in some cases because you didn't find what you'd lost. Nobody likes that.

The Lord Jesus Christ describes those who don't know Him as "lost" people. He wants them to be found. In the Scripture reading for this lesson, you read three parables that Jesus told about lost things. He presented these parables because the Pharisees thought that He shouldn't be so concerned about lost people. The parables teach why we should be concerned about them and how we can show that concern.

In the first parable, Jesus told about a sheep that wandered away from the flock (Luke 15:4–7). It was in serious danger because it could easily fall into a ravine or be killed by a wild animal. When people wander away from God, they're also in danger. Satan will try to destroy them through sin. Your friends and relatives who have never been saved are in that kind of danger. They need you to show them the way to Christ. You can do this by living the right kind of life and telling them the gospel.

In the second parable, the Lord talked about a woman who had lost a coin in her house. When people lose money, they usually look hard for it. That's what this woman did. The coin she lost was worth a lot—a whole day's wages. This would be like losing a hundred-dollar bill today. Lost money is not worth anything; it is useless until it is found. Lost people are useless to God, but He still loves them. If you'll find them by giving them the gospel, they can live worthwhile, useful lives.

The last parable that Jesus presented in response to the Pharisees was about a lost son who got some money from his father and left home. He wasted the money and began to think about home. While he'd been at home, he couldn't wait to get away. When he got away, he realized that home wasn't such a bad place after all. He decided to go home and ask his father to

The shepherd went to great lengths, enduring inconvenience, discomfort, fatigue, and danger, to rescue that one little lamb.

181

Lesson 51
Seeking the Lost

Theme	Parables About Lost Things
Scripture	Luke 15:1–32
Memory Work	Luke 15:10

Approach to the Lesson

Theme: Having the mind of Christ results in a deep and abiding concern for those who don't know Him. This concern results in specific efforts to communicate the gospel to them.

Rationale: Jesus once prayed about His followers, "As thou hast sent me into the world, even so have I also sent them into the world" (John 17:18). Earlier in His ministry He stated, "For the Son of man is come to save that which was lost" (Matt. 18:11). Soulwinning should have priority in the life of the Christian. No believer can be a true disciple and not share Christ's burden for those who have not heard the gospel. Impress on your students the need to make evangelism a priority. Emphasize that they do not have to be saved for a certain amount of time, nor do they have to be a certain age. They can win souls now.

Background: The Lord taught the parables about the three lost things during His last year of public ministry. This year is often called "the year of opposition"

Objectives

KNOWLEDGE (concepts students need to grasp)	the reason for this parable (the improper attitude toward sinners manifested by the religious establishment)
	that all three parables emphasize the same truth (the importance of winning the unsaved)
APPLICATION (principles students should put into practice)	Christ's emphasis in soulwinning was on the importance of the individual lost person.
	Soulwinning has an edifying effect on the Christian and the church as a whole.
	Isolating ourselves from lost people is dangerous.
	We should be aggressively optimistic in witnessing for Christ.

because the Jewish leaders opposed Him fiercely during this time. This parable is a response to the Pharisees' accusations against the Lord because of His constant efforts to gain followers. He often did this by associating with them in their homes over meals (Luke 7:34).

During a time of preaching in Jerusalem Jesus had encountered serious resistance. He had left the area temporarily and traveled east to Perea, where the confrontation recorded in Luke 15:1–3 took place. When the passage mentions "all the publicans and sinners," it is referring to all the tax collectors and disreputable people in that region. Jesus was enjoying considerable success in His evangelistic ministry with these people.

Neither of these groups was appreciated by the Pharisees. The *publicans* were Jews who had purchased the right to collect taxes from their fellow Jews for the Roman empire. They were viewed as religiously and politically disloyal because of their activities and were generally perceived as dishonest. The *sinners* were Jews who did not concern themselves with following either the law or the minute religious regulations developed by the rabbis. The Pharisees viewed social contact with these people as polluting, so it's not surprising that the religious leaders would slander the Lord for His involvement with these outcasts.

Outline

 ## The Lesson

I. The Lost Are Directionless (Luke 15:4–7)

In Israel, pastureland was scarce. The plateau region is often bounded by cliffs or canyons. The shepherd was personally responsible for the sheep, usually a flock of the sheep belonging to a whole village. In the parable of the lost sheep, there were at least two shepherds, since one left the main flock to search for the lost sheep. When he found it, he carried it on his shoulders back to his home in the village, where general rejoicing prevailed.

This is the time to impress your students on the terrible danger the unsaved are in. Their friends and relatives who do not know Christ are wasting the valuable time and energy of their lives, making no progress toward heaven, but rather drifting toward hell.

People without Christ are wandering, directionless, and in grave danger of destruction. The Devil, like a roaring lion, walks around looking for someone he can destroy (1 Pet. 5:8). People need to be led back to the Overseer and Shepherd of their souls (1 Pet. 2:25).

The Lord makes some important applications from the parable. When He states, "Likewise joy shall be in heaven over one sinner that repenteth" (Luke 15:7), He is emphasizing the joy it brings to the heart of God when even one person is converted. The ninety-nine righteous people who need no repentance represent the Pharisees, who viewed themselves as free from any need to turn from sin.

Begin to build in your students a keen understanding of the importance of one person brought to God and taught in the Christian faith. Quantity is not the Lord's emphasis. Our vision for lost people must be as wide as the world, but realistically our personal practice will always be to win them one by one.

allow him to work on their farm as just a hired servant. But when he arrived home, his father forgave him completely for the wrong he'd done and accepted him back as a son.

Twice the father described the son as dead but alive again. When you help someone come to Christ, you're helping him come to life in his relationship with God. Before a person turns from his sins, he's dead as far as God is concerned. God isn't pleased with anything he does or says. But when you explain the gospel and he believes in the Lord Jesus, he immediately comes to life spiritually and becomes part of the family of God.

In these parables, the Lord described lost people as directionless, worthless, and lifeless. When they are saved, though, everything in their lives changes. You can be part of what brings about that change in people by being a witness for the Lord Jesus Christ.

These parables also tell how to be a good witness for Christ. You must be persistent. You shouldn't become discouraged and give up in your witnessing. The shepherd, the woman, and the father all refused to give up on what they had lost.

These parables teach us that we should be optimistic about our witnessing for Christ. Each lost item in these parables was found. Some people who are lost will be found by the Lord Jesus through our witnessing.

Are You Looking for Lost People?

You need to be concerned about people who don't know Jesus Christ as Savior. Show this concern by telling them about what He's done for them by His death on the cross.

The lost one is the most important one. The shepherd was concerned about the lost sheep, not the ninety-nine that he had. The woman was concerned about the one piece of silver that was lost, not the nine coins she still had. The father was deeply concerned over the lost son, though he loved his other son as well. How concerned are you about lost people?

182

II. The Lost Are Valueless (Luke 15:8–10)

The lost coin was a silver drachma, a little more than one day's wage in that day. Such a coin could buy a sheep or pay one-fifth of the price for an ox, one of the largest domesticated animals in the Middle East. The loss of such a coin would have been a serious blow. In the homes of poor Israelites, a coin dropped on the dirt floor could easily have been lost. The houses were usually dimly lit by one or two small windows. The woman diligently searched for the coin until she found it. As with the shepherd, she called her neighbors together so that they could rejoice over her good news.

Our Lord makes the same application of this parable as of the first: joy abounds in the presence of the angels of God over one sinner who repents. Note that in this case the angels are the ones rejoicing. One of the privileges we enjoy is that of proclaiming the gospel to the lost. The angelic army does not enjoy this opportunity. However, they do take great interest in our work of evangelism.

Help your students grasp the overwhelming significance of this truth. The angels enjoy greater intelligence, mobility, and power than we; yet it is not their task to win the unsaved to Christ. The task belongs to the students you are teaching. Challenge them with this responsibility.

The use of the coin in this parable is suggestive. Although normally a valuable object, when the coin was lost it was valueless for practical purposes. But the finding

Do You Remember?

1. How many sheep was the shepherd responsible for and how many strayed away? _____
   Out of one hundred, one had wandered away.

2. Where did the shepherd take the lost sheep when he found it? *back home* _____

3. How many pieces of silver did the woman lose? *one* _____

4. How did the younger son spend his money? _____
   He wasted it on "riotous living."

5. How did he support himself after his money was spent? *by feeding pigs* _____

6. What did he plan to do when he returned to his father? _____
   ask to be hired as a servant

7. How did the father treat him when he returned? _____
   He welcomed him with kindness and treated him as a son.

8. Why was the older brother angry? _____
   He was not treated as royally as his brother even though he had been faithful.

183

---

of the coin restored its value. Although God has endowed the unsaved with many priceless abilities and personality traits, as long as they are lost, they are valueless (from a spiritual perspective) to God and to others. At the moment of salvation, however, a person becomes of great value and usefulness to God (Philem. 11).

III. The Lost Are Spiritually Dead (Luke 15:11–32)

The parable of the prodigal son has been called "the greatest short story in the world." With pathos and power, it pictures the restoration of a lost soul to God. The father represents God; the prodigal son, repentant sinners; the elder son, the Pharisees. The prodigal son rebelled against his home and determined to live independently. He asked his father for his share of the inheritance; as the younger son, he was entitled to one-third. He soon wasted it all in "riotous living." (This is the source of the common name for this parable since *prodigal* means "wasteful" rather than "wayward," as many people assume.) To support himself during the ensuing famine, he took a job tending swine, a degrading position for a Jew since pigs are unclean animals. He got so hungry that he wanted to eat the same stuff he was feeding to the pigs—the long bean-shaped pods of the carob tree, a food containing a small amount of sugar and occasionally eaten by the poorest classes of people.

The sinful state symbolized here is characterized by (1) departure from God, (2) waste, (3) need, (4) bondage (Rom. 6:16), (5) dissatisfaction, and (6) death. The father twice speaks of his son as having been dead (15:24, 32).

In cultures where voodoo is prevalent, a *zombie* is a person who supposedly has died and come back to life, living in a stupor as if on drugs. People who are unsaved are spiritual zombies: alive but dead in terms of their sensitivity to God and His will. They are not alive to the reality of the spiritual realm and the claims of God on their lives. The light of the gospel must shine into their lives to awaken them out of their spiritual darkness.

When the son returned, there was great rejoicing in the household. The answer to the problem of waning enthusiasm in a local church is the conversion of the lost. No substitute will suffice.

Just as exuberant joy follows the birth of a baby, so it will follow the birth of someone into the family of God. Few things will make you or your students happier about being a Christian than winning an unsaved person to Christ.

In the second part of the parable, the focus shifts to the older brother, who was angry, boastful, and complaining. This brother pictures the Pharisees' attitude toward the common people who had received the gospel. They resented the fact that these people were received into the kingdom. In his resentment the older brother refused to enter the father's house. This was exactly what the Pharisees did in response to Jesus's message; even though the Father pleaded with them, they stood outside His house.

The pride of students who have grown up in Christian homes, good churches, and Christian schools may keep them from admitting that they are sinners who need to repent and be saved. Address this issue directly with your students, since many of them are in these circumstances.

IV. The Lost Can Be Found

Luke 15 teaches us the qualities of a good soulwinner by repeating certain elements in the parables. Notice that both the shepherd and the woman persisted until they found what they were looking for. Likewise the father constantly longed for the return of his son.

Stress to your students the quality of aggressiveness characterized by persistence as necessary in the life of an effective soulwinner.

Another attitude is optimism. Elsewhere the New Testament teaches that only a percentage of those to whom we preach will be saved (Matt. 13:18–23). Knowing this fact helps us to be realistic in our evangelistic endeavors. On the other hand, Luke 15 shows everything that was lost being found. A positive attitude toward witnessing is being encouraged. Not everyone will respond positively to our message, but some will!

 Extra Activities

Discussion: Discuss the following three-point approach to witnessing:

1. "May I show you from the Bible how to know God and to know that your sins are forgiven?"
2. "The Bible teaches that all have sinned and that sin causes death" (Rom. 3:23; 6:23).
3. "The Bible teaches that Jesus Christ can save us from our sins and give us eternal life" (Rom. 6:23; 10:13).

Testimonies: Have one or two of your students give testimonies about their witnessing experiences. If they can't provide testimonies, draw from your own experience.

Survey: When you begin this lesson, have your students write "Yes" or "No" to the following two questions:

1. Have you ever witnessed to one of your unsaved friends?
2. Has anyone ever been saved because of your witness for Christ?

Post the results of this survey at the end of the lesson. Of course, do not ask your students to put their names on their responses.

Field trip: Plan a special trip to a children's home, nursing home, or park in the community. To prepare for the trip, supply your students with tracts and have them role-play witnessing to each other using the plan above.

Lesson 52
Loving Others

THEME	The Good Samaritan
SCRIPTURE	Luke 10:25–37
MEMORY WORK	Luke 10:27

 Approach to the Lesson

Theme: The second greatest commandment is to love others as ourselves. Our love for God should result in love for others. This love manifests itself in the choice to sacrifice ourselves for the good of others. This giving is without any thought of return. God, by His power, enables the Christian to love this way. He is the source of this love because God Himself is love.

Rationale: Few teens actively seek to help others—even their friends. If an opportunity presents itself, they may act; but they normally do not go out of their way to find ways to help. Encourage them to look aggressively for opportunities to live out their faith by helping those in need.

Background: The parable of the good Samaritan is recorded only in Luke. Many of Jesus's parables have a future prophetic application or a reference to Israel in the past. This is only one of several that have a present meaning for Israel. It is primarily practical. Of course, the application is timeless, so it's as relevant to us as it was to the original hearers.

 The Lesson

I. Unlimited Love (Luke 10:25–29)

The lawyer (scribe) attended a meeting where Jesus was teaching. To attract His attention, the lawyer stood and tested Jesus with a question. Apparently he was trying to check Christ's skill in interpreting the law. It is also possible, as on other occasions in the Gospels, that he was trying to trap Jesus. When the man asked what he should do to inherit eternal life, Jesus responded by asking him what was written in the law. Perhaps He pointed to the phylactery on the lawyer's forehead or wrist as He asked the question. The lawyer responded by quoting Deuteronomy 6:5 (cf. Lev. 19:18), a verse carried inside the phylactery. Jesus

commended him for his answer, but the lawyer asked for further clarification.

The verse the lawyer quoted teaches an all-consuming love for God (as explained in Lesson 1), but he added an element that doesn't actually appear in the Hebrew text—loving God with all the mind. But Jesus concurred with his analysis because we are to dedicate all our thoughts and intellectual gifts to the Lord. We are also to love our neighbors as ourselves. The term used to describe our love for our neighbors is the same one used to describe our love for God. It is a giving, sacrificial, self-forgetful spirit that results in action for the good of a chosen person.

Unsatisfied that he had not trapped Jesus by his initial question, the lawyer then asked who his neighbor was. He was still trying to put Christ on the spot by testing His ability to interpret the law. Jesus responded by telling the story of the good Samaritan.

II. Superior Love (Luke 10:30–35)

The setting for the parable was the road between Jerusalem (2,400 feet above sea level) and Jericho (1,200 feet below sea level), a distance of about twenty-one miles. A traveler literally went down when traveling to Jericho. The narrow, winding road was noted for thieves. Jerome (fifth century AD) wrote that it was called "the red, or bloody, way." The man of the parable fell prey to thieves and was left "half dead."

Objectives

KNOWLEDGE (concepts students need to grasp)	the meaning of Christian love
	who they are responsible to love
APPLICATION (principles students should put into practice)	No amount of religious activity can take the place of love for others.
	People in physical need present an opportunity to demonstrate Christian love.
	The closest "neighbors" we have are our family members. They deserve our love.
	Our neighbors are not only those we know, but anyone with whom we come in contact who is in need.
	Love is giving, and the best gift is the gospel.

Outline

(Luke 10:25–37)
I. Unlimited love (25–29)
II. Superior love (30–35)
III. Far-reaching love (36–37)

A priest passed by the wounded man. Priests were supposed to act as intermediaries between God and man although by the time of Christ their corruption prevented them from acting as God's representatives. They were chosen from Aaron's descendants, members of the tribe of Levi. King David had divided them into twenty-four groups, each serving a week at a time. During the times they were not serving, they were free to return to their homes in other cities. This priest may have been returning to his home in Jericho after completing his service in the temple. In any case he saw the wounded man but did not stop. This is a sad commentary on the religious leadership of the time. If he was returning home from service in the temple, where he was seeking to fulfill the greatest command, the scene is even more pathetic. After praising God and serving Him in the holy temple, he left a needy man in the ditch.

> Our faith cannot be a Jekyll/Hyde faith. We cannot be loving and self-sacrificial toward God and then heartless toward our fellow human beings.

The next to come by was a Levite. The Levites were from the non-Aaronic families of the tribe of Levi. They were responsible for teaching the Law to the people and assisting the priests by guarding the temple, cleaning it, baking in connection with the sacrifices, and helping with the slaughter of animals. They too served only part of their time at the temple, remaining at home for the rest of the year. At the time of Christ, the Levites had become formal and legalistic. This one stopped to look at the

The student text pages for this lesson begin on the next page.

wounded man but then continued on his way, no doubt rationalizing away his obligation.

This lawyer needed to learn an important lesson from a person he viewed as a social outcast. To love others is to fulfill the second greatest commandment, second only to a man's love for God Himself.

Next came a Samaritan. The Samaritans were a mixed-race group that emerged after the Assyrian Emperor Sargon II's capture of the Northern Kingdom in 721 BC. He took the upper class of Israel captive and replaced it with slaves from other nations. From the intermarriage of these slaves with the remaining Israelites came the Samaritans. The idolatrous worship of the Samaritans caused great bitterness between the southern Jews and the Samaritans. When the Samaritans offered to help the Israelites rebuild the temple, they were rejected (Ezra 4:3). From that time on, hostility existed between the two groups, each having nothing to do with the other.

For this Samaritan to help the wounded Jew was a distinct act of mercy. That he was not rich seems evident from the fact that he provided only "two pence" (two days' wages) to care for the man. Though a Samaritan, he was more willing to help the wounded man than the religious leaders were.

III. Far-Reaching Love (Luke 10:36–37)

After relating this story, Jesus posed a question to the lawyer. The obvious answer was that anyone in need of help is our neighbor and is to be loved. The Samaritan bound up the man's wounds, took care of him, took him to the inn, and paid for his keep. This man on the side of the road, beaten and half-dead, was there through no fault of his own. He had been viciously attacked and robbed. Many who are poor are not in that condition because of foolish decisions or waste; they are in that state by uncontrollable human circumstance or injustice. They need help, and we must give it, especially to believers (Gal. 6:10). A person's spiritual need is the most important need, but close behind follow the other necessities of life. We must not and cannot forget those needs.

Bible Expressions to Understand

lawyer—one skilled in the Old Testament Law; usually a scribe
Levites—descendants of the tribe of Levi, set apart for the care of the tabernacle and later the temple
Samaritan—a person from Samaria; held in low regard by the Jews

A young lady in New York City was attacked and killed late at night while returning home. The many people who heard the girl's cries and even saw the murder from their apartment windows did nothing. The most common excuse was, "I didn't want to get involved." In another incident a woman was knocked to the sidewalk accidentally, breaking her leg. For almost an hour she pleaded with bankers, lawyers, stockbrokers, and other passersby to help her. Finally, a taxi driver helped her into his cab and took her to a hospital.

Why would people ignore others in need? Is this behavior typical only of modern America, or has it been characteristic of other people at other times. Does everyone act this way toward those needing help?

Twenty-first-century Americans aren't the only such people. Jesus's parable of the good Samaritan shows that even the religious leadership of that day was callous. In this parable a priest and a Levite, both religious leaders of the time, ignored a man who'd been robbed and beaten along the road to Jericho. Later a Samaritan, a natural enemy of the Jews, saw the man. He stopped, cared for the man's wounds, and carried him on his own animal to the nearest inn for further medical attention. The Samaritan gave money to the innkeeper, telling him to take care of the wounded man. If he needed to spend more, the Samaritan promised that he would pay any additional costs when he came again.

What reason did the Samaritan have for responding differently than the Jews? He understood the importance of loving others. You cannot love God and hate other people at the same time. In fact, you should focus on meeting the needs of other people

The phrase "good Samaritan" is never used in Scripture, but because of this parable the word *samaritan* now often connotes someone who helps people (not a despised ethnic minority as it did in Jesus's day).

184

Following the example of the Samaritan, we must love by doing, and not just by saying or feeling. Love is not to be limited by social class or race.

as a primary way to show your love for God. When your brother or sister is sick and jobs around the house need to be done, you should do those things well, without being asked. If your grandmother needs her house painted, take some time in the summer and do it without pay. If the man next door is ill and needs someone to keep his lawn cut, volunteer! Where there's a need, meet it. Don't think someone else will. If no one does and you wait, the opportunity may pass you by. Show your love for others now.

Whose Needs Have You Ignored Today?

The second greatest commandment in the Bible is to love others as we love ourselves. Our love for God should result in love for others. This love is a deliberate choice to sacrifice ourselves for the good of others. To unselfishly meet the needs of another is to love. This giving is without thought of return. God grants the Christian the ability to love this way. He's the source of this love because He is love.

Do You Remember?

1. Who tested Jesus with a question in this passage? _a lawyer (probably a scribe)_

2. What single word summarizes the whole Old Testament Law? _love_

3. Where was the man going when he was wounded by the thieves? _Jericho_

4. Who first passed by the wounded man? _a priest_

5. Who was the next man to pass the wounded man? _a Levite_

6. Who stopped to help the man? _a Samaritan_

7. How much money did the Samaritan give the innkeeper? _enough to take care of the man; two pence_

8. What promise did the Samaritan make to the innkeeper? _If the innkeeper spent more money, he would pay him when he returned._

185

✳ Extra Activities

Discussion: Have a panel discussion on the seven times Jesus was tested by questions from the Jewish leaders who were trying to trap Him. Looking at these passages will show your students that Jesus could not be trapped, even by the sharpest and most intellectually astute people of His time. You should be the moderator of the discussion, which means you will ask questions of each of three participants you select from the class. To prevent embarrassment, select the students ahead of time, give them the passages below, and guide them in searching out what Jesus was being tempted about and how He answered.

Speaker #1—Matt. 16:14
(Luke 11:16–23; Mark 8:10–12); Matt. 19:3–9 (Mark 10:1–9)

Speaker #2—Matt. 22:23–33
(Mark 12:18–27; Luke 20:27–38); Matt. 22:15–22 (Mark 12:14–17; Luke 20:19–26)

Speaker #3—Mark 11:27–33
(Matt. 21:23–27; Luke 20:1–8; John 8:3–11)

These events show the enmity between truth and error. The Jews continually sought to trap Jesus, either by enticing Him to deny the authority of the Old Testament or by forcing Him to take a position against Roman authority. Yet He was able to avoid their plots each time. The questions also show how difficult it is for an unsaved person to comprehend spiritual truth (1 Cor. 2:14).

Writing: Have each student write one page about a special ministry his church has to the needy. If his church does not have such a ministry, then the paper may be written as a suggestion of what could be done.

Field trip: Take your students to a poverty-stricken part of your community or a neighboring community. Prepare them by reading to them about specific cases of poverty and destitution in this country. You can find many resources and statistics on the Internet. Remind your students that the greatest human need is spiritual. Meeting people's physical needs may be a means to winning them to Christ.

Map 6
Modern Israel

Israel today is quite different from the Israel of Jesus's time, but the places where He lived, taught His followers, and performed miracles are still there.

[Note: Students will need to study or refer to this map in order to complete Map Exercise 4 (on the CD).]

Israel Past and Present

Many of Christ's parables are based on scenes from everyday life in first-century Palestine. In many ways, Israel today parallels Israel at the time of Christ. Many of the cities to which Christ traveled are still there today. The terrain is basically the same even though agricultural activity has increased in recent years because of irrigation.

For the most part, Israel today occupies the same area as it did in Christ's day. The width of the country varies from only a few miles wide in the north and the south to seventy miles across at its widest point. Similar in size to the small state of New Hampshire, Israel occupies about eight thousand square miles with a population of 6.8 million people.

Modern Israel is marked by cultural diversity, as it was in Christ's time. In those days Greek was the language of commerce and diplomacy in Israel. Rome ruled there, imposing its taxes, coinage, armies, and rulers. Today hundreds of thousands of Jews have returned to their homeland, bringing with them the native languages and cultures of Europe,

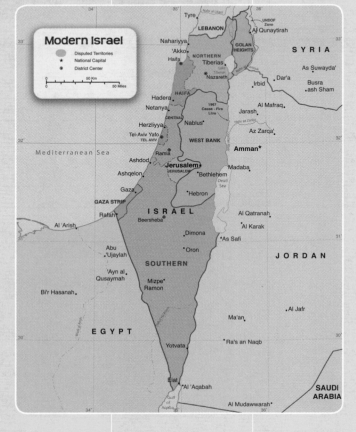

Modern Israel

- Disputed Territories
- ★ National Capital
- • District Center

0 — 50 Km
0 — 50 Miles

186

the Americas, Africa, and Asia. Israel is still strongly influenced by other nations.

Religious diversity within Palestine is as strong as it was in Christ's time. The Samaritans, a half-Jewish people with a competing religion, annoyed pure Jews in the first century, as is evident in the story of the woman at the well (John 4). Today Israel faces the "Palestinian question." Arab Palestinians, who once were almost the only residents of the land, now number 5.3 million (counting those in the occupied territories of the Gaza Strip and the West Bank), a "nation within a nation." In fact, the Palestinian population outnumbers the Jewish population. As Muslims, the Palestinian Arabs are viewed much as the Samaritans were. The majority of them live in the West Bank area, near where the Samaritans lived in Christ's time.

When Rome ruled Israel, there was great political unrest. The Jews resented being under a Gentile power. Some had hoped that, as the Messiah, Jesus would deliver them from political bondage (Luke 24:21). Today there's again a lot of political unrest in Israel. Although Israel is no longer under foreign oppressors, it has to be on constant military alert. All young men and women serve in the military. The unrest is caused by the resentment of the surrounding Arab nations toward Israel's treatment of the Arab Palestinians.

Biblical prophecy teaches that one day Israel will undergo severe trials—"the time of Jacob's trouble." At the close of those days, the Lord will come again to defeat the nations and deliver Israel (Rev. 19:1–16). He'll then reign over the earth for one thousand years. What the Jews of Christ's day hoped He would do for them, He'll one day yet do.

A final way modern Israel reflects the mood of Israel in Christ's day is in its Messianic expectations. Although modern Israel is far from being a thoroughly religious nation, there are signs of a return to basic Jewish beliefs. Rabbis are an integral part of the judicial system. Stricter Sabbath laws have been instituted. The Cohanim (priests) are studying about the offering of animal sacrifices in case the temple is rebuilt.

Some Jews believe their Messiah will come to the town of Zefat, northwest of the Sea of Galilee. Each Friday hundreds gather there to await His coming.

As for location, they're not too far off. According to the Bible, He will come to Armageddon, in the plains of Jezreel southwest of Zefat, but He Who will come won't be the one they now expect. He'll be Jesus Christ of Nazareth, Who was rejected and crucified two thousand years ago. "And they shall look upon me whom they have pierced" (Zech. 12:10). He came the first time as the Savior, bringing spiritual deliverance to those who would believe in Him. The second time He'll come as King of Kings and Lord of Lords, bringing political deliverance to Israel and establishing His millennial kingdom on the earth.

According to prophecies in the Bible, the Jezreel Valley—now a fertile agricultural area—will be the site of the end-times Battle of Armageddon.

187

Lesson 53
Forgiving Others

THEME	The Unforgiving Servant
SCRIPTURE	Matthew 18:15–35 (Luke 17:3–4)
MEMORY WORK	Matthew 18:21–22

 Approach to the Lesson

Theme: No one lives without being mistreated. How should a person respond to these wrongs? Forgiveness is the Christian's rule in responding to offenses. He must pardon the offense and renounce anger and resentment toward the wrongdoer. The basis for this approach is the way God deals with us. He forgives every one of our transgressions. Repeatedly He pardons us for our wrongs as we confess them and repent. He restores us to close fellowship with Him.

Rationale: Most young people can see that it is wrong to be angry with someone without a cause. They find it much more difficult to understand, however, that they shouldn't hold a grudge even for clear and real wrongs committed against them. Challenge them to cultivate a spirit of forgiveness that responds on the basis of the way God has treated them, and not the way others treat them.

Background: Forgiveness is the oil of human relations. Without forgiveness, bitterness and anger cause intolerable friction among Christians and non-Christians

Objectives

KNOWLEDGE (concepts students need to grasp)	the meaning of forgiveness
	the steps to follow in granting forgiveness
	the unreasonableness of withholding forgiveness
APPLICATION (principles students should put into practice)	When a friend sins against you, you must confront him, bring him to see his wrong, and forgive him.
	If a person sins against you repeatedly, you must forgive him repeatedly.
	When you have been offended, you should forgive the offender because of Christ's forgiveness for you.

Bible Expressions to Understand

heathen—non-Christian
publican—a Jew who collected taxes for the Roman government
talent—the largest Hebrew monetary unit; probably 3,000 shekels or about 1,500 ounces
pence—(plural of *penny*) a denarius, a day's wage

Jason's problems didn't begin as his fault. Candy was his girlfriend, and he treated her right. But Steve, a classmate, was also interested in Candy, and his methods weren't exactly honest. He started a rumor that Jason had been telling some pretty bad stories about his dates with Candy. Jason hadn't, of course, and there hadn't been anything wrong to tell about, but Candy heard the rumor, and that was the end of their relationship. Not long after that, Steve and Candy were seeing each other often.

Jason was bitter about what had happened. One time after soccer practice, he picked a fight with Steve and was almost kicked out of school for it. He hated the idea of talking to Steve or even seeing him. As graduation neared, Jason was making plans to attend a Christian college and study engineering—at least until he found out that Steve was planning to attend the same college.

On the night of graduation, many of the seniors got together for a party at a classmate's house. Steve ruined a conversation by making a cutting remark about Jason's grades in senior math. Jason went outside to cool off. The longer he sat there, the angrier he got. *I've had all I can take from him*, he thought. Some friends tried to get him to come back inside and join the group, but he wouldn't. Finally, after an hour, he returned to the party.

Steve's folks had given him a new car for graduation. When the party was over,

he left with Candy to take her home. As they wound their way along a mountain road, a rabbit shot into the road just ahead. Instinctively Steve swerved, and then the brakes failed. Candy screamed. The car rolled seven times down a seventy-foot embankment, smashing trees as it went. An elderly couple who lived nearby heard the crash and called 911.

Sometimes unforgiveness has tragic, unforeseen consequences. Scripture warns us to avoid it, "lest any root of bitterness springing up trouble you, and thereby many be defiled" (Heb. 12:15).

188

alike. The unbeliever has neither the spiritual motivation (God's forgiveness) nor the spiritual strength (God's grace) to forgive others. Believers have both.

The Lord gave His disciples thorough instruction on forgiveness. Nearing the midpoint of His third year of public ministry, He addressed the issue while at Capernaum in Galilee.

⭐ The Lesson

I. Steps to Forgiveness (Matt. 18:15–17)

The Scriptures outline a four-step process for dealing with a brother who has sinned against you. The goal of this process is forgiveness and restoration, not just discipline. A believer should never wish

for the excommunication of a brother from the body of Christ.

The first step is to go alone to that brother and confront him with his wrongdoing. Privacy in such a meeting is essential for openness and honesty. Privacy alone is not enough, however. The Christian must take great care in broaching the subject. A caustic, condemning spirit is not in order, of course, because it would alienate rather than heal. The offended brother should explain the wrong, including a clear statement of the biblical principle that has been violated. The only necessary response is an admission of wrongdoing, a contrite attitude, and a willingness to make restitution. If the offending brother rationalizes away his sin or flatly refuses to admit it, then another step is necessary.

Outline

(Matt. 18:15–35)
I. Steps to forgiveness
   (15–17)
II. Church discipline
   (18–20)
III. Failure to forgive
   (21–35)

EMTs arrived on the scene in minutes and rushed both young people to the hospital. Candy had a broken arm and a serious cut on her face. She was shaken up but alive. Steve, however, never even regained consciousness.

The funeral was difficult. Candy couldn't attend. A week after the accident, the police talked to her in the hospital. After a few minutes she broke down, sobbing, "Why didn't the brakes work? The car was brand new!" Those words launched an investigation of the wreckage. The brake line had been cut intentionally. Several guys remembered the argument between Jason and Steve. One had seen Jason tampering with the car but hadn't thought much about it at the time.

The months that followed were torture for Jason. He hadn't intended for something this terrible to happen. He hadn't thought the small cut in Steve's brake line would cause the brakes to fail completely. Instead of going off to college, Jason ended up behind bars for the next several years.

Why did he do it? Where did his problem begin? Jason's tragic experience is one example of what can happen when someone is offended and doesn't confront the offender and forgive him. Jason never confronted Steve about the lie he told. His anger grew. He wouldn't forgive Steve, and ultimately he killed him. Anger and bitterness don't always end up this way. Sometimes the results are not as bad. Through forgiveness, however, this whole story could have been rewritten. Steve would be alive, Candy wouldn't have an ugly scar on her face, and Jason would be in a Christian college studying engineering.

Jesus taught the importance of handling offenses the right way. Confrontation and forgiveness is the only way to deal with them. The Lord said that the offended person should privately talk the matter over with the one who offended him in hopes of restoring peace. If that isn't successful, one or two witnesses should come along to verify the conversation. If the offender won't listen to them, the trouble should be shared with the entire church. As a final step, the offender should be excluded from the church and treated as

though he were unsaved. God will stand behind the decision of His people in matters of this kind. It doesn't matter how small the group is; God has promised to answer their prayers for guidance. By His Holy Spirit, He's present in their gatherings.

Peter's curiosity was aroused by this teaching on forgiveness, and he asked the Lord, "How oft shall my brother sin against me, and I forgive him?" (Matt. 18:21). He suggested that seven times would be enough. However, Jesus told him that this wasn't enough. Forgiveness should be extended not just seven times but "seventy times seven" times.

Jesus illustrated this truth with the parable of the unmerciful servant. A certain king called one of his servants to account for an enormous debt (comparable to millions of dollars). When the servant proved unable to pay, the king commanded that he and his family should be sold into slavery and his possessions confiscated. The servant, however, fell down before the king and pleaded for mercy. "Lord, have patience with me, and I'll pay you the full amount," the servant cried. The king was so moved by the plea that he completely forgave the debt.

The servant then went out and happened to run into a fellow servant who owed him a relatively small amount. Grabbing him by the throat, he harshly

Jesus admonished His disciples: "If ye forgive not men their trespasses, neither will your Father forgive your trespasses" (Matt. 6:15).

189

The second step brings a third and possibly a fourth party into the situation. Following the advice given in Deuteronomy 19:15, the one or two witnesses will hear the conversation to substantiate the claims of the offended party if the final step has to be taken. The weight of numbers is also an advantage. Confrontation by two or three men is strong action. The presence of the witnesses also helps ensure the reasonableness of the position. If the offended brother has no case, it will probably die in this stage.

If the offender still does not respond, then the matter must be brought to the attention of the congregation of which these two brothers are a part. The mere mention of this step to a God-fearing man should

be enough to bring him back to the Lord and a right relationship to his brother.

The fourth and final step is that the offender must be rejected from the fellowship and treated as an unsaved person. This may seem like extreme action, but if the man's attitude toward sin is as light as his reaction suggests, then the action is not extreme at all. He is acting like an unconverted person and should be treated accordingly. There should be no vindictiveness in this action; the goal is still restoration and forgiveness.

Human relations can be complex. What one person views as a gross offense may be merely a difference of taste or legitimate conviction to another. Everyone should be fully persuaded in his own mind on questionable subjects. This is the right of the

individual. He is answerable for his actions and conscience before God. This four-step procedure should be used only when a person has clearly sinned by violating Scripture.

Encourage your students to follow this biblical procedure. It precludes holding grudges and refusing to communicate, thereby bettering relationships.

II. Church Discipline (Matt. 18:18–20)

Christ next justified a remarkably forceful action the church is to take in this procedure. The church has the right and the responsibility to bind (judge offenders) and to loose (restore them to fellowship when they confess their wrong).

As a safeguard against high-handed treatment by church leaders, however, the Lord stated that the church must reach a consensus on the problem. Yet only two, the smallest conceivable group, may comprise the correcting body. To encourage the saints in this sober and awesome responsibility, the Lord promised His presence: "For where two or three are gathered together in my name, there am I in the midst of them" (18:20). If a church is trying to be faithful in helping its membership maintain personal purity, the Lord will be with them. The Lord's presence is more important than the presence of a Christian who will not admit his sin and get right with God. Taking action against members who sin may cause the size of the congregation to dwindle, but better to be a small church that has the Lord's presence than a vast congregation without Him.

III. Failure to Forgive (Matt. 18:21–35)

Peter asked how often he had to forgive someone who sinned against him, mentioning seven times as a maximum. On the basis of Amos 2:6 the rabbis taught that it was necessary to forgive a person only three times: "When a man sins the first time, he is pardoned; the second time, he is pardoned;

the third time, he is pardoned; the fourth time, he is not pardoned" (Babylonian Talmud). Jesus, however, corrected Peter's generous suggestion that seven times was enough. He said that an offender should be forgiven "seventy times seven," or 490 times. In other words, no limit is to be put on forgiveness.

To underscore the unreasonableness of failing to forgive, Jesus presented the parable of the unmerciful servant. Discussion of the steps to forgiveness and the church's authority over an offender is pointless if no one is willing to forgive in the first place.

> Young people wrestle with the problem of forgiveness. They hold grudges, look for ways to get even, and generally despise anyone who has wronged them. Slander for the purpose of revenge is not uncommon in Christian schools. This sin should not be viewed lightly. What is practiced in the halls of Christian schools today will become the practice in the church sanctuaries tomorrow. Although young people are not quick to forgive, they are quick to protest if the greatest leniency is not extended to them. Both these excesses can be corrected by applying this parable.

The unjust servant owed his master ten thousand talents, which would have been equivalent to several million dollars. (One talent was about six thousand drachma, almost twenty years' pay for the average working man in that day.) He could not pay the debt. The king commanded that the man, his wife, his children, and his possessions be sold to pay the debt. The man pleaded for mercy and, surprisingly, received it. The king forgave the entire debt.

Not long after, this same servant encountered another servant who owed him a comparatively small amount. (One *penny* or denarius, was an average day's pay according to Matthew 20:2. Since the servant owed *an hundred pence*, the debt would have amounted to a few thousand dollars in today's economy.) Despite this servant's pleas for mercy, the unjust servant remained unmoved, demanding that he be sent to jail for his failure to pay. The unreasonableness of this servant is easy to see against the backdrop of the king's recent forgiveness.

When the king heard of the unjust servant's actions, he responded by having the man thrown in jail and kept there until his debts were paid. The Lord's closing words are sobering: no forgiveness for others means no forgiveness for us.

ordered him to pay up. The servant fell at his feet and pleaded for time to pay. The unmerciful servant rejected the appeal, however, and ordered him to be sent to the debtor's prison until the debt was paid. The king, filled with anger when he heard about his servant's wickedness, commanded that he also be sent to prison until his debts were paid.

If you've been forgiven for many things by your heavenly Father, you should be willing to forgive your Christian brothers and sisters as well. Scripture warns that if you don't have a sincere spirit of forgiveness toward them, your Father in heaven won't forgive you.

Are You Holding Any Grudges?

You should never allow someone else's sin to infect you. If someone has sinned against you or somehow offended you, go to him in private and work it out, as the Bible commands. If he apologizes, you must forgive him. Even if he is unwilling to admit his wrong and ask forgiveness, you must forgive him. No one could ever sin against you as much as you have sinned against God, and yet God has forgiven you for everything.

Do You Remember?

1. What are the four steps to follow in solving a conflict between Christians?
   (1) Talk the matter over with the offender.
   (2) Include one or two witnesses to verify your conversation.
   (3) Share the trouble with the entire church.
   (4) Exclude the offender from the church.

2. How do we know that the prayers of the church will be answered?
   God has promised to answer them.

3. How many times should we forgive a Christian brother? *Seventy times seven (490) means that we should forgive someone without setting a limit.*

4. What first happened to the servant who owed a large debt?
   He was forgiven his debt.

5. How did he treat the servant who owed him a lot less?
   He would not forgive him but demanded that he pay.

6. How did the king punish him for his lack of mercy?
   He commanded that he be sent to prison until he could pay.

7. What was the lesson that Jesus taught through this parable?
   If we do not forgive others, God will not forgive us.

190

For any Christian to be unforgiving of others is just as unreasonable. The King of Kings has granted us forgiveness for our sins; how can we refuse that same forgiveness to our fellow servants?

✳ Extra Activity

Role-play: Pick four students to help you enact a case of church discipline as described in Matthew 18. Assign one student to the role of the offender, who has told a lie about the offended. Assign another student to the role of the offended. The remaining two will be the two witnesses for the second step of the disciplinary procedure. You will play the part of the pastor, and the rest of the class will represent the congregation.

Stress before the role-play that the purpose of confrontation and disciplinary action is forgiveness and restoration. Meet with the participants to explain to them what to say and how to respond throughout the demonstration. Have the offender remain unrepentant so that the entire procedure can be demonstrated.

Humility  L.54

Read: Matthew 20:1–16;
Luke 14:7–11; 18:9–14

Memorize: Luke 14:11

Bible Expressions to Understand

householder—landowner
penny—a denarius, a day's wage
steward—one who manages another's household or business; usually a trusted servant
chief rooms, highest rooms—seats of honor
lowest room—seat of least honor
extortioner—one who takes from another out of greed

Napoleon Bonaparte was born on Corsica, an island off the coast of France. His father died when he was a young man, and Napoleon became the head of the family when he was only sixteen. He soon entered a military academy. He wasn't an outstanding student. Out of a group of fifty-two, he was eighth from the bottom—not a particularly good start.

However, in his military career Napoleon was exceptionally intelligent, prompt in decision making, and diligent. But the quality that stood out the most was his ambition. He wanted to be powerful and important. Through plotting, scheming, and hard work, he became the ruler of France by the time he was thirty. Five years later he was crowned emperor of France, a title he thought up for himself. Through his military victories, he forced most of the countries of Europe to become his subjects or allies.

Napoleon's desire for greatness drove him to expand France's power even more. With a huge army of 435,000 men, he attacked Russia. The severe cold of the Russian winter, however, worked against him, and he returned with barely 10,000 men fit for combat. Knowing the weakened condition of his army, several of the nations he'd conquered rebelled against him. Soon France was being attacked by so many countries that Napoleon was forced to give up the throne and live in exile on the island of Elba.

Soon Napoleon gathered an army and tried to regain his power. He was defeated for the last time by the British at Waterloo. He was then sent to the island of St. Helena, from which he never escaped. He died at age fifty-two, not knowing the where-

abouts of his own wife and son, and was buried in a grave marked only "Here lies."

Napoleon was a man of great ability, but his character was seriously flawed by his lack of humility.

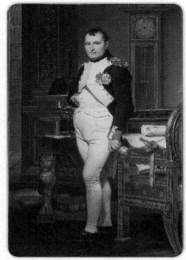

Ironically, Napoleon said, "Great ambition is the passion of a great character. Those endowed with it may perform either very good actions or very bad ones; all depends upon the principles which direct them."

(David, Jacques-Louis, "The Emperor Napoleon in His Study at the Tuileries," Samuel H. Kress collection, Image © 2005 Board of Trustees, National Gallery of Art, Washington)

191

Lesson 54

Humility

THEME	Parables Teaching Humility
SCRIPTURE	Matthew 20:1–16; Luke 14:7–11; 18:9–14
MEMORY WORK	Luke 14:11

 ## Approach to the Lesson

Theme: Humility is grateful recognition that every gift and grace is a result of God's goodness. It is not demonstrated by a constant denigration of our capacities and abilities; the truly humble Christian is

submissive to the Lord's commands, appreciates the good in others, and doesn't seek honor or recognition for himself. Jesus is the prime example of humility. He left His honored position in heaven for the role of a servant and suffered a humiliating death to accomplish our salvation.

Rationale: A natural consequence of succumbing to peer pressure is the desire to promote self in the eyes of one's peers. Teens, who usually value the opinions of their peers more than any other age group, especially need to be reminded that they shouldn't get caught up in self-promotion.

Background: The three parables considered in this lesson are about the workers in the vineyard (Matt. 20:1–16), the low seat at the wedding (Luke 14:7–11), and the Pharisee and the publican (Luke 18:9–14).

Objectives

KNOWLEDGE (concepts students need to grasp)	the importance of the settings of the three parables teaching humility: vocational (a vineyard), social (a dinner), and religious (the temple)
	the contrasting positions of the Pharisees and the publicans
APPLICATION (principles students should put into practice)	A humble person does not complain because greater honor or responsibility is given to others.
	A humble person avoids bragging about his own accomplishments.
	A humble person does not conclude that he is righteous by comparing himself to others who seem less godly.

Both the parables recorded in Luke end with the saying, "For whosoever exalteth himself shall be abased; and he that humbleth himself shall be exalted" (Luke 14:11; cf. 18:14). The parable of the workers in the vineyard ends with the idea that the first shall be last and the last shall be first (Matt. 20:16). These statements say essentially the same thing: God elevates humble people and humbles proud people. Each parable treats a slightly different dimension of the subject of humility.

 ## The Lesson

I. Humility and Contentment (Matt. 20:1–16)

In this parable the Lord discusses the kingdom of heaven. He is explaining, in part, what a person under the dominion of Christ can expect in the present.

God is just (20:1–7). The first part of the parable teaches that God always does what is right in the service He allows His servants to perform. The householder (landowner) went to find workers for his vineyard. A group of men agreed to work for him for the day for a *penny* (a denarius, which was a standard day's wage). At 9:00 a.m. he hired more men and told them only that they would be paid a fair wage. At noon and at 3:00 p.m. he hired more workers on the same basis. About 5:00 p.m. he found some men who had not been working at all. He asked them why they were not working, and they said that no one had hired them. He then hired them, promising them a fair but unspecified wage.

Outline

I. Humility and contentment
   (Matt. 20:1–16)
   A. God is just (1–7).
   B. We accept God's rewards
      (8–16).
II. Humility and honor (Luke 14:7–11)
III. Humility and righteousness
   (Luke 18:9–14)

These workers did not perform equal work; some worked much longer than others. They were also working under different conditions because some worked later in the day when it was not as hot. We see that the servant of the Lord does not decide the terms of his service; that is the Lord's prerogative. Not all believers labor for equally long periods or in equally difficult circumstances.

We accept God's rewards (20:8–16). The second part of this parable teaches that the humble Christian accepts God's rewards as right. He is content with whatever God gives. The employer rewarded those who worked only one hour with a whole day's wage. What prompted the householder to do this is not clear. The application that Christ draws is that the last shall be first and the first shall be last. In other words, those least deserving according to outward evidence receive a reward equivalent to those who seem to have done much more in the service of God. The Lord is generous to those who humbly serve him.

Those who had worked all day were embittered by what they thought was unfair treatment. They received what they had agreed on, but they thought they should have received more, and they complained forcefully. They said they had borne the burden of the day. The term for *burden* means an extreme burden, almost beyond what a person can bear. They also said they had endured the heat of the day. This may be a reference to the burning east wind characteristic of Palestine.

To all this complaining the householder responded that they had received what he had agreed to pay them. The Lord is always just in the way He treats His servants. The standard against which that justice is measured is His omniscience and wisdom, not His treatment of others. One servant of the Lord mustn't look to another servant's experience to determine how the Lord should treat him. Every believer must

His pride caused his life to end in disgrace. As Solomon said, "Pride goeth before destruction, and an haughty spirit before a fall" (Prov. 16:18). Napoleon had ignored the truth that "by humility and the fear of the Lord are riches, and honour, and life" (Prov. 22:4). The Lord Jesus Christ taught, "For whosoever exalteth himself shall be abased; and he that humbleth himself shall be exalted" (Luke 14:11).

Jesus used three parables to teach about humility. Each taught a different aspect of this quality. What is humility? It's the opposite of pride, which is an exaggerated view of one's abilities and importance. Humility, then, doesn't mean thinking there's nothing good about yourself, but rather it's accepting that every ability and good quality you possess is a gift from God and is to be used for His glory.

In the parable of the workers in the vineyard, the Lord Jesus taught that a humble Christian is content with whatever God gives him. The first group of workers agreed on their wages. The manager told the rest they would get a fair wage. When the day's work was over, everyone was paid the same. The men who had worked the longest complained because they thought they'd been treated unfairly. Yet they were given what the landowner had agreed to give them. He'd simply been generous with those who had worked less. The workers shouldn't have compared themselves to each other. If they hadn't, they wouldn't have become envious.

To contrast extreme pride and appropriate humility, Jesus talked about a respected Pharisee and a despised publican worshiping.

192

God doesn't treat all His servants alike. He has the right to give differing responsibilities and differing rewards to them. If a Christian is humble, he accepts from the Lord whatever He gives and expects no more. He's content. The proud Christian is constantly frustrated, feeling he deserves more. He's envious of others who have a better situation.

God has given you what you need. He's given you the right amount of intelligence, the right family, and the right teacher. Be grateful. Recognize that God didn't have to give you anything, but out of His generosity He has given you so much.

Jesus presented the parable of the low seat at the wedding to teach that a humble Christian avoids honoring himself. The honored guests at a wedding feast were assigned special places to sit. To rush in and try to get one of those seats when it isn't assigned to you is foolish. The host would tell you to sit somewhere else, probably in a less important place not occupied yet. Jesus said that the best approach is to find an unimportant place to sit in the beginning and let the host place you in an honored position if he wants to.

Doing things to make other people think you're important is pride. What you do may be innocent in itself. The issue is the motive or reason you act the way you do. If you play a sport to make other people think you're important, you're playing for the wrong reason. If you answer questions in class to show people how smart you are, then you're proud, not humble. If you dress the way you do so others will think highly of you, that's not humility.

Pride and humility are attitudes of the heart. Sometimes others can tell why you do what you do, but often no one knows but you and the Lord. If you're humble and don't try to make others think you're important, God will make sure you are properly recognized. He wants people to respect you for your abilities and accomplishments. Trust Him to bring you honor in His own time.

In the parable of the Pharisee and the publican, Jesus showed that a humble person trusts in Christ's righteousness, not his own. The proud Pharisee thought well of himself. He thought he wasn't as bad as the tax collector who was at the temple praying when he was. But God wasn't impressed with his good works. The man was deceived; he thought he was good because he did better than others. This isn't true righteousness. The issue wasn't how good

fulfill his own responsibilities. He must also be fully satisfied with the Lord's will and reward. If it were not for the grace of Christ, there would be no service at all and no reward at all. The humble believer is grateful for the opportunities of service He allows and the rewards He sends, as many or as few as they may be. Envy has no place in the service of the Lord. The Lord's goodness to others should never be a source of irritation, but a source of rejoicing.

Your students are probably beginning to do a lot of comparing of themselves with others. Bitterness often takes root in the early teen years because the young person concludes that God has not been fair to him. He feels that he deserves better parents, a better church, better friends, and a better personal appearance. All these attitudes are a subtle

form of pride, resulting in ingratitude. The student reasons, *I am special, so everything should be just as I want it. I deserve it.* The main purpose Jesus had for telling this parable was to combat the attitude of pride.

II. Humility and Honor (Luke 14:7–11)

The parable of the low seat at the wedding teaches that a humble Christian avoids honoring himself. Jesus had gone to eat at the home of a chief Pharisee on the Sabbath, and a group of Pharisees and scribes were also there. Jesus healed a man suffering with dropsy to show these people that human need takes precedence over Sabbath observance. Then He turned His attention to another spiritual problem these Jews had—pride. Pride seeks honor for self above

he was compared to others, but what he was in his heart and how good he was compared to God.

By contrast, the publican was so humbled by his sin that he begged God for mercy. He's the picture of the attitude necessary for salvation. A person must humbly admit that there's nothing in him that makes him acceptable to God. All his gifts, abilities, and works are merely results of God's goodness and are tainted by sin. Only God can wash away that sin by the work of Christ.

If you've come to the place the publican reached and asked Christ to save you, then you've been made spiritually clean in God's eyes. As a Christian you should continue in grateful dependence on Christ and His goodness. This is true humility.

Are You Proud of Your Humility?

You're a humble Christian if you know that all that's good about you is by God's grace. You're honest about your good qualities, but you recognize them as gifts, and you don't talk about them to other people. You're grateful to Christ for His generosity. Because you're humble, you're content with whatever God gives you. You're not frustrated, thinking that you deserve better. You don't try to bring honor to yourself by what you do. Above all, you've turned to Christ to trust His work of saving you. You continue to trust His grace for deliverance from sin and for power to serve in a way that glorifies Him.

Do You Remember?

1. How much did the householder pay those who had worked just an hour? _____
   one penny; a full day's wage

2. Why did the householder pay only one penny to those who worked all day? _____
   That was the wage they had agreed to.

3. What did those who had put in a full day's work complain about? _____
   They were not paid more than those who worked one hour.

4. On what occasion did Jesus present the parable of the low seat at the wedding? _____
   He had gone to eat at the home of one of the Pharisees and saw proud men vying
   for the important places to sit around the table.

5. What did Jesus recommend to those coming to the wedding? _____
   to sit in a low seat

6. What happens to a person who exalts himself? *He will be humbled.*

7. What happens to a person who humbles himself? *He will be exalted.*

8. How often did the proud Pharisee say he fasted? *twice a week*

9. What did the Pharisee think of himself compared to the publican? *that he was much better*

10. What was the prayer of the publican? *"God be merciful to me a sinner."*

193

---

others. Jesus, noticing how each of those who came to the house tried to sit in as high a position of honor at the table as he could, responded with this parable teaching that honoring oneself leads to humiliation. At a wedding feast the positions of honor in seating were always given at the discretion of the host, not on the basis of the assertiveness of those attending. The danger of taking the highest *room* or "seat" was that you could be moved to a lower seat, and the humiliation would be well-deserved. Any demonstration of pride is inappropriate, regardless of the circumstances.

The Lord further taught that humbling yourself brings honor. Instead of seeking a position of honor, it is wise to take the position of least honor. If you are then elevated to a place of honor, others do not resent it, but rather respect you for it.

The conclusion is that the one who lifts himself up will be put down but the one who humbles himself will be honored. The Old Testament states, "Pride goeth before destruction, and an haughty spirit before a fall" (Prov. 16:18). "By humility and the fear of the Lord are riches, and honour, and life" (Prov. 22:4). Twice the New Testament alludes to Proverbs 3:34—"Surely he scorneth the scorners: but he giveth grace unto the lowly" (cf. James 4:6 and 1 Pet. 5:5).

Often students are placed in competitive circumstances academically and athletically that can lead them into pride in their accomplishments. "Every good gift and every perfect gift is from above, and cometh down from the Father of lights, with whom is no variableness, neither shadow of turning" (James 1:17). So why should any Christian be proud? (See I Cor. 4:7.)

III. Humility and Righteousness (Luke 18:9–14)

The parable of the Pharisee and the publican is a vivid portrait from the first century. The stark contrast in the parable teaches that the humble man is not self-righteous but rather trusts in God for mercy. The Lord first taught that self-righteousness, a form of pride, comes from comparing yourself with others. Such was the error of the Pharisee. This man's standard of righteousness was not the law of God, but the sinfulness of others. While he stood praying in the temple near a publican, he rehearsed how outstanding he was compared to others. He was not an extortioner, one who took from others by any means possible, including violence. Nor was he unjust, ethically unscrupulous. Of course, he was not an adulterer. But most important, he was not a traitor to Israel, a collector of taxes for the oppressive Roman government. Positively speaking, he fasted often, following the Pharisaical practice of two fasts a week, on Thursday and Monday. (Thursday was supposedly the day Moses went up on Mount Sinai to receive the Law; Monday, the day he returned with it. To fast on these two days was a special mark of holiness.) He also tithed everything he had; he gave a tenth of all his income.

What was wrong with this Pharisee's conception of righteousness? He seemed to feel so righteous that he didn't need God. He acknowledged no need for God's mercy, no need for God's grace, no need for salvation in Christ. This man's problem was the sin of measuring himself by a false standard. The result was a self-righteousness that was particularly repugnant to God.

In contrast to the Pharisee, the publican was so disturbed in his conscience over his sins that he could not even look up to heaven in prayer. All he could do was throw himself on the mercy of God and admit that he was a sinner. There was no pretense here. Somehow this man, who in practice had little concern for religion, had been freed from religion-induced false righteousness. He understood that relationship with God takes priority over outward religiosity. Measured against his understanding of God's expectations, he was a sinner, one who had missed the true spiritual purpose of his life. Coming to the end of himself, he found the mercy of God. The Lord stated that a man with a repentant heart, as demonstrated by the publican, would be freed from the guilt of his sin.

Your students must understand that righteousness comes only from Christ. Any other mentality is pharisaism and unacceptable to God. You are saved not because of who you are. You are saved because of trusting who Christ is. This attitude must continue throughout the Christian experience, not just at the outset. Shall we begin in faith and then continue by the works of the Law (Gal. 3:3)? No, we must always trust only Christ.

✳ Extra Activities

Discussion: From each group below, have your students choose the Bible character who failed to demonstrate humility and explain how. If they cannot come up with the right answer, give them the reference to look up. This may be used as a competitive Scripture search exercise.

Who failed to show humility?

1. Joshua, Samson, or Moses
   Samson because he showed off his strength (Judg. 16:1–3)

2. Peter, Samuel, or Paul
   Peter because he said he would never deny the Lord (Matt 26:31–35)

3. Isaiah, Elijah, or Jeremiah
   Elijah because he thought he was the only faithful person left in Israel (1 Kings 19:8–14)

4. Barnabas, Stephen, or James and John
   James and John because they thought they deserved to be greatest among the disciples in Christ's future kingdom (Mark 10:35–45)

5. Judas, Silas, or Thomas
   Judas because he would not accept reproof from the Lord (Matt. 26:6–16)

Case study: Have your students listen to this case study and answer the questions.

Three friends—Sharon, Patty, and Melissa—were in the same biology class. Mrs. Stuber, their teacher, had been reminding the class for two weeks that a unit test was coming on Friday. After class on Wednesday, the girls planned to go to Patty's house to study together.

Near the end of the day, Sharon decided she didn't want to go. She said she knew she was going to get an A on the test since she always got A's. Patty and Melissa went to study. Patty wanted to do well on the test; she knew it would please her parents and the Lord.

After the test, Sharon said, "I made an A on my test! I knew I would." Patty said, "Well, how high was your score? I'll bet my 96 was higher." Melissa didn't say anything. What Sharon and Patty never found out was that Melissa had done better than both of them.

1. Who was the first person in the story to violate the standard of Christian humility? How?
   Sharon; by boasting about her general performance on biology tests

2. Who demonstrated humility in this story? How?
   Melissa; by not boasting

3. What should Patty have done differently?
   She should not have invited comparison with the other girls by stating her score.

Memory work: Review Luke 14:11 aloud in class. Have your students read it together twice from their Bibles. Then put the first letter of each word in the verse on the board and review the verse three times. Erase half the letters and go over the verse twice. Erase the rest of the letters, and say the verse twice.

Lesson 55

Being Ready for His Coming

THEME	Preparation for Christ's Return
SCRIPTURE	Matthew 24:43–51; 25:1–13; Mark 13:34–37; Luke 12:35–40
MEMORY WORK	Matthew 25:13

Approach to the Lesson

Theme: Just as certainly as Christ came in fulfillment of prophecy the first time, so He will come again. This is the clear message of the New Testament. Jesus Himself prophesied His coming through parables. For the believer the return of Christ will be a time of physical transformation—what Christians often call "the Rapture" of the church. Saints living on the earth will be caught up to meet Christ in the air. They will be preceded by a great resurrection of the bodies of departed saints who have been with the Lord in heaven. Their physical bodies will be reconstituted and reunited with their souls.

The promise of this event is a source of comfort and hope for the believer since it means that finally he will be in the presence of the Lord (1 Thess. 4:15–18). For the ungodly the Rapture will be a strange and inexplicable phenomenon. Seven years of judgment will begin soon after that point. Finally, Christ will come in glory, subdue the world, rule it for a thousand years, defeat the remaining forces of wickedness, and then judge the unsaved one last time. For the unsaved the Second Coming is the sealing of their doom. For the Christian it is the beginning of uninterrupted blessing.

Rationale: The best way to make this lesson practical is to stress the imminency of Christ's return. He will come while we are carrying on our usual daily activities. Will we be ashamed?

Background: This lesson synthesizes the teaching of five parables concerning the Second Coming:

1. The lord returning from a wedding (Luke 12:35–38)
2. The goodman and the thief (Matt. 24:43–44; Luke 12:39–40)
3. The wise and the wicked servants (Matt. 24:45–51; Luke 12:41–48)
4. The ten virgins (Matt. 25:1–13)
5. The faithful doorkeeper (Mark 13:34–37)

Even though in some points these parables are distinctive, combined they give the believer a strategy for anticipating the Lord's return. The first part of the lesson gives background explanation helpful in understanding each parable's primary teachings. The last two sections develop these teachings.

The Lesson

I. Parables about Christ's Return

The lord returning from the wedding (Luke 12:35–38). This parable is introduced by an exhortation to be ready for service. The lord returns from a wedding at night. The servants are ready and waiting for him. As soon as he knocks on the door, they open it. Implied is the fact that the door is securely shut from the inside, and the lord could not let himself in. Any lord would be grateful for faithful servants like these, who are ready at his return. The lord will change clothes and serve them in gratitude.

The spiritual lesson to learn from this parable is that readiness is always expected of believers, whether it's convenient or inconvenient. The Lord will meet that readiness with appropriate gratitude.

The goodman and the thief (Matt. 24:43–44; Luke 12:39–40). This parable speaks of a landowner who has his house broken into. If he had known when the thief was going to come, he would not have allowed it to happen. The unexpected time

Objectives

KNOWLEDGE (concepts students need to grasp)	what the main characters in each of the parables in this lesson represent
	that the Lord's return will occur suddenly
APPLICATION (principles students should put into practice)	We should watch for Christ's coming.
	Attempting to predict the date of the Lord's return is futile and unbiblical.
	We must be prepared for the Lord's return by being saved, serving Christ, and watching for His coming.

Outline

I. Parables about Christ's return
  A. The lord returning from the wedding (Luke 12:35–38)
  B. The goodman and the thief (Matt. 24:43–44; Luke 12:39–40)
  C. The wise and the wicked servants (Matt. 24:45–51; Luke 12:41–48)
  D. The ten virgins (Matt. 25:1–13)
  E. The faithful doorkeeper (Mark 13:34–37)
II. Timing of Christ's return
  A. Delayed
  B. Uncertain
  C. Sudden
III. Preparing for Christ's return
  A. Salvation
  B. Service
  C. Watchfulness

of the thief's coming naturally gave him an advantage. Even though the thief is reprehensible, the point is his unexpected arrival, not his character. For this reason the illustration is entirely appropriate for the Lord's Second Coming.

We should prepare ourselves for the Lord's coming because it will occur unexpectedly (Luke 12:40).

The wise and the wicked servants (Matt. 24:45–51; Luke 12:41–48). The accounts of this parable in Matthew and Luke are virtually identical. (Since the account in Luke is slightly longer, references are from it.) The first segment of the parable describes a steward who faithfully executes his lord's will. This man has been given the responsibility of paying all the employees. The term *meat* can mean "food" or "a living," and so can be properly understood as remuneration for work. The man who is faithful will receive greater responsibility as a reward.

This teaching is parallel to the Christian's experience as a steward of God's grace in this life: If he is faithful, he can expect a greater reward in eternity.

> **The student text pages for this lesson begin on the next page.**

In contrast, the wicked servant assumed that his lord would not return soon. He beat the other servants and spent his time getting drunk. When the lord returns, this servant will be assigned a place with the unbelievers. The term translated *unbelievers* can also be translated "unfaithful." The man was unfaithful in what the lord gave him to do and would be dealt with appropriately. He could also expect to be *cut asunder*, i.e., to face physical punishment.

Spiritually, unbelievers can expect severe punishment from the Lord when He returns.

The parable next discusses earthly servants who were unfaithful to their masters, but to different degrees. The one who knew what he was supposed to do and refused experiences the more serious punishment. The servant disobeying out of ignorance receives less punishment.

Here is the Lord's standard for judging unbelievers. Those who have more knowledge of God and greater opportunity to respond and refuse it will be judged more severely than those with less knowledge and opportunity.

The ten virgins (Matt. 25:1–13). The setting is a wedding. In first-century Palestine a wedding ceremony was held at the bride's home. It was brief, sometimes accompanied by a meal. Then a procession went to the groom's home for a great feast. Often many of the wedding guests would meet the procession along the way. If it was at night, everyone had to be prepared with his own torch or lamp to light the way. Without light it would be difficult to find their way through the dark streets.

In this parable ten virgins, probably friends of the bride, were waiting for the procession. To prepare, half had their rag torches doused with oil so they would light easily, and they had extra oil in a container in case they had difficulty getting their torches lit. The foolish virgins had perhaps doused their torches but had no additional oil. They all waited patiently for the long-delayed procession.

When the call came that the procession was on its way, the women with oil lit their torches and were ready. The foolish virgins could not get their torches lit and asked for some oil from the others. They refused in case their own torches went out and told the others to go buy oil. While they were buying, the procession reached the

Bible Expressions to Understand

goodman of the house—homeowner
cut asunder—cut in pieces; punish severely
virgin—a morally pure, unmarried woman
vessels with their lamps—small containers of olive oil for fuel
trimmed their lamps—prepared and lit their torches
porter—doorkeeper

What do Jamaican land crabs and Atlantic eels have in common? Instinct prompts them to go certain places at certain times—without fail.

Each year Jamaican land crabs leave the rocky crevices in which they live and travel to beaches to mate. They follow a certain path, allowing nothing to get in their way. They'll climb over rocks and even houses until they reach their destination. They do this at the same time every year without fail.

The Atlantic eel spends most of its life in the ponds and the streams of Europe and North America. Suddenly, after years of living in the same place, it leaves and swims to a spot south of Bermuda. There it descends into the deep ocean, never to return. Some time later, thousands of clear, tiny, wormlike creatures with bulging black eyes come floating to the surface. Growing stronger, these baby eels begin their swim back to the homes of their parents in North America and Europe. At a certain point in life, Atlantic eels do this without fail.

Just as these animals perform their characteristic rituals without fail, Christ will come again without fail as He has promised (John 14:3; Matt. 24:35). Christ cannot and will not violate His Word. For Christians, Christ's return will be a time of great blessing. For the ungodly, it will be a time of judgment.

According to 1 Thessalonaians 4:14–17, the Lord Jesus will miraculously take all believers off the earth. All believers who have died will have their bodies resurrected. This will begin a time of release from sin and reward for all believers. The Lord's coming should be something every Christian looks forward to with great excitement. What can you know about it before it happens? The five parables you read for this lesson give some information that will help you answer that question.

All the parables discuss the timing of the Lord's coming. Since He's delayed His coming by some two thousand years, you may be inclined not to think about it much. You may reason that if the Lord has waited this long, He'll probably continue to wait. These parables teach that you should be waiting for the Lord's return expectantly regardless of the seeming delay.

These parables also teach that the exact time of the event is uncertain. No other event has to occur as a fulfillment of prophecy before the Rapture of the church. That's the next thing on God's prophetic agenda. At the same time, hurricanes, floods, earthquakes, and other natural catastrophes are no indication that the Lord's coming is especially near. Only the Father in heaven knows the exact time.

When the Lord does return for the saints, it'll be a sudden event. Paul described it as occurring in a moment or a twinkling of an eye. In His parables the Lord Jesus said that the event would come suddenly, catching people by surprise. Now's the time to prepare for the Lord's coming. When it occurs, there will be no time to prepare.

194

bridegroom's house and everyone went in, shutting the door behind them. When the foolish virgins finally made it to the house, they were refused entrance because the groom did not know them and probably was suspicious because of their lateness.

The faithful doorkeeper (Mark 13:34–37). This parable (not found in the other gospels) briefly illustrates the varying responsibilities the Lord gives His followers while He is in heaven. The Lord pictures Himself as a landowner who gives some of His servants authority, others laboring positions, and one the job of the *porter* ("doorkeeper"), who was commanded to watch. The Lord then generalized the porter's responsibility as applying to all His servants; they were all to watch for the landowner's unexpected return.

II. Timing of Christ's Return

Delayed. The New Testament stressed that the Lord's coming would be delayed. The proper response to this delay is continued faithfulness. Even with this delay, the believer is to continue to expect Jesus to return. In the parable of the wise and the wicked servants, the wicked servant said in his heart, "My lord delayeth his coming" (Matt. 24:48) and began to live in wickedness. He saw the lord's delay as an excuse for a poor spiritual life. As the bridegroom in the parable of the ten virgins tarried, five remained unprepared (Matt. 25:3–5). And in the parable of the faithful doorkeeper, the fact that the master took a long journey did not excuse unfaithfulness on the part of the servants (Mark 13:34).

What opportunity of eternal significance did the foolish virgins fail to prepare for?

will be true of many after the Lord comes and takes His saints to heaven. The Scriptures teach that now is the day for you to be saved. Before you know it, the time of salvation will be past.

If you're already saved, you can continue to prepare by faithfully serving Christ. This is what the faithful servant did. He wasn't like the neglectful, rebellious servant. When the lord returned, the faithful servant was doing what he had been told to do. In another parable a man went into a far country and left directions for some to have authority, others to work, and another to be a doorkeeper. The servants were expected to work while the master was gone. Idleness isn't the Lord's will. This is the time for you to be serving the Lord.

Trusting Christ as your Savior and serving Him faithfully are crucial steps in your preparation for the Lord's return. Yet there's one other step you can take—developing a spirit of watchfulness. Look forward to the return of Christ. Watch for it, and conduct your life as if it'll happen any moment. This will help keep you from sin and will increase your love for Christ. By focusing on the return of Christ and the kingdom, you'll be less tempted to love the world.

What If It Were Today?

Just as certainly as Christ came in fulfillment of prophecy the first time, He'll come again. Jesus Himself prophesied about His coming through parables. If you're a believer at the time of the Lord's coming, you'll be transformed physically, released from sin, and rewarded for your labors. Though you cannot know exactly when Christ will return, you should always be serving Him and watching for His arrival for you. Your prayers should be like John's at the end of Revelation: "Even so, come, Lord Jesus" (Rev. 22:20).

How can you prepare for Christ's coming? The most important preparation is to be saved. No one can prepare for you. Because the five foolish virgins hadn't prepared their torches for the wedding procession, no one could help them when the procession came. The others couldn't give them their oil; the foolish virgins had to get some for themselves. Their unpreparedness cost them the opportunity to go to the wedding feast. They couldn't get in late. This

195

which is imminency. It does not matter when the Lord will return. The believer is to yearn for His return and serve as if it will happen today.

Sudden. The suddenness of the return is another point these parables stress. Therefore, we should be watchful. For the wicked servant it was an unhappy day when the lord suddenly appeared (Matt. 24:50). The virgins were dozing when suddenly the procession was upon them (Matt. 25:5). In applying the parable of the faithful doorkeeper, the Lord commanded the porter to watch "lest coming suddenly he find you sleeping" (Mark 13:36). The Rapture and resurrection of the saints is described as shockingly sudden. Paul wrote, "In a moment, in the twinkling of an eye, at the last trump: for the trumpet shall sound, and the dead shall be raised incorruptible, and we shall be changed" (1 Cor. 15:52). Jesus said, "And, behold, I come quickly; and my reward is with me, to give every man according as his work shall be" (Rev. 22:12).

When the Lord returns, He will come so swiftly that no one except believers will be prepared. This is an incentive to prepare now. There will be no time for preparation then.

III. Preparing for Christ's Return

Since the unknown timing of the Lord's return offers a strong incentive to prepare for it, the logical question is, "How, then, does a person prepare for the Lord's return?" These five parables answer that question in the following three ways.

Salvation. A person must first trust Christ as his Savior. The difference between the wise and foolish virgins was the personal preparation of the former. When the foolish asked the wise to give them oil, the wise virgins told them to go buy some for themselves (Matt. 25:9). At first glance this may seem heartless, but there was wisdom in it. Certain preparations can be made only by each person doing them for himself.

Service. To be prepared for Christ's return, a Christian must be serving Christ. The wise servant was faithfully doing what the lord had told him (Matt. 24:46). He had been given authority, and he was faithfully exercising it. The man who took the long journey, representing the Lord, gave authority to some, work to others, and the job of doorkeeping to another (Mark 13:34). Each was expected to do his job faithfully until the return. This is a picture of the church

Uncertain. These parables also stress the uncertainty of the timing of the Lord's return. The proper response to this uncertainty is faithfulness, watchfulness, and readiness. These proper responses are emphasized in several of the parables. The wicked and the wise servants responded differently to this uncertainty (Matt. 24:46, 50): the one worked steadily, while the other was unfaithful. All the ten virgins slept while waiting the uncertain arrival of the wedding procession (Matt. 25:5). In applying the parable Jesus said, "Watch therefore, for ye know neither the day nor the hour wherein the Son of man cometh" (Matt. 25:13). Similarly, from the parable of the faithful doorkeeper, Christ made the application, "Watch ye therefore: for ye know not when the master of the house cometh,

at even, or at midnight, or at the cock-crowing, or in the morning: lest coming suddenly he find you sleeping" (Mark 3:35–36). The thrust of the parable of the goodman and the thief is that the homeowner is uncertain of the time of the thief's coming. "Be ye therefore ready also: for the Son of man cometh at an hour when ye think not" (Luke 12:40).

No one knows the day or hour of the Lord's return. The Lord said, "But of that day and that hour knoweth no man, no, not the angels which are in heaven, neither the Son, but the Father" (Mark 13:32). How strange that people claim to predict the time of this return when it is concealed even from the Son of God Himself. Their conjectures are unbiblical in two ways: first, Scripture teaches that they cannot know; second, they violate the spirit of the teaching, as we wait for our Lord—each working faithfully for Christ and expecting His return.

Watchfulness. A last step in preparation is a spirit of watchfulness. The heart pounds and spirits rise at the anticipation of a friend's arrival. When plans are laid and necessities purchased, enthusiasm grows. Why? The change of routine is refreshing; the point of view and conversation of the visitor are stimulating.

> The believer has every reason to watch in excited anticipation. What an experience to forever be listening to Christ explain the inexplicable, to marvel at His word and character, to enjoy His commendation and the new expanses of service He assigns. All these things await the believer. The prayer of John is the prayer of every faithful saint: "Even so, come, Lord Jesus" (Rev. 22:20).

These parables teach that the Christian is to have this kind of anticipation. The sin of the wicked servant was in part that he was not watching (Matt. 24:50). The mistake of the unwise virgins was that they prepared somewhat and then became careless and inattentive (Matt. 25:3). In the parable of the faithful doorkeeper, Jesus exhorted, "Watch ye therefore: for ye know not when the master of the house cometh, at even, or at midnight, or at the cockcrowing, or in the morning" (Mark 13:35). The servants awaiting their lord's return from the wedding were watching for him (Luke 12:37), whereas the mistake of the homeowner who was robbed was that he did not watch (Luke 12:39).

✳ Extra Activity

Question and answer: Use the following series of questions and answers to arouse interest in the lesson.

a. When will Christ return for believers?
We don't know.

b. What will happen just before the Rapture of the saints on earth?
the resurrection of the saints who have died

c. Where is the word *rapture* found in the Bible?
It is not found in the Bible. It is derived from a Latin word that translates the Greek word for "caught up" or "caught away."

d. How long will the Rapture take?
a moment of time, a twinkling of an eye, a split second

e. What are Christians supposed to do until Christ comes?
serve faithfully and watch for Him

Do You Remember?

1. Why did the owner of the house not prevent the thief from breaking in? _____
   He didn't know when the thief was coming.

2. According to the parable of the goodman and the thief (Matt. 24:43–44), why should the believer be ready for the Lord's coming? _____
   because of the uncertainty of the time of the Lord's return

3. What will happen to the wicked servant because of his unfaithfulness? _____
   He will be appointed a place with the hypocrites, where there will be weeping and gnashing of teeth.

4. Who do the five prepared virgins represent? *Christians*

5. Who do the five unprepared virgins represent? *the unsaved*

6. Who does the bridegroom represent? *Christ*

7. Who does the porter represent? *the watchful Christian*

8. Who do the servants who waited for their lord to return from a wedding represent? _____
   faithful Christians

9. What will happen to those who know the Lord's will and choose not to do it? _____
   They will receive severe punishment.

10. What will happen to those who fail to do the Lord's will because of ignorance? _____
    They will receive less punishment.

196

Expecting a Reward L.56

Read: Luke 19:11–27   Memorize: Luke 19:26

Bible Expressions to Understand

pound—a unit of currency (Greek *mina*)
usury—lending money or trading at a reasonable rate of interest

If you're a Christian, you will live in heaven for all eternity. What are you going to do with all that time? Will you be lying around strumming a harp and floating on a fluffy cloud? Is there anything you can do now to make sure heaven will be an enjoyable experience, or is that all decided for you by someone else? These are important questions. The parable of the pounds answers them.

Near the end of Christ's ministry, some of His disciples thought that He was going to establish His kingdom at that time. To prepare them for the fact that His earthly kingdom would not yet come, Jesus told the the following story.

The third servant had carefully kept the money entrusted to him by the master, not wasting it or losing it. Why was he evaluated as "unfaithful"?

A nobleman took a long journey into a distant country. Before he left, he charged his servants to serve him faithfully while he was gone. Each of them was given one pound (*mina*) to invest. (A *mina* was about three months' wages for a typical laborer.)

When the man returned, he called in his servants for an accounting. The first servant had gained ten pounds through his investments. His lord commended and rewarded him in proportion to his success. The second servant had gained five pounds through his investments. He likewise was rewarded in proportion to his success. The third servant, however, had been unfaithful while his lord was gone. He brought back only the original amount, saying that he had been afraid that he would lose it during his master's absence. Instead of investing it, he had wrapped it carefully in a cloth and protected it.

His lord was angry. He condemned the lazy servant for his failure to try anything. At the least, he pointed out, the servant could have drawn interest on the money from the bank. He commanded other servants to take away the pound from the unfaithful servant and give it to the first servant, who had demonstrated great faithfulness by his work. He then stated a general principle: those who are unfaithful to him will lose even that which they have. It will be given to those who are faithful.

In this parable the master represents the Lord Jesus Christ; the servants are Christians; and the master's enemies represent the unsaved. The servants all receive the same amount of money to use while the master is gone. The picture is of a group of Christians all being granted the same opportunity and ability. This does not teach that all Christians have the same opportunities and abilities for service in this life. However, one Christian who has the same amount of opportunity and ability as another

197

Lesson 56
Expecting a Reward

THEME	The Parable of the Pounds
SCRIPTURE	Luke 19:11–27
MEMORY WORK	Luke 19:26

 Approach to the Lesson

Theme: This life is a time when the Christian proves his faithfulness to Christ in service. If he is steadfast and fulfills his responsibilities, he will be rewarded for it with greater responsibility in heaven. The

degree to which the believer is productive determines the degree of his reward. If two individuals are given equal opportunity and ability, the one who excels in faithfulness will receive the greater reward. This truth motivates the Christian to maximum usefulness in Christ's service, and it offers hope for the future. Although our efforts may go largely unappreciated in this life, the future holds the promise of great reward.

Rationale: Young people respond well to rewards. Impress on them that their whole lives will determine a reward, one with eternal effects.

Background: Just after the visit to Zacchaeus's house, and before the last week of His life, Jesus presented the parable of the pounds. Some of His disciples thought that His rule in this world and their reward

Objectives

KNOWLEDGE (concepts students need to grasp)	what faithfulness means
	what the characters in this parable represent
APPLICATION (principles students should put into practice)	The standard by which a Christian measures his faithfulness is his ability and opportunity, not that of another.
	Unfaithfulness will bring loss of opportunity for service and reward in heaven.
	The enemies of Christ will be punished for their rebellion.
	Love for Christ should be the primary motive for service.

as participants in that kingdom would occur in the near future (Luke 19:11). To clear up their misunderstanding, He presented this parable.

This parable not only clarifies the sequence of events after the Lord's death, but it is also rich in instruction concerning the future reward of saints. Other Scriptures teach that Christians who are given different degrees of opportunity and ability for service will be rewarded equally if they are equally faithful (Matt. 25:14–30; 1 Cor. 4:2). The Bible teaches that the judgment seat of Christ is a time of reward for the believer (1 Cor. 3:13–15; 2 Cor. 5:10). Christians will never face eternal punishment for sin since Jesus took all of God's wrath for our sins on the cross (Ps. 103:12; Isa. 53:5; Jer. 31:34).

The Lesson

I. Christ Ascends to Heaven (Luke 19:12–14)

The nobleman in this passage represents the Lord. His ascension is part of what we call His exaltation. On His return to heaven, He received all the rights to His future earthly and eternal kingdom (Eph. 1:20–23). The right to judge, to rule, and to be worshiped were all His by virtue of His acts of Creation and Redemption (Rev. 4:11; 5:9).

Before his departure the nobleman called ten servants together and gave each a pound to use while he was gone. A pound was literally a *mna* (or *mina*), equal to one hundred drachmas, a little more than three months' salary in New Testament times. The lord then commanded them, "Occupy till I come" i.e., be involved in trading or

Outline

banking practices. More generally, the idea was for them to do something productive with what had been given them.

Later, the citizens of the country over which he ruled sent a message that they wanted nothing to do with his rule and would rebel against it. These citizens represent the unsaved world, which rejects Christ's rule. Day by day the world sends its message to heaven, "We will not have this man to reign over us" (Luke 19:14).

> The world will never submit to Christ. The Christian should not expect the world to submit to His dominion in the future or in the present. The world has always rejected Christian principles and practices and always will (Rom. 1:19-22).

II. Christ Returns and Rewards Faithful Christians (Luke 19:15-19)

When the nobleman returned, he called the servants in to give an account of what they had accomplished by trading. This pictures the Lord's evaluation of the works of the righteous and the subsequent reward for their labors.

The first servant had managed to increase his single pound tenfold. The nobleman called him a good servant and granted him authority over ten cities. This servant's industriousness earned him greater opportunity for the future.

> The industrious believer who uses his opportunities wisely will be granted great responsibility in heaven. Heaven is pictured here as a place, not of inactivity, but of service. Active, productive people know that the greatest satisfactions in life come not from inactivity and ease, but from hard work and accomplishment. With boundless energy, freed from the bondage of time, the believer who is faithful in this life will know the exhilaration of great opportunity and responsibility in heaven. The satisfaction of great accomplishments for Christ will be ours throughout eternity.

The second servant had increased his pound fivefold. His commendation was

may be more faithful than his fellow Christians. If he is, he'll receive a greater reward—greater opportunity and responsibility in heaven. Heaven's not a place of doing nothing. There will be service there. This service will never tire us out but will be a source of great satisfaction and joy.

This parable also teaches that a person may be a Christian and waste his life. The one servant did nothing with what was given to him. He didn't invest what he had for the master. He received no reward. God has given you a mind, your health, and opportunities for training and service. How are you going to use these gifts? If you use them for God, He'll usually increase your opportunities for service in this life. He'll certainly increase those opportunities in the future life. If you waste all of what God has entrusted you with, your actions will affect your life in eternity. The servant disobeyed his master; he should have done something with that money. If you live your life without any concern for what God wants out of your life, you're just like that servant.

This parable also presents the enemies of the master, who didn't want him to rule over them. They were determined to rebel. This is a picture of the lost. They don't want the Lord to rule over them; they want to rule themselves. The Bible teaches that they'll be punished according to their wicked works. Some will be punished more than others, but they will all be punished. Your friends who aren't Christians are not wise, and they're not to be envied. They aren't investing their lives the right way. You should give the good news about Jesus Christ and pray that they'll trust Him as their Savior.

Are You Laying Up Treasure In Heaven?

More than anything else, the Lord's love for you should cause you to serve Him. Though the Lord has already given every Christian far more than he deserves in salvation, He also promises rewards in heaven. These rewards will be big or small, depending on the believer's faithfulness. Little faithfulness will mean little reward; great faithfulness will mean great reward. These rewards will help make heaven an exciting place with great opportunities for service and accomplishment. With limitless time and energy, you'll be able to serve God exuberantly. But you'll have those opportunities only if you're faithful in this life.

Do You Remember?

1. Why did the Lord present the parable of the pounds? _to teach His followers that their rewards would be given during a future kingdom_

2. Who does the nobleman represent? _Jesus_

3. Who do the servants represent? _Christians_

4. Who do the enemies represent? _the unsaved_

5. What did the nobleman give each of his servants? _one pound_

6. What did the wicked servant do with his money? _hid it in a cloth_

7. Who was the wicked servant's pound entrusted to? _the servant who had invested his pound and gained ten_

198

not as great as the first's, nor was the authority granted him as extensive, but he was rewarded with authority over five cities. This was still a considerable increase over his previous responsibility.

III. Christ Rebukes Unfaithful Christians (Luke 19:20-26)

Only one other servant is reckoned with in the parable. We can assume that the other seven prospered and were rewarded in varying degrees. The last servant represents those who profess Christ but do not produce works that are fitting for Christians. The servants had been commanded to do something with what had been given to them. Instead this servant took the money and hid it in a cloth. His reason was weak at best, and it became the clear basis for

the lord's rebuke. The man said he feared the master because he was an austere man. Since the master was strict and expected much out of those in his employ, the servant should have done something more with the money. The master asked why he did not at least put the money in the bank and earn interest (usury) from it. If the man was not going to involve himself in trading to get a significant gain on his investment, then he should have put it in a bank.

Perhaps the servant acted out of self-preservation. Knowing that the citizenry had voiced their intentions to rebel, the servant planned to have a little something hidden away when the populace confiscated the king's property. This servant was appropriately described as wicked. He was wicked for not earning money for the master and for taking steps to keep the money himself.

The action taken against the wicked servant was severe. He had his pound taken away and given to the man who had ten. The other servants questioned the action, to which the lord responded that the one who has proved himself faithful will have more entrusted to him, but the one who does nothing will lose what opportunity he had.

It is clear from this passage that there is a suffering of loss at the time of reward. Is this punishment? Not in the sense of punishment for sin; however, there is the loss of what could have been.

One alternative explanation for the loss is that this servant was a servant only in name and not in heart. Thus he represents a hypocrite, one who professes to know the Lord but in truth does not. The problem with this explanation is that the passage doesn't mention actual retribution for his sin.

IV. Christ Punishes the Unsaved (Luke 19:27)

The last reckoning by the new king was with the enemies who had spoken against him. They were brought before him and killed. This is a picture of the Great White Throne Judgment (Rev. 20:11–15). Just as the righteous will receive differing rewards based on their faithfulness, so the wicked will receive varying degrees of punishment based on their wickedness; they will be judged according to their works. The judgment of the wicked is not a time when a vindictive God vents His anger against those He hates. It is a time when justice is finally done (Rom. 12:19). All wrongs will be made right. All sin will be dealt with by an appropriate punishment, never excessive, never too lenient.

 Extra Activities

Quiz: Give a diagnostic quiz to measure your students' understanding of the doctrine of future reward, to increase their interest in the subject, and to provide them with a guide to correct their misunderstandings.

1. Will the righteous be rewarded and the wicked be punished at the same time?
   No; the righteous are rewarded at the judgment seat of Christ, whereas the wicked are sentenced at the Great White Throne Judgment.

2. On what basis will a Christian be rewarded?
   his faithfulness

3. What Bible passages teach that some Christians will get more reward than others?
   Luke 19:11–27
   1 Corinthians 3:13–15
   2 Corinthians 5:9–10

4. What is the Christian's reward in heaven?
   greater opportunity and responsibility for service

5. What should be the believer's greatest motivation for service to Christ?
   his love for Christ in response to Christ's love for him

Storytelling: This lesson provides an opportunity to tell an inspiring story about an Olympic athlete who gains reward. These stories can be located easily at a public library. They appear frequently in periodicals and on websites, and in some cases whole biographies have been written. The reference librarian can speed up the process of locating some. Beginning the lesson with such a story should create a lot of interest.

Lesson 57

Faithfulness Until He Comes

Theme	The Parable of the Talents
Scripture	Matthew 25:14–30
Memory Work	Matthew 25:21

 Approach to the Lesson

Theme: When a person becomes a part of the family of God, the heavenly Father gives him tasks to perform. He does not give all believers equal ability or equal responsibility for service. What He does give is equal opportunity and ability to be faithful in whatever he has been given to do. Faithfulness is what the Lord desires above all else. When the Lord returns, He will reward the saints according to their faithfulness. No matter how different the abilities and responsibilities are, those who are faithful will be rewarded.

Faithfulness grows out of a love for Christ that originates in salvation. Those who don't know the Lord as their Savior will not be faithful and will be judged with eternal condemnation.

Rationale: Many students think that the aim in life is ease. Challenge them to see life as an opportunity for work and accomplishment.

Background: The parable of the talents is part of the Olivet Discourse. The Gospels record this discourse in Matthew 24–25, Mark 13, and Luke 21:4–36. Together these chapters give us the most important eschatological teaching in the Gospels. One must understand these sections to understand the prophetic teaching of the New Testament.

The parable of the talents, like others in the Olivet Discourse, emphasizes the certain return of the Lord. Believers learn that they are to be ready for the Lord's return. They will be ready if they are faithfully serving Him every day. The parable instructs us how to live under the authority of the Lord as our King.

An important teaching aid, a copy of the chart from page 200 of the student text, is found on the CD.

 The Lesson

I. Responsibilities Given (Matt. 25:14–15)

The Lord began this parable by introducing a man who prepared to travel into a far country. The purpose of the journey is not stated, but the man represents the Lord. He is the One Who rewards His servants and punishes the unfaithful. The far country symbolizes heaven, the place to which Jesus ascended.

The opportunities for service occur during the time of the master's absence, which represents the current era—the church age. This age, between the first and second advents of Christ, is an age of service. The New Testament variously describes the Christian's service as an athletic contest, farming, and a military conflict. In every case the analogy suggests hard work and sacrifice for the sake of the kingdom. The day of rest will come, but it hasn't yet.

> Life for a Christian is serious business; it should not be spent in worthless activity and entertainment. Occasionally rest and diversion are needed (Mark 6:31), but these times are for renewal of strength and presence of mind to continue in faithful service. They are a means to an end, not an end in themselves.

The opportunities for service in this age vary according to the recipients' abilities. One man received five talents; another, two; and another, one. The value of a talent is difficult to establish. Some have suggested that it represents about six thousand

Objectives

Knowledge (concepts students need to grasp)	what a *talent* represents
	the identity of the man who went into a far country
	the identity of the unprofitable servant
Application (principles students should put into practice)	Not everyone is given equal opportunity or ability to serve the Lord.
	Christ wants us to serve Him until He comes again.
	Some who profess to be servants of the Lord are not really saved; therefore, they are not faithful in their service.
	Faithful servants will be rewarded.

Outline

(Matt. 25:14–30)
I. Responsibilities given (14–15)
II. Responsibilities taken (16–18)
III. Faithfulness rewarded (19–30)

denarii, or roughly the salary of a laborer for twenty years. What is indisputable is that the values were great. The amount of responsibility varied, yet they were all significant.

The Lord grants natural talents and spiritual gifts to His servants as He wills. The Scriptures teach, "If any man speak, let him speak as the oracles of God; if any man minister, let him do it as of the ability which God giveth: that God in all things may be glorified through Jesus Christ, to whom be praise and dominion for ever and ever" (1 Pet. 4:11). He above all others knows what His servants are capable of accomplishing. He has the right to grant whatever responsibilities best match the capacities of His followers. Responsibility always represents an opportunity for service and accomplishment.

> The inclination to measure our own success or failure against others is a terrible mistake. The Lord never intended for us to compare ourselves to others. The only standard against which we should measure ourselves is our faithfulness to the will of God. As Paul writes, "For we dare not make ourselves of the number, or compare ourselves with some that commend themselves: but they measuring themselves by themselves, and comparing themselves among themselves, are not wise" (2 Cor. 10:12).

II. Responsibilities Taken (Matt. 25:16–18)

Two of the three servants were faithful in using the resources God put at their disposal. One took his five talents and gained five more through wise investment. Likewise, the one given two talents gained two more through careful management. What did these two servants have in common? They responsibly used what they were given.

> Every ability, gift, and circumstance is to be used to the fullest for the glory of Christ. This is faithfulness in service.

In contrast to these two servants, the third squandered his opportunity. He was not faithful with what had been given him,

Faithfulness Until He Comes

Read: Matthew 25:14–30 Memorize: Matthew 25:21

Bible Expressions to Understand

talent—a large sum of money
strawed—scattered
exchangers—bankers
usury—lending money and charging interest

At one time, the Persian Empire stretched thousands of miles from India to Turkey and down to Egypt. On the western edge of this vast territory was a small group of Greek cities. Each city had its own government and its own army, and they spent a lot of their time fighting each other. Yet when mighty Persia threatened Greece, the Greek cities banded together to resist. In 480 BC, with an army of about 150,000 men and over 300 ships, the Persian king Xerxes attacked Greece.

The pass at Thermopylae was later the site of other important Greek battles (against the Gauls in 279 BC and against the Syrians in 191 BC).

To halt the Persians, the Greeks sent an army of only 7,000 men to a narrow mountain pass called Thermopylae. The Greeks were commanded by Leonidas, king of Sparta. The backbone of his army was 300 fierce, well-trained Spartan soldiers.

The disciplined Greeks fought ferociously and turned back every Persian attack. The second day, Xerxes sent in his "Immortals," the finest troops in the Persian army. The Greeks defeated them as well, holding the pass. Then Xerxes received some unexpected help. A Greek traitor showed the Persians a mountain trail around the Greek forces. When Leonidas realized that his position was now hopeless, he ordered most of his army to retreat. Fewer than 2,000 men stayed behind to delay the Persians so that the rest could escape. Leonidas and the 300 Spartan soldiers remained with them because their Spartan sense of honor would not allow them to leave a post that they had been ordered to guard. Rather than waiting for the Persians, the Greeks attacked first. They fought with their spears until their spears were broken. Then they fought with their swords until their swords were broken. Then they fought with their fists and even their teeth until they could fight no more. In the end, most of the small Greek army, including Leonidas and all of his 300 Spartans, lay dead at Thermopylae. The other Greeks did not forget their sacrifice. They rallied to defeat the

199

---

a responsibility perfectly suited to his abilities. Not as great an opportunity as those enjoyed by the others, it nonetheless was invaluable. And the servant did not simply ignore what he had been given; he purposefully took the talent and buried it in the ground. The money was set aside for another day and another purpose. He would not conform himself to the will of the lord in either timing or task. This is rebellion, not just neglect.

Conduct like the third servant's raises sober questions about a supposed believer's spiritual state. If he does not want the Lord's timing and the Lord's will, what does he want in life? Perhaps he is really serving another lord.

III. Faithfulness Rewarded (Matt. 25:19–30)

All those who are faithful receive rewards. After a long time the lord returned to see how his servants were faring with what he had given them. To the servant who had earned five more talents the lord gave a commendation. He promised him greater responsibility and favor in the future. To the servant who had earned two more talents the same commendation and promise were given. These men had different abilities; they had different responsibilities. In the end, however, they received the same kind of reward for their faithfulness. The lord promised both they would become rulers over "many things," but he didn't specify how many in either case. The

difference wasn't as important as the fact that they were both rewarded.

Is this example of reward in the future establishing a law that is also true in this life? Will a man who is faithful with what has been granted him receive greater responsibility and the favor of the one for whom he labors? Often this is the case. Those in the Lord's work who are faithful with their opportunities usually receive greater responsibilities in this life.

Stress to your students that in any case, what they do in the present with what God has given them will affect their future.

Primarily, though, this parable is teaching about reward in the future life. This is a reward of increased usefulness and favor in the Lord's eyes. Any Christian who has hungered and thirsted after righteousness knows that this is a wonderful reward. The ability to obey the Lord more fully and please Him is the aim of the Christian life, achieving ultimate fulfillment in heaven. Heaven will not be a place of idleness and boredom, but of productive service and excitement. These verses indicate that what we do with our stewardship in this life determines the extent of our stewardship in the next life. The guiding principle that determines our future reward is faithfulness.

In contrast to the rewards of the faithful, punishment is given to the unfaithful. The man who had been given the one talent was afraid that the master would take all the profit he earned or be harsh with him if he lost the talent, so out of fear he buried it. The master called the servant wicked and slothful. Considering the duration of the lord's absence, this servant perhaps thought the lord would never return. If he invested in the name of his master, he thought he would never get anything out of the money. So instead he hid it, to dig it up later for his own use. Furthermore, his excuse was not logical. If he had really been concerned about the austere character of the master, he could have invested the money with bankers (*exchangers*) and earned interest (*usury*) on it, giving himself a secure and effortless way of earning a profit.

The judgment on the wicked servant was twofold. First, all that could have been his was lost forever. This wicked servant represents lost people. The Lord gives them remarkable abilities out of His goodness. He is prepared at the moment of their conversion to grant them spiritual gifts and opportunities commensurate with the abilities He has granted. The Lord must get His work accomplished through faithful servants, however, because the unsaved reject Him and His gifts.

Second, the wicked man loses his own soul. All who profess the Lord but by their works deny Him are destined for eternal condemnation. This condemnation stems not from any vindictiveness on the Lord's part, but from His unfailing justice. The Judge of all the earth will do right (Gen. 18:25).

The condemnation is described as outer darkness, emphasizing the total absence of ethical understanding. In hell there is no appreciation of righteousness and truth, which are often symbolized by light in the Bible. Worst of all, the Lord Jesus, the Light of the World, is not present in hell. This is darkness in the most severe sense. The place of punishment is also described as a place of weeping and gnashing of teeth. People weep when there is no hope; weeping comes when they are in the throes of tragedy and can see no way out. The gnashing or grinding of the teeth suggests agony and suffering.

Persians and drove them from Greece. A monument erected at Thermopylae had an inscription that said:

> Go tell the Spartans, thou that passest by,
> That here, obedient to their laws, we lie.

The Lord Jesus taught about this kind of endurance and faithfulness in service through His parable of the talents. Before leaving on a long trip, a wealthy man called in his servants. So that his money would not be unproductive while he was gone, he distributed it to the servants. To one he gave five talents; to a second, two talents; and to a third, one talent. Each servant received an amount that his ability would allow him to invest wisely.

While the man was gone, the first servant doubled his five talents through various business pursuits. The second servant also doubled his two talents. But the third servant took his talent and buried it in the ground so no one would steal it. When the wealthy man returned, he called his servants in for an accounting. When he heard the report of the first servant, he was pleased and rewarded him by giving him even greater responsibilities. Likewise, at the report of the second servant, the master was pleased and increased his responsibilities.

The third servant came forward apologetically. He justified his lack of success by stating that he feared his master's anger. The wealthy man was furious. He pointed out that, at the very least, the servant could have put the talent in a bank and drawn interest on it. Because he'd been unfaithful, his talent was taken away from him and given to the servant who had earned five talents with his investments.

You should learn several lessons from this parable. First, the Lord has given every believer responsibilities he's to live up to. Just as the man assigned duties to his servants, so Christ has given them to us. We're to be faithful in our service to Him by using what He's given us. What do you enjoy doing most in life? Playing basketball? Snowboarding? Cheering at a ball game? Playing computer games? Talking with a friend? All these things are fine, but they're not the important things in life. These are pastimes for relaxation. They should never become our goals in life.

Christ wants you to serve Him faithfully as the goal of your life. At times serving the Lord can be enjoyable or fun, but pleasure isn't the major purpose of life. Sometimes serving God is difficult and even unpleasant. Still, you must be faithful.

The second lesson is that God doesn't give everyone the same abilities. Why? He's concerned about faithfulness in whatever you're given to do. Are you and your best friend just alike? Of course not. He may have musical ability you don't have. You may have athletic ability she doesn't have. She may be a good speaker while you may not be. Some of your friends may be more intelligent than you are. The master in the parable gave one servant five talents, another two, and another one. He did this because they had differing abilities. Was he fair in treating them this way? Yes, because all he expected was

PARABLES OF THE POUNDS AND TALENTS COMPARED

Ideas Found in the Parables	The Parable of the Pounds (Luke 19:11–27)	The Parable of the Talents (Matt. 25:14–30)
Level of ability	Different for each servant	Different for each servant
Amount of responsibility	Same for each servant	Different for each servant
Number of faithful servants	All but one	All but one
Degree of fruitfulness	Different proportions	Same proportions
Reward for faithfulness	Proportionate	Equal
Consequences of unfaithfulness	Loss of what he had	Loss of what he had
	Enemies killed	Servant cast out

200

faithfulness with what had been given to them. Christ is fair to us because all He expects is faithfulness in our service to Him.

Since Christians have varying abilities and responsibilities, not everyone will accomplish the same amount of service. The servants in the parable didn't, and neither will we. Never compare yourself to other people. Compare yourself to the standard of what God expects from you. That standard consists of the abilities and opportunities you have. If God has given you a lot of ability, then you might become proud or begin to think badly of others. God resists proud people. Scripture teaches that every good and perfect gift comes down from God to us—so we have no basis for being proud.

This parable also teaches that the future will bring a time of reward for those who are faithful. The servants who were faithful received the same reward. They were commended by the master for their faithfulness and promised greater responsibility and his favor. This is the reward that faithful Christians can look forward to. Their reward will be greater responsibility in heaven and an abiding sense of God's favor. Heaven is not a place of idleness. It will be a place of service, excitement, and encouragement from Christ.

This parable teaches one last sobering lesson. Some who claim to be servants of Christ prove by their works that they're not. They squander their abilities and opportunities just like the unfaithful servant. They don't respect and love the Lord Jesus

Christ. They think of Him just as the wicked and slothful servant in the parable thought of his master—as an unreasonable, harsh person.

The destiny of the lost person who pretends to be a servant of Christ is sad. He loses all his opportunity for service and usefulness to God in eternity. He also faces eternal punishment. In hell he lives in his sin forever, suffering and mourning over his hopeless condition. The only way to avoid this is by salvation through faith in Christ.

What Kind of Servant Will You Be?

You have special abilities that God has given you. He's also given you opportunities to serve Him that no one else enjoys. Now is the time for you to begin a life of faithful service to Christ. If you do what God has given you to do with the abilities He's given, He'll reward you. In heaven you'll have greater ability and responsibility. The best thing is that you'll enjoy the encouragement of the Lord Jesus Christ in your service forever.

✳ Extra Activity

Discussion: The following Scripture passages suggest several qualities of a faithful servant. Have your students look them up and cite the quality in each passage. Make the Scripture search competitive, allowing the student who first locates the quality in each passage to state that quality to the class. Explain each quality after the students identify it.

Deuteronomy 10:12
serve with all your heart

Joshua 24:14
serve in sincerity and truth

1 Chronicles 28:9
serve with a perfect heart and a willing mind

Psalm 2:11
serve with fear

Psalm 100:2
serve with gladness

Acts 20:19
serve with humility

Romans 7:6
serve with newness of spirit

Romans 12:11
serve with a fervent spirit

2 Timothy 1:3
serve with a pure conscience

Hebrews 12:28
serve with reverence and godly fear

Do You Remember?

1. Why did the master give his servants money? _____
   because he was going away, and he wanted his money to be put to use

2. Why were some servants given greater responsibility than others? _____
   They had more ability.

3. What commendation did the servant who was entrusted with five talents receive from the master? _____
   "Well done, thou good and faithful servant."

4. What commendation did the servant who was entrusted with two talents receive for his labors? _____
   "Well done, good and faithful servant."

5. Why did the man who received the one talent not use it faithfully? _____
   He was wicked, slothful, and selfish.

6. Who received the wicked servant's talent? _____
   the first servant

7. To whom should the wicked servant have given his talent? _____
   the exchangers or bankers

8. Where was the wicked servant to be thrown? _____
   into outer darkness, where there was weeping and gnashing of teeth

202

Verse(s)	Lesson
Isaiah 53:6	12
Matthew	
1:23	8
2:1–2	37
3:17	9
5:5	4
5:7	6
5:16	14
5:17	15
5:48	16
6:1	17
6:33	18
7:12	19
7:13–14	20
12:34–35	25
13:23	47
13:52	48
16:24	30
18:21–22	53
19:26	31
23:11–12	36
25:13	55
25:21	57
26:10–11	34
26:41	39
Mark	
5:19	45
10:44	32
Luke	
4:4	10
5:10b–11	43
9:35	11

Verse(s)	Lesson
Luke (continued)	
10:27	52
11:9–10	27
12:15	50
14:11	54
15:10	51
16:10	49
16:23	23
19:26	56
John	
1:14, 16	2
1:29	33
2:17	5
3:6–7	21
6:35	24
10:10–11	26
11:25a–26	46
15:5	29
16:13	28
18:37–38	40
20:30–31	41
1 Cor. 15:1, 20	13
Col. 3:8–10	1
1 Thess. 5:18	44
1 Timothy 3:16	3
Hebrews 11:6	42
James	
1:8	38
3:7	35
1 Peter 1:15–16	7
1 John 2:15–17	22

Scripture Index

Topical Index

The following agencies and individuals have furnished materials to meet the photographic needs of this textbook. We wish to express our gratitude to them for their important contribution. (Page numbers refer to the student text.)

Unit 1

odd Bolen/BiblePlaces.com ii (top right, top left), 4 op); Unusual Films ii (bottom), 5 (top left); Greg Moss (top, middle), 7; © 2005 Map Resources. All Rights eserved iii (bottom right), 5 (bottom); Scala/Art esource 4 (bottom)

Unit 2

hotoDisc/Getty Images 12 (bottom left), 13 (bottom ght), 22 (both); Library of Congress 12 (middle), 14; 2005 Map Resources. All Rights Reserved 13 (bottom ft), 25 (top)

Unit 3

2005 Map Resources. All Rights Reserved 29; Shrine the Book; photo © The Israel Museum, Jerusalem 32; PattyBrdarPhoto.com 38; *Christ Leaving the Praeto- um*, Gustave Doré, from the Bob Jones University ollection 42; *Historic Views of the Holy Land: the 60's: Photographs of Charles Lee Feinberg*, www. bleplaces.com, 2004 47

Unit 4

hotoDisc/Getty Images 50 (top left, bottom middle), 67; 2005 Hemera Technologies, Inc. All Rights Reserved (top right), 72; © 2005 iStockphotos, Inc. 50 (bottom t), 51 (middle), 61, 65 (top); Library of Congress 51 p left), 58; WEC International 51 (bottom left), 66; dd Bolen/BiblePlaces.com 51 (bottom right), 64 (top), –65

Unit 5

Tor Eigeland/Saudi Aramco World/PADIA 76 (both), 94; NASA 77, 81; Todd Bolen/BiblePlaces.com 92; © Chuck Doswell/Visuals Unlimited 100

Unit 6

© 2005 Jupiterimagescorporation/photos.com 112 (top), 117; Todd Bolen/BiblePlaces.com 112 (bottom), 132 (all), 133 (both); PhotoDisc/Getty Images 113 (left), 114 (right); Library of Congress 113 (right), 114 (left)

Unit 7

© Adam Jones/Visuals Unlimited 159

Unit 8

Todd Bolen/BiblePlaces.com 171, 187; © 2005 Map Resources. All Rights Reserved 186; National Gallery of Art 191

GETTING STARTED

Viewing the supplemental material on the CD requires an Adobe Acrobat Reader compatible with version 5.0 or higher. Various versions of Acrobat Reader for Windows are provided on the CD. Acrobat Reader for Macintosh operating systems, Acrobat Reader in language other than English, and the most recent version of Acrobat Reader for Windows are available for free download at www. acrobat.com. Internet access is required.

Installing Adobe Acrobat Reader for Windows

1. Insert the CD. If the CD does not start automatically, use Windows Explorer to open the CD's file listing.
2. Double-click on Startup.exe and follow the installation instructions on the screen.

Installing Adobe Acrobat Reader for Macintosh (requires Internet access)

1. Insert the CD. Open the "Reader" folder and then the "Mac" folder.
2. Double-click on the appropriate installation file for your operating system version.
3. Double-click on the file that is copied to your computer, and follow the installation instructions on the screen.

END USER LICENSE AGREEMENT

CAREFULLY READ THE FOLLOWING TERMS AND CONDITIONS BEFORE USING THIS PRODUCT. IT CONTAINS SOFTWARE AND OTHER MATERIALS, THE USE OF WHICH IS LICENSED BY BJU PRESS TO YOU, THE ORIGINAL END USER, FOR YOUR USE ONLY AS SET FORTH BELOW. IF YOU DO NOT AGREE TO THE TERMS AND CONDITIONS OF THIS AGREEMENT, DO NOT USE THE SOFTWARE OR MATERIALS CONTAINED ON THIS CD-ROM. USING ANY PART OF THE SOFTWARE OR MATERIALS INDICATES THAT YOU ACCEPT THESE TERMS.

BJU Press ("Licensor") grants you a non-exclusive license ("License") for the software ("Software") and documents ("Documents") contained on this electronic medium, and any derivative works created in your use of the Documents. The Software, Documents, and derivative works of the Documents are hereafter collectively referred to as the "Product." The Product is subject to protection under copyright laws and other intellectual property laws of the United States and other jurisdictions.

You may

1. use the Product on a single computer at any one time;
2. use the Product on more than one computer provided only one copy is used at a time or provided that copies used at the same time are used by the teacher and his or her designated assistant only;
3. use the Product on a network provided that each user accessing the Product through the network has lawfully obtained a licensed copy of the Product or is a designated assistant of a licensed user;
4. make one copy of the Product for archival or backup purposes;
5. create derivative works from the Documents as part of the normal use of the Documents.

The Product is the sole and exclusive property of Licensor. Other than classroom distribution, you may not reproduce, redistribute, retransmit, modify, publish, or exploit any part of the Product, or permit a third party to do any of the foregoing, without permission of Licensor. You may not sell, rent, lease, give access to, modify, alter, decompile, disassemble, translate, or reverse engineer the Product.

LIMITED WARRANTY: Licensor warrants that the media on which the Product is supplied will be free from defect in material and workmanship under normal use for a period of 90 days from the date of delivery to you. If the Product or media do not perform as warranted in this paragraph, Licensor will, at its option, correct or replace the Product or defective media to comply with the warranty given in this paragraph. Licensor does not warrant that all program defects will be corrected, that the operation of the Product will be uninterrupted or error free, or that the Product will be compatible with your computer.

Use of the Product to access the Internet may not include safeguards relative to copyright, ownership, decency, reliability, and integrity of content, and is at your own risk. You will be responsible for providing and maintaining all equipment and services required to use and access the Internet.

In the event that you fail to comply with any term or condition in the License Agreement, the License will terminate immediately without notice to you and Licensor may pursue all appropriate legal remedies.

WARRANTIES EXCLUSIVE: THE FOREGOING WARRANTIES AND REMEDIES ARE EXCLUSIVE AND IN LIEU OF ALL OTHER WARRANTIES, EXPRE OR IMPLIED, INCLUDING WARRANTII OF MERCHANTABILITY, FITNESS FOR A PARTICULAR PURPOSE, CORRESPONDENCE WITH DESCRIPTION, AN NON-INFRINGEMENT, ALL OF WHICH ARE EXPRESSLY DISCLAIMED BY LICENSOR AND ITS SUPPLIERS.

LIMITATION OF LIABILITY: NEITHER LICENSOR NOR ITS SUPPLIERS SHALL BE LIABLE FOR INCIDENTAL, CONSEQUENTIAL, INDIRECT, OF SPECIAL DAMAGES OF ANY KIND, LO OF INFORMATION OR DATA, OR OTHI FINANCIAL LOSS ARISING OUT OF OI IN CONNECTION WITH THE SALE OR USE OF THE PRODUCT, WHETHER BASED IN CONTRACT, TORT (INCLUD ING NEGLIGENCE) OR ANY OTHER THEORY, EVEN IF LICENSOR HAS BEI ADVISED OF THE POSSIBILITY OF SUCH DAMAGES. LICENSOR'S ENTIF LIABILITY SHALL BE LIMITED TO REPLACEMENT, REPAIR, OR REFUND OF THE PURCHASE PRICE PAID, AT LICENSOR'S OPTION.

DISCLAIMER: Some countries, state or provinces do not allow the exclusion or limitation of implied warranties or the limi tation of incidental or consequential damag so the above limitations and exclusions may be limited in their application to you. Whe implied warranties may not be excluded in their entirety, they will be limited to the du tion of the applicable written warranty. Thi warranty gives you specific legal rights; yo may have other rights that may vary depen ing on local law. Your statutory rights are n affected.

GOVERNING LAW: This License Agreement shall be governed by the laws the State of South Carolina, U.S.A., and by the laws of the United States, without rega to any rule of law that might provide for th application of another or different law. The United Nations Convention on Contracts fe the International Sale of Goods is hereby excluded in its entirety from application to this License Agreement.

SEVERABILITY: In the event that a provision of this License Agreement is fou to be invalid, illegal, or unenforceable, th validity, legality, and enforceability of any the remaining provisions shall not in any v be affected or impaired.